W9-AOQ-976

Plays by Four Tragedians

Plays by Four Tragedians

Edited by

LOUIS GLORFELD
University of Denver

TOM E. KAKONIS
Wisconsin State University

JAMES C. WILCOX
Northern Illinois University

Charles E. Merrill Publishing Company
Columbus, Ohio
A Bell & Howell Company

Copyright © 1968 by CHARLES E. MERRILL PUBLISHING COMPANY, Columbus, Ohio. All rights reserved. No part of this book may be reproduced in any form or by any process without permission in writing from the publisher.

Library of Congress Catalog Number: 68-22235

1 2 3 4 5 6 7 8 9 10—72 71 70 69 68

Printed in the United States of America

PREFACE

The principal justification for the addition of *Plays by Four Tragedians* to the burgeoning ranks of drama anthologies lies in its versatility. This book can be profitably used at several levels in the study of dramatic literature. It can serve as either a corollary reader in introductory and survey courses, or as the primary text in an advanced class in drama.

Another facet of this versatility arises from the selections of dramatists and their plays. The literary era bounded by classical tragedy on the one hand and realistic and naturalistic tragedy on the other witnessed the evolution of an entirely new concept of the tragic form. Each of the plays in this collection demonstrates a certain contribution to that evolution. Beyond this, the choices reflect a two-fold purpose on the part of the editors: to include an early and a later play by each of the four dramatists, and to show through our selection the maturing process of the playwright and the direction of this process.

The apparatus appended to each of the four sections includes both discussion questions and writing topics. In keeping with the emphasis on versatility, the broadest possible range of questions has been supplied, from a very fundamental treatment of plot and character to a more sophisticated exploration of theme and dramatic technique. We feel that such a range helps meet the particular needs of student and instructor and at the same time provides a general direction for the study of drama as an independent form of literary art. In addition, a comprehensive bibliography and research topics have been included for the purpose of an in depth study of the most significant scholarship and criticism available on the four dramatists considered.

CONTENTS

Plays by Four Tragedians

Introduction

I The Reading of Drama

Drama, as one of the several means of telling a story, is rarely the exclusive property of the field of literature. The theatre arts—acting, directing, stage designing—all can claim their legitimate share of the total art of the performed play. But in this text we are concerned only with the experience of reading drama; in other words, with direct communication between the playwright and his audience. It may be argued that the printed pages which comprise a play are not a play at all until the combined efforts of author, producer, director, and actors have been shaped into a performance, made viable upon the stage. This objection is not entirely valid, for theatre is, by its very nature, a representational and interpretative art. That is, between the audience and the dramatist lie a host of interpreters (these same directors, actors, set designers, and many others) who produce what is ultimately a representation of the playwright's script. No two such representations are ever the same, and it is quite unlikely that any one performance ever captures just the proper nuances of meaning the playwright himself intended. Thus it is that while the play-reader sacrifices something of the vivid immediacy of a theatrical performance, he makes up for the loss through his uninterpreted, uncluttered communication with the playwright's work itself. All of which is to say that while drama can certainly survive without the theatre, the reverse is not at all the case.

But if he is to appreciate that personal vision which, hopefully, emerges from the totality of the dramatist's art, the reader of plays must be exceptionally trained and perceptive. He must be capable of a complete response: intellectual, imaginative, emotional. He must never forget that the dramatist is indeed writing his play for performance by actors on a stage. There are, of course, exceptions to this assertion, and it is well to mention them at this time. Dramatic poems such as Milton's *Samson Agonistes* and Hardy's *The Dynasts*—closet-dramas, as they are called—were intended for the reader rather than the theatre audience. However commendable these plays may be for their poetic

1

merit, they have a minimal importance in the history of drama. To study them is not to study the dramatic genre. Another, more significant, exception is the trend pioneered by Ibsen and Shaw, a trend toward the inclusion of elaborate stage directions and lengthy prefaces which can in no way be translated into the terms of a performance. By including these non-dramatic elements, the playwright avails himself of some of the freedom of the novelist and sidesteps the primary limitation imposed upon him by his chosen form: the restriction of authorial comment on action, characters, setting, and theme.

If the closet-drama is seldom encountered and lengthy prefaces and elaborate stage direction are comparatively recent developments, then the reader who hopes to understand the literary achievement of drama must familiarize himself with certain rudiments and conventions of that art. A brief explanation of the most notable of those fundamentals follows. (The student is referred to the glossary for a more comprehensive treatment of dramatic terminology.)

Basic to any discussion of drama is the concept of *plot*. Plot is the sequential arrangement of incidents in the play, providing a coherent progression from beginning to conclusion. If a play is, as Aristotle suggests, a patterning of language, character, event, and spectacle, then it is the dramatist's task to blend these several elements into the unified whole which best conveys his theme. In doing so, he must solve certain problems which writers in other genres never face. Not the least of these problems has to do with point of view. Unlike the novelist, for example, the playwright must always remain out of the picture. He cannot, like a Fielding or Thackeray or Eliot, interrupt the plot to comment on the action at hand. He cannot, in the usual sense, look into the minds of his characters and explore their innermost thoughts and feelings (except, of course, through the medium of the soliloquy, which is, in a sense, a peek into the mind of the character). He cannot provide any direct description, and any expository material must come from the mouths of his characters. Finally, he cannot explain or elaborate upon his theme; the play itself must be its own explanation. Naturally, the reader of drama has the advantage of seeing the stage directions and any other form of authorial commentary which may accompany the printed play, but he should be aware of the fact that such information and interpretation partakes of the technique of prose fiction and is not, strictly, dramatic.

Given these numerous restrictions, how does the dramatist proceed in the shaping of his plot? Most plots fall into four formal divisions: *exposition, complication, reversal,* and *denouement*. Broadly, the purpose of the *exposition* is, as the term implies, to inform the audience.

It must inform them of the time and place of the action, of who the characters are and their relationships with each other, and of what has occurred prior to the initial scene that is vital in the understanding of the events to come. It must, in effect, supply all the information necessary to fix the characters in time and space, and to set in motion the chain of events about to be unfolded.

The *complication* deals primarily with those events and, as a rule, comprises the bulk of the play. Complication, like exposition, tends to define itself. The playwright poses a problem for one or more of his characters; he introduces a conflicting force or sets his characters into conflict among themselves. Whatever form it may take, that conflict builds toward a major crisis, generally called the climax. At this point the principal character makes a crucial decision, or an event beyond his control occurs, in which case the decision or event inexorably fixes the outcome of the play.

The *reversal* grows out of the climactic event or decision. It is so termed because the protagonist's fortune alters as a result of his choice or lack of choice. In a comedy his fortune changes from bad to good, in a tragedy from good to bad. The reversal, then, is that culminating point of the complication at which the plot is, for better or worse, resolved.

The function of the *denouement* is to demonstrate the consequences of the reversal. It is, essentially, a tying together of any loose strands of the play, and a hint or implication of what *could* follow were the play to continue beyond the final act.

It must be added that these four divisions of plot are rarely distinct in any given play. That is, the play in which the reader can single out an act or scene as pure complication or reversal is likely to be mechanical at best and not of the highest order of dramatic literature. In the works of the finest playwrights plot is a complex and structured blending of these arbitrarily defined sub-elements. It is a blending that allows for subtle overlapping or alternation of any of the parts. The reader must bear in mind that these divisions, then, are merely bases for analysis. He must be as flexible in his critical use of the terms as the accomplished dramatist is in the practical application of them.

Plot arranges in coherent fashion the incidents of the play, but that arrangement and those incidents must all contribute to the essence of the dramatic experience, *conflict*. The French critic, Ferdinand Brunetière, has observed: "In drama or farce, what we ask of the character, is the spectacle of a *will* striving toward a goal, and conscious of the means which it employs." In other words, what Brunetière suggests as the vital ingredient of any play is that contest or opposition of forces generally known as the conflict. Such forces can take a variety of forms, some elemental, some extremely ambiguous and complex. One character physically at odds with another is a simple kind of conflict. More subtle (and vastly more rewarding as literature) is that conflict in which a character clashes with either an external force, nature, society, "the gods," or an internal force, such as pride, jealousy, or fear. Whatever form the conflict may take, it remains the fundamental dramatic element upon which all other functions of the play depend.

The quality of *suspense* is an example of this dependency. Suspense obviously must be generated by the conflict, and it is instructive to note in this connection why some conflicts (and hence some plays) can be judged more rewarding than others. The suspense which focuses the reader's attention on "how things come out" is considerably different from that which absorbs his interest in the events themselves. In the former case a surface concern is created over the outcome of the conflict, and thus it is that such plays are rarely of interest after the first reading or viewing. But in the latter case suspense outlasts a knowledge of the resolution of the conflict, and this is perhaps one of the most significant characteristics of great drama. An *Oedipus Rex* or an *Othello* suffers nothing in rereading. These plays, like all superior drama, take on a new dimension with each reading, and what may be lost in excitement or thrills is made up for by the fuller enjoyment and understanding of the playwright's insights into human experience.

Those insights are represented in part through fine *characterization*, another equally significant trait of superior drama. The requirements for successful characterization in the drama are essentially the same requirements as in prose fiction: consistency, motivation, and plausibility. Thus a well-realized character is one whose actions grow naturally and inevitably out of the personality established for him early in the play. If he has been depicted as a proud person he must act pridefully throughout the play; any sudden reversal to an unexplained or unprepared-for humility is out of keeping with the reader's conception of him and is a violation of consistency. Such reversals can occur, but these changes must be reconciled to the character as presented early in the play. This reconcilement becomes a problem in motivation; it is nothing more than the revelation of how and why a person either changes or remains as he is. Finally, plausibility requires a balanced and full presentation of a character. The writer must convince us that the character is or could be a real person, with all the strengths and weaknesses that expression implies.

However, the playwright is bound by time limitations in a way that a novelist is not. Consequently he is more likely to employ type or stock characters, figures whose actions, speech, and appearance signal a predetermined response in the audience and the reader. Full or round character development is usually reserved for the most important figures in the play, on some occasions for the *protagonist* only. The protagonist is the focal figure in the drama, around whom the central action and the conflict revolve. In the finest drama the protagonist is a developing character; that is, as a direct result of the conflict he comes to a deeper understanding or a new awareness either of himself or of some facet of the world around him.

The dramatist has open to him three means of portraying character, the same means by which we come to know and judge people in our own lives. The first of these methods is through what others say about the particular character, a method usually employed in exposition. The second and third methods are what the character himself says and what he does respectively. As a rule, these latter two are much more important means of delineating character, for as in life, we tend to judge people chiefly on the basis of their words and their actions.

Action is always vital in the performance of a play, for it is a major means of expressing emotion. However, action can never reveal thought; if the dramatist wants to communicate ideas or to draw subtle variations in character, he must depend upon his most fundamental tool, *dialogue*. Dialogue has certain obvious dramatic functions, but only one requires comment here. Any dramatist that aims at literary excellence attempts to infuse the language of his play with stylistic beauty. This explains in part why earlier dramatists wrote in verse, for poetry traditionally is the means of imparting a lyric beauty to speech. Verse dialogue required audience acceptance of the dramatic convention of a group of people who spoke naturally and easefully in poetic language; such acceptance is rarely accorded the modern dramatist, who (with certain notable exceptions) has abandoned verse and strives for vividness, lucidity, and an illusion of reality in language. At the same time, it is worth observing that however "realistic" dialogue may be, it never fully imitates everyday speech, which is too halting, too repetitious, in fact too bumbling to ever be effective on the stage. The careful reader will discover that even dialogue which appears to be most prosaic has a concise directness and a charm seldom found in ordinary conversation.

There remains only to consider *dramatic conventions*, those conditions which the playwright and his audience tacitly agree to accept as "real" when they clearly violate the most elementary notions of reality. What dramatic conventions require, in effect, is an ability to accept the imaginative world as real, and their demands are considerably heavier on the theater-going audience than upon the reader. For example, in witnessing a play the audience is first asked to believe that the actors are really the people they pretend to be, and that the stage before them is some strange three-walled room whose fourth wall has somehow, magically and conveniently, been whisked away for their viewing pleasure. Both audience and reader are expected never to cavil when characters who are obviously foreigners speak a refined and beautiful—often poetic—English. And when twenty years elapse between curtains, the play-goer or reader is scarcely troubled.

Conventions constantly shift and change. What is in vogue in one era is obsolete in the next and, conceivably, may be the "bold experiment" of a subsequent age. The point is that the reader who wishes to appreciate thoroughly the drama of the past must learn a certain tolerance for conventions strange to him. This same reader may find the Greek chorus and the Shakespearean soliloquy naive and less than realistic, but he must approach these and other unfamiliar conventions with an attitude of objective inquiry if he hopes ever to understand their function and contribution to the particular drama they enrich.

The fundamentals of drama discussed in this introduction apply to any kind of play, regardless of its sub-genre. Farce, melodrama, comedy, problem play, tragedy—all are plotted, all set characters in some sort of conflict, all conform to the conventions of their age and their special type. The serious student of drama would be well-advised to use these fundamentals judiciously in his reading and analysis of the plays in this text, and of any other plays he encounters; for it is doubtless safe to say that we enjoy best that which we understand.

II Tragedy

The two major categories of drama are comedy and tragedy. In this book we are concerned only with the latter and with its development through the work of four tragedians who have contributed immeasurably to the art of tragedy. Of course, there are a number of other categories besides these two, and there is considerable mixing of the several types, so much so that we seldom find a single example of an absolutely pure comedy or tragedy. All the same, the two represent the balancing extremes of dramatic types, and so it is important to undertake a definition of that type we propose to work with here.

The kinds of emotion a play arouses in the spectator and reader determine its genre or type. In the *Poetics* Aristotle made the classic statement on the tragic emotions, and it is worth quoting that section most often referred to:

A perfect tragedy should imitate actions which excite pity and fear, this being the distinctive function of tragic imitation. It follows plainly, in the first place, that the change of fortune presented must not be the spectacle of virtuous man brought from prosperity to adversity, for this moves neither pity nor fear; it merely shocks us. Nor, again, that of a bad man passing from adversity to prosperity, for nothing can be more alien to the spirit of Tragedy; it possesses no single tragic quality; it neither satisfies the moral sense nor calls forth pity or fear. Nor, again, should the downfall of an utter villain be exhibited. A plot of this kind would doubtless satisfy the moral sense, but it would inspire neither pity nor fear; for pity is aroused by unmerited misfortune, fear by the misfortune of a man like ourselves. Such an event, therefore, will be neither pitiful nor terrible. There remains, then, the character between these two extremes—that of a man who is not eminently good and just, yet whose misfortune is brought about not by vice or depravity, but by some error or frailty. He must be one who is highly renowned and prosperous—a personage like Oedipus, Thyestes, or other illustrious men of such families. (Translated by S. H. Butcher)

This statement, abundantly qualified and interpreted, has been accepted by critics for well over two thousand years; and while it is not to be considered as axiomatic as physical law, it is easily the best single guideline we have for understanding tragic drama. However, the use of the terms pity and fear require further comment.

In *Tragedy*, his excellent study of Aristotle's dramatic theory, F. L. Lucas emphasizes the role of purgation (*catharsis*). Thus the pity and fear aroused serve as a sort of emotional safety valve to reduce audience passions to a normal, healthy balance. There are some who feel that admiration could well be substituted for fear as one of the fundamental tragic emotions, thereby stressing the ethical insight gained by the protagonist as a direct result of his personal misfortune.

Pity, fear, and perhaps admiration are the emotions elicited by all great tragedy; however, through the ages there have been varying attitudes toward tragic drama. All forms of drama have their origin in religious ritual. Greek drama—the ultimate source of all Western drama—grew out of the worship of the god of wine and vegetation, Dionysus. For the Greeks, tragedy came to represent the sufferings of Dionysus, but as the art of drama developed in the Periclean age (the fifth century B.C.) tragedy came to imply any play that dealt with the serious actions of serious characters. Thus for Aristotle tragedy need not necessarily have an unhappy ending, though in practice such conclusions were almost always employed.

During the Middle Ages, when the connection between the word tragedy and the stage was very tenuous, the unhappy ending became an essential part of the definition of the term. That trait was carried over in the revival of drama during the Renaissance, and has been associated with tragedy ever since. At the same time, in a rush of romantic exuberance, the English dramatists of the Renaissance broke from the confines of traditional tragic form to create a body of work that stands as the pinnacle of achievement in Western literature. Unlike the Greeks, who were close enough to the ritualistic origins of drama to retain a certain stylized formality in their work, the Elizabethans could and did break with the old established dramatic patterns to give full vent to their imaginations. And when, as in the case of Shakespeare, imagination is coupled with a penetrating insight into the human condition, the end result is genius.

Most readers feel that modern tragedy has never attained the heights of either the Greek or the Elizabethan. There are many, indeed, who would deny the label tragic to the serious drama written in the past one hundred years. This drama has its beginnings primarily in the work of two nineteenth century Scandinavian playwrights, Henrik Ibsen and August Strindberg, whose plays were so different from the earlier forms of tragedy that it is probably unfair, if not impossible, to judge them by the same set of standards. With Ibsen in particular, those traits now common to a considerable body of contemporary tragedy were developed and refined: realistic prose dialogue; a common man or woman as protagonist; a conflict that centers on psychological character study, or on a social problem, or on a mingling of both.

For all the changes tragedy has undergone over the centuries, there are certain general principles that have remained constant. The tragic hero, for one thing, must demonstrate strength of character. He need no longer be a "highly renowned and prosperous" personage, and he will always have his share of weaknesses and frailties, but he must be capable of a spirited resistance against whatever antagonist is selected to bring him to grief. And that antagonist must never be so completely overwhelming as to render the tragic hero powerless from the start. There must be a chance, however slim, for the protagonist to triumph over his apparent destiny. Further, the role of destiny or fate must be carefully balanced against the protagonist's characterization. That is, his fate must somehow proceed from his character; he must be at least partly responsible for the disaster that befalls him. This responsibility adds the important dimension of the problem of moral awareness to what would otherwise be little more than the dramatic working out of a bleak determinism. Finally—and most nebulous of all—the greatest tragedy inspires in the reader a sense of identification with the tragic hero. In doing so, it achieves that quality so easy to invoke and so difficult to define—universality. The tragic hero's struggle and misfortune strike some responsive chord in us (if we are perceptive enough and sensitive enough) so that regardless of the disparity in time or place or language or custom, we can vicariously share in and understand his suffering and his glory.

What glory, one may ask, can be found in a dramatized tale of agony, woe, and ultimate defeat? The question is a legitimate one and deserves an answer, for most people find life grim enough without subjecting themselves to a playwright's black imagination. But the question, as put, is also a loaded one, and it displays an ignorance of the purpose and execution of a tragic drama. For though the tragic hero is most often overcome by the antagonistic (and frequently evil) forces that confront him, those forces are rarely left triumphant over anything more than his physical person. The best tragedy always offers us an astute comment upon humanity. It demonstrates that the downfall of the individual man is perhaps inevitable, that weakness, stupidity, frailty, pride—*some* flaw in character or *some* error in judgment must finally defeat him. But paradoxically, any tragedy worthy of the name also concludes on a note of affirmation of faith in the human spirit, in the greatness of man in the face of inescapable calamity. The outward defeat of the tragic hero is tempered by the inner victory he attains, a victory of personal insight, spiritual awakening, moral awareness, or possibly some combination of all three. So it is that the critic Joseph Wood Krutch can assert: "All works of art which deserve their name have a happy end." And so it is that great tragedy will never inspire pessimism or gloom, but rather a quality of faith that transcends despair.

Sophocles

Greek drama grows directly out of religious ceremony, and even at its artistic height its function was primarily a religious one. The purpose of tragedy was to enrich the religious experience through the combined arts of music, poetry, acting, and the dance. The plays themselves were performed only at two annual religious festivals. Almost without exception, the dramatists took their plots from the myths of heroes and gods familiar to their audience.

Because of this close tie with the religious culture, some of the conventions of Greek tragedy may seem mystifying to the reader encountering the plays for the first time. He should realize, first of all, that music and dancing were intrinsic parts of the drama, though they were later subordinated to the action of the play and its poetry. The principal vehicle for the music and the dance was the group of twelve to fifteen persons who comprised the chorus. Choric odes had their origin in the Dionysiac dithyramb, a choral dance in honor of the god Dionysus; and in the later drama they continued to be sung or chanted as the group moved rhythmically about the stage. The chorus also had other, more dramatic, functions. It served at times as a kind of composite character who represented common humanity. Frequently it acted as a foil to the protagonist. And always it provided a means for the dramatist to comment philosophically on the action of the play.

The physical construction of the Greek theater had much to do with the form and conventions of the drama itself. The theater was built in a semicircle on the side of a hill (it is not inappropriate to compare it with our modern stadium). The action of the play took place in the center of this semicircle, in a level area known as the orchestra. At the back of the stage stood an elaborate, two-storied building with several doors serving as entrances and exits. Most significant of all, the Greek theater had no drop curtains. As a result of this, the scene was rarely changed, the duration of the action was generally limited to one day, the complexity of the plot was minimized and the action confined to those episodes very near the conclusion of the story. As a further result of such practices (and they were nothing more than practices or customs which can be traced to the limitations of the Greek theater) the so-called unities of time, place, and action were *described* by Aristotle and misconstrued by a host of his interpreters as rules or axioms for the tragic drama. Greek tragedy owes no small share of its near perfect symmetry, artful simplicity, and compression of dramatic effect to the physical makeup of its theater.

Sophocles (c.496-c.406 B.C.): A Biographical Note. Sophocles was born near Athens and his life span coincided almost exactly with the Periclean or "Golden" age of that city. He was one of the most prolific and popular of the Greek tragedians, writing over one hundred plays (though only seven survive) and winning more than eighteen first prizes for his work. The plays of Sophocles represent all that is great about Greek tragedy. They demonstrate the coupling of flawless technique—structure, proportion, restraint—with a profound insight into the plight of man.

OEDIPUS THE KING

Sophocles
Translated by J. T. Sheppard

Characters

OEDIPUS, *King of Thebes, son of Laïus, reputed son of Polybus.*
JOCASTA, *widow of Laïus, now wife of Oedipus.*
CREON, *her brother, a prince of Thebes.*
TEIRESIAS, *a blind soothsayer.*
A PRIEST OF ZEUS.
A MESSENGER *from Corinth.*
A HERDSMAN.
A MESSENGER *from the Palace.*
ANTIGONE and ISMENE, *children of Oedipus.*
CHORUS OF THEBAN CITIZENS.
SUPPLIANTS, GUARDS, *and* SERVANTS.

An open place before the Royal Palace at Thebes. Enter a company of suppliants, old men, youths, and children, who take their places at the altars before the Palace. Enter to them, from the Palace, OEDIPUS.

OEDIPUS: My children, sons of Cadmus and his care,
Why thus, in suppliant session, with the boughs

Reprinted with permission of Cambridge University Press for Sophocles' *Oedipus the King,* translated by J. T. Sheppard.

Enwreathed for prayer, throng you about my feet,
While Thebes is filled with incense, filled with hymns
To the Healer, Phoebus, and with lamentation?—
Whereof I would not hear the tale, my children,
From other lips than yours. Look! I am here,
I, who am called 'the All-Famous Oedipus'!

   Tell me, old priest, you who by age are fit
To speak for these, in what mood stand ye here—
Of panic—or good courage? Speak! For I,
You know, would give all aid. Hard were my heart,
Pitying not such a petitioning.

A PRIEST: King, Master of my country, Oedipus,
You see us, in our several ages, ranged
About your altars. Some are not yet fledged
For long flight, others old and bowed with years,
Priests—I of Zeus—and yonder, of our youth
A chosen band. Thebes, garlanded for prayer,
Sits in the markets, at the shrines of Pallas,
And by Ismenus' oracle of fire.

   With your own eyes you see, the storm is grown
Too strong, and Thebes can no more lift her head
Out of the waves, clear from the surge of death.
A blight is on her budding fruit, a blight
On pastured cattle, and the barren pangs
Of women: and the fiery fever-god
Hath struck his blow—Pestilence sweeps the city,
Empties the house of Cadmus and makes rich
With tears and wailings the black house of Death.

   We count you not a god, I and these children,
That thus we seek your hearth. Of human kind
We judge you first in the common accident
Of fate; in the traffic of the gods with man
Greatest of men;—who came to Cadmus' town
And loosed the knot and quit us of the toll
To that grim singer paid. No hint from us,
No schooling, your own wit, touched by some god,
Men say and think, raised us and gave us life.
So now, great Oedipus, mighty in the world,
We stand and pray. If you have any knowledge
From god or man, find help! The tried man's thought,
And his alone, springs to the live event!

Oh, noblest among men, raise up our state!
Oh, have a care! To-day for that past zeal
Our country calls you Saviour. Shall your sway
Be thus remembered—that you raised us high
Only to fall? Not so! Lift up our state
Securely, not to fall. With promise good
You brought us fortune. Be the same to-day!
Would you be Prince, as you are Master, here?
Better to master men than empty walls.
The desolate ship is nothing, ramparts nothing,
Deserted, with no men to people them.

OEDIPUS: Alas, my sons! I know with what desire
You seek me. Well I know the hurt whereby
You all are stricken—and not one of you
So far from health as I. Your several griefs
Are single and particular, but my soul
Mourns for myself, for you, and for all Thebes.

You rouse not one that sleeps. Through many tears
And many searchings on the paths of thought,
By anxious care, at last, one way of cure
I found:—and put in action. . . . I have sent
Menoeceus' son, Creon, my own wife's brother,
To ask of Phoebus, in his Pythian shrine,
'By word or deed how shall I rescue Thebes?'

And when I mark the distance and the time,
It troubles me—what does he? Very long—
Beyond his time, he lingers. . . . When he comes,
Then call me base if I put not in act
What thing soever Phoebus showeth me.

PRIEST: Good words and seasonable. In good time—
Look! my companions tell me, Creon comes!

OEDIPUS: O King Apollo, as his looks are glad
So may he bring us glad and saving fortune.

PRIEST: I think he bears us good. Else were his head
Not thus enwreathed, thick with the clustered laurel.

OEDIPUS: He is in earshot. We'll not think, but know! (*He raises his voice as* CREON *approaches.*)
Prince, and my kinsman, son of Menoeceus, speak!
What message bring you for us from the god?

CREON: Good news! I count all news as fortunate,
However hard, that issues forth in good.

OEDIPUS: 'Tis a response that finds me undismayed,
And yet not overbold. What says the god?
CREON: If you would hear now, with this company
Here present, I will speak—or go within?
OEDIPUS: Speak it to all, since it is their distress
I care for—aye, more than for my own life.
CREON: So be it. As I heard from the god, I speak.
Phoebus the King enjoins with clear command:

> *A fell pollution, fed on Theban soil,*
> *Ye shall drive out, not feed it past all cure,*

OEDIPUS: How drive it out? In what way came misfortune?
CREON: There must be banishment, or blood for blood
Be paid. 'Tis murder brings the tempest on us.
OEDIPUS: Blood—for what blood? Whose fate revealeth he?
CREON: My Lord, in former days, our land was ruled—
Before you governed us—by Laïus.
OEDIPUS: I know—men tell me so—I never saw him.
CREON: He fell. Apollo chargeth us to strike
His murderers, whoe'er they be, with vengeance.
OEDIPUS: The task is hard. How can we hope to track
A crime so ancient? Where can they be found?
CREON: Here, said the god, in Thebes. To seek is oft
To find—neglected, all escapes the light.
OEDIPUS: Was it in Thebes, or on the countryside
Of Thebes, the King was murdered, or abroad?
CREON: Abroad, on sacred mission, as he said,
He started—then, as he went, returned no more.
OEDIPUS: Came none with news? Came none who journeyed with him
Back, to report, that you might learn and act?
CREON: All slain. . . . One panic-stricken fugitive
Told naught that he saw—knew naught—save one thing only.
OEDIPUS: What thing? One clue, disclosing many more,
The first small promise grasped, may teach us all.
CREON: Robbers, he told us, met the King and slew him—
Not just one man, but a great company.
OEDIPUS: What brought the robber . . . what, unless 'twas pay, . . .
Something contrived from Thebes! . . . to such a deed?
CREON: Some thoughts of that there were. Yet, in our troubles,
For Laïus dead no man arose with aid.
OEDIPUS: Some thoughts! For a King dead! A pressing trouble,
To put you off with less than certainty!
CREON: It was the Sphinx—whose riddling song constrained us

To leave the unknown unknown, and face the present.
OEDIPUS: Then I'll go back and fetch all to the light!
'Tis very just in Phoebus—and in you
'Tis a just zeal for the cause of that slain man.
And right it is in me that ye shall see me
Fighting that cause for Phoebus and for Thebes.
 Not for some distant unknown friend,—myself,
For my own sake, I'll drive this evil out,
Since he that slew this King were fain perchance
Again, by the same hand, to strike . . . at me!
So, fighting for your King, I serve myself.
 Come then, my children, lift your prayerful boughs,
And leave the altar-steps. Up! No delay!
Go, someone, gather Cadmus' people here!
I will do all. Then as the god gives aid,
We'll find Good Luck . . . or else calamity! (*Exit.*)
PRIEST: Up, children, let us go! The King's own word,
You hear it, grants the boon for which we came.
Now Phoebus, who sent the oracle,
Himself to stay the plague and save us all.

 The SUPPLIANTS *leave the altars. The* THEBAN CITIZENS, *summoned
 by the King's messengers, gather in front of the Palace.*

CHORUS: Glad Message of the voice of Zeus,
From golden Pytho travelling to splendid Thebes, what burden bring-
  est thou?
 Eager, am I, afraid, heart-shaken with fear of thee—
 (Healer, Apollo of Delos, God of the Cry, give ear!)
 Shaken with reverent fear. Is it some new task to be done?
Or is it some ancient debt thou wilt sweep in the fulness of time to the
  payment?
Tell me thy secret, Oracle deathless, Daughter of golden Hope!
 First call we on the child of Zeus,
Deathless Athene; then on her that guards our land, her Sister,
  Artemis,
 Lady of Good Report, whose throne is our market place;
 Aye, and Apollo! I cry thee, Shooter of Arrows, hear!
 Three that are strong to deliver, appear! Great Fighters of Death,
Now, if in ancient times, when calamity threatened, ye came to help us,
Sweeping afar the flame of affliction,—strike, as of old, to-day!

II

Alas! Alas! Beyond all reckoning
My myriad sorrows!
All my people sick to death, yet in my mind
No shaft of wit, no weapon to fight the death.
The fruits of the mighty mother Earth increase not.
Women from their tempest of cries and travail-pangs
Struggle in vain . . . no birth-joy followeth.
As a bird on the wing, to the west, to the coast of the sunset god
Look, 'tis the soul of the dead that flies to the dark, nay, soul upon
soul,
Rushing, rushing, swifter and stronger in flight than the race of
implacable fire,

Myriads, alas, beyond all recokoning,—
A city dying!
None has pity. On the ground they lie, unwept,
Spreading contagious death; and among them wives
That wail, but not for them, aye, and grey mothers
Flocking the altar with cries, now here, now there,
Shrilling their scream of prayer . . . for their own lives.
And a shout goeth up to the Healer; and, cleaving the air like fire.
Flashes the Paean, above those voices that wail in a piping tune.
Rescue! Rescue! Golden One! Send us the light of thy rescuing, Daugh-
ter of Zeus!

III

Turn to flight that savage War-God, warring not with shield and spear,
But with fire he burneth when his battle-cry is loud,
Turn him back and drive him with a rushing into flight,
For away, to exile, far, far away from Thebes,
To the great sea-palace of Amphitrite,
Perchance to the waves of the Thracian sea and his own barbaric shore
He spareth us not. Is there aught that the night has left?
Lo! Day cometh up to destroy.
King and Lord, O Zeus, of the lightning fires,
Father of all! Thine is the Might. Take up the bolt and slay!

Phoebus, King Lycean, I would see thee string thy golden bow,
  Raining on the monster for our succour and defence
  Shafts unconquered. I would see the flashing of the fires
  From the torch of Artemis, that blazeth on the hills
      When she scours her mountains of Lycia.
And another I call, the Golden-Crowned, and his name is a name of
      Thebes;
    He is ruddy with wine, and his cry is the triumph cry,
      And his train are the Maenades;—
    Come, great Bacchus, come! With a splendour of light,
    Blazing for us, strike at the god cursed among gods, and save!

Re-enter OEDIPUS.

OEDIPUS: You pray! And for your prayer . . . release, perchance,
And succour you shall find; if you will aid
My nursing of this malady, and attend,
Obedient, to the words which I shall speak
Touching a story strange to me. I stand
A stranger to the fact, could not have proved it,
A foreigner, with no hint to guide me to it,
Yet now, a Theban among Thebans, speak
To you, to Thebes, my solemn proclamation.
  Is there among you one who knows what hand
Did murder Laïus, son of Labdacus?
That man I charge unfold the truth to me.
Say that he fear by utterance to bring
Himself in accusation . . . why, his payment
Shall not be harsh; he shall depart unharmed.
Doth any know another, citizen
Or stranger, guilty? Hide it not. Reward
I'll pay, and Thebes shall add her gratitude.
  What! You are silent still? If any fear
For a friend or for himself, and will not speak,
Then I must play my part. Attend what follows.
This man, whoe'er he be, from all the land
Whose government and sway is mine, I make
An outlaw. None shall speak to him, no roof
Shall shelter. In your sacrifice and prayer
Give him no place, nor in drink-offerings,
But drive him out of doors . . . for it is he

Pollutes us, as the oracle Pythian
Of Phoebus hath to-day revealed to me.

   Thus I take up my fight for the dead man's cause
And for the god, adding this malediction
Upon the secret criminal—came the blow
By one man's hand, or aid of many hands—
As was the deed, so be his life, accurst!
Further, if, with my knowledge, in my house
He harbour at my hearth, on mine own head
Fall every imprecation here pronounced.

   On you I lay my charge. Observe this ban
For my sake and the god's, and for your country
Now sunk in ruin, desolate, god-forsaken.
Why—such a business, even had the gods
Not moved therein, 'twas ill to leave uncleansed.
A noble gentleman, a King had perished . . .
Matter enough for probing. Well, you failed.
To-day, since I am King where he was King,
The husband of his bride, from whose one womb,
Had he been blest with progeny, had sprung
Near pledges of our bond, his fruit and mine . . .
Not so . . . fell Fortune leapt upon her prey,
And slew him. Therefore I will fight for him
As for my father; face all issues; try
All means, to find the slayer, and avenge
That child of Labdacus and Polydorus,
Agenor's offspring and great Cadmus' son.

   If any shirk this task, I pray the gods
Give to their land no increase, make their wives
Barren, and with the like calamities,
Nay, worse than ours to-day, so let them perish.

   On you, the rest of Thebes, who make my will
Your own—may Righteousness, who fights for us,
And all the gods wait on you still with good.

CHORUS: O King, as bound beneath thy curse I speak.
I neither slew, nor can I point to him
That slew. The quest . . . Apollo, he that sent
The oracle, should tell who is the man.

OEDIPUS: 'Twere just. Yet lives there any man so strong,
Can force unwilling gods to do his will?

CHORUS: I think, the second best . . . if I may speak . . .

OEDIPUS: Aye, if you have a third best, speak it! speak it!

CHORUS: The great Teiresias, more than other men,
Sees as great Phoebus sees. From him, great King,
The searcher of this case were best instructed.
OEDIPUS: There I have not been slothful. I have sent—
Creon advising—I have sent for him
Twice . . . It is very strange . . . Is he not yet come?
CHORUS: Well, well. The rest's old vague unmeaning talk.
OEDIPUS: What talk? What talk? I must neglect no hint.
CHORUS: He died, they said, at the hand of travellers.
OEDIPUS: I heard it too. And he that saw . . . none sees him!
CHORUS: Nay, if he have the touch of fear, he'll not
Abide thy dreadful curse. He needs must speak.
OEDIPUS: Phrases to frighten him that dared the doing?
CHORUS: Yet hath he his accuser. See! They bring
The sacred prophet hither, in whose soul,
As in no other mortal's, liveth truth.

Enter TEIRESIAS, *led by a boy.*

OEDIPUS: Teiresias, thou that judgest all the signs
That move in heaven and earth—the secret things,
And all that men may learn—thine eyes are blind,
Yet canst thou feel our city's plight, whereof
Thou are the champion, in whom alone,
Prophet and Prince, we find our saving help!
Phoebus hath sent—perchance my messengers
Spoke not of it—this answer to our sending.
One only way brings riddance of the plague:—
To find, and kill or banish, them that killed
King Laïus. Come! Be lavish of thy skill.
By hint of birds, by all thy mantic arts,
Up! Save thyself and me, save Thebes, and heal
All the pollution of that murdered King!
See, we are in thy hands. 'Tis good to serve
Thy fellows by all means, with all thou hast.
TEIRESIAS: Ah me! It is but sorrow to be wise
When wisdom profits not. All this I knew,
Yet missed the meaning. Else I had not come.
OEDIPUS: Why, what is this? How heavily thou comest!
TEIRESIAS: Dismiss me home. Be ruled by me. The load
Will lighter press on thee, as mine on me.
OEDIPUS: Dost thou refuse us? In thy words I find

Small love for Thebes, thy nurse, and for her law.

TEIRESIAS: 'Tis that I see thy own word quit the path
Of safety, and I would not follow thee.

OEDIPUS: Oh, if thy wisdom knows, turn not away!
We kneel to thee. All are thy suppliants.

TEIRESIAS: For none of you is wise, and none shall know
From me this evil . . . call it mine, not thine!

OEDIPUS: Thou knowest? And thou will not tell? Thy mind
Is set, to play us false, and ruin Thebes?

TEIRESIAS: I spare myself and thee. Why question me?
'Tis useless, for I will not answer thee.

OEDIPUS: Not answer me! So, scoundrel! . . . Thou wouldst heat
A stone. . . . Thou wilt not? Can we wring from thee
Nothing but stubborn hopeless heartlessness?

TEIRESIAS: My stubborn heart thou chidest, and the wrath
To which thy own is mated, canst not see.

OEDIPUS: Have I no cause for anger? Who unmoved
Could brook the slight such answers put on Thebes?

TEIRESIAS: Though I hide all in silence, all must come.

OEDIPUS: Why, if all must, more cause to tell me all.

TEIRESIAS: I speak no more. So, if it pleasure thee,
Rage on in the full fury of thy wrath!

OEDIPUS: Aye, so I will—speak out my wrath, and spare
No jot of all I see. Listen! I see
In thee the plotter of the deed, in thee,
Save for the blow, the doer. Hadst thou eyes,
Then had I said—the killing too was thine.

TEIRESIAS: So! Is it so?—I bid thee, by the words
Of thy decree abiding, from this day
That lights thee now, speak not to these or me:
Since thou art foul, and thou pollutest Thebes.

OEDIPUS: So bold, so shameless? Can you dare to launch
Such impudent malice, and still look for safety?

TEIRESIAS: Safe am I now. The truth in me is strong.

OEDIPUS: The truth? Who taught it you? 'Twas not your art.

TEIRESIAS: Thyself. I would not speak. Thou madest me.

OEDIPUS: Once more. What was it? I must have it plain.

TEIRESIAS: Spoke I not plainly? Art thou tempting me?

OEDIPUS: I am not sure I took it. Speak again.

TEIRESIAS: Thou seekest, and thou art, the murderer!

OEDIPUS: A second time that slander! You shall rue it.

TEIRESIAS: Shall I add more to make thee rage the more?

OEDIPUS: Add all you will. Say on. 'Tis wasted breath.
TEIRESIAS: I tell thee, with thy dearest, knowing nought,
Thou liv'st in shame, seeing not thine own ill.
OEDIPUS: You talk and talk and fear no punishment?
TEIRESIAS: Aye, none, if there be any strength in truth.
OEDIPUS: 'Tis strong enough for all, but not for thee.
Blind eyes, blind ears, blind heart, thou hast it not.
TEIRESIAS: And *thou* hast . . . misery, this to mock in me
Which soon shall make all present mock at thee.
OEDIPUS: Night, endless night is on thee. How canst thou
Hurt me or any man that see the light?
TIERESIAS: Thou art not doomed to fall by me. Apollo,
Who worketh out this end, sufficeth thee—
OEDIPUS: —Creon!—Was this invention his, or thine?—
TEIRESIAS: Nor is thy ruin Creon. 'Tis thyself!
OEDIPUS: O Wealth, O Kingship and thou, gift of Wit
That conquers in life's rivalry of skill,
What hate, what envy come with you! For this,
The government, put in my hand by Thebes,
A gift I asked not,—can it be for this;
Creon, the true, Creon, so long my friend,
Can plot my overthrow, can creep and scheme
And set on me this tricking fraud, this quack,
This crafty magic-monger—quick to spy
Ill-gotten gain, but blind in prophecy.
Aye . . . Where have you shown skill? Come, tell me.
   Where?
When that fell bitch was here with riddling hymn
Why were you silent? Not one word or hint
To save this people? Why? That puzzle cried
For mantic skill, not common human wit;
And skill, as all men saw, you had it not;
No birds, no god informed you. I, the fool,
Ignorant Oedipus,—no birds to teach me—
Must come, and hit the truth, and stop the song;—
The man whom you would banish—in the thought
To make yourself a place—by Creon's throne!
You and your plotter will not find, I think,
Blood-hunting pays! You have the look of age:
Else, your own pain should teach you what you are!
CHORUS: We think the prophet's word came but from wrath,
And, as we think, O King, from wrath thine own.

We need not this. Our need is thought, how best
Resolve the god's decree, how best fulfill it.
TEIRESIAS: Though thou be master, thou must brook one right's
Equality—reply! Speech yet is mine,
Since I am not thy slave, nor Creon's man
And client, but the slave of Loxias.

   I speak then. Thou hast taunted me for blind,
Thou, who hast eyes and dost not see the ill
Thou standest in, the ill that shares thy house,—
Dost know whose child thou art?—nor see that hate
Is thine from thy own kin, here and below.
Twin-scourged, a mother's Fury and thy father's,
Swift, fatal, dogging thee, shall drive thee forth,
Till thou, that seest so true, see only night,
And cry with cries that every place shall harbour,
And all Cithaeron ring back to thee,
When thou shalt know thy Marriage . . . and the end
Of that blithe bridal-voyage, whose port is death!

   Full many other evils that thou know'st not
Shall pull thee down from pride and level thee
With thy own brood, aye, with the thing thou art!

   So then, rail on at Creon: if thou wilt,
Rail on at me who speak: yet know that thou
Must perish, and no man so terribly.
OEDIPUS: Can this be borne? This, and from such as he?
Go, and destruction take thee! Hence! Away!
Quick! . . . Leave my house . . . begone the way thou camest.
TEIRESIAS: That way I had not come hadst thou not called me.
OEDIPUS: I little thought to hear such folly; else
I had made little haste to summon thee.
TEIRESIAS: Such as thou say'st I am; for thee a fool,
But for thy parents that begat thee, wise.
OEDIPUS: My parents! Stay! Who is my father? . . . Speak!
TEIRESIAS: This day shall give thee birth and shall destroy thee.
OEDIPUS: Riddles again! All subtle and all vague!
TEIRESIAS: Thou can'st read riddles as none other can.
OEDIPUS: Aye, taunt me there! There thou shalt find me great.
TEIRESIAS: 'Tis just that Luck of thine hath ruined thee.
OEDIPUS: What matter? I saved Thebes, and I care nothing.
TEIRESIAS: Then I will go. Come, lad, conduct me hence.
OEDIPUS: Aye. Bid him take thee hence. Here thou dost clog
And hinder—once well sped, wilt harm no more!

TEIRESIAS: I go, yet speak my message, fearing not
Thee and thy frown. No way canst thou destroy me.
Wherefore I tell thee . . . He whom thou this while
Hast sought with threatenings and with publishings
Of Laïus' murder—that same man is here,
Now called a stranger in our midst, but soon
He shall be known, a Theban born, yet find
Small pleasure in it. Blind, that once had sight,
A beggar, once so rich, in a foreign land
A wanderer, with a staff groping his way,
He shall be known—the brother of the sons
He fathered; to the woman out of whom
He sprang, both son and husband;—and the sire
Whose bed he fouled, he murdered! Get thee in,
And think, and think. Then, if thou find'st I lie,
Then say I have no wit for prophecy! (*Exit* TEIRESIAS. OEDIPUS, *deeply moved, withdraws into the Palace.*)

CHORUS: Who is the man of wrong, seen by the Delphian Crag
     oracular?
  Seen and guilty—blood on his hand—from a sin unspeakable!
        Now shall he fly!
     Swifter, stronger than horses of storm,
        Fly! It is time!
Armed with the fire and the lightning, the Child of Zeus leapeth upon
     him:
     After the god swarm the dreadful Fates unerring.
     Swift as a flame of light, leapeth a Voice, from the snows
        Parnassian,
    Voice of Phoebus, hunting the sinner that lurks invisible.
        Lost in the wild,
     Rock and forest and cavernous haunt
        Rangeth the bull,
Lost and alone—to escape from the words that fly, swift from Apollo's
     Oracle shrine:—stinging words that swarm and die not.
        The prophet wise, reader of bird and sign,
           Terribly moveth me.
        I cannot deny. I cannot approve. I knew not what to say.
       I brood and waver. I know not the truth of the day or the morrow.
I know not any quarrel that the Labdacids have, or have ever had, with
     the son of Polybus,
     Nor proof to make me stand against the praise men give to
     Oedipus,

Though I fight for the Labdacids, to avenge the King's strange
death,

The only Wise, Zeus and Apollo, know
Truth and the way of man,

They know! Can a prophet know? Can a man know more than
common men?
No proof is found. Yet a man may be wiser, I know, than his
fellow.
Until the charge be proven good, let the world cry "Guilty," never will
I consent with it.
We saw the maid of fatal wing: we know the helper.
Wise and true
To the city of Thebes, he came. I will never call him false.

Enter CREON.

CREON: Good citizens, news of a monstrous charge
Spoken by Oedipus the King against me
Brings me indignant here. Can he believe
That I am guilty in this perilous time
Of act or word conducing to his hurt?
I care no more for life, with such a tale
Abroad—no vexing trifle, but a charge
Of great concern and import—to be called
By you, my country, and my friends, a traitor!
CHORUS: It was not reasoned judgment, but the stress,
Perhaps, of anger, forced the bitter words.
CREON: So, then, the words were uttered, that I plotted
And won the seer to make his tale a lie?
CHORUS: 'Twas spoken so. I know not with what thought.
CREON: Was the mind steady, was the eye unchanged,
When the King spoke against my loyalty?
CHORUS: I know not. What my masters do, I see not.

Enter OEDIPUS.

Look! In good time, the King himself is come!
OEDIPUS: Fellow, what brings you here? Are you so bold,
Unblushingly to venture to the house
Of him you would destroy, proved murderer,
Brigand, and traitor, that would steal my throne?

Tell me, come, tell me. When you plotted this,
Seemed I a fool or coward? Did you think
I should not see the crime so cunningly
Preparing, or could see and not prevent?
What! Without friends or money did you hunt
A Kingdom? 'Twas a foolish enterprise.
Kingdoms are caught by numbers and by gold!
CREON: This right I bid thee do. As thou hast spoken,
So hear me. Then, when thou hast knowledge, judge.
OEDIPUS: Glib art thou . . . and I slow to learn—from thee,
In whom I find so harsh an enemy.
CREON: This one thing first, this one thing let me say—
OEDIPUS: This one thing never—that thou art not false.
CREON: Nay, if you think unreasoned stubbornness
A thing to value, 'tis an evil thought.
OEDIPUS: Nay, if you think to do your kinsman wrong
And scape the penalty . . . 'tis a mad thought.
CREON: Aye, true, and justly spoken. But the hurt
You think that I have done you, tell it me.
OEDIPUS: Did you, or did you not, urge me 'twas best
To summon his grand reverence, the prophet?
CREON: Even as I first advised, so I think still.
OEDIPUS: How long ago, tell me did Laïus . . .
CREON: What, that he did? I have not understood.
OEDIPUS: Pass, by that stroke that slew him, from men's sight?
CREON: 'Tis a long count of many long-sped days.
OEDIPUS: This prophet—well! Was he in practice then?
CREON: Honoured as now, wise as he is to-day.
OEDIPUS: So? In those days spoke he at all of me?
CREON: Never, when I was present, aught of thee.
OEDIPUS: And did you make no question for the dead?
CREON: Question, be sure, we made—but had no answer.
OEDIPUS: That day this wise man did not breathe it! Why?
CREON: I know not. Where I am not wise, I speak not.
OEDIPUS: One thing you know.—Be wise, then, and confess it.
CREON: What is it? If I know I'll not deny.
OEDIPUS: Had you not been with him, he had not hinted
My name, my compassing of Laïus' fall.
CREON: Doth he so? You best know. Nay, let me ask,
And do you answer, as I answered you.
OEDIPUS: Ask! You will never prove me murderer!
CREON: First, then:—is not your wedded wife my sister?
OEDIPUS: A truth allowed and not deniable!

CREON: Joint partner of your honours and your lands?
OEDIPUS: Freely she has her every wish of me.
CREON: Am not I third, in equal partnership?
OEDIPUS: Aye, and 'tis that proves thee a traitor friend.
CREON: No! Reason with thyself, as reason I,
And, first, consider—Who would be a King
That lives with terrors, when he might sleep sound,
Knowing no fear, and wield the selfsame sway?
Not such an one as I. My nature craves
To live a King's life, not to be a King:—
And so think all who know what Wisdom is.
Through you, all unafraid, I win my will;
To crown me were to lay constraints on me.
What can the despot's throne confer more sweet
Than peaceful sway and princely influence?
When all clean gains of honourable life
Are mine, must I run mad, and thirst for more?
"Good-day" cries all the world, and open-armed
Greets me! The King's own suitors call for me,
Since that way lies success! What? Leave all this,
To win that Nothing? No, Disloyalty
Were neither reason nor good policy.
My nature holds no lust for that high thought,
And loathes the man who puts that thought in act.
    Thus you may prove it—go to Pytho: ask
If well and truly I have brought my message:
Or thus—discover plot or plan wherein
The seer and I joined council—I'll pronounce
The sentence, add my voice to thine, for death!
Only, on vague suspicion charge me not.
It is not fair, it is not just, for nothing
To call a true man false, a false man true!
To cast a good friend off—it is as if
You cast the very life you love away.
    Well, Time shall teach you surely. For 'tis Time,
And only Time, can prove a true man's worth,
Where one short day discovers villainy!
CHORUS: Good words, O King, for one that hath a care
To scape a fall. Hot thoughts are dangerous!
OEDIPUS: Ah! Where a secret plotter to his end
Moves hot, as hotly must I counter him.
Shall I sit still and bide his time? My all

Were lost, in error mazed, and his work done.
CREON: Come then. What is your will? To cast me forth . . .
OEDIPUS: Not so! My will is death, not banishment.
CREON: Still so unmoved? Can you not trust my word?
OEDIPUS: No, you must prove the folly of ambition!
CREON: Have you such wisdom?
OEDIPUS: I can play my hand!
CREON: But should play fair with me! . . .
OEDIPUS: —who are so false!
CREON: If you are blinded. . .
OEDIPUS: Still I must be King!
CREON: Better unkinged, than Tyrant. . .
OEDIPUS: Thebes—my Thebes!
CREON: *My* Thebes, as thine! Both are her citizens!
CHORUS: Peace, princes! See where from the palace comes
Jocasta, in your time of need. With her
Turn into good the evil of this quarrel.

Enter JOCASTA.

JOCASTA: O foolish! foolish! Why this rioting
Of ill-conditioned words? For shame, with Thebes
So suffering, to open private sores!
    Come in! . . . Go, Creon, home! . . . You must not turn
What matters nothing into a great wrong.
CREON: Sister, your husband Oedipus claims right
To do me grievous wrong—his fatal choice,
To thrust me from my country, or to slay me!
OEDIPUS: Aye, wife, 'tis true. I find him practising
Against my person craft and treachery.
CREON: An oath! If aught in all this charge be true,
Desert me good! May my own oath destroy me!
JOCASTA: Believe, believe him, Oedipus! Respect
My prayer, and these, thy friends, that pray to thee,
And, if not these, that oath's solemnity!

I

CHORUS: King, we are thy suppliants, Yield, be kind, be wise.
OEDIPUS: What would you have me yield?

CHORUS: Spurn not him that never yet was false, and now is strong in his great oath.
OEDIPUS: Know you the thing you ask?
CHORUS: We know.
OEDIPUS: Speak on!
CHORUS: Thy friend, so terribly bound by his oath to truth,
      For mere suspicion's sake,
   Cast not away, blamed and disgraced.
OEDIPUS: Be not deceived. As thus you ask, for me
You ask destruction, or my flight from Thebes.

CHORUS: Never! By him that is prince of the gods, the Sun,
      If that thought be in us,
    Hopeless, godless, friendless, may we perish!
Not so! Our hearts are heavy. The land we love is perishing.
And now shall a hurt yourselves have made be added to the wrong?

OEDIPUS: So! Let him go . . . though I be slain for it,
Or shamed, and violently thrust from Thebes.
It is your pleading voice, 'tis not his oath,
Hath moved me. Him I shall hate where'er he be.
CREON: You yield, but still you hate; and as you pass
From passion, you are hard. 'Tis very plain.
Such men—'tis just—reap for themselves most pain!
OEDIPUS: Go! Get you gone, and leave me!
CREON: I will go!
You know not, pity not. These trust me still, and know! (*Exit* CREON.)

II

CHORUS: Lady, stay no longer! Take your lord within. 'Tis time!
JOCASTA: First tell me what has happened.
CHORUS: Words that bred conjecture lacking knowledge, charges whose injustice galls.
JOCASTA: Came they from both?
CHORUS: From both.
JOCASTA: Tell me, what words?
CHORUS: Enough! Already the land is afflicted sore!
     For me, enough that strife
   Fell, as it fell. There let it lie!

OEDIPUS: See where it leads you, though the thought was kind,
To stay my hand and blunt my purposes.

CHORUS: King, we have told it thee often, again we tell.
                Could we put thee from us,
            Call us fools and bankrupt of all wisdom.
Not so! When this dear land on a sea of woes was perishing,
You brought her a wind of Fortune. Steer the ship once more safe
home!

JOCASTA: I pray you, husband, give me also leave
To know the cause of this so steadfast wrath.
OEDIPUS: I'll tell it. You are more to me than these.
'Twas Creon, and his plotting for my hurt.
JOCASTA: Speak on, my lord. Make charge and quarrel plain.
OEDIPUS: He says I am the murderer of Laïus.
JOCASTA: Of his own knowledge? Or on evidence?
OEDIPUS: No, he has brought a rascal prophet in
To speak, and save his own lips from the lie!
JOCASTA: Then leave these thoughts. . . . Listen to me and learn,
Listen . . . I'll give my proof.—On soothsaying
Nothing depends. An oracle once came
To Laïus—I'll not say it came from Phoebus,
But from his ministers—that he should die
Some day, slain by a son of him and me.
Now, the King . . . strangers, robbers murdered him,
So runs report, at a place where three roads meet.
And the child, not yet three days from the birth,
He took, and pierced his ankles, fettered him,
And cast him out to die on the barren hills.
Phoebus fulfilled not that; made not the son
His father's murderer; wrought not the thing
That haunted Laïus, death by that son's hand.
So dread, so false was prophecy! And you
Regard it not. The god will easily
Bring to the light whate'er he seeks and wills.
OEDIPUS: Wife, as I heard you speak, within my soul
What trouble stirred! What fearful doubt was born!
JOCASTA: What moves you to speak thus? What is your fear?
OEDIPUS: I seemed to hear you say that Laïus
Was murdered at a place where three roads meet.
JOCASTA: So it was said, and so it still is said.

OEDIPUS: Tell me the country where this thing was done?

JOCASTA: Phocis the land is called, where meet the roads
That run from Delphi and from Daulia.

OEDIPUS: Tell me how long ago?

JOCASTA: 'Twas publishéd
Just before you were known as King in Thebes.

OEDIPUS: O Zeus, what is it thou wilt do with me!

JOCASTA: What is it, Oedipus, in this, that moves you?

OEDIPUS: Ask nothing yet. Tell me of Laïus—
What was his stature? Tell me, how old was he?

JOCASTA: Tall, and his hair turning to grey, his shape
Not unlike yours—

OEDIPUS: My curse! Oh, ignorant!
Alas! I see it was myself I cursed.

JOCASTA: Speak! When I look at you I am afraid—

OEDIPUS: My thoughts are heavy. Had the prophet eyes
Help me to make it clear: one answer more—

JOCASTA: I am afraid, but ask! If I know, I'll tell.

OEDIPUS: How travelled Laïus? Went he out, alone,
Or, like a King, with retinue and guard?

JOCASTA: They were five, five in all, and one of them
A herald—and one chariot for the King.

OEDIPUS: All out, alas! All clear! Come, tell me, wife,
Who brought the news? Who gave you that report?

JOCASTA: One servant who alone escaped alive.

OEDIPUS: Where is that servant now? Here, in my house?

JOCASTA: No, no! He is not here. When he came home,
And saw you on the throne, and Laïus dead,
He touched me by the hand, beseeching me
To send him out into some pasture lands
Far off, to live far from the sight of Thebes.
And I—I sent him—he deservèd, my lord,
Though but a slave, as much, nay more, than this.

OEDIPUS: Come, we must have him back, and instantly!

JOCASTA: 'Tis easy. . . . Yet—What would you with the man?

OEDIPUS: I fear myself, dear wife; I fear that I
Have said too much, and therefore I must see him.

JOCASTA: Then he shall come. Yet, have not I some claim
To know the thought that so afflicts my lord?

OEDIPUS: I'll not refuse that claim, so deep am I
Gone in forebodings. None so close as you,
To learn what ways of destiny are mine.

My father was of Corinth, Polybus;
My mother Merope, Dorian. As a prince
I lived at first in Corinth, till there fell
A stroke of Fortune, very strange, and yet
Not worth such passion as it moved in me.
Some fellow, at a banquet, flown with wine,
Called me my father's bastard, drunkenly;
And I was angry, yet for that one day
Held myself back, though hardly. Then I sought
Mother and father, questioning; and they
Were hot in their resentment of the taunt;
And I was glad to see them angry. Still
It rankled, and I felt the rumour grow.
I told my parents nothing, but set out
For Pytho. Phoebus, for my journey's pains,
Gave me no clue—dismissed me—yet flashed forth,
In words most strange and sad and horrible:—
'Thou shalt defile thy mother, show mankind
A brood by thee begot intolerable,
And shalt be thy own father's murderer.'
    When this I heard, I fled. Where Corinth lay
Henceforth I guessed but by the stars. My road
Was exile, where I might escape the sight
Of that foul oracle's shame fulfilled on me.
    And as I went, I came to that same land
In which you tell me that your King was slain.
    Wife, I will tell you all the truth. I passed
Close by that meeting of three ways, and there
A herald met me, and a man that drove
Steeds and a car, even as you have said.
The leader and the old man too were fain
To thrust me rudely from the road. But I,
When one that led the horses jostled me,
Struck him in anger. This the old man saw,
And, from the car—watching for me to pass—
Dashed down his forking goad full on my head—
But paid me double for it. Instantly,
Out from the car, my staff and this right hand
Smote him and hurled him backward to the ground,
And all of them I slew.
                          If there be aught
That makes that stranger one with Laïus,

There lives no wretch to-day so sad as I,
Nor ever can be one more scorned of heaven
Than I, whom none may welcome, citizen
Or stranger, to his home; nor speak to me;
But only drive me out. And this—'twas I,
No other, on myself invoked this curse.
These hands, by which he died, pollute his bed
And her that shared it. Am I vile enough?
Am I not all uncleanness. I must fly;
And, though I fly from Thebes, must never set
My foot in my own country, never see
My people there, or else I must be joined
In marriage with my mother, and must kill
My father, Polybus, that got and reared me.
   If any judge my life and find therein
Malignant stars at work, he hath the truth.
   No, No! Ye pure and awful gods, forbid
That I should see that day! Oh, let me pass
Out from the world of men, before my doom
Of living set so foul a blot on me!

CHORUS: O King, we fear thy words, yet bid thee hope,
Till he that saw the deed bring certainty.

OEDIPUS: Why—hope, one little hope, remains. 'Tis this:—
To wait that herdsman's coming; nothing more.

JOCASTA: What—if he comes—what would you have of him?

OEDIPUS: Listen, and I will tell you. If it prove
He speaks as you have spoken, I am saved.

JOCASTA: Tell me, what was it in my words?

OEDIPUS: You said
This was his tale, that robbers slew the King,
Robbers. If he confirm it, if he speak
Of robbers still, it was not I, not I,
That slew. One man is not a company.
But if he names one lonely wayfarer,
Then the deed sways to me, and all is true.

JOCASTA: No. It is certain. When he brought his news
He told it thus. Not I alone, but all
The city heard. He cannot take it back.
And should he swerve a little from his story,
He cannot show, my King, that Laïus died
As prophets would have had him. Loxias
Declared a son of mine must murder him;—

And then that poor lost creature never lived
To kill him. Long ere that, my child was dead.
Since that, for all the soothsayers can tell,
I go straight on, I look not left nor right.
OEDIPUS: 'Tis well. 'Tis very well. And yet—that slave—
Send for him. Have him fetched. Do not neglect it.
JOCASTA: I'll send without delay. Let us go in.
I will do nothing, nothing, but to please you. (*Exeunt* OEDIPUS *and*
.   JOCASTA.)

CHORUS: Be the prize of all my days
        In every word, in every deed,
            Purity, with Reverence.
    Laws thereof are set before us.
                In the heights they move.
        They were born where Heaven is,
        And Olympus fathered them.
        Mortal parent have they none.
    Nor shall man's forgetfulness ever make them sleep.
        A god in them is great. He grows not old.

        Insolence it is that breeds
    A tyrant, Insolence enriched
        Overmuch with vanities,
    Gains unmeet, that give no profit.
                So he climbs the height,
        So down to a destiny
        Evil utterly he leaps,
        Where there is no help at all.
    True Ambition, for the State, quench it not, O God!
        Apollo, still in thee is my defence.

        True Ambition, yes! But if a man
            Tread the ways of Arrogance;
    Fear not Justice, honour not the gods enshrined;
        Evil take him; Ruin be the prize
                Of his fatal pride!
        If his gain be gain of wrong,
        If he know not reverence,
        If in vanity he dare profane
            Sanctities inviolate,

Then from the arrows of the gods what mortal man shall save his
soul alive?
If doings such as these be countenanced,
What mean religion's holy dance and hymn?

No more shall I seek in reverence
Earth's inviolate Central Shrine;
No more go to Abai, nor Olympia;
If before all eyes the oracle
Fit not the event!
Zeus, if thou art rightly named,
King and Master over all,
Save thine honour! Let not this escape
Thine eternal governance!
Look to thy oracles of old concerning Laïus; put to nought by
man,
They fade, nor is Apollo glorified
In worship any more. Religion dies!

Enter JOCASTA.

JOCASTA: Princes of Thebes, the thought has come to me
To seek the temples of the gods with boughs
Of supplication and these offerings
Of incense. Oedipus, much overwrought,
And every way distracted, cannot judge
The present sanely by the past, but lends
All ears to every voice that bids him fear.
So, since my words are spent in vain, I come
To thee, Apollo—thou art near to us,
Lycean!—and I pray thee, take the gift,
And grant some clean way of deliverance!
We are afraid; for Oedipus, the guide
And captain of us all, runs mad with fear.

Enter a MESSENGER *from Corinth.*

MESSENGER: Can you direct me, strangers, to the house
Of Oedipus, your Master?—Better still,
Perchance you know where I may find the King?
CHORUS: This is the house, and he within. The Queen,
His wife and mother of his home, is here.

MESSENGER: His wife, and blest with offspring! Happiness
Wait on her always, and on all her home!
JOCASTA: I wish you happy too. Your gracious speech
Deserves no less. Tell me, with what request
You are come hither, or what news you bring.
MESSENGER: Lady, good news for him and all his house.
JOCASTA: Why, what good news is this? Who sent you here?
MESSENGER: I come from Corinth, and have that to tell
I think will please, though it be partly sad.
JOCASTA: How can a sad tale please? Come, tell it me!
MESSENGER: The people of that country, so men said,
Will choose him monarch of Corinthia.
JOCASTA: What? Is old Polybus no longer King?
MESSENGER: No longer King. Death has him in the grave.
JOCASTA: Dead! Say you so? Oedipus' father dead?
MESSENGER: If he be not so, may I die myself!
JOCASTA: Quick! To your master, girl; tell him this news!
O oracles of the gods, where are you now!
This was the man that Oedipus so feared
To slay, he needs must leave his country. Dead!
And 'tis not Oedipus, but Fortune slew him!

Enter OEDIPUS.

OEDIPUS: Tell me, Jocasta, wife of my dear love,
Why you have called me hither, out of doors.
JOCASTA: Let this man speak; and as you listen, judge
The issue of the god's grand oracles!
OEDIPUS: This man, who is he? What has he to tell?
JOCASTA: He comes from Corinth, and will tell you this:—
Polybus is no more. Your father's dead.
OEDIPUS: What! Is this true, sir? Answer for yourself!
MESSENGER: If this must needs come first in my report,
'Tis true enough. King Polybus is dead.
OEDIPUS: By treachery? Or did sickness visit him?
MESSENGER: A little shift of the scale, and old men sleep.
OEDIPUS: Ah! My poor father died, you say, by sickness?
MESSENGER: Yes, and by reason of his length of days.
OEDIPUS: Ah, me! Wife, why should any man regard
The Delphic Hearth oracular, and the birds
That scream above us—guides, whose evidence
Doomed me to kill my father, who is dead,

Yes, buried underground, and I stand here,
And have not touched my weapon.—Stay! Perchance
'Twas grief for me. I may have slain him so.
Anyhow, he is dead, and to his grave
Has carried all these oracles—worth nothing!
JOCASTA: Worth nothing. Did I not tell you so long since?
OEDIPUS: You told me, but my fears misguided me.
JOCASTA: Banish your fears, and think no more of them.
OEDIPUS: No, no! Should I not fear my mother's bed?
JOCASTA: Why, what should a man fear? Luck governs all!
There's no foreknowledge, and no providence!
Take life at random. Live as best you can.
That's the best way. What! Fear that you may wed
Your mother? Many a man has dreamt as much,
And so may you! The man who values least
Such scruples, lives his life most easily.
OEDIPUS: All this were well enough, that you have said,
Were not my mother living. Though your words
Be true, my mother lives, and I must fear.
JOCASTA: Your father's death at least is a great hope.
OEDIPUS: Yes, but she lives, and I am still afraid.
MESSENGER: What woman is the cause of all these terrors?
OEDIPUS: Merope, sir, that dwelt with Polybus.
MESSENGER: What find you both to fear in Merope?
OEDIPUS: An oracle from the gods, most terrible.
MESSENGER: May it be told, or did the gods forbid?
OEDIPUS: No, you may hear it. Phoebus hath said that I
Must come to know my mother's body, come
To shed with my own hand my father's blood.
Therefore I have put Corinth this long time
Far from me. Fortune has been kind, and yet
To see a parent's face is best of all.
MESSENGER: Was this the fear that drove you from your home?
OEDIPUS: This, and my will never to slay my father.
MESSENGER: Then since I only came to serve you, sir,
Why should I hesitate to end your fear?
OEDIPUS: Ah! If you could, you should be well rewarded!
MESSENGER: Why, that was my chief thought in coming here,
To do myself some good when you come home.
OEDIPUS: No, where my parents are, I'll not return!
MESSENGER: Son, I can see, you know not what you do.
OEDIPUS: 'Fore God, what mean you, sir? Say what you know.

MESSENGER: If this be all that frightens you from home!—

OEDIPUS: All? 'Tis the fear Apollo may prove true—

MESSENGER: And you polluted, and your parents wronged?

OEDIPUS: Aye, it is that, good man! Always that fear!

MESSENGER: Can you not see the folly of such fancies?

OEDIPUS: Folly? Why folly, since I am their son?

MESSENGER: Because King Polybus was nothing to you!

OEDIPUS: How now? The father that begot me, nothing?

MESSENGER: No more, no less, than I who speak to you!

OEDIPUS: How should my father rank with nought—with you?

MESSENGER: He never was your father, nor am I.

OEDIPUS: His reason, then, for calling me his son?

MESSENGER: You were a gift. He had you from these arms.

OEDIPUS: He gave that great love to a stranger's child?

MESSENGER: Because he had none of his own to love.

OEDIPUS: So. Did you buy this child,—or was it yours?

MESSENGER: I found you where Cithaeron's valleys wind.

OEDIPUS: Our Theban hills! What made you travel here?

MESSENGER: Once on these very hills I kept my flocks.

OEDIPUS: A shepherd? Travelling to earn your wages?

MESSENGER: Yes, but your saviour too, my son, that day!

OEDIPUS: What ailed me, that you found me in distress?

MESSENGER: Ask your own feet. They best can answer that.

OEDIPUS: No, no! Why name that old familiar hurt?

MESSENGER: I set you free. Your feet were pinned together!

OEDIPUS: A brand of shame, alas! from infancy!

MESSENGER: And from that fortune comes the name you bear.

OEDIPUS: Who named me? Father or mother? Speak!

MESSENGER: I know not. He that gave you to me—may!

OEDIPUS: You found me not? You had me from another?

MESSENGER: Another shepherd bade me take you. True.

OEDIPUS: What shepherd? Can you tell me? Do you know?

MESSENGER: I think they called him one of Laïus' people.

OEDIPUS: Laïus? The same that once was King in Thebes?

MESSENGER: Aye. 'Twas the same. For him he shepherded.

OEDIPUS: Ah! Could I find him! Is he still alive?

MESSENGER: You best can tell, you, natives of the place!

OEDIPUS: Has any man here present knowledge of
The shepherd he describes? Has any seen,
Or here or in the pastures, such an one?
Speak! It is time for full discovery!

CHORUS: I think, my lord, he means that countryman

Whose presence you desired. But there is none,
Perchance, can tell you better than the Queen.
OEDIPUS: You heard him, wife. Think you he means the man
Whom we await already? Was it he?
JOCASTA: What matter what he means? Oh, take no heed,
And waste no thoughts, I beg you, on such tales.
OEDIPUS: For me it is not possible—to hold
Such clues as these, and leave my secret so.
JOCASTA: No! By the gods, no; leave it, if you care
For your own life. I suffer. 'Tis enough.
OEDIPUS: Take heart. *Your* noble blood is safe, although
I prove thrice bastard, and three times a slave!
JOCASTA: Yet, I beseech you, yield, and ask no more.
OEDIPUS: I cannot yield my right to know the truth.
JOCASTA: And yet I speak—I think—but for your good.
OEDIPUS: And this same good, I find, grows tedious.
JOCASTA: Alas! I pray you may not know yourself.
OEDIPUS: Go, someone, fetch the herdsman! Let the Queen
Enjoy her pride in her fine family!
JOCASTA: O Wretched, Wretched utterly! That name
I give you, and henceforth no other name! (*Exit.*)
CHORUS: Why went the Queen so swiftly, Oedipus,
As by some anguish moved? Alas! I fear
Lest from that silence something ill break forth.
OEDIPUS: Break what break will! My will shall be to see
My origin however mean! For her,
She is a woman, proud, and woman's pride
Likes not perhaps a husband humbly got!

   I am Luck's child. Deeming myself her son,
I shall not be disowned. She lavishes
Good gifts upon me, she's my nature's mother!
Her moons, my cousins, watched my littleness
Wax and grow great. I'll not deny my nature
But be myself and prove my origin.

CHORUS: To-morrow brings full moon!
         All hail, Cithaeron! Hail!
   If there be wit in me, or any prophet-power,
         To-morrow bringeth thee
      Fresh glory. Oedipus the King
      Shall sing thy praise and call thee his!
         His mother and his nurse!

All Thebes shall dance to thee, and hymn thy hill,
Because it is well-pleasing to the King.
Apollo, hear us! Be this thing thy pleasure too!

Who is thy mother, child?
Is it a maid, perchance,
Of that fair family that grows not old with years,
Embraced upon the hills
By roving Pan? Or else a bride
Of Loxias, who loveth well
All upland pasturage?
Did Hermes, or that dweller on the hills,
Bacchus, from one of Helicon's bright Nymphs,
His chosen playmates, take the child for his delight?

OEDIPUS: If I may guess—I never met the man—
I think, good friends, yonder I see the herd
Whom we so long have sought. His many years
Confirm it, for they tally with the years
Of this our other witness; and the guides
I know for men of mine. Can *you*, perchance,
Be certain? You have seen, and know the man.

Enter HERDSMAN.

CHORUS: Indeed I know him. Laïus trusted him,
Though but a shepherd, more than other men.
OEDIPUS: This question first to you, Corinthian:—
Is this the man you mean?
MESSENGER: Aye, this is he.
OEDIPUS: Look hither, sir, and answer everything
That I shall ask. Were you once Laïus' man?
HERDSMAN: I was, a house-bred servant, no bought slave!
OEDIPUS: What was your work? What was your way of life?
HERDSMAN: The chief part of my life I kept the flocks.
OEDIPUS: Which were the regions where you camped the most?
HERDSMAN: Cithaeron—or sometimes the country round.
OEDIPUS: Ah, then you know this man? You saw him there?
HERDSMAN: I saw him? Saw him when? What man, my lord?
OEDIPUS: Yonder!—Did nothing ever pass between you?
HERDSMAN: No—speaking out of hand, from memory.
MESSENGER: Small wonder he forgets! Come, I'll remind

His ignorance, my lord. I make no doubt
He knows that once around Cithaeron's hills
He tended his two flocks—I had but one—
Yet served for company three summer-times,
The six long months from spring to autumn nights.
And when at last the winter came, I drove
Down to my farm, and he to Laïus' folds.
Was it so done as I have said, or no?
HERDSMAN: 'Tis very long ago. Yes, it is true.
MESSENGER: Now tell me this:—You know you gave me once
A boy, to rear him as a child of mine?
HERDSMAN: What do you mean? Why do you ask me?
MESSENGER: Why?
Because, my friend, that child is now your King!
HERDSMAN: A curse upon you! Silence! Hold your peace.
OEDIPUS: No, no! You must not chide him, sir! 'Tis you
That should be chid, not he, for speaking so.
HERDSMAN: Nay, good my master, what is my offence?
OEDIPUS: This: that you answer nothing—of the child.
HERDSMAN: 'Tis nothing. He knows nothing. 'Tis but talk.
OEDIPUS: You will not speak to please me? Pain shall make you!
HERDSMAN: No! By the gods, hurt me not! I am old.
OEDIPUS: Come, one of you. Quick! Fasten back his arms!
HERDSMAN: O Wretched, Wretched! Why? What would you know?
OEDIPUS: Did you, or did you not, give him the child?
HERDSMAN: I gave it him. Would I had died that day.
OEDIPUS: This day you shall, unless you speak the truth.
HERDSMAN: Alas! And if I speak, 'tis worse, far worse.
OEDIPUS: Ah! So the fellow means to trifle with us!
HERDSMAN: No, No! I have confessed I gave it him.
OEDIPUS: How came you by it? Was the child your own?
HERDSMAN: It was not mine. Another gave it me.
OEDIPUS: Another? Who, and of what house in Thebes?
HERDSMAN: Nay, for the gods' love, Master, ask no more.
OEDIPUS: Make me repeat my question, and you die!
HERDSMAN: The answer is:—a child of Laïus' house.
OEDIPUS: Slave born? Or kinsman to the royal blood?
HERDSMAN: Alas!
So it has come, the thing I dread to tell.
OEDIPUS: The thing I dread to hear. Yet I must hear it.
HERDSMAN: Thus then:—they said 'twas . . . Laïus' son. . . . And yet
Perhaps Jocasta best can answer that.

OEDIPUS: Jocasta gave it you?
HERDSMAN: She gave it me.
OEDIPUS: For what?
HERDSMAN: She bade me do away with it.
OEDIPUS: Its mother! Could she?
HERDSMAN: Fearing prophecies—
OEDIPUS: What prophecies?
HERDSMAN: His father he must kill!
OEDIPUS: And yet you let this old man take him? Why?
HERDSMAN: 'Twas pity, sir. I thought: he dwells afar,
And takes him to some distant home. But he
Saved him to suffer! If you are the child
He saith, no man is more unfortunate.
OEDIPUS: Alas! It comes! It comes! And all is true!
Light! Let me look my last on thee, for I
Stand naked now. Shamefully was I born:
In shame I wedded: to my shame I slew. (*Exeunt all except the*
    CHORUS.)

CHORUS: Ah! Generations of mankind!
Living, I count your life as nothingness.
    None hath more of happiness,
    None that mortal is, than this:
    But to seem to be and then,
        Having seemed, to fail.
    Thine, O unhappy Oedipus,
    Thine is the fatal destiny,
That bids me call no mortal creature blest.

    Zeus! To the very height of wit
He shot, and won the prize of perfect life;
    Conqueror that slew the maid,
    Who, with crooked claw and tongue
    Riddling, brought us death, when he
        Rose and gave us life.
    That day it was that hailed thee King,
    Preferred above mankind in state
And honour, Master of the Might of Thebes.

    To-day, alas! no tale so sad as thine!
        No man whom changing life hath lodged
So close with Hell, and all her plagues, and all her sorrowing!

Woe for the fame of Oedipus!
For the Son hath lain where the Father lay,
And the bride of one is the bride of both.
How could the field that the father sowed endure him
So silently so long?

Time knoweth all. Spite of they purposing,
Time hath discovered thee, to judge
The monstrous mating that defiled the father through the son.
Woe for the babe that Laïus got.
And I would I never had looked on thee,
And the songs I sing are a dirge for thee.
This is the end of the matter: he that saved me,
Hath made me desolate.

Enter a MESSENGER *from the Palace.*

MESSENGER: Great Lords, that keep the dignities of Thebes,
What doings must ye hear, what sights must see,
And oh! what grief must bear, if ye are true
To Cadmus and the breed of Labdacus!
Can Ister or can Phasis wash this house—
I trow not—, with their waters, from the guilt
It hides? . . . Yet soon shall publish to the light
Fresh, not unpurposed evil. 'Tis the woe
That we ourselves have compassed, hurts the most.
CHORUS: That which we knew already, was enough
For lamentation. What have you besides?
MESSENGER: This is the briefest tale for me to tell,
For you to hear:—your Queen Jocasta's dead.
CHORUS: Alas! Poor lady! Dead! What was the cause?
MESSENGER: She died by her own hand. Of what befell
The worst is not for you, who saw it not.
Yet shall you hear, so much as memory
Remains in me, the sad Queen's tragedy.
   When in her passionate agony she passed
Beyond those portals, straight to her bridal-room
She ran, and ever tore her hair the while;
Clashed fast the doors behind her; and within,
Cried to her husband Laïus in the grave,
With mention of that seed whereby he sowed
Death for himself, and left to her a son

To get on her fresh children, shamefully.
So wept she for her bridal's double woe,
Husband of husband got, and child of child.
And after that—I know not how—she died.

    We could not mark her sorrows to the end,
For, with a shout, Oedipus broke on us,
And all had eyes for him. Hither he rushed
And thither. For a sword he begged, and cried:
"Where is that wife that mothered in one womb
Her husband and his children! Show her me!
No wife of mine!" As thus he raged, some god—
'Twas none of us—guided him where she lay.
And he, as guided, with a terrible shout,
Leapt at her double door; free of the bolts
Burst back the yielding bar,—and was within.
And there we saw Jocasta. By a noose
Of swaying cords, caught and entwined, she hung.

    He too has seen her—with a moaning cry
Looses the hanging trap, and on the ground
Has laid her. Then—Oh, sight most terrible!—
He snatched the golden brooches from the Queen,
With which her robe was fastened, lifted them,
And struck. Deep to the very founts of sight
He smote, and vowed those eyes no more should see
The wrongs he suffered, and the wrong he did.
"Henceforth," he cried, "be dark!—since ye have seen
Whom ye should ne'er have seen, and never knew
Them that I longed to find." So chanted he,
And raised the pins again, and yet again,
And every time struck home. Blood from the eyes
Sprinkled his beard, and still fresh clammy drops
Welled in a shower unceasing, nay, a storm
With blood for rain, and hail of clotting gore.

    So from these twain hath evil broken; so
    Are wife and husband mingled in one woe.
Justly their ancient happiness was known
For happiness indeed; and lo! to-day—
Tears and Disasters, Death and Shame, and all
The ills the world hath names for—all are here.

CHORUS: And hath he found some respite now from pain?
MESSENGER: He shouts, and bids open the doors, and show
To all his Thebes this father-murderer,

This mother- . . . Leave the word. It is not clean.
He would be gone from Thebes, nor stay to see
His home accursèd by the curse he swore;
Yet hath he not the strength. He needs a guide,
Seeing his griefs are more than man can bear.

   Nay, he himself will show you. Look! The gates
Fall open, and the sight that you shall see
Is such that even hate must pity it.

Enter OEDIPUS, *blind.*

CHORUS: O sight for all the world to see
          Most terrible! O suffering
Of all mine eyes have seen most terrible!
          Alas! What Fury came on thee?
          What evil Spirit, from afar,
          O Oedipus! O Wretched!
            Leapt on thee, to destroy?

          I cannot even Alas! look
          Upon thy face, though much I have
          To ask of thee, and much to hear,
            Aye, and to see—I cannot!
            Such terror is in thee!

OEDIPUS: Alas! O Wretched! Whither go
          My steps? My voice? It seems to float
            Far, far away from me.
          Alas! Curse of my Life, how far
            Thy leap hath carried thee!
CHORUS: To sorrows none can bear to see or hear.

OEDIPUS: Ah! The cloud!
Visitor unspeakable! Darkness upon me horrible!
Unconquerable! Cloud that may not ever pass away!
            Alas!
And yet again, alas! How deep they stab—
These throbbing pains, and all those memories.
CHORUS: Where such afflictions are, I marvel not,
If soul and body made one doubled woe.

OEDIPUS: Ah! My friend!
Still remains thy friendship. Still thine is the help that comforts me,

And kindness, that can look upon these dreadful eyes unchanged.
                    Ah me!
My friend, I feel thy presence. Though mine eyes
Be darkened, yet I hear thy voice, and know.
CHORUS: Oh, dreadful deed! How wert thou steeled to quench
Thy vision thus? What Spirit came on thee?

OEDIPUS: Apollo! 'Twas Apollo, friends,
Willed the evil, willed, and brought the agony to pass!
          And yet the hand that struck was mine, mine only,
               wretched.
          Why should I see, whose eyes
     Had no more any good to look upon?
CHORUS: 'Twas even as thou sayest.
OEDIPUS: Aye. For me . . . Nothing is left for sight.
                    Nor anything to love:
     Nor shall the sound of greetings any more
               Fall pleasant on my ear.
   Away! Away! Out of the land, away!
     Banishment, Banishment! Fatal am I, accursed,
          And the hate on me, as on no man else, of the gods!
CHORUS: Unhappy in thy fortune and the wit
That shows it thee. Would thou hadst never known.
OEDIPUS: A curse upon the hand that loosed
     In the wilderness the cruel fetters of my feet,
          Rescued me, gave me life! Ah! Cruel was his pity,
               Since, had I died, so much
          I had not harmed myself and all I love.
CHORUS: Aye, even so 'twere better.
OEDIPUS: Aye, for life never had led me then
                    To shed my father's blood;
          Men had not called me husband of the wife
                    That bore me in the womb.
   But now—but now—Godless am I, the son
          Born of impurity, mate of my father's bed,
               And if worse there be, I am Oedipus! It is mine!
CHORUS: In this I know not how to call thee wise,
For better wert thou dead than living—blind.

OEDIPUS: Nay, give me no more counsel. Bid me not
Believe my deed, thus done, is not well done.
I know 'tis well. When I had passed the grave,
How could those eyes have met my father's gaze,

Or my unhappy mother's—since on both
I have done wrongs beyond all other wrong?
Or live and see my children?—Children born
As they were born! What pleasure in that sight?
None for these eyes of mine, for ever, none.
Nor in the sight of Thebes, her castles, shrines
And images of the gods, whereof, alas!
I robbed myself—myself, I spoke that word,
I that she bred and nurtured, I her prince,
And bade her thrust the sinner out, the man
Proved of the gods polluted—Laïus' son.
When such a stain by my own evidence
Was on me, could I raise my eyes to them?
No! Had I means to stop my ears, and choke
The wells of sound, I had not held my hand,
But closed my body like a prison-house
To hearing as to sight. Sweet for the mind
To dwell withdrawn, where troubles could not come.

    Cithaeron! Ah, why didst thou welcome me?
Why, when thou hadst me there, didst thou not kill,
Never to show the world myself—my birth!

    O Polybus, and Corinth, and the home
Men called my father's ancient house, what sores
Festered beneath that beauty that ye reared,
Discovered now, sin out of sin begot.

    O ye three roads, O secret mountain-glen,
Trees, and a pathway narrowed to the place
Where met the three, do you remember me?
I gave you blood to drink, my father's blood,
And so my own! Do you remember that?
The deed I wrought for you? Then, how I passed
Hither to other deeds?

              O Marriage-bed
That gave me birth, and, having borne me, gave
Fresh children to your seed, and showed the world
Father, son, brother, mingled and confused,
Bride, mother, wife in one, and all the shame
Of deeds the foulest ever known to man.

    No. Silence for a deed so ill to do
Is better. Therefore lead me hence, away!
To hide me or to kill. Or to the sea
Cast me, where you shall look on me no more.

Come! Design to touch me, though I am a man
Accurséd. Yield! Fear nothing! Mine are woes
That no man else, but I alone, must bear.

Enter CREON, *attended.*

CHORUS: Nay, for your prayer, look! in good season comes
Creon, for act or counsel. In your place
He stands, the sole protector of the land.
OEDIPUS: Alas! What words have I for him? What plea
That I can justify? Since all the past
Stands proved, and shows me only false to him.
CREON: I come not, Oedipus, in mockery.
Nor with reproach for evils that are past.—
Nay, if ye have no reverence for man,
Have ye no shame before our Lord the Sun,
Who feeds the world with light, to show unveiled
A thing polluted so, that neither Earth
Nor Light nor Heaven's rain may welcome it.
Stay not. Convey him quickly to his home:
Save his own kindred, none should see nor hear—
So piety enjoins—a kinsman's woe.
OEDIPUS: Ah, since thou hast belied my thought and come
As noblest among men to me, so vile,
Grant me one boon, for thine own weal, not mine.
CREON: What is thy prayer? What boon can I bestow?
OEDIPUS: Cast me from Thebes, aye, cast me quickly forth
Where none may see, and no man speak with me.
CREON: This had I done, be sure, save that I first
Would ask the god what thing is right to do.
OEDIPUS: His word was published, and 'twas plain:—'Destroy
The guilty one, the parricide!'—'tis I!
CREON: So runs the word; and yet, to ask the god
For guidance in such utter need is best.
OEDIPUS: What? Will you ask for one so lost as I?
CREON: Surely, and you will now believe the god.
OEDIPUS: Aye, and on thee I lay this charge, this prayer:
For her that is within make burial
As pleaseth thee. 'Tis fitting. She is thine.
For me, ah! never doom this land of Thebes,
My father's town, to harbour me alive.
Leave me to haunt the mountains, where the name

.

Is known of my Cithaeron—proper tomb
By mother and by father set apart
For me, their living child. So let me die
Their victim still that would have slain me there.
   And yet this much I know. There is no hurt
Nor sickness that can end me. Since from death
I lived, it was to finish some strange woe. . . .
  So let my Fortune, where it goeth, go!
But for my children, Creon,—for the sons
Think not at all. Men are they; anywhere
Can live, and find sufficiency for life.
But for my sad daughters, that dear pair
That never found my table spread apart
From then, nor missed their comrade, but must share
Always the very food their father had:
Be all your care for them. Oh! Best of all,
Let me but touch them, and so weep my full.
Grant it, my prince,
O noble spirit, grant it. But one touch,
And I could think them mine, as when I saw.

              Enter ANTIGONE *and* ISMENE.

Ah! What is this?
That sound? Oh, can it be? Are these my loves,
Weeping? Has Creon pitied me, and fetched
The children of my dearest love to me?
Can it be true?
CREON: 'Tis true; 'twas I so ordered it. I knew
The joy thou hadst in them. 'Tis with thee still.
OEDIPUS: Be happy, and for treading this good way
A kinder fate than mine defend thy steps.
Children, where are you? Come. Ah, come to me!
These arms that wait you are your brother's arms,
Their kindness bade these eyes that were so bright,
Your father's eyes, to see as now they see,
Because 'tis known, my children, ignorant
And blind, your father sowed where he was got.
   For you I weep, for you. I have not strength
To see you, only thoughts of all the life
That waits you in the cruel world of men.
No gathering of Thebes, no festival

That you shall visit, but shall send you home
With tears, instead of happy holiday.
And when you come to marriage-days, ah! then
Who will be found to wed you? Who so brave
Will shoulder such reproach of shame as I
Put on my parents, and must leave with you?
Is any woe left out? Your father killed
His father, took the mother of his life
And sowed the seed on her, begetting you
From the same womb whereof himself was born.
This your reproach must be. Lives there a man,
Children, to wed you? None, alas! 'Tis plain:
Unwedded and unfruitful must you die.
   Son of Menoeceus, thou art left to them,
Their only father now, for we, their own,
Who gave them life, are dead. Suffer not these,
That are thy kin, beggared and husbandless
To wander, laid as low as I am laid.
Have pity on them. See how young they are,
And, save for thy good part, all desolate.
Promise me, loyal friend. Give me thy hand
In token of it. Children, out of much
I might have told you, could you understand,
Take this one counsel: be your prayer to live.
Where fortune's modest measure is, a life
That shall be better than your father's was.

CREON: It is enough! Go in! Shed no more tears, but go!
OEDIPUS: I would not, yet must yield.
CREON: Measure in all is best.
OEDIPUS: Know you the pledge I crave?
CREON: Speak it, and I shall know.
OEDIPUS: This:—that you banish me!
CREON: That is the gods' to give.
OEDIPUS: The gods reject me!
CREON: Then, perchance, you *shall* have banishment.
OEDIPUS: You promise?
CREON: Knowing not, 'tis not my wont to speak.
OEDIPUS: Then take me, take me, hence!
CREON: Come! Quit your children. Come!
OEDIPUS: No! No! You shall not.
CREON: Ah! Seek not the mastery
In all. Too brief, alas! have proved your masteries.

CHORUS: Look, ye who dwell in Thebes. This man was Oedipus.
That Mighty King, who knew the riddle's mystery,
Whom all the city envied, Fortune's favourite.
Behold, in the event, the storm of his calamities,
And, being mortal, think on that last day of death,
Which all must see, and speak of no man's happiness
Till, without sorrow, he hath passed the goal of life. (*Exeunt omnes.*)

STUDY AND DISCUSSION QUESTIONS*

1. (Scene I) Analyze the first speech of Oedipus. What is its tone? Does it indicate anything about the political position of the speaker? How does it characterize him? What is the function of the priest? How does he regard Oedipus? Why does the priest remind Oedipus of his past glories? What is the significance of the conversation between Creon and Oedipus? Why has the investigation of Laius' murder been delayed? What do the comments of the Chorus contribute to this scene?

2. (Scene II) What is Oedipus' reaction to the prayer offered by the Chorus at the end of the first scene? What is the function of Teiresias at this point in the play? Why is Oedipus suspicious of Teiresias? Analyze Teiresias' first speech. What is his attitude toward knowledge and wisdom? How does Oedipus react to this attitude? What motivates Teiresias to tell what he knows? Why does Oedipus place such great importance on solving the riddle of the Sphinx? What function does the Chorus perform after the bitter argument between Oedipus and Teiresias?

3. (Scene III) At the beginning of the third scene Creon's speech is filled with images of sight (this kind of imagery is, in fact, found throughout the play). What is the purpose of this imagery? Is there any change in the character of Oedipus in his dialogue with Creon? What is the significance of Jocasta's revealing the oracle at this point in the action? How does Oedipus react to this revelation? What is the role of the Chorus at the conclusion of the scene?

---

* Questions 1-5 reflect the breaks in the action of the play that follow the speeches of the Chorus. For purposes of discussion we shall call them scenes even though they are not so designated in the play.

4. (Scene IV) What is the meaning of Jocasta's prayer at the beginning of the scene? What is the function of the messenger from Corinth? When does Jocasta realize the truth? What is her reaction to this knowledge? In this scene Oedipus' pride (*hubris*) seems to be at its peak. Single out the speeches that demonstrate this. How do the comments of the Chorus underscore the protagonist's pride?

5. (Scene V) This scene is broken down into three parts—the entrance of the herdsman, the entrance of the Second Messenger, and the final catastrophe. What is the function of the herdsman? How does the repetitive effect of Oedipus' attempts to gain information from reluctant informants effect the tragedy? What is the Second Messenger's role? How do the images of eyesight function in the last few speeches of Oedipus? What is Creon's reaction to Oedipus? Why is the scene with the children included? What is the point of Creon's last speech? What seems to be the implication of the final speech of the Chorus?

6. Sophocles is known for his use of dramatic irony (see Glossary). For example, Oedipus says that he will conduct a search for the murderer of the King as he would if Laius were his own father. Discuss some of the other ironies in the play. How does the dramatist make use of the fact that the audience already knows the story of Oedipus?

7. In the *Poetics* Aristotle says that the protagonist of a tragedy should be an individual of high rank worthy of respect and admiration but with some fault of character which results in and causes the tragic disaster. In this respect the protagonist is in some way responsible for the events that destroy him. Does the character of Oedipus satisfy Aristotle's definition? Be sure to view him in his various roles—King, father, husband.

8. One way of reading the play is to see it as a tragedy of fate. Trace the events that show how Oedipus tries to avoid his destiny. What does this indicate about the nature of the universe as Sophocles understands it? Does this struggle enhance the stature of Oedipus' tragedy?

9. It is generally accepted that Sophocles has one of the most effective styles in dramatic literature. One way to analyze style is to isolate and analyze most of the elements of which it is composed—the choice and use of words, their sound qualities, their order, the structure of clause and sentence, the use of figures of speech and thought. Read the first few speeches in the play and analyze the style in terms of the approach suggested above.

10. The critic H. D. F. Kitto suggests that the antagonist in the play is the "underlying laws" that man encounters. In this sense the play could be read in religious terms, since a world-order does exist for Sophocles. Hence, the play or the actions "are part of the whole pattern of life; that in spite of things that we can neither understand nor justify—life is not chaos." If this is the way the play should be read, then what role does Apollo play in the tragedy? Why is Oedipus punished in the end? What is life like, then, in the Sophoclean world?

WRITING TOPICS

1. The action of the play centers on a quest for the reasons why evil beset the state, but in the end it becomes a quest for self-knowledge. Write an essay tracing the movement from the external quest for reasons to the internal search for knowledge.

2. Write an essay defining the character of Oedipus—analyze his personality in terms of attitude, statement, thought, and action. *Or* write an essay establishing the *function* of the minor characters (Jocasta, Creon, the Chorus, the Messengers, and Teiresias).

3. One of the dramatic techniques that is very effective in Sophocles' plays is the use of "dramatic irony." Write an essay analyzing the relationship between the technique of irony and the structure.

4. Write an essay on what you consider an important theme or interpretation of *Oedipus the King*.

ANTIGONE

Sophocles
Translated by Sir Richard C. Jebb

Persons of the Drama

ANTIGONE \
ISMENE } *daughters of Oedipus.*

CREON, *King of Thebes.*

EURYDICE, *his wife.*

HAEMON, *his son.*

TEIRESIAS, *the blind prophet.*

GUARD, *set to watch the corpse of Polyneices.*

FIRST MESSENGER.

SECOND MESSENGER, *from the house.*

CHORUS OF THEBAN ELDERS.

Scene, *Before the Royal Palace at Thebes*

ANTIGONE: Ismene, sister, mine own dear sister, knowest thou what ill there is, of all bequeathed by Oedipus, that Zeus fulfils not for us twain while we live? Nothing painful is there, nothing fraught with ruin, no shame, no dishonor, that I have not seen in thy woes and mine.

And now what new edict is this of which they tell, that our Captain hath just published to all Thebes? Knowest thou aught? Hast thou heard? Or is it hidden from thee that our friends are threatened with the doom of our foes?

ISMENE: No word of friends, Antigone, gladsome or painful, hath come to me, since we two sisters were bereft of brothers twain, killed in one day by a twofold blow; and since in this last night the Argive host hath fled, I know no more, whether my fortune be brighter, or more grievous.

ANTIGONE: I knew it well, and therefore sought to bring thee beyond the gates of the court, that thou mightest hear alone.

ISMENE: What is it? 'Tis plain that thou are brooding on some dark tidings.

ANTIGONE: What, hath not Creon destined our brothers, the one to honored burial, the other to unburied shame? Eteocles, they say, with due observance of right and custom, he hath laid in the earth, for his honor among the dead below. But the hapless corpse of Polyneices—as rumor saith, it hath been published to the town that none shall entomb him or mourn, but leave unwept, unsepulchred, a welcome store for the birds, as they espy him, to feast on at will.

Such, 'tis said, that the good Creon hath set forth for thee and for me,—yes, for *me*,—and is coming hither to proclaim it clearly to those who know it not; nor counts the matter light, but, whoso disobeys in aught, his doom is death by stoning before all the folk. Thou knowest it now; and thou wilt soon show whether thou art nobly bred, or the base daughter of a noble line.

ISMENE: Poor sister,—and if things stand thus, what could I help to do or undo?

ANTIGONE: Consider if thou wilt share the toil and the deed.

ISMENE: In what venture? What can be thy meaning?

ANTIGONE: Wilt thou aid this hand to lift the dead?

ISMENE: Thou wouldst bury him,—when 'tis forbidden to Thebes?

ANTIGONE: I will do my part,—and thine, if thou wilt not,—to a brother. False to him will I never be found.

ISMENE: Ah, over-bold! when Creon hath forbidden?

ANTIGONE: Nay, he hath no right to keep me from mine own.

ISMENE: Ah me! think, sister, how our father perished, amid hate and scorn, when sins bared by his own search had moved him to strike both eyes with self-blinding hand; then the mother wife, two names in one, with twisted noose did despite unto her life; and last, our two brothers in one day,—each shedding, hapless one, a kinsman's blood,—wrought out with mutual hands their common doom. And now *we* in turn—we two left all alone—think how we shall perish, more miserably than all the rest, if, in defiance of the law, we brave a king's decree or his powers. Nay, we must remember, first, that we were born women, as who should not strive with men; next, that we are ruled of the stronger, so that we must obey in these things, and in things yet sorer. I, therefore, asking the Spirits Infernal to pardon, seeing that force is put on me herein, will hearken to our rulers; for 'tis witless to be over busy.

ANTIGONE: I will not urge thee,—no, nor, if thou yet shouldst have the mind, wouldst thou be welcome as a worker with *me*. Nay, be what thou wilt; but I will bury him: well for me to die in doing that. I shall rest, a loved one with him whom I have loved, sinless in my crime; for I owe a longer allegiance to the dead than to the living: in that world I shall abide for ever. But if *thou* wilt, be guilty of dishonoring laws which the gods have established in honor.

ISMENE: I do them no dishonor; but to defy the State,—I have no strength for that.

ANTIGONE: Such be thy plea:—I, then, will go to heap the earth above the brother whom I love.

ISMENE: Alas, unhappy one! How I fear for thee!

ANTIGONE: Fear not for me: guide thine own fate aright.

ISMENE: At least, then, disclose this plan to none, but hide it closely, —and so, too, will I.

ANTIGONE: Oh, denounce it! Thou wilt be far more hateful for thy silence, if thou proclaim not these things to all.

ISMENE: Thou hast a hot heart for chilling deeds.

ANTIGONE: I know that I please where I am most bound to please.

ISMENE: Aye, if thou canst; but thou wouldst what thou canst not.

ANTIGONE: Why, then, when my strength fails, I shall have done.

ISMENE: A hopeless quest should not be made at all.

ANTIGONE: If thus thou speakest, thou wilt have hatred from me, and will justly be subject to the lasting hatred of the dead. But leave me, and the folly that is mine alone, to suffer this dread thing; for I shall not suffer aught so dreadful as an ignoble death.

ISMENE: Go, then, if thou must; and of this be sure,—that, though thine errand is foolish, to thy dear ones thou art truly dear. (*Exit* ANTIGONE *on the spectator's left.* ISMENE *retires into the palace by one of the two side-doors*)

Strophe 1.

CHORUS[1]: Beam of the sun, fairest light that ever dawned on Thebè of the seven gates, thou hast shone forth at last, eye of golden day, arisen above Dircè's streams! The warrior of the white shield, who came from Argos in his panoply, hath been stirred by thee to headlong flight, in swifter career.

---

[1] Composed of Theban Senators.

Who set forth against our land by reason of the vexed claims of Polyneices; and, like shrill-screaming eagle, he flew over into our land, in
snow-white pinion sheathed, with an armèd throng, and with plu-
mage of helms.

Antistrophe 1.

He paused above our dwellings; he ravened around our sevenfold portals with spears athirst for blood; but he went hence, or ever his jaws
were glutted with our gore, or the Fire-god's pine-fed flame had
seized our crown of towers. So fierce was the noise of battle raised
behind him, a thing too hard for him to conquer, as he wrestled with
his dragon foe.

For Zeus utterly abhors the boasts of a proud tongue; and when he
beheld them coming on in a great stream, in the haughty pride of
clanging gold, he smote with brandished fire one who was now hast-
ing to shout victory at his goal upon our ramparts.

Strophe 2.

Swung down, he fell on the earth with a crash, torch in hand, he who
so lately, in the frenzy of the mad onset, was raging against us with
the blasts of his tempestuous hate. But those threats fared not as he
hoped; and to other foes the mighty War-god dispensed their several
dooms, dealing havoc around, a mighty helper at our need.

For seven captains at seven gates, matched against seven, left the tribute
of their panoplies to Zeus who turns the battle; save those two of
cruel fate, who, born of one sire and one mother, set against each
other their twain conquering spears, and are sharers in a common
death.

Antistrophe 2.

But since Victory of glorious name hath come to us, with joy responsive
to the joy of Thebè whose chariots are many, let us enjoy forgetful-
ness after the late wars, and visit all the temples of the gods with
night-long dance and song; and may Bacchus be our leader, whose
dancing shakes the land of Thebè.

But lo, the king of the land comes yonder, Creon, son of Menoeceus,
our new ruler by the new fortunes that the gods have given; what

counsel is he pondering, that he hath proposed this special conference of elders, summoned by his general mandate?

Enter CREON, *from the central doors of the palace, in the garb of king; with two attendants.*

CREON: Sirs, the vessel of our State, after being tossed on wild waves, hath once more been safely steadied by the gods: and ye, out of all the folk, have been called apart by my summons, because I knew, first of all, how true and constant was your reverence for the royal power of Laïus; how, again, when Oedipus was ruler of our land, and when he had perished, your steadfast loyalty still upheld their children. Since, then, his sons have fallen in one day by a twofold doom,—each smitten by the other, each stained with a brother's blood,—I now possess the throne and all its powers by nearness of kinship to the dead.

No man can be fully known, in soul and spirit and mind, until he hath been seen versed in rule and law-giving. For if any, being supreme guide of the State, cleaves not to the best counsels, but, through some fear, keeps his lips locked, I hold, and have ever held, him most base; and if any makes a friend of more account than his fatherland, that man hath no place in my regard. For I—be Zeus my witness, who sees all things always—would not be silent if I saw ruin, instead of safety, coming to the citizens; nor would I ever deem the country's foe a friend to myself; remembering this, that our country is the ship that bears us safe, and that only while she prospers in our voyage can we make true friends.

Such are the rules by which I guard this city's greatness. And in accord with them is the edict which I have now published to the folk touching the sons of Oedipus;—that Eteocles, who hath fallen fighting for our city, in all renown of arms, shall be entombed, and crowned with every rite that follows the noblest dead to their rest. But for his brother, Polyneices,—who came back from exile, and sought to consume utterly with fire the city of his fathers and the shrines of his fathers' gods,— sought to taste of kindred blood, and to lead the remnant into slavery; —touching this man, it hath been proclaimed to our people that none shall grace him with sepulture or lament, but leave him unburied, a corpse for birds and dogs to eat, a ghastly sight of shame.

Such the spirit of my dealing; and never, by deed of mine, shall the wicked stand in honor before the just; but whoso hath good will to Thebes, he shall be honored of me, in his life and in his death.

CHORUS: Such is thy pleasure, Creon, son of Menoeceus, touching this city's foe, and its friend; and thou hast power, I ween, to take what order thou wilt, both for the dead, and for all us who live.

CREON: See, then, that ye be guardians of the mandate.

CHORUS: Lay the burden of this task on some younger man.

CREON: Nay, watchers of the corpse have been found.

CHORUS: What, then, is this further charge that thou wouldst give?

CREON: That ye side not with the breakers of these commands.

CHORUS: No man is so foolish that he is enamored of death.

CREON: In sooth, that is the meed; yet lucre hath oft ruined men through their hopes.

Enter GUARD.

GUARD: My liege, I will not say that I come breathless from speed, or that I have plied a nimble foot; for often did my thoughts make me pause, and wheel round in my path, to return. My mind was holding large discourse with me; "Fool, why goest thou to thy certain doom?" "Wretch, tarrying again? And if Creon hears this from another, must not thou smart for it?" So debating, I went on my way with lagging steps, and thus a short road was made long. At last, however, it carried the day that I should come hither—to thee; and, though my tale be nought, yet will I tell it; for I come with a good grip on one hope,— that I can suffer nothing but what is my fate.

CREON: And what is it that disquiets thee thus?

GUARD: I wish to tell thee first about myself—I did not do the deed—I did not see the doer—it were not right that I should come to any harm.

CREON: Thou hast a shrewd eye for thy mark; well dost thou fence thyself round against the blame:—clearly thou hast some strange thing to tell.

GUARD: Aye, truly; dread news makes one pause long.

CREON: Then tell it, wilt thou, and so get thee gone?

GUARD: Well, this is it.—The corpse—some one hath just given it burial, and gone away,—after sprinkling thirsty dust on the flesh, with such other rites as piety enjoins.

CREON: What sayest thou? What living man hath dared this deed?

GUARD: I know not; no stroke of pickaxe was seen there, no earth thrown up by mattock; the ground was hard and dry, unbroken, without track of wheels; the doer was one who had left no trace. And when the first day-watchman showed it to us, sore wonder fell on all. The dead man was veiled from us; not shut within a tomb, but lightly strewn with dust, as by the hand of one who shunned a curse. And no sign met the eye as though any beast of prey or any dog had come nigh to him, or torn him.

Then evil words flew fast and loud among us, guard accusing guard;

and it would e'en have come to blows at last, nor was there any to hinder. Every man was the culprit, and no one was convicted, but all disclaimed knowledge of the deed. And we were ready to take red-hot iron in our hands;—to walk through fire;—to make oath by the gods that we had not done the deed,—that we were not privy to the planning or the doing.

At last, when all our searching was fruitless, one spake, who made us all bend our faces on the earth in fear; for we saw not how we could gainsay him, or escape mischance if we obeyed. His counsel was that this deed must be reported to thee, and not hidden. And this seemed best; and the lot doomed my hapless self to win this prize. So here I stand,—as unwelcome as unwilling, well I wot; for no man delights in the bearer of bad news.

CHORUS: O king, my thoughts have long been whispering, can this deed, perchance, be e'en the work of gods?

CREON: Cease, ere thy words fill me utterly with wrath, lest thou be found at once an old man and foolish. For thou sayest what is not to be borne, in saying that the gods have care for this corpse. Was it for high reward of trusty service that they sought to hide his nakedness, who came to burn their pillared shrines and sacred treasures, to burn their land, and scatter its laws to the winds? Or dost thou behold the gods honoring the wicked? It cannot be. No! From the first there were certain in the town that muttered against me, chafing at this edict, wagging their heads in secret; and kept not their necks duly under the yoke, like men contented with my sway.

'Tis by them, well I know, that these have been beguiled and bribed to do this deed. Nothing so evil as money ever grew to be current among men. This lays cities low, this drives men from their homes, this trains and warps honest souls till they set themselves to works of shame; this still teaches folk to practice villainies, and to know every godless deed.

But all the men who wrought this thing for hire have made it sure that, soon or late, they shall pay the price. Now, as Zeus still hath my reverence, know this—I tell it thee on my oath:—If ye find not the very author of this burial, and produce him before mine eyes, death alone shall not be enough for you, till first, hung up alive, ye have revealed this outrage,—that henceforth ye may thieve with better knowledge whence lucre should be won, and learn that it is not well to love gain from every source. For thou wilt find that ill-gotten pelf brings more men to ruin than to weal.

GUARD: May I speak? Or shall I just turn and go?

CREON: Knowest thou not that even now thy voice offends?

GUARD: Is thy smart in the ears, or in the soul?

CREON: And why wouldst thou define the seat of my pain?

GUARD: The doer vexes thy mind, but I, thine ears.

CREON: Ah, thou art a born babbler, 'tis well seen.

GUARD: May be, but never the doer of this deed.

CREON: Yea, and more,—the seller of thy life for silver.

GUARD: Alas! 'Tis sad, truly, that he who judges should misjudge.

CREON: Let thy fancy play with "judgment" as it will;—but, if ye show me not the doers of these things, ye shall avow that dastardly gains work sorrows. (*Exit*)

GUARD: Well, may he be found! so 'twere best. But, be he caught or be he not—fortune must settle that—truly thou wilt not see me here again. Saved, even now, beyond hope and thought, I owe the gods great thanks. (*Exit*)

Strophe 1.

CHORUS: Wonders are many, and none is more wonderful than man; the power that crosses the white sea, driven by the stormy south-wind, making a path under surges that threaten to engulf him; and Earth, the eldest of the gods, the immortal, the unwearied, doth he wear, turning the soil with the offspring of horses, as the ploughs go to and fro from year to year.

Antistrophe 1.

And the light-hearted race of birds, and the tribes of savage beasts, and the sea-brood of the deep, he snares in the meshes of his woven toils, he leads captive, man excellent in wit. And he masters by his arts the beast whose lair is in the wilds, who roams the hills; he tames the horse of shaggy mane, he puts the yoke upon its neck, he tames the tireless mountain bull.

Strophe 2.

And speech, and wind-swift thought, and all the moods that mould a state, hath he taught himself; and how to flee the arrows of the frost, when 'tis hard lodging under the clear sky, and the arrows of the rushing rain; yea, he hath resource for all; without resource he meets nothing that must come: only against Death shall he call for aid in vain; but from baffling maladies he hath devised escapes.

Antistrophe 2.

Cunning beyond fancy's dream is the fertile skill which brings him, now to evil, now to good. When he honors the laws of the land, and that justice which he hath sworn by the gods to uphold, proudly stands his city: no city hath he who, for his rashness, dwells with sin. Never may he share my hearth, never think my thoughts, who doth these things!

Enter the GUARD *on the spectators' left, leading in* ANTIGONE.

What portent from the gods is this?—my soul is amazed. I know her—how can I deny that yon maiden is Antigone?

O hapless, and child of hapless sire,—of Oedipus! What means this? Thou brought a prisoner?—thou, disloyal to the king's laws, and taken in folly?

GUARD: Here she is, the doer of the deed:—we caught this girl burying him:—but where is Creon?

CHORUS: Lo, he comes forth again from the house, at our need.

CREON: What is it? What hath chanced, that makes my coming timely?

GUARD: O king, against nothing should men pledge their word; for the after-thought belies the first intent. I could have vowed that I should not soon be here again,—scared by thy threats, with which I had just been lashed: but,—since the joy that surprises and transcends our hopes is like in fulness to no other pleasure,—I have come, though 'tis in breach of my sworn oath, bringing this maid; who was taken showing grace to the dead. This time there was no casting of lots; no, this luck hath fallen to me, and to none else. And now, sire, take her thyself, question her, examine her, as thou wilt; but I have a right to free and final quittance of this trouble.

CREON: And thy prisoner here—how and whence hast thou taken her?

GUARD: She was burying the man; thou knowest all.

CREON: Dost thou mean what thou sayest? Dost thou speak aright?

GUARD: I saw her burying the corpse that thou hadst forbidden to bury. Is that plain and clear?

CREON: And how was she seen? how taken in the act?

GUARD: It befell on this wise. When we had come to the place,—with those dread menaces of thine upon us,—we swept away all the dust that covered the corpse, and bared the dank body well; and then sat us down on the brow of the hill, to windward, heedful that the smell from him should not strike us; every man was wide awake, and kept his neighbor alert with torrents of threats, if any one should be careless of this task.

So went it, until the sun's bright orb stood in mid heaven, and the heat began to burn: and then suddenly a whirlwind lifted from the earth a storm of dust, a trouble in the sky, and filled the plain, marring all the leafage of its woods; and the wide air was choked therewith: we closed our eyes, and bore the plague from the gods.

And when, after a long while, this storm had passed, the maid was seen; and she cried aloud with the sharp cry of a bird in its bitterness, —even as when, within the empty nest, it sees the bed stripped of its nestlings. So she also, when she saw the corpse bare, lifted up a voice of wailing, and called down curses on the doers of that deed. And straightway she brought thirsty dust in her hands; and from a shapely ewer of bronze, held high, with thrice-poured drink-offering she crowned the dead.

We rushed forward when we saw it, and at once closed upon our quarry, who was in no wise dismayed. Then we taxed her with her past and present doings; and she stood not on denial of aught,—at once to my joy and to my pain. To have escaped from ills one's self is a great joy; but 'tis painful to bring friends to ill. Howbeit, all such things are of less account to me than mine own safety.

CREON: Thou—thou whose face is bent to earth—dost thou avow, or disavow, this deed?

ANTIGONE: I avow it; I make no denial.

CREON: (*To* GUARD) Thou canst betake thee whither thou wilt, free and clear of a grave charge. (*Exit* GUARD)

(*To* ANTIGONE) Now, tell me thou—not in many words, but briefly— knewest thou that an edict had forbidden this?

ANTIGONE: I knew it: could I help it? It was public.

CREON: And thou didst indeed dare to transgress that law?

ANTIGONE: Yes; for it was not Zeus that had published me that edict; not such are the laws set among men by the Justice who dwells with the gods below; nor deemed I that thy decrees were of such force, that a mortal could override the unwritten and unfailing statutes of heaven. For their life is not of to-day or yesterday, but from all time, and no man knows when they were first put forth.

Not through dread of any human pride could I answer to the gods for breaking *these*. Die I must,—I knew that well (how should I not?)— even without thy edicts. But if I am to die before my time, I count that a gain: for when any one lives, as I do, compassed about with evils, can such an one find aught but gain in death?

So for me to meet this doom is trifling grief; but if I had suffered my mother's son to lie in death an unburied corpse, that would have grieved me; for this, I am not grieved. And if my present deeds are foolish in thy sight, it may be that a foolish judge arraigns my folly.

CHORUS: The maid shows herself passionate child of passionate sire, and knows not how to bend before troubles.

CREON: Yet I would have thee know that o'er-stubborn spirits are most often humbled; 'tis the stiffest iron, baked to hardness in the fire, that thou shalt oftenest see snapped and shivered; and I have known horses that show temper brought to order by a little curb; there is no room for pride, when thou art thy neighbor's slave.—This girl was already versed in insolence when she transgressed the laws that had been set forth; and, that done, lo, a second insult,—to vaunt of this, and exult in her deed.

Now verily I am no man, she is the man, if this victory shall rest with her, and bring no penalty. No! be she sister's child, or nearer to me in blood than any that worships Zeus at the altar of our house,— she and her kinsfolk shall not avoid a doom most dire; for indeed I charge that other with a like share in the plotting of this burial.

And summon her—for I saw her e'en now within,—raving, and not mistress of her wits. So oft, before the deed, the mind stands self-convicted in its treason, when folks are plotting mischief in the dark. But verily this, too, is hateful,—when one who hath been caught in wickedness then seeks to make the crime a glory.

ANTIGONE: Wouldst thou do more than take and slay me?

CREON: No more, indeed; having that, I have all.

ANTIGONE: Why then dost thou delay? In thy discourse there is nought that pleases me,—never may there be!—and so my words must needs be unpleasing to thee. And yet, for glory—whence could I have won a nobler, than by giving burial to mine own brother? All here would own that they thought it well, were not their lips sealed by fear. But royalty, blest in so much besides, hath the power to do and say what it will.

CREON: Thou differest from all these Thebans in that view.

ANTIGONE: These also share it; but they curb their tongues for thee.

CREON: And art thou not ashamed to act apart from them?

ANTIGONE: No; there is nothing shameful in piety to a brother.

CREON: Was it not a brother, too, that died in the opposite cause?

ANTIGONE: Brother by the same mother and the same sire.

CREON: Why, then, dost thou render a grace that is impious in his sight?

ANTIGONE: The dead man will not say that he so deems it.

CREON: Yea, if thou makest him but equal in honor with the wicked.

ANTIGONE: It was his brother, not his slave, that perished.

CREON: Wasting this land; while *he* fell as its champion.

ANTIGONE: Nevertheless, Hades desires these rites.

CREON: But the good desires not a like portion with the evil.

ANTIGONE: Who knows but this seems blameless in the world below?

CREON: A foe is never a friend—not even in death.

ANTIGONE: 'Tis not my nature to join in hating, but in loving.

CREON: Pass, then, to the world of the dead, and, if thou must needs love, love them. While I live, no woman shall rule me.

Enter ISMENE *from the house, led in by two attendants.*

CHORUS: Lo, yonder Ismene comes forth, shedding such tears as fond sisters weep; a cloud upon her brow casts its shadow over her darkly-flushing face, and breaks in rain on her fair cheek.

CREON: And thou, who, lurking like a viper in my house, wast secretly draining my life-blood, while I knew not that I was nurturing two pests, to rise against my throne—come, tell me now, wilt thou also confess thy part in this burial, or wilt thou forswear all knowledge of it?

ISMENE: I have done the deed,—if she allows my claim,—and share the burden of the charge.

ANTIGONE: Nay, justice will not suffer thee to do that: thou didst not consent to the deed, nor did I give thee part in it.

ISMENE: But, now that ills beset thee, I am not ashamed to sail the sea of trouble at thy side.

ANTIGONE: Whose was the deed, Hades and the dead are witnesses: a friend in words is not the friend I love.

ISMENE: Nay, sister, reject me not, but let me die with thee, and duly honor the dead.

ANTIGONE: Share not thou my death, nor claim deeds to which thou hast not put thy hand: my death will suffice.

ISMENE: And what life is dear to me, bereft of thee?

ANTIGONE: Ask Creon; all thy care is for him.

ISMENE: Why vex me thus, when it avails thee nought?

ANTIGONE: Indeed, if I mock, 'tis with pain that I mock thee.

ISMENE: Tell me,—how can I serve thee, even now?

ANTIGONE: Save thyself: I grudge not thy escape.

ISMENE: Ah, woe is me! And shall I have no share in thy fate?

ANTIGONE: Thy choice was to live; mine, to die.

ISMENE: At least thy choice was not made without my protest.

ANTIGONE: One world approved thy wisdom; another, mine.

ISMENE: Howbeit, the offence is the same for both of us.

ANTIGONE: Be of good cheer; thou livest; but my life hath long been given to death, that so I might serve the dead.

CREON: Lo, one of these maidens hath newly shown herself foolish, as the other hath been since her life began.

ISMENE: Yea, O king, such reason as nature may have given abides not with the unfortunate, but goes astray.

CREON: Thine did, when thou chosest vile deeds with the vile.

ISMENE: What life could I endure, without her presence?

CREON: Nay, speak not of her "presence"; she lives no more.

ISMENE: But wilt thou slay the betrothed of thine own son?

CREON: Nay, there are other fields for him to plough.

ISMENE: But there can never be such love as bound him to her.

CREON: I like not an evil wife for my son.

ANTIGONE: Haemon, beloved! How thy father wrongs thee!

CREON: Enough, enough of thee and of thy marriage!

CHORUS: Wilt thou indeed rob thy son of this maiden?

CREON: 'Tis Death that shall stay these bridals for me.

CHORUS: 'Tis determined, it seems, that she shall die.

CREON: Determined, yes, for thee and for me.—(*To the two attendants*) No more delay—servants, take them within! Henceforth they must be women, and not range at large; for verily even the bold seek to fly, when they see Death now closing on their life. (*Exeunt attendants, guarding* ANTIGONE *and* ISMENE.—CREON *remains*)

CHORUS: Blest are they whose days have not tasted of evil. For when a house hath once been shaken from heaven, there the curse fails nevermore, passing from life to life of the race; even as, when the surge is driven over the darkness of the deep by the fierce breath of Thracian sea-winds, it rolls up the black sand from the depths, and there is a sullen roar from wind-vexed headlands that front the blows of the storm.

I see that from olden time the sorrows in the house of the Labdacidae are heaped upon the sorrows of the dead; and generation is not freed by generation, but some god strikes them down, and the race hath no deliverance.

For now that hope of which the light had been spread above the last root of the house of Oedipus—that hope, in turn, is brought low—by the blood-stained dust due to the gods infernal, and by folly in speech, and frenzy at the heart.

Thy power, O Zeus, what human trespass can limit? That power which neither Sleep, the all-ensnaring, nor the untiring months of the gods can master; but thou, a ruler to whom time brings not old age, dwellest in the dazzling splendor of Olympus.

And through the future, near and far, as through the past, shall this law hold good: Nothing that is vast enters into the life of mortals without a curse.

For that hope whose wanderings are so wide is to many men a comfort, but to many a false lure of giddy desires; and the disappointment comes on one who knoweth nought till he burn his foot against the hot fire.

For with wisdom hath some one given forth the famous saying, that evil seems good, soon or late, to him whose mind the god draws to mischief; and but for the briefest space doth he fare free of woe.

But lo, Haemon, the last of thy sons;—comes he grieving for the doom of his promised bride, Antigone, and bitter for the baffled hope of his marriage?

Enter HAEMON.

CREON: We shall know soon, better than seers could tell us.—My son, hearing the fixed doom of thy betrothed, art thou come in rage against thy father? Or have I thy good will, act how I may?

HAEMON: Father, I am thine; and thou, in thy wisdom, tracest for me rules which I shall follow. No marriage shall be deemed by me a greater gain than thy good guidance.

CREON: Yea, this, my son, should be thy heart's fixed law,—in all things to obey thy father's will. 'Tis for this that men pray to see dutiful children grow up around them in their homes,—that such may requite their father's foe with evil, and honor, as their father doth, his friend. But he who begets unprofitable children—what shall we say that he hath sown, but troubles for himself, and much triumph for his foes? Then do not thou, my son, at pleasure's beck, dethrone thy reason for a woman's sake; knowing that this is a joy that soon grows cold in clasping arms,—an evil woman to share thy bed and thy home. For what wound could strike deeper than a false friend? Nay, with loathing, and as if she were thine enemy, let this girl go to find a husband in the house of Hades. For since I have taken her, alone of all the city, in open disobedience, I will not make myself a liar to my people—I will slay her.

So let her appeal as she will to the majesty of kindred blood. If I am to nurture mine own kindred in naughtiness, needs must I bear with it in aliens. He who does his duty in his own household will be found righteous in the State also. But if any one transgresses, and does violence to the laws, or thinks to dictate to his rulers, such an one can win no praise from me. No, whomsoever the city may appoint, that man must be obeyed, in little things and great, in just things and unjust;

and I should feel sure that one who thus obeys would be a good ruler no less than a good subject, and in the storm of spears would stand his ground where he was set, loyal and dauntless at his comrade's side.

But disobedience is the worst of evils. This it is that ruins cities; this makes homes desolate; by this, the ranks of allies are broken into headlong rout; but, of the lives whose course is fair, the greater part owes safety to obedience. Therefore we must support the cause of order, and in no wise suffer a woman to worst us. Better to fall from power, if we must, by a man's hand; then we should not be called weaker than a woman.

CHORUS: To us, unless our years have stolen our wit, thou seemest to say wisely what thou sayest.

HAEMON: Father, the gods implant reason in men, the highest of all things that we call our own. Not mine the skill—far from me be the quest!—to say wherein thou speakest not aright; and yet another man, too, might have some useful thought. At least, it is my natural office to watch, on thy behalf, all that men say, or do, or find to blame. For the dread of thy frown forbids the citizen to speak such words as would offend thine ear; but I can hear these murmurs in the dark, these moanings of the city for this maiden; "no woman," they say, "ever merited her doom less,—none ever was to die so shamefully for deeds so glorious as hers; who, when her own brother had fallen in bloody strife, would not leave him unburied, to be devoured by carrion dogs, or by any bird:—deserves not *she* the meed of golden honor?"

Such is the darkling rumor that spreads in secret. For me, my father, no treasure is so precious as thy welfare. What, indeed, is a nobler ornament for children than a prospering sire's fair fame, or for sire than son's? Wear not, then, one mood only in thyself; think not that thy word, and thine alone, must be right. For if any man thinks that he alone is wise,—that in speech, or in mind, he hath no peer,—such a soul, when laid open, is ever found empty.

No, though a man be wise, 'tis no shame for him to learn many things, and to bend in season. Seest thou, beside the wintry torrent's course, how the trees that yield to it save every twig, while the stiff-necked perish root and branch? And even thus he who keeps the sheet of his sail taut, and never slackens it, upsets his boat, and finishes his voyage with keel uppermost.

Nay, forego thy wrath; permit thyself to change. For if I, a younger man, may offer my thought, it were far best, I ween, that men should be all-wise by nature; but, otherwise—and oft the scale inclines not so —'tis good also to learn from those who speak aright.

CHORUS: Sire, 'tis meet that thou shouldest profit by his words, if he speaks aught in season, and thou, Haemon, by thy father's; for on both parts there hath been wise speech.

CREON: Men of my age—are we indeed to be schooled, then, by men of his?

HAEMON: In nothing that is not right; but if I am young, thou shouldest look to my merits, not to my years.

CREON: Is it a merit to honor the unruly?

HAEMON: I could wish no one to show respect for evil-doers.

CREON: Then is not she tainted with that malady?

HAEMON: Our Theban folk, with one voice, denies it.

CREON: Shall Thebes prescribe to me how I must rule?

HAEMON: See, there thou hast spoken like a youth indeed.

CREON: Am I to rule this land by other judgment than mine own?

HAEMON: That is no city, which belongs to one man.

CREON: Is not the city held to be the ruler's?

HAEMON: Thou wouldst make a good monarch of a desert.

CREON: This boy, it seems, is the woman's champion.

HAEMON: If thou art a woman; indeed, my care is for thee.

CREON: Shameless, at open feud with thy father!

HAEMON: Nay, I see thee offending against justice.

CREON: Do I offend, when I respect mine own prerogatives?

HAEMON: Thou dost not respect them, when thou tramplest on the gods' honors.

CREON: O dastard nature, yielding place to woman!

HAEMON: Thou wilt never find me yield to baseness.

CREON: All thy words, at least, plead for that girl.

HAEMON: And for thee, and for me, and for the gods below.

CREON: Thou canst never marry her, on this side the grave.

HAEMON: Then she must die, and in death destroy another.

CREON: How! doth thy boldness run to open threats?

HAEMON: What threat is it, to combat vain resolves?

CREON: Thou shalt rue thy witless teaching of wisdom.

HAEMON: Wert thou not my father, I would have called thee unwise.

CREON: Thou woman's slave, use not wheedling speech with me.

HAEMON: Thou wouldest speak, and then hear no reply?

CREON: Sayest thou so? Now, by the heaven above us—be sure of it—thou shalt smart for taunting me in this opprobrious strain. Bring forth that hated thing, that she may die forthwith in his presence—before his eyes—at her bridegroom's side!

HAEMON: No, not at my side—never think it—shall she perish; nor shalt thou ever set eyes more upon my face:—rave, then, with such friends as can endure thee. (*Exit* HAEMON)

CHORUS: The man is gone, O king, in angry haste; a youthful mind, when stung, is fierce.

CREON: Let him do, or dream, more than man—good speed to him!— But he shall not save these two girls from their doom.

CHORUS: Dost thou indeed purpose to slay both?

CREON: Not her whose hands are pure: thou sayest well.

CHORUS: And by what doom mean'st thou to slay the other?

CREON: I will take her where the path is loneliest, and hide her, living, in a rocky vault, with so much food set forth as piety prescribes, that the city may avoid a public stain. And there, praying to Hades, the only god whom she worships, perchance she will obtain release from death; or else will learn, at last, though late, that it is lost labor to revere the dead. (*Exit* CREON)

Strophe.

CHORUS: Love, unconquered in the fight, Love, who makest havoc of wealth, who keepest thy vigil on the soft cheek of a maiden; thou roamest over the sea, and among the homes of dwellers in the wilds; no immortal can escape thee, nor any among men whose life is for a day; and he to whom thou hast come is mad.

Antistrophe.

The just themselves have their minds warped by thee to wrong, for their ruin: 'tis thou that hast stirred up this present strife of kinsmen; victorious is the love-kindling light from the eyes of the fair bride; it is a power enthroned in sway beside the eternal laws; for there the goddess Aphrodite is working her unconquerable will.

But now I also am carried beyond the bounds of loyalty, and can no more keep back the streaming tears, when I see Antigone thus passing to the bridal chamber where all are laid to rest.

Strophe 1.

ANTIGONE: See me, citizens of my fatherland, setting forth on my last way, looking my last on the sunlight that is for me no more; no, Hades who gives sleep to all leads me living to Acheron's shore; who have had no portion in the chant that brings the bride, nor hath any song been mine for the crowning of bridals; whom the lord of the Dark Lake shall wed.

CHORUS: Glorious, therefore, and with praise, thou departest to that deep place of the dead: wasting sickness hath not smitten thee; thou hast not found the wages of the sword; no, mistress of thine own fate, and still alive, thou shalt pass to Hades, as no other of mortal kind hath passed.

Antistrophe 1.

ANTIGONE: I have heard in other days how dread a doom befell our Phrygian guest, the daughter of Tantalus, on the Sipylian heights; how, like clinging ivy, the growth of stone subdued her; and the rains fail not, as men tell, from her wasting form, nor fails the snow, while beneath her weeping lids the tears bedew her bosom; and most like to hers is the fate that brings me to my rest.

CHORUS: Yet she was a goddess, thou knowest, and born of gods; we are mortals, and of mortal race. But 'tis great renown for a woman who hath perished that she should have shared the doom of the godlike, in her life, and afterward in death.

Strophe 2.

ANTIGONE: Ah, I am mocked! In the name of our fathers' gods, can ye not wait till I am gone,—must ye taunt me to my face, O my city, and ye, her wealthy sons? Ah, fount of Dircè, and thou holy ground of Thebè whose chariots are many; ye, at least, will bear me witness, in what sort, unwept of friends, and by what laws I pass to the rock-closed prison of my strange tomb, ah me unhappy! who have no home on the earth or in the shades, no home with the living or with the dead.

Strophe 3.

CHORUS: Thou hast rushed forward to the utmost verge of daring; and against that throne where Justice sits on high thou hast fallen, my daughter, with a grievous fall. But in this ordeal thou art paying, haply, for thy father's sin.

Antistrophe 2.

ANTIGONE: Thou hast touched on my bitterest thought,—awaking the ever-new lament for my sire and for all the doom given to us, the famed house of Labdacus. Alas for the horrors of the mother's bed! alas for the wretched mother's slumber at the side of her own son,— and my sire! From what manner of parents did I take my miserable being! And to them I go thus, accursed, unwed, to share their home. Alas, my brother, ill-starred in thy marriage, in thy death thou hast undone my life!

Antistrophe 3.

CHORUS: Reverent action claims a certain praise for reverence; but an offence against power cannot be brooked by him who hath power in his keeping. Thy self-willed temper hath wrought thy ruin.

Epode.

ANTIGONE: Unwept, unfriended, without marriage-song, I am led forth in my sorrow on this journey that can be delayed no more. No longer, hapless one, may I behold yon day-star's sacred eye; but for my fate no tear is shed, no friend makes moan.

CREON: Know ye not that songs and wailings before death would never cease, if it profited to utter them? Away with her—away! And when ye have enclosed her, according to my word, in her vaulted grave, leave her alone, forlorn—whether she wishes to die, or to live a buried life in such a home. Our hands are clean as touching this maiden. But this is certain—she shall be deprived of her sojourn in the light.

ANTIGONE: Tomb, bridal-chamber, eternal prison in the caverned rock, whither I go to find mine own, those many who have perished, and whom Persephone hath received among the dead! Last of all shall I pass thither, and far most miserably of all, before the term of my life is spent. But I cherish good hope that my coming will be welcome to my father, and pleasant to thee, my mother, and welcome, brother, to thee; for, when ye died, with mine own hands I washed and dressed you, and poured drink-offerings at your graves; and now, Polyneices, 'tis for tending thy corpse that I win such recompense as this.

[And yet I honored thee, as the wise will deem, rightly. Never, had I been a mother of children, or if a husband had been mouldering in death, would I have taken this task upon me in the city's despite. What law, ye ask, is my warrant for that word? The husband lost, another might have been found, and child from another, to replace the first-born; but, father and mother hidden with Hades, no brother's life could ever bloom for me again. Such was the law whereby I held thee first in honor; but Creon deemed me guilty of error therein, and of outrage, ah brother mine! And now he leads me thus, a captive in his hands; no bridal bed, no bridal song hath been mine, no joy of marriage, no portion in the nurture of children; but thus, forlorn of friends, unhappy one, I go living to the vaults of death.]

And what law of heaven have I transgressed? Why, hapless one, should I look to the gods any more,—what ally should I invoke,—when by piety I have earned the name of impious? Nay, then, if these things are pleasing to the gods, when I have suffered my doom, I shall come to know my sin; but if the sin is with my judges, I could wish them no fuller measure of evil than they, on their part, mete wrongfully to me.

CHORUS: Still the same tempest of the soul vexes this maiden with the same fierce gusts.

CREON: Then for this shall her guards have cause to rue their slowness.

ANTIGONE: Ah me! that word hath come very near to death.

CREON: I can cheer thee with no hope that this doom is not thus to be fulfilled.

ANTIGONE: O city of my fathers in the land of Thebè! O ye gods, eldest of our race!—they lead me hence—now, now—they tarry not! Behold me, princes of Thebes, the last daughter of the house of your kings,—see what I suffer, and from whom, because I feared to cast away the fear of Heaven! (ANTIGONE *is led away by the guards*)

Strophe 1.

CHORUS: Even thus endured Danaë in her beauty to change the light of day for brass-bound walls; and in that chamber, secret as the grave, she was held close prisoner; yet was she of a proud lineage, O my daughter, and charged with the keeping of the seed of Zeus, that fell in the golden rain.

But dreadful is the mysterious power of fate; there is no deliverance from it by wealth or by war, by fenced city, or dark, sea-beaten ships.

Antistrophe 1.

And bonds tamed the son of Dryas, swift to wrath, that king of the Edonians; so paid he for his frenzied taunts, when, by the will of Dionysus, he was pent in a rocky prison. There the fierce exuberance of his madness slowly passed away. That man learned to know the god, whom in his frenzy he had provoked with mockeries; for he had sought to quell the god-possessed women, and the Bacchanalian fire; and he angered the Muses that love the flute.

Strophe 2.

And by the waters of the Dark Rocks, the waters of the twofold sea, are the shores of Bosporus, and Thracian Salmydessus; where Ares, neighbor to the city, saw the accurst, blinding wound dealt to the two sons of Phineus by his fierce wife,—the wound that brought darkness to those vengeance-craving orbs, smitten with her bloody hands, smitten with her shuttle for a dagger.

Antistrophe 2.

Pining in their misery, they bewailed their cruel doom, those sons of a mother hapless in her marriage; but she traced her descent from the ancient line of the Erechtheidae; and in far-distant caves she was nursed amid her father's storms, that child of Boreas, swift as a steed over the steep hills, a daughter of gods; yet upon her also the gray Fates bore hard, my daughter.

Enter TEIRESIAS, *led by a boy, on the spectators' right.*

TEIRESIAS: Princes of Thebes, we have come with linked steps, both served by the eyes of one; for thus, by a guide's help, the blind must walk.

CREON: And what, aged Teiresias, are thy tidings?

TEIRESIAS: I will tell thee; and do thou hearken to the seer.

CREON: Indeed, it has not been my wont to slight thy counsel.

TEIRESIAS: Therefore didst thou steer our city's course aright.

CREON: I have felt, and can attest, thy benefits.

TEIRESIAS: Mark that now, once more, thou standest on fate's fine edge.

CREON: What means this? How I shudder at thy message!

TEIRESIAS: Thou wilt learn, when thou hearest the warnings of mine art. As I took my place on mine old seat of augury, where all birds have been wont to gather within my ken, I heard a strange voice among them; they were screaming with dire, feverish rage, that drowned their language in a jargon; and I knew that they were rending each other with their talons, murderously; the whirr of wings told no doubtful tale.

Forthwith, in fear, I essayed burnt-sacrifice on a duly kindled altar: but from my offerings the Fire-god showed no flame; a dank moisture, oozing from the thigh-flesh, trickled forth upon the embers, and smoked, and sputtered; the gall was scattered to the air; and the streaming thighs lay bared of the fat that had been wrapped round them.

Such was the failure of the rites by which I vainly asked a sign, as from this boy I learned; for he is my guide, as I am guide to others. And 'tis thy counsel that hath brought this sickness on our State. For the altars of our city and of our hearths have been tainted, one and all, by birds and dogs, with carrion from the hapless corpse, the son of Oedipus: and therefore the gods no more accept prayer and sacrifice at our hands, or the flame of meat-offering; nor doth any bird give a clear sign by its shrill cry, for they have tasted the fatness of a slain man's blood.

Think, then, on these things, my son. All men are liable to err; but when an error hath been made, that man is no longer witless or unblest who heals the ill into which he hath fallen, and remains not stubborn.

Self-will, we know, incurs the charge of folly. Nay, allow the claim of the dead; stab not the fallen; what prowess is it to slay the slain anew? I have sought thy good, and for thy good I speak: and never is it sweeter to learn from a good counselor than when he counsels for thine own gain.

CREON: Old man, ye all shoot your shafts at me, as archers at the butts;—ye must needs practice on me with seer-craft also;—aye, the seer-tribe hath long trafficked in me, and made me their merchandise. Gain your gains, drive your trade, if ye list, in the silver-gold of Sardis and the gold of India; but ye shall not hide that man in the grave,— no, though the eagles of Zeus should bear the carrion morsels to their Master's throne—no, not for dread of that defilement will I suffer his burial:—for well I know that no mortal can defile the gods.—But, aged Teiresias, the wisest fall with a shameful fall, when they clothe shameful thoughts in fair words, for lucre's sake.

TEIRESIAS: Alas! Doth any man know, doth any consider . . .

CREON: Whereof? What general truth dost thou announce?

TEIRESIAS: How precious, above all wealth, is good counsel.

CREON: As folly, I think, is the worst mischief.

TEIRESIAS: Yet thou art tainted with that distemper.

CREON: I would not answer the seer with a taunt.

TEIRESIAS: But thou dost, in saying that I prophesy falsely.

CREON: Well, the prophet-tribe was ever fond of money.

TEIRESIAS: And the race bred of tyrants loves base gain.

CREON: Knowest thou that thy speech is spoken of thy king?

TEIRESIAS: I know it; for through me thou hast saved Thebes.

CREON: Thou art a wise seer; but thou lovest evil deeds.

TEIRESIAS: Thou wilt rouse me to utter the dread secret in my soul.

CREON: Out with it!—Only speak it not for gain.

TEIRESIAS: Indeed, methinks, I shall not,—as touching thee.

CREON: Know that thou shalt not trade on my resolve.

TEIRESIAS: Then know thou—aye, know it well—that thou shalt not live through many more courses of the sun's swift chariot, ere one begotten of thine own loins shall have been given by thee, a corpse for corpses; because thou hast thrust children of the sunlight to the shades, and ruthlessly lodged a living soul in the grave; but keepest in this world one who belongs to the gods infernal, a corpse unburied, unhonored, all unhallowed. In such thou hast no part, nor have the gods above, but this is a violence done to them by thee. Therefore the avenging destroyers lie in wait for thee, the Furies of Hades and of the gods, that thou mayest be taken in these same ills.

And mark well if I speak these things as a hireling. A time not long to be delayed shall awaken the wailing of men and of women in thy house. And a tumult of hatred against thee stirs all the cities whose mangled sons had the burial-rite from dogs, or from wild beasts, or from some winged bird that bore a polluting breath to each city that contains the hearths of the dead.

Such arrows for thy heart—since thou provokest me—have I launched at thee, archer-like, in my anger,—such sure arrows, of which thou shalt not escape the smart.—Boy, lead me home, that he may spend his rage on younger men, and learn to keep a tongue more temperate, and to bear within his breast a better mind than now he bears. (*Exit* TEIRESIAS)

CHORUS: The man hath gone, O king, with dread prophecies. And, since the hair on his head, once dark, hath been white, I know that he hath never been a false prophet to our city.

CREON: I, too, know it well, and am troubled in soul. 'Tis dire to yield; but, by resistance, to smite my pride with ruin—this, too, is a dire choice.

CHORUS: Son of Menoeceus, it behooves thee to take wise counsel.

CREON: What should I do, then? Speak, and I will obey.

CHORUS: Go thou, and free the maiden from her rocky chamber, and make a tomb for the unburied dead.

CREON: And this is thy counsel? Thou wouldst have me yield?

CHORUS: Yea, King, and with all speed; for swift harms from the gods cut short the folly of men.

CREON: Ah me, 'tis hard, but I resign my cherished resolve,—I obey. We must not wage a vain war with destiny.

CHORUS: Go, thou, and do these things; leave them not to others.

CREON: Even as I am I'll go:—on, on, my servants, each and all of you,

—take axes in your hands, and hasten to the ground that ye see yonder! Since our judgment hath taken this turn, I will be present to unloose her, as I myself bound her. My heart misgives me, 'tis best to keep the established laws, even to life's end.

Strophe 1.

CHORUS: O thou of many names, glory of the Cadmeian bride, off-spring of loud-thundering Zeus! thou who watchest over famed Italia, and reignest, where all guests are welcomed, in the sheltered plain of Eleusinian Deô! O Bacchus, dweller in Thebè, mother-city of Bacchants, by the softly-gliding stream of Ismenus, on the soil where the fierce dragon's teeth were sown!

Antistrophe 1.

Thou hast been seen where torch-flames glare through smoke, above the crests of the twin peaks, where move the Corycian nymphs, thy votaries, hard by Castalia's stream.

Thou comest from the ivy-mantled slopes of Nysa's hills, and from the shore green with many-clustered vines, while thy name is lifted up on strains of more than mortal power, as thou visitest the ways of Thebè:

Strophe 2.

Thebè, of all cities, thou holdest first in honor, thou, and thy mother whom the lightning smote; and now, when all our people is captive to a violent plague, come thou with healing feet over the Parnassian height, or over the moaning strait!

Antistrophe 2.

O thou with whom the stars rejoice as they move, the stars whose breath is fire; O master of the voices of the night; son begotten of Zeus; appear, O king, with thine attendant Thyiads, who in night-long frenzy dance before thee, the giver of good gifts, Iacchus!

Enter MESSENGER, *on the spectators' left hand.*

MESSENGER: Dwellers by the house of Cadmus and of Amphion, there is no estate of mortal life that I would ever praise or blame as settled.

Fortune raises and Fortune humbles the lucky or unlucky from day to day, and no one can prophesy to men concerning those things which are established. For Creon was blest once, as I count bliss; he had saved this land of Cadmus from its foes; he was clothed with sole dominion in the land; he reigned, the glorious sire of princely children. And now all hath been lost. For when a man hath forfeited his pleasures, I count him not as living,—I hold him but a breathing corpse. Heap up riches in thy house, if thou wilt; live in kingly state; yet, if there be no gladness therewith, I would not give the shadow of a vapor for all the rest, compared with joy.

CHORUS: And what is this new grief that thou hast to tell for our princes?

MESSENGER: Death; and the living are guilty for the dead.

CHORUS: And who is the slayer? Who the stricken? Speak.

MESSENGER: Haemon hath perished; his blood hath been shed by no stranger.

CHORUS: By his father's hand, or by his own?

MESSENGER: By his own, in wrath with his sire for the murder.

CHORUS: O prophet, how true, then, hast thou proved thy word!

MESSENGER: These things stand thus; ye must consider of the rest.

CHORUS: Lo, I see the hapless Eurydicè, Creon's wife, approaching; she comes from the house by chance, haply,—or because she knows the tidings of her son.

Enter EURYDICÈ.

EURYDICÈ: People of Thebes, I heard your words as I was going forth, to salute the goddess Pallas with my prayers. Even as I was loosing the fastenings of the gate, to open it, the message of a household woe smote on mine ear: I sank back, terror-stricken, into the arms of my handmaids, and my senses fled. But say again what the tidings were; I shall hear them as one who is no stranger to sorrow.

MESSENGER: Dear lady, I will witness of what I saw, and will leave no word of the truth untold. Why, indeed, should I soothe thee with words in which I must presently be found false? Truth is ever best.—I attended thy lord as his guide to the furthest part of the plain, where the body of Polyneices, torn by dogs, still lay unpitied. We prayed the goddess of the roads, and Pluto, in mercy to restrain their wrath; we washed the dead with holy washing; and with freshly-plucked boughs we solemnly burned such relics as there were. We raised a high mound of his native earth; and then we turned away to enter the maiden's nuptial chamber with rocky couch, the caverned mansion of the bride of Death. And, from afar off, one of us heard a voice of loud wailing at that bride's unhallowed bower; and came to tell our master Creon.

And as the king drew nearer, doubtful sounds of a bitter cry floated around him; he groaned, and said in accents of anguish, "Wretched that I am, can my foreboding be true? Am I going on the woefullest way that ever I went? My son's voice greets me.—Go, my servants,— haste ye nearer, and when ye have reached the tomb, pass through the gap, where the stones have been wrenched away, to the cell's very mouth,—and look, and see if 'tis Haemon's voice that I know, or if mine ear is cheated by the gods."

This search, at our despairing master's word, we went to make; and in the furthest part of the tomb we descried *her* hanging by the neck, slung by a thread-wrought halter of fine linen; while *he* was embracing her with arms thrown around her waist,—bewailing the loss of his bride who is with the dead, and his father's deeds, and his own ill-starred love.

But his father, when he saw him, cried aloud with a dread cry and went in, and called to him with a voice of wailing:—"Unhappy, what a deed hast thou done! What thought hath come to thee? What manner of mischance hath marred thy reason? Come forth, my child! I pray thee—I implore!" But the boy glared at him with fierce eyes, spat in his face, and, without a word of answer, drew his cross-hilted sword:— as his father rushed forth in flight, he missed his aim;—then, hapless one, wroth with himself, he straightway leaned with all his weight against his sword, and drove it, half its length, into his side; and, while sense lingered, he clasped the maiden to his faint embrace, and, as he gasped, sent forth on her pale cheek the swift stream of the oozing blood.

Corpse enfolding corpse he lies; he hath won his nuptial rites, poor youth, not here, yet in the halls of Death; and he hath witnessed to mankind that, of all curses which cleave to man, ill counsel is the sovereign curse. (EURYDICÈ *retires into the house*)

CHORUS: What wouldst thou augur from this? The lady hath turned back, and is gone, without a word, good or evil.

MESSENGER: I, too, am startled; yet I nourish the hope that, at these sore tidings of her son, she cannot deign to give her sorrow public vent, but in the privacy of the house will set her handmaids to mourn the household grief. For she is not untaught of discretion, that she should err.

CHORUS: I know not; but to me, at least, a strained silence seems to portend peril, no less than vain abundance of lament.

MESSENGER: Well, I will enter the house, and learn whether indeed she is not hiding some repressed purpose in the depths of a passionate heart. Yea, thou sayest well: excess of silence, too, may have a perilous meaning. (*Exit* MESSENGER)

Enter CREON, *on the spectators' left, with attendants, carrying the shrouded body of* HAEMON *on a bier*

CHORUS: Lo, yonder the king himself draws near, bearing that which tells too clear a tale,—the work of no stranger's madness,—if we may say it,—but of his own misdeeds.

Strophe 1.

CREON: Woe for the sins of a darkened soul, stubborn sins, fraught with death! Ah, ye behold us, the sire who hath slain, the son who hath perished! Woe is me, for the wretched blindness of my counsels! Alas, my son, thou hast died in thy youth, by a timeless doom, woe is me!—thy spirit hath fled,—not by thy folly, but by mine own!

Strophe 2.

CHORUS: Ah me, how all too late thou seemest to see the right!
CREON: Ah me, I have learned the bitter lesson! But then, methinks, oh then, some god smote me from above with crushing weight, and hurled me into ways of cruelty, woe is me,—overthrowing and trampling on my joy! Woe, woe, for the troublous toils of men!

Enter MESSENGER *from the house*

MESSENGER: Sire, thou hast come, methinks, as one whose hands are not empty, but who hath store laid up besides; thou bearest yonder burden with thee; and thou art soon to look upon the woes within thy house.
CREON: And what worse ill is yet to follow upon ills?
MESSENGER: Thy queen hath died, true mother of yon corpse—ah, hapless lady!—by blows newly dealt.

Antistrophe 1.

CREON: Oh Hades, all-receiving, whom no sacrifice can appease! Hast thou, then, no mercy for me? O thou herald of evil, bitter tidings, what word dost thou utter? Alas, I was already as dead, and thou hast smitten me anew! What sayest thou, my son? What is this new message that thou bringest—woe, woe is me!—of a wife's doom,—of slaughter heaped on slaughter?

CHORUS: Thou canst behold: 'tis no longer hidden within. (*The doors of the palace are opened, and the corpse of* EURYDICÈ *is disclosed*)

Antistrophe 2.

CREON: Ah me,—yonder I behold a new, a second woe! What destiny, ah what, can yet await me? I have but now raised my son in my arms, —and there, again, I see a corpse before me! Alas, alas, unhappy mother! Alas, my child!

MESSENGER: There, at the altar, self-stabbed with a keen knife, she suffered her darkening eyes to close, when she had wailed for the noble fate of Megareus who died before, and then for his fate who lies there,—and when, with her last breath, she had invoked evil fortunes upon thee, the slayer of thy sons.

Strophe 3.

CREON: Woe, woe! I thrill with dread. Is there none to strike me to the heart with two-edged sword?—O miserable that I am, and steeped in miserable anguish!

MESSENGER: Yea, both this son's doom, and that other's, were laid to thy charge by her whose corpse thou seest.

CREON: And what was the manner of the violent deed by which she passed away?

MESSENGER: Her own hand struck her to the heart, when she had learned her son's sorely lamented fate.

Strophe 4.

CREON: And what was the manner of the fixed on any other of mortal kind, for my acquittal! I, even I, was thy slayer, wretched that I am —I own the truth. Lead me away, O my servants, lead me hence with all speed, whose life is but as death!

CHORUS: Thy counsels are good, if there can be good with ills; briefest is best, when trouble is in our path.

Antistrophe 3.

CREON: Oh, let it come, let it appear, that fairest of fates for me, that brings my last day,—aye, best fate of all! Oh, let it come, that I may never look upon tomorrow's light.

CHORUS: These things are in the future; present tasks claim our care: the ordering of the future rests where it should rest.

CREON: All my desires, at least, were summed in that prayer.

CHORUS: Pray thou no more; for mortals have no escape from destined woe.

Antistrophe 4.

CREON: Lead me away, I pray you; a rash, foolish man; who have slain thee, ah my son, unwittingly, and thee, too, my wife—unhappy that I am! I know not which way I should bend my gaze, or where I should seek support; for all is amiss with that which is in my hands,— and yonder, again, a crushing fate hath leapt upon my head. (*As* CREON *is being conducted into the house, the Coryphaeus speaks the closing verses*)

CHORUS: Wisdom is the supreme part of happiness; and reverence towards the gods must be inviolate. Great words of prideful men are ever punished with great blows, and, in old age, teach the chastened to be wise.

STUDY AND DISCUSSION QUESTIONS*

1. (Scene I) What purpose does the Prologue serve? What is Ismene's dramatic function? Analyze the speech of the Chorus. Is there any relationship between what they discuss and the preceding conversation between Antigone and Ismene? Does Antigone's background give any clue to her character? Analyze Creon's speech. How does he interpret the motives of others? What is the central conflict between Creon and Antigone? In the first Choral Ode what is the attitude expressed toward Man?

2. (Scene II) Why does a whirlwind hide Antigone's movements when she returns to bury the body? What are the reasons she gives Creon for burying her brother? Both Creon and Antigone defend their actions on the basis of "the law." What is this law? Why is Ismene willing to share the guilt with her sister? In the second Choral

---

* Questions 1-5 reflect the breaks in the action of the play that follow the speeches of the Chorus. For purposes of discussion we shall call them scenes even though they are not so designated in the play.

Ode what explanation does the Chorus give for the disaster that befalls Antigone?

3. (Scene III) What function does Haemon play? Why has he not appeared until this scene? What reasons does he give to Creon for delaying the sentence imposed on Antigone? Why does Creon reject Haemon's arguments? What thematic purpose is served in the third Choral Ode?

4. (Scene IV) What is Antigone's reaction to the comments of the Chorus as she awaits her death? What parallel does the story of Niobe have with Antigone's impending death? Has Antigone's state of mind altered since the last scene? What does the Chorus mean when it says, "But in this ordeal thou art paying, haply, for thy father's sin"? What is the significance of the arrangements Creon makes for Antigone's death? In the fourth Choral Ode the Chorus tells a series of tragic tales. What is the importance of these tales at this particular time?

5. What dramatic function does Teiresias serve? Why does Creon initially refuse to accept his recommendations? Why does he change his mind? Is it significant that the prophet is blind? Why does the Chorus accept the prophecy of Teiresias without question? Why does Creon change his mind concerning the death sentence? What is the significance of Eurydice's death? Why does Creon order the burial of Polyneices before he releases Antigone? Is the punishment Creon receives justifiable?

6. Cedric H. Whitman (*Sophocles, a Study of Heroic Humanism*) says that "the *Antigone* unquestionably reflects one of the earliest phases of the rift between city and citizen; Creon, drawn in tyrannical or oligarchic colors, embodies the moral atrophy of civic institutions, while the heroine herself presents the ideal of individual moral perception." Discuss this interpretation in terms of the action in the play.

7. H. D. F. Kitto (*Form and Meaning in Drama*) sees as the basis of the conflict Creon's failure to recognize the consequences of not allowing the burial of the body. Kitto construes this act as "an offence against Nature herself, against the laws of the gods, against the constitution of the universe—they are the same thing." How does Antigone's position confirm this view? Discuss.

8. Using the bases of analysis suggested in question 9 under *Oedipus*, study the use of figurative language in the first scene. What is

being compared in the metaphors and similes? Point out examples of antithesis (the balancing of two contrasted words, ideas, or phrases against each other) and anaphora (the repetition of a word or phrase at the beginning of several successive verses, clauses) in this scene.

9. Much of the action in both *Oedipus the King* and *Antigone* is developed through the use of messengers. Compare their various uses in relation to the structure. Sophocles also employs other characters very effectively in both plays. Compare and contrast the roles of the Chorus, Creon, and Teiresias in the two tragedies.

WRITING TOPICS

1. Write an essay arguing for or against Creon as a sympathetic character; that is, whether or not he is justified in his actions. *Or* develop an essay analyzing the character of Antigone in terms of her attitude and actions. *Or* write an essay establishing the dramatic function of the minor characters (Ismene, Haemon, Eurydice, and Teiresias).

2. Write an essay developing the theme suggested by either Cedric H. Whitman or H. D. F. Kitto arguing for or against these suggested interpretations.

3. Write an essay establishing the character of the Chorus in *Antigone* and (if possible) compare and contrast it with the Chorus in *Oedipus.*

4. Write an essay in which the antagonistic elements in *Oedipus* and *Antigone* are compared and contrasted. *Or* discuss the use of mythological figures in the two plays.

Shakespeare

Elizabethan drama flourished during one of the most prosperous and vital periods in English history. At the time Shakespeare wrote, England enjoyed a national unity and solidarity previously unknown, commerce was developing rapidly, and men's geographic and intellectual horizons were widening at an unprecedented rate. The English Renaissance had stimulated a new interest in literature, art, and the achievements of the past. At the same time, old ideas and traditions were breaking up—witness the Reformation—and men were no longer reluctant to experiment.

In drama, however, the Elizabethan audience, like the Greek, was less insistent upon originality than upon the effective re-telling of familiar stories. For the most part the dramatists took as their models the work of the classical Roman dramatists, notably Plautus and Seneca, whose plays are not representative of the finest in ancient drama. Elizabethans were largely ignorant of Greek tragedy, but in another respect it is perhaps just as well, for the Greek qualities of restraint and symmetry were scarcely in keeping with their audience's tastes, and, perhaps, with their own natural temper.

The audience was a fascinatingly amorphous group, and just as the Greek theater influenced the form of Greek drama, the Elizabethan audience dictated something of the form and content of the Elizabethan drama. The typical audience was composed of gentlemen, clerks, fops, tradesmen, dandies, and the lowly groundlings. Its tastes ran to intricately plotted plays full of suspense, spectacle, surprise, and violence. The crude tragedy-of-blood, with its revenge motif, its ghosts, and its corpse-littered concluding scene, was a particular favorite. But while this audience cared little for subtle ideas, it did care a great deal about character, and its dual preoccupation with story and characterization is reflected in the work of Shakespeare and his contemporaries.

The Elizabethan theater was much different from the Greek, and because it too influenced the form of the drama played out upon its boards, it merits a brief description here. The several London theaters varied in shape from square to round, but most of them had certain physical characteristics in common. For example, in all but the winter theaters only the galleries and rear stage were roofed; the pit, where the groundlings stood throughout the performance, was without cover of any sort. The stage itself consisted of three parts: front, back, and upper level. Front stage projected into the middle of the theater and was the scene of most of the action. It was surrounded on three sides by spectators, who for a good share of the play had the actors performing in their very midst. Back stage was generally used to represent another scene, frequently a background scene, such as a house, a forest, or a cave. The upper stage often served as a balcony, or in dramas of war as a wall or tower. The significant fact is that the Elizabethan stage had no drop curtains (though the back stage did have a draw curtain). Consequently the playwright could and did shift his scene with extraordinary frequency merely by sending some actors off one area of the stage and immediately bringing others on another. With so many scenes and characters, a detailed, loosely woven plot could be performed with relative ease, hence the complexity of the typical Elizabethan story.

Elizabethan tragedy bears little surface resemblance to the tragedy of the Greeks. Where the latter is stylized, logical, and restrained, the former is robust, energetic, and above everything else imaginative. Shakespeare and his fellow dramatists shaped their plays from the raw materials of violent passions and rude humours. They wrote for a special audience and catered to its tastes. Yet it is to their everlasting credit that the type of tragedy they created ranks as the greatest in the English tradition, and in the minds of many readers it rivals and even surpasses the finest work of the Greeks.

Shakespeare (1564-1616): A Biographical Note. A vast amount of scholarship has been devoted to the life and work of William Shakespeare, however, we know surprisingly little about the man himself. We know he was born in the small town of Stratford, at eighteen he married Ann Hathaway, eight years his senior, and sometime around 1588 he went to London to seek his fortune. In London he wrote some of the finest poetry in the English language, and became active in the theater as actor and playwright. His reputation and his fortune grew, and by 1600 he was one of the most popular playwrights in London. Approximately eleven years later he was able to retire, a wealthy and successful man. Shakespeare was that rare sort of artist who could at one and the same time contrive to appeal to popular tastes and satisfy his own standards of excellence. His name has become synonymous with literary greatness.

ROMEO AND JULIET

William Shakespeare
Edited by Hardin Craig

Dramatis Personae

ESCALUS, *prince of Verona.*
PARIS, *a young nobleman, kinsman to the prince.*
MONTAGUE,⎱ *heads of two houses at variance*
CAPULET, ⎰ *with each other.*
An old man, cousin to Capulet.
ROMEO, *son to Montague.*
MERCUTIO, *kinsman to the prince, and friend to Romeo.*
BENVOLIO, *nephew to Montague, and friend to Romeo.*
TYBALT, *nephew to Lady Capulet.*
FRIAR LAURENCE,⎱ *Franciscans.*
FRIAR JOHN, ⎰
BALTHASAR, *servant to Romeo.*
SAMPSON,⎱ *servants to Capulet.*
GREGORY, ⎰
PETER, *servant to Juliet's nurse.*
ABRAHAM, *servant to Montague.*
AN APOTHECARY.
Three Musicians.
Page to Paris; another Page; an Officer.
LADY MONTAGUE, *wife to Montague.*

Reprinted from *An Introduction to Shakespeare*, edited by Hardin Craig. Copyright 1952 by Scott, Foresman and Company.

LADY CAPULET, *wife to Capulet.*
JULIET, *daughter to Capulet.*
Nurse to Juliet.
Citizens of Verona; several Men and Women, relations to both houses;
Maskers, Guards, Watchmen, and Attendants.
CHORUS.

Scene, *Verona: Mantua.*

PROLOGUE

Two households, both alike in dignity,
    In fair Verona, where we lay our scene,
From ancient grudge break to new mutiny,
    Where civil blood makes civil hands unclean.
From forth the fatal loins of these two foes
    A pair of star-cross'd lovers take their life;
Whose misadventured piteous overthrows
    Do with their death bury their parents' strife.
The fearful passage of their death-mark'd love,
    And the continuance of their parents' rage,   10
Which, but their children's end, nought could remove,
    Is now the two hours' traffic of our stage;
The which if you with patient ears attend,
What here shall miss, our toil shall strive to mend.

PROLOGUE. The prologue is in the form of a Shakespearean sonnet, three quatrains and a couplet of five-foot iambic verse.

3. *mutiny*, state of discord.

6. *star-cross'd*, thwarted by destiny. Shakespeare shows in this play particularly, and throughout his plays generally, the current belief in the power of the stars. The idea blends with that of divine providence.

9. *fearful*, full of fear. *passage*, progress.

12. *two hours' traffic of our stage*. This line is one of a small number of references which enable us to tell the length of time occupied by a Shakespearean play. If the time was nearer two hours than three, the play must have been rapidly recited, with little loss of time between scenes. The bareness of the stage and the lack of a curtain would have contributed to the speed of presentation.

ACT I.

Scene I, *Verona. A public place.*

Enter SAMPSON *and* GREGORY *of the house of Capulet, armed with swords and bucklers.*

SAM: Gregory, o' my word, we'll not carry coals.

GRE: No, for then we should be colliers.

SAM: I mean, an we be in choler, we'll draw.

GRE: Ay, while you live, draw your neck out o' the collar.

SAM: I strike quickly, being moved.

GRE: But thou art not quickly moved to strike.

SAM: A dog of the house of Montague moves me.   10

GRE: To move is to stir; and to be valiant is to stand: therefore, if thou art moved, thou runn'st away.

SAM: A dog of that house shall move me to stand: I will take the wall of any man or maid of Montague's.

GRE: That shows thee a weak slave; for the weakest goes to the wall.

SAM: True; and therefore women, being the weaker vessels, are ever thrust to the wall: therefore I will push Montague's men from the wall, and thrust his maids to the wall.

GRE: The quarrel is between our masters and us their men.

SAM: 'Tis all one, I will show myself a tyrant: when I have fought with the men, I will be cruel with the maids, and cut off their heads.

GRE: The heads of the maids?   29

SAM: Ay, the heads of the maids, or their maidenheads; take it in what sense thou wilt.

GRE: They must take it in sense that feel it.

SAM: Me they shall feel while I am able to stand: and 'tis known I am a pretty piece of flesh.

ACT I. SCENE I. This scene serves to give us the atmosphere of the whole play, an atmosphere of feud. Sampson is a stupid bully, Gregory a merry one.

1. *carry coals,* endure insults; the word play is on the dirty trade of the collier.

4. *choler,* one of the four humors, productive of anger.

6. *collar,* halter.

10. *moves,* incites.

15. *take the wall,* take the side of the walk nearest the wall, an act of discourtesy.

GRE: 'Tis well thou art not fish; if thou hadst, thou hadst been poor John. Draw thy tool; here comes two of the house of the Montagues.

SAM: My naked weapon is out: quarrel, I will back thee.   40

GRE: How! turn thy back and run?

SAM: Fear me not.

GRE: No, marry; I fear thee!

SAM: Let us take the law of our sides; let them begin.

GRE: I will frown as I pass by, and let them take it as they list.

SAM: Nay, as they dare. I will bite my thumb at them; which is a disgrace to them, if they bear it.   50

Enter ABRAHAM *and* BALTHASAR.

ABR: Do you bite your thumb at us, sir?

SAM: I do bite my thumb, sir.

ABR: Do you bite your thumb at us, sir?

SAM: (*Aside to* GRE.) Is the law of our side, if I say ay?

GRE: No.

SAM: No, sir, I do not bite my thumb at you, sir, but I bite my thumb, sir.

GRE: Do you quarrel, sir?

ABR: Quarrel, sir! no, sir.   60

SAM: If you do, sir, I am for you: I serve as good a man as you.

ABR: No better.

SAM: Well, sir.

GRE: Say 'better:' here comes one of my master's kinsmen.

SAM: Yes, better, sir.

ABR: You lie.

SAM: Draw, if you be men. Gregory, remember thy swashing   70
blow. (*They fight.*)

Enter BENVOLIO.

BEN: Part, fools!
Put up your swords; you know not what you do. (*Beats down their swords.*)

---

37. *poor John*, hake salted and dried—a poor kind of food.
42. *Fear*, mistrust.
43. *marry*, mild oath; originally an oath by the Virgin Mary.
47. *list*, please.
48. *bite my thumb*, an insulting gesture.
70. *swashing*, crushing.

Enter TYBALT.

TYB: What, art thou drawn among these heartless hinds? Turn thee,
Benvolio, look upon thy death.
BEN: I do but keep the peace: put up thy sword,
Or manage it to part these men with me.
TYB: What, drawn, and talk of peace! I hate the word,
As I hate hell, all Montagues, and thee:
Have at thee, coward! (*They fight.*)

Enter several of both houses, who join the fray; then enter CITI-
ZENS, *with clubs.*

FIRST CIT: Clubs, bills, and partisans! strike! beat them down!   80
Down with the Capulets! down with the Montagues!

Enter CAPULET *in his gown, and* LADY CAPULET.

CAP: What noise is this? Give me my long sword, ho!
LA. CAP: A crutch, a crutch! why call you for a sword?
CAP: My sword, I say! Old Montague is come,
And flourishes his blade in spite of me.

Enter MONTAGUE *and* LADY MONTAGUE.

MON: Thou villain Capulet,—Hold me not, let me go.
LA. MON: Thou shalt not stir a foot to seek a foe.

Enter PRINCE, *with* ATTENDANTS.

PRIN: Rebellious subjects, enemies to peace,
Profaners of this neighbour-stained steel,—
Will they not hear? What, ho! you men, you beasts,   90
That quench the fire of your pernicious rage
With purple fountains issuing from your veins,

---

73. *drawn*, with drawn sword. *heartless hinds*, cowardly menials. Tybalt's spirit is
irreconcilable throughout.
79. *Have at thee*, I shall attack thee, defend thyself.
80. *Clubs, bills, and partisans*, a rallying cry of London apprentices. *Bills* and
partisans were long-handled spears with cutting blades.
83. *crutch*, i.e., a crutch would befit him better than a sword.

On pain of torture, from those bloody hands
Throw your mistemper'd weapons to the ground,
And hear the sentence of your moved prince.
Three civil brawls, bred of an airy word,
By thee, old Capulet, and Montague,
Have thrice disturb'd the quiet of our streets,
And made Verona's ancient citizens
Cast by their grave beseeming ornaments,   100
To wield old partisans, in hands as old,
Canker'd with peace, to part your canker'd hate:
If ever you disturb our streets again,
Your lives shall pay the forfeit of the peace.
For this time, all the rest depart away:
You, Capulet, shall go along with me:
And, Montague, come you this afternoon,
To know our further pleasure in this case,
To old Free-town, our common judgement-place.
Once more, on pain of death, all men depart. (*Exeunt all*   110
but MONTAGUE, LADY MONTAGUE, *and* BENVOLIO.)
MON: Who set this ancient quarrel new abroach?
Speak, nephew, were you by when it began?
BEN: Here were the servants of your adversary,
And yours, close fighting ere I did approach:
I drew to part them: in the instant came
The fiery Tybalt, with his sword prepared,
Which, as he breathed defiance to my ears,
He swung about his head and cut the winds,
Who nothing hurt withal hiss'd him in scorn:
While we were interchanging thrusts and blows,   120
Came more and more and fought on part and part,
Till the prince came, who parted either part.
LA. MON: O, where is Romeo? saw you him to-day?
Right glad I am he was not at this fray.
BEN: Madam, an hour before the worshipp'd sun
Peer'd forth the golden window of the east,
A troubled mind drave me to walk abroad;
Where, underneath the grove of sycamore
That westward rooteth from the city's side,

---

102. *Canker'd . . . canker'd*, corroded . . . malignant.
109. *Free-town*, Villa Franca in Brooke's poem *Romeus and Juliet*.
111. *set . . . abroach*, reopened.
119. *nothing*, not at all. *withal*, with this.
127. *drave*, drove; archaic preterit.

So early walking did I see your son: 130
Towards him I made, but he was ware of me
And stole into the covert of the wood:
I, measuring his affections by my own,
That most are busied when they're most alone,
Pursued my humour not pursuing his,
And gladly shunn'd who gladly fled from me.
MON: Many a morning hath he there been seen,
With tears augmenting the fresh morning's dew,
Adding to clouds more clouds with his deep sighs;
But all so soon as the all-cheering sun 140
Should in the furthest east begin to draw
The shady curtains from Aurora's bed,
Away from light steals home my heavy son,
And private in his chamber pens himself,
Shuts up his windows, locks fair daylight out
And makes himself an artificial night:
Black and portentous must this humour prove,
Unless good counsel may the cause remove.
BEN: My noble uncle, do you know the cause?
MON: I neither know it nor can learn of him. 150
BEN: Have you importuned him by any means?
MON: Both by myself and many other friends:
But he, his own affections' counsellor,
Is to himself—I will not say how true—
But to himself so secret and so close,
So far from sounding and discovery,
As is the bud bit with an envious worm,
Ere he can spread his sweet leaves to the air,
Or dedicate his beauty to the sun.
Could we but learn from whence his sorrows grow, 160
We would as willingly give cure as know.

Enter ROMEO.

BEN: See, where he comes: so please you, step aside;
I'll know his grievance, or be much denied.

---

133. *affections*, wishes, inclination.
135. *humour*, mood, whim.
143. *heavy*, sad.
151. *means*, agency.
155. *close*, secret, private.
157. *envious*, malicious.
163. *denied*, refused.

MON: I would thou wert so happy by thy stay,
To hear true shrift. Come, madam, let's away. (*Exeunt* MONTAGUE *and*
LADY.)
BEN: Good morrow, cousin.
ROM: Is the day so young?
BEN: But new struck nine.
ROM: Ay me! sad hours seem long.
Was that my father that went hence so fast?
BEN: It was. What sadness lengthens Romeo's hours?
ROM: Not having that, which, having, makes them short.
BEN: In love?   171
ROM: Out—
BEN: Of love?
ROM: Out of her favour, where I am in love.
BEN: Alas, that love, so gentle in his view,
Should be so tyrannous and rough in proof!
ROM: Alas, that love, whose view is muffled still,
Should, without eyes, see pathways to his will!
Where shall we dine? O me! What fray was here?
Yet tell me not, for I have heard it all.   180
Here 's much to do with hate, but more with love.
Why, then, O brawling love! O loving hate!
O any thing, of nothing first create!
O heavy lightness! serious vanity!
Mis-shapen chaos of well-seeming forms!
Feather of lead, bright smoke, cold fire, sick health!
Still-waking sleep, that is not what it is!
This love feel I, that feel no love in this.
Dost thou not laugh?
BEN: No, coz, I rather weep.
ROM: Good heart, at what?
BEN: At thy good heart's oppression.   190
ROM: Why, such is love's transgression.

_____

165. *shrift*, confession.
166. *morrow*, morning. *cousin*, any relative not belonging to one's immediate
family.
168. *Was . . . fast.* This line is matter of fact, not sentimental like Romeo's other
utterances. See also line 179.
174. *favour*, good will, liking.
176. *proof*, experience.
181-188. *Here 's . . . this.* These lines, abounding in paradoxical phrases called
oxymoron, such as *loving hate, cold fire*, are characteristic of artificial love poetry.
They indicate Romeo's sentimentality.

Griefs of mine own lie heavy in my breast,
Which thou wilt propagate, to have it prest
With more of thine: this love that thou hast shown
Doth add more grief to too much of mine own.
Love is a smoke raised with the fume of sighs;
Being purged, a fire sparkling in lovers' eyes;
Being vex'd, a sea nourish'd with lovers' tears:
What is it else? a madness most discreet,
A choking gall and a preserving sweet.   200
Farewell, my coz.
BEN: Soft! I will go along;
An if you leave me so, you do me wrong.
ROM: Tut, I have lost myself; I am not here;
This is not Romeo, he 's some other where.
BEN: Tell me in sadness, who is that you love.
ROM: What, shall I groan and tell thee?
BEN: Groan! why, no:
But sadly tell me who.
ROM: Bid a sick man in sadness make his will:
Ah, word ill urged to one that is so ill!
In sadness, cousin, I do love a woman.   210
BEN: I aim'd so near, when I supposed you loved.
ROM: A right good mark-man! And she 's fair I love.
BEN: A right fair mark, fair coz, is soonest hit.
ROM: Well, in that hit you miss: she'll not be hit
With Cupid's arrow; she hath Dian's wit;
And, in strong proof of chastity well arm'd,
From love's weak childish bow she lives unharm'd.
She will not stay the siege of loving terms,
Nor bide the encounter of assailing eyes,
Nor ope her lap to saint-seducing gold: 220
O, she is rich in beauty, only poor,
That when she dies with beauty dies her store.
BEN: Then she hath sworn that she will still live chaste?
ROM: She hath, and in that sparing makes huge waste,

---

193. *propagate*, increase.
208. *sadness*, seriousness.
212. *fair*, beautiful.
213. *fair*, clear, distinct.
216. *proof*, impenetrable armor.
218. *stay*, withstand.
222. *store*. She will die without children and therefore her beauty will die with her.

For beauty starved with her severity
Cuts beauty off from all posterity.
She is too fair, too wise, wisely too fair,
To merit bliss by making me despair:
She hath forsworn to love, and in that vow
Do I live dead that live to tell it now.　　　　　　　　230
BEN:　Be ruled by me, forget to think of her.
ROM:　O, teach me how I should forget to think.
BEN:　By giving liberty unto thine eyes;
Examine other beauties.
ROM:　　　　　　　'Tis the way
To call hers exquisite, in question more:
These happy masks that kiss fair ladies' brows
Being black put us in mind they hide the fair;
He that is strucken blind cannot forget
The precious treasure of his eyesight lost:
Show me a mistress that is passing fair,　　　　　　　　240
What doth her beauty serve, but as a note
Where I may read who pass'd that passing fair?
Farewell: thou canst not teach me to forget.
BEN:　I'll pay that doctrine, or else die in debt. (*Exeunt.*)

Scene II, *A street.*

Enter CAPULET, PARIS, *and* SERVANT.

CAP:　But Montague is bound as well as I,
In penalty alike; and 'tis not hard, I think,
For men so old as we to keep the peace.
PAR:　Of honourable reckoning are you both;
And pity 'tis you lived at odds so long.
But now, my lord, what say you to my suit?
CAP:　But saying o'er what I have said before:

---

225. *starved*, allowed to die.
235. *in question more*, into greater consideration.
240. *passing*, surpassingly.
244. *pay that doctrine*, give that instruction.
SCENE II. 4. *reckoning*, estimation, repute.

My child is yet a stranger in the world;
She hath not seen the change of fourteen years;
Let two more summers wither in their pride,   10
Ere we may think her ripe to be a bride.
PAR: Younger than she are happy mothers made.
CAP: And too soon marr'd are those so early made.
The earth hath swallow'd all my hopes but she,
She is the hopeful lady of my earth:
But woo her, gentle Paris, get her heart,
My will to her consent is but a part;
An she agree, within her scope of choice
Lies my consent and fair according voice.
This night I hold an old accustom'd feast,   20
Whereto I have invited many a guest,
Such as I love; and you, among the store,
One more, most welcome, makes my number more.
At my poor house look to behold this night
Earth-treading stars that make dark heaven light:
Such comfort as do lusty young men feel
When well-apparell'd April on the heel
Of limping winter treads, even such delight
Among fresh female buds shall you this night
Inherit at my house; hear all, all see,   30
And like her most whose merit most shall be:
†Which on more view, of many mine being one
May stand in number, though in reckoning none.
Come, go with me. (*To* SERV., *giving a paper.*) Go, sirrah, trudge about
Through fair Verona; find those persons out
Whose names are written there, and to them say,

---

8. *stranger in the world.* Capulet's reluctance is largely a matter of manners.

15. *lady . . . earth,* i.e., she is the heir of his estate or more probably, his only hope in the world.

17. *My . . . part.* This is also a conventional statement, since Capulet has no idea of letting Juliet have her way.

18. *An,* if. *scope,* limit.

25. *Earth-treading . . . light,* stars on earth that illuminate the dark heavens with their beams.

29. *female,* so Q_1; Q_2 and F read *fennel,* which can be justified by the circumstance that fennel was thought to have the power of awakening passion.

32-33. *Which . . . none.* Capulet may mean that his daughter will lose her identity by being swallowed up in a number of others. He is punning on the saying, "one is no number." The Arden editor places a comma after *of* and dashes after *many* and *one.* He explains *reckoning* to mean "estimation" (as in line 4, above), with word play, i.e., "counting heads."

34. *sirrah,* customary form of address to servants.

My house and welcome on their pleasure stay. (*Exeunt*　　　37
CAPULET *and* PARIS.)
SERV:　Find them out whose names are written here! It is written, that
the shoemaker should meddle with his yard, and the tailor with his
last, the fisher with his pencil, and the painter with his nets; but I am
sent to find those persons whose names are here writ, and can never
find what names the writing person hath here writ. I must to the
learned.—In good time.　　　　　　　　　　　　　　　　　　45

Enter BENVOLIO and ROMEO.

BEN:　Tut, man, one fire burns out another's burning,
　One pain is lessen'd by another's anguish;
Turn giddy, and be holp by backward turning;
　One desperate grief cures with another's languish:
Take thou some new infection to thy eye,　　　　.　　　50
And the rank poison of the old will die.
ROM:　Your plaintain-leaf is excellent for that.
BEN:　For what, I pray thee?
ROM:　　　　　　　　For your broken shin.
BEN:　Why, Romeo, art thou mad?
ROM:　Not mad, but bound more than a madman is;
Shut up in prison, kept without my food,
Whipp'd and tormented and—God-den, good fellow.
SERV:　God gi' god-den. I pray, sir, can you read?
ROM:　Ay, mine own fortune in my misery.　　　　　　60
SERV:　Perhaps you have learned it without book: but, I pray, can you
read any thing you see?
ROM:　Ay, if I know the letters and the language.
SERV:　Ye say honestly: rest you merry!
ROM:　Stay, fellow; I can read. (*Reads*.)
'Signior Martino and his wife and daughters; County Anselme and
his beauteous sisters; the lady widow of Vitruvio; Signior Placentio and
his lovely nieces; Mercutio and his brother Valentine; mine uncle
Capulet, his wife, and daughters; my fair niece Rosaline; Livia; Signior
Valentio and his cousin Tybalt; Lucio and the lively Helena.'　　74
A fair assembly: whither should they come?
SERV:　Up.

---

46. *one . . . burning.* Cf. the proverb, "fire drives out fire."
48. *holp*, helped.
51. *rank*, corrupt.
57. *God-den*, good evening. *fellow*, usual term for a servant.

ROM: Whither?

SERV: To supper; to our house.

ROM: Whose house?

SERV: My master's.   80

ROM: Indeed, I should have asked you that before.

SERV: Now I'll tell you without asking: my master is the great rich Capulet; and if you be not of the house of Montagues, I pray, come and crush a cup of wine. Rest you merry! (*Exit.*)

BEN: At this same ancient feast of Capulet's
Sups the fair Rosaline whom thou so lovest,
With all the admired beauties of Verona:
Go thither; and, with unattainted eye,   90
Compare her face with some that I shall show,
And I will make thee think thy swan a crow.

ROM: When the devout religion of mine eye
  Maintains such falsehood, then turn tears to fires;
And these, who often drown'd could never die,
  Transparent heretics, be burnt for liars!
One fairer than my love! the all-seeing sun
Ne'er saw her match since first the world begun.

BEN: Tut, you saw her fair, none else being by,
Herself poised with herself in either eye: 100
But in that crystal scales let there be weigh'd
Your lady's love against some other maid
That I will show you shining at this feast,
And she shall scant show well that now shows best.

ROM: I'll go along, no such sight to be shown,
But to rejoice in splendour of mine own. (*Exeunt.*)

Scene III, *A room in Capulet's house.*

Enter LADY CAPULET *and* NURSE.

LA. CAP: Nurse, where 's my daughter? call her forth to me.

NURSE: Now, by my maidenhead, at twelve year old,

---

86. *crush a cup of wine,* drink a cup of wine. Cf. "crack a bottle."
87. *ancient,* customary.
89. *admired,* wondered at.
90. *unattained,* impartial.
95. *these,* i.e., these eyes.

I bade her come. What, lamb! what, ladybird!
God forbid! Where 's this girl? What, Juliet!

Enter JULIET.

JUL: How now! who calls?
NURSE: Your mother.
JUL: Madam, I am here.
What is your will?
LA. CAP: This is the matter:—Nurse, give leave awhile,
We must talk in secret:—nurse, come back again;
I have remember'd me, thou 's hear our counsel.
Thou know'st my daughter 's of a pretty age.   10
NURSE: Faith, I can tell her age unto an hour.
LA. CAP: She 's not fourteen.
NURSE: I'll lay fourteen of my teeth,—
And yet, to my teen be it spoken, I have but four,—
She is not fourteen. How long is it now
To Lammas-tide?
LA. CAP: A fortnight and odd days.
NURSE: Even or odd, of all days in the year,
Come Lammas-eve at night shall she be fourteen.
Susan and she—God rest all Christian souls!—
Were of an age: well, Susan is with God;
She was too good for me: but, as I said,   20
On Lammas-eve at night shall she be fourteen;
That shall she, marry; I remember it well.
'Tis since the earthquake now eleven years;
And she was wean'd,—I never shall forget it,—
Of all the days of the year, upon that day:
For I had then laid wormwood to my dug,
Sitting in the sun under the dove-house wall;
My lord and you were then at Mantua:—
Nay, I do bear a brain:—but, as I said,

SCENE III. 7. *give leave*, leave us.
9. *thou 's*, thou shalt.
10. *pretty*, moderately great.
13. *teen*, sorrow; with play on *fourteen*.
15. *Lammas-tide*, August 1.
23. *'Tis . . . years*. It has been thought that Shakespeare was alluding in this line
to a famous earthquake in 1580 and was, therefore, writing in 1591.
29. *bear a brain*. The nurse prides herself on her memory.

When it did taste the wormwood on the nipple   30
Of my dug and felt it bitter, pretty fool,
To see it tetchy and fall out with the dug!
'Shake' quoth the dove-house: 'twas no need, I trow,
To bid me trudge:
And since that time it is eleven years;
For then she could stand alone; nay, by the rood,
She could have run and waddled all about;
For even the day before, she broke her brow:
And then my husband—God be with his soul!
A' was a merry man—took up the child: 40
'Yea,' quoth he, 'dost thou fall upon thy face?
Thou wilt fall backward when thou hast more wit;
Wilt thou not, Jule?' and, by my holidame,
The pretty wretch left crying and said 'Ay.'
To see, now, how a jest shall come about!
I warrant, an I should live a thousand years,
I never should forget it: 'Wilt thou not, Jule?' quoth he;
And, pretty fool, it stinted and said 'Ay.'
LA. CAP: Enough of this; I pray thee, hold thy peace.
NURSE: Yes, madam: yet I cannot choose but laugh,   50
To think it should leave crying and say 'Ay.'
And yet, I warrant, it had upon it brow
A bump as big as a young cockerel's stone;
A parlous knock; and it cried bitterly:
'Yea,' quoth my husband, 'fall'st upon thy face?
Thou wilt fall backward when thou comest to age;
Wilt thou not, Jule?' it stinted and said 'Ay.'
JUL: And stint thou too, I pray thee, nurse, say I.
NURSE: Peace, I have done. God mark thee to his grace!
Thou wast the prettiest babe that e'er I nursed: 60
An I might live to see thee married once,
I have my wish.
LA. CAP: Marry, that 'marry' is the very theme
I came to talk of. Tell me, daughter Juliet,

---

30. *wormwood*, an herb noted for bitterness, from which absinthe is derived.
31. *fool*, term of endearment.
32. *tetchy*, fretful.
33. *trow*, believe.
40. *A'*, he.
43. *holidame*, same as "halidom," a relic or holy thing.
48. *stinted*, ceased.
52. *it*, so QqF; Globe: *its;* possessive case.

How stands your disposition to be married?
JUL: It is an honour that I dream not of.
NURSE: An honour! were not I thine only nurse,
I would say thou hadst suck'd wisdom from thy teat.
LA. CAP: Well, think of marriage now; younger than you, 70
Here in Verona, ladies of esteem,
Are made already mothers: by my count,
I was your mother much upon these years
That you are now a maid. Thus then in brief:
The valiant Paris seeks you for his love.
NURSE: A man, young lady! lady, such a man
As all the world—why, he 's a man of wax.
LA. CAP: Verona's summer hath not such a flower.
NURSE: Nay, he 's a flower; in faith, a very flower.
LA. CAP: What say you? can you love the gentleman?
This night you shall behold him at our feast; 80
Read o'er the volume of young Paris' face
And find delight writ there with beauty's pen;
Examine every married lineament
And see how one another lends content,
And what obscured in this fair volume lies
Find written in the margent of his eyes.
This precious book of love, this unbound lover,
To beautify him, only lacks a cover:
The fish lives in the sea, and 'tis much pride
For fair without the fair within to hide: 90
That book in many's eyes doth share the glory,
That in gold clasps locks in the golden story;
So shall you share all that he doth possess,
By having him, making yourself no less.
NURSE: No less! nay, bigger; women grow by men.
LA. CAP: Speak briefly, can you like of Paris' love?
JUL: I'll look to like, if looking liking move:
But no more deep will I endart mine eye
Than your consent gives strength to make it fly. 99

---

76. *a man of wax*, such as one would picture in wax, i.e., handsome.
83. *married*, harmonized into mutual helpfulness (Hudson).
86. *margent*, commentary or marginal gloss.
89. *fish lives in the sea*. The figure of speech is of the binding of a book; since fishskins were used to cover books, this "unbound lover" is yet to be made complete.
97-99. *I'll . . . fly*. Juliet's attitude is one of proper obedience such as would be expected in the morals of the time.

Enter a SERVANT.

SERV: Madam, the guests are come, supper served up, you called, my young lady asked for, the nurse cursed in the pantry, and every thing in extremity. I must hence to wait; I beseech you, follow straight.
LA. CAP: We follow thee. (*Exit* SERVANT.) Juliet, the county stays. 105
NURSE: Go, girl, seek happy nights to happy days. (*Exeunt.*)

Scene IV, *A street.*

Enter ROMEO, MERCUTIO, BENVOLIO, *with five or six* MASKERS, TORCH-BEARERS, *and others.*

RON: What, shall this speech be spoke for our excuse?
Or shall we on without apology?
BEN: The date is out of such prolixity:
We'll have no Cupid hoodwink'd with a scarf,
Bearing a Tartar's painted bow of lath,
Scaring the ladies like a crow-keeper;
Nor no without-book prologue, faintly spoke
After the prompter, for our entrance:
But let them measure us by what they will;
We'll measure them a measure, and be gone. 10
ROM: Give me a torch: I am not for this ambling;
Being but heavy, I will bear the light.
MER: Nay, gentle Romeo, we must have you dance.
ROM: Not I, believe me: you have dancing shoes
With nimble soles: I have a soul of lead
So stakes me to the ground I cannot move.

---

105. *county*, count.
SCENE IV. 1. *speech*. The older fashion was for maskers to be preceded by a messenger with a set speech, but *the date is out* for *such prolixity*.
4. *hoodwink'd*, blindfolded.
5. *Tartar's painted bow*. Tartar's bows are said to have resembled the old Roman bow with which Cupid was pictured.
6. *crow-keeper*, scarecrow.
10. *measure . . . measure*, perform a dance.
11. *ambling*, walking affectedly; used contemptuously of dancing.

MER: You are a lover; borrow Cupid's wings,
And soar with them above a common bound.
ROM: I am too sore enpierced with his shaft
To soar with his light feathers, and so bound,   20
I cannot bound a pitch above dull woe:
Under love's heavy burden do I sink.
MER: And, to sink in it, should you burden love;
Too great oppression for a tender thing.
ROM: Is love a tender thing? it is too rough,
Too rude, too boisterous, and it pricks like thorn.
MER: If love be rough with you, be rough with love;
Prick love for pricking, and you beat love down.
Give me a case to put my visage in:
A visor for a visor! what care I   30
What curious eye doth quote deformities?
Here are the beetle brows shall blush for me.
BEN: Come, knock and enter; and no sooner in,
But every man betake him to his legs.
ROM: A torch for me: let wantons light of heart
Tickle the senseless rushes with their heels,
For I am proverb'd with a grandsire phrase;
I'll be a candle-holder, and look on.
The game was ne'er so fair, and I am done.
MER: Tut, dun 's the mouse, the constable's own word: 40
If thou art dun, we'll draw thee from the mire
Of this sir-reverence love, wherein thou stick'st
Up to the ears. Come, we burn daylight, ho!
ROM: Nay, that 's not so.
MER: I mean, sir, in delay
We waste our lights in vain, like lamps by day.
Take our good meaning, for our judgement sits
Five times in that ere once in our five wits.

---

21. *pitch*, height.
30. *visor*, a mask, for an ugly masklike face.
31. *quote*, take notice of.
36. *rushes*. Rushes were used for floor coverings.
38. *candle-holder*, an allusion to the proverb "A good candle-holder (i.e., a mere onlooker) is a good gamester."
40. *dun 's the mouse*, a common phrase usually taken to mean "keep still." *Dun* (l. 41) alludes to a Christmas game, "Dun is in the mire," in which a heavy log was lifted by the players.
42. *sir-reverence*, corruption of "save-reverence" (*salve-reverentia*), an apology for something improper.
47. *five wits*, the five faculties, usually given as common wit, imagination, fantasy, judgment, and reason.

ROM: And we mean well in going to this mask;
But 'tis no wit to go.
MER: Why, may one ask?
ROM: I dream'd a dream to-night.
MER: And so did I.   50
ROM: Well, what was yours?
MER: That dreamers often lie.
ROM: In bed asleep, while they do dream things true.
MER: O, then, I see Queen Mab hath been with you.
She is the fairies' midwife, and she comes
In shape no bigger than an agate-stone
On the fore-finger of an alderman,
Drawn with a team of little atomies
Athwart men's noses as they lie asleep;
Her waggon-spokes made of long spinners' legs,
The cover of the wings of grasshoppers,   60
The traces of the smallest spider's web,
The collars of the moonshine's watery beams,
Her whip of cricket's bone, the lash of film,
Her waggoner a small grey-coated gnat,
Not half so big as a round little worm
Prick'd from the lazy finger of a maid;
Her chariot is an empty hazel-nut
Made by the joiner squirrel or old grub,
Time out o' mind the fairies' coachmakers.
And in this state she gallops night by night   70
Through lovers' brains, and then they dream of love;
O'er courtiers' knees, that dream on court'sies straight,
O'er lawyers' fingers, who straight dream on fees,
O'er ladies' lips, who straight on kisses dream,
Which oft the angry Mab with blisters plagues,
Because their breaths with sweetmeats tainted are:
Sometime she gallops o'er a courtier's nose,.

---

53. *Queen Mab*, a name of Celtic origin for the fairy queen. Mercutio's famous speech interested the audience, no doubt, and certainly added to the sum of fairy mythology, but has little connection with plot or character.
57. *atomies*, tiny creatures.
59. *spinners'*, spiders'.
63. *film*, gossamer thread.
64. *waggoner*, coachman.
65. *worm*. This alludes to an ancient and no doubt useful superstition that "worms breed in the fingers of the idle."
70. *state*, pomp, dignity.
73. *straight*, immediately.
77. *Sometime*, from time to time, sometimes.

And then dreams he of smelling out a suit;
And sometime comes she with a tithe-pig's tail
Tickling a parson's nose as a' lies asleep,   80
Then dreams he of another benefice:
Sometime she driveth o'er a soldier's neck,
And then dreams he of cutting foreign throats,
Of breaches, ambuscadoes, Spanish blades,
Of healths five-fathom deep; and then anon
Drums in his ear, at which he starts and wakes,
And being thus frighted swears a prayer or two
And sleeps again. This is that very Mab
That plats the manes of horses in the night,
And bakes the elf-locks in foul sluttish hairs,   90
Which once untangled much misfortune bodes:
This is the hag, when maids lie on their backs,
That presses them and learns them first to bear,
Making them women of good carriage:
This is she—
ROM: Peace, peace, Mercutio, peace!
Thou talk'st of nothing.
MER: True, I talk of dreams,
Which are the children of an idle brain,
Begot of nothing but vain fantasy,
Which is as thin of substance as the air
And more inconstant than the wind, who wooes   100
Even now the frozen bosom of the north,
And, being anger'd, puffs away from thence,
Turning his face to the dew-dropping south.
BEN: This wind, you talk of, blows us from ourselves;
Supper is done, and we shall come too late.
ROM: I fear, too early: for my mind misgives
Some consequence yet hanging in the stars
Shall bitterly begin his fearful date
With this night's revels and expire the term

---

78. *suit*, a request or plea at court.
79. *tithe-pig's tail*. This alludes to the tenth pig given the parson as a church tax.
84. *Spanish blades*, swords made at Toledo in Spain.
85. *anon*, by and by.
89. *plats the manes of horses*, an allusion to the familiar superstition of "witches' stirrups," tangles in the manes of horses.
93. *learns*, teaches.
98. *vain*, empty, foolish. *fantasy*, imagination.
108. *date*, time, period.
109. *expire* (transitive), bring to an end.

Of a despised life closed in my breast 110
By some vile forfeit of untimely death.
But He, that hath the steerage of my course,
Direct my sail! On, lusty gentlemen.
BEN: Strike, drum. (*Exeunt.*)

Scene V, *A hall in Capulet's house.*

MUSICIANS *waiting. Enter* SERVINGMEN, *with napkins.*

FIRST SERV: Where 's Potpan, that he helps not to take away?
He shift a trencher? he scrape a trencher!
SEC. SERV: When good manners shall lie all in one or two men's hands
and they unwashed too, 'tis a foul thing.
FIRST SERV: Away with the joint-stools, remove the court-cupboard,
look to the plate. Good thou, save me a piece of marchpane; and, as
thou lovest me, let the porter let in Susan Grindstone and Nell. An-
tony, and Potpan! 11
SEC. SERV: Ay, boy, ready.
FIRST SERV: You are looked for and called for, asked for and sought
for, in the great chamber.
SEC. SERV: We cannot be here and there too. Cheerly, boys; be brisk
awhile, and the longer liver take all.

Enter CAPULET, *with* JULIET *and others of his house, meeting the*
GUESTS *and* MASKERS.

CAP: Welcome, gentlemen! ladies that have their toes
Unplagued with corns will have a bout with you.
Ah ha, my mistresses! which of you all 20
Will now deny to dance? she that makes dainty,
She, I'll swear, hath corns; am I come near ye now?
Welcome, gentlemen! I have seen the day
That I have worn a visor and could tell

SCENE V. 2. *trencher*, wooden dish or plate; Poptan is too proud to shift trenchers.
7. *joint-stools*, stools, properly those made by a joiner.
8. *court-cupboard*, sideboard.
9. *marchpane*, cake made from sugar and almonds.
17. *longer . . . all*, proverbial expression.
21. *makes dainty*, hesitates from affectation to dance.

A whispering tale in a fair lady's ear,
Such as would please: 'tis gone, 'tis gone, 'tis gone:
You are welcome, gentlemen! Come, musicians, play.
A hall, a hall! give room! and foot it, girls. (*Music plays, and
they dance.*)
More light, you knaves; and turn the tables up,
And quench the fire, the room is grown too hot.   30
Ah, sirrah, this unlook'd-for sport comes well.
Nay, sit, nay, sit, good cousin Capulet;
For you and I are past our dancing days:
How long is 't now since last yourself and I
Were in a mask?
SEC. CAP: By 'r lady, thirty years.
CAP: What, man! 'tis not so much, 'tis not so much:
'Tis since the nuptial of Lucentio,
Come pentecost as quickly as it will,
Some five and twenty years; and then we mask'd.
SEC. CAP: 'Tis more, 'tis more: his son is elder, sir;   40
His son is thirty.
CAP: Will you tell me that?
His son was but a ward two years ago.
ROM: (*To a* SERVINGMAN) What lady is that, which doth enrich
the hand
Of yonder knight?
SERV: I know not, sir.
ROM: O, she doth teach the torches to burn bright!
It seems she hangs upon the cheek of night
Like a rich jewel in an Ethiope's ear;
Beauty too rich for use, for earth too dear!
So shows a snowy dove trooping with crows,   50
As yonder lady o'er her fellows shows.
The measure done, I'll watch her place of stand,
And, touching hers, make blessed my rude hand.

---

28. *A hall!* Make room!
29. *turn the tables up.* Tables were probably made of hinged leaves and placed on trestles. They were put aside for dancing.
38. *pentecost,* a festival in honor of the descent of the Holy Spirit, seventh Sunday after Easter.
42. *ward,* a minor under guardianship.
46-55. *O . . . night.* Romeo's love is love at first sight, a type of perfect love provided for in Elizabethan psychological doctrine and, no doubt, in life. That love is the inciting force of the drama.
49. *dear,* precious.

Did my heart love till now? forswear it, sight!
For I ne'er saw true beauty till this night.
TYB: This, by his voice, should be a Montague.
Fetch me my rapier, boy. What dares the slave
Come hither, cover'd with an antic face,
To fleer and scorn at our solemnity?
Now, by the stock and honour of my kin,   60
To strike him dead I hold it not a sin.
CAP: Why, how now, kinsman! wherefore storm you so?
TYB: Uncle, this is a Montague, our foe,
A villain that is hither come in spite,
To scorn at our solemnity this night.
CAP: Young Romeo is it?
TYB: 'Tis he, that villain Romeo.
CAP: Content thee, gentle coz, let him alone;
He bears him like a portly gentleman;
And, to say truth, Verona brags of him
To be a virtuous and well govern'd youth: 70
I would not for the wealth of all the town
Here in my house do him disparagement:
Therefore be patient, take no note of him:
It is my will, the which if thou respect,
Show a fair presence and put off these frowns,
An ill-beseeming semblance for a feast.
TYB: It fits, when such a villain is a guest:
I'll not endure him.
CAP: He shall be endured:
What, goodman boy! I say, he shall: go to;
Am I the master here, or you? go to.   80
You'll not endure him! God shall mend my soul!
You'll make a mutiny among my guests!
You will set cock-a-hoop! you'll be the man!

---

57. *Fetch me my rapier*. This speech of Tybalt's is in immediate contrast to the happy sentiment of Romeo's speech and brings the elements of love and hate together.
58. *antic*, fantastic.
59. *fleer*, to look mockingly.
68. *portly*, of an excellent bearing.
74. *respect*, regard.
79. *goodman boy*, a belittling ironical epithet. Capulet has a spirit more reconcilable than that of Tybalt. *go to*, expression of impatience.
82. *mutiny*, quarrel, strife.
83. *cock-a-hoop*, complete disorder.

TYB: Why, uncle, 'tis a shame.
CAP: Go to, go to;
You are a saucy boy: is 't so, indeed?
This trick may chance to scathe you, I know what:
You must contrary me! marry, 'tis time.
Well said, my hearts! You are a princox; go:
Be quiet, or—More light, more light! For shame!
I'll make you quiet. What, cheerly, my hearts!   90
TYB: Patience perforce with wilful choler meeting
Makes my flesh tremble in their different greeting.
I will withdraw: but this intrusion shall
Now seeming sweet convert to bitter gall. (*Exit.*)
ROM: (*To* JULIET) If I profane with my unworthiest hand
    This holy shrine, the gentle fine is this:
My lips, two blushing pilgrims, ready stand
    To smooth that rough touch with a tender kiss.
JUL: Good pilgrim, you do wrong your hand too much,
    Which mannerly devotion shows in this;   100
For saints have hands that pilgrims' hands do touch,
    And palm to palm is holy palmers' kiss.
ROM: Have not saints lips, and holy palmers too?
JUL: Ay, pilgrim, lips that they must use in prayer.
ROM: O, then, dear saint, let lips do what hands do;
    They pray, grant thou, lest faith turn to despair.
JUL: Saints do not move, though grant for prayers' sake.
ROM: Then move not, while my prayer's effect I take.
Thus from my lips, by yours, my sin is purged.
JUL: Then have my lips the sin that they have took.   110
ROM: Sin from my lips? O trespass sweetly urged!
    Give me my sin again.
JUL: You kiss by the book.
NURSE: Madam, your mother craves a word with you.
ROM: What is her mother?

---

86. *scathe*, injure.
88. *princox*, pert, saucy boy.
91. *Patience perforce*, patience upon compulsion; *patience* is a general word for self-control.
94. *convert*, change (to).
95-108. *If . . . take.* These lines are in the form of a sonnet. They afford an example of Shakespeare's early exuberance in poetic style.
99. *pilgrim.* Romeo was masquerading as a pilgrim or palmer.
112. *by the book*, according to rule.

NURSE: Marry, bachelor,
Her mother is the lady of the house,
And a good lady, and a wise and virtuous:
I nursed her daughter, that you talk'd withal;
I tell you, he that can lay hold of her
Shall have the chinks.
ROM: Is she a Capulet?
O dear account! my life is my foe's debt. 120
BEN: Away, be gone; the sport is at the best.
ROM: Ay, so I fear; the more is my unrest.
CAP: Nay, gentlemen, prepare not to be gone;
We have a trifling foolish banquet towards.
Is it e'en so? why, then, I thank you all;
I thank you, honest gentlemen; good night.
More torches here! Come on then, let 's to bed.
Ah, sirrah, by my fay, it waxes late:
I'll to my rest. (*Exeunt all but* JULIET *and* NURSE.)
JUL: Come hither, nurse. What is yond gentleman? 130
NURSE: The son and heir of old Tiberio.
JUL: What 's he that now is going out of door?
NURSE: Marry, that, I think, be young Petrucio.
JUL: What 's he that follows there, that would not dance?
NURSE: I know not.
JUL: Go, ask his name: if he be married,
My grave is like to be my wedding bed.
NURSE: His name is Romeo, and a Montague;
The only son of your great enemy.
JUL: My only love sprung from my only hate! 140
Too early seen unknown, and known too late!
Prodigious birth of love it is to me,
That I must love a loathed enemy.
NURSE: What 's this? what 's this?
JUL: A rhyme I learn'd even now
Of one I danced withal. (*One calls within* JULIET.)
NURSE: Anon, anon!
Come, let 's away; the strangers all are gone. (*Exeunt.*)

---

119. *chinks,* money.
120. *my foe's debt,* due to my foe, at his mercy.
124. *foolish,* insignificant. *banquet,* dessert. *towards,* in preparation.
128. *fay,* faith.

ACT II.

PROLOGUE.

Enter CHORUS.

CHOR:　Now old desire doth in his death-bed lie,
　And young affection gapes to be his heir;
That fair for which love groan'd for and would die,
　With tender Juliet match'd, is now not fair.
Now Romeo is beloved and loves again,
　Alike bewitched by the charm of looks,
But to his foe supposed he must complain,
　And she steal love's sweet bait from fearful hooks:
Being held a foe, he may not have access
　To breathe such vows as lovers use to swear;　　　　　10
And she as much in love, her means much less
　To meet her new-beloved any where:
But passion lends them power, time means, to meet,
Tempering extremities with extreme sweet. (*Exit.*)

Scene I, *A lane by the wall of Capulet's orchard.*

Enter ROMEO.

ROM:　Can I go forward when my heart is here?
Turn back, dull earth, and find thy centre out. (*He climbs the wall, and leaps down within it.*)

ACT II. PROLOGUE. 3. *fair*, beautiful woman, beloved; allusion to Rosaline, the lady with whom Romeo had fancied himself in love before he met Juliet.
10. *use to swear*, are in the habit of swearing.
13. *passion*, feeling of love.
SCENE I. 2. *dull earth*, Romeo himself. *thy centre*, Juliet. The figure of speech is that of man as a microcosm or little world.

Enter BENVOLIO *and* MERCUTIO.

BEN: Romeo! my cousin Romeo!
MER: He is wise;
And, on my life, hath stol'n him home to bed.
BEN: He ran this way, and leap'd this orchard wall:
Call, good Mercutio.
MER: Nay, I'll conjure too.
Romeo! humours! madman! passion! lover!
Appear thou in the likeness of a sigh:
Speak but one rhyme, and I am satisfied;
Cry but 'Ay me!' pronounce but 'love' and 'dove;'   10
Speak to my gossip Venus one fair word,
One nick-name for her purblind son and heir,
Young Adam Cupid, he that shot so trim,
When King Cophetua loved the beggar-maid!
He heareth not, he stirreth not, he moveth not;
The ape is dead, and I must conjure him.
I conjure thee by Rosaline's bright eyes,
By her high forehead and her scarlet lip,
By her fine foot, straight leg and quivering thigh
And the demesnes that there adjacent lie.   20
That in thy likeness thou appear to us!
BEN: An if he hear thee, thou wilt anger him.
MER: This cannot anger him: 'twould anger him
To raise a spirit in his mistress' circle
Of some strange nature, letting it there stand
Till she had laid it and conjured it down;
That were some spite: my invocation
Is fair and honest, and in his mistress' name
I conjure only but to raise up him.

---

6. *conjure*, utter an incantation.
12. *purblind*, completely blind.
13. *Adam*, Upton's conjecture; Qq and F: *Abraham*. It is thought that *Adam* may refer to Adam Bell, a famous archer in the old ballads; *Abraham* is a form of "abram" or "auburn," which would refer to Cupid's flaxen hair.
14. *King Cophetua*, reference to the ballad *King Cophetua and the Beggar Maid*.
16. *ape*, used as a term of endearment.
20. *demesnes*, regions.
22. *An if*, if.
25. *strange*, belonging to another person.
27. *spite*, injury.
28. *honest*, chaste.

BEN: Come, he hath hid himself among these trees,   30
To be consorted with the humorous night:
Blind is his love and best befits the dark.
MER: If love be blind, love cannot hit the mark.
Now will he sit under a medlar tree,
And wish his mistress were that kind of fruit
As maids call medlars, when they laugh alone.
O, Romeo, that she were, O, that she were
An open et cætera, thou a poperin pear!
Romeo, good night: I'll to my truckle-bed;
This field-bed is too cold for me to sleep: 40
Come, shall we go?
BEN: Go, then; for 'tis in vain
To seek him here that means not to be found. (*Exeunt.*)

Scene II, *Capulet's orchard.*

Enter ROMEO.

ROM: He jests at scars that never felt a wound.

JULIET *appears above at a window*

But, soft! what light through yonder window breaks?
It is the east, and Juliet is the sun.
Arise, fair sun, and kill the envious moon,
Who is already sick and pale with grief,
That thou her maid art far more fair than she:
Be not her maid, since she is envious;
Her vestal livery is but sick and green

---

31. *consorted*, associated. *humorous*, moist; also, influenced by humor or mood.
34. *medlar*, the fruit of the *Mespilus germanica*, edible only when partly decayed.
38. *poperin*, variety of pear; derived from the Flemish town *Poperinghe* in Flanders.
39. *truckle-bed*, a bed on casters to be shoved under a standing bed.
40. *field-bed*, large bed; here, the ground.
SCENE II. There is no break in the action. Romeo must have been standing on the front stage behind some obstruction to represent the garden wall. He speaks at once, then turns to observe Juliet.
8. *sick and green*, of a wan and sickly complexion; cf. "greensickness."

And none but fools do wear it; cast it off.
It is my lady, O, it is my love! 10
O, that she knew she were!
She speaks, yet she says nothing: what of that?
Her eye discourses; I will answer it.
I am too bold, 'tis not to me she speaks:
Two of the fairest stars in all the heaven,
Having some business, do entreat her eyes
To twinkle in their spheres till they return.
What if her eyes were there, they in her head?
The brightness of her cheek would shame those stars,
As daylight doth a lamp; her eyes in heaven 20
Would through the airy region stream so bright
That birds would sing and think it were not night.
See, how she leans her cheek upon her hand!
O, that I were a glove upon that hand,
That I might touch that cheek!
JUL: Ay me!
ROM: She speaks:
O, speak again, bright angel! for thou art
As glorious to this night, being o'er my head,
As is a winged messenger of heaven
Unto the white-upturned wondering eyes
Of mortals that fall back to gaze on him 30
When he bestrides the lazy-pacing clouds
And sails upon the bosom of the air.
JUL: O Romeo, Romeo! wherefore art thou Romeo?
Deny thy father and refuse thy name;
Or, if thou wilt not, be but sworn my love,
And I'll no longer be a Capulet.
ROM: (*Aside*) Shall I hear more, or shall I speak at this?
JUL: 'Tis but thy name that is my enemy;
Thou art thyself, though not a Montague.
What 's Montague? it is nor hand, nor foot, 40
Nor arm, nor face, nor any other part
Belonging to a man. O, be some other name!
What 's in a name? that which we call a rose

---

13. *discourses*, speaks.
17. *spheres*, transparent concentric shells supposed to carry the heavenly bodies with them in their revolution around the earth.
30. *mortals*, human beings.
39. *though . . . Montague*, i.e., even if thou wert not a Montague.

By any other name would smell as sweet;
So Romeo would, were he not Romeo call'd,
Retain that dear perfection which he owes
Without that title. Romeo, doff thy name,
And for that name which is no part of thee
Take all myself.
ROM: I take thee at thy word:
Call me but love, and I'll be new baptized;   50
Henceforth I never will be Romeo.
JUL: What man art thou that thus bescreen'd in night
So stumblest on my counsel?
ROM: By a name
I know not how to tell thee who I am:
My name, dear saint, is hateful to myself,
Because it is an enemy to thee;
Had I it written, I would tear the word.
JUL: My ears have not yet drunk a hundred words
Of that tongue's utterance, yet I know the sound:
Art thou not Romeo and a Montague?   60
ROM: Neither, fair saint, if either thee dislike.
JUL: How camest thou hither, tell me, and wherefore?
The orchard walls are high and hard to climb,
And the place death, considering who thou art,
If any of my kinsmen find thee here.
ROM: With love's light wings did I o'erperch these walls;
For stony limits cannot hold love out,
And what love can do that dares love attempt;
Therefore thy kinsmen are no let to me.
JUL: If they do see thee, they will murder thee.   70
ROM: Alack, there lies more peril in thine eye
Than twenty of their swords: look thou but sweet,
And I am proof against their enmity.
JUL: I would not for the world they saw thee here.
ROM: I have night's cloak to hide me from their sight;
And but thou love me, let them find me here:
My life were better ended by their hate,
Than death prorogued, wanting of thy love.

---

46. *owes*, owns.
53. *counsel*, secret thought.
61. *dislike*, displease.
66. *o'er-perch*, fly over and perch beyond.
69. *let*, hindrance.
78. *prorogued*, postponed. *wanting*, lacking.

JUL: By whose direction found'st thou out this place?
ROM: By love, who first did prompt me to inquire;   80
He lent me counsel and I lent him eyes.
I am no pilot; yet, wert thou as far
As that vast shore wash'd with the farthest sea,
I would adventure for such merchandise.
JUL: Thou know'st the mask of night is on my face,
Else would a maiden blush bepaint my cheek
For that which thou hast heard me speak tonight.
Fain would I dwell on form, fain, fain deny
What I have spoke: but farewell compliment!
Dost thou love me? I know thou wilt say 'Ay,'   90
And I will take thy word: yet, if thou swear'st,
Thou mayst prove false; at lovers' perjuries,
They say, Jove laughs. O gentle Romeo,
If thou dost love, pronounce it faithfully:
Or if thou think'st I am too quickly won,
I'll frown and be perverse and say thee nay,
So thou wilt woo; but else, not for the world.
In truth, fair Montague, I am too fond,
And therefore thou mayst think my 'haviour light:
But trust me, gentleman, I'll prove more true   100
Than those that have more cunning to be strange.
I should have been more strange, I must confess,
But that thou overheard'st, ere I was ware,
My true love's passion; therefore pardon me,
And not impute this yielding to light love,
Which the dark night hath so discovered.
ROM: Lady, by yonder blessed moon I swear
That tips with silver all these fruit-tree tops—
JUL: O, swear not by the moon, the inconstant moon,
That monthly changes in her circled orb,   110
Lest that thy love prove likewise variable.
ROM: What shall I swear by?
JUL: Do not swear at all;
Or, if thou wilt, swear by thy gracious self,
Which is the god of my idolatry,

---

89. *compliment*, punctiliousness, ceremony.
98. *fond*, foolish, infatuated.
101. *strange*, reserved.
105. *light*, frivolous, wanting in steadiness.
106. *discovered*, revealed.
110. *orb*, equivalent to *sphere;* see above, line 17.

And I'll believe thee.
ROM: If my heart's dear love—
JUL: Well, do not swear: although I joy in thee,
I have no joy of this contract to-night:
It is too rash, too unadvised, too sudden;
Too like the lightning, which doth cease to be
Ere one can say 'It lightens.' Sweet, good night!   120
This bud of love, by summer's ripening breath,
May prove a beauteous flower when next we meet.
Good night, good night! as sweet repose and rest
Come to thy heart as that within my breast!
ROM: O, wilt thou leave me so unsatisfied?
JUL: What satisfaction canst thou have to-night?
ROM: The exchange of thy love's faithful vow for mine.
JUL: I gave thee mine before thou didst request it:
And yet I would it were to give again.
ROM: Wouldst thou withdraw it? for what purpose, love?
JUL: But to be frank, and give it thee again.   131
And yet I wish but for the thing I have:
My bounty is as boundless as the sea,
My love as deep; the more I give to thee,
The more I have, for both are infinite. (NURSE *calls within.*)
I hear some noise within; dear love, adieu!
Anon, good nurse! Sweet Montague, be true.
Stay but a little, I will come again. (*Exit, above.*)
ROM: O blessed, blessed night! I am afeard,
Being in night, all this is but a dream,   140
Too flattering-sweet to be substantial.

Re-enter JULIET, *above.*

JUL: Three words, dear Romeo, and good night indeed.
If that thy bent of love be honourable,
Thy purpose marriage, send me word to-morrow,
By one that I'll procure to come to thee,
Where and what time thou wilt perform the rite;
And all my fortunes at thy foot I'll lay
And follow thee my lord throughout the world.

---

131. *frank*, liberal, bounteous.
143. *bent*, purpose; from the idea of the tension of a bow.
145. *procure*, cause.

NURSE: (*Within*) Madam!

JUL: I come, anon.—But if thou mean'st not well, 150
I do beseech thee—

NURSE: (*Within*) Madam!

JUL: By and by, I come:—
To cease thy suit, and leave me to my grief:
To-morrow will I send.

ROM: So thrive my soul—

JUL: A thousand times good night! (*Exit, above.*)

ROM: A thousand times the worse, to want thy light.
Love goes toward love, as schoolboys from their books,
But love from love, toward school with heavy looks. (*Retiring.*)

Re-enter JULIET, *above.*

JUL: Hist! Romeo, hist! O, for a falconer's voice,
To lure this tassel-gentle back again! 160
Bondage is hoarse, and may not speak aloud;
Else would I tear the cave where Echo lies,
And make her airy tongue more hoarse than mine,
With repetition of my Romeo's name.

ROM: It is my soul that calls upon my name:
How silver-sweet sound lovers' tongues by night,
Like softest music to attending ears!

JUL: Romeo!

ROM: My dear?

JUL: At what o'clock to-morrow
Shall I send to thee?

ROM: At the hour of nine.

JUL: I will not fail: 'tis twenty years till then. 170
I have forgot why I did call thee back.

ROM: Let me stand here till thou remember it.

JUL: I shall forget, to have thee still stand there,
Remembering how I love thy company.

ROM: And I'll still stay, to have thee still forget,
Forgetting any other home but this.

JUL: 'Tis almost morning; I would have thee gone:
And yet no further than a wanton's bird;

151. *By and by*, immediately.
160. *tassel-gentle*, tercel-gentle, the male of the goshawk.
173. *still*, always.
178. *wanton's*, of one apt to jest and play.

Who lets it hop a little from her hand,
Like a poor prisoner in his twisted gyves,   180
And with a silk thread plucks it back again,
So loving-jealous of his liberty.
ROM: I would I were thy bird.
JUL: Sweet, so would I:
Yet I should kill thee with much cherishing.
Good night, good night! parting is such sweet sorrow,
That I shall say good night till it be morrow. (*Exit, above.*)
ROM: Sleep dwell upon thine eyes, peace in thy breast!
Would I were sleep and peace, so sweet to rest!
Hence will I to my ghostly father's cell,
His help to crave, and my dear hap to tell. (*Exit*)   190

Scene III, *Friar Laurence's cell.*

Enter FRIAR LAURENCE, *with a basket.*

FRI. L: The grey-eyed morn smiles on the frowning night,
Chequering the eastern clouds with streaks of light,
And flecked darkness like a drunkard reels
From forth day's path and Titan's fiery wheels:
Now, ere the sun advance his burning eye,
The day to cheer and night's dank dew to dry,
I must up-fill this osier cage of ours
With baleful weeds and precious-juiced flowers.
The earth that 's nature's mother is her tomb;
What is her burying grave that is her womb,   10
And from her womb children of divers kind
We sucking on her natural bosom find,
Many for many virtues excellent,
None but for some and yet all different.
O, mickle is the powerful grace that lies

---

180. *gyves*, fetters.
189. *ghostly*, spiritual.
190. *dear hap*, good fortune.
SCENE III. 3. *flecked*, dappled.
4. *Titan's*. Helios, the sun god, was a descendant of the race of Titans.
7. *osier cage*, willow basket.
15. *mickle*, great. *grace*, beneficent virtue.

In herbs, plants, stones, and their true qualities:
For nought so vile that on the earth doth live
But to the earth some special good doth give,
Nor aught so good but strain'd from that fair use
Revolts from true birth, stumbling on abuse: 20
Virtue itself turns vice, being misapplied;
And vice sometimes by action dignified.
Within the infant rind of this small flower
Poison hath residence and medicine power:
For this, being smelt, with that part cheers each part;
Being tasted, slays all senses with the heart.
Two such opposed kings encamp them still
In man as well as herbs, grace and rude will;
And where the worser is predominant,
Full soon the canker death eats up that plant.   30

Enter ROMEO.

ROM: Good morrow, father.
FRI. L: Benedicite!
What early tongue so sweet saluteth me?
Young son, it argues a distemper'd head
So soon to bid good morrow to thy bed:
Care keeps his watch in every old man's eye,
And where care lodges, sleep will never lie;
But where unbruised youth with unstuff'd brain
Doth couch his limbs, there golden sleep doth reign:
Therefore thy earliness doth me assure
Thou art up-roused by some distemperature;   40
Or if not so, then here I hit it right,
Our Romeo hath not been in bed to-night.
ROM: That last is true; the sweeter rest was mine.
FRI. L: God pardon sin! wast thou with Rosaline?
ROM: With Rosaline, my ghostly father? no;
I have forgot that name, and that name's woe.
FRI. L: That 's my good son: but where hast thou been, then?

---

16. *qualities,* properties.
25. *that part,* the odorous quality.
30. *canker,* cankerworm.
33. *distemper'd,* ill; a reference to a state of the humors in the body.
34. *morrow,* morning.
37. *unstuff'd,* not overcharged; another reference to the state of the humors.

ROM: I'll tell thee, ere thou ask it me again.
I have been feasting with mine enemy,
Where on a sudden one hath wounded me,   50
That's by me wounded: both our remedies
Within thy help and holy physic lies:
I bear no hatred, blessed man, for, lo,
My intercession likewise steads my foe.
FRI. L: Be plain, good son, and homely in thy drift;
Riddling confession finds but riddling shrift.
ROM: Then plainly know my heart's dear love is set
On the fair daughter of rich Capulet:
As mine on hers, so hers is set on mine;
And all combined, save what thou must combine   60
By holy marriage: when and where and how
We met, we woo'd and made exchange of vow,
I'll tell thee as we pass; but this I pray,
That thou consent to marry us to-day.
FRI. L: Holy Saint Francis, what a change is here!
Is Rosaline, whom thou didst love so dear,
So soon forsaken? young men's love then lies
Not truly in their hearts, but in their eyes.
Jesu Maria, what a deal of brine
Hath wash'd thy sallow cheeks for Rosaline!   70
How much salt water thrown away in waste,
To season love, that of it doth not taste!
The sun not yet thy sighs from heaven clears,
Thy old groans ring yet in my ancient ears;
Lo, here upon thy cheek the stain doth sit
Of an old tear that is not wash'd off yet:
If e'er thou wast thyself and these woes thine,
Thou and these woes were all for Rosaline:
And art thou changed? pronounce this sentence then,
Women may fall, when there's no strength in men.   80
ROM: Thou chid'st me oft for loving Rosaline.
FRI. L: For doting, not for loving, pupil mine.
ROM: And bad'st me bury love.
FRI. L: Not in a grave,
To lay one in, another out to have.

---

52. *physic*, medicine, healing property. *lies*, one of many instances of third person plural in *-s;* see Abbott, *A Shakesperian Grammar*, 333.
54. *steads*, helps.

ROM: I pray thee, chide not: she whom I love now
Doth grace for grace and love for love allow;
The other did not so.
FRI. L: O, she knew well
Thy love did read by rote and could not spell.
But come, young waverer, come, go with me,
In one respect I'll thy assistant be;   90
For this alliance may so happy prove,
To turn your households' rancour to pure love.
ROM: O, let us hence; I stand on sudden haste.
FRI. L: Wisely and slow; they stumble that run fast. (*Exeunt.*)

Scene IV, *A street.*

Enter BENVOLIO *and* MERCUTIO.

MER: Where the devil should this Romeo be?
Came he not home to-night?
BEN: Not to his father's; I spoke with his man.
MER: Ah, that same pale hard-hearted wench, that Rosaline,
Torments him so, that he will sure run mad.
BEN: Tybalt, the kinsman of old Capulet,
Hath sent a letter to his father's house.
MER: A challenge, on my life.
BEN: Romeo will answer it.
MER: Any man that can write may answer a letter.   10
BEN: Nay, he will answer the letter's master, how he dares, being
dared.
MER: Alas, poor Romeo! he is already dead; stabbed with a white
wench's black eye; shot through the ear with a love-song; the very pin
of his heart cleft with the blind bow-boy's butt-shaft: and is he a man
to encounter Tybalt?   17
BEN: Why, what is Tybalt?
MER: More than prince of cats, I can tell you. O, he is the courageous

---

88. *did read by rote,* was merely a matter of repeating conventional expressions
of love.
93. *stand on,* am in a position calling for.
SCENE IV. 15. *pin,* peg in the center of a target.
16. *butt-shaft,* an unbarbed arrow, used by Cupid.
19. *prince of cats.* The name of the king of cats in *Reynard the Fox* was Tybalt.

captain of complements. He fights as you sing prick-song, keeps time, distance, and proportion; rests me his minim rest, one, two, and the third in your bosom: the very butcher of a silk button, a duellist, a duellist; a gentleman of the very first house, of the first and second cause: ah, the immortal passado! the punto reverso! the hai! 27

BEN: The what?

MER: The pox of such antic, lisping, affecting fantasticoes; these new tuners of accents! 'By Jesu, a very good blade! a very tall man! a very good whore!' Why, is not this a lamentable thing, grandsire, that we should be thus afflicted with these strange flies, these fashion-mongers, these perdona-mi's, who stand so much on the new form, that they cannot sit at ease on the old bench? O, their bones, their bones! 37

Enter ROMEO.

BEN: Here comes Romeo, here comes Romeo.

MER: Without his roe, like a dried herring: O flesh, flesh, how art thou fishified! Now is he for the numbers that Petrarch flowed in: Laura to his lady was but a kitchen-wench; marry, she had a better love to be-rhyme her; Dido a dowdy; Cleopatra a gipsy; Helen and Hero hildings and harlots; Thisbe a grey eye or so, but not to the purpose. Signior Romeo, bon jour! there 's a French salutation to your French slop. You gave us the counterfeit fairly last night.

ROM: Good morrow to you both. What counterfeit did I give you? 50

MER: The slip, sir, the slip; can you not conceive?

---

20. *captain of complements,* master of ceremony and outward show.
21. *prick-song,* music written out.
22. *proportion,* rhythm.
23. *minim,* half measure in music.
24. *butcher of a silk button,* one able to strike a button on his adversary's person.
26. *first house,* possibly of the best school of fencing. *first and second cause,* ready to quarrel for a trifle; probably an allusion to the supposed code of quarreling.
27. *passado,* forward thrust. *punto reverso,* back-handed stroke. *hai,* home thrust.
30. *fantasticoes,* coxcombs.
31. *accents,* language. *tall,* fine.
35. *flies,* affected persons. *fashion-mongers,* those affecting gentility by following fashion. *perdona-mi's,* Italian for "pardon me's"; a reference to the affectation of using foreign phrases.
36-37. *form . . . bench. Form* means both "fashion" and "bench."
37. *bones,* French *bon* with play on English "bone."
39. *Without his roe,* sometimes explained as a pun on first syllable of Romeo's name, in which case the last syllables might be taken as an expression of woe.
41. *Petrarch,* Italian poet of the Renaissance who addressed his sonnets to Laura.
45. *hildings,* good-for-nothings.
48. *slop,* loose trousers of French fashion. *fairly,* handsomely.
51. *slip.* Counterfeit coins were called "slips."

ROM: Pardon, good Mercutio, my business was great; and in such a case as mine a man may strain courtesy.

MER: That 's as much as to say, such a case as yours constrains a man to bow in the hams.

ROM: Meaning, to court'sy.

MER: Thou hast most kindly hit it.

ROM: A most courteous exposition.   60

MER: Nay, I am the very pink of courtesy.

ROM: Pink for flower.

MER: Right.

ROM: Why, then is my pump well flowered.

MER: Well said: follow me this jest now till thou hast worn out thy pump, that when the single sole of it is worn, the jest may remain after the wearing sole singular.

ROM: O single-soled jest, solely singular for the singleness!   70

MER: Come between us, good Benvolio; my wits faint.

ROM: Switch and spurs, switch and spurs; or I'll cry a match.

MER: Nay, if thy wits run the wild-goose chase, I have done, for thou hast more of the wild-goose in one of thy wits than, I am sure, I have in my whole five: was I with you there for the goose?

ROM: Thou wast never with me for any thing when thou wast not there for the goose.

MER: I will bite thee by the ear for that jest.

ROM: Nay, good goose, bite not.   82

MER: Thy wit is a very bitter sweeting; it is a most sharp sauce.

ROM: And is it not well served in to a sweet goose?

MER: O, here 's a wit of cheveril, that stretches from an inch narrow to an ell broad!

ROM: I stretch it out for that word 'broad;' which added to the goose, proves thee far and wide a broad goose.   91

MER: Why, is not this better now than groaning for love? now art thou sociable, now art thou Romeo; now art thou what thou art, by art

---

56. *case*, mask.

59. *kindly*, naturally.

64. *is . . . flowered*. The pump is pinked or perforated in ornamental figures.

69. *single-soled*, thin; contemptible, with pun on "soul."

70. *singleness*, feebleness.

74. *cry a match*, claim a victory.

75. *wild-goose chase*, a horse race in which the leading rider might force his competitors to follow him wherever he went.

83. *sweeting*, probably a pun on an apple called the "sweeting."

87. *cheveril*, kid leather.

91. *broad goose*, possibly means that Mercurio is known far and wide as a goose

as well as by nature: for this drivelling love is like a great natural, that runs lolling up and down to hide his bauble in a hole.

BEN: Stop there, stop there.

MER: Thou desirest me to stop in my tale against the hair.

BEN: Thou wouldst else have made thy tale large.

MER: O, thou art deceived; I would have made it short: for I was come to the whole depth of my tale; and meant, indeed, to occupy the argument no longer.

ROM: Here 's goodly gear!

Enter NURSE *and* PETER.

MER: A sail, a sail!

BEN: Two, two; a shirt and a smock.

NURSE: Peter!   110

PETER: Anon!

NURSE: My fan, Peter.

MER: Good Peter, to hide her face; for her fan 's the fairer face.

NURSE: God ye good morrow, gentlemen.

MER: God ye good den, fair gentlewoman.

NURSE: Is it good den?

MER: 'Tis no less, I tell you, for the bawdy hand of the dial is now upon the prick of noon.

NURSE: Out upon you! what a man are you!   120

ROM: One, gentlewoman, that God hath made for himself to mar.

NURSE: By my troth, it is well said; 'for himself to mar,' quoth a'? Gentlemen, can any of you tell me where I may find the young Romeo?

ROM: I can tell you; but young Romeo will be older when you have found him than he was when you sought him: I am the youngest of that name, for fault of a worse.

NURSE: You say well.   130

MER: Yea, is the worst well? very well took, i' faith; wisely, wisely.

NURSE: If you be he, sir, I desire some confidence with you.

BEN: She will indite him to some supper.

---

96. *natural*, idiot.

100. *against the hair*, against the grain.

102. *large*, unrestrained, with play on the sense of extension.

107. *gear*, general word meaning "substance" or "stuff."

109. *a shirt . . . smock*, a man and a woman.

119. *prick*, point on the dial of a clock.

120. *Out upon you*, expression of indignation.

124. *quoth a'*, said he; a sarcastic echoing of something said.

134. *confidence*, the nurse's mistake for "conference."

135. *indite*, Benvolio's malapropism for "invite."

MER: A bawd, a bawd, a bawd! So ho!

ROM: What hast thou found?

MER: No hare, sir; unless a hare, sir, in a lenten pie, that is something stale and hoar ere it be spent. (*Sings.*)

> An old hare hoar,   141
> And an old hare hoar,
> Is very good meat in lent:
> But a hare that is hoar
> Is too much for a score,
> When it hoars ere it be spent.

Romeo, will you come to your father's? we'll to dinner, thither.

ROM: I will follow you.

MER: Farewell, ancient lady; farewell (*singing*) 'lady, lady,   151 lady.' (*Exeunt Mercutio and Benvolio.*)

NURSE: Marry, farewell! I pray you, sir, what saucy merchant was this, that was so full of his ropery?

ROM: A gentleman, nurse, that loves to hear himself talk, and will speak more in a minute than he will stand to in a month.   157

NURSE: An a' speak any thing against me, I'll take him down, an a' were lustier than he is, and twenty such Jacks; and if I cannot, I'll find those that shall. Scurvy knave! I am none of his flirt-gills; I am none of his skains-mates. And thou must stand by too, and suffer every knave to use me at his pleasure?

PETER: I saw no man use you at his pleasure; if I had, my weapon should quickly have been out, I warrant you: I dare draw as soon as another man, if I see occasion in a good quarrel, and the law on my side.   169

NURSE: Now, afore God, I am so vexed, that every part about me quivers. Scurvy knave! Pray you, sir, a word: and as I told you, my young lady bade me inquire you out; what she bade me say, I will keep to myself: but first let me tell ye, if ye should lead her into a fool's paradise, as they say, it were a very gross kind of behaviour, as they say: for the gentlewoman is young; and, therefore, if you should deal double

---

138. *hare*, used as a slang word for "courtesan."

144. *hoar*, moldy.

151. '*lady, lady, lady,*' refrain from the ballad *Chaste Susanna*.

153. *mechant*, fellow.

154. *ropery*, the nurse's mistake for "roguery."

160. *Jacks*, used as a term of disparagement.

162. *flirt-gills*, loose women.

163. *skains-mates*, not well understood; sometimes connected with "skein" (of thread) or with "skain," a dagger.

with her, truly it were an ill thing to be offered to any gentlewoman,
and very weak dealing.   181
ROM: Nurse, commend me to thy lady and mistress. I protest unto
thee—
NURSE: Good heart, and, i' faith, I will tell her as much: Lord, Lord,
she will be a joyful woman.
ROM: What wilt thou tell her, nurse? thou dost not mark me.
NURSE: I will tell her, sir, that you do protest; which, as I take it, is a
gentlemanlike offer.
ROM: Bid her devise   191
Some means to come to shrift this afternoon;
And there she shall at Friar Laurence' cell
Be shrived and married. Here is for thy pains.
NURSE: No, truly, sir; not a penny.
ROM: Go to; I say you shall.
NURSE: This afternoon, sir? well, she shall be there.
ROM: And stay, good nurse, behind the abbey wall:
Within this hour my man shall be with thee,   200
And bring thee cords made like a tackled stair;
Which to the high top-gallant of my joy
Must be my convoy in the secret night.
Farewell; be trusty, and I'll quit thy pains:
Farewell; commend me to thy mistress.
NURSE: Now God in heaven bless thee! Hark you, sir.
ROM: What say'st thou, my dear nurse?
NURSE: Is your man secret? Did you ne'er hear say,
Two may keep counsel, putting one away?
ROM: I warrant thee, my man 's as true as steel.   210
NURSE: Well, sir; my mistress is the sweetest lady—Lord, Lord! when
'twas a little prating thing:—O, there is a nobleman in town, one Paris,
that would fain lay knife aboard; but she, good soul, had as lief see a
toad, a very toad, as see him. I anger her sometimes and tell her that
Paris is the properer man; but, I'll warrant you, when I say so, she

---

183. *protest*, vow.
188. *mark*, attend to.
201. *tackled stair*, rope ladder.
202. *top-gallant*, summit.
203. *convoy*, a thing that conducts.
204. *quit*, reward, requite.
208. *secret*, trustworthy.
216. *lay . . . aboard*, board, grapple, as in a sea fight.
217. *properer*, handsomer.

looks as pale as any clout in the versal world. Doth not rosemary and
Romeo begin both with a letter?   220

ROM: Ay, nurse; what of that? both with an R.

NURSE: Ah, mocker! that 's the dog's name; R is for the—No; I know
it begins with some other letter:—and she hath the prettiest sententious
of it, of you and rosemary, that it would do you good to hear it.

ROM: Commend me to thy lady.

NURSE: Ay, a thousand times. (*Exit* ROMEO.) Peter!   230

PET: Anon!

NURSE: Peter, take my fan, and go before, and apace. (*Exeunt.*)

Scene V, *Capulet's orchard.*

Enter JULIET.

JUL: The clock struck nine when I did send the nurse;
In half an hour she promised to return.
Perchance she cannot meet him: that 's not so.
O, she is lame! love's heralds should be thoughts,
Which ten times faster glide than the sun's beams,
Driving back shadows over louring hills:
Therefore do nimble-pinion'd doves draw love,
And therefore hath the wind-swift Cupid wings.
Now is the sun upon the highmost hill
Of this day's journey, and from nine till twelve   10
Is three long hours, yet she is not come.
Had she affections and warm youthful blood,
She would be as swift in motion as a ball;
My words would bandy her to my sweet love,
And his to me:
†But old folks, many feign as they were dead;

---

219. *clout,* rag; a proverbial expression. *versal,* universal.
220. *a,* the same.
223. *the dog's name.* The letter *R* was thought to resemble the dog's growl.
226. *sententious.* The nurse probably means "sentence," pithy saying.
SCENE V. 7. *love,* Venus, whose chariot was drawn by doves.
9. *highmost,* highest; used of the sun's position.
14. *bandy,* toss to and fro.
16. *many,* Johnson: *marry.*

Unwieldy, slow, heavy and pale as lead.
O God, she comes!

Enter NURSE *and* PETER.

O honey nurse, what news?
Hast thou met with him? Send thy man away.
NURSE: Peter, stay at the gate. (*Exit* PETER.)   20
JUL: Now, good sweet nurse,—O Lord, why look'st thou sad?
Though news be sad, yet tell them merrily;
If good, thou shamest the music of sweet news
By playing it to me with so sour a face.
NURSE: I am a-weary, give me leave awhile:
Fie, how my bones ache! what a jaunce have I had!
JUL: I would thou hadst my bones, and I thy news.
Nay, come, I pray thee, speak; good, good nurse, speak.
NURSE: Jesu, what haste? can you not stay awhile?
Do you not see that I am out of breath?   30
JUL: How art thou out of breath, when thou hast breath
To say to me that thou art out of breath?
The excuse that thou dost make in this delay
Is longer than the tale thou dost excuse.
Is thy news good, or bad? answer to that;
Say either, and I'll stay the circumstance:
Let me be satisfied, is 't good or bad?
NURSE: Well, you have made a simple choice; you know not how to
choose a man: Romeo! no, not he; though his face be better than any
man's, yet his leg excels all men's; and for a hand, and a foot, and a
body, though they be not to be talked on, yet they are past compare:
he is not the flower of courtesy, but, I'll warrant him, as gentle as a
lamb. Go thy ways, wench; serve God. What, have you dined at
home?   46
JUL: No, no: but all this did I know before.
What says he of our marriage? what of that?
NURSE: Lord, how my head aches! what a head have I!
It beats as it would fall in twenty pieces.   50
My back o' t' other side,—O my back, my back!

25. *give me leave*, let me alone.
26. *jaunce*, running to and fro; so Q₂; Globe: *jaunt*.
34. *excuse*, put off by making excuses.
36. *stay the circumstance*, await details.

Beshrew your heart for sending me about,
To catch my death with jaunting up and down!
JUL: I' faith, I am sorry that thou art not well.
Sweet, sweet, sweet nurse, tell me, what says my love?
NURSE: Your love says, like an honest gentleman, and a courteous, and
a kind, and a handsome, and, I warrant, a virtuous,—Where is your
mother?
JUL: Where is my mother! why, she is within;   60
Where should she be? How oddly thou repliest!
'Your love says, like an honest gentleman,
Where is your mother?'
NURSE: O God's lady dear!
Are you so hot? marry, come up, I trow;
Is this the poultice for my aching bones?
Henceforward do your messages yourself.
JUL: Here 's such a coil! come, what says Romeo?
NURSE: Have you got leave to go to shrift to-day?
JUL: I have.
NURSE: Then hie you hence to Friar Laurence' cell;   70
There stays a husband to make you a wife:
Now comes the wanton blood up in your cheeks,
They'll be in scarlet straight at any news.
Hie you to church; I must another way,
To fetch a ladder, by the which your love
Must climb a bird's nest soon when it is dark:
I am the drudge and toil in your delight,
But you shall bear the burden soon at night.
Go; I'll to dinner; hie you to the cell.   79
JUL: Hie to high fortune! Honest nurse, farewell. (*Exeunt.*)

Scene VI, *Friar Laurence's cell.*

Enter FRIAR LAURENCE *and* ROMEO.

FRI. L: So smile the heavens upon this holy act,
That after hours with sorrow chide us not!

---

52. *Beshrew,* common objurgation meaning "ill-luck."
64. *come up,* expressive of impatience like "go to."
67. *coil,* turmoil, bustle.
74. *Hie,* hasten.

ROM: Amen, amen! but come what sorrow can,
It cannot countervail the exchange of joy
That one short minute gives me in her sight:
Do thou but close our hands with holy words,
Then love-devouring death do what he dare;
It is enough I may but call her mine.
FRI. L: These violent delights have violent ends
And in their triumph die, like fire and powder,   10
Which as they kiss consume: the sweetest honey
Is loathsome in his own deliciousness
And in the taste confounds the appetite:
Therefore love moderately; long love doth so;
Too swift arrives as tardy as too slow.

Enter JULIET.

Here comes the lady: O, so light a foot
Will ne'er wear out the everlasting flint:
A lover may bestride the gossamer
That idles in the wanton summer air,
And yet not fall; so light is vanity.   20
JUL: Good even to my ghostly confessor.
FRI. L: Romeo shall thank thee, daughter, for us both.
JUL: As much to him, else is his thanks too much.
ROM: Ah, Juliet, if the measure of thy joy
Be heap'd like mine and that thy skill be more
To blazon it, then sweeten with thy breath
This neighbour air, and let rich music's tongue
Unfold the imagined happiness that both
Receive in either by this dear encounter.
JUL: Conceit, more rich in matter than in words,   30
Brags of his substance, not of ornament:
They are but beggars that can count their worth;
But my true love is grown to such excess
I cannot sum up sum of half my wealth.

SCENE VI. 4. *countervail*, equal.
9. *These violent delights*, etc., expresses a premonition of evil.
13. *confounds*, destroys.
17. *wear . . . flint*. The friar thinks of the roughness and sharpness of life's way.
18. *gossamer*, spider's thread.
26. *blazon*, heraldic term meaning "to describe" or "to set forth."
28. *Unfold*, make known.
30. *Conceit*, imagination, thought.

FRI. L: Come, come with me, and we will make short work;
For, by your leaves, you shall not stay alone
Till holy church incorporate two in one. (*Exeunt.*)

ACT III.

Scene I, *A public place.*

Enter MERCUTIO, BENVOLIO, PAGE, *and* SERVANTS.

BEN: I pray thee, good Mercutio, let 's retire:
The day is hot, the Capulets abroad,
And, if we meet, we shall not scape a brawl;
For now, these hot days, is the mad blood stirring.
MER: Thou art like one of those fellows that when he enters the confines of a tavern claps me his sword upon the table and says 'God send me no need of thee!' and by the operation of the second cup draws it on the drawer, when indeed there is no need.   10
BEN: Am I like such a fellow?
MER: Come, come, thou art as hot a Jack in thy mood as any in Italy, and as soon moved to be moody, and as soon moody to be moved.
BEN: And what to?
MER: Nay, an there were two such, we should have none shortly, for one would kill the other. Thou! why, thou wilt quarrel with a man that hath a hair more, or a hair less, in his beard, than thou hast: thou wilt quarrel with a man for cracking nuts, having no other reason but because thou hast hazel eyes: what eye but such an eye would spy out such a quarrel? Thy head is as full of quarrels as an egg is full of meat, and yet thy head hath been beaten as addle as an egg for quarrelling: thou hast quarrelled with a man for coughing in the street, because he hath wakened thy dog that hath lain asleep in the sun: didst thou not fall out with a tailor for wearing his new doublet before Easter? with

---

ACT III. SCENE I. 2. *The day is hot.* This offers a little touch of Italian atmosphere.
8. *operation*, effect. Mercutio's charges of quarrelsomeness against the peaceful Benvolio are, of course, ironical.
14. *moody*, angry.

another, for tying his new shoes with old riband? and yet thou wilt
tutor me from quarrelling!   33
BEN: An I were so apt to quarrel as thou art, any man should buy the
fee-simple of my life for an hour and a quarter.
MER: The fee simple! O simple!
BEN: By my head, here come the Capulets.
MER: By my heel, I care not.

Enter TYBALT *and others.*

TYB: Follow me close, for I will speak to them.   40
Gentlemen, good den: a word with one of you.
MER: And but one word with one of us? couple it with something;
make it a word and a blow.
TYB: You shall find me apt enough to that, sir, an you will give me
occasion.
MER: Could you not take some occasion without giving?
TYB: Mercutio, thou consort'st with Romeo,—
MER: Consort! what, dost thou make us minstrels? an thou make min-
strels of us, look to hear nothing but discords: here 's my fiddlestick;
here 's that shall make you dance. 'Zounds, consort!   52
BEN: We talk here in the public haunt of men:
Either withdraw unto some private place,
And reason coldly of your grievances,
Or else depart; here all eyes gaze on us.
MER: Men's eyes were made to look, and let them gaze;
I will not budge for no man's pleasure, I.

Enter ROMEO.

TYB: Well, peace be with you, sir: here comes my man.
MER: But I'll be hang'd, sir, if he wear your livery: 60
Marry, go before to field, he'll be your follower;
Your worship in that sense may call him 'man.'
TYB: Romeo, the hate I bear thee can afford
No better term than this,—thou art a villain.
ROM: Tybalt, the reason that I have to love thee
Doth much excuse the appertaining rage

---

47. *consort'st. To consort* meant "to accompany" and also "to attend or wait upon."
52. *'Zounds,* a modified form of the oath, "by God's wounds."
61. *field,* field of encounter.

To such a greeting: villain am I none;
Therefore farewell; I see thou know'st me not.

TYB: Boy, this shall not excuse the injuries
That thou hast done me; therefore turn and draw.   70

ROM: I do protest, I never injured thee,
But love thee better than thou canst devise,
Till thou shalt know the reason of my love:
And so, good Capulet,—which name I tender
As dearly as my own,—be satisfied.

MER: O calm, dishonourable, vile submission!
Alla stoccata carries it away. (*Draws.*)
Tybalt, you rat-catcher, will you walk?

TYB: What wouldst thou have with me?   79

MER: Good king of cats, nothing but one of your nine lives; that I
mean to make bold withal, and, as you shall use me hereafter, dry-beat
the rest of the eight. Will you pluck your sword out of his pilcher by
the ears? make haste, lest mine be about your ears ere it be out.

TYB: I am for you. (*Drawing.*)

ROM: Gentle Mercutio, put thy rapier up.

MER: Come, sir, your passado. (*They fight.*)

ROM: Draw, Benvolio; beat down their weapons.
Gentlemen, for shame, forbear this outrage!   90
Tybalt, Mercutio, the prince expressly hath
Forbidden bandying in Verona streets:
Hold, Tybalt! good Mercutio! (TYBALT *under* ROMEO's *arm stabs* MER-
CUTIO, *and flies with his followers.*)

MER: I am hurt.
A plague o' both your houses! I am sped.
Is he gone, and hath nothing?

BEN: What, art thou hurt?

MER: Ay, ay, a scratch, a scratch; marry, 'tis enough.
Where is my page? Go, villain, fetch a surgeon. (*Exit* PAGE.)

ROM: Courage, man; the hurt cannot be much.   98

MER: No, 'tis not so deep as a well, nor so wide as a church-door; but
'tis enough, 'twill serve: ask for me tomorrow, and you shall find me a

---

77. *Alla stoccata*, Italian, "with the thrust"; i.e., the fencing master wins the victory.
78. *rat-catcher*, an allusion to Tybalt as king of cats (see II, iv, 19).
81. *make bold*, make free with.
83. *dry-beat*, beat soundly.
84. *pilcher*, scabbard.
88. *passado*, forward thrust; used derisively.
94. *sped*, done for.

grave man. I am peppered, I warrant, for this world. A plague o' both
your houses! 'Zounds, a dog, a rat, a mouse, a cat, to scratch a man to
death! a braggart, a rogue, a villain, that fights by the book of arithmetic! Why the devil came you between us? I was hurt under your arm.

ROM: I thought all for the best.

MER: Help me into some house, Benvolio,   110
Or I shall faint. A plague o' both your houses!
They have made worms' meat of me: I have it,
And soundly too: your houses! (*Exeunt* MERCUTIO *and* BENVOLIO.)

ROM: This gentleman, the prince's near ally,
My very friend, hath got his mortal hurt
In my behalf; my reputation stain'd
With Tybalt's slander,—Tybalt, that an hour
Hath been my kinsman! O sweet Juliet,
Thy beauty hath made me effeminate
And in my temper soften'd valour's steel!   120

Re-enter BENVOLIO.

BEN: O Romeo, Romeo, brave Mercutio's dead!
That gallant spirit hath aspired the clouds,
Which too untimely here did scorn the earth.

ROM: This day's black fate on moe days doth depend;
This but begins the woe others must end.

BEN: Here comes the furious Tybalt back again.

ROM: Alive, in triumph! and Mercutio slain!
Away to heaven, respective lenity,
And fire-eyed fury be my conduct now!

Re-enter TYBALT.

Now, Tybalt, take the villain back again,   130
That late thou gavest me; for Mercutio's soul
Is but a little way above our heads,

---

102. *grave man.* Mercutio thus makes puns with his last breath.
106. *by the book of arithmetic,* merely by theory. Back of the whole scene lies a
current controversy between the old broadsword style of fencing and the new
French style of rapier fencing.
114. *ally,* kinsman.
115. *very,* true.
124. *moe,* more; so Q₂F; Globe: *more.*
128. *respective lenity,* considerate gentleness.
129. *conduct,* guide.

Staying for thine to keep him company:
Either thou, or I, or both, must go with him.

TYB: Thou, wretched boy, that didst consort him here,
Shalt with him hence.

ROM: This shall determine that. (*They fight;* TYBALT
falls.)

BEN: Romeo, away, be gone!
The citizens are up, and Tybalt slain.
Stand not amazed: the prince will doom thee death,
If thou art taken: hence, be gone, away!   140

ROM: O, I am fortune's fool!

BEN: Why dost thou stay? (*Exit* ROMEO.)

Enter CITIZENS, *etc.*

FIRST CIT: Which way ran he that kill'd Mercutio?
Tybalt, that murderer, which way ran he?

BEN: There lies that Tybalt.

FIRST CIT: Up, sir, go with me;
I charge thee in the prince's name, obey.

Enter PRINCE, *attended;* MONTAGUE, CAPULET, *their* WIVES, *and*
OTHERS.

PRIN: Where are the vile beginners of this fray?

BEN: O noble prince, I can discover all
The unlucky manage of this fatal brawl:
There lies the man, slain by young Romeo,
That slew thy kinsman, brave Mercutio.   150

LA. CAP: Tybalt, my cousin! O my brother's child!
O prince! O cousin! husband! O, the blood is spilt
Of my dear kinsman! Prince, as thou art true,
For blood of ours, shed blood of Montague.
O cousin, cousin!

PRIN: Benvolio, who began this bloody fray?

BEN: Tybalt, here slain, whom Romeo's hand did slay;

---

139. *doom,* adjudge.

141. *fortune's fool.* At this crucial moment in the play Romeo again alludes to
destiny. The fact that in normal human circumstances neither he nor any man
could hardly, irrespective of consequences, have done otherwise than he did uni-
versalizes his tragedy.

148. *manage,* management.

Romeo that spoke him fair, bade him bethink
How nice the quarrel was, and urged withal
Your high displeasure: all this uttered   160
With gentle breath, calm look, knees humbly bow'd,
Could not take truce with the unruly spleen
Of Tybalt deaf to peace, but that he tilts
With piercing steel at bold Mercutio's breast,
Who, all as hot, turns deadly point to point,
And, with a martial scorn, with one hand beats
Cold death aside, and with the other sends
It back to Tybalt, whose dexterity
Retorts it: Romeo he cries aloud,
'Hold, friends! friends, part!' and, swifter than his tongue,
His agile arm beats down their fatal points,   171
And 'twixt them rushes; underneath whose arm
An envious thrust from Tybalt hit the life
Of stout Mercutio, and then Tybalt fled;
But by and by comes back to Romeo,
Who had but newly entertain'd revenge,
And to 't they go like lightning, for, ere I
Could draw to part them, was stout Tybalt slain,
And, as he fell, did Romeo turn and fly.
This is the truth, or let Benvolio die.   180
LA. CAP: He is a kinsman to the Montague;
Affection makes him false; he speaks not true:
Some twenty of them fought in this black strife,
And all those twenty could but kill one life.
I beg for justice, which thou, prince, must give;
Romeo slew Tybalt, Romeo must not live.
PRIN: Romeo slew him, he slew Mercutio;
Who now the price of his dear blood doth owe?
MON: Not Romeo, prince, he was Mercutio's friend;
His fault concludes but what the law should end,   190
The life of Tybalt.
PRIN: And for that offence

---

158. *fair*, civilly.
159. *nice*, trivial.
162. *take truce*, make peace. *unruly spleen*, ungovernable rage.
163. *tilts*, strikes.
169. *Retorts*, throws back upon his adversary.
173. *envious*, i.e., Tybalt's blow was a malicious one.
176. *entertain'd*, harbored thoughts of.

Immediately we do exile him hence:
I have an interest in your hate's proceeding,
My blood for your rude brawls doth lie a-bleeding;
But I'll amerce you with so strong a fine
That you shall all repent the loss of mine:
I will be deaf to pleading and excuses;
Nor tears nor prayers shall purchase out abuses:
Therefore use none: let Romeo hence in haste,
Else, when he 's found, that hour is his last.   200
Bear hence this body and attend our will:
Mercy but murders, pardoning those that kill. (*Exeunt.*)

Scene II, *Capulet's orchard.*

Enter JULIET.

JUL: Gallop apace, you fiery-footed steeds,
Towards Phœbus' lodging: such a waggoner
As Phæthon would whip you to the west,
And bring in cloudy night immediately.
Spread thy close curtain, love-performing night,
That runaways' eyes may wink, and Romeo
Leap to these arms, untalk'd of and unseen.
Lovers can see to do their amorous rites
By their own beauties; or, if love be blind,
It best agrees with night. Come, civil night,   10
Thou sober-suited matron, all in black,
And learn me how to lose a winning match,
Play'd for a pair of stainless maidenhoods:
Hood my unmann'd blood, bating in my cheeks,

---

195. *amerce,* punish by fine.
198. *purchase out,* redeem, exempt from penalty. *abuses,* misdeeds.
SCENE II. 3. *Phæthon,* son of Helios, who was allowed to assume the reins of the sun for a day; not being able to restrain the steeds, he had to be slain by the thunderbolt of Jupiter in order that the universe might not be destroyed.
6. *runaways' eyes,* a famous crux of which there is no satisfactory explanation. The allusion to Phæthon (l. 3) may here be repeated. *wink,* shut.
10. *civil,* well-ordered.
14. *Hood,* cover; term in falconry. The hawk's eyes were covered so that it would not bate, or beat the wings. *unmann'd,* another term in falconry meaning "untamed."

With thy black mantle; till strange love, grown bold,
Think true love acted simple modesty.
Come, night; come, Romeo; come, thou day in night;
For thou wilt lie upon the wings of night
Whiter than new snow on a raven's back.
Come, gentle night, come, loving, black-brow'd night,   20
Give me my Romeo; and, when he shall die,
Take him and cut him out in little stars,
And he will make the face of heaven so fine
That all the world will be in love with night
And pay no worship to the garish sun.
O, I have bought the mansion of a love,
But not possess'd it, and, though I am sold,
Not yet enjoy'd: so tedious is this day
As is the night before some festival
To an impatient child that hath new robes   30
And may not wear them. O, here comes my nurse,
And she brings news; and every tongue that speaks
But Romeo's name speaks heavenly eloquence.

Enter NURSE, *with cords.*

Now, nurse, what news? What hast thou there? the cords
That Romeo bid thee fetch?
NURSE: Ay, ay, the cords. (*Throws them down.*)
JUL: Ay me! what news? why dost thou wring thy hands?
NURSE: Ay, well-a-day! he 's dead, he 's dead, he 's dead!
We are undone, lady, we are undone!
Alack the day! he 's gone, he 's kill'd, he 's dead!
JUL: Can heaven be so envious?
NURSE: Romeo can,   40
Though heaven cannot: O Romeo, Romeo!
Who ever would have thought it? Romeo!
JUL: What devil art thou, that dost torment me thus?
This torture should be roar'd in dismal hell.
Hath Romeo slain himself? say thou but 'I,'
And that bare vowel 'I' shall poison more
Than the death-darting eye of cockatrice:

---

25. *garish,* gaudy, showy.
38. *undone,* ruined.
45. *'I,'* ay, yes.
47. *cockatrice,* basilisk, a fabulous serpent which could kill by its look.

I am not I, if there be such an I;
Or those eyes shut, that make thee answer 'I.'
If he be slain, say 'I'; or if not, no: 50
Brief sounds determine of my weal or woe.
NURSE: I saw the wound, I saw it with mine eyes,—
God save the mark!—here on his manly breast:
A piteous corse, a bloody piteous corse;
Pale, pale as ashes, all bedaub'd in blood,
All in gore-blood; I swounded at the sight.
JUL: O, break, my heart! poor bankrupt, break at once!
To prison, eyes, ne'er look on liberty!
Vile earth, to earth resign; end motion here;
And thou and Romeo press one heavy bier!   60
NURSE: O Tybalt, Tybalt, the best friend I had!
O courteous Tybalt! honest gentleman!
That ever I should live to see thee dead!
JUL: What storm is this that blows so contrary?
Is Romeo slaughter'd, and is Tybalt dead?
My dear-loved cousin, and my dearer lord?
Then, dreadful trumpet, sound the general doom!
For who is living, if those two are gone?
NURSE: Tybalt is gone, and Romeo banished;
Romeo that kill'd him, he is banished.   70
JUL: O God! did Romeo's hand shed Tybalt's blood?
NURSE: It did, it did; alas the day, it did!
JUL: O serpent heart, hid with a flowering face!
Did ever dragon keep so fair a cave?
Beautiful tyrant! fiend angelical!
Dove-feather'd raven! wolvish-ravening lamb!
Despised substance of divinest show!
Just opposite to what thou justly seem'st,
A damned saint, an honourable villain!
O nature, what hadst thou to do in hell,   80
When thou didst bower the spirit of a fiend
In mortal paradise of such sweet flesh?
Was ever book containing such vile matter

---

51. *determine of*, decide.
53. *God save the mark*, God forbid; a familiar oath originally intended to avert ill omen.
56. *gore-blood*, clotted blood.
59. *motion*, power of movement.
81. *bower*, give lodging to.

So fairly bound? O, that deceit should dwell
In such a gorgeous palace!

NURSE: There 's no trust,
No faith, no honesty in men; all perjured,
All forsworn, all naught, all dissemblers.
Ah, where 's my man? give me some aqua vitæ:
These griefs, these woes, these sorrows make me old.
Shame come to Romeo!

JUL: Blister'd be thy tongue   90
For such a wish! he was not born to shame:
Upon his brow shame is ashamed to sit;
For 'tis a throne where honour may be crown'd
Sole monarch of the universal earth.
O, what a beast was I to chide at him!

NURSE: Will you speak well of him that kill'd your cousin?

JUL: Shall I speak ill of him that is my husband?
Ah, poor my lord, what tongue shall smooth thy name,
When I, thy three-hours wife, have mangled it?
But, wherefore, villain, didst thou kill my cousin?   100
That villain cousin would have kill'd my husband:
Back, foolish tears, back to your native spring;
Your tributary drops belong to woe,
Which you, mistaking, offer up to joy.
My husband lives, that Tybalt would have slain;
And Tybalt 's dead, that would have slain my husband:
All this is comfort; wherefore weep I then?
Some word there was, worser than Tybalt's death,
That murder'd me: I would forget it fain;
But, O, it presses to my memory,   110
Like damned guilty deeds to sinners' minds:
'Tybalt is dead, and Romeo—banished;'
That 'banished,' that one word 'banished,'
Hath slain ten thousand Tybalts. Tybalt's death
Was woe enough, if it had ended there:
Or, if sour woe delights in fellowship
And needly will be rank'd with other griefs,
Why follow'd not, when she said 'Tybalt 's dead,'
Thy father, or thy mother, nay, or both,

---

87. *naught*, worthless.
88. *aqua vitæ*, distilled spirit.
117. *needly*, of necessity.

Which modern lamentation might have moved? 120
But with a rearward following Tybalt's death,
'Romeo is banished,' to speak that word,
Is father, mother, Tybalt, Romeo, Juliet,
All slain, all dead. 'Romeo is banished!'
There is no end, no limit, measure, bound,
In that word's death; no words can that woe sound.
Where is my father, and my mother, nurse?
NURSE: Weeping and wailing over Tybalt's corse:
Will you go to them? I will bring you thither.
JUL: Wash they his wounds with tears: mine shall be spent,
When theirs are dry, for Romeo's banishment. 131
Take up those cords: poor ropes, you are beguiled,
Both you and I; for Romeo is exiled:
He made you for a highway to my bed;
But I, a maid, die maiden-widowed.
Come, cords, come, nurse; I'll to my wedding-bed;
And death, not Romeo, take my maidenhead!
NURSE: Hie to your chamber: I'll find Romeo
To comfort you: I wot well where he is.
Hark ye, your Romeo will be here at night: 140
I'll to him; he is hid at Laurence' cell.
JUL: O, find him! give this ring to my true knight,
And bid him come to take his last farewell. (*Exeunt.*)

Scene III, *Friar Laurence's cell.*

Enter FRIAR LAURENCE.

FRI. L: Romeo, come forth; come forth, thou fearful man:
Affliction is enamour'd of thy parts,
And thou art wedded to calamity.

Enter ROMEO.

ROM: Father, what news? what is the prince's doom?
What sorrow craves acquaintance at my hand,

---

120. *modern,* ordinary.
121. *rearward,* rear guard.
139. *wot,* know.

That I yet know not?

FRI. L: Too familiar
Is my dear son with such sour company:
I bring thee tidings of the prince's doom.

ROM: What less than dooms-day is the prince's doom?

FRI. L: A gentler judgement vanish'd from his lips,   10
Not body's death, but body's banishment.

ROM: Ha, banishment! be merciful, say 'death;'
For exile hath more terror in his look,
Much more than death: do not say 'banishment.'

FRI. L: Hence from Verona art thou banished:
Be patient, for the world is broad and wide.

ROM: There is no world without Verona walls,
But purgatory, torture, hell itself.
Hence-banished is banish'd from the world,
And world's exile is death: then banished,   20
Is death mis-term'd; calling death banishment,
Thou cutt'st my head off with a golden axe,
And smilest upon the stroke that murders me.

FRI. L: O deadly sin! O rude unthankfulness!
Thy fault our law calls death; but the kind prince,
Taking thy part, hath rush'd aside the law,
And turn'd that black word death to banishment:
This is dear mercy, and thou seest it not.

ROM: 'Tis torture, and not mercy: heaven is here,
Where Juliet lives; and every cat and dog   30
And little mouse, every unworthy thing,
Live here in heaven and may look on her;
But Romeo may not; more validity,
More honourable state, more courtship lives
In carrion-flies than Romeo: they may seize
On the white wonder of dear Juliet's hand
And steal immortal blessing from her lips,
Who, even in pure and vestal modesty,
Still blush, as thinking their own kisses sin;
But Romeo may not; he is banished: 40

SCENE III. 10. *vanish'd*, issued.
26. *rush'd*, thrust (aside).
28. *dear*, rare, unusual; or kind, generous.
33. *validity*, value.
34. *courtship*, both courtliness and wooing.

Flies may do this, but I from this must fly:
They are free men, but I am banished.
And say'st thou yet that exile is not death?
Hadst thou no poison mix'd, no sharp-ground knife,
No sudden mean of death, though ne'er so mean,
But 'banished' to kill me?—'banished'?
O friar, the damned use that word in hell;
Howlings attend it: how hast thou the heart,
Being a divine, a ghostly confessor,
A sin-absolver, and my friend profess'd,   50
To mangle me with that word 'banished'?
FRI. L: Thou fond mad man, hear me but speak a word.
ROM: O, thou wilt speak again of banishment.
FRI. L: I'll give thee armour to keep off that word;
Adversity's sweet milk, philosophy,
To comfort thee, though thou art banished.
ROM: Yet 'banished'? Hang up philosophy!
Unless philosophy can make a Juliet,
Displant a town, reverse a prince's doom,
It helps not, it prevails not: talk no more.   60
FRI. L: O, then I see that madmen have no ears.
ROM: How should they, when that wise men have no eyes?
FRI. L: Let me dispute with thee of thy estate.
ROM: Thou canst not speak of that thou dost not feel:
Wert thou as young as I, Juliet thy love,
An hour but married, Tybalt murdered,
Doting like me and like me banished,
Then mightst thou speak, then mightst thou tear thy hair,
And fall upon the ground, as I do now,
Taking the measure of an unmade grave. (*Knocking within.*)
FRI. L: Arise; one knocks; good Romeo, hide thyself.   71
ROM: Not I; unless the breath of heart-sick groans,
Mist-like, infold me from the search of eyes. (*Knocking.*)
FRI. L: Hark, how they knock! Who's there? Romeo, arise;
Thou wilt be taken. Stay awhile! Stand up; (*Knocking.*)
Run to my study. By and by! God's will,
What simpleness is this! I come, I come! (*Knocking.*)
Who knocks so hard? whence come you? what's your will?

---

45. *mean . . . mean*, means . . . base.
63. *dispute*, reason. *estate*, situation.

NURSE: (*Within*) Let me come in, and you shall know my errand;
I come from Lady Juliet.
FRI. L: Welcome, then.   80

Enter NURSE.

NURSE: O holy friar, O, tell me, holy friar,
Where is my lady's lord, where 's Romeo?
FRI. L: There on the ground, with his own tears made drunk.
NURSE: O, he is even in my mistress' case,
Just in her case! O woful sympathy!
Piteous predicament! Even so lies she,
Blubbering and weeping, weeping and blubbering.
Stand up, stand up; stand, an you be a man:
For Juliet's sake, for her sake, rise and stand;
Why should you fall into so deep an O?   90
ROM: Nurse!
NURSE: Ah sir! ah sir! Well, death 's the end of all.
ROM: Spakest thou of Juliet? how is it with her?
Doth she not think me an old murderer,
Now I have stain'd the childhood of our joy
With blood removed but little from her own?
Where is she? and how doth she? and what says
My conceal'd lady to our cancell'd love?
NURSE: O, she says nothing, sir, but weeps and weeps;
And now falls on her bed; and then starts up,   100
And Tybalt calls; and then on Romeo cries,
And then down falls again.
ROM: As if that name,
Shot from the deadly level of a gun,
Did murder her; as that name's cursed hand
Murder'd her kinsman. O, tell me, friar, tell me,
In what vile part of this anatomy
Doth my name lodge? tell me that I may sack
The hateful mansion. (*Drawing his sword.*)
FRI. L: Hold thy desperate hand:

---

86. *predicament*, condition, situation.
90. *O*, lamentation.
94. *old* (colloquial), real, actual.
98. *conceal'd lady*, secretly married wife.
103. *level*, aim.
107. *sack*, destroy.

Art thou a man? thy form cries out thou art:
Thy tears are womanish; thy wild acts denote   110
The unreasonable fury of a beast:
Unseemly woman in a seeming man!
Or ill-beseeming beast in seeming both!
Thou hast amazed me: by my holy order,
I thought thy disposition better temper'd.
Hast thou slain Tybalt? wilt thou slay thyself?
And slay thy lady too that lives in thee,
By doing damned hate upon thyself?
Why rail'st thou on thy birth, the heaven, and earth?
Since birth, and heaven, and earth, all three do meet   120
In thee at once; which thou at once wouldst lose.
Fie, fie, thou shamest thy shape, thy love, thy wit;
Which, like a usurer, abound'st in all,
And usest none in that true use indeed
Which should bedeck thy shape, thy love, thy wit:
Thy noble shape is but a form of wax,
Digressing from the valour of a man;
Thy dear love sworn but hollow perjury,
Killing that love which thou hast vow'd to cherish;
Thy wit, that ornament to shape and love,   130
Mis-shapen in the conduct of them both,   .
Like powder in a skilless soldier's flask,
Is set a-fire by thine own ignorance,
And thou dismember'd with thine own defence.
What, rouse thee, man! thy Juliet is alive,
For whose dear sake thou wast but lately dead;
There art thou happy: Tybalt would kill thee,
But thou slew'st Tybalt; there art thou happy too:
The law that threaten'd death becomes thy friend
And turns it to exile; there art thou happy: 140
A pack of blessings lights upon thy back;
Happiness courts thee in her best array;
But, like a misbehaved and sullen wench,
Thou pout'st upon thy fortune and thy love:
Take heed, take heed, for such die miserable.
Go, get thee to thy love, as was decreed,
Ascend her chamber, hence and comfort her:
But look thou stay not till the watch be set,
For then thou canst not pass to Mantua;
Where thou shalt live, till we can find a time   150

To blaze your marriage, reconcile your friends,
Beg pardon of the prince, and call thee back
With twenty hundred thousand times more joy
Than thou went'st forth in lamentation.
Go before, nurse: commend me to thy lady;
And bid her hasten all the house to bed,
Which heavy sorrow makes them apt unto:
Romeo is coming.
NURSE: O Lord, I could have stay'd here all the night
To hear good counsel: O, what learning is!   160
My lord, I'll tell my lady you will come.
ROM: Do so, and bid my sweet prepare to chide.
NURSE: Here, sir, a ring she bid me give you, sir:
Hie you, make haste, for it grows very late. (*Exit.*)
ROM: How well my comfort is revived by this!
FRI. L: Go hence; good night; and here stands all your state:
Either be gone before the watch be set,
Or by the break of day disguised from hence:
Sojourn in Mantua; I'll find out your man,
And he shall signify from time to time   170
Every good hap to you that chances here:
Give me thy hand; 'tis late: farewell; good night.
ROM: But that a joy past joy calls out on me,
It were a grief, so brief to part with thee:
Farewell. (*Exeunt.*)

Scene IV, *A room in Capulet's house.*

Enter CAPULET, LADY CAPULET, *and* PARIS.

CAP: Things have fall'n out, sir, so unluckily,
That we have had no time to move our daughter:
Look you, she loved her kinsman Tybalt dearly,
And so did I:—Well, we were born to die.
'Tis very late, she'll not come down to-night:
I promise you, but for your company,
I would have been a-bed an hour ago.

———————

151. *blaze*, publish, divulge.
157. *apt*, ready, inclined.
166. *here stands all your state*, your fortune depends on what follows.

PAR: These times of woe afford no time to woo.
Madam, good night: commend me to your daughter.
LA. CAP: I will, and know her mind early to-morrow;   10
To-night she is mew'd up to her heaviness.
CAP: Sir Paris, I will make a desperate tender
Of my child's love: I think she will be ruled
In all respects by me; nay, more, I doubt it not.
Wife, go you to her ere you go to bed;
Acquaint her here of my son Paris' love;
And bid her, mark you me, on Wednesday next—
But, soft! what day is this?
PAR: Monday, my lord.
CAP: Monday! ha, ha! Well, Wednesday is too soon,
O' Thursday let it be: o' Thursday, tell her,   20
She shall be married to this noble earl.
Will you be ready? do you like this haste?
We'll keep no great ado,—a friend or two;
For, hark you, Tybalt being slain so late,
It may be thought we held him carelessly,
Being our kinsman, if we revel much:
Therefore we'll have some half a dozen friends,
And there an end. But what say you to Thursday?
PAR: My lord, I would that Thursday were to-morrow.
CAP: Well, get you gone: o' Thursday be it, then.   30
Go you to Juliet ere you go to bed,
Prepare her, wife, against this wedding-day.
Farewell, my lord. Light to my chamber, ho!
Afore me! it is so very very late,
That we may call it early by and by.
Good night. (*Exeunt.*)

Scene V, *Capulet's orchard.*

Enter ROMEO *and* JULIET *above, at the window.*

JUL: Wilt thou be gone? it is not yet near day:
It was the nightingale, and not the lark,

SCENE IV. 11. *mew'd,* cooped.
12. *desperate tender,* rash offer.
25. *held,* regarded.
34. *Afore me,* by my life.

That pierced the fearful hollow of thine ear;
Nightly she sings on yond pomegranate-tree:
Believe me, love, it was the nightingale.
ROM: It was the lark, the herald of the morn,
No nightingale: look, love, what envious streaks
Do lace the severing clouds in yonder east:
Night's candles are burnt out, and jocund day
Stands tiptoe on the misty mountain tops.   10
I must be gone and live, or stay and die.
JUL: Yond light is not day-light, I know it, I:
It is some meteor that the sun exhales,
To be to thee this night a torch-bearer,
And light thee on thy way to Mantua:
Therefore stay yet; thou need'st not to be gone.
ROM: Let me be ta'en, let me be put to death;
I am content, so thou wilt have it so.
I'll say yon grey is not the morning's eye,
'Tis but the pale reflex of Cynthia's brow;   20
Nor that is not the lark, whose notes do beat
The vaulty heaven so high above our heads:
I have more care to stay than will to go:
Come, death, and welcome! Juliet wills it so.
How is 't, my soul? let 's talk; it is not day.
JUL: It is, it is: hie hence, be gone, away!
It is the lark that sings so out of tune,
Straining harsh discords and unpleasing sharps.
Some say the lark makes sweet division;
This doth not so, for she divideth us: 30
Some say the lark and loathed toad change eyes;
O, now I would they had changed voices too!
Since arm from arm that voice doth us affray,
Hunting thee hence with hunt's-up to the day.
O, now be gone; more light and light it grows.
ROM: More light and light; more dark and dark our woes!

SCENE V. 8. *lace*, stripe.
20. *Cynthia's*, the moon's.
28. *sharps*, high notes.
29. *division*, melody.
31. *change eyes*, an allusion to a popular saying that the toad and the lark had changed eyes, since the lark has ugly eyes and the toad beautiful ones.
33. *affray*, frighten away.
34. *hunt's-up*, a song or tune to awaken huntsmen.

Enter NURSE, *to the chamber.*

NURSE: Madam!

JUL: Nurse?

NURSE: Your lady mother is coming to your chamber:

The day is broke; be wary, look about. (*Exit.*)   40

JUL: Then, window, let day in, and let life out.

ROM: Farewell, farewell! one kiss, and I'll descend. (*He goeth down.*)

JUL: Art thou gone so? love, lord, ay, husband, friend!

I must hear from thee every day in the hour,

For in a minute there are many days:

O, by this count I shall be much in years

Ere I again behold my Romeo!

ROM: Farewell!

I will omit no opportunity

That may convey my greetings, love, to thee.   50

JUL: O, think'st thou we shall ever meet again?

ROM: I doubt it not; and all these woes shall serve

For sweet discourses in our time to come.

JUL: O God, I have an ill-divining soul!

Methinks I see thee, now thou art below,

As one dead in the bottom of a tomb:

Either my eyesight fails, or thou look'st pale.

ROM: And trust me, love, in my eye so do you:

Dry sorrow drinks our blood. Adieu, adieu! (*Exit.*)

JUL: O fortune, fortune! all men call thee fickle: 60

If thou art fickle, what dost thou with him

That is renown'd for faith? Be fickle, fortune;

For then, I hope, thou wilt not keep him long,

But send him back.

LA. CAP: (*Within*) Ho, daughter! are you up?

JUL: Who is 't that calls? is it my lady mother?

Is she not down so late, or up so early?

What unaccustom'd cause procures her hither?

Enter LADY CAPULET.

---

57. *fails*, errs.

59. *Dry sorrow*. The heat of the body in sorrow and despair was thought to descend into the bowels and dry up the blood.

67. *down*, in bed.

68. *procures*, induces to come.

LA. CAP: Why, how now, Juliet!

JUL: Madam, I am not well.

LA. CAP: Evermore weeping for your cousin's death?   70
What, wilt thou wash him from his grave with tears?
An if thou couldst, thou couldst not make him live;
Therefore, have done: some grief shows much of love;
But much of grief shows still some want of wit.

JUL: Yet let me weep for such a feeling loss.

LA. CAP: So shall you feel the loss, but not the friend
Which you weep for.

JUL: Feeling so the loss,
I cannot choose but ever weep the friend.

LA. CAP: Well, girl, thou weep'st not so much for his death,
As that the villain lives which slaughter'd him.   80

JUL: What villain, madam?

LA. CAP: That same villain, Romeo.

JUL: (*Aside*) Villain and he be many miles asunder.—
God pardon him! I do, with all my heart;
And yet no man like he doth grieve my heart.

LA. CAP: That is, because the traitor murderer lives.

JUL: Ay, madam, from the reach of these my hands:
Would none but I might venge my cousin's death!

LA. CAP: We will have vengeance for it, fear thou not:
Then weep no more. I'll send to one in Mantua,
Where that same banish'd runagate doth live,   90
Shall give him such an unaccustom'd dram,
That he shall soon keep Tybalt company:
And then, I hope, thou wilt be satisfied.

JUL: Indeed, I never shall be satisfied
With Romeo, till I behold him—dead—
Is my poor heart so for a kinsman vex'd:
Madam, if you could find out but a man
To bear a poison, I would temper it;
That Romeo should, upon receipt thereof,
Soon sleep in quiet. O, how my heart abhors   100
To hear him named, and cannot come to him,
To wreak the love I bore my cousin

---

84. *like*, so much as.

90. *runagate*, vagabond.

95. *dead*. This word is placed between the clauses so that it can be understood with either what precedes or what follows it.

98. *temper*, used equivocally, meaning "to mix" or "to alloy."

Upon his body that hath slaughter'd him!
LA. CAP: Find thou the means, and I'll find such a man.
But now I'll tell thee joyful tidings, girl.
JUL: And joy comes well in such a needy time:
What are they, I beseech your ladyship?
LA. CAP: Well, well, thou hast a careful father, child;
One who, to put thee from thy heaviness,
Hath sorted out a sudden day of joy,   110
That thou expect'st not nor I look'd not for.
JUL: Madam, in happy time, what day is that?
LA. CAP: Marry, my child, early next Thursday morn,
The gallant, young and noble gentleman,
The County Paris, at Saint Peter's Church,
Shall happily make thee there a joyful bride.
JUL: Now, by Saint Peter's Church and Peter too,
He shall not make me there a joyful bride.
I wonder at this haste; that I must wed
Ere he, that should be husband, comes to woo.   120
I pray you, tell my lord and father, madam,
I will not marry yet; and, when I do, I swear,
It shall be Romeo, whom you know I hate,
Rather than Paris. These are news indeed!
LA. CAP: Here comes your father; tell him so yourself,
And see how he will take it at your hands.

Enter CAPULET *and* NURSE.

CAP: When the sun sets, the air doth drizzle dew;
But for the sunset of my brother's son
It rains downright.
How now! a conduit, girl? what, still in tears?   130
Evermore showering? In one little body
Thou counterfeit'st a bark, a sea, a wind;
For still thy eyes, which I may call the sea,
Do ebb and flow with tears; the bark thy body is,
Sailing in this salt flood; the winds, thy sighs;
Who, raging with thy tears, and they with them,
Without a sudden calm, will overset

---

108. *careful*, provident.
112. *in happy time*, a vague expression like "by the way."
130. *conduit*, water pipe.

Thy tempest-tossed body. How now, wife!
Have you deliver'd to her our decree?
LA. CAP: Ay, sir; but she will none, she gives you thanks.
I would the fool were married to her grave!   141
CAP: Soft! take me with you, take me with you, wife.
How! will she none? doth she not give us thanks?
Is she not proud? doth she not count her blest,
Unworthy as she is, that we have wrought
So worthy a gentleman to be her bridegroom?
JUL: Not proud, you have; but thankful, that you have:
Proud can I never be of what I hate;
But thankful even for hate, that is meant love.
CAP: How now, how now, chop-logic! What is this?   150
'Proud,' and 'I thank you,' and 'I thank you not;'
And yet 'not proud:' mistress minion, you,
Thank me no thankings, nor proud me no prouds,
But fettle your fine joints 'gainst Thursday next,
To go with Paris to Saint Peter's Church,
Or I will drag thee on a hurdle thither.
Out, you green-sickness carrion! out, you baggage!
You tallow-face!
LA. CAP: Fie, fie! what, are you mad?
JUL: Good father, I beseech you on my knees,
Hear me with patience but to speak a word.   160
CAP: Hang thee, young baggage! disobedient wretch!
I tell thee what: get thee to church o' Thursday,
Or never after look me in the face:
Speak not, reply not, do not answer me;
My fingers itch. Wife, we scarce thought us blest
That God had lent us but this only child;
But now I see this one is one too much,
And that we have a curse in having her:

---

140. *will none*, refuses it.
142. *take me with you*, let me understand you.
145. *wrought*, procured.
150. *choplogic*, a shallow and sophistical arguer.
152. *minion*, favored or pampered person.
154. *fettle*, make ready.
156. *hurdle*, a conveyance for criminals.
157. *green-sickness*, an anemic ailment of young women; it suggests Juliet's paleness.
161. *baggage*, worthless woman.
165. *My . . . itch*, I have a mind to strike.

Out on her, hilding!

NURSE: God in heaven bless her!

You are to blame, my lord, to rate her so.   170

CAP: And why, my lady wisdom? hold your tongue,

Good prudence; smatter with your gossips, go.

NURSE: I speak no treason.

CAP: O, God ye god-den.

NURSE: May not one speak?

CAP: Peace, you mumbling fool!

Utter your gravity o'er a gossip's bowl;

For here we need it not.

LA. CAP: You are too hot.

CAP: †God's bread! it makes me mad:

†Day, night, hour, tide, time, work, play,

Alone, in company, still my care hath been

To have her match'd: and having now provided   180

A gentleman of noble parentage,

Of fair demesnes, youthful, and nobly train'd,

Stuff'd, as they say, with honourable parts,

Proportion'd as one's thought would wish a man;

And then to have a wretched puling fool,

A whining mammet, in her fortune's tender,

To answer 'I'll not wed; I cannot love,

I am too young; I pray you, pardon me.'

But, an you will not wed, I'll pardon you:

Graze where you will, you shall not house with me: 190

Look to 't, think on 't, I do not use to jest.

Thursday is near; lay hand on heart, advise:

An you be mine, I'll give you to my friend;

An you be not, hang, beg, starve, die in the streets,

For, by my soul, I'll ne'er acknowledge thee,

Nor what is mine shall never do thee good:

Trust to 't, bethink you; I'll not be forsworn. (*Exit.*)

JUL: Is there no pity sitting in the clouds,

That sees into the bottom of my grief?

O, sweet my mother, cast me not away!   200

---

169. *hilding,* good-for-nothing.
170. *rate,* berate, scold.
172. *smatter,* chatter.
175. *gravity,* wisdom; used contemptuously.
177. *God's bread,* an oath by the sacrament.
186. *mammet,* doll. *fortune's tender,* offer of good fortune.

Delay this marriage for a month,. a week;
Or, if you do not, make the bridal bed
In that dim monument where Tybalt lies.
LA. CAP: Talk not to me, for I'll not speak a word:
Do as thou wilt, for I have done with thee. (*Exit.*)
JUL: O God!—O nurse, how shall this be prevented?
My husband is on earth, my faith in heaven;
How shall that faith return again to earth,
Unless that husband send it me from heaven
By leaving earth? comfort me, counsel me.   210
Alack, alack, that heaven should practise stratagems
Upon so soft a subject as myself!
What say'st thou? hast thou not a word of joy?
Some comfort, nurse.
NURSE: Faith, here it is.
Romeo is banish'd; and all the world to nothing,
That he dares ne'er come back to challenge you;
Or, if he do, it needs must be by stealth.
Then, since the case so stands as now it doth,
I think it best you married with the county.
O, he 's a lovely gentleman!   220
Romeo 's a dishclout to him: an eagle, madam,
Hath not so green, so quick, so fair an eye
As Paris hath. Beshrew my very heart,
I think you are happy in this second match,
For it excels your first: or if it did not,
Your first is dead; or 'twere as good he were,
As living here and you no use of him.
JUL: Speakest thou from thy heart?
NURSE: And from my soul too;
Or else beshrew them both.
JUL: Amen!
NURSE: What?
JUL: Well, thou hast comforted me marvellous much.   230
Go in; and tell my lady I am gone,
Having displeased my father, to Laurence' cell,
To make confession and to be absolved.
NURSE: Marry, I will; and this is wisely done. (*Exit.*)

---

207. *my faith in heaven.* Juliet refers to her marriage vows.
211. *practise*, scheme, contrive. *stratagems*, dreadful deeds.
222. *green.* Green was an admired color for eyes. *quick*, lively.

JUL: Ancient damnation! O most wicked fiend!
Is it more sin to wish me thus forsworn,
Or to dispraise my lord with that same tongue
Which she hath praised him with above compare
So many thousand times? Go, counsellor;
Thou and my bosom henceforth shall be twain.   240
I'll to the friar, to know his remedy:
If all else fail, myself have power to die. (*Exit.*)

ACT IV.

Scene I, *Friar Laurence's cell.*

Enter FRIAR LAURENCE *and* PARIS.

FRI. L: On Thursday, sir? the time is very short.
PAR: My father Capulet will have it so;
And I am nothing slow to slack his haste.
FRI. L: You say you do not know the lady's mind:
Uneven is the course, I like it not.
PAR: Immoderately she weeps for Tybalt's death,
And therefore have I little talk'd of love;
For Venus smiles not in a house of tears.
Now, sir, her father counts it dangerous
That she doth give her sorrow so much sway,   10
And in his wisdom hastes our marriage,
To stop the inundation of her tears;
Which, too much minded by herself alone,
May be put from her by society:
Now do you know the reason of this haste.
FRI. L: (*Aside*) I would I knew not why it should be slow'd.
Look, sir, here comes the lady towards my cell.

Enter JULIET.

ACT IV. SCENE I. 3. *slack,* slacken.
5. *Uneven,* not straightforward.
13. *minded,* perceived, noticed.

PAR: Happily met, my lady and my wife!

JUL: That may be, sir, when I may be a wife.

PAR: That may be must be, love, on Thursday next.   20

JUL: What must be shall be.

FRI. L: That 's a certain text.

PAR: Come you to make confession to this father?

JUL: To answer that, I should confess to you.

PAR: Do not deny to him that you love me.

JUL: I will confess to you that I love him.

PAR: So will ye, I am sure, that you love me.

JUL: If I do so, it will be of more price,
Being spoke behind your back, than to your face.

PAR: Poor soul, thy face is much abused with tears.

JUL: The tears have got small victory by that;   30
For it was bad enough before their spite.

PAR: Thou wrong'st it, more than tears, with that report.

JUL: That is no slander, sir, which is a truth;
And what I spake, I spake it to my face.

PAR: Thy face is mine, and thou hast slander'd it.

JUL: It may be so, for it is not mine own.
Are you at leisure, holy father, now;
Or shall I come to you at evening mass?

FRI. L: My leisure serves me, pensive daughter, now.
My lord, we must entreat the time alone.   40

PAR: God shield I should disturb devotion!
Juliet, on Thursday early will I rouse ye:
Till then, adieu; and keep this holy kiss. (*Exit.*)

JUL: O, shut the door! and when thou hast done so,
Come weep with me; past hope, past cure, past help!

FRI. L: Ah, Juliet, I already know thy grief;
It strains me past the compass of my wits:
I hear thou must, and nothing may prorogue it,
On Thursday next be married to this county.

JUL: Tell me not, friar, that thou hear'st of this,   50
Unless thou tell me how I may prevent it:
If, in thy wisdom, thou canst give no help,
Do thou but call my resolution wise,
And with this knife I'll help it presently.

---

40. *entreat*, ask to have.
41. *shield*, prevent (that).
54. *presently*, at once.

God join'd my heart and Romeo's, thou our hands;
And ere this hand, by thee to Romeo seal'd,
Shall be the label to another deed,
Or my true heart with treacherous revolt
Turn to another, this shall slay them both:
Therefore, out of thy long-experienced time,   60
Give me some present counsel, or, behold,
'Twixt my extremes and me this bloody knife
Shall play the umpire, arbitrating that
Which the commission of thy years and art
Could to no issue of true honour bring.
Be not so long to speak; I long to die,
If what thou speak'st speak not of remedy.
FRI. L: Hold, daughter: I do spy a kind of hope,
Which craves as desperate an execution
As that is desperate which we would prevent.   70
If, rather than to marry County Paris,
Thou hast the strength of will to slay thyself,
Then is it likely thou wilt undertake
A thing like death to chide away this shame,
That copest with death himself to scape from it;
And, if thou darest, I'll give thee remedy.
JUL: O, bid me leap, rather than marry Paris,
From off the battlements of yonder tower;
Or walk in thievish ways; or bid me lurk
Where serpents are; chain me with roaring bears;   80
Or shut me nightly in a charnel-house,
O'er-cover'd quite with dead men's rattling bones,
With reeky shanks and yellow chapless skulls;
Or bid me go into a new-made grave
And hide me with a dead man in his shroud;
Things that, to hear them told, have made me tremble;
And I will do it without fear or doubt,
To live an unstain'd wife to my sweet love.
FRI. L: Hold, then; go home, be merry, give consent

---

57. *label,* a strip attached to a deed to carry the seal.

61. *present,* instant.

62. *extremes,* extreme difficulties.

64. *commission,* authority.

75. *copest,* encounterest.

81. *charnel-house,* a room or vault where bodies or bones of the dead were deposited.

83. *reeky,* malodorous. *chapless,* without the lower jaw.

To marry Paris: Wednesday is to-morrow: 90
To-morrow night look that thou lie alone;
Let not thy nurse lie with thee in thy chamber:
Take thou this vial, being then in bed,
And this distilled liquor drink thou off;
When presently through all thy veins shall run
A cold and drowsy humour, for no pulse
Shall keep his native progress, but surcease:
No warmth, no breath, shall testify thou livest;
The roses in thy lips and cheeks shall fade
To paly ashes, thy eyes' windows fall,   100
Like death, when he shuts up the day of life;
Each part, deprived of supple government,
Shall, stiff and stark and cold, appear like death:
And in this borrow'd likeness of shrunk death
Thou shalt continue two and forty hours,
And then awake as from a pleasant sleep.
Now, when the bridegroom in the morning comes
To rouse thee from thy bed, there art thou dead:
Then, as the manner of our country is,
In thy best robes uncover'd on the bier   110
Thou shalt be borne to that same ancient vault
Where all the kindred of the Capulets lie.
In the mean time, against thou shalt awake,
Shall Romeo by my letters know our drift,
And hither shall he come: and he and I
Will watch thy waking, and that very night
Shall Romeo bear thee hence to Mantua.
And this shall free thee from this present shame;
If no inconstant toy, nor womanish fear,
Abate thy valour in the acting it.   120
JUL: Give me, give me! O, tell not me of fear!
FRI. L: Hold; get you gone, be strong and prosperous
In this resolve: I'll send a friar with speed
To Mantua, with my letters to thy lord.
JUL: Love give me strength! and strength shall help afford.
Farewell, dear father! (*Exeunt.*)

---

97. *surcease*, cease, stop.
113. *against*, in expectation of the time.
119. *toy*, idle fancy.
120. *Abate*, diminish.

Scene II, *Hall in Capulet's house.*

Enter CAPULET, LADY CAPULET, NURSE, *and two* SERVINGMEN.

CAP: So many guests invite as here are writ. (*Exit* FIRST SERVANT.)
Sirrah, go hire me twenty cunning cooks.
SEC. SERV: You shall have none ill, sir; for I'll try if they can lick their
fingers.
CAP: How canst thou try them so?
SEC. SERV: Marry, sir, 'tis an ill cook that cannot lick his own fingers:
therefore he that cannot lick his fingers goes not with me.
CAP: Go, be gone. (*Exit* SEC. SERVANT.)
We shall be much unfurnish'd for this time.   10
What, is my daughter gone to Friar Laurence?
NURSE: Ay, forsooth.
CAP: Well, he may chance to do some good on her:
A peevish self-will'd harlotry it is.
NURSE: See where she comes from shrift with merry look.

Enter JULIET.

CAP: How now, my headstrong! where have you been gadding?
JUL: Where I have learn'd me to repent the sin
Of disobedient opposition
To you and your behests, and am enjoin'd
By holy Laurence to fall prostrate here,   20
And beg your pardon: pardon, I beseech you!
Henceforward I am ever ruled by you.
CAP: Send for the county; go tell him of this:
I'll have this knot knit up to-morrow morning.
JUL: I met the youthful lord at Laurence' cell;
And gave him what becomed love I might,
Not stepping o'er the bounds of modesty.
CAP: Why, I am glad on 't; this is well: stand up:

SCENE II. 6-7. *ill . . . fingers,* a proverb given in John Heywood's *Proverbs.*
14. *peevish,* silly. *harlotry,* hussy.
26. *becomed,* befitting.

This is as 't should be. Let me see the county;
Ay, marry, go, I say, and fetch him hither.   30
Now, afore God! this reverend holy friar,
All our whole city is much bound to him.
JUL: Nurse, will you go with me into my closet,
To help me sort such needful ornaments
As you think fit to furnish me to-morrow?
LA. CAP: No, not till Thursday; there is time enough.
CAP: Go, nurse, go with her: we'll to church to-morrow. (*Exeunt*
JULIET *and* NURSE.)
LA. CAP: We shall be short in our provision:
'Tis now near night.
CAP: Tush, I will stir about,
And all things shall be well, I warrant thee, wife: 40
Go thou to Juliet, help to deck up her;
I'll not to bed to-night; let me alone;
I'll play the housewife for this once. What, ho!
They are all forth. Well, I will walk myself
To County Paris, to prepare him up
Against to-morrow: my heart is wondrous light,
Since this same wayward girl is so reclaim'd. (*Exeunt.*)

Scene III, *Juliet's chamber.*

Enter JULIET *and* NURSE.

JUL: Ay, those attires are best: but, gentle nurse,
I pray thee, leave me to myself to-night;
For I have need of many orisons
To move the heavens to smile upon my state,
Which, well thou know'st, is cross and full of sin.

Enter LADY CAPULET.

LA. CAP: What, are you busy, ho? need you my help?
JUL: No, madam; we have cull'd such necessaries
As are behoveful for our state to-morrow:

---

33. *closet*, private room.
35. *furnish*, fit out.
SCENE III. 3. *orisons*, prayers.
5. *cross*, contrary.
8. *behoveful*, needful.

So please you, let me now be left alone,
And let the nurse this night sit up with you;   10
For, I am sure, you have your hands full all,
In this so sudden business.
LA. CAP: Good night:
Get thee to bed, and rest; for thou hast need. (*Exeunt* LADY CAPULET
and NURSE.)
JUL: Farewell! God knows when we shall meet again.
I have a faint cold fear thrills through my veins,
That almost freezes up the heat of life:
I'll call them back again to comfort me:
Nurse! What should she do here?
My dismal scene I needs must act alone. Come, vial.   20
What if this mixture do not work at all?
Shall I be married then to-morrow morning?
No, no: this shall forbid it: lie thou there. (*Laying down her dagger.*)
What if it be a poison, which the friar
Subtly hath minister'd to have me dead,
Lest in this marriage he should be dishonour'd,
Because he married me before to Romeo?
I fear it is; and yet, methinks, it should not,
For he hath still been tried a holy man.
How if, when I am laid into the tomb,   30
I wake before the time that Romeo
Come to redeem me? there 's a fearful point!
Shall I not, then, be stifled in the vault,
To whose foul mouth no healthsome air breathes in,
And there die strangled ere my Romeo comes?
Or, if I live, is it not very like,
The horrible conceit of death and night,
Together with the terror of the place,—
As in a vault, an ancient receptacle,
Where, for these many hundred years, the bones   40
Of all my buried ancestors are pack'd:
Where bloody Tybalt, yet but green in earth,
Lies festering in his shroud; where, as they say,
At some hours in the night spirits resort;—
Alack, alack, is it not like that I,

---

25. *minister'd*, administered (something healing or the reverse).
29. *still*, ever, always. *tried*, proved. After this line, Q₁: *I will not entertain so bad a thought.*
39. *As*, namely.
42. *green*, fresh, i.e., just buried.

So early waking, what with loathsome smells,
And shrieks like mandrakes' torn out of the earth,
That living mortals, hearing them, run mad:—
O, if I wake, shall I not be distraught,
Environed with all these hideous fears?   50
And madly play with my forefathers' joints?
And pluck the mangled Tybalt from his shroud?
And, in this rage, with some great kinsman's bone,
As with a club, dash out my desperate brains?
O, look! methinks I see my cousin's ghost
Seeking out Romeo, that did spit his body
Upon a rapier's point: stay, Tybalt, stay!
Romeo, I come! this do I drink to thee. (*She falls upon her bed, within the curtains.*)

Scene IV, *Hall in Capulet's house.*

Enter LADY CAPULET *and* NURSE.

LA. CAP: Hold, take these keys, and fetch more spices, nurse.
NURSE: They call for dates and quinces in the pastry.

Enter CAPULET.

CAP: Come, stir, stir, stir! the second cock hath crow'd,
The curfew-bell hath rung, 'tis three o'clock:
Look to the baked meats, good Angelica:
Spare not for cost.
NURSE: Go, you cot-quean, go,
Get you to bed; faith, you'll be sick to-morrow
For this night's watching.

---

47. *mandrakes'*. Mandragora or mandrake was a narcotic plant, the root of which resembled the human form; it was fabled to utter a shriek when torn from the ground.
50. *fears*, objects of fear.
53. *rage*, madness.
SCENE IV. 2. *pastry*, room in which pastry was made.
4. *curfew-bell*, apparently rung at other times than at curfew.
5. *baked meats*, pies, pastry.
6. *cot-quean*, a man who acts the housewife.
8. *watching*, being awake.

CAP: No, not a whit: what! I have watch'd ere now
All night for lesser cause, and ne'er been sick.   10
LA. CAP: Ay, you have been a mouse-hunt in your time;
But I will watch you from such watching now. (*Exeunt* LADY CAPULET
and NURSE.)
CAP: A jealous-hood, a jealous-hood!

Enter three or four SERVINGMEN, *with spits, logs, and baskets.*

Now, fellow,
What 's there?
FIRST SERV: Things for the cook, sir; but I know not what.
CAP: Make haste, make haste. (*Exit* FIRST SERV.) Sirrah, fetch drier
logs:
Call Peter, he will show thee where they are.
SEC. SERV: I have a head, sir, that will find out logs,
And never trouble Peter for the matter. (*Exit.*)
CAP: Mass, and well said; a merry whoreson, ha!
Thou shalt be logger-head. Good faith, 'tis day: 20
The county will be here with music straight,
For so he said he would: I hear him near. (*Music within.*)
Nurse! Wife! What, ho! What, nurse, I say!

Re-enter NURSE.

Go waken Juliet, go and trim her up;
I'll go and chat with Paris; hie, make haste,
Make haste; the bridegroom he is come already:
Make haste, I say. (*Exeunt.*)

Scene V, *Juliet's chamber.*

Enter NURSE.

NURSE: Mistress! what, mistress! Juliet! fast, I warrant her, she:
Why, lamb! why, lady! fie, you slug-a-bed!

---

11. *mouse-hunt*, pursuer of women.
13. *jealous-hood*, jealousy.
19. *Mass*, by the Mass.
20. *logger-head*, blockhead.
SCENE V. 1. *fast*, fast asleep.

Why, love, I say! madam! sweet-heart! why, bride!
What, not a word? you take your pennyworths now;
Sleep for a week; for the next night, I warrant,
The County Paris hath set up his rest,
That you shall rest but little. God forgive me,
Marry, and amen, how sound is she asleep!
I must needs wake her. Madam, madam, madam!
Ay, let the county take you in your bed;   10
He'll fright you up, i' faith. Will it not be? (*Undraws the curtains.*)
What, dress'd! and in your clothes! and down again!
I must needs wake you: Lady! lady! lady!
Alas, alas! Help, help! my lady 's dead!
O, well-a-day, that ever I was born!
Some aqua vitæ, ho! My lord! my lady!

Enter LADY CAPULET.

LA. CAP: What noise is here?
NURSE: O lamentable day!
LA. CAP: What is the matter?
NURSE: Look, look! O heavy day!
LA. CAP: O me, O me! My child, my only life,
Revive, look up, or I will die with thee!   20
Help, help! Call help.

Enter CAPULET.

CAP: For shame, bring Juliet forth; her lord is come.
NURSE: She 's dead, deceased, she 's dead; alack the day!
LA. CAP: Alack the day, she 's dead, she 's dead, she 's dead!
CAP: Ha! let me see her: out, alas! she 's cold;
Her blood is settled, and her joints are stiff;
Life and these lips have long been separated:
Death lies on her like an untimely frost
Upon the sweetest flower of all the field.
NURSE: O lamentable day!
LA. CAP: O woful time!   30

---

4. *pennyworths*, little bits.
6. *set up his rest*, a phrase from the game of primero meaning to complete your hand and wager on it; hence, to be resolved.
26. *settled*, probably congealed.

CAP: Death, that hath ta'en her hence to make me wail,
Ties up my tongue, and will not let me speak.

Enter FRIAR LAURENCE *and* PARIS, *with* MUSICIANS.

FRI. L: Come, is the bride ready to go to church?
CAP: Ready to go, but never to return.
O son! the night before thy wedding-day
Hath Death lain with thy wife. There she lies,
Flower as she was, deflowered by him.
Death is my son-in-law, Death is my heir;
My daughter he hath wedded: I will die,
And leave him all; life, living, all is Death's.   40
PAR: Have I thought long to see this morning's face,
And doth it give me such a sight as this?
LA. CAP: Accursed, unhappy, wretched, hateful day!
Most miserable hour that e'er time saw
In lasting labour of his pilgrimage!
But one, poor one, one poor and loving child,
But one thing to rejoice and solace in,
And cruel death hath catch'd it from my sight!
NURSE: O woe! O woful, woful, woful day!
Most lamentable day, most woful day,   50
That ever, ever, I did yet behold!
O day! O day! O day! O hateful day!
Never was seen so black a day as this:
O woful day, O woful day!
PAR: Beguiled, divorced, wronged, spited, slain!
Most detestable death, by thee beguiled,
By cruel cruel thee quite overthrown!
O love! O life! not life, but love in death!
CAP: Despised, distressed, hated, martyr'd, kill'd!
Uncomfortable time, why camest thou now   60
To murder, murder our solemnity?
O child! O child! my soul, and not my child!
Dead art thou! Alack! my child is dead;
And with my child my joys are buried.
FRI. L: Peace, ho, for shame! confusion's cure lives not
In these confusions. Heaven and yourself

---

41. *thought long,* looked forward to.
43. *unhappy,* fatal.
61. *solemnity,* festivity.
65. *confusion's,* destruction's.

Had part in this fair maid; now heaven hath all,
And all the better is it for the maid:
Your part in her you could not keep from death,
But heaven keeps his part in eternal life.   70
The most you sought was her promotion;
For 'twas your heaven she should be advanced:
And weep ye now, seeing she is advanced
Above the clouds, as high as heaven itself?
O, in this love, you love your child so ill,
That you run mad, seeing that she is well:
She 's not well married that lives married long;
But she 's best married that dies married young.
Dry up your tears, and stick your rosemary
On this fair corse; and, as the custom is,   80
In all her best array bear her to church:
For though fond nature bids us all lament,
Yet nature's tears are reason's merriment.
CAP: All things that we ordained festival,
Turn from their office to black funeral;
Our instruments to melancholy bells,
Our wedding cheer to a sad burial feast,
Our solemn hymns to sullen dirges change,
Our bridal flowers serve for a buried corse,
And all things change them to the contrary.   90
FRI. L: Sir, go you in; and, madam, go with him;
And go, Sir Paris; every one prepare
To follow this fair corse unto her grave:
The heavens do lour upon you for some ill;
Move them no more by crossing their high will. (*Exeunt* CAPULET, LADY
CAPULET, PARIS, *and* FRIAR.)
FIRST MUS: Faith, we may put up our pipes, and be gone.
NURSE: Honest good fellows, ah, put up. put up;
For, well you know, this is a pitiful case. (*Exit.*)
FIRST MUS: Ay, by my troth, the case may be amended.   101

---

72. *advanced. Advance* meant both "promote in worldly affairs" and "lift or raise up."

79. *rosemary*, symbol of immortality and enduring love; therefore used at both funerals and weddings.

83. *Yet . . . merriment.* Nature is here used as the opposite of reason.

84. *ordained festival*, intended to be festive.

101. *amended*, bettered. *Stage Direction: Enter Peter.* Q₂ has *Enter Will Kemp.* This well-known comic actor was a member of Shakespeare's company and evidently played this part. His name was written in probably by the prompter; hence one argues that Q₂ was set up from a playhouse copy.

Enter PETER.

PET: Musicians, O, musicians, 'Heart's ease, Heart's ease:'
O, an you will have me live, play 'Heart's ease.'
FIRST MUS: Why 'Heart's ease'?
PET: O, musicians, because my heart itself plays 'My heart is full of woe:' O, play me some merry dump, to comfort me.
FIRST MUS: Not a dump we; 'tis no time to play now.   110
PET: You will not, then?
FIRST MUS: No.
PET: I will then give it you soundly.
FIRST MUS: What will you give us?
PET: No money, on my faith, but the gleek; I will give you the minstrel.
FIRST MUS: Then will I give you the serving-creature.
PET: Then will I lay the serving-creature's dagger on your pate. I will carry no crotchets: I'll re you, I'll fa you; do you note me?   121
FIRST MUS: An you re us and fa us, you note us.
SEC. MUS: Pray you, put up your dagger, and put out your wit.
PET: Then have at you with my wit! I will dry-beat you with an iron wit, and put up my iron dagger. Answer me like men:
    'When griping grief the heart doth wound,
        And doleful dumps the mind oppress,
    Then music with her silver sound'—   130
why 'silver sound'? why 'music with her silver sound'? What say you, Simon Catling?
FIRST MUS: Marry, sir, because silver hath a sweet sound.
PET: Pretty! What say you, Hugh Rebeck?
SEC. MUS: I say 'silver sound,' because musicians sound for silver.
PET: Pretty too! What say you, James Soundpost?

---

102. *'Heart's ease,'* popular tune, as also *'My heart is full of woe,'* line 107.
108. *dump,* mournful tune.
115. *gleek,* jest, gibe.
116. *give . . . minstrel,* call you a minstrel, which word still suggested mere entertainer or jester.
120. *carry,* endure. *crotchets,* meaning both "quarter notes" and "whims."
122. *note,* set to music; used punningly.
124. *put out,* exert.
128-130. *'When . . . sound.'* This is a part of a song by Richard Edwards preserved in the *Paradise of Daintie Devices* (1576).
132. *Catling.* A catling was a small lutestring made of catgut.
135. *Rebeck.* A rebeck was a fiddle with three strings.
139. *Soundpost.* A soundpost is the pillar or peg which supports the body of a stringed instrument.

THIRD MUS: Faith, I know not what to say.   140
PET: O, I cry you mercy; you are the singer: I will say for you. It is 'music with her silver sound,' because musicians have no gold for sounding:
  'Then music with her silver sound
    With speedy help doth lend redress.' (*Exit.*)
FIRST MUS: What a pestilent knave is this same!
SEC. MUS: Hang him, Jack! Come, we'll in here; tarry for the mourners, and stay dinner. (*Exeunt.*)

ACT V.

Scene I, *Mantua. A street.*

Enter ROMEO.

ROM: If I may trust the flattering truth of sleep,
My dreams presage some joyful news at hand:
My bosom's lord sits lightly in his throne;
And all this day an unaccustom'd spirit
Lifts me above the ground with cheerful thoughts.
I dreamt my lady came and found me dead—
Strange dream, that gives a dead man leave to think!—
And breathed such life with kisses in my lips,
That I revived, and was an emperor.
Ah me! how sweet is love itself possess'd,   10
When but love's shadows are so rich in joy!

Enter BALTHASAR, *booted.*

News from Verona!—How now, Balthasar!
Dost thou not bring me letters from the friar?

---

141. *cry you mercy,* beg your pardon.
143. *sounding,* playing music.
150. *stay dinner,* wait until after dinner.
ACT V. SCENE I. 1. *flattering,* illusive.
2. *presage some joyful news.* The premonition here is ironical.
3. *bosom's lord,* heart.
11. *shadows,* phantoms.

How doth my lady? Is my father well?
How fares my Juliet? that I ask again;
For nothing can be ill, if she be well.
BAL: Then she is well, and nothing can be ill:
Her body sleeps in Capels' monument,
And her immortal part with angels lives.
I saw her laid low in her kindred's vault,   20
And presently took post to tell it you:
O, pardon me for bringing these ill news,
Since you did leave it for my office, sir.
ROM: Is it even so? then I defy you, stars!
Thou know'st my lodging: get me ink and paper,
And hire post-horses; I will hence to-night.
BAL: I do beseech you, sir, have patience:
Your looks are pale and wild, and do import
Some misadventure.
ROM: Tush, thou art deceived:
Leave me, and do the thing I bid thee do.   30
Hast thou no letters to me from the friar?
BAL: No, my good lord.
ROM: No matter: get thee gone,
And hire those horses; I'll be with thee straight. (*Exit* BALTHASAR.)
Well, Juliet, I will lie with thee to-night.
Let 's see for means: O mischief, thou art swift
To enter in the thoughts of desperate men!
I do remember an apothecary,—
And hereabouts he dwells,—which late I noted
In tatter'd weeds, with overwhelming brows,
Culling of simples; meagre were his looks,   40
Sharp misery had worn him to the bones:
And in his needy shop a tortoise hung,
An alligator stuff'd, and other skins
Of ill-shaped fishes; and about his shelves
A beggarly account of empty boxes,
Green earthen pots, bladders and musty seeds,

---

21. *took post,* started with post horses.
24. *then I defy you, stars.* The fatalism of this utterance is in keeping with the other references to destiny in the play.
32. *straight,* immediately.
39. *weeds,* clothes. *overwhelming,* overhanging.
40. *simples,* medicinal herbs.
45. *beggarly account,* poor array.

Remnants of packthread and old cakes of roses,
Were thinly scatter'd, to make up a show.
Noting this penury, to myself I said
'An if a man did need a poison now,   50
Whose sale is present death in Mantua,
Here lives a caitiff wretch would sell it him.'
O, this same thought did but forerun my need;
And this same needy man must sell it me.
As I remember, this should be the house.
Being holiday, the beggar's shop is shut.
What, ho! apothecary!

Enter APOTHECARY.

AP: Who calls so loud?
ROM: Come hither, man. I see that thou art poor:
Hold, there is forty ducats: let me have
A dram of poison, such soon-speeding gear   60
As will disperse itself through all the veins
That the life-weary taker may fall dead
And that the trunk may be discharged of breath
As violently as hasty powder fired
Doth hurry from the fatal cannon's womb.
AP: Such mortal drugs I have; but Mantua's law
Is death to any he that utters them.
ROM: Art thou so bare and full of wretchedness,
And fear'st to die? famine is in thy cheeks,
Need and oppression starveth in thine eyes,   70
Contempt and beggary hangs upon thy back;
The world is not thy friend nor the world's law;
The world affords no law to make thee rich;
Then be not poor, but break it, and take this.
AP: My poverty, but not my will, consents.
ROM: I pay thy poverty, and not thy will.
AP: Put this in any liquid thing you will,
And drink it off; and, if you had the strength

---

47. *cakes of roses*, rose petals caked to be used as perfume.
52. *caitiff*, poor.
59. *ducats*, coins, usually gold, of varying value.
60. *soon-speeding gear*, quick-acting stuff.
63. *trunk*, body.
67. *utters*, issues, gives out.
70. *starveth*, show hunger.

Of twenty men, it would dispatch you straight.

ROM: There is thy gold, worse poison to men's souls,   80
Doing more murders in this loathsome world,
Than these poor compounds that thou mayst not sell.
I sell thee poison; thou hast sold me none.
Farewell: buy food, and get thyself in flesh.
Come, cordial and not poison, go with me
To Juliet's grave; for there must I use thee. (*Exeunt.*)

Scene II, *Friar Laurence's cell.*

Enter FRIAR JOHN.

FRI. J: Holy Franciscan friar! brother, ho!

Enter FRIAR LAURENCE.

FRI. L: This same should be the voice of Friar John.
Welcome from Mantua: what says Romeo?
Or, if his mind be writ, give me his letter.
FRI. J: Going to find a bare-foot brother out,
One of our order, to associate me,
Here in this city visiting the sick,
And finding him, the searchers of the town,
Suspecting that we both were in a house
Where the infectious pestilence did reign,   10
Seal'd up the doors, and would not let us forth;
So that my speed to Mantua there was stay'd.
FRI. L: Who bare my letter, then, to Romeo?
FRI. J: I could not send it,—here it is again,—
Nor get a messenger to bring it thee,
So fearful were they of infection.
FRI. L: Unhappy fortune! by my brotherhood,
The letter was not nice but full of charge

80-86. *There . . . thee,* a passage of general reflection but slightly connected with
the action and having no special appropriateness to Romeo.
SCENE II. 4. *mind,* thoughts, message.
6. *associate,* accompany.
8. *searchers,* officers of the pestilence.
18. *nice,* unimportant, casual. *charge,* importance.

Of dear import, and the neglecting it
May do much danger. Friar John, go hence;   20
Get me an iron crow, and bring it straight
Unto my cell.
FRI. J: Brother, I'll go and bring it thee. (*Exit.*)
FRI. L: Now must I to the monument alone;
Within this three hours will fair Juliet wake:
She will beshrew me much that Romeo
Hath had no notice of these accidents;
But I will write again to Mantua,
And keep her at my cell till Romeo come;
Poor living corse, closed in a dead man's tomb! (*Exit.*)   30

Scene III, *A churchyard; in it a tomb belonging to the Capulets.*

Enter PARIS, *and his* PAGE *bearing flowers and a torch.*

PAR: Give me thy torch, boy: hence, and stand aloof:
Yet put it out, for I would not be seen.
Under yond yew-trees lay thee all along,
Holding thine ear close to the hollow ground;
So shall no foot upon the churchyard tread,
Being loose, unfirm, with digging up of graves,
But thou shalt hear it: whistle then to me,
As signal that thou hear'st something approach.
Give me those flowers. Do as I bid thee, go.
PAGE: (*Aside*) I am almost afraid to stand alone   10
Here in the churchyard; yet I will adventure. (*Retires.*)
PAR: Sweet flower, with flowers thy bridal bed I strew,—
    O woe! thy canopy is dust and stones;—
Which with sweet water nightly I will dew,
    Or, wanting that, with tears distill'd by moans:
The obsequies that I for thee will keep
    Nightly shall be to strew thy grave and weep. (*The* PAGE *whistles.*)
The boy gives warning something doth approach.

---

19. *dear import,* dire or grievous significance.
21. *iron crow,* crowbar.
SCENE III. 3. *all along,* at full length.
16. *obsequies,* dutiful acts performed in memory of the dead.

What cursed foot wanders this way to-night,
To cross my obsequies and true love's rite?   20
What, with a torch! muffle me, night, awhile. (*Retires.*)

Enter ROMEO *and* BALTHASAR, *with a torch, mattock.*

ROM: Give me that mattock and the wrenching iron.
Hold, take this letter; early in the morning
See thou deliver it to my lord and father.
Give me the light: upon thy life, I charge thee,
Whate'er thou hear'st or seest, stand all aloof,
And do not interrupt me in my course.
Why I descend into this bed of death,
Is partly to behold my lady's face;
But chiefly to take thence from her dead finger   30
A precious ring, a ring that I must use
In dear employment: therefore hence, be gone:
But if thou, jealous, dost return to pry
In what I further shall intend to do,
By heaven, I will tear thee joint by joint
And strew this hungry churchyard with thy limbs:
The time and my intents are savage-wild,
More fierce and more inexorable far
Than empty tigers or the roaring sea.
BAL: I will be gone, sir, and not trouble you.   40
ROM: So shalt thou show me friendship. Take thou that:
Live, and be prosperous: and farewell, good fellow.
BAL: (*Aside*) For all this same, I'll hide me hereabout:
His looks I fear, and his intents I doubt. (*Retires.*)
ROM: Thou detestable maw, thou womb of death,
Gorged with the dearest morsel of the earth,
Thus I enforce thy rotten jaws to open,
And, in despite, I'll cram thee with more food! (*Opens the tomb.*)
PAR: This is that banish'd haughty Montague,
That murder'd my love's cousin, with which grief,   50
It is supposed, the fair creature died;
And here is come to do some villanous shame

---

21. *muffle*, hide. *mattock*, pickax.
33. *jealous*, suspicious.
44. *doubt*, suspect.
45-48. *Thou . . . food.* The words of these lines seem to echo the wrenching of
the door.

To the dead bodies: I will apprehend him (*Comes forward.*)
Stop thy unhallow'd toil, vile Montague!
Can vengeance be pursued further than death?
Condemned villain, I do apprehend thee:
Obey, and go with me; for thou must die.
ROM: I must indeed; and therefore came I hither.
Good gentle youth, tempt not a desperate man;
Fly hence, and leave me: think upon these gone;   60
Let them affright thee. I beseech thee, youth,
Put not another sin upon my head,
By urging me to fury: O, be gone!
By heaven, I love thee better than myself;
For I come hither arm'd against myself:
Stay not, be gone; live, and hereafter say,
A madman's mercy bade thee run away.
PAR: I do defy thy conjurations,
And apprehend thee for a felon here.
ROM: Wilt thou provoke me? then have at thee, boy! (*They fight.*) 70
PAGE: O Lord, they fight! I will go call the watch. (*Exit.*)
PAR: O, I am slain! (*Falls.*) If thou be merciful,
Open the tomb, lay me with Juliet. (*Dies.*)
ROM: In faith, I will. Let me peruse this face.
Mercutio's kinsman, noble County Paris!
What said my man, when my betossed soul
Did not attend him as we rode? I think
He told me Paris should have married Juliet:
Said he not so? or did I dream it so?
Or am I mad, hearing him talk of Juliet,   80
To think it was so? O, give me thy hand,
One writ with me in sour misfortune's book!
I'll bury thee in a triumphant grave;
A grave? O, no! a lantern, slaughter'd youth,
For here lies Juliet, and her beauty makes
This vault a feasting presence full of light.
Death, lie thou there, by a dead man interr'd. (*Laying* PARIS *in the tomb.*)
How oft when men are at the point of death
Have they been merry! which their keepers call

------

68. *conjurations*, solemn appeals, which seem perhaps like incantations.
74. *peruse*, scrutinize.
84. *lantern*, a turret full of windows.
86. *presence*, presence chamber.

A lightning before death: O, how may I 90
Call this a lightning? O my love! my wife!
Death, that hath suck'd the honey of thy breath,
Hath had no power yet upon thy beauty:
Thou art not conquer'd; beauty's ensign yet
Is crimson in thy lips and in thy cheeks,
And death's pale flag is not advanced there.
Tybalt, liest thou there in thy bloody sheet?
O, what more favour can I do to thee,
Than with that hand that cut thy youth in twain
To sunder his that was thine enemy? 100
Forgive me, cousin! Ah, dear Juliet,
Why art thou yet so fair? shall I believe
That unsubstantial death is amorous,
And that the lean abhorred monster keeps
Thee here in dark to be his paramour?
For fear of that, I still will stay with thee;
And never from this palace of dim night
Depart again: here, here will I remain
With worms that are thy chamber-maids; O, here
Will I set up my everlasting rest, 110
And shake the yoke of inauspicious stars
From this world-wearied flesh. Eyes, look your last!
Arms, take your last embrace! and, lips, O you
The doors of breath, seal with a righteous kiss
A dateless bargain to engrossing death!
Come, bitter conduct, come, unsavoury guide!
Thou desperate pilot, now at once run on
The dashing rocks thy sea-sick weary bark!
Here 's to my love! (*Drinks.*) O true apothecary!
Thy drugs are quick. Thus with a kiss I die. (*Dies.*) 120

Enter, at the other end of the churchyard, FRIAR LAURENCE, *with a
lantern, crow, and spade.*

FRI. L: Saint Francis be my speed! how oft to-night
Have my old feet stumbled at graves! Who 's there?

---

90. *lightning*, a shedding of light; also, a revival of the spirits.
110. *set . . . rest.* See IV, v, 6. The meaning is, "make my final determination,"
with allusion also to the idea of repose.
115. *dateless*, everlasting. *engrossing*, monopolizing.
121. *speed*, protector and assistant.
122. *stumbled at graves*, a bad omen.

BAL: Here 's one, a friend, and one that knows you well.

FRI. L: Bliss be upon you! Tell me, good my friend,
What torch is yond, that vainly lends his light
To grubs and eyeless skulls? as I discern,
It burneth in the Capels' monument.

BAL: It doth so, holy sir; and there 's my master,
One that you love.

FRI. L: Who is it?

BAL: Romeo.

FRI. L: How long hath he been there?

BAL: Full half an hour.   130

FRI. L: Go with me to the vault.

BAL: I dare not, sir:
My master knows not but I am gone hence;
And fearfully did menace me with death,
If I did stay to look on his intents.

FRI. L: Stay, then; I'll go alone. Fear comes upon me:
O, much I fear some ill unlucky thing.

BAL: As I did sleep under this yew-tree here,
I dreamt my master and another fought,
And that my master slew him.

FRI. L: Romeo! (*Advances.*)
Alack, alack, what blood is this, which stains   140
The stony entrance of this sepulchre?
What mean these masterless and gory swords
To lie discolour'd by this place of peace? (*Enters the tomb.*)
Romeo! O, pale! Who else? what, Paris too?
And steep'd in blood? Ah, what an unkind hour
Is guilty of this lamentable chance!
The lady stirs. (JULIET *wakes.*)

JUL: O comfortable friar! where is my lord?
I do remember well where I should be,
And there I am. Where is my Romeo? (*Noise within.*)   150

FRI. L: I hear some noise. Lady, come from that nest
Of death, contagion, and unnatural sleep:
A greater power than we can contradict
Hath thwarted our intents. Come, come away.
Thy husband in thy bosom there lies dead;
And Paris too. Come, I'll dispose of thee

---

126. *grubs*, wormlike larvae, which would, of course, be blind.
137. *yew-*, so Pope; Q₂F: *yong*.

Among a sisterhood of holy nuns:
Stay not to question, for the watch is coming;
Come, go, good Juliet (*Noise again*), I dare no longer stay.
JUL: Go, get thee hence, for I will not away. (*Exit* FRI. L.)
What's here? a cup, closed in my true love's hand?   161
Poison, I see, hath been his timeless end:
O churl! drunk all, and left no friendly drop
To help me after? I will kiss thy lips;
Haply some poison yet doth hang on them,
To make me die with a restorative. (*Kisses him.*)
Thy lips are warm.
FIRST WATCH: (*Within*) Lead, boy: which way?
JUL: Yea, noise? then I'll be brief. O happy dagger! (*Snatching*   169
Romeo's dagger.)
This is thy sheath (*Stabs herself*); there rust, and let me die. (*Falls on
Romeo's body, and dies.*)

Enter WATCH, *with the* PAGE *of* PARIS.

PAGE: This is the place; there, where the torch doth burn.
FIRST WATCH: The ground is bloody; search about the churchyard:
Go, some of you, whoe'er you find attach.
Pitiful sight! here lies the county slain;
And Juliet bleeding, warm, and newly dead,
Who here hath lain these two days buried.
Go, tell the prince: run to the Capulets:
Raise up the Montagues: some others search:
We see the ground whereon these woes do lie;
But the true ground of all these piteous woes   180
We cannot without circumstance descry.

Re-enter some of the WATCH, *with* BALTHASAR.

SEC. WATCH: Here's Romeo's man; we found him in the churchyard.
FIRST WATCH: Hold him in safety, till the prince come hither.

Re-enter others of the WATCH, *with* FRIAR LAURENCE.

---

162. *timeless*, everlasting, or untimely.
163. *churl*, ill-mannered fellow.
165. *Haply*, perhaps.
173. *attach*, arrest.
180. *ground*, cause.

THIRD WATCH: Here is a friar, that trembles, sighs, and weeps:
We took his mattock and this spade from him,
As he was coming from this churchyard side.
FIRST WATCH: A great suspicion: stay the friar too.

Enter the PRINCE *and* ATTENDANTS.

PRINCE: What misadventure is so early up,
That calls our person from our morning's rest?

Enter CAPULET, LADY CAPULET, *and* OTHERS.

CAP: What should it be, that they so shriek abroad?   190
LA. CAP: The people in the street cry Romeo,
Some Juliet, and some Paris; and all run,
With open outcry, toward our monument.
PRINCE: What fear is this which startles in our ears?
FIRST WATCH: Sovereign, here lies the County Paris slain;
And Romeo dead; and Juliet, dead before,
Warm and new kill'd.
PRINCE: Search, seek, and know how this foul murder comes.
FIRST WATCH: Here is a friar, and slaughter'd Romeo's man;
With instruments upon them, fit to open   200
These dead men's tombs.
CAP: O heavens! O wife, look how our daughter bleeds!
This dagger hath mista'en,—for, lo, his house
Is empty on the back of Montague,—
And it mis-sheathed in my daughter's bosom!
LA. CAP: O me! this sight of death is as a bell,
That warns my old age to a sepulchre.

Enter MONTAGUE *and* OTHERS.

PRINCE: Come, Montague; for thou art early up,
To see thy son and heir more early down.
MON: Alas, my liege, my wife is dead tonight;   210
Grief of my son's exile hath stopp'd her breath:
What further woe conspires against mine age?
PRINCE: Look, and thou shalt see.
MON: O thou untaught! what manners is in this,

---

203. *house,* scabbard.

To press before thy father to a grave?
PRINCE: Seal up the mouth of outrage for a while,
Till we can clear these ambiguities,
And know their spring, their head, their true descent;
And then will I be general of your woes,
And lead you even to death: meantime forbear, 220
And let mischance be slave to patience.
Bring forth the parties of suspicion.
FRI. L: I am the greatest, able to do least,
Yet most suspected, as the time and place
Doth make against me, of this direful murder:
And here I stand, both to impeach and purge
Myself condemned and myself excused.
PRINCE: Then say at once what thou dost know in this,
FRI. L: I will be brief, for my short date of breath
Is not so long as is a tedious tale. 230
Romeo, there dead, was husband to that Juliet;
And she, there dead, that Romeo's faithful wife:
I married them; and their stol'n marriage-day
Was Tybalt's dooms-day, whose untimely death
Banish'd the new-made bridegroom from this city,
For whom, and not for Tybalt, Juliet pined.
You, to remove that siege of grief from her,
Betroth'd and would have married her perforce
To County Paris: then comes she to me,
And, with wild looks, bid me devise some mean 240
To rid her from this second marriage,
Or in my cell there would she kill herself.
Then gave I her, so tutor'd by my art,
A sleeping potion; which so took effect
As I intended, for it wrought on her
The form of death: meantime I writ to Romeo,
That he should hither come as this dire night,
To help to take her from her borrow'd grave,
Being the time the potion's force should cease.
But he which bore my letter, Friar John, 250
Was stay'd by accident, and yesternight
Return'd my letter back. Then all alone

---

216. *mouth of outrage*, outcry.
226. *purge*, purify, cleanse.
247. *as this*, this very.

At the prefixed hour of her waking,
Came I to take her from her kindred's vault;
Meaning to keep her closely at my cell,
Till I conveniently could send to Romeo:
But when I came, some minute ere the time
Of her awaking, here untimely lay
The noble Paris and true Romeo dead.
She wakes; and I entreated her come forth,   260
And bear this work of heaven with patience:
But then a noise did scare me from the tomb;
And she, too desperate, would not go with me,
But, as it seems, did violence on herself.
All this I know; and to the marriage
Her nurse is privy: and, if aught in this
Miscarried by my fault, let my old life
Be sacrificed, some hour before his time,
Unto the rigour of severest law.
PRINCE: We still have known thee for a holy man.   270
Where 's Romeo's man? what can he say in this?
BAL: I brought my master news of Juliet's death;
And then in post he came from Mantua
To this same place, to this same monument.
This letter he early bid me give his father,
And threaten'd me with death, going in the vault,
If I departed not and left him there.
PRINCE: Give me the letter; I will look on it.
Where is the county's page, that raised the watch?
Sirrah, what made your master in this place?   280
PAGE: He came with flowers to strew his lady's grave;
And bid me stand aloof, and so I did:
Anon comes one with light to ope the tomb;
And by and by my master drew on him;
And then I ran away to call the watch.
PRINCE: This letter doth make good the friar's words,
Their course of love, the tidings of her death:
And here he writes that he did buy a poison
Of a poor 'pothecary, and therewithal
Came to this vault to die, and lie with Juliet.   290

---

253. *prefixed*, agreed upon previously.
255. *closely*, secretly.
273. *post*, haste.

Where be these enemies? Capulet! Montague!
See, what a scourge is laid upon your hate,
That heaven finds means to kill your joys with love.
And I for winking at your discords too
Have lost a brace of kinsmen: all are punish'd.
CAP: O brother Montague, give me thy hand:
This is my daughter's jointure, for no more
Can I demand.
MON: But I can give thee more:
For I will raise her statue in pure gold;
That while Verona by that name is known,   300
There shall no figure at such rate be set
As that of true and faithful Juliet.
CAP: As rich shall Romeo's by his lady's lie;
Poor sacrifices of our enmity!
PRINCE: A glooming peace this morning with it brings;
   The sun, for sorrow, will not show his head:
Go hence, to have more talk of these sad things;
   Some shall be pardon'd, and some punished:
For never was a story of more woe
Than this of Juliet and her Romeo. (*Exeunt.*)   310

STUDY AND DISCUSSION QUESTIONS

1.   (Prologue and Act I) The first two acts are introduced with a prologue while the last three are not. What is the function of the prologue to the first act? The opening scene is considered a "patterned
opening" in which most of the characters are introduced. What is
the purpose of introducing all of the major characters except
Romeo and Juliet at this time? Is the cause of the feud ever mentioned? With the entrance of Romeo, the subject of love is introduced. Is there any indication in Romeo's dialogue that he is really
not in love at this time? What is the dramatic function of Paris?
What is the significance of the chance encounter between the
Capulet servant and Romeo? What is the role of the Nurse? Of
Mercutio? Of Benvolio? What motivates Romeo to go to the party?

297. *jointure*, marriage portion.
301. *rate*, value.

2. (Act II) Note carefully Romeo's description of Juliet. What imagery does he use? What is the structural significance of Romeo overhearing Juliet's confessions of love? Why is Friar Laurence first seen in his garden? What is his motive for marrying Romeo and Juliet? What is the purpose of the warning the Friar gives Romeo when the latter urges haste? In the war of wits between Romeo and Mercutio, who wins?

3. (Act III) Act III, scene 1, is the meeting of the young men (Paris excepted) in the tragedy. What is ironic about the conflict among these men? What part does the weather play in the fight? Why is Tybalt so bent on a duel with Romeo? Why does Romeo fight knowing that he will be punished by the Prince? In this Act there are some distinct differences drawn between the Capulets and the Montagues. What are these differences and how do they contribute to the impending tragedy?

4. (Act IV) What is the significance of the meeting between Juliet and Paris in Friar Laurence's cell? What is the purpose of the scene between Capulet and the cooks (Act IV, scene 2)? Why does Capulet change the date of the wedding? Why does Friar Laurence devise the feigned death plot? What are some of the doubts Juliet has about taking the poison? What is the dramatic function of Act IV, scene 4?

5. (Act V) While in Mantua, Romeo has a dream. What is the implication of that dream? It seems that in Shakespeare's plays dreams always come true. What effect does this have as a dramatic technique? Why does Paris attack Romeo at the tomb? When Juliet awakens and finds Romeo dead what does Friar Laurence suggest? What effect does the tragedy have on the two families? What does this suggest about the power of love as Shakespeare conceives it?

6. Often Shakespeare employs a number of minor characters to help the reader understand more clearly the protagonist or central character. Such characters usually fall into two categories: foil characters, who develop the protagonist through contrast, and parallel characters, who reinforce him through analogy. Discuss the function of the following characters in terms of the above criteria: Benvolio, Mercutio, Paris, Tybalt, and the Nurse.

7. The operation of Fate seems to be an intregal aspect of the thematic as well as structural development of the play. For instance, Capulet's forgetting that his servant is illiterate sets up the scene in which the servant asks Romeo to read the list. There are several similar situations in the course of the actions. Discuss the role of chance or fate in *Romeo and Juliet*.

8. The imagery in all of Shakespeare's plays is very important and often helps to explain the psychological state of mind of a character. In *Romeo and Juliet* why is it significant that the lovers generally meet under the guise of darkness? What imagery is associated with the two lovers when they talk and think about each other? Can you find any oxymorons (a figure of speech in which contradictory terms are brought together for emphasis)? What is the meaning of the Prince's last speech?

9. There are several possible explanations for the cause of the tragedy. One is Romeo and Juliet's character. In what ways do their characters lead to the tragic consequences? Another is the lack of foresight and understanding on the part of the elders. Discuss this second possibility.

10. If you have read *Oedipus,* discuss the uses of dramatic irony used by Sophocles and Shakespeare in relation to their tragedies.

WRITING TOPICS

1. Throughout the play the lovers seem to realize the danger of their actions, but the importance of these realizations is lost in the passion of their love. Write an essay discussing the warnings they receive both externally and internally.

2. Write an essay analyzing Shakespeare's attitude toward love as represented in *Romeo and Juliet.* Be sure to include the nature of the imagery and the characterization of the two lovers in terms of their growing maturity.

3. Develop an essay based on the premise that *Romeo and Juliet* is a tragedy of circumstance in which the two lovers fall prey to preordained events over which they have no control.

4. Write an essay tracing the function of dreams in *Romeo and Juliet. Or* trace the use of letters as a dramatic technique.

5. Compare and contrast one of the following aspects of Shakespeare's work with that of Sophocles: the use of minor characters, the use of dramatic irony, the use of imagery, the use of Fate.

OTHELLO

William Shakespeare
Edited by Thomas Marc Parrott

The Names of the Actors

DUKE OF VENICE.

BRABANTIO, *father to* DESDEMONA.

GRATIANO, } *two noble Venetians.*
LUDOVICO,

OTHELLO, *the Moor.*

CASSIO, *an honourable lieutenant.*

IAGO, *a villain.*

RODERIGO, *a gulled gentleman.*

MONTANO, *governor of Cyprus.*

CLOWN.

DESDEMONA, *wife to* OTHELLO.

EMILIA, *wife to* IAGO.

BIANCA, *a courtezan.*

SENATORS, GENTLEMEN OF CYPRUS, SAILORS, OFFICERS, MESSENGER, HERALD, MUSICIANS, *and* ATTENDANTS.

[This list appears at the end of the play in the Folio.]

Reprinted with the permission of Charles Scribner's Sons from *Shakespeare: Twenty-three Plays and Sonnets,* pp. 730-772, edited by Thomas Marc Parrott. Copyright 1938, 1953 Charles Scribner's Sons.

189

SCENE: *Venice; Cyprus.*

ACT I.

Scene I, *Venice. A street.*

Enter RODERIGO *and* IAGO.

ROD: Tush, never tell me! I take it much unkindly
That thou, Iago, who hast had my purse
As if the strings were thine, shouldst know of this.
IAGO: 'Sblood, but you will not hear me.
If ever I did dream of such a matter,   5
Abhor me.
ROD·   Thou told'st·me thou didst hold him in thy hate.
IAGO: Despise me, if I do not. Three great ones of the city,
In personal suit to make me his lieutenant,
Off-capp'd to him; and, by the faith of man,   10
I know my price; I am worth no worse a place.
But he, as loving his own pride and purposes,
Evades them with a bombast circumstance
Horribly stuff'd with epithets of war;
And, in conclusion,   15
Nonsuits my mediators; for, "Certes," says he,
"I have already chose my officer."
And what was he?
Forsooth, a great arithmetician,
One Michael Cassio, a Florentine,   20
(A fellow almost damn'd in a fair wife)

---

3. *this*, Desdemona's elopement.
10. *Off-capp'd*, doffed their caps.
13. *bombast circumstance*, inflated circumlocution.
16. *Nonsuits*, rejects the suit of.
21. Cassio has no wife in the play. In the source he has a lady (*una donna*) in his house, who may or may not be his wife. Shakespeare may have planned to give Cassio a wife and later have changed his mind. Some editors read *life*, interpreting "fair life" as meaning a civilian's life.

.

That never set a squadron in the field,
Nor the division of a battle knows
More than a spinster, unless the bookish theoric,
Wherein the toged consuls can propose   25
As masterly as he. Mere prattle without practice
Is all his soldiership. But he, sir, had the election;
And I, of whom his eyes had seen the proof
At Rhodes, at Cyprus, and on other grounds
Christian and heathen, must be be-lee'd and calm'd   30
By debitor and creditor; this counter-caster,
He, in good time, must his lieutenant be,
And I—God bless the mark!—his Moorship's ancient.
ROD: By heaven, I rather would have been his hangman.
IAGO: Why, there 's no remedy. 'T is the curse of service,   35
Preferment goes by letter and affection,
And not by old gradation, where each second
Stood heir to the first. Now, sir, be judge yourself
Whether I in any just term am affin'd
To love the Moor.   40
ROD: I would not follow him then.
IAGO: O, sir, content you;
I follow him to serve my turn upon him.
We cannot all be masters, nor all masters
Cannot be truly follow'd. You shall mark   45
Many a duteous and knee-crooking knave,
That, doting on his own obsequious bondage,
Wears out his time, much like his master's ass,
For nought but provender, and when he 's old, cashier'd.
Whip me such honest knaves. Others there are   50
Who, trimm'd in forms and visages of duty,
Keep yet their hearts attending on themselves,

---

23. *division,* disposition of troops.
24. *theoric,* theory.
25. *toged,* wearing the toga, a mark of civilian office. *consuls,* senators.
29. *Rhodes, Cyprus,* islands in the Mediterranean, outposts in the wars between Venice and the Turks.
31. *counter-caster,* contemptuous term for "accountant."
33. *God bless the mark,* an ironical apology for mentioning so mean and profane a thing as himself. *ancient,* standard bearer.
36. *letter,* i.e., of recommendation.
37. *old gradation,* established seniority.
39. *affin'd,* bound.
49. *cashier'd,* dismissed.
51. *visages,* outward semblances.

And, throwing but shows of service on their lords,
Do well thrive by 'em, and when they have lin'd their coats
Do themselves homage. These fellows have some soul;   55
And such a one do I profess myself. For, sir,
It is as sure as you are Roderigo,
Were I the Moor, I would not be Iago:
In following him, I follow but myself;
Heaven is my judge, not I for love and duty,   60
But seeming so, for my peculiar end;
For when my outward action does demonstrate
The native act and figure of my heart
In compliment extern, 't is not long after
But I will wear my heart upon my sleeve   65
For daws to peck at: I am not what I am.
ROD: What a full fortune does the thick-lips owe,
If he can carry 't thus!
IAGO: Call up her father,
Rouse him; make after him, poison his delight,   70
Proclaim him in the streets. Incense her kinsmen,
And, though he in a fertile climate dwell,
Plague him with flies; though that his joy be joy,
Yet throw such changes of vexation on 't,
As it may lose some colour.   75
ROD: Here is her father's house; I 'll call aloud.
IAGO: Do, with like timorous accent and dire yell
As when, by night and negligence, the fire
Is spied in populous cities.
ROD: What, ho, Brabantio! Signior Brabantio, ho!   80
IAGO: Awake! what, ho, Brabantio! thieves! thieves!
Look to your house, your daughter, and your bags!
Thieves! thieves!

Enter BRABANTIO *above, at a window.*

BRA: What is the reason of this terrible summons?
What is the matter there?   85
ROD: Signior, is all your family within?

---

54. *lin'd their coats*, filled their pockets.
61. *peculiar*, private.
64. *compliment extern*, outward civility.
67. *thick-lips*, i.e., negro. *owe*, own.
77. *timorous*, terrifying.

IAGO: Are your doors lock'd?
BRA: Why, wherefore ask you this?
IAGO: 'Zounds, sir, you 're robb'd! For shame, put on your gown;
Your heart is burst, you have lost half your soul;   90
Even now, now, very now, an old black ram
Is tupping your white ewe. Arise, arise!
Awake the snorting citizens with the bell,
Or else the devil will make a grandsire of you.
Arise, I say!   95
BRA: What, have you lost your wits?
ROD: Most reverend signior, do you know my voice?
BRA: Not I. What are you?
ROD: My name is Roderigo.
BRA: The worser welcome;   100
I have charg'd thee not to haunt about my doors:
In honest plainness thou hast heard me say
My daughter is not for thee; and now, in madness,
Being full of supper and distempering draughts,
Upon malicious bravery dost thou come   105
To start my quiet.
ROD: Sir, sir, sir,—
BRA: But thou must needs be sure
My spirits and my place have in them power
To make this bitter to thee.   110
ROD: Patience, good sir.
BRA: What tell'st thou me of robbing? This is Venice;
My house is not a grange.
ROD: Most grave Brabantio,
In simple and pure soul I come to you.   115
IAGO: 'Zounds, sir, you are one of those that will not serve God, if
the devil bid you. Because we come to do you service and you think we
are ruffians, you 'll have your daughter covered with a Barbary horse;
you 'll have your nephews neigh to you; you 'll have coursers for
cousins, and gennets for germans.   120
BRA: What profane wretch art thou?

---

93. *snorting*, snoring.
104. *distempering*, intoxicating.
105. *bravery*, bravado.
106. *start*, disturb.
113. *grange*, remote farm-house.
119. *nephews*, grandsons.
120. *gennets*, Spanish horses. *germans*, near relatives.

IAGO: I am one, sir, that comes to tell you your daughter and the Moor are now making the beast with two backs.

BRA: Thou art a villain.

IAGO: You are—a senator.   125

BRA: This thou shalt answer. I know thee, Roderigo.

ROD: Sir, I will answer anything. But, I beseech you,
If 't be your pleasure and most wise consent,
(As partly I find it is) that your fair daughter,
At this odd-even and dull watch o' th' night,   130
Transported, with no worse nor better guard
But with a knave of common hire, a gondolier,
To the gross clasps of a lascivious Moor,—
If this be known to you and your allowance,
We then have done you bold and saucy wrongs;   135
But if you know not this, my manners tell me
We have your wrong rebuke. Do not believe
That, from the sense of all civility,
I thus would play and trifle with your reverence.
Your daughter, if you have not given her leave,   140
I say again, hath made a gross revolt;
Tying her duty, beauty, wit, and fortunes
In an extravagant and wheeling stranger
Of here and everywhere. Straight satisfy yourself.
If she be in her chamber or your house,   145
Let loose on me the justice of the state
For thus deluding you.

BRA: Strike on the tinder, ho!
Give me a taper! Call up all my people!
This accident is not unlike my dream;   150
Belief of it oppresses me already.
Light, I say! light! (*Exit.*)

IAGO: Farewell; for I must leave you.
It seems not meet, nor wholesome to my place,
To be produc'd—as, if I stay, I shall—   155
Against the Moor; for, I do know, the state,

---

130. *odd-even*, i.e., between twelve and one.
134. *allowance*, what you approve.
138. *from*, contrary to.
143. *extravagant and wheeling*, itinerant and roving.
148. *tinder*, scorched linen kept in a metal box and ignited as need arose by a flint and steel.

However this may gall him with some check,
Cannot with safety cast him, for he 's embark'd
With such loud reason to the Cyprus wars,
Which even now stands in act, that, for their souls,   160
Another of his fathom they have none,
To lead their business; in which regard,
Though I do hate him as I do hell-pains,
Yet, for necessity of present life,
I must show out a flag and sign of love,   165
Which is indeed but sign. That you shall surely find him,
Lead to the Sagittary the raised search;
And there will I be with him. So, farewell. (*Exit.*)

    Enter BRABANTIO *in his night-gown, and* SERVANTS *with torches.*

BRA: It is too true an evil; gone she is;
And what 's to come of my despised time   170
Is nought but bitterness. Now, Roderigo,
Where didst thou see her? O unhappy girl!
With the Moor, say'st thou? Who would be a father!
How didst thou know 't was she? O, she deceives me
Past thought! What said she to you? Get moe tapers;   175
Raise all my kindred. Are they married, think you?
ROD: Truly, I think they are.
BRA: O heaven! How got she out? O treason of the blood!
Fathers, from hence trust not your daughters' minds
By what you see them act. Is there not charms   180
By which the property of youth and maidhood
May be abus'd? Have you not read, Roderigo,
Of some such thing?
ROD: Yes, sir, I have indeed.
BRA: Call up my brother. O, would you had had her!   185
Some one way, some another. Do you know
Where we may apprehend her and the Moor?
ROD: I think I can discover him, if you please

---

157. *check*, rebuke.
158. *cast*, dismiss.
161. *fathom*, capacity.
167. *the Sagittary*, probably an inn.
181. *property*, nature.
182. *abus'd*, deceived.

To get good guard and go along with me.
BRA: Pray you, lead on. At every house I 'll call;   190
I may command at most. Get weapons, ho!
And raise some special officers of night.
On, good Roderigo; I 'll deserve your pains. (*Exeunt.*)

Scene II, *Another street.*

Enter OTHELLO, IAGO, *and* ATTENDANTS *with torches.*

IAGO: Though in the trade of war I have slain men,
Yet do I hold it very stuff o' th' conscience
To do no contriv'd murder: I lack iniquity
Sometimes to do me service. Nine or ten times
I had thought to have yerk'd him here under the ribs.   5
OTH: 'T is better as it is.
IAGO: Nay, but he prated,
And spoke such scurvy and provoking terms
Against your honour
That, with the little godliness I have,   10
I did full hard forbear him. But, I pray you, sir,
Are you fast married? Be assur'd of this,
That the magnifico is much belov'd,
And hath in his effect a voice potential
As double as the Duke's: he will divorce you;   15
Or put upon you what restraint or grievance
The law, with all his might to enforce it on,
Will give him cable.
OTH: Let him do his spite;
My services which I have done the signiory   20
Shall out-tongue his complaints. 'T is yet to know,—
Which, when I know that boasting is an honour,
I shall promulgate—I fetch my life and being
From men of royal siege, and my demerits

SCENE II. 5. *yerk'd*, stabbed.
13. *magnifico*, Venetian senator.
15. *double*, weighty.
18. *cable*, rope, i.e., power.
20. *signiory*, Venetian senate.
24. *siege*, rank, lit., seat. *demerits*, deserts.

May speak unbonneted to as proud a fortune 25
As this that I have reach'd; for know, Iago,
But that I love the gentle Desdemona,
I would not my unhoused free condition
Put into circumscription and confine
For the sea's worth. But, look! what lights come yond? 30

Enter CASSIO, *with lights,* OFFICERS, *and torches.*

IAGO: Those are the raised father and his friends.
You were best go in.
OTH: Not I; I must be found.
My parts, my title, and my perfect soul
Shall manifest me rightly. Is it they? 35
IAGO: By Janus, I think no.
OTH: The servants of the Duke, and my lieutenant!
The goodness of the night upon you, friends!
What is the news?
CAS: The Duke does greet you, general, 40
And he requires your haste-post-haste appearance,
Even on the instant.
OTH: What is the matter, think you?
CAS: Something from Cyprus, as I may divine;
It is a business of some heat. The galleys 45
Have sent a dozen sequent messengers
This very night at one another's heels,
And many of the consuls, rais'd and met,
Are at the Duke's already. You have been hotly call'd for;
When, being not at your lodging to be found, 50
The Senate hath sent about three several quests
To search you out.
OTH: 'T is well I am found by you.
I will but spend a word here in the house,
And go with you. (*Exit.*) 55
CAS: Ancient, what makes he here?
IAGO: Faith, he to-night hath boarded a land carack:
If it proves lawful prize, he 's made for ever.

---

25. *unbonneted*, with hat off, i.e., with all courtesy.
28. *unhoused*, unhampered.
45. *heat*, urgency. *galleys*, naval officers.
46. *sequent*, successive.
57. *carack*, large merchantman.

CAS: I do not understand.
IAGO: He 's married.   60
CAS: To who?

Re-enter OTHELLO.

IAGO: Marry, to—Come, captain, will you go?
OTH: Have with you.
CAS: Here comes another troop to seek for you.

Enter BRABANTIO, RODERIGO, *and* OFFICERS *with torches and weapons.*

IAGO: It is Brabantio. General, be advis'd;   65
He comes to bad intent.
OTH: Holla! stand there!
ROD: Signior, it is the Moor.
BRA: Down with him, thief! (*They draw on both sides.*)
IAGO: You, Roderigo! come, sir, I am for you.   70
OTH: Keep up your bright swords, for the dew will rust them.
Good signior, you shall more command with years
Than with your weapons.
BRA: O thou foul thief, where hast thou stow'd my daughter?
Damn'd as thou art, thou hast enchanted her;   75
For I 'll refer me to all things of sense,
If she in chains of magic were not bound,
Whether a maid so tender, fair, and happy,
So opposite to marriage that she shunn'd
The wealthy curled darlings of our nation,   80
Would ever have, t' incur a general mock,
Run from her guardage to the sooty bosom
Of such a thing as thou—to fear, not to delight.
Judge me the world, if 't is not gross in sense
That thou hast practis'd on her with foul charms,   85
Abus'd her delicate youth with drugs or minerals
That weakens motion. I 'll have 't disputed on;
'T is probable, and palpable to thinking.
I therefore apprehend and do attach thee

---

79. *opposite to,* averse to.
82. *guardage,* guardianship.
84. *gross in sense,* obvious.
87. *motion,* power of movement. *disputed on,* argued in court.

For an abuser of the world, a practiser   90
Of arts inhibited and out of warrant.
Lay hold upon him; if he do resist,
Subdue him at his peril.
OTH: Hold your hands,
Both you of my inclining, and the rest.   95
Were it my cue to fight, I should have known it
Without a prompter. Where will you that I go
To answer this your charge?
BRA: To prison, till fit time
Of law and course of direct session   100
Call thee to answer.
OTH: What if I do obey?
How may the Duke be therewith satisfied,
Whose messengers are here about my side
Upon some present business of the state   105
To bring me to him?
OFF: 'T is true, most worthy signior.
The Duke 's in council; and your noble self,
I am sure, is sent for.
BRA: How? the Duke in council?   110
In this time of the night? Bring him away;
Mine 's not an idle cause. The Duke himself,
Or any of my brothers of the state,
Cannot but feel this wrong as 't were their own;
For if such actions may have passage free,   115
Bond-slaves and pagans shall our statesmen be. (*Exeunt.*)

Scene III, *A council-chamber.*

The DUKE *and* SENATORS *set at a table, with lights,* OFFICERS *and*
ATTENDANTS.

DUKE: There is no composition in these news
That gives them credit.

---

90. *abuser,* corrupter.
91. *inhibited,* prohibited.
100. *course . . . session,* regular legal procedure.
SCENE III. 1. *composition,* consistency.

1. SEN: Indeed, they are disproportioned;
My letters say a hundred and seven galleys.
DUKE: And mine, a hundred forty.   5
2. SEN: And mine, two hundred!
But though they jump not on a just account,—
As in these cases, where the aim reports,
'T is oft with difference—yet do they all confirm
A Turkish fleet, and bearing up to Cyprus.   10
DUKE: Nay, it is possible enough to judgement.
I do not so secure me in the error
But the main article I do approve
In fearful sense.
SAILOR: (*Within.*) What, ho! what, ho! what, ho!   15

Enter a SAILOR.

OFF: A messenger from the galleys.
DUKE: Now, what 's the business?
SAIL: The Turkish preparation makes for Rhodes;
So was I bid report here to the state
By Signior Angelo.   20
DUKE: How say you by this change?
1. SEN: This cannot be,
By no assay of reason. 'T is a pageant,
To keep us in false gaze. When we consider
Th' importancy of Cyprus to the Turk,   25
And let ourselves again but understand
That, as it more concerns the Turk than Rhodes,
So may he with more facile question bear it,
For that it stands not in such warlike brace,
But altogether lacks th' abilities   30
That Rhodes is dress'd in; if we make thought of this,
We must not think the Turk is so unskilful
To leave that latest which concerns him first,
Neglecting an attempt of ease and gain

---

7. *jump*, agree. *just*, exact.
8. *the aim reports*, the report is based on conjecture.
12-14. *I do not . . . sense*, I am not so much reassured by this discrepancy as not
to believe and fear the essential fact, i.e., the threatened attack.
23. *assay of reason*, reasonable test. *pageant*, pretence.
28. *more . . . it*, carry it with easier contest.
29. *brace*, defense.

To wake and wage a danger profitless. 35
DUKE: Nay, in all confidence, he 's not for Rhodes.
OFF: Here is more news.

Enter a MESSENGER.

MESS: The Ottomites, reverend and gracious,
Steering with due course toward the isle of Rhodes,
Have there injointed them with an after fleet. 40
1. SEN: Ay, so I thought. How many, as you guess?
MESS: Of thirty sail; and now they do re-stem
Their backward course, bearing with frank appearance
Their purposes toward Cyprus. Signior Montano,
Your trusty and most valiant servitor, 45
With his free duty recommends you thus,
And prays you to believe him.
DUKE: 'T is certain, then, for Cyprus.
Marcus Luccicos, is not he in town?
1. SEN: He 's now in Florence. 50
DUKE: Write from us to him; post-post-haste dispatch.
1. SEN: Here comes Brabantio and the valiant Moor.

Enter BRABANTIO, OTHELLO, CASSIO, IAGO, RODERIGO, *and* OFFICERS.

DUKE: Valiant Othello, we must straight employ you
Against the general enemy Ottoman.
(*To* BRABANTIO.) I did not see you; welcome, gentle signior; 55
We lack'd your counsel and your help to-night.
BRA: So did I yours. Good your Grace, pardon me;
Neither my place nor aught I heard of business
Hath rais'd me from my bed, nor doth the general care
Take hold on me; for my particular grief 60
Is of so flood-gate and o'erbearing nature
That it engluts and swallows other sorrows
And it is still itself.
DUKE: Why, what 's the matter?
BRA: My daughter! O, my daughter! 65
SEN: Dead?

---

35. *wage*, risk.
40. *after*, sent after.
42. *re-stem*, steer back.

BRA: Ay, to me;
She is abus'd, stol'n from me, and corrupted
By spells and medicines bought of mountebanks;
For nature so preposterously to err,   70
Being not deficient, blind, or lame of sense,
Sans witchcraft could not.
DUKE: Whoe'er he be that in this foul proceeding
Hath thus beguil'd your daughter of herself
And you of her, the bloody book of law   75
You shall yourself read in the bitter letter
After your own sense, yea, though our proper son
Stood in your action.
BRA: Humbly I thank your Grace.
Here is the man,—this Moor, whom now, it seems,   80
Your special mandate for the state affairs
Hath hither brought.
ALL: We are very sorry for 't.
DUKE: (*To* OTHELLO.) What, in your own part, can you say to this?
BRA: Nothing, but this is so.   85
OTH: Most potent, grave, and reverend signiors,
My very noble and approv'd good masters,
That I have ta'en away this old man's daughter,
It is most true; true, I have married her:
The very head and front of my offending   90
Hath this extent, no more. Rude am I in my speech,
And little bless'd with the soft phrase of peace;
For since these arms of mine had seven years' pith
Till now, some nine moons wasted, they have us'd
Their dearest action in the tented field,   95
And little of this great world can I speak
More than pertains to feats of broils and battle,
And therefore little shall I grace my cause
In speaking for myself. Yet, by your gracious patience,
I will a round unvarnish'd tale deliver   100
Of my whole course of love; what drugs, what charms,
What conjuration and what mighty magic,
(For such proceeding I am charg'd withal,)
I won his daughter.

---

69. *mountebanks,* quacks.
73. *Sans,* without.
78. *Stood in,* were the object of.

BRA: A maiden never bold;   105
Of spirit so still and quiet, that her motion
Blush'd at herself; and she, in spite of nature,
Of years, of country, credit, everything,
To fall in love with what she fear'd to look on!
It is a judgement maim'd and most imperfect   110
That will confess perfection so could err
Against all rules of nature, and must be driven
To find out practices of cunning hell,
Why this should be. I therefore vouch again
That with some mixtures powerful o'er the blood,   115
Or with some dram conjur'd to this effect,
He wrought upon her.
DUKE: To vouch this is no proof,
Without more wider and more overt test
Than these thin habits and poor likelihoods   120
Of modern seeming do prefer against him.
1. SEN: But, Othello, speak.
Did you by indirect and forced courses
Subdue and poison this young maid's affections?
Or came it by request and such fair question   125
As soul to soul affordeth?
OTH: I do beseech you,
Send for the lady to the Sagittary,
And let her speak of me before her father;
If you do find me foul in her report,   130
The trust, the office I do hold of you,
Not only take away, but let your sentence
Even fall upon my life.
DUKE: Fetch Desdemona hither. (*Exeunt two or three.*)
OTH: Ancient, conduct them; you best know the place. (*Exit* IAGO.)
And, till she come, as truly as to heaven   136
I do confess the vices of my blood,
So justly to your grave ears I 'll present
How I did thrive in this fair lady's love,
And she in mine.   140
DUKE: Say it, Othello.
OTH: Her father lov'd me; oft invited me;

---

106. *motion*, inward impulse.
120. *thin habits*, superficial appearances.
121. *modern*, trivial.

Still question'd me the story of my life
From year to year, the battles, sieges, fortunes,
That I have pass'd.   145
I ran it through, even from my boyish days,
To th' very moment that he bade me tell it.
Wherein I spoke of most disastrous chances,
Of moving accidents by flood and field,
Of hair-breadth scapes i' th' imminent deadly breach, 150
Of being taken by the insolent foe
And sold to slavery, of my redemption thence
And portance in my travellers' history;
Wherein of antres vast and deserts idle,
Rough quarries, rocks, and hills whose heads touch heaven, 155
It was my hint to speak,—such was my process,—
And of the Cannibals that each other eat,
The Anthropophagi, and men whose heads
Do grow beneath their shoulders. This to hear
Would Desdemona seriously incline;   160
But still the house-affairs would draw her thence,
Which ever as she could with haste dispatch,
She 'd come again, and with a greedy ear
Devour up my discourse: which I observing,
Took once a pliant hour, and found good means   165
To draw from her a prayer of earnest heart
That I would all my pilgrimage dilate,
Whereof by parcels she had something heard,
But not intentively. I did consent,
And often did beguile her of her tears   170
When I did speak of some distressful stroke
That my youth suffer'd. My story being done,
She gave me for my pains a world of sighs.
She swore, in faith, 't was strange, 't was passing strange,
'T was pitiful, 't was wondrous pitiful.   175
She wish'd she had not heard it; yet she wish'd
That Heaven had made her such a man. She thank'd me,

---

150. *imminent*, overhanging.
153. *portance*, conduct.
154. *antres*, caves. *idle*, barren.
156. *hint*, occasion. *process*, order (of events).
158. *Anthropophagi*, man-eaters.
165. *pliant*, convenient.
167. *dilate*, relate in full.
169. *intentively*, attentively.

And bade me, if I had a friend that lov'd her,
I should but teach him how to tell my story,
And that would woo her. Upon this hint I spake: 180
She lov'd me for the dangers I had pass'd,
And I lov'd her that she did pity them.
This only is the witchcraft I have us'd.
Here comes the lady; let her witness it.

Enter DESDEMONA, IAGO, *and* ATTENDANTS.

DUKE: I think this tale would win my daughter too.   185
Good Brabantio,
Take up this mangled matter at the best;
Men do their broken weapons rather use
Than their bare hands.
BRA: I pray you, hear her speak.   190
If she confess that she was half the wooer,
Destruction on my head, if my bad blame
Light on the man! Come hither, gentle mistress.
Do you perceive in all this noble company
Where most you owe obedience?   195
DES: My noble father,
I do perceive here a divided duty.
To you I am bound for life and education;
My life and education both do learn me
How to respect you; you are lord of all my duty;   200
I am hitherto your daughter. But here 's my husband;
And so much duty as my mother show'd
To you, preferring you before her father,
So much I challenge that I may profess
Due to the Moor, my lord.   205
BRA: God be with you! I have done.
Please it your Grace, on to the state-affairs.
I had rather to adopt a child than get it.
Come hither, Moor.
I here do give thee that with all my heart   210
Which, but thou hast already, with all my heart
I would keep from thee. For your sake, jewel,
I am glad at soul I have no other child;

---

187. *at the best*, as well as possible.

For thy escape would teach me tyranny,
To hang clogs on them. I have done, my lord.   215
DUKE: Let me speak like yourself, and lay a sentence,
Which, as a grise or step, may help these lovers
Into your favour.
When remedies are past, the griefs are ended
By seeing the worst, which late on hopes depended.   220
To mourn a mischief that is past and gone
Is the next way to draw new mischief on.
What cannot be preserv'd when fortune takes,
Patience her injury a mockery makes.
The robb'd that smiles steals something from the thief;
He robs himself that spends a bootless grief.   225
BRA: So let the Turk of Cyprus us beguile;
We lose it not, so long as we can smile.
He bears the sentence well that nothing bears
But the free comfort which from thence he hears,
But he bears both the sentence and the sorrow   230
That, to pay grief, must of poor patience borrow.
These sentences, to sugar, or to gall,
Being strong on both sides, are equivocal:
But words are words; I never yet did hear
That the bruis'd heart was pierced through the ear.   235
I humbly beseech you, proceed to th' affairs of state.
DUKE: The Turk with a most mighty prepation makes for Cyprus.
Othello, the fortitude of the place is best known to you; and though we
have there a substitute of most allowed sufficiency, yet opinion, a sov-
ereign mistress of effects, throws a more safer voice on you: you [240
must therefore be content to slubber the gloss of your new fortunes
with this more stubborn and boisterous expedition.
OTH: The tyrant custom, most grave senators,
Hath made the flinty and steel couch of war
My thrice-driven bed of down. I do agnize   245

---

216. *like yourself*, as you should.
217. *grise*, degree.
225. *bootless*, useless.
229. *free comfort*, freely-given consolation.
232. *sentences*, moral aphorisms.
233. *equivocal*, equivalent.
238. *fortitude*, strength.
239. *allowed*, acknowledged; *opinion*, reputation.
241. *slubber*, sully.
245. *thrice-driven*, thrice-winnowed. *agnize*, acknowledge.

A natural and prompt alacrity
I find in hardness, and do undertake
These present wars against the Ottomites.
Most humbly therefore bending to your state,
I crave fit disposition for my wife,   250
Due reference of place and exhibition,
With such accommodation and besort
As levels with her breeding.
DUKE: If you please,
Be 't at her father's.   255
BRA: I 'll not have it so.
OTH: Nor I.
DES: Nor I; I would not there reside,
To put my father in impatient thoughts
By being in his eye. Most gracious duke,   260
To my unfolding lend your prosperous ear;
And let me find a charter in your voice,
T' assist my simpleness.
DUKE: What would you, Desdemona?
DES: That I did love the Moor to live with him,   265
My downright violence and storm of fortunes
May trumpet to the world. My heart 's subdued
Even to the very quality of my lord:
I saw Othello's visage in his mind,
And to his honours and his valiant parts   270
Did I my soul and fortunes consecrate.
So that, dear lords, if I be left behind,
A moth of peace, and he go to the war,
The rites for which I love him are bereft me,
And I a heavy interim shall support   275
By his dear absence. Let me go with him.
OTH: Let her have your voice.
Vouch with me, Heaven, I therefore beg it not
To please the palate of my appetite,

_____

247. *hardness,* hardship.
251. *exhibition,* allowance.
252. *besort,* attendance.
253. *levels with,* suits.
261. *prosperous,* propitious.
262. *charter,* privilege.
266. The headlong and violent way of taking my fortunes by storm.
276. *dear,* deeply felt.

Nor to comply with heat, the young affects   280
In my defunct and proper satisfaction,
But to be free and bounteous to her mind;
And Heaven defend your good souls, that you think
I will your serious and great business scant
When she is with me. No, when light-wing'd toys   285
Of feather'd Cupid seel with wanton dullness
My speculative and offic'd instruments
That my disports corrupt and taint my business,
Let housewives make a skillet of my helm,
And all indign and base adversities   290
Make head against my estimation!
DUKE: Be it as you shall privately determine,
Either for her stay or going: th' affair cries haste,
And speed must answer it.
1. SEN: You must away to-night.   295
DES: To-night, my lord?
DUKE: This night.
OTH: With all my heart.
DUKE: At nine i' th' morning here we 'll meet again.
Othello, leave some officer behind,   300
And he shall our commission bring to you,
And such things else of quality and respect
As doth import you.
OTH: So please your Grace, my ancient;
A man he is of honesty and trust: 305
To his conveyance I assign my wife,
With what else needful your good Grace shall think
To be sent after me.
DUKE: Let it be so.
Good-night to every one. (*To* BRABANTIO.) And, noble signior,   310
If virtue no delighted beauty lack,

280-281. *affects . . . satisfaction*, a difficult passage. The text may be corrupt; but the sense is plain: Othello wishes to take his wife with him not to gratify his sensual desires but to comply with her request.

283. *defend*, forbid.

285. *toys*, trifles.

286. *seel*, blind, a term in falconry. Hawks were partly blinded by sewing up their eyelids.

287. *speculative and offic'd instruments*, visual and active powers.

290. *indign*, unworthy.

291. *estimation*, reputation.

303. *import*, concern.

311. *delighted*, delightful.

Your son-in-law is far more fair than black.

1. SEN: Adieu, brave Moor; use Desdemona well.

BRA: Look to her, Moor, if thou hast eyes to see;
She has deceiv'd her father, and may thee. (*Exeunt* DUKE, BRABANTIO,
SENATORS, OFFICERS.)   315

OTH: My life upon her faith! Honest Iago,
My Desdemona must I leave to thee.
I prithee, let thy wife attend on her;
And bring them after in the best advantage.
Come, Desdemona; I have but an hour   320
Of love, of worldly matters and direction,
To spend with thee. We must obey the time. (*Exeunt* OTHELLO *and*
DESDEMONA.)

ROD: Iago,—

IAGO: What say'st thou, noble heart?

ROD: What will I do, think'st thou?   325

IAGO: Why, go to bed, and sleep.

ROD: I will incontinently drown myself.

IAGO: If thou dost, I shall never love thee after. Why, thou silly
gentleman!

ROD: It is silliness to live when to live is torment; and then have we a
prescription to die when Death is our physician.   331

IAGO: O villanous! I have looked upon the world for four times seven
years; and since I could distinguish betwixt a benefit and an injury, I
never found man that knew how to love himself. Ere I would say I
would drown myself for the love of a guinea-hen, I would change my
humanity with a baboon.   336

ROD: What should I do? I confess it is my shame to be so fond, but it
is not in my virtue to amend it.

IAGO: Virtue! a fig! 't is in ourselves that we are thus or thus. Our
bodies are our gardens, to the which our wills are gardeners; so [340
that if we will plant nettles, or sow lettuce, set hyssop and weed up
thyme, supply it with one gender of herbs, or distract it with many,
either to have it sterile with idleness, or manured with industry, why,
the power and corrigible authority of this lies in our wills. If the balance of our lives had not one scale of reason to poise another of [345
sensuality, the blood and baseness of our natures would conduct us to
most preposterous conclusions. But we have reason to cool our raging

---

319. *advantage*, opportunity.
327. *incontinently*, immediately.
342. *gender*, kind.
344. *corrigible authority*, correcting control.

motions, our carnal stings, our unbitted lusts, whereof I take this that
you call love to be a sect or scion.

ROD: It cannot be.   350

IAGO: It is merely a lust of the blood and a permission of the will.
Come, be a man. Drown thyself? drown cats and blind puppies. I have
professed me thy friend, and I confess me knit to thy deserving with
cables of perdurable toughness; I could never better stead thee than
now. Put money in thy purse; follow thou the wars; defeat thy [355
favour with an usurped beard. I say, put money in thy purse. It cannot
be long that Desdemona should continue her love to the Moor,—put
money in thy purse,—nor he his to her. It was a violent commencement
in her, and thou shalt see an answerable sequestration: put but money
in thy purse. These Moors are changeable in their wills;—fill thy [360
purse with money;—the food that to him now is as luscious as locusts,
shall be to him shortly as bitter as coloquintida. She must change for
youth; when she is sated with his body, she will find the error of her
choice—she must have change, she must—therefore put money in thy
purse. If thou wilt needs damn thyself, do it a more delicate way [365
than drowning. Make all the money thou canst. If sanctimony and a
frail vow betwixt an erring barbarian and a super-subtle Venetian be
not too hard for my wits and all the tribe of hell, thou shalt enjoy her;
therefore make money. A pox of drowning thyself! it is clean out of the
way. Seek thou rather to be hanged in compassing thy joy than to be
drowned and go without her.   371

ROD: Wilt thou be fast to my hopes, if I depend on the issue?

IAGO: Thou art sure of me—go, make money—I have told thee often,
and I re-tell thee again and again, I hate the Moor. My cause is hearted;
thine hath no less reason. Let us be conjunctive in our revenge [375
against him. If thou canst cuckold him, thou dost thyself a pleasure, me
a sport. There are many events in the womb of time which will be de-
livered. Traverse! go, provide thy money. We will have more of this
to-morrow. Adieu.

---

348. *motions*, sexual appetites.
349. *sect or scion*, cutting or shoot.
354. *stead*, help.
355-356. *defeat thy favour*, disguise thy face.
359. *answerable sequestration*, corresponding rupture.
361. *locusts*, thought to be eaten by Moors.
362. *coloquintida*, colocynth, a bitter fruit.
367. *erring*, vagrant.
374. *hearted*, fixed in the heart.
375. *conjunctive*, united.
378. *Traverse*, forward march.

ROD: Where shall we meet i' th' morning? 380
IAGO: At my lodging.
ROD: I 'll be with thee betimes.
IAGO: Go to; farewell. Do you hear, Roderigo?
ROD: What say you?
IAGO: No more of drowning, do you hear? 385
ROD: I am chang'd; I 'll go sell all my land. (*Exit.*)
IAGO: Thus do I ever make my fool my purse;
For I mine own gain'd knowledge should profane
If I would time expend with such a snipe
But for my sport and profit. I hate the Moor; 390
And it is thought abroad that 'twixt my sheets
He has done my office. I know not if 't be true;
But I, for mere suspicion in that kind,
Will do as if for surety. He holds me well;
The better shall my purpose work on him. 395
Cassio 's a proper man: let me see now:
To get his place and to plume up my will
In double knavery—How, how?—Let 's see:—
After some time, to abuse Othello's ear
That he is too familiar with his wife. 400
He hath a person and a smooth dispose
To be suspected, fram'd to make women false.
The Moor is of a free and open nature,
That thinks men honest that but seem to be so,
And will as tenderly be led by th' nose 405
As asses are.
I have 't. It is engender'd. Hell and night
Must bring this monstrous birth to the world's light. (*Exit.*)

ACT II.

Scene I, *A sea-port in Cyprus. An open place.*

Enter MONTANO *and two* GENTLEMEN.

---

389. *snipe*, woodcock, fool.
396. *proper*, handsome.
397. *plume up*, make triumph.
401. *dispose*, disposition.

MON: What from the cape can you discern at sea?
1. GENT: Nothing at all; it is a high-wrought flood.
I cannot, 'twixt the heaven and the main,
Descry a sail.
MON: Methinks the wind hath spoke aloud at land;   5
A fuller blast ne'er shook our battlements:
If it hath ruffian'd so upon the sea,
What ribs of oak, when mountains melt on them,
Can hold the mortise? What shall we hear of this?
2. GENT: A segregation of the Turkish fleet: 10
For do but stand upon the foaming shore,
The chidden billow seems to pelt the clouds;
The wind-shak'd surge, with high and monstrous mane,
Seems to cast water on the burning bear
And quench the guards of th' ever-fixed pole: 15
I never did like molestation view
On the enchafed flood.
MON: If that the Turkish fleet
Be not enshelter'd and embay'd, they are drown'd;
It is impossible to bear it out.   20

Enter a third GENTLEMAN.

3. GENT: News, lads! our wars are done.
The desperate tempest hath so bang'd the Turks,
That their designment halts. A noble ship of Venice
Hath seen a grievous wreck and sufferance
On most part of their fleet.   25
MON: How? is this true?
3. GENT: The ship is here put in,
A Veronesa; Michael Cassio,
Lieutenant to the warlike Moor Othello,
Is come on shore; the Moor himself at sea,   30
And is in full commission here for Cyprus.
MON: I am glad on 't; 't is a worthy governor.

ACT II. SCENE I. 9. *hold the mortise*, remain jointed.
10. *segregation*, dispersion.
15. *guards*, two stars in the constellation of the Little Bear. *pole*, pole-star.
16. *molestation*, disturbance.
23. *designment*, enterprise.
24. *sufferance*, disaster.
28. *A Veronesa*, a ship equipped by Verona, then a town subject to Venice.

3. GENT: But this same Cassio, though he speak of comfort
Touching the Turkish loss, yet he looks sadly,
And prays the Moor be safe; for they were parted   35
With foul and violent tempest.
MON: Pray heavens he be;
For I have serv'd him, and the man commands
Like a full soldier. Let 's to the seaside, ho!
As well to see the vessel that 's come in   40
As to throw out our eyes for brave Othello,
Even till we make the main and th' aerial blue
An indistinct regard.
3. GENT: Come, let 's do so:
For every minute is expectancy   45
Of more arrivance.

Enter CASSIO.

CAS: Thanks, you the valiant of this warlike isle,
That so approve the Moor! O, let the heavens
Give him defence against the elements,
For I have lost him on a dangerous sea.   50
MON: Is he well shipp'd?
CAS: His bark is stoutly timber'd, and his pilot
Of very expert and approv'd allowance;
Therefore my hopes, not surfeited to death,
Stand in bold cure. (*Within,*) "A sail, a sail, a sail!"   55

Enter a MESSENGER.

CAS: What noise?
MESS: The town is empty; on the brow o' th' sea
Stand ranks of people, and they cry, "A sail!"
CAS: My hopes do shape him for the governor. (*A shot.*)
2. GENT: They do discharge their shot of courtesy.   60
Our friends at least.
CAS: I pray you, sir, go forth,
And give us truth who 't is that is arriv'd.

---

39. *full,* thorough.
43. *regard,* view.
46. *arrivance,* arrival.
53. *approv'd allowance,* established skill.
54-55. *not . . . cure,* not being overindulged stand in expectation of fulfilment.

2. GENT: I shall. (*Exit.*)
MON: But, good lieutenant, is your general wiv'd?   65
CAS: Most fortunately: he hath achiev'd a maid
That paragons description and wild fame;
One that excels the quirks of blazoning pens,
And in th' essential vesture of creation
Does tire the ingener.   70

Re-enter second GENTLEMAN.

How now? who has put in?
2. GENT: 'T is one Iago, ancient to the general.
CAS: Has had most favourable and happy speed:
Tempests themselves, high seas, and howling winds,
The gutter'd rocks and congregated sands,   75
Traitors ensteep'd to clog the guiltless keel,
As having sense of beauty do omit
Their mortal natures, letting go safely by
The divine Desdemona.
MON: What is she?   80
CAS: She that I spake of, our great captain's captain,
Left in the conduct of the bold Iago,
Whose footing here anticipates our thoughts
A se'nnight's speed. Great Jove, Othello guard,
And swell his sail with thine own powerful breath,   85
That he may bless this bay with his tall ship,
Make love's quick pants in Desdemona's arms,
Give renew'd fire to our extincted spirits,
And bring all Cyprus comfort!

Enter DESDEMONA, EMILIA, IAGO, RODERIGO, *and* ATTENDANTS.

O, behold,   90
The riches of the ship is come on shore!
You men of Cyprus, let her have your knees.

---

67. *paragons*, excels.
68. *quirks*, conceits. *blazoning*, praising.
69. *essential vesture of creation*, real endowments.
70. *ingener*, inventor (of praises).
75. *gutter'd*, jagged.
76. *ensteep'd*, submerged.
78. *mortal*, deadly.

Hail to thee, lady! and the grace of heaven,
Before, behind thee, and on every hand,
Enwheel thee round! 95
DES: I thank you, valiant Cassio.
What tidings can you tell me of my lord?
CAS: He is not yet arriv'd; nor know I aught
But that he 's well and will be shortly here.
DES: O, but I fear—How lost you company? 100
CAS: The great contention of the sea and skies
Parted our fellowship.—But, hark! a sail. (*Within,*) "A sail, a sail!"
(*Guns heard.*)
2. GENT: They give their greeting to the citadel:
This likewise is a friend.
CAS: See for the news. (*Exit* GENTLEMAN.) 105
Good ancient, you are welcome. (*To* EMILIA.) Welcome, mistress.
Let it not gall your patience, good Iago,
That I extend my manners; 't is my breeding
That gives me this bold show of courtesy. (*Kissing her.*)
IAGO: Sir, would she give you so much of her lips 110
As of her tongue she oft bestows on me,
You 'd have enough.
DES: Alas, she has no speech.
IAGO: In faith, too much;
I find it still, when I have list to sleep. 115
Marry, before your ladyship, I grant,
She puts her tongue a little in her heart,
And chides with thinking.
EMIL: You have little cause to say so.
IAGO: Come on, come on; you are pictures out of doors, 120
Bells in your parlours, wild-cats in your kitchens,
Saints in your injuries, devils being offended,
Players in your housewifery, and housewives in your beds.
DES: O, fie upon thee, slanderer!
IAGO: Nay, it is true, or else I am a Turk. 125
You rise to play and go to bed to work.
EMIL: You shall not write my praise.
IAGO: No, let me not.
DES: What wouldst thou write of me, if thou shouldst praise me?

---

95. *Enwheel,* encompass.
122. *Saints in your injuries,* say spiteful things with a sanctimonious air.
123. *Players,* triflers. *housewives,* hussies.

IAGO: O gentle lady, do not put me to 't;   130
For I am nothing, if not critical.
DES: Come on, assay.—There 's one gone to the harbour?
IAGO: Ay, madam.
DES: I am not merry; but I do beguile
The thing I am, by seeming otherwise.—   135
Come, how wouldst thou praise me?
IAGO: I am about it; but indeed my invention
Comes from my pate as birdlime does from frieze;
It plucks out brains and all. But my Muse labours,
And thus she is deliver'd: 140

> If she be fair and wise, fairness and wit,
> The one 's for use, the other useth it.

DES: Well prais'd! How if she be black and witty?
IAGO:

> If she be black, and thereto have a wit,
> She 'll find a white that shall her blackness fit.

DES: Worse and worse.   146
EMIL: How if fair and foolish?
IAGO:
> She never yet was foolish that was fair;
> For even her folly help'd her to an heir.

DES: These are old fond paradoxes to make fools laugh i' th' alehouse.
What miserable praise hast thou for her that 's foul and foolish? [151
IAGO:
> There 's none so foul and foolish thereunto,
> But does foul pranks which fair and wise ones do.

DES: O heavy ignorance! thou praisest the worst best. But what praise
couldst thou bestow on a deserving woman indeed, one that, in [155
the authority of her merit, did justly put on the vouch of very malice
itself?
IAGO:
> She that was ever fair and never proud,
> Had tongue at will and yet was never loud,
> Never lack'd gold and yet went never gay,

---

138. *birdlime*, sticky substance for catching birds. *frieze*, coarse woolen cloth.
145. *white*, (1) white. (2) wight, person.
150. *fond*, foolish.
156. *put on the vouch*, challenge the testimony.

Fled from her wish and yet said, "Now I may"; 160
She that being anger'd, her revenge being nigh,
Bade her wrong stay and her displeasure fly;
She that in wisdom never was so frail
To change the cod's head for the salmon's tail;
She that could think and ne'er disclose her mind 165
See suitors following and not look behind,
She was a wight, if ever such wights were,—

DES: To do what?
IAGO:
To suckle fools and chronicle small beer.

DES: O most lame and impotent conclusion! Do not learn of him, [170
Emilia, though he be thy husband. How say you, Cassio? Is he not a
most profane and liberal counsellor?
CAS: He speaks home, madam: you may relish him more in the soldier
than in the scholar. 174
IAGO: (*Aside.*) He takes her by the palm; ay, well said, whisper. With
as little a web as this will I ensnare as great a fly as Cassio. Ay, smile
upon her, do; I will gyve thee in thine own courtship.—You say true;
't is so, indeed.—If such tricks as these strip you out of your lieuten-
antry, it had been better you had not kissed your three fingers so oft,
which now again you are most apt to play the sir in. Very good; [180
well kissed! an excellent curtsy! 'T is so, indeed. Yet again your fingers
to your lips? Would they were clyster-pipes for your sake! (*Trumpet
within.*)—The Moor! I know his trumpet.
CAS: 'T is truly so.
DES: Let 's meet him and receive him. 185
CAS: Lo, where he comes!

Enter OTHELLO *and* ATTENDANTS.

OTH: O my fair warrior!
DES: My dear Othello!
OTH: It gives me wonder great as my content
To see you here before me. O my soul's joy! 190
If after every tempest come such calms,

---

169. *chronicle small beer,* keep small household accounts.
172. *liberal,* licentious.
177. *gyve,* fetter.
180. *sir,* gallant.
182. *clyster-pipes,* tubes used for medical injections.

May the winds blow till they have waken'd death!
And let the labouring bark climb hills of seas
Olympus-high, and duck again as low
As hell 's from heaven! If it were now to die,   195
'T were now to be most happy; for, I fear,
My soul hath her content so absolute
That not another comfort like to this
Succeeds in unknown fate.
DES: The heavens forbid   200
But that our loves and comforts should increase,
Even as our days do grow!
OTH: Amen to that, sweet powers!
I cannot speak enough of this content;
It stops me here; it is too much of joy.   205
And this, and this, the greatest discords be (*They kiss.*)
That e'er our hearts shall make!
IAGO: (*Aside.*) O, you are well tun'd now!
But I 'll set down the pegs that make this music,
As honest as I am.   210
OTH: Come, let us to the castle.
News, friends: our wars are done, the Turks are drown'd.
How does my old acquaintance of this isle?
Honey, you shall be well desir'd in Cyprus;
I have found great love amongst them. O my sweet,   215
I prattle out of fashion, and I dote
In mine own comforts. I prithee, good Iago,
Go to the bay and disembark my coffers:
Bring thou the master to the citadel;
He is a good one, and his worthiness   220
Does challenge much respect. Come, Desdemona,
Once more, well met at Cyprus. (*Exeunt* OTHELLO, DESDEMONA *and*
ATTENDANTS.)
IAGO: Do thou meet me presently at the harbour. Come hither. If thou
be'st valiant,—as, they say, base men being in love have then a nobility
in their natures more than is native to them,—list me. The lieu- [225
tenant to-night watches on the court of guard;—first, I must tell thee
this: Desdemona is directly in love with him.

---

209. *set down the pegs*, loosen the pegs and so untune the strings.
214. *desir'd*, loved.
219. *master*, ship's master.
226. *court of guard*, main guard-house.

ROD: With him? why, 't is not possible.

IAGO: Lay thy finger thus, and let thy soul be instructed. Mark me with what violence she first loved the Moor, but for bragging and [230 telling her fantastical lies. To love him still for prating,—let not thy discreet heart think it. Her eye must be fed; and what delight shall she have to look on the devil? When the blood is made dull with the act of sport, there should be, again to inflame it, and to give satiety a fresh appetite, loveliness in favour, sympathy in years, manners, and [235 beauties; all which the Moor is defective in. Now, for want of these required conveniences, her delicate tenderness will find itself abused, begin to heave the gorge, disrelish and abhor the Moor; very nature will instruct her in it and compel her to some second choice. Now, sir, this granted,—as it is a most pregnant and unforced position—who [240 stands so eminent in the degree of this fortune as Cassio does? a knave very voluble; no further conscionable than in putting on the mere form of civil and humane seeming, for the better compassing of his salt and most hidden loose affection? Why, none; why, none; a slipper and subtle knave, a finder of occasion, that has an eye can stamp and [245 counterfeit advantages, though true advantage never present itself; a devilish knave. Besides, the knave is handsome, young, and hath all those requisites in him that folly and green minds look after; a pestilent complete knave, and the woman hath found him already.   [249

ROD: I cannot believe that in her; she 's full of most blessed condition.

IAGO: Blessed fig's-end! The wine she drinks is made of grapes. If she had been blessed, she would never have loved the Moor. Blessed pudding! Didst thou not see her paddle with the palm of his hand? Didst not mark that?

ROD: Yes, that I did; but that was but courtesy.   255

IAGO: Lechery, by this hand; an index and obscure prologue to the history of lust and foul thoughts. They met so near with their lips that their breaths embraced together. Villanous thoughts, Roderigo! When these mutualities so marshal the way, hard at hand comes the master and main exercise, th' incorporate conclusion. Pish! But, sir, be [260 you ruled by me; I have brought you from Venice. Watch you to-night; for the command, I 'll lay 't upon you. Cassio knows you not: I 'll not

---

238. *heave the gorge*, be nauseated.
240. *pregnant*, evident.
242. *conscionable*, conscientious.
243. *salt*, lewd.
244. *slipper*, slippery.
250. *condition*, qualities.

be far from you. Do you find some occasion to anger Cassio, either by
speaking too loud, or tainting his discipline; or from what other course
you please, which the time shall more favourably minister.   265
ROD: Well?
IAGO: Sir, he 's rash and very sudden in choler, and haply may strike
at you: provoke him, that he may; for even out of that will I cause
these of Cyprus to mutiny, whose qualification shall come into no true
taste again but by the displanting of Cassio. So shall you have a [270
shorter journey to your desires by the means I shall then have to prefer
them; and the impediment most profitably removed, without the which
there were no expectation of our prosperity.
ROD: I will do this, if you can bring it to any opportunity.
IAGO: I warrant thee. Meet me by and by at the citadel; I must fetch
his necessaries ashore. Farewell.   276
ROD: Adieu. (*Exit.*)
IAGO: That Cassio loves her, I do well believe 't;
That she loves him, 't is apt and of great credit;
The Moor, howbeit that I endure him not,   280
Is of a constant, loving, noble nature,
And I dare think he 'll prove to Desdemona
A most dear husband. Now, I do love her too;
Not out of absolute lust, though peradventure
I stand accountant for as great a sin,   285
But partly led to diet my revenge,
For that I do suspect the lusty Moor
Hath leap'd into my seat; the thought whereof
Doth, like a poisonous mineral, gnaw my inwards;
And nothing can or shall content my soul   290
Till I am even'd with him, wife for wife;
Or failing so, yet that I put the Moor
At least into a jealousy so strong
That judgement cannot cure. Which thing to do,
If this poor trash of Venice, whom I trash   295
For his quick hunting, stand the putting on,
I 'll have our Michael Cassio on the hip,
Abuse him to the Moor in the rank garb—
For I fear Cassio with my night-cap too—

264. *tainting*, discrediting.
269. *qualification*, appeasement.
279. *apt*, natural. *of great credit*, very credible.
295. *trash*, worthless fellow. *trash*, check, a hunting term.
298. *rank garb*, coarse fashion.

Make the Moor thank me, love me, and reward me,   300
For making him egregiously an ass
And practising upon his peace and quiet
Even to madness. 'T is here, but yet confus'd;
Knavery's plain face is never seen till us'd. (*Exit.*)

Scene II, *A street.*

Enter OTHELLO'S HERALD, *with a proclamation.* PEOPLE *following.*

HER: It is Othello's pleasure, our noble and valiant general, that, upon certain tidings now arrived importing the mere perdition of the Turkish fleet, every man put himself into triumph; some to dance, some to make bonfires, each man to what sport and revels his addiction leads him; for, beside these beneficial news, it is the celebration of [5 his nuptial. So much was his pleasure should be proclaimed. All offices are open, and there is full liberty of feasting from this present hour of five till the bell have told eleven. Heaven bless the isle of Cyprus and our noble general Othello! (*Exeunt.*)

Scene III, *A hall in the castle.*

Enter OTHELLO, DESDEMONA, CASSIO, *and* ATTENDANTS.

OTH: Good Michael, look you to the guard to-night:
Let 's teach ourselves that honourable stop,
Not to outsport discretion.
CAS: Iago hath direction what to do;
But, notwithstanding, with my personal eye   5
Will I look to 't.
OTH: Iago is most honest.
Michael, good-night; to-morrow with your earliest
Let me have speech with you. (*To* DESDEMONA.) Come, my dear love,

---

SCENE II. 2. *mere perdition*, complete loss.
6. *offices*, storerooms and kitchens.

The purchase made, the fruits are to ensue;   10
That profit 's yet to come 'tween me and you.
Good-night. (*Exeunt* OTHELLO, DESDEMONA, *and* ATTENDANTS.)

Enter IAGO.

CAS: Welcome, Iago; we must to the watch.

IAGO: Not this hour, lieutenant; 't is not yet ten o' th' clock. Our general cast us thus early for the love of his Desdemona; who let us not [15 therefore blame: he hath not yet made wanton the night with her; and she is sport for Jove.

CAS: She 's a most exquisite lady.

IAGO: And, I 'll warrant her, full of game.

CAS: Indeed, she 's a most fresh and delicate creature.   20

IAGO: What an eye she has! Methinks it sounds a parley to provocation.

CAS: An inviting eye; and yet methinks right modest.

IAGO: And when she speaks, is it not an alarum to love?

CAS: She is indeed perfection.   24

IAGO: Well, happiness to their sheets! Come, lieutenant, I have a stoup of wine; and here without are a brace of Cyprus gallants that would fain have a measure to the health of black Othello.

CAS: Not to-night, good Iago: I have very poor and unhappy brains for drinking; I could well wish courtesy would invent some other custom of entertainment.   30

IAGO: O, they are our friends: but one cup;
I 'll drink for you.

CAS: I have drunk but one cup to-night, and that was craftily qualified too, and, behold, what innovation it makes here. I am unfortunate in the infirmity, and dare not task my weakness with any more.   35

IAGO: What, man! 't is a night of revels: the gallants desire it.

CAS: Where are they?

IAGO: Here at the door; I pray you, call them in.

CAS: I 'll do 't; but it dislikes me. (*Exit.*)

IAGO: If I can fasten but one cup upon him,   40
With that which he hath drunk to-night already,
He 'll be as full of quarrel and offence
As my young mistress' dog. Now, my sick fool Roderigo,

SCENE III. 15. *cast*, dismissed.
26. *stoup*, large measure.
33. *craftily qualified*, slyly diluted.
34. *innovation*, change for the worst.

Whom love hath turn'd almost the wrong side out,
To Desdemona hath to-night carous'd 45
Potations pottle-deep; and he 's to watch:
Three lads of Cyprus, noble swelling spirits
That hold their honours in a wary distance,
The very elements of this warlike isle,
Have I to-night fluster'd with flowing cups, 50
And they watch too. Now, 'mongst this flock of drunkards
Am I to put our Cassio in some action
That may offend the isle. But here they come.

Re-enter CASSIO, *with him* MONTANO *and* GENTLEMEN. SERVANTS *follow with wine.*

If consequence do but approve my dream,
My boat sails freely, both with wind and stream. 55
CAS: 'Fore God, they have given me a rouse already.
MON: Good faith, a little one; not past a pint, as I am a soldier.
IAGO: Some wine, ho! (*Sings.*)

And let me the canakin clink. 60
And let me the canakin clink.
A soldier 's a man;
O, man's life 's but a span;
Why, then, let a soldier drink.

Some wine, boys!
CAS: 'Fore God, an excellent song. 65
IAGO: I learned it in England, where, indeed, they are most potent in potting; your Dane, your German, and your swag-bellied Hollander—Drink, ho!—are nothing to your English.
CAS: Is your Englishman so exquisite in his drinking? 69
IAGO: Why, he drinks you, with facility, your Dane dead drunk; he sweats not to overthrow your Almain; he gives your Hollander a vomit ere the next pottle can be filled.
CAS: To the health of our general!
MON: I am for it, lieutenant; and I 'll do you justice.
IAGO: O sweet England! 75

46. *pottle-deep,* to the bottom of the tankard.
48. *hold . . . distance,* i.e., are easily provoked to a quarrel.
49. *elements,* i.e., typical inhabitants.
56. *rouse,* bumper.
71. *Almain,* German.

> King Stephen was and-a worthy peer,
>   His breeches cost him but a crown;
> He held them sixpence all too dear,
>   With that he call'd the tailor lown.
>
> He was a wight of high renown,   80
>   And thou art but of low degree.
> 'T is pride that pulls the country down;
>   And take thy auld cloak about thee.

Some wine, ho!

CAS: Why, this is a more exquisite song than the other.   85

IAGO: Will you hear 't again?

CAS: No; for I hold him to be unworthy of his place that does those things. Well, God's above all; and there be souls must be saved, and there be souls must not be saved.

IAGO: It 's true, good lieutenant.   90

CAS: For mine own part,—no offence to the general, nor any man of quality— I hope to be saved.

IAGO: And so do I too, lieutenant.

CAS: Ay, but, by your leave, not before me; the lieutenant is to be saved before the ancient. Let 's have no more of this; let 's to our affairs. —God forgive us our sins!—Gentlemen, let 's look to our business. [95 Do not think, gentlemen, I am drunk. This is my ancient; this is my right hand, and this is my left. I am not drunk now; I can stand well enough, and I speak well enough.

GENT: Excellent well.

CAS: Why, very well then; you must not think then that I am [100 drunk. (*Exit.*)

MON: To th' platform, masters; come, let 's set the watch.

IAGO: You see this fellow that is gone before:
He is a soldier fit to stand by Cæsar
And give direction; and do but see his vice.
'T is to his virtue a just equinox,   105
The one as long as the other; 't is pity of him.
I fear the trust Othello puts him in,
On some odd time of his infirmity,
Will shake this island.

MON: But is he often thus?   110

IAGO: 'T is evermore his prologue to his sleep.

---

79. *lown,* lout.
105. *just equinox,* exact counterpart.

He 'll watch the horologe a double set,
If drink rock not his cradle.
MON: It were well
The general were put in mind of it.   115
Perhaps he sees it not; or his good nature
Prizes the virtue that appears in Cassio,
And looks not on his evils. Is not this true?

Enter RODERIGO.

IAGO: (*Aside to him.*) How now, Roderigo!
I pray you, after the lieutenant; go. (*Exit* RODERIGO.)   120
MON: And 't is great pity that the noble Moor
Should hazard such a place as his own second
With one of an ingraft infirmity:
It were an honest action to say
So to the Moor.   125
IAGO: Not I, for this fair island.
I do love Cassio well; and would do much
To cure him of this evil.—But, hark! what noise? (*Cry within*) "Help!
help!"

Re-enter CASSIO, *pursuing* RODERIGO.

CAS: 'Zounds, you rogue! you rascal!
MON: What 's the matter, lieutenant?   130
CAS: A knave teach me my duty!
I 'll beat the knave into a twiggen bottle.
ROD: Beat me?
CAS: Dost thou prate, rogue? (*Striking* RODERIGO.)
MON: Nay, good lieutenant; (*Staying him.*)   135
I pray you, sir, hold your hand.
CAS: Let me go, sir,
Or I 'll knock you o'er the mazzard.
MON: Come, come, you 're drunk.
CAS: Drunk! (*They fight.*)   140
IAGO: (*Aside to* RODERIGO.) Away, I say; go out, and cry a mutiny. (*Exit*
RODERIGO.)

---

112. *horologe a double set*, the clock twice around.
132. *twiggen bottle*, bottle covered with wickerwork.
138. *mazzard*, head.

Nay, good lieutenant,—God's will, gentlemen;—
Help, ho!—Lieutenant,—sir,—Montano,—sir;—
Help, masters!—Here 's a goodly watch indeed! (*A bell rings.*)
Who 's that which rings the bell?—Diablo, ho!   145
The town will rise. God's will, lieutenant, hold!
You will be sham'd for ever.

Re-enter OTHELLO *and* ATTENDANTS.

OTH: What is the matter here?
MON: 'Zounds, I bleed still; I am hurt to th' death. He dies!
OTH: Hold, for your lives!   150
IAGO: Hold, ho! Lieutenant,—sir,—Montano,—gentlemen,—
Have you forgot all.sense of place and duty?
Hold! the general speaks to you; hold, for shame!
OTH: Why, how now, ho! from whence ariseth this?
Are we turn'd Turks, and to ourselves do that   155
Which Heaven hath forbid the Ottomites?
For Christian shame, put by this barbarous brawl.
He that stirs next to carve for his own rage
Holds his soul light; he dies upon his motion.
Silence that dreadful bell; it frights the isle   160
From her propriety. What is the matter, masters?
Honest Iago, that looks dead with grieving,
Speak, who began this? On thy love, I charge thee.
IAGO: I do not know: friends all but now, even now,
In quarter, and in terms like bride and groom   165
Devesting them for bed; and then, but now—
As if some planet had unwitted men—
Swords out, and tilting one at other's breast,
In opposition bloody. I cannot speak
Any beginning to this peevish odds;   170
And would in action glorious I had lost
Those legs that brought me to a part of it!
OTH: How comes it, Michael, you are thus forgot?
CAS: I pray you, pardon me; I cannot speak.
OTH: Worthy Montano, you were wont to be civil;   175
The gravity and stillness of your youth

---

158. *to carve,* to indulge himself.
159. *upon his motion,* as soon as he moves.
165. *quarter,* concord.
170. *peevish odds,* silly quarrel.

The world hath noted, and your name is great
In mouths of wisest censure. What 's the matter,
That you unlace your reputation thus,
And spend your rich opinion for the name   180
Of a night-brawler? Give me answer to it.
MON: Worthy Othello, I am hurt to danger.
Your officer, Iago, can inform you—
While I spare speech, which something now offends me—
Of all that I do know; nor know I aught   185
By me that 's said or done amiss this night,
Unless self-charity be sometimes a vice,
And to defend ourselves it be a sin
When violence assails us.
OTH: Now, by heaven,   190
My blood begins my safer guides to rule;
And passion, having my best judgement collied,
Assays to lead the way. If I once stir
Or do but lift this arm, the best of you
Shall sink in my rebuke. Give me to know   195
How this foul rout began, who set it on;
And he that is approv'd in this offence,
Though he had twinn'd with me, both at a birth,
Shall lose me. What! in a town of war,
Yet wild, the people's hearts brimful of fear,   200
To manage private and domestic quarrel,
In night, and on the court and guard of safety!
'T is monstrous. Iago, who began 't?
MON: If partially affin'd, or leagued in office,
Thou dost deliver more or less than truth,   205
Thou art no soldier.
IAGO: Touch me not so near.
I had rather have this tongue cut from my mouth
Than it should do offence to Michael Cassio;
Yet, I persuade myself, to speak the truth   210
Shall nothing wrong him. Thus it is, general:
Montano and myself being in speech,

---

178. *censure*, judgment.
180. *rich opinion*, valuable reputation.
184. *offends*, pains.
192. *collied*, obscured.
197. *approv'd*, implicated.
204. *partially affin'd*, made partial by any relationship.

There comes a fellow crying out for help;
And Cassio following him with determin'd sword
To execute upon him. Sir, this gentleman   215
Steps in to Cassio and entreats his pause;
Myself the crying fellow did pursue,
Lest by his clamour—as it so fell out—
The town might fall in fright. He, swift of foot,
Outran my purpose; and I return'd the rather   220
For that I heard the clink and fall of swords,
And Cassio high in oath; which till to-night
I ne'er might say before. When I came back—
For this was brief—I found them close together,
At blow and thrust; even as again they were   225
When you yourself did part them.
More of this matter cannot I report.
But men are men; the best sometimes forget.
Though Cassio did some little wrong to him,
As men in rage strike those that wish them best,   230
Yet surely Cassio, I believe, receiv'd
From him that fled some strange indignity
Which patience could not pass.
OTH: I know, Iago,
Thy honesty and love doth mince this matter,   235
Making it light to Cassio. Cassio, I love thee;
But never more be officer of mine.

Re-enter DESDEMONA, *attended.*

Look, if my gentle love be not rais'd up!
I'll make thee an example.
DES: What's the matter, dear?   240
OTH: All's well now, sweeting; come away to bed.
Sir, for your hurts, myself will be your surgeon.—
Lead him off. (*To* MONTANO, *who is led off.*)
Iago, look with care about the town,
And silence those whom this vile brawl distracted.   245
Come, Desdemona; 't is the soldiers' life
To have their balmy slumbers wak'd with strife. (*Exeunt all but* IAGO *and* CASSIO.)
IAGO: What, are you hurt, lieutenant?
CAS: Ay, past all surgery.

IAGO: Marry, God forbid! 250

CAS: Reputation, reputation, reputation! O, I have lost my reputation! I have lost the immortal part of myself, and what remains is bestial. My reputation, Iago, my reputation!

IAGO: As I am an honest man, I thought you had received some bodily wound; there is more sense in that than in reputation. Reputation [255 is an idle and most false imposition; oft got without merit, and lost without deserving. You have lost no reputation at all, unless you repute yourself such a loser. What, man! there are more ways to recover the general again. You are but now cast in his mood, a punishment more in policy than in malice; even so as one would beat his offenceless dog to affright an imperious lion. Sue to him again, and he 's yours. 261

CAS: I will rather sue to be despised than to deceive so good a commander with so slight, so drunken, and so indiscreet an officer. Drunk? and speak parrot? and squabble? swagger? swear? and discourse fustian with one's own shadow? O thou invisible spirit of wine, if thou hast no name to be known by, let us call thee devil! 266

IAGO: What was he that you followed with your sword? What had he done to you?

CAS: I know not.

IAGO: Is 't possible? 270

CAS: I remember a mass of things, but nothing distinctly; a quarrel, but nothing wherefore. O God, that men should put an enemy in their mouths to steal away their brains! That we should, with joy, pleasance, revel, and applause, transform ourselves into beasts!

IAGO: Why, but you are now well enough. How came you thus 275 recovered?

CAS: It hath pleased the devil drunkenness to give place to the devil wrath: one unperfectness shows me another, to make me frankly despise myself. 279

IAGO: Come, you are too severe a moraler. As the time, the place, and the condition of this country stands, I could heartily wish this had not befallen; but since it is as it is, mend it for your own good.

CAS: I will ask him for my place again; he shall tell me I am a drunkard! Had I as many mouths as Hydra, such an answer would stop them all. To be now a sensible man, by and by a fool, and presently a beast! O strange! Every inordinate cup is unblessed and the ingredient is a devil. 287

---

255. *sense*, feeling.
264. *speak parrot*, talk nonsense. *fustian*, high-sounding nonsense.

IAGO: Come, come, good wine is a good familiar creature, if it be well used; exclaim no more against it. And, good lieutenant, I think you think I love you.   290

CAS: I have well approved it, sir. I drunk!

IAGO: You or any man living may be drunk at a time, man. I 'll tell you what you shall do. Our general's wife is now the general;—I may say so in this respect, for that he hath devoted and given up himself to the contemplation, mark, and denotement of her parts and graces; [295 —confess yourself freely to her; importune her help to put you in your place again. She is of so free, so kind, so apt, so blessed a disposition, she holds it a vice in her goodness not to do more than she is requested. This broken joint between you and her husband entreat her to splinter; and, my fortunes against any lay worth naming, this crack of your love shall grow stronger than it was before.   301

CAS: You advise me well.

IAGO: I protest, in the sincerity of love and honest kindness.

CAS: I think it freely; and betimes in the morning I will beseech the virtuous Desdemona to undertake for me. I am desperate of my fortunes if they check me here.   306

IAGO: You are in the right. Good-night, lieutenant; I must to the watch.

CAS: Good-night, honest Iago. (*Exit.*)

IAGO: And what 's he then that says I play the villain?   310
When this advice is free I give and honest,
Probal to thinking and indeed the course
To win the Moor again? For 't is most easy
The inclining Desdemona to subdue
In any honest suit; she 's fram'd as fruitful   315
As the free elements. And then for her
To win the Moor, were 't to renounce his baptism,
All seals and symbols of redeemed sin,
His soul is so enfetter'd to her love,
That she may make, unmake, do what she list,   320
Even as her appetite shall play the god
With his weak function. How am I then a villain
To counsel Cassio to this parallel course,
Directly to his good? Divinity of hell!

---

299. *splinter*, bind with splints.
300. *lay*, wager.
312. *Probal*, probable.
315. *fruitful*, bountiful.

When devils will the blackest sins put on,   325
They do suggest at first with heavenly shows,
As I do now; for whiles this honest fool
Plies Desdemona to repair his fortunes
And she for him pleads strongly to the Moor,
I 'll pour this pestilence into his ear,   330
That she repeals him for her body's lust;
And by how much she strives to do him good,
She shall undo her credit with the Moor.
So will I turn her virtue into pitch,
And out of her own goodness make the net   335
That shall enmesh them all.

Re-enter RODERIGO.

How now, Roderigo!
ROD: I do follow here in the chase, not like a hound that hunts, but
one that fills up the cry. My money is almost spent; I have been to-
night exceedingly well cudgelled; and I think the issue will be, I [340
shall have so much experience for my pains; and so, with no money at
all and a little more wit, return again to Venice.
IAGO: How poor are they that have not patience!
What wound did ever heal but by degrees?
Thou know'st we work by wit, and not by witchcraft;   345
And wit depends on dilatory time.
Does 't not go well? Cassio hath beaten thee,
And thou, by that small hurt, hast cashier'd Cassio.
Though other things grow fair against the sun,
Yet fruits that blossom first will first be ripe.   350
Content thyself a while. By the mass, 't is morning;
Pleasure and action make the hours seem short.
Retire thee; go where thou art billeted:
Away, I say; thou shalt know more hereafter.
Nay, get thee gone. (*Exit* RODERIGO.) Two things are to be done: 355
My wife must move for Cassio to her mistress;
I 'll set her on;
Myself the while to draw the Moor apart,

---

325. *put on*, instigate.
326. *suggest*, tempt.
331. *repeals*, seeks to recall him.
339. *cry*, pack. Hounds were admired for their voices as well as for hunting qualities.

And bring him jump when he may Cassio find
Soliciting his wife. Ay, that 's the way;   360
Dull not device by coldness and delay. (*Exit.*)

ACT III.

Scene I, *Before the castle.*

Enter CASSIO, *with* MUSICIANS.

CAS: Masters, play here; I will content your pains;
Something that 's brief; and bid "Good morrow, General." (*They play.*)

Enter CLOWN.

CLO: Why, masters, have your instruments been in Naples, that they
speak i' th' nose thus?
1. MUS: How, sir, how?   5
CLO: Are these, I pray you, wind-instruments?
1. MUS: Ay, marry, are they, sir.
CLO: O, thereby hangs a tail.
1. MUS: Whereby hangs a tale, sir?   9
CLO: Marry, sir, by many a wind-instrument that I know. But, masters,
here 's money for you; and the General so likes your music, that he
desires you, of all loves, to make no more noise with it.
1. MUS: Well, sir, we will not.
CLO: If you have any music that may not be heard, to 't again; but, as
they say, to hear music the General does not greatly care.   15
1. MUS: We have none such, sir.
CLO: Then put up your pipes in your bag, for I 'll away. Go, vanish
into air, away! (*Exeunt* MUSICIANS.)
CAS: Dost thou hear, mine honest friend?
CLO: No, I hear not your honest friend; I hear you.   20
CAS: Prithee, keep up thy quillets. There 's a poor piece of gold for
thee: if the gentlewoman that attends the general's wife be stirring, tell

---

359. *jump,* exactly.
ACT III. SCENE I. 1. *content,* reward.
21. *quillets,* quibbles.

her there 's one Cassio entreats her a little favour of speech. Wilt thou do this?

CLO: She is stirring, sir: if she will stir hither, I shall seem to notify unto her. 26

CAS: Do, good my friend. (*Exit* CLOWN.)

Enter IAGO.

In happy time, Iago.

IAGO: You have not been a-bed, then?

CAS: Why, no; the day had broke 30
Before we parted. I have made bold, Iago,
To send in to your wife. My suit to her
Is, that she will to virtuous Desdemona
Procure me some access.

IAGO: I 'll send her to you presently; 35
And I 'll devise a mean to draw the Moor
Out of the way, that your converse and business
May be more free.

CAS: I humbly thank you for 't. (*Exit* IAGO.) I never knew
A Florentine more kind and honest. 40

Enter EMILIA.

EMIL: Good morrow, good lieutenant: I am sorry
For your displeasure; but all will sure be well.
The General and his wife are talking of it,
And she speaks for you stoutly. The Moor replies,
That he you hurt is of great fame in Cyprus 45
And great affinity, and that in wholesome wisdom
He might not but refuse you; but he protests he loves you,
And needs no other suitor but his likings
To take the safest occasion by the front
To bring you in again. 50

CAS: Yet, I beseech you,
If you think fit, or that it may be done,
Give me advantage of some brief discourse
With Desdemon alone.

42. *displeasure,* disfavor incurred.
46. *affinity,* family connections.
49. *front,* forelock.

234 Plays by Four Tragedians

EMIL: Pray you, come in.   55
I will bestow you where you shall have time
To speak your bosom freely.
CAS: I am much bound to you. (*Exeunt.*)

Scene II, *A room in the castle.*

Enter OTHELLO, IAGO, *and* GENTLEMEN.

OTH: These letters give, Iago, to the pilot;
And by him do my duties to the Senate.
That done, I will be walking on the works;
Repair there to me.
IAGO: Well, my good lord, I 'll do 't.   5
OTH: This fortification, gentlemen, shall we see 't?
GENT: We 'll wait upon your lordship. (*Exeunt.*)

Scene III, *The garden of the castle.*

Enter DESDEMONA, CASSIO, *and* EMILIA.

DES: Be thou assur'd, good Cassio, I will do
All my abilities in thy behalf.
EMIL: Good madam, do: I warrant it grieves my husband
As if the cause were his.
DES: O, that 's an honest fellow. Do not doubt, Cassio,   5
But I will have my lord and you again
As friendly as you were.
CAS: Bounteous madam,
Whatever shall become of Michael Cassio,
He 's never anything but your true servant.   10
DES: I know 't; I thank you. You do love my lord;
You have known him long; and be you well assur'd
He shall in strangeness stand no farther off

SCENE III. 13. *strangeness*, aloofness.

Than in a politic distance.

CAS: Ay, but, lady,   15
That policy may either last so long,
Or feed upon such nice and waterish diet,
Or breed itself so out of circumstances,
That, I being absent and my place suppli'd,
My general will forget my love and service.   20

DES: Do not doubt that; before Emilia here
I give thee warrant of thy place. Assure thee,
If I do vow a friendship, I 'll perform it
To the last article. My lord shall never rest;
I 'll watch him tame, and talk him out of patience;   25
His bed shall seem a school, his board a shrift;
I 'll intermingle everything he does
With Cassio's suit: therefore be merry, Cassio;
For thy solicitor shall rather die
Than give thy cause away.   30

Enter OTHELLO *and* IAGO.

EMIL: Madam, here comes my lord.
CAS: Madam, I 'll take my leave.
DES: Why, stay, and hear me speak.
CAS: Madam, not now; I am very ill at ease,
Unfit for mine own purposes.   35
DES: Well, do your discretion. (*Exit* CASSIO.)
IAGO: Ha! I like not that.
OTH: What dost thou say?
IAGO: Nothing, my lord; or if—I know not what.
OTH: Was not that Cassio parted from my wife?   40
IAGO: Cassio, my lord! No, sure, I cannot think it,
That he would steal away so guilty-like,
Seeing your coming.
OTH: I do believe 't was he.
DES: How now, my lord!   45
I have been talking with a suitor here,
A man that languishes in your displeasure.
OTH: Who is 't you mean?

---

25. *watch him tame,* keep him awake until he submits (method used in the training of hawks).
26. *shrift,* confessional.

DES: Why, your lieutenant, Cassio. Good my lord,
If I have any grace or power to move you,   50
His present reconciliation take;
For if he be not one that truly loves you,
That errs in ignorance and not in cunning,
I have no judgement in an honest face.
I prithee, call him back.   55
OTH: Went he hence now?
DES: Yes, faith; so humbled
That he hath left part of his grief with me,
To suffer with him. Good love, call him back.
OTH: Not now, sweet Desdemon; some other time.   60
DES: But shall 't be shortly?
OTH: The sooner, sweet, for you.
DES: Shall 't be to-night at supper?
OTH: No, not to-night.
DES: To-morrow dinner, then?   65
OTH: I shall not dine at home;
I meet the captains at the citadel.
DES: Why, then, to-morrow night; on Tuesday morn;
On Tuesday morn, or night; on Wednesday morn.
I prithee, name the time, but let it not   70
Exceed three days. In faith, he 's penitent;
And yet his trespass, in our common reason—
Save that, they say, the wars must make example
Out of their best—is not almost a fault
T' incur a private check. When shall he come?   75
Tell me, Othello. I wonder in my soul,
What you would ask me, that I should deny,
Or stand so mamm'ring on. What! Michael Cassio,
That came a-wooing with you, and so many a time,
When I have spoke of you dispraisingly,   80
Hath ta'en your part,—to have so much to do
To bring him in! Trust me, I could do much,—
OTH: Prithee, no more; let him come when he will
I will deny thee nothing.
DES: Why, this is not a boon.   85
'T is as I should entreat you wear your gloves,

---

74. *not almost*, scarcely.
75. *check*, rebuke.
78. *mamm'ring*, hesitating.

Or feed on nourishing dishes, or keep you warm,
Or sue to you to do a peculiar profit
To your own person. Nay, when I have a suit
Wherein I mean to touch your love indeed, 90
It shall be full of poise and difficult weight
And fearful to be granted.
OTH: I will deny thee nothing;
Whereon, I do beseech thee, grant me this,
To leave me but a little to myself. 95
DES: Shall I deny you? No. Farewell, my lord.
OTH: Farewell, my Desdemona; I 'll come to thee straight.
DES: Emilia, come.—Be as your fancies teach you;
Whate'er you be, I am obedient. (*Exeunt* DESDEMONA *and* EMILIA.)
OTH: Excellent wretch! Perdition catch my soul, 100
But I do love thee! and when I love thee not,
Chaos is come again.
IAGO: My noble lord,—
OTH: What dost thou say, Iago?
IAGO: Did Michael Cassio, when you woo'd my lady, 105
Know of your love?
OTH: He did, from first to last. Why dost thou ask?
IAGO: But for a satisfaction of my thought;
No further harm.
OTH: Why of thy thought, Iago? 110
IAGO: I did not think he had been acquainted with her.
OTH: O, yes; and went between us very oft.
IAGO: Indeed!
OTH: Indeed! ay, indeed. Discern'st thou aught in that?
Is he not honest? 115
IAGO: Honest, my lord?
OTH: Honest! ay, honest.
IAGO: My lord, for aught I know.
OTH: What dost thou think?
IAGO: Think, my lord? 120
OTH: Think, my lord!
By heaven, he echoes me,
As if there were some monster in his thought
Too hideous to be shown.—Thou dost mean something:
I heard thee say even now, thou lik'st not that, 125

---

91. *poise,* counterpoise.
100. *wretch,* term of affection often mingled with pity.

When Cassio left my wife. What didst not like?
And when I told thee he was of my counsel,
Of my whole course of wooing, thou criedst, "Indeed!"
And didst contract and purse thy brow together,
As if thou then hadst shut up in thy brain   130
Some horrible conceit. If thou dost love me,
Show me thy thought.
IAGO: My lord, you know I love you.
OTH: I think thou dost;
And, for I know thou 'rt full of love and honesty,   135
And weigh'st thy words before thou giv'st them breath,
Therefore these stops of thine fright me the more;
For such things in a false disloyal knave
Are tricks of custom; but in a man that 's just
They 're close delations, working from the heart   140
That passion cannot rule.
IAGO: For Michael Cassio,
I dare be sworn I think that he is honest.
OTH: I think so too.
IAGO: Men should be what they seem;   145
Or those that be not, would they might seem none!
OTH: Certain, men should be what they seem.
IAGO: Why, then, I think Cassio 's an honest man.
OTH: Nay, yet there 's more in this.
I prithee, speak to me as to thy thinkings,   150
As thou dost ruminate, and give thy worst of thoughts
The worst of words.
IAGO: Good my lord, pardon me.
Though I am bound to every act of duty,
I am not bound to that all slaves are free to.   155
Utter my thoughts? Why, say they are vile and false;
As where 's that palace whereinto foul things
Sometimes intrude not? Who has a breast so pure
But some uncleanly apprehensions
Keep leets and law-days and in sessions sit   160
With meditations lawful?
OTH: Thou dost conspire against thy friend, Iago,
If thou but think'st him wrong'd and mak'st his ear

---

127. *of my counsel,* in my confidence.
140. *close delations,* secret accusations.
150. *as . . . thinkings,* as frankly as to thine own thoughts.
160. *leets,* days on which court is held.

A stranger to thy thoughts.

IAGO: I do beseech you—   165
Though I perchance am vicious in my guess,
As, I confess, it is my nature's plague
To spy into abuses, and oft my jealousy
Shapes faults that are not—that your wisdom yet,
From one that so imperfectly conceits,   170
Would take no notice, nor build yourself a trouble
Out of his scattering and unsure observance.
It were not for your quiet nor your good,
Nor for my manhood, honesty, and wisdom,
To let you know my thoughts.   175

OTH: What dost thou mean?

IAGO: Good name in man and woman, dear my lord,
Is the immediate jewel of their souls.
Who steals my purse steals trash; 't is something, nothing;
'T was mine, 't is his, and has been slave to thousands;   180
But he that filches from me my good name
Robs me of that which not enriches him,
And makes me poor indeed.

OTH: By heaven, I 'll know thy thoughts.

IAGO: You cannot, if my heart were in your hand;   185
Nor shall not, whilst 't is in my custody.

OTH: Ha!

IAGO: O, beware, my lord, of jealousy;
It is the green-ey'd monster which doth mock
The meat it feeds on. That cuckold lives in bliss   190
Who, certain of his fate, loves not his wronger;
But, O, what damned minutes tells he o'er
Who dotes, yet doubts, suspects, yet strongly loves!

OTH: O misery!

IAGO: Poor and content is rich and rich enough,   195
But riches fineless is as poor as winter
To him that ever fears he shall be poor.
Good heaven, the souls of all my tribe defend
From jealousy!

OTH: Why, why is this?   200

---

166. *vicious*, wrong.
168. *jealousy*, suspicion.
170. *conceits*, imagines.
172. *scattering*, random.
196. *fineless*, boundless.

Think'st thou I 'd make a life of jealousy,
To follow still the changes of the moon
With fresh suspicions? No! to be once in doubt
Is once to be resolv'd: exchange me for a goat,
When I shall turn the business of my soul   205
To such exsufflicate and blown surmises,
Matching thy inference. 'T is not to make me jealous
To say my wife is fair, feeds well, loves company,
Is free of speech, sings, plays, and dances well;
Where virtue is, these are more virtuous;   210
Nor from mine own weak merits will I draw
The smallest fear or doubt of her revolt;
For she had eyes, and chose me. No, Iago;
I 'll see before I doubt; when I doubt, prove;
And on the proof, there is no more but this,—   215
Away at once with love or jealousy!
IAGO: I am glad of this, for now I shall have reason
To show the love and duty that I bear you
With franker spirit; therefore, as I am bound,
Receive it from me. I speak not yet of proof.   220
Look to your wife; observe her well with Cassio;
Wear your eyes thus, not jealous nor secure:
I would not have your free and noble nature,
Out of self-bounty, be abus'd; look to 't.
I know our country disposition well;   225
In Venice they do let God see the pranks
They dare not show their husbands. Their best conscience
Is not to leave 't undone, but keep 't unknown.
OTH: Dost thou say so?
IAGO: She did deceive her father, marrying you;   230
And when she seem'd to shake and fear your looks,
She lov'd them most.
OTH: And so she did.
IAGO: Why, go to then.
She that, so young, could give out such a seeming,   235
To seel her father's eyes up close as oak—
He thought 't was witchcraft—but I am much to blame.
I humbly do beseech you of your pardon

---

206. *exsufflicate and blown,* insubstantial and inflated, like a bubble.
222. *secure,* careless.
224. *self-bounty,* innate generosity.

For too much loving you.

OTH: I am bound to thee for ever.   240

IAGO: I see this hath a little dash'd your spirits.

OTH: Not a jot, not a jot.

IAGO: I' faith, I fear it has.

I hope you will consider what is spoke

Comes from my love. But I do see you 're mov'd.   245

I am to pray you not to strain my speech

To grosser issues nor to larger reach

Than to suspicion.

OTH: I will not.

IAGO: Should you do so, my lord,   250

My speech should fall into such vile success

Which my thoughts aim'd not at. Cassio 's my worthy friend,—

My lord, I see you 're mov'd.

OTH: No, not much mov'd.

I do not think but Desdemona 's honest.   255

IAGO: Long live she so; and long live you to think so!

OTH: And yet, how nature erring from itself,—

IAGO: Ay, there 's the point; as—to be bold with you—

Not to affect many proposed matches

Of her own clime, complexion, and degree,   ·   260

Whereto we see in all things nature tends—

Foh! one may smell in such, a will most rank,

Foul disproportions, thoughts unnatural.

But pardon me; I do not in position

Distinctly speak of her; though I may fear   265

Her will, recoiling to her better judgement,

May fall to match you with her country forms,

And happily repent.

OTH: Farewell, farewell!

If more thou dost perceive, let me know more;   270

Set on thy wife to observe. Leave me, Iago.

IAGO: (*Going.*) My lord, I take my leave.

OTH: Why did I marry? This honest creature doubtless

Sees and knows more, much more, than he unfolds.

IAGO: (*Returning.*) My lord, I would I might entreat your honour

To scan this thing no farther; leave it to time.   276

---

251. *success*, results.

255. *honest*, chaste.

262. *will*, desire. *rank*, foul.

264. *position*, formal assertion.

Although 't is fit that Cassio have his place,
For, sure, he fills it up with great ability,
Yet, if you please to hold him off a while,
You shall by that perceive him and his means: 280
Note if your lady strain his entertainment
With any strong or vehement importunity;
Much will be seen in that. In the mean time,
Let me be thought too busy in my fears—
As worthy cause I have to fear I am—   285
And hold her free, I do beseech your honour.
OTH: Fear not my government.
IAGO: I once more take my leave. (*Exit.*)
OTH: This fellow 's of exceeding honesty,
And knows all qualities, with a learned spirit,   290
Of human dealings. If I do prove her haggard,
Though that her jesses were my dear heartstrings,
I 'd whistle her off and let her down the wind
To prey at fortune. Haply, for I am black
And have not those soft parts of conversation   295
That chamberers have, or for I am declin'd
Into the vale of years,—yet that 's not much—
She 's gone. I am abus'd; and my relief
Must be to loathe her. O curse of marriage,
That we can call these delicate creatures ours,   300
And not their appetites! I had rather be a toad
And live upon the vapour of a dungeon,
Than keep a corner in the thing I love
For others' uses. Yet, 't is the plague of great ones;
Prerogativ'd are they less than the base: 305
'T is destiny unshunnable, like death.
Even then this forked plague is fated to us
When we do quicken. Look where she comes.

Re-enter DESDEMONA *and* EMILIA.

---

281. *strain his entertainment*, over-urge his reinstatement.
286. *free*, i.e., from guilt.
287. *government*, self-control.
291. *haggard*, wild, untamed (used of hawks).
292. *jesses*, strings by which hawks were held.
293. *down the wind*, i.e., go free (trained hawks flew against the wind).
295. *conversation*, social intercourse.
296. *chamberers*, courtiers.
307. *forked plague*, horns of a cuckold.
308. *quicken*, begin to live.

If she be false, O, then heaven mocks itself!
I 'll not believe 't.   310
DES: How now, my dear Othello!
Your dinner, and the generous islanders
By you invited, do attend your presence.
OTH: I am to blame.
DES: Why do you speak so faintly?   315
Are you not well?
OTH: I have a pain upon my forehead here.
DES: Faith, that 's with watching; 't will away again.
Let me but bind it hard, within this hour
It will be well.   320
OTH: Your napkin is too little; (*He puts the handkerchief
from him; and it drops.*)
Let it alone. Come, I 'll go in with you.
DES: I am very sorry that you are not well. (*Exeunt* OTHELLO *and*
DESDEMONA.)
EMIL: I am glad I have found this napkin;
This was her first remembrance from the Moor: 325
My wayward husband hath a hundred times
Woo'd me to steal it; but she so loves the token,
For he conjur'd her she should ever keep it,
That she reserves it evermore about her
To kiss and talk to. I 'll have the work ta'en out,   330
And give 't Iago. What he will do with it
Heaven knows, not I;
I nothing but to please his fantasy.

Re-enter IAGO.

IAGO: How now! what do you here alone?
EMIL: Do not you chide; I have a thing for you.   335
IAGO: A thing for me? It is a common thing—
EMIL: Ha!
IAGO: To have a foolish wife.
EMIL: O, is that all? What will you give me now

---

312. *generous,* well-born.
318. *watching,* lying awake.
321. *napkin,* handkerchief.
326. *wayward,* wilful.
329. *reserves,* keeps.
330. *work ta'en out,* embroidery copied.
333. *fantasy,* whim.

244. Plays by Four Tragedians

For that same handkerchief?   340
IAGO: What handkerchief?
EMIL: What handkerchief!
Why, that the Moor first gave to Desdemona;
That which so often you did bid me steal.
IAGO: Hast stol'n it from her?   345
EMIL: No, faith; she let it drop by negligence,
And, to th' advantage, I, being here, took 't up.
Look, here it is.
IAGO: A good wench; give it me.
EMIL: What will you do with 't, that you have been so earnest 350
To have me filch it?
IAGO: (*Snatching it.*) Why, what is that to you?
EMIL: If it be not for some purpose of import,
Give 't me again. Poor lady, she 'll run mad
When she shall lack it.
IAGO: Be not acknown on 't; I have use for it.   355
Go, leave me. (*Exit* EMILIA.)
I will in Cassio's lodging lose this napkin,
And let him find it. Trifles light as air
Are to the jealous confirmations strong
As proofs of holy writ; this may do something.   360
The Moor already changes with my poison:
Dangerous conceits are, in their nature, poisons,
Which at the first are scarce found to distaste,
But with a little act upon the blood,
Burn like the mines of sulphur. I did say so.

Re-enter OTHELLO.

Look, where he comes! Not poppy, nor mandragora,   365
Nor all the drowsy syrups of the world
Shall ever medicine thee to that sweet sleep
Which thou ow'dst yesterday.
OTH: Ha! ha! false to me?
IAGO: Why, how now, General! no more of that.   370
OTH: Avaunt! be gone! thou hast set me on the rack.
I swear 't is better to be much abus'd

---

347. *to th' advantage,* opportunely.
355. *Be not acknown,* do not admit knowledge of it.
365. *mandragora,* a soporific drug.
368. *ow'dst,* ownedst.

Than but to know 't a little.

IAGO: How now, my lord!

OTH: What sense had I of her stol'n hours of lust?   375

I saw 't not, thought it not, it harm'd not me:

I slept the next night well, fed well, was free and merry;

I found not Cassio's kisses on her lips:

He that is robb'd, not wanting what is stol'n,

Let him not know 't, and he 's not robb'd at all.   380

IAGO: I am sorry to hear this.

OTH: I had been happy, if the general camp,

Pioners and all, had tasted her sweet body,

So I had nothing known. O, now, for ever

Farewell the tranquil mind! farewell content!   385

Farewell the plumed troop, and the big wars, .

That makes ambition virtue! O, farewell!

Farewell the neighing steed, and the shrill trump,

The spirit-stirring drum, th' ear-piercing fife,

The royal banner, and all quality,   390

Pride, pomp, and circumstance of glorious war!

And, O you mortal engines, whose rude throats

Th' immortal Jove's dread clamours counterfeit,

Farewell! Othello's occupation 's gone!

IAGO: Is 't possible, my lord?   395

OTH: Villain, be sure thou prove my love a whore,

Be sure of it; give me the ocular proof;

Or, by the worth of mine eternal soul,

Thou hadst been better have been born a dog

Than answer my wak'd wrath!   400

IAGO: Is 't come to this?

OTH: Make me to see 't; or, at the least, so prove it,

That the probation bear no hinge nor loop

To hang a doubt on; or woe upon thy life!

IAGO: My noble lord,—   405

OTH: If thou dost slander her and torture me,

Never pray more; abandon all remorse;

On horror's head horrors accumulate;

Do deeds to make heaven weep, all earth amaz'd;

For nothing canst thou to damnation add   410

---

383. *Pioners*, pioneers, sappers.
391. *circumstance*, ceremony.
403. *probation*, proof.

246 Plays by Four Tragedians

Greater than that.
IAGO: O grace! O Heaven forgive me!
Are you a man? Have you a soul or sense?
God buy you; take mine office. O wretched fool,
That lov'st to make thine honesty a vice!   415
O monstrous world! Take note, take note, O world,
To be direct and honest is not safe.
I thank you for this profit; and from hence
I 'll love no friend, sith love breeds such offence.
OTH: Nay, stay. Thou shouldst be honest.   420
IAGO: I should be wise, for honesty 's a fool
And loses that it works for.
OTH: By the world,
I think my wife be honest and think she is not;
I think that thou art just and think thou art not.
I 'll have some proof. Her name, that was as fresh   425
As Dian's visage, is now begrim'd and black
As mine own face. If there be cords, or knives,
Poison, or fire, or suffocating streams,
I 'll not endure it. Would I were satisfied!
IAGO: I see, sir, you are eaten up with passion;   430
I do repent me that I put it to you.
You would be satisfied?
OTH: Would! nay, I will.
IAGO: And may; but, how? How satisfied, my lord?
Would you, the supervisor, grossly gape on—   435
Behold her tupp'd?
OTH: Death and damnation! O!
IAGO: It were a tedious difficulty, I think,
To bring them to that prospect; damn them then,
If ever mortal eyes do see them bolster   440
More than their own! What then? How then?
What shall I say? Where 's satisfaction?
It is impossible you should see this,
Were they as prime as goats, as hot as monkeys,
As salt as wolves in pride, and fools as gross   445
As ignorance made drunk. But yet, I say,
If imputation and strong circumstances,
Which lead directly to the door of truth,

---

418. profit, profitable lesson.
444. prime, lecherous.

Will give you satisfaction, you might have 't.

OTH: Give me a living reason she 's disloyal. 450

IAGO: I do not like the office;
But, sith I am enter'd in this cause so far,
Prick'd to 't by foolish honesty and love,
I will go on. I lay with Cassio lately;
And, being troubled with a raging tooth, 455
I could not sleep.
There are a kind of men so loose of soul,
That in their sleeps will mutter their affairs;
One of this kind is Cassio.
In sleep I heard him say, "Sweet Desdemona, 460
Let us be wary, let us hide our loves";
And then, sir, would he gripe and wring my hand,
Cry, "O sweet creature!" and then kiss me hard,
As if he pluck'd up kisses by the roots
That grew upon my lips; then laid his leg 465
Over my thigh, and sigh'd and kiss'd; and then
Cried, "Cursed fate that gave thee to the Moor!"

OTH: O monstrous! monstrous!

IAGO: Nay, this was but his dream.

OTH: But this denoted a foregone conclusion. 470
'T is a shrewd doubt, though it be but a dream.

IAGO: And this may help to thicken other proofs
That do demonstrate thinly.

OTH: I 'll tear her all to pieces.

IAGO: Nay, but be wise; yet we see nothing done. 475
She may be honest yet. Tell me but this,
Have you not sometimes seen a handkerchief
Spotted with strawberries in your wife's hand?

OTH: I gave her such a one; 't was my first gift.

IAGO: I know not that; but such a handkerchief— 480
I am sure it was your wife's—did I to-day
See Cassio wipe his beard with.

OTH: If it be that,—

IAGO: If it be that, or any that was hers,
It speaks against her with the other proofs. 485

OTH: O, that the slave had forty thousand lives!

---

453. *Prick'd,* incited.
470. *foregone conclusion,* a previous experience.
471. *shrewd doubt,* strong ground for suspecting evil.

One is too poor, too weak for my revenge.
Now do I see 't is true. Look here, Iago;
All my fond love thus do I blow to heaven.
'T is gone.   490
Arise, black vengeance, from the hollow hell!
Yield up, O love, thy crown and hearted throne
To tyrannous hate! Swell, bosom, with thy fraught,
For 't is of aspics' tongues!
IAGO: Yet be content.   495
OTH: O, blood, blood, blood!
IAGO: Patience, I say; your mind perhaps may change.
OTH: Never, Iago. Like to the Pontic Sea,
Whose icy current and compulsive course
Ne'er feels retiring ebb, but keeps due on   500
To the Propontic and the Hellespont,
Even so my bloody thoughts, with violent pace,
Shall ne'er look back, ne'er ebb to humble love,
Till that a capable and wide revenge
Swallow them up. Now, by yond marble heaven,   505
In the due reverence of a sacred vow
I here engage my words. (*Kneels.*)
IAGO: Do not rise yet.
Witness, you ever-burning lights above.
You elements that clip us round about, (*Kneels.*)   510
Witness that here Iago doth give up
The execution of his wit, hands, heart,
The wrong'd Othello's service! Let him command,
And to obey shall be in me remorse,
What bloody business ever. (*They rise.*)   515
OTH: I greet thy love,
Not with vain thanks, but with acceptance bounteous,
And will upon the instant put thee to 't:
Within these three days let me hear thee say
That Cassio 's not alive.   520
IAGO: My friend is dead; 't is done at your request.

---

493. *fraught,* freight.
494. *aspics',* asps'.
498. *Pontic sea,* Black Sea.
504. *capable,* capacious.
510. *clip,* surround.
512. *execution,* performance.
514. *remorse,* matter of conscience.

But let her live.

OTH: Damn her, lewd minx! O, damn her!
Come, go with me apart; I will withdraw
To furnish me with some swift means of death   525
For the fair devil. Now art thou my lieutenant.

IAGO: I am your own for ever. (*Exeunt.*)

Scene IV, *Before the castle.*

Enter DESDEMONA, EMILIA, *and* CLOWN.

DES: Do you know, sirrah, where Lieutenant Cassio lies?

CLO: I dare not say he lies anywhere.

DES: Why, man?

CLO: He 's a soldier, and for me to say a soldier lies, 't is stabbing.

DES: Go to! Where lodges he?   5

CLO: To tell you where he lodges, is to tell you where I lie.

DES: Can anything be made of this?

CLO: I know not where he lodges, and for me to devise a lodging and
say he lies here or he lies there, were to lie in mine own throat.

DES: Can you inquire him out, and be edified by report?   10

CLO: I will catechize the world for him; that is, make questions, and
by them answer.

DES: Seek him, bid him come hither. Tell him I have moved my lord
on his behalf, and hope all will be well.

CLO: To do this is within the compass of man's wit; and therefore I
will attempt the doing it. (*Exit.*)   16

DES: Where should I lose the handkerchief, Emilia?

EMIL: I know not, madam.

DES: Believe me, I had rather have lost my purse
Full of crusadoes; and, but my noble Moor   20
Is true of mind and made of no such baseness
As jealous creatures are, it were enough
To put him to ill thinking.

EMIL: Is he not jealous?

SCENE IV. 1. *lies,* resides.
17. *should,* could.
20. *crusadoes,* Portuguese gold coins stamped with a cross.

DES: Who, he? I think the sun where he was born   25
Drew all such humours from him.
EMIL: Look, where he comes.

Enter OTHELLO.

DES: I will not leave him now till Cassio
Be call'd to him.—How is 't with you, my lord?
OTH: Well, my good lady. (*Aside.*) O, hardness to dissemble!—   30
How do you, Desdemona?
DES: Well, my good lord.
OTH: Give me your hand. This hand is moist, my lady.
DES: It yet hath felt no age nor known no sorrow.
OTH: This argues fruitfulness and liberal heart;   35
Hot, hot, and moist. This hand of yours requires
A sequester from liberty, fasting and prayer,
Much castigation, exercise devout;
For here 's a young and sweating devil here,
That commonly rebels. 'T is a good hand,   40
A frank one.
DES: You may, indeed, say so;
For 't was that hand that gave away my heart.
OTH: A liberal hand. The hearts of old gave hands;
But our new heraldry is hands, not hearts.   45
DES: I cannot speak of this. Come now, your promise.
OTH: What promise, chuck?
DES: I have sent to bid Cassio come speak with you.
OTH: I have a salt and sorry rheum offends me;
Lend me thy handkerchief.   50
DES: Here, my lord.
OTH: That which I gave you.
DES: I have it not about me.
OTH: Not?
DES: No, faith, my lord.   55
OTH: That 's a fault. That handkerchief
Did an Egyptian to my mother give;
She was a charmer, and could almost read

---

35. *fruitfulness*, generosity.
37. *sequester*, sequestration.
49. *sorry*, painful.
57. *Egyptian*, gypsy.
58. *charmer*, sorceress.

The thoughts of people. She told her, while she kept it
'T would make her amiable and subdue my father 60
Entirely to her love, but if she lost it,
Or made a gift of it, my father's eye
Should hold her loathed and his spirits should hunt
After new fancies. She, dying, gave it me;
And bid me, when my fate would have me wiv'd, 65
To give it her. I did so; and take heed on 't;
Make it a darling like your precious eye.
To lose 't or give 't away were such perdition
As nothing else could match.
DES: Is 't possible? 70
OTH: 'T is true; there 's magic in the web of it.
A sibyl, that had number'd in the world
The sun to course two hundred compasses,
In her prophetic fury sew'd the work;
The worms were hallowed that did breed the silk; 75
And it was dy'd in mummy which the skilful
Conserv'd of maidens' hearts.
DES: Indeed! is 't true?
OTH: Most veritable; therefore look to 't well.
DES: Then would to God that I had never seen 't! 80
OTH: Ha! wherefore?
DES: Why do you speak so startingly and rash?
OTH: Is 't lost? Is 't gone? Speak, is 't out o' the way?
DES: Heaven bless us!
OTH: Say you? 85
DES: It is not lost; but what an if it were?
OTH: How?
DES: I say, it is not lost.
OTH: Fetch 't, let me see 't.
DES: Why, so I can, sir, but I will not now. 90
This is a trick to put me from my suit:
Pray you, let Cassio be receiv'd again.
OTH: Fetch me the handkerchief; my mind misgives.
DES: Come, come;
You 'll never meet a more sufficient man. 95
OTH: The handkerchief!

---

60. *amiable*, lovable.
76. *in mummy*, embalming fluid that oozed from mummies.
77. *conserv'd*, preserved out of.
82. *startingly*, abruptly.

DES:	I pray, talk me of Cassio.
OTH:	The handkerchief!
DES:	A man that all his time

Hath founded his good fortunes on your love, 100
Shar'd dangers with you,—

OTH:	The handkerchief!
DES:	I' faith, you are to blame.
OTH:	'Zounds! (*Exit* OTHELLO.)
EMIL:	Is not this man jealous? 105
DES:	I ne'er saw this before.

Sure, there 's some wonder in this handkerchief;
I am most unhappy in the loss of it.

EMIL: 'T is not a year or two shows us a man:
They are all but stomachs, and we all but food; 110
They eat us hungerly, and when they are full
They belch us.

Enter CASSIO *and* IAGO.

Look you, Cassio and my husband!
IAGO: There is no other way, 't is she must do 't;
And, lo, the happiness! Go, and importune her. 115
DES: How now, good Cassio! what 's the news with you?
CAS: Madam, my former suit. I do beseech you
That by your virtuous means I may again
Exist, and be a member of his love
Whom I with all the office of my heart 120
Entirely honour: I would not be delay'd.
If my offence be of such mortal kind
That nor my service past, nor present sorrows,
Nor purpos'd merit in futurity
Can ransom me into his love again, 125
But to know so must be my benefit;
So shall I clothe me in a forc'd content,
And shut myself up in some other course,
To fortune's alms.
DES: Alas, thrice-gentle Cassio! 130
My advocation is not now in tune;

---

115. *happiness,* lucky chance.
118. *virtuous,* effective.
131. *advocation,* advocacy.

My lord is not my lord, nor should I know him
Were he in favour as in humour alter'd.
So help me every spirit sanctified
As I have spoken for you all my best   135
And stood within the blank of his displeasure
For my free speech! You must a while be patient.
What I can do I will; and more I will
Than for myself I dare. Let that suffice you.
IAGO: Is my lord angry?   140
EMIL: He went hence but now,
And certainly in strange unquietness.
IAGO: Can he be angry? I have seen the cannon
When it hath blown his ranks into the air,
And, like the devil, from his very arm   145
Puff'd his own brother—and can he be angry?
Something of moment then. I will go meet him.
There 's matter in 't indeed, if he be angry. (*Exit* IAGO.)
DES: I prithee, do so. Something, sure, of state,
Either from Venice, or some unhatch'd practice   150
Made demonstrable here in Cyprus to him,
Hath puddled his clear spirit; and in such cases
Men's natures wrangle with inferior things,
Though great ones are their object. 'T is even so;
For let our finger ache, and it indues   155
Our other healthful members even to a sense
Of pain. Nay, we must think men are not gods,
Nor of them look for such observancy
As fits the bridal. Beshrew me much, Emilia,
I was, unhandsome warrior as I am,   160
Arraigning his unkindness with my soul;
But now I find I had suborn'd the witness,
And he 's indicted falsely.
EMIL: Pray Heaven it be state-matters, as you think,
And no conception nor no jealous toy   165
Concerning you.

---

136. *blank*, range, lit., white spot in the target.
150. *unhatch'd practice*, undeveloped plot.
152. *puddled*, made muddy, troubled.
155. *indues*, endows.
158. *observancy*, devoted attention.
160. *unhandsome*, unfair.
165. *toy*, whim.

DES: Alas the day! I never gave him cause.
EMIL: But jealous souls will not be answer'd so;
They are not ever jealous for the cause,
But jealous for they 're jealous. It is a monster   170
Begot upon itself, born on itself.
DES: Heaven keep that monster from Othello's mind!
EMIL: Lady, amen.
DES: I will go seek him. Cassio, walk hereabout;
If I do find him fit, I 'll move your suit   175
And seek to effect it to my uttermost.
CAS: I humbly thank your ladyship. (*Exeunt* DESDEMONA *and* EMILIA.)

Enter BIANCA.

BIAN: Save you, friend Cassio!
CAS: What make you from home?
How is it with you, my most fair Bianca?   180
I' faith, sweet love, I was coming to your house.
BIAN: And I was going to your lodging, Cassio.
What, keep a week away? seven days and nights?
Eightscore eight hours? and lovers' absent hours,
More tedious than the dial eightscore times?   185
O weary reck'ning!
CAS: Pardon me, Bianca.
I have this while with leaden thoughts been press'd;
But I shall, in a more continuate time,
Strike off this score of absence. Sweet Bianca, (*Giving her* DESDEMONA'S
handkerchief.)
Take me this work out.   191
BIAN: O Cassio, whence came this?
This is some token from a newer friend;
To the felt absence now I feel a cause.
Is 't come to this? Well, well.   195
CAS: Go to, woman!
Throw your vile guesses in the devil's teeth,
From whence you have them. You are jealous now
That this is from some mistress, some remembrance.
No, by my faith, Bianca.   200
BIAN: Why, whose is it?
CAS: I know not, sweet; I found it in my chamber.

---

189. *continuate*, uninterrupted.

I like the work well; ere it be demanded—
As like enough it will—I 'd have it copied.
Take it, and do 't; and leave me for this time.   205
BIAN: Leave you! Wherefore?
CAS: I do attend here on the General;
And think it no addition, nor my wish,
To have him see me woman'd.
BIAN: Why, I pray you?   210
CAS: Not that I love you not.
BIAN: But that you do not love me.
I pray you, bring me on the way a little,
And say if I shall see you soon at night.
CAS: 'T is but a little way that I can bring you,   215
For I attend here; but I 'll see you soon.
BIAN: 'T is very good; I must be circumstanc'd. (*Exeunt.*)

ACT IV.

Scene I, *Cyprus. Before the castle.*

Enter OTHELLO *and* IAGO.

IAGO: Will you think so?
OTH: Think so, Iago!
IAGO: What,
To kiss in private?
OTH: An unauthoriz'd kiss.   5
IAGO: Or to be naked with her friend in bed
An hour or more, not meaning any harm?
OTH: Naked in bed, Iago, and not mean harm!
It is hypocrisy against the devil:
They that mean virtuously, and yet do so,   10
The devil their virtue tempts, and they tempt heaven.
IAGO: If they do nothing, 't is a venial slip;

---

208. *addition,* mark of distinction.
217. *be circumstanc'd,* yield to circumstances.
ACT IV. SCENE I. 9. *hypocrisy,* so to appear to sin without sinning.

But if I give my wife a handkerchief,—
OTH: What then?
IAGO: Why, then, 't is hers, my lord; and, being hers,   15
She may, I think, bestow 't on any man.
OTH: She is protectress of her honour too;
May she give that?
IAGO: Her honour is an essence that 's not seen;
They have it very oft that have it not: 20
But, for the handkerchief,—
OTH: By heaven, I would most gladly have forgot it.
Thou said'st—O, it comes o'er my memory,
As doth the raven o'er the infected house,
Boding to all—he had my handkerchief.   25
IAGO: Ay, what of that?
OTH: That 's not so good now.
IAGO: What
If I had said I had seen him do you wrong?
Or heard him say,—as knaves be such abroad,   30
Who having, by their own importunate suit,
Or voluntary dotage of some mistress,
Convinced or supplied them, cannot choose
But they must blab—
OTH: Hath he said anything?   35
IAGO: He hath, my lord; but be you well assur'd,
No more than he 'll unswear.
OTH: What hath he said?
IAGO: Faith, that he did—I know not what he did.
OTH: What? what?   40
IAGO: Lie—
OTH: With her?
IAGO: With her, on her; what you will.
OTH: Lie with her! lie on her! We say lie on her, when they belie her.
Lie with her! 'Zounds, that 's fulsome!—Handkerchief—confessions [45
—handkerchief!—To confess, and be hanged for his labour;—first, to be
hanged, and then to confess.—I tremble at it. Nature would not invest
herself in such shadowing passion without some instruction. It is not
words that shakes me thus. Pish! Noses, ears, and lips.—Is 't possible?—
Confess—handkerchief!—O devil! (*Falls in a trance.*)   50

---

33. *Convinced or supplied*, overcome or satisfied.
47-48. *Nature . . . instruction*, passion would not fill my mind with so many images unless they represented not mere words but actual facts.

IAGO: Work on,
My medicine, work! Thus credulous fools are caught;
And many worthy and chaste dames even thus,
All guiltless, meet reproach.—What, ho! my lord!
My lord, I say! Othello!   55

Enter CASSIO.

How now, Cassio!
CAS: What 's the matter?
IAGO: My lord is fall'n into an epilepsy.
This is his second fit; he had one yesterday.
CAS: Rub him about the temples.   60
IAGO: No, forbear;
The lethargy must have his quiet course;
If not, he foams at mouth and by and by
Breaks out to savage madness. Look, he stirs.
Do you withdraw yourself a little while,   65
He will recover straight: when he is gone,
I would on great occasion speak with you. (*Exit Cassio.*)
How is it, general? Have you not hurt your head?
OTH: Dost thou mock me?
IAGO: I mock you not, by heaven.   70
Would you would bear your fortune like a man!
OTH: A horned man 's a monster and a beast.
IAGO: There 's many a beast then in a populous city,
And many a civil monster.
OTH: Did he confess it?   75
IAGO: Good sir, be a man;
Think every bearded fellow that 's but yok'd
May draw with you. There 's millions now alive
That nightly lie in those unproper beds
Which they dare swear peculiar; your case is better.   80
O, 't is the spite of hell, the fiend's arch-mock,
To lip a wanton in a secure couch,
And to suppose her chaste! No, let me know;
And knowing what I am, I know what she shall be.
OTH: O, thou art wise; 't is certain.   85

---

72. *horned man,* a cuckold.
74. *civil,* civilized.
79. *unproper,* not their own.
80. *peculiar,* their very own.

IAGO: Stand you a while apart;
Confine yourself but in a patient list.
Whilst you were here o'erwhelmed with your grief—
A passion most unsuiting such a man—
Cassio came hither. I shifted him away,   90
And laid good 'scuse upon your ecstasy;
Bade him anon return and here speak with me,
The which he promis'd. Do but encave yourself,
And mark the fleers, the gibes, and notable scorns,
That dwell in every region of his face;   95
For I will make him tell the tale anew,
Where, how, how oft, how long ago, and when
He hath, and is again to cope your wife.
I say, but mark his gesture. Marry, patience;
Or I shall say you 're all in all in spleen,   100
And nothing of a man.
OTH: Dost thou hear, Iago?
I will be found most cunning in my patience;
But—dost thou hear?—most bloody.
IAGO: That 's not amiss;   105
But yet keep time in all. Will you withdraw? (OTHELLO *retires*.)
Now will I question Cassio of Bianca,
A housewife that by selling her desires
Buys herself bread and clothes. It is a creature
That dotes on Cassio;—as 't is the strumpet's plague   110
To beguile many and be beguil'd by one;—
He, when he hears of her, cannot refrain
From the excess of laughter. Here he comes:

Re-enter CASSIO.

As he shall smile, Othello shall go mad;
And his unbookish jealousy must construe   115
Poor Cassio's smiles, gestures, and light behaviours
Quite in the wrong. How do you, lieutenant?
CAS: The worser that you give me the addition

---

87. *patient list*, confines of patience.
91. *ecstasy*, fainting fit.
93. *encave*, hide.
100. *spleen*, anger.
115. *unbookist*, ignorant.
118. *addition*, title.

Whose want even kills me.

IAGO: Ply Desdemona well, and you are sure on 't.   120
Now, if this suit lay in Bianca's power,
How quickly should you speed!

CAS: Alas, poor caitiff!

OTH: Look, how he laughs already!

IAGO: I never knew a woman love man so.   125

CAS: Alas, poor rogue! I think, i' faith, she loves me.

OTH: Now he denies it faintly, and laughs it out.

IAGO: Do you hear, Cassio?

OTH: Now he importunes him
To tell it o'er. Go to; well said, well said.   130

IAGO: She gives it out that you shall marry her.
Do you intend it?

CAS: Ha, ha, ha!

OTH: Do ye triumph, Roman? Do you triumph?

CAS: I marry her! What? a customer! Prithee, bear some charity to my
wit; do not think it so unwholesome. Ha, ha, ha!   136

OTH: So, so, so, so; they laugh that wins.

IAGO: Faith, the cry goes that you shall marry her.

CAS: Prithee, say true.   140

IAGO: I am a very villain else.

OTH: Have you scor'd me? Well.

CAS: This is the monkey's own giving out. She is persuaded I will
marry her, out of her own love and flattery, not out of my promise.

OTH: Iago beckons me; now he begins the story.   145

CAS: She was here even now; she haunts me in every place. I was the
other day talking on the sea-bank with certain Venetians; and thither
comes the bauble, and, by this hand, she falls me thus about my neck—

OTH: Crying, "O dear Cassio!" as it were; his gesture imports it.   149

CAS: So hangs, and lolls, and weeps upon me; so shakes and pulls me.
Ha, ha, ha!

OTH: Now he tells how she plucked him to my chamber. O, I see that
nose of yours, but not that dog I shall throw it to.

CAS: Well, I must leave her company.

IAGO: Before me! look, where she comes.   155

Enter BIANCA.

---

134. *Roman,* suggested by "triumph."
135. *customer,* harlot.
142. *scor'd,* branded.
148. *bauble,* plaything.

CAS: 'T is such another fitchew! Marry, a perfumed one.—What do you mean by this haunting of me?

BIAN: Let the devil and his dam haunt you! What did you mean by that same handkerchief you gave me even now? I was a fine fool to take it. I must take out the work?—A likely piece of work, that you [160 should find it in your chamber, and know not who left it there! This is some minx's token, and I must take out the work? There; give it your hobby-horse: wheresoever you had it, I 'll take out no work on 't.

CAS: How now, my sweet Bianca! how now! how now!

OTH: By heaven, that should be my handkerchief!   165

BIAN: If you 'll come to supper to-night, you may; if you will not, come when you are next prepared for. (*Exit.*)

IAGO: After her, after her.

CAS: Faith, I must; she 'll rail in the streets else.

IAGO: Will you sup there?   170

CAS: Faith, I intend so.

IAGO: Well, I may chance to see you; for I would very fain speak with you.

CAS: Prithee, come; will you?

IAGO: Go to; say no more. (*Exit* CASSIO.)   175

OTH: (*Advancing.*) How shall I murder him, Iago?

IAGO: Did you perceive how he laughed at his vice?

OTH: O Iago!

IAGO: And did you see the handkerchief?

OTH: Was that mine?   180

IAGO: Yours, by this hand: and to see how he prizes the foolish woman your wife! She gave it him, and he hath given it his whore.

OTH: I would have him nine years a-killing. A fine woman! a fair woman! a sweet woman!

IAGO: Nay, you must forget that.   185

OTH: Ay, let her rot, and perish, and be damned to-night; for she shall not live. No, my heart is turned to stone; I strike it, and it hurts my hand. O, the world hath not a sweeter creature! She might lie by an emperor's side and command him tasks.

IAGO: Nay, that 's not your way.   190

OTH: Hang her! I do but say what she is. So delicate with her needle! an admirable musician! O! she will sing the savageness out of a bear: of so high and plenteous wit and invention!

IAGO: She 's the worse for all this.   194

---

156. *fitchew*, polecat.
163. *hobby-horse*, lover, used contemptuously.

OTH: O, a thousand thousand times! And then, of so gentle a condition!

IAGO: Ay, too gentle.

OTH: Nay, that 's certain. But yet the pity of it, Iago! O Iago, the pity of it, Iago!

IAGO: If you are so fond over her iniquity, give her patent to offend; for, if it touch not you, it comes near nobody.   200

OTH: I will chop her into messes. Cuckold me!

IAGO: O, 't is foul in her.

OTH: With mine officer!

IAGO: That 's fouler.   204

OTH: Get me some poison, Iago, this night. I 'll not expostulate with her, lest her body and beauty unprovide my mind again. This night, Iago.

IAGO: Do it not with poison; strangle her in her bed, even the bed she hath contaminated.

OTH: Good, good; the justice of it pleases; very good.   210

IAGO: And for Cassio, let me be his undertaker: you shall hear more by midnight.

OTH: Excellent good! (*A trumpet.*)
          What trumpet is that same?

IAGO: Something from Venice sure.   215

Enter LODOVICO, DESDEMONA, *and* ATTENDANTS.

          'T is Lodovico.
Come from the Duke; and, see, your wife is with him.

LOD: God save you, worthy General!

OTH: With all my heart, sir.   219

LOD: The Duke and senators of Venice greet you. (*Gives him a letter.*)

OTH: I kiss the instrument of their pleasures. (*Opens the letter, and reads.*)

DES: And what 's the news, good cousin Lodovico?

IAGO: I am very glad to see you, signior;
Welcome to Cyprus.

LOD: I thank you. How does Lieutenant Cassio?   225

IAGO: Lives, sir.

DES: Cousin, there 's fall'n between him and my lord

---

195. *condition*, disposition.
206. *unprovide*, weaken.
211. *undertaker*, dispatcher.

An unkind breach; but you shall make all well.

OTH: Are you sure of that?

DES: My lord!   230

OTH: (*Reads.*) "This fail you not to do, as you will"—

LOD: He did not call; he 's busy in the paper.
Is there division 'twixt my lord and Cassio?

DES: A most unhappy one. I would do much
T' atone them, for the love I bear to Cassio.   235

OTH: Fire and brimstone!

DES: My lord?

OTH: Are you wise?

DES: What, is he angry?

LOD: May be the letter mov'd him;   240
For, as I think, they do command him home,
Deputing Cassio in his government.

DES: Trust me, I am glad on 't.

OTH: Indeed!

DES: My lord?   245

OTH: I am glad to see you mad.

DES: Why, sweet Othello,—

OTH: (*Striking her.*) Devil!

DES: I have not deserv'd this.

LOD: My lord, this would not be believ'd in Venice   250
Though I should swear I saw 't. 'T is very much.
Make her amends: she weeps.

OTH: O devil, devil!
If that the earth could teem with woman's tears,
Each drop she falls would prove a crocodile.   255
Out of my sight!

DES: I will not stay to offend you. (*Going.*)

LOD: Truly, an obedient lady:
I do beseech your lordship, call her back.

OTH: Mistress!   260

DES: My lord?

OTH: What would you with her, sir?

LOD: Who, I, my lord?

OTH: Ay; you did wish that I would make her turn.
Sir, she can turn, and turn, and yet go on,

---

235. *atone*, bring together.

242. *Deputing*, substituting.

254. *teem*, engender. Refers to belief that the crocodile wept hypocritical tears over its victims.

And turn again; and she can weep, sir, weep;   265
And she 's obedient, as you say, obedient,
Very obedient. Proceed you in your tears.
Concerning this, sir,—O well-painted passion!—
I am commanded home.—Get you away;
I 'll send for you anon.—Sir, I obey the mandate,   270
And will return to Venice.—Hence, avaunt!—(*Exit* DESDEMONA.)
Cassio shall have my place. And, sir, to-night,
I do entreat that we may sup together.
You are welcome, sir, to Cyprus.—Goats and monkeys! (*Exit.*)
LOD: Is this the noble Moor whom our full Senate   275
Call all in all sufficient? Is this the nature
Whom passion could not shake? whose solid virtue
The shot of accident nor dart of chance
Could neither graze nor pierce?
IAGO: He is much chang'd.   280
LOD: Are his wits safe? Is he not light of brain?
IAGO: He 's that he is; I may not breathe my censure
What he might be. If what he might he is not,
I would to heaven he were!
LOD: What, strike his wife!   285
IAGO: Faith, that was not so well; yet would I knew
That stroke would prove the worst!
LOD: Is it his use?
Or did the letters work upon his blood,
And new-create this fault?   290
IAGO: Alas, alas!
It is not honesty in me to speak
What I have seen and known. You shall observe him,
And his own courses will denote him so
That I may save my speech: do but go after,   295
And mark how he continues.
LOD: I am sorry that I am deceiv'd in him. (*Exeunt.*)

Scene II, *A room in the castle.*

Enter OTHELLO *and* EMILIA.

---

268. *well-painted*, well-simulated.
282. *censure*, judgment.

OTH: You have seen nothing then?

EMIL: Nor ever heard, nor ever did suspect.

OTH: Yes, you have seen Cassio and she together.

EMIL: But then I saw no harm, and then I heard

Each syllable that breath made up between them.   5

OTH: What, did they never whisper?

EMIL: Never, my lord.

OTH: Nor send you out o' th' way?

EMIL: Never.

OTH: To fetch her fan, her gloves, her mask, nor nothing?   10

EMIL: Never, my lord.

OTH: That 's strange.

EMIL: I durst, my lord, to wager she is honest,

Lay down my soul at stake: if you think other,

Remove your thought; it doth abuse your bosom.   15

If any wretch have put this in your head,

Let Heaven requite it with the serpent's curse!

For, if she be not honest, chaste, and true,

There 's no man happy; the purest of their wives

Is foul as slander.   20

OTH: Bid her come hither; go. (*Exit* EMILIA.)

She says enough; yet she 's a simple bawd

That cannot say as much. This is a subtle whore,

A closet lock and key of villanous secrets;

And yet she 'll kneel and pray; I have seen her do 't.   25

Enter DESDEMONA *with* EMILIA.

DES: My lord, what is your will?

OTH: Pray, chuck, come hither.

DES: What is your pleasure?

OTH: Let me see your eyes;   30

Look in my face.

DES: What horrible fancy 's this?

OTH: (*To* EMILIA.) Some of your function, mistress;

Leave procreants alone and shut the door;

Cough, or cry "hem," if anybody come.   35

Your mystery, your mystery; nay, dispatch. (*Exit* EMILIA.)

DES: Upon my knees, what doth your speech import?

SCENE II. 33. *Some of your function*, do your office, i.e., as bawd.
36. *mystery*, trade.

I understand a fury in your words,
But not the words.

OTH: Why, what art thou?   40

DES: Your wife, my lord; your true and loyal wife.

OTH: Come, swear it, damn thyself,
Lest, being like one of heaven, the devils themselves
Should fear to seize thee; therefore be double damn'd,
Swear thou art honest.   45

DES: Heaven doth truly know it.

OTH: Heaven truly knows that thou art false as hell.

DES: To whom, my lord? With whom? How am I false?

OTH: Ah, Desdemon! Away! away! away!

DES: Alas the heavy day! Why do you weep?   50
Am I the motive of these tears, my lord?
If haply you my father do suspect
An instrument of this your calling back,
Lay not your blame on me: if you have lost him,
Why, I have lost him too.   55

OTH: Had it pleas'd Heaven
To try me with affliction; had they rain'd
All kinds of sores and shames on my bare head,
Steep'd me in poverty to the very lips,
Given to captivity me and my utmost hopes,   60
I should have found in some place of my soul
A drop of patience; but, alas, to make me
A fixed figure for the time of scorn
To point his slow unmoving finger at!
Yet could I bear that too, well, very well;   65
But there, where I have garner'd up my heart,
Where either I must live, or bear no life;
The fountain from the which my current runs,
Or else dries up; to be discarded thence!
Or keep it as a cistern for foul toads   70
To knot and gender in! Turn thy complexion there,
Patience, thou young and rose-lipp'd cherubin,
Ay, there look grim as hell!

DES: I hope my noble lord esteems me honest.

OTH: O, ay; as summer flies are in the shambles,   75

---

63. *time of scorn*, scorn of the age.
64. *slow unmoving*, moving so slowly as not be be observed.
71. *Turn thy complexion*, change thy color.

That quicken even with blowing. O thou weed,
Who art so lovely fair and smell'st so sweet
That the sense aches at thee, would thou hadst ne'er been born!
DES: Alas, what ignorant sin have I committed?
OTH: Was this fair paper, this most goodly book,   80
Made to write "whore" upon? What committed?
Committed! O thou public commoner!
I should make very forges of my cheeks,
That would to cinders burn up modesty,
Did I but speak thy deeds. What committed?   85
Heaven stops the nose at it, and the moon winks,
The bawdy wind, that kisses all it meets,
Is hush'd within the hollow mine of earth,
And will not hear it. What committed!
Impudent strumpet!   90
DES: By heaven, you do me wrong.
OTH: Are not you a strumpet?
DES: No, as I am a Christian.
If to preserve this vessel for my lord
From any other foul unlawful touch   95
Be not to be a strumpet, I am none.
OTH: What, not a whore?
DES: No, as I shall be sav'd.
OTH: Is 't possible?
DES: O, Heaven forgive us!   100
OTH: I cry you mercy, then.
I took you for that cunning whore of Venice
That married with Othello.—You, mistress,

Re-enter EMILIA.

That have the office opposite to Saint Peter,
And keeps the gate of hell! You, you, ay, you!   105
We have done our course; there 's money for your pains.
I pray you, turn the key and keep our counsel. (*Exit.*)
EMIL: Alas, what does this gentleman conceive?
How do you, madam? How do you, my good lady?

---

76. *quicken . . . blowing,* are impregnated again as soon as they lay their eggs.
82. *commoner,* prostitute.
86. *winks,* shuts her eyes.
94. *this vessel,* this body of mine.

DES: Faith, half asleep.   110
EMIL: Good madam, what 's the matter with my lord?
DES: With who?
EMIL: Why, with my lord, madam.
DES: Who is thy lord?
EMIL: He that is yours, sweet lady.   115
DES: I have none: do not talk to me, Emilia;
I cannot weep, nor answers have I none
But what should go by water. Prithee, tonight
Lay on my bed my wedding sheets, remember;
And call thy husband hither.   120
EMIL: Here 's a change indeed! (*Exit.*)
DES: 'T is meet I should be us'd so, very meet.
How have I been behav'd, that he might stick
The small'st opinion on my least misuse?

Re-enter EMILIA *with* IAGO.

IAGO: What is your pleasure, madam? How is 't with you?   125
DES: I cannot tell. Those that do teach young babes
Do it with gentle means and easy tasks.
He might have chid me so; for, in good faith,
I am a child to chiding.
IAGO: What 's the matter, lady?   130
EMIL: Alas, Iago, my lord hath so bewhor'd her,
Thrown such despite and heavy terms upon her,
That true hearts cannot bear.
DES: Am I that name, Iago?
IAGO: What name, fair lady?   135
DES: Such as she said my lord did say I was.
EMIL: He call'd her whore: a beggar in his drink
Could not have laid such terms upon his callet.
IAGO: Why did he so?
DES: I do not know; I am sure I am none such.   140
IAGO: Do not weep, do not weep. Alas the day!
EMIL: Hath she forsook so many noble matches,
Her father and her country and her friends,
To be call'd whore? Would it not make one weep?

118. *go by water*, be expressed in tears.
124. *small'st opinion on my least misuse*, the least censure on my slightest misdemeanor.
138. *callet*, whore.

DES: It is my wretched fortune.   145
IAGO: Beshrew him for 't!
How comes this trick upon him?
DES: Nay, Heaven doth know.
EMIL: I will be hang'd, if some eternal villain,
Some busy and insinuating rogue,   150
Some cogging, cozening slave, to get some office,
Have not devis'd this slander: I 'll be hang'd else.
IAGO: Fie, there is no such man; it is impossible.
DES: If any such there be, Heaven pardon him!
EMIL: A halter pardon him and hell gnaw his bones!   155
Why should he call her whore? Who keeps her company?
What place? what time? what form? what likelihood?
The Moor 's abus'd by some most villanous knave,
Some base notorious knave, some scurvy fellow.
O heaven, that such companions thou 'dst unfold,   160
And put in every honest hand a whip
To lash the rascals naked through the world
Even from the east to th' west!
IAGO: Speak within door.
EMIL: O, fie upon them! Some such squire he was   165
That turn'd your wit the seamy side without,
And made you to suspect me with the Moor.
IAGO: You are a fool; go to.
DES: Alas, Iago,
What shall I do to win my lord again?   170
Good friend, go to him; for, by this light of heaven,
I know not how I lost him. Here I kneel:
If e'er my will did trespass 'gainst his love,
Either in discourse of thought or actual deed,
Or that mine eyes, mine ears, or any sense   175
Delighted them in any other form;
Or that I do not yet, and ever did,
And ever will—though he do shake me off
To beggarly divorcement—love him dearly,
Comfort forswear me! Unkindness may do much;   180
And his unkindness may defeat my life,

---

151. *cogging*, lying. *cozening*, cheating.
160. *unfold*, expose.
164. *within door*, not so loud.
174. *discourse*, range.
181. *defeat*, destroy.

But never taint my love. I cannot say "whore."
It does abhor me now I speak the word;
To do the act that might the addition earn
Not the world's mass of vanity could make me.   185
IAGO: I pray you, be content; 't is but his humour.
The business of the state does him offence,
And he does chide with you.
DES: If 't were no other,—
IAGO: It is but so, I warrant. (*trumpets within.*)   190
Hark, how these instruments summon to supper!
The messengers of Venice stays the meat.
Go in, and weep not; all things shall be well. (*Exeunt* DESDEMONA *and*
EMILIA.)

Enter RODERIGO.

How now, Roderigo!
ROD: I do not find that thou deal'st justly with me.   195
IAGO: What in the contrary?
ROD: Every day thou daff'st me with some device, Iago; and rather, as
it seems to me now, keep'st from me all conveniency than suppliest me
with the least advantage of hope. I will indeed no longer endure it, nor
am I yet persuaded to put up in peace what already I have foolishly
suffered.   201
IAGO: Will you hear me, Roderigo?
ROD: Faith, I have heard too much, for your words and performances
are no kin together.
IAGO: You charge me most unjustly.   205
ROD: With nought but truth. I have wasted myself out of my means.
The jewels you have had from me to deliver Desdemona would half
have corrupted a votarist. You have told me she hath received them and
returned me expectations and comforts of sudden respect and acquaint-
ance, but I find none.   210
IAGO: Well; go to; very well.
ROD: Very well! go to! I cannot go to, man; nor 't is not very well. By

---

184. *addition*, title, name of whore.
185. *vanity*, finery.
192. *stays the meat*, wait for supper.
197. *daff'st me*, puttest me off.
198. *conveniency*, opportunity.
208. *votarist*, nun.
209. *sudden respect*, immediate notice.

this hand, I say 't is scurvy, and begin to find myself fopped in it.

IAGO: Very well.   214

ROD: I tell you 't is not very well. I will make myself known to Desdemona: if she will return me my jewels, I will give over my suit and repent my unlawful solicitation; if not, assure yourself I will seek satisfaction of you.

IAGO: You have said now.   219

ROD: Ay, and said nothing but what I protest intendment of doing.

IAGO: Why, now I see there 's mettle in thee, and even from this instant do build on thee a better opinion than ever before. Give me thy
hand, Roderigo: thou hast taken against me a most just exception; but
yet, I protest, I have dealt most directly in thy affair.

ROD: It hath not appeared.   225

IAGO: I grant indeed it hath not appeared, and your suspicion is not
without wit and judgement. But Roderigo, if thou hast that in thee indeed, which I have greater reason to believe now than ever—I mean
purpose, courage, and valour—this night show it. If thou the next night
following enjoy not Desdemona, take me from this world with treachery and devise engines for my life.   231

ROD: Well, what is it? Is it within reason and compass?

IAGO: Sir, there is especial commission come from Venice to depute
Cassio in Othello's place.

ROD: Is that true? Why, then Othello and Desdemona return again to
Venice.   236

IAGO: O, no; he goes into Mauritania and takes away with him the
fair Desdemona, unless his abode be lingered here by some accident;
wherein none can be so determinate as the removing of Cassio.

ROD: How do you mean, removing him?   240

IAGO: Why, by making him uncapable of Othello's place; knocking
out his brains.

ROD: And that you would have me to do?

IAGO: Ay, if you dare do yourself a profit and a right. He sups to-night
with a harlotry, and thither will I go to him; he knows not yet of [245
his honourable fortune. If you will watch his going thence, which I will
fashion to fall out between twelve and one, you may take him at your
pleasure. I will be near to second your attempt, and he shall fall between us. Come, stand not amazed at it, but go along with me; I will

---

213. *fopped*, duped.
224. *directly*, in a straightforward manner.
231. *engines for*, contrivances against.
239. *determinate*, decisive.
245. *harlotry*, harlot.

show you such a necessity in his death that you shall think yourself
bound to put it on him. It is now high suppertime, and the night grows
to waste. About it.   252

ROD: I will hear further reason for this.

IAGO: And you shall be satisfied. (*Exeunt.*)

Scene III, *Another room in the castle.*

.

Enter OTHELLO, LODOVICO, DESDEMONA, EMILIA, *and* ATTENDANTS.

LOD: I do beseech you, sir, trouble yourself no further.

OTH: O, pardon me; 't will do me good to walk.

LOD: Madam, good-night; I humbly thank your ladyship.

DES: Your honour is most welcome.

OTH: Will you walk, sir?   5
O, Desdemona,—

DES: My lord?

OTH: Get you to bed on th' instant; I will be returned forthwith. Dismiss your attendant there. Look 't be done.

DES: I will, my lord. (*Exeunt* OTHELLO, LODOVICO, *and* ATTENDANTS.) 10

EMIL: How goes it now? He looks gentler than he did.

DES: He says he will return incontinent;
And hath commanded me to go to bed,
And bade me to dismiss you.

EMIL: Dismiss me?   15

DES: It was his bidding; therefore, good Emilia,
Give me my nightly wearing, and adieu.
We must not now displease him.

EMIL: I would you had never seen him!

DES: So would not I: my love doth so approve him,   20
That even his stubbornness, his checks, his frowns,—
Prithee, unpin me,—have grace and favour in them.

EMIL: I have laid those sheets you bade me on the bed.

DES: All 's one. Good faith, how foolish are our minds!
If I do die before thee, prithee, shroud me   25
In one of those same sheets.

251-252. *grows to waste,* is wasting away.
SCENE III. 12. *incontinent,* immediately.
21. *stubbornness,* harshness.

EMIL: Come, come, you talk.
DES: My mother had a maid call'd Barbara;
She was in love, and he she lov'd prov'd mad
And did forsake her. She had a song of "willow";   30
An old thing 't was, but it express'd her fortune,
And she died singing it. That song to-night
Will not go from my mind; I have much to do
But to go hang my head all at one side
And sing it like poor Barbara. Prithee, dispatch.   35
EMIL: Shall I go fetch your night-gown?
DES: No, unpin me here.
This Lodovico is a proper man.
EMIL: A very handsome man.
DES: He speaks well.   40
EMIL: I know a lady in Venice would have walked barefoot to Pales-
tine for a touch of his nether lip.
DES: (*Singing.*)
    The poor soul sat sighing by a sycamore tree,
      Sing all a green willow;
    Her hand on her bosom, her head on her knee,   45
      Sing willow, willow, willow.
    The fresh streams ran by her, and murmur'd her moans;
      Sing willow, willow, willow;
    Her salt tears fell from her, and soften'd the stones;
      Sing willow, willow, willow;   50

Lay by these;—
(*Singing.*) "*Willow, willow;*"—
Prithee, hie thee; he 'll come anon;—
(*Singing.*)
    Sing all a green willow must be my garland.
    Let nobody blame him, his scorn I approve,—   55
Nay, that 's not next.—Hark! who is 't that knocks?
EMIL: It 's the wind.
DES: (*Singing.*)
    I call'd my love false love; but what said he then?
      Sing willow, willow, willow.
    If I court moe women, you'll couch with moe men.—   60
So, get thee gone; good-night. Mine eyes do itch;

---

29. *prov'd mad*, turned wild, inconstant.
36. *night-gown*, dressing gown.
43. Desdemona's song is a popular ballad, altered by Shapespeare to fit the situation.

Doth that bode weeping?

EMIL: 'T is neither here nor there.

DES: I have heard it said so. O, these men, these men!

Dost thou in conscience think,—tell me, Emilia,—   65

That there be women do abuse their husbands

In such gross kind?

EMIL: There be some such, no question.

DES: Wouldst thou do such a deed for all the world?

EMIL: Why, would not you?   70

DES: No, by this heavenly light!

EMIL: Nor I neither by this heavenly light;

I might do 't as well i' th' dark.

DES: Wouldst thou do such a deed for all the world?

EMIL: The world 's a huge thing; it is a great price   75

For a small vice.

DES: In troth, I think thou wouldst not.

EMIL: In troth, I think I should; and undo 't when I had done. Marry,
I would not do such a thing for a joint-ring, nor for measures of lawn,
nor for gowns, petticoats, nor caps, nor any petty exhibition; but, [80
for all the whole world,—'ud's pity, who would not make her husband
a cuckold to make him a monarch? I should venture purgatory for 't.

DES: Beshrew me, if I would do such a wrong

For the whole world.   84

EMIL: Why, the wrong is but a wrong i' th' world; and having the
world for your labour, 't is a wrong in your own world, and you might
quickly make it right.

DES: I do not think there is any such woman.

EMIL: Yes, a dozen; and as many to th' vantage as would store the
world they play'd for.   90

But I do think it is their husbands' faults

If wives do fall. Say that they slack their duties

And pour our treasures into foreign laps,

Or else break out in peevish jealousies,

Throwing restraint upon us; or say they strike us,   95

Or scant our former having in despite;

Why, we have galls, and though we have some grace,

---

79. *joint-ring*, ring made of interlocking halves, a favorite love-token.
80. *exhibition*, stipend.
89. *to th' vantage*, to boot.
94. *peevish*, foolish.
96. *having*, allowance.
97. *galls*, resentment.

Yet have we some revenge. Let husbands know
Their wives have sense like them; they see and smell
And have their palates both for sweet and sour   100
As husband have. What is it that they do
When they change us for others? Is it sport?
I think it is. And doth affection breed it?
I think it doth. Is 't frailty that thus errs?
It is so too. And have not we affections,   105
Desires for sport, and frailty, as men have?
Then let them use us well; else let them know,
The ills we do, their ills instruct us so.
DES: Good-night, good-night. Heaven me such uses send,
Not to pick bad from bad, but by bad mend. (*Exeunt.*)   110

ACT V.

Scene I, *Cyprus. A street.*

Enter IAGO *and* RODERIGO.

IAGO: Here, stand behind this bulk; straight will he come:
Wear thy good rapier bare, and put it home.
Quick, quick; fear nothing; I 'll be at thy elbow.
It makes us, or it mars us; think on that,
And fix most firm thy resolution.   5
ROD: Be near at hand; I may miscarry in 't.
IAGO: Here, at thy hand; be bold, and take thy stand. (*Retires.*)
ROD: I have no great devotion to the deed,
And yet he hath given me satisfying reasons:
'T is but a man gone. Forth, my sword: he dies.   10
IAGO: I have rubb'd this young quat almost to the sense,
And he grows angry. Now, whether he kill Cassio,
Or Cassio him, or each do kill the other,
Every way makes my gain. Live Roderigo,

---

99. *sense*, feeling.
ACT V, SCENE I. 1. *bulk*, projecting part of a building.
11. *quat*, pimple. *sense*, quick.

He calls me to a restitution large   15
Of gold and jewels that I bobb'd from him,
As gifts to Desdemona;
It must not be. If Cassio do remain,
He hath a daily beauty in his life
That makes me ugly; and, besides, the Moor   20
May unfold me to him; there stand I in much peril.
No, he must die. Be 't so. I hear him coming.

Enter CASSIO.

ROD: I know his gait, 't is he.—Villain, thou diest! (*Makes a pass at* CASSIO.)
CAS: That thrust had been mine enemy indeed,
But that my coat is better than thou know'st.   25
I will make proof of thine. (*Draws, and wounds* RODERIGO.)
ROD: O, I am slain. (IAGO *from behind wounds* CASSIO *in the leg, and exit.*)
CAS: I am maim'd for ever. Help, ho! murder! murder! (*Falls.*)

Enter OTHELLO.

OTH: The voice of Cassio! Iago keeps his word.
ROD: O, villain that I am!   30
OTH: It is even so.
CAS: O, help, ho! light! a surgeon!
OTH: 'T is he!—O brave Iago, honest and just,
That hast such noble sense of thy friends' wrong!
Thou teachest me. Minion, your dear lies dead,   35
And your unblest fate hies; strumpet, I come.
Forth of my heart those charms, thine eyes, are blotted;
Thy bed, lust-stain'd, shall with lust's blood be spotted. (*Exit.*)

Enter LODOVICO *and* GRATIANO.

CAS: What, ho! no watch? no passage? Murder! murder!
GRA: 'T is some mischance; the voice is very direful.   40
CAS: O, help!

---

16. *bobb'd,* cheated.
25. *coat,* i.e., of mail worn under outer garments.
35. *Minion,* hussy.
39. *passage,* passers-by.

LOD: Hark!

ROD: O wretched villain!

LOD: Two or three groan. It is a heavy night,

These may be counterfeits; let 's think 't unsafe   45

To come in to the cry without more help.

ROD: Nobody come? Then shall I bleed to death.

Re-enter IAGO, *with a light.*

LOD: Hark!

GRA: Here 's one comes in his shirt, with light and weapons.

IAGO: Who 's there? Whose noise is this that cries on murder?   50

LOD: We do not know.

IAGO: Do not you hear a cry?

CAS: Here, here! for Heaven's sake, help me!

IAGO: What 's the matter?

GRA: This is Othello's ancient, as I take it.   55

LOD: The same indeed; a very valiant fellow.

IAGO: What are you here that cry so grievously?

CAS: Iago? O, I am spoil'd, undone by villains!

Give me some help.

IAGO: O me, lieutenant! what villains have done this?   60

CAS: I think that one of them is hereabout,

And cannot make away.

IAGO: O treacherous villains!

What are you there?—Come in, and give some help. (*To* LODOVICO *and*

GRATIANO.)

ROD: O, help me there!   65

CAS: That 's one of them.

IAGO: O murderous slave! O villain! (*Stabs* RODERIGO.)

ROD: O damn'd Iago! O inhuman dog!

IAGO: Kill men i' th' dark!—Where be these bloody thieves?—

How silent in this town!—Ho! murder! murder!—   70

What may you be? Are you of good or evil?

LOD: As you shall prove us, praise us.

IAGO: Signior Lodovico?

LOD: He, sir.

IAGO: I cry you mercy. Here 's Cassio hurt by villains.   75

GRA: Cassio!

---

44. *heavy*, thick, cloudy.

50. *cries on*, cries out.

IAGO: How is 't, brother!
CAS: My leg is cut in two.
IAGO: Marry, heaven forbid!
Light, gentlemen! I 'll bind it with my shirt.   80

Enter BIANCA.

BIAN: What is the matter, ho? Who is 't that cried?
IAGO: Who is 't that cried!
BIAN: O my dear Cassio! my sweet Cassio!
O Cassio, Cassio, Cassio!
IAGO: O notable strumpet! Cassio, may you suspect   85
Who they should be that have thus mangled you?
CAS: No.
GRA: I am sorry to find you thus; I have been to seek you.
IAGO: Lend me a garter. So. O, for a chair,
To bear him easily hence!   90
BIAN: Alas, he faints! O Cassio, Cassio, Cassio!
IAGO: Gentlemen all, I do suspect this trash
To be a party in this injury.
Patience a while, good Cassio. Come, come;
Lend me a light. Know we this face or no?   95
Alas, my friend and my dear countryman
Roderigo! No:—yes, sure:—O heaven! Roderigo.
GRA: What, of Venice?
IAGO: Even he, sir; did you know him?
GRA: Know him? ay.   100
IAGO: Signior Gratiano? I cry your gentle pardon;
These bloody accidents must excuse my manners,
That so neglected you.
GRA: I am glad to see you.
IAGO: How do you, Cassio? O, a chair, a chair!   105
GRA: Roderigo!
IAGO: He, he, 't is he. (*A chair brought in.*)
O, that 's well said; the chair.
Some good man bear him carefully from hence;
I 'll fetch the General's surgeon. (*To* BIANCA.) For you, mistress,   110
Save you your labour. He that lies slain here, Cassio,
Was my dear friend. What malice was between you?

---

89. *chair*, sedan chair.
92. *trash*, i.e., Bianca.
108. *said*, done.

CAS: None in the world; nor do I know the man.
IAGO: (*To* BIAN.) What, look you pale? O, bear him out o' th' air.
(CASSIO *and* RODERIGO *are borne off.*)
Stay you, good gentlemen. Look you pale, mistress?   115
Do you perceive the gastness of her eye?
Nay, if you stare, we shall hear more anon.
Behold her well; I pray you, look upon her.
Do you see, gentlemen? Nay, guiltiness will speak,
Though tongues were out of use.   120

Enter EMILIA.

EMIL: Alas, what 's the matter? What 's the matter, husband?
IAGO: Cassio hath here been set on in the dark
By Roderigo and fellows that are scap'd.
He 's almost slain, and Roderigo dead.
EMIL: Alas, good gentlemen! alas, good Cassio!   125
IAGO: This is the fruits of whoring. Prithee, Emilia,
Go know of Cassio where he supp'd to-night.
(*To* BIANCA.) What, do you shake at that?
BIAN: He supp'd at my house; but I therefore shake not.
IAGO: O, did he so? I charge you, go with me.   130
EMIL: Oh, fie upon thee, strumpet!
BIAN: I am no strumpet, but of life as honest
As you that thus abuse me.
EMIL: As I? Fie upon thee!
IAGO: Kind gentlemen, let 's go see poor Cassio dress'd.   135
Come, mistress, you must tell 's another tale.
Emilia, run you to the citadel,
And tell my lord and lady what hath happ'd.
Will you go on afore? (*Aside.*) This is the night
That either makes me or fordoes me quite. (*Exeunt.*)   140

Scene II, *A bedchamber in the castle:* DESDEMONA *in bed asleep.*

Enter OTHELLO *with a light.*

OTH: It is the cause, it is the cause, my soul,—
Let me not name it to you, you chaste stars!—

---

116. *gastness*, ghastliness.
140. *fordoes*, destroys.

It is the cause. Yet I 'll not shed her blood,
Nor scar that whiter skin of hers than snow,
And smooth as monumental alabaster.   5
Yet she must die, else she 'll betray more men.
Put out the light, and then put out the light:
If I quench thee, thou flaming minister,
I can again thy former light restore,
Should I repent me; but once put out thy light,   10
Thou cunning'st pattern of excelling nature,
I know not where is that Promethean heat
That can thy light relume. When I have pluck'd the rose
I cannot give it vital growth again,
It needs must wither; I 'll smell it on the tree. (*Kisses her.*) 15
Oh, balmy breath, that dost almost persuade
Justice to break her sword! One more, one more.
Be thus when thou art dead, and I will kill thee
And love thee after. One more, and that 's the last;
So sweet was ne'er so fatal. I must weep,   20
But they are cruel tears: this sorrow 's heavenly;
It strikes where it doth love. She wakes.
DES: Who 's there? Othello?
OTH: Ay, Desdemona.
DES: Will you come to bed, my lord?   25
OTH: Have you pray'd to-night, Desdemon?
DES: Ay, my lord.
OTH: If you bethink yourself of any crime
Unreconcil'd as yet to heaven and grace,
Solicit for it straight.   30
DES: Alack, my lord, what may you mean by that?
OTH: Well, do it, and be brief; I will walk by.
I would not kill thy unprepared spirit;
No; heaven forfend! I would not kill thy soul.
DES: Talk you of killing?   35
OTH: Ay, I do.
DES: Then heaven
Have mercy on me!

SCENE II. 12. *Promethean heat,* divine fire (stolen by Prometheus from heaven).
13. *relume,* rekindle.
21. *this sorrow's heavenly,* because it results from a punishment divine in its justice.
32. *by,* aside.
34. *forfend,* forbid.

OTH: Amen, with all my heart!
DES: If you say so, I hope you will not kill me.   40
OTH: Hum!
DES: And yet I fear you; for you 're fatal then
When your eyes roll so. Why I should fear I know not,
Since guiltiness I know not; but yet I feel I fear.
OTH: Think on thy sins.   45
DES: They are loves I bear to you.
OTH: Ay, and for that thou diest.
DES: That death 's unnatural that kills for loving.
Alas, why gnaw you so your nether lip?
Some bloody passion shakes your very frame.   50
These are portents; but yet I hope, I hope,
They do not point on me.
OTH: Peace, and be still!
DES: I will so. What 's the matter?
OTH: That handkerchief which I so lov'd and gave thee   55
Thou gav'st to Cassio.
DES: No, by my life and soul!
Send for the man, and ask him.
OTH: Sweet soul, take heed,
Take heed of perjury; thou art on thy deathbed.   60
DES: Ay, but not yet to die.
OTH: Yes, presently:
Therefore confess thee freely of thy sin;
For to deny each article with oath
Cannot remove nor choke the strong conception   65
That I do groan withal. Thou art to die.
DES: Then Lord have mercy on me!
OTH: I say, amen.
DES: And have you mercy too! I never did
Offend you in my life; never lov'd Cassio   70
But with such general warranty of heaven
As I might love; I never gave him token.
OTH: By heaven, I saw my handkerchief in 's hand.
O perjur'd woman! thou dost stone my heart,
And makes me call what I intend to do   75
A murder, which I thought a sacrifice.
I saw the handkerchief.

---

65. *conception*, intention.
74. *stone*, turn to stone.

DES: He found it then;
I never gave it him: send for him hither;
Let him confess a truth.   80
OTH: He hath confess'd.
DES: What, my lord?
OTH: That he hath us'd thee.
DES: How? unlawfully?
OTH: Ay.   85
DES: He will not say so.
OTH: No, his mouth is stopp'd;
Honest Iago hath ta'en order for 't.
DES: O! my fear interprets. What, is he dead?
OTH: Had all his hairs been lives, my great revenge   90
Had stomach for them all.
DES: Alas! he is betray'd and I undone.
OTH: Out, strumpet! weep'st thou for him to my face?
DES: O, banish me, my lord, but kill me not!
OTH: Down, strumpet!   95
DES: Kill me to-morrow; let me live to-night!
OTH: Nay, if you strive,—
DES: But half an hour!
OTH: Being done, there is no pause.
DES: But while I say one prayer!   100
OTH: It is too late. (*He smothers her.*)
EMIL: (*At the door.*) My lord, my lord! What, ho! my lord, my lord!
OTH: What noise is this? Not dead? not yet quite dead?
I that am cruel am yet merciful;
I would not have thee linger in thy pain.   105
So, so.
EMIL: (*Within.*) What, ho! my lord, my lord!
OTH: Who 's there?
EMIL: (*Within.*) O, good my lord, I would speak a word with you!
OTH: Yes:—'t is Emilia.—By and by.— She 's dead.   110
'T is like she comes to speak of Cassio's death.
The noise was high. Ha! no more moving?
Still as the grave. Shall she come in? Were 't good?—
I think she stirs again:—no. What 's best to do?
If she come in, she 'll sure speak to my wife.   115

---

88. *ta'en order*, made arrangements.
91. *stomach*, appetite.
99. *Being . . . pause*, now that it is being done, there can be no delay.

My wife! my wife! what wife? I have no wife.
O, insupportable! O heavy hour!
Methinks it should be now a huge eclipse
Of sun and moon, and that th' affrighted globe
Did yawn at alteration.   120
EMIL: (*Within.*) I do beseech you
That I may speak with you, O, good my lord!
OTH: I had forgot thee. O, come in, Emilia.
Soft; by and by.—Let me the curtains draw.—
Where art thou? (*Opens the door.*)   125

Enter EMILIA.

What 's the matter with thee now?
EMIL: O, my good lord, yonder 's foul murders done!
OTH: What, now?
EMIL: But now, my lord.
OTH: It is the very error of the moon;   130
She comes more nearer earth than she was wont,
And makes men mad.
EMIL: Cassio, my lord, hath kill'd a young Venetian
Call'd Roderigo.
OTH: Roderigo kill'd!   135
And Cassio kill'd!
EMIL: No, Cassio is not kill'd.
OTH: Not Cassio kill'd! Then murder 's out of tune,
And sweet revenge grows harsh.
DES: O, falsely, falsely murder'd!   140
EMIL: O Lord, what cry is that?
OTH: That! what?
EMIL: Out, and alas! that was my lady's voice.
Help! help, ho! help! O lady, speak again!
Sweet Desdemona! O sweet mistress, speak!   145
DES: A guiltless death I die.
EMIL: O, who hath done this deed?
DES: Nobody; I myself. Farewell!
Commend me to my kind lord. O, farewell! (*Dies.*)
OTH: Why, how should she be murder'd?   150

---

120. *yawn at alteration*, gape with amazement at the change. Earthquakes were
supposed to accompany eclipses.
130. *error*, aberration, wandering from her orbit.

EMIL: Alas, who knows?
OTH: You hear her say herself, it was not I.
EMIL: She said so; I must needs report the truth.
OTH: She 's like a liar, gone to burning hell.
'T was I that kill'd her.   155
EMIL: O, the more angel she,
And you the blacker devil!
OTH: She turn'd to folly, and she was a whore.
EMIL: Thou dost belie her, and thou art a devil.
OTH: She was false as water.   160
EMIL: Thou art rash as fire, to say
That she was false: O, she was heavenly true!
OTH: Cassio did tup her; ask thy husband else.
O, I were damn'd beneath all depth in hell
But that I did proceed upon just grounds   165
To this extremity. Thy husband knew it all.
EMIL: My husband?
OTH: Thy husband.
EMIL: That she was false to wedlock?
OTH: Ay, with Cassio. Nay, had she been true,   170
If Heaven would make me such another world
Of one entire and perfect chrysolite,
I 'd not have sold her for it.
EMIL: My husband?
OTH: Ay, 't was he that told me on her first.   175
An honest man he is, and hates the slime
That sticks on filthy deeds.
EMIL: My husband?
OTH: What needs this iterance, woman? I say thy husband.
EMIL: O mistress, villainy hath made mocks with love!   180
My husband say that she was false?
OTH: He, woman;
I say thy husband; dost understand the word?
My friend, thy husband, honest, honest Iago.
EMIL: If he say so, may his pernicious soul   185
Rot half a grain a day! He lies to th' heart:
She was too fond of her most filthy bargain.
OTH: Ha!

---

158. *folly*, wantonness.
172. *chrysolite*, precious stone; according to Pliny the largest and costliest of gems.
180. *villainy . . . love*, villainy hath made sport of deceived love.

EMIL: Do thy worst!
This deed of thine is no more worthy heaven   190
Than thou wast worthy her.
OTH: Peace, you were best.
EMIL: Thou hast not half that power to do me harm
As I have to be hurt. O gull! O dolt!
As ignorant as dirt! Thou hast done a deed—   195
I care not for thy sword; I 'll make thee known,
Though I lost twenty lives.—Help! help, ho! help!
The Moor hath kill'd my mistress! Murder! murder!

Enter MONTANO, GRATIANO, IAGO, *and others.*

MON: What is the matter? How now, General!
EMIL: O, are you come, Iago? You have done well,   200
That men must lay their murders on your neck.
GRA: What is the matter?
EMIL: Disprove this villain, if thou be'st a man.
He says thou told'st him that his wife was false:
I know thou didst not, thou 'rt not such a villain.   205
Speak, for my heart is full.
IAGO: I told him what I thought, and told no more
Than what he found himself was apt and true.
EMIL: But did you ever tell him she was false?
IAGO: I did.   210
EMIL: You told a lie, an odious, damned lie;
Upon my soul, a lie, a wicked lie.
She false with Cassio!—did you say with Cassio?
IAGO: With Cassio, mistress. Go to, charm your tongue.
EMIL: I will not charm my tongue; I am bound to speak.   215
My mistress here lies murdered in her bed,—
ALL: O heavens forfend!
EMIL: And your reports have set the murderer on.
OTH: Nay, stare not, masters; it is true, indeed.
GRA: 'T is a strange truth.   220
MON: O monstrous act!
EMIL: Villainy, villainy, villainy!
I think upon 't, I think: I smell 't,—O villainy!

---

208. *apt*, natural.
214. *charm*, silence with a charm.

I thought so then,—I 'll kill myself for grief—
O villainy, villainy!   225
IAGO: What, are you mad? I charge you, get you home.
EMIL: Good gentlemen, let me have leave to speak;
'T is proper I obey him, but not now.
Perchance, Iago, I will ne'er go home.
OTH: O! O! O! (*He falls on the bed.*)   230
EMIL: Nay, lay thee down and roar;
For thou hast kill'd the sweetest innocent
That e'er did lift up eye.
OTH: (*Rising.*) O, she was foul!
I scarce did know you, uncle; there lies your niece,   235
Whose breath, indeed, these hands have newly stopp'd.
I know this act shows horrible and grim.
GRA: Poor Desdemon! I am glad thy father 's dead:
Thy match was mortal to him, and pure grief
Shore his old thread in twain. Did he live now,   240
This sight would make him do a desperate turn,
Yea, curse his better angel from his side,
And fall to reprobance.
OTH: 'T is pitiful; but yet Iago knows
That she with Cassio hath the act of shame   245
A thousand times committed. Cassio confess'd it;
And she did gratify his amorous works
With that recognizance and pledge of love
Which I first gave her: I saw it in his hand;
It was a handkerchief, an antique token   250
My father gave my mother.
EMIL: O God! O heavenly God!
IAGO: 'Zounds, hold your peace.
EMIL: 'T will out, 't will out! I peace!
No, I will speak as liberal as the north: 255
Let Heaven and men and devils, let them all,
All, all, cry shame against me, yet I 'll speak.
IAGO: Be wise, and get you home.
EMIL: I will not. (IAGO *offers to stab* EMILIA.)
GRA: Fie!   260

---

224. *then*, see IV, II, 149ff, above.
243. *reprobance*, eternal damnation.
248. *recognizance*, token.
255. *liberal as the north*, as unrestrainedly as the north-wind.

Your sword upon a woman?

EMIL: O thou dull Moor! that handkerchief thou speak'st of
I found by fortune and did give my husband;
For often, with a solemn earnestness,
More than indeed belong'd to such a trifle,   265
He begg'd of me to steal it.

IAGO: Villanous whore!

EMIL: She give it Cassio! No, alas! I found it,
And I did give 't my husband.

IAGO: Filth, thou liest!   270

EMIL: By heaven, I do not, I do not, gentlemen.
O murderous coxcomb! what should such a fool
Do with so good a wife?

OTH: I am there no stones in heaven
But what serves for the thunder?—Precious villain! (*He runs at* IAGO:
IAGO *kills his wife.*)

GRA: The woman falls; sure, he hath kill'd his wife.   276

EMIL: Ay, ay! O, lay me by my mistress' side. (*Exit* IAGO.)

GRA: He 's gone, but his wife 's kill'd.

MON: 'T is a notorious villain. Take you this weapon
Which I have here recover'd from the Moor: 280
Come, guard the door without; let him not pass,
But kill him rather. I 'll after that same villain,
For 't is a damned slave. (*Exeunt* MONTANO *and* GRATIANO.)

OTH: I am not valiant neither,
But every puny whipster gets my sword.   285
But why should honour outlive honesty?
Let it go all.

EMIL: What did thy song bode, lady?
Hark, canst thou hear me? I will play the swan,
And die in music. (*Singing.*) "Willow, willow, willow!"—   290
Moor, she was chaste; she lov'd thee, cruel Moor;
So come my soul to bliss, as I speak true;
So speaking as I think, alas, I die. (*Dies.*)

OTH: I have another weapon in this chamber;
It was a sword of Spain, the ice-brook's temper,—   295
O, here it is. Uncle, I must come forth.

GRA: (*Within.*) If thou attempt it, it will cost thee dear:

---

274. *stones,* it was thought that thunder was accompanied by a stone or bolt from heaven.

285. *whipster,* stripling, lit., boy who whips a top.

295. *ice-brook's temper,* tempered in icy water.

Thou hast no weapon, and perforce must suffer.

OTH:　　Look in upon me then and speak with me,

Or, naked as I am, I will assault thee.　　　　　　　　　　300

Re-enter GRATIANO.

GRA:　　What is the matter?

OTH:　　　　　　　Behold, I have a weapon;

A better never did itself sustain

Upon a soldier's thigh. I have seen the day　　　　　　305

That, with this little arm this good sword,

I have made my way through more impediments

Than twenty times your stop. But, O vain boast!

Who can control his fate? 't is not so now.

Be not afraid though you do see me weapon'd;　　　　　310

Here is my journey's end, here is my butt

And very sea-mark of my utmost sail.

Do you go back dismay'd? 'T is a lost fear;

Man but a rush against Othello's breast

And he retires. Where should Othello go?　　　　　　315

Now, how dost thou look now? O ill-starr'd wench!

Pale as thy smock! when we shall meet at compt,

This look of thine will hurl my soul from heaven,

And fiends will snatch at it. Cold, cold, my girl!

Even like thy chastity. O cursed, cursed slave!　　　　320

Whip me, ye devils,

From the possession of this heavenly sight!

Blow me about in winds! roast me in sulphur!

Wash me in steep-down gulfs of liquid fire!

O Desdemona, Desdemona! dead!　　　　　　　　　　325

Oh! Oh! Oh!

Enter LODOVICO, MONTANO, CASSIO *carried in a chair, and* OFFICERS, *with* IAGO *prisoner.*

LOD:　　Where is this rash and most unfortunate man?

OTH:　　That 's he that was Othello; here I am.

LOD:　　Where is that viper? Bring the villain forth.

---

300. *naked,* unarmed.

308. *your stop,* your power to stop me.

311. *butt,* goal.

312. *sea-mark,* beacon, limit.

317. *compt,* reckoning, i.e., the Day of Judgment.

OTH: I look down towards his feet; but that 's a fable.   330
If that thou be'st a devil, I cannot kill thee. (*Wounds* IAGO.)
LOD: Wrench his sword from him.
IAGO: I bleed, sir; but not kill'd.
OTH: I am not sorry neither. I 'd have thee live;
For, in my sense, 't is happiness to die.   335
LOD: O thou Othello, that wert once so good,
Fallen in the practice of a cursed slave,
What shall be said to thee?
OTH: Why, anything.
An honourable murderer, if you will;   340
For nought did I in hate, but all in honour.
LOD: This wretch hath part confess'd his villainy.
Did you and he consent in Cassio's death?
OTH: Ay.
CAS: Dear General, I never gave you cause.   345
OTH: I do believe it, and I ask your pardon.
Will you, I pray, demand that demi-devil
Why he hath thus ensnar'd my soul and body?
IAGO: Demand me nothing; what you know, you know.
From this time forth I never will speak word.   350
LOD: What, not to pray?
GRA: Torments will ope your lips.
OTH: Well, thou dost best.
LOD: Sir, you shall understand what hath befall'n,
Which, as I think, you know not. Here is a letter   355
Found in the pocket of the slain Roderigo,
And here another. The one of them imports
The death of Cassio to be undertook
By Roderigo.
OTH: O villain!   360
CAS: Most heathenish and most gross!
LOD: Now here 's another discontented paper,
Found in his pocket too; and this, it seems,
Roderigo meant t' have sent this damned villain;
But that belike Iago in the interim   365
Came in and satisfi'd him.
OTH: O thou pernicious caitiff!—

---

330. *I look . . . feet*, i.e., to see if they are cloven like the Devil's.
337. *in the practice*, into the power of the stratagems.
343. *consent in*, conspire together.
362. *discontented*, expressing dissatisfaction.

How came you, Cassio, by that handkerchief
That was my wife's?
CAS: I found it in my chamber;   370
And he himself confess'd but even now
That there he dropp'd it for a special purpose
Which wrought to his desire.
OTH: O fool! fool! fool!
CAS: There is besides in Roderigo's letter,   375
How he upbraids Iago, that he made him
Brave me upon the watch, whereon it came
That I was cast; and even but now he spake,
After long seeming dead, Iago hurt him,
Iago set him on.   380
LOD: You must forsake this room, and go with us.
Your power and your command is taken off,
And Cassio rules in Cyprus. For this slave,
If there be any cunning cruelty   .
That can torment him much and hold him long,   385
It shall be his. You shall close prisoner rest,
Till that the nature of your fault be known
To the Venetian state. Come, bring away.
OTH: Soft you; a word or two before you go.
I have done the state some service, and they know 't.   390
No more of that. I pray you, in your letters,
When you shall these unlucky deeds relate,
Speak of me as I am; nothing extenuate,
Nor set down aught in malice. Then must you speak
Of one that lov'd not wisely but too well;   395
Of one not easily jealous, but being wrought
Perplex'd in the extreme; of one whose hand,
Like the base Indian, threw a pearl away
Richer than all his tribe; of one whose subdued eyes,
Albeit unused to the melting mood,   400
Drops tears as fast as the Arabian trees
Their medicinal gum. Set you down this;
And say besides, that in Aleppo once,
Where a malignant and a turban'd Turk
Beat a Venetian and traduc'd the state,   405

---

382. *taken off*, removed.
397. *Perplex'd*, distraught.
398. *base Indian*, i.e., who through ignorance despises jewels.
403. *Aleppo*, a Syrian town where Venice had special trading privileges.

I took by th' throat the circumcised dog,
And smote him, thus. (*Stabs himself.*)
LOD: O bloody period!
GRA: All that 's spoke is marr'd.
OTH: I kiss'd thee ere I kill'd thee: no way but this,   410
Killing myself, to die upon a kiss. (*Falls on the bed, and dies.*)
CAS: This did I fear, but thought he had no weapon;
For he was great of heart.
LOD: (*To* IAGO.) O Spartan dog,
More fell than anguish, hunger, or the sea!   415
Look on the tragic loading of this bed;
This is thy work. The object poisons sight;
Let it be hid. Gratiano, keep the house,
And seize upon the fortunes of the Moor,
For they succeed on you. To you, lord governor,   420
Remains the censure of this hellish villain;
The time, the place, the torture. O, enforce it!
Myself will straight aboard; and to the state
This heavy act with heavy heart relate. (*Exeunt.*)

STUDY AND DISCUSSION QUESTIONS

1.   (Act I) What is the purpose of the dialogue between Roderigo and
     Iago? How does Iago feel about Othello? What function does
     Brabantio serve? What is the significance of the scene in the coun-
     cil chamber? What logic does Iago use to attain Roderigo's serv-
     ices?

2.   (Act II) The critic Alvin Kernan suggests that the change in setting
     from Venice to Cyprus emphasizes a change "from organized so-
     ciety to a condition much closer to raw nature, and from collective
     life to the life of the solitary individual." What is the society like
     in Venice? In Cyprus? What individuals seem to be particularly
     affected by this geographical change? Is there any significance in
     the fact that Othello is a Moor? Does the storm at the beginning

---

408. *period*, end.
414. *Spartan dog*, bloodhound.
419. *seize upon*, take legal possession of.
421. *censure*, legal sentence.

of this act have any symbolic significance? Why is Iago so successful in his manipulation of Cassio?

3. (Act III) Many critics feel that the central crisis of the play occurs in this act. Point out specifically the scene and the lines which lead them to this conclusion. What is the basis of Othello's breakdown? What purpose does Emilia serve? What are the mystical and symbolic functions of the handkerchief? What role do these functions play in characterizing Othello? What is the dramatic role of Bianca?

4. (Act IV) Winifred M. T. Notwottny ("Justice and Love in *Othello*") says, "it is in Act IV that the nature of the action affords indisputable proof that Shakespeare has in this play a unified design . . . that satisfactorily explains Shakespeare's choice of episodes." Trace the events in the fourth act that show the conflict that exists in Othello's mind.

5. (Act V) Is there a change in Othello's character from the fourth to the fifth acts? If so, what causes this change? What is meant by Othello's comment, "Then must you speak / Of one that lov'd not wisely but too well."?

6. One way of revealing character is through the imagery associated with it. Wolfgang H. Clemen (*The Development of Shakespeare's Imagery*) suggests that one "consider the subject matter of the images, and ask whether the objects and themes occurring in the imagery stand in a significant relation to the character of the person using the image." Do the images contained in the lines of Iago and Othello generally refer to themselves? What are the objects they name frequently? What do these images and objects suggest about the respective characters?

7. *Othello* is among the most carefully constructed of Shakespeare's plays. One element of the construction is the balancing of characters through either similarity or contrast. Discuss some characters that seem parallel or contrasted. What is the purpose of this technique?

8. There have been a great many interpretations of Iago's role in the play. For example, E. E. Stoll (*Othello: Tragedy of Effect*) sees Iago as Fate or the Devil, while Coleridge ("The Motiveless Villain") thinks of Iago as a "preconceiving experimenter, a passionless character" who uses "moral feelings and qualities only as prudential ends to means." Blanche Cole (*Shakespeare's Four Giants*) suggests

that Iago has a "psychopathic personality." Still another view by William Hazlitt (*"Othello* as Tragedy and the Character of Iago") places Iago in a "class of characters, common to Shakespeare and at the same time particular to him; whose heads are as acute and active as their hearts are hard and callous." Discuss these four views in relation to your own interpretation of Iago's role.

9. Like Iago, Othello's character has been the object of much critical writing. A. C. Bradley (*Shakespearian Tragedy*) says, "Othello is, in one sense of the word, by far the most romantic figure among Shakespeare's heroes; and he is so partly from the strange life of war and adventure which he has lived from childhood. He is not merely a romantic figure; his own nature is romantic." Leo Kirschbaum (*English Literary History*) feels that Othello is a very noble puppet who evinces no psychological consistency in his passage from love to sudden jealousy and who must fall because of the dramatic device that everyone trusts the villain. Robert B. Heilman (*Magic in the Web: Action and Language in Othello*) says, "Othello is the least heroic of Shakespeare's tragic heroes." Discuss these comments in light of your own understanding of Othello's character.

10. Discuss through comparison and contrast the following themes and techniques of *Othello* and *Romeo and Juliet:* (a) the use of dramatic irony, (b) the characteristics of love that are common to both plays, (c) the antagonistic forces, (d) the use of imagery, (e) the use of society.

WRITING TOPICS

1. Write an essay defining the character of either Othello or Iago (analyze their personalities in terms of action, thoughts, and imagery). *Or* write an essay explaining the dramatic function of the minor characters in *Othello.*
acters in *Othello.*

2. There are several possible themes in the play. Choose one of the following (or one of your own) and develop it into an essay: (a) organized society vs. nature, (b) love and justice, (c) the rational vs. the irrational.

3. Harold C. Goddard (*The Meaning of Shakespeare*) suggests that *Othello* is a play about war. Write an essay developing this thesis in relation to the characters and the action.

4. Write an essay analyzing the use Shakespeare makes of dramatic irony or imagery in *Othello*. If you have read *Romeo and Juliet* or one of Sophocles' plays, compare or contrast the uses of one of these techniques.

5. In *Oedipus* and *Othello* the protagonists come to understand the nature of their actions through an ordeal of self-knowledge. Write an essay explaining the revelation of self-knowledge in *Othello* and *Oedipus* as a characteristic experience of the tragic hero. *Or* write an essay comparing the use of Fate in *Romeo and Juliet* with that in *Othello*, or the use of Fate in *Oedipus* with that in *Othello*.

Ibsen

Contemporary drama—and tragedy in particular—is so radically different from anything written in the past that it requires a considerable adjustment of the old set of standards for critical judgment (by contemporary we intend the drama from approximately 1850 to the present). There are many critics who maintain that ours is one of the great ages of dramatic art, and they point to the extensiveness, variety, and durability of modern drama as evidence of its vitality. On the other hand, a critic of the stature of Joseph Wood Krutch can find in modern tragedy only a reflection of all that is base and mean in modern life. Before he can arrive at his own judgment, the reader must understand something of the physical aspects of the theater and the intellectual trends that have influenced the leading dramatists of the contemporary period.

Since the middle of the nineteenth century the stage has undergone the several changes that have resulted in what we call our picture-frame stage. The forestage of the Elizabethan theater has disappeared. Modern lighting techniques contribute to the picture-frame impression, into which the actor fits as though he were a segment of the picture. The visual illusion created is highly effective, but the actors now are removed from close contact with the audience. During a performance they appear to be going about their business oblivious of the presence of the audience, and a gulf exists between them and the spectators.

The importance of this gulf cannot be overestimated. Now the audience observes the drama with a certain detachment, where it once had participated more intimately in the action of the play. The playwright is unlikely ever to employ the soliloquy or the aside, for his characters can no longer easily take the audience into their confidence. With the increasing stress on "natural" behavior on stage, occasioned at least in part by the physical layout of the theater, much of the high-sounding rhetoric of the older verse drama has given way to a colloquial, if often artful, prose.

"Natural behavior" is merely another way of saying realism or fidelity to fact. This quality above all, was the goal of the dramatists of the late nineteenth century. There are numerous reasons for the drift toward realism and all of them are associated with the intellectual climate of the time. Virtually every facet of modern culture, from politics to sociology, found its way into the drama. As a result, playwrights began to work with subjects and ideas taken from the everyday lives of their audience. Even more significant was the influence of the scientific temper. The scientific frame of mind had already left its mark on the naturalistic novel of the last half of the nineteenth century, and the dramatist learned from the fiction writer to seek for greater verisimilitude, naturalness, and attention to precise detail. ·

Realism manifested itself in several clearly recognizable traits in modern drama. As mentioned above, poetry was largely replaced by prose dialogue, and most dramatists felt that prose was a proper medium for exalted as well as comic emotions. In the interest of creating more realistic background and characterization, playwrights began to provide elaborate stage directions for their plays. The audience could not, of course, benefit directly from this authorial description and comment, but the effect on the production was often notable and the play reader benefited immensely. The playwright himself began to adopt an objective stance toward his material. Influenced by the cool "distance" of the scientist, he avoided moral judgments of any sort and treated his characters with a matter-of-fact detachment. Finally, the subject matter of modern drama came increasingly to center upon social problems. Many dramatists accepted the doctrine that character is to a great extent the product of social factors, and in their plays they began probing those social and environmental causes of human behavior and, by extension, of the human condition.

Modern drama, then, deals most often with the common man and his environment; modern tragedy with his sense of isolation in a world without apparent purpose or meaning. There is none of the heroic grandeur of the Greeks or Elizabethans here, but there is perhaps a closer touch with whatever may be deemed heroic in everyday life.

Ibsen (1828-1906): A Biographical Note. Henrik Ibsen was born in a small town in southern Norway. His once prosperous parents lost their money when he was a boy, and at sixteen he was apprenticed to an apothecary for a long and tedious five years. Later he made his way to the capital, and the following year became director of a little theater in Bergen. As part of his contract, he wrote a play a year, and in this fashion his theatrical career began. That career can be divided roughly into three periods: romantic drama, 1850-1873; realistic drama, 1877-1890; and symbolist-drama, 1888-1899. Ibsen's realistic drama brought him international fame, and he is best known today for the plays written during that period.

GHOSTS

Henrik Ibsen
Translated from the Norwegian by William Archer

Characters

MRS. HELEN ALVING, *widow of Captain Alving, late Chamberlain to the King.*
OSWALD ALVING, *her son, a painter.*
PASTOR MANDERS.
JACOB ENGSTRAND, *a carpenter.*
REGINA ENGSTRAND, *Mrs. Alving's maid.*

The action takes place at Mrs. Alving's country house, beside one of the large fjords in Western Norway.

ACT I

A spacious garden-room, with one door to the left, and two doors to the right. In the middle of the room a round table, with chairs about it. On the table lie books, periodicals, and newspapers. In the foreground to the left a window, and by it a small sofa, with a work-table in front of it. In the background, the room is con-

Ghosts is reprinted with the permission of Charles Scribner's Sons from Volume VII of *The Collected Works of Henrik Ibsen*, translated by William Archer (1906, 1907).

tinued into a somewhat narrower conservatory, the walls of which are formed by large panes of glass. In the right-hand wall of the conservatory is a door leading down into the garden. Through the glass wall a gloomy fjord-landscape is faintly visible, veiled by steady rain. ENGSTRAND, *the carpenter, who has a club foot, stands by the garden door. His left leg is somewhat bent; he has a clump of wood under the sole of his boot.* REGINA, *with an empty garden syringe in her hand, hinders him from advancing.*

REGINA: (*In a low voice*) What do you want? Stop where you are. You're positively dripping.

ENGSTRAND: It's the Lord's own rain, my girl.

REGINA: It's the devil's rain, *I* say.

ENGSTRAND: Lord, how you talk, Regina. (*Limps a step or two forward into the room*) It's just this as I wanted to say—

REGINA: Don't clatter so with that foot of yours, I tell you! The young master's asleep upstairs.

ENGSTRAND: Asleep? In the middle of the day?

REGINA: It's no business of yours.

ENGSTRAND: I was out on the loose last night—

REGINA: I can quite believe that.

ENGSTRAND: Yes, we're weak vessels, we poor mortals, my girl—

REGINA: So it seems.

ENGSTRAND: —and temptations are manifold in this world, you see. But all the same, I was hard at work, God knows, at half-past five this morning.

REGINA: Very well; only be off now. I won't stop here and have *rendezvous* with you.

ENGSTRAND: What do you say you won't have?

REGINA: I won't have any one find you here; so just you go about your business.

ENGSTRAND: (*Advances a step or two*) Blest if I go before I've had a talk with you. This afternoon I shall have finished my work at the school-house, and then I shall take to-night's boat and be off home to the town.

REGINA: (*Mutters*) Pleasant journey to you!

ENGSTRAND: Thank you, my child. To-morrow the Orphanage is to be opened, and then there'll be fine doings, no doubt, and plenty of intoxicating drink going, you know. And nobody shall say of Jacob Engstrand that he can't keep out of temptation's way.

REGINA: Oh!

ENGSTRAND: You see, there's to be heaps of grand folks here to-morrow. Pastor Manders is expected from town, too.

REGINA: He's coming to-day.

ENGSTRAND: There, you see! And I should be cursedly sorry if he found out anything against me, don't you understand?

REGINA: Oho! is that your game?

ENGSTRAND: Is what my game?

REGINA: (*Looking hard at him*) What are you going to fool Pastor Manders into doing, this time?

ENGSTRAND: Sh! sh! Are you crazy? Do *I* want to fool Pastor Manders? Oh no! Pastor Manders has been far too good a friend to me for that. But I just wanted to say, you know—that I mean to be off home again to-night.

REGINA: The sooner the better, say I.

ENGSTRAND: Yes, but I want you with me, Regina.

REGINA: (*Open-mouthed*) You want me—? What are you talking about?

ENGSTRAND: I want you to come home with me, I say.

REGINA: (*Scornfully*) Never in this world shall you get me home with you.

ENGSTRAND: Oh, we'll see about that.

REGINA: Yes, you may be sure we'll see about it! Me, that have been brought up by a lady like Mrs. Alving! Me, that am treated almost as a daughter here! Is it me you want to go home with you?—to a house like yours? For shame!

ENGSTRAND: What the devil do you mean? Do you set yourself up against your father, you hussy?

REGINA: (*Mutters without looking at him*) You've said often enough I was no concern of yours.

ENGSTRAND: Pooh! Why should you bother about that—

REGINA: Haven't you many a time sworn at me and called me a—? *Fi donc!*

ENGSTRAND: Curse me, now, if ever I used such an ugly word.

REGINA: Oh, I remember very well what word you used.

ENGSTRAND: Well, but that was only when I was a bit on with drink. Temptations are manifold in this world, Regina.

REGINA: Ugh!

ENGSTRAND: And besides, it was when your mother was that aggravating—I had to find something to twit her with, my child. She was always setting up for a fine lady. (*Mimics*) "Let me go, Engstrand; let me be. Remember I was three years in Chamberlain Alving's family at Rosenvold." (*Laughs*) Mercy on us! She could never forget that the Captain was made a Chamberlain while she was in service here.

REGINA: Poor mother! you very soon tormented her into her grave.

ENGSTRAND: (*With a twist of his shoulders*) Oh, of course! I'm to have the blame for everything.

REGINA: (*Turns away; half aloud*) Ugh—! And that leg too!

ENGSTRAND: What do you say, my child?

REGINA: *Pied de mouton.*

ENGSTRAND: Is that English, eh?

REGINA: Yes.

ENGSTRAND: Ay, ay; you've picked up some learning out here; and that may come in useful now, Regina.

REGINA: (*After a short silence*) What do you want with me in town?

ENGSTRAND: Can you ask what a father wants with his only child? A'n't I a lonely, forlorn widower?

REGINA: Oh, don't try on any nonsense like that with me! Why do you want me?

ENGSTRAND: Well, let me tell you, I've been thinking of setting up in a new line of business.

REGINA: (*Contemptuously*) You've tried that often enough, and much good you've done with it.

ENGSTRAND: Yes, but this time you shall see, Regina! Devil take me—

REGINA: (*Stamps*) Stop your swearing!

ENGSTRAND: Hush, hush; you're right enough there, my girl. What I wanted to say was just this—I've laid by a very tidy pile from this Orphanage job.

REGINA: Have you? That's a good thing for you.

ENGSTRAND: What can a man spend his ha'pence on here in this country hole?

REGINA: Well, what then?

ENGSTRAND: Why, you see, I thought of putting the money into some paying speculation. I thought of a sort of a sailor's tavern—

REGINA: Pah!

ENGSTRAND: A regular high-class affair, of course; not any sort of pig-sty for common sailors. No! damn it! it would be for captains and mates, and—and—regular swells, you know.

REGINA: And I was to—?

ENGSTRAND: You were to help, to be sure. Only for the look of the thing, you understand. Devil a bit of hard work shall you have, my girl. You shall do exactly what you like.

REGINA: Oh, indeed!

ENGSTRAND: But there must be a petticoat in the house; that's as clear as daylight. For I want to have it a bit lively-like in the evenings, with singing and dancing, and so on. You must remember they're weary wanderers on the ocean of life. (*Nearer*) Now don't be a fool and stand in your own light, Regina. What's to become of you out here? Your mistress has given you a lot of learning; but what good is that to you? You're to look after the children at the new Orphanage, I hear. Is that the sort of thing for you, eh? Are you so dead set on wearing your life out for a pack of dirty brats?

REGINA: No; if things go as I want them to—Well there's no saying— there's no saying.

ENGSTRAND: What do you mean by "there's no saying"?

REGINA: Never you mind.—How much money have you saved?

ENGSTRAND: What with one thing and another, a matter of seven or eight hundred crowns.

REGINA: That's not so bad.

ENGSTRAND: It's enough to make a start with, my girl.

REGINA: Aren't you thinking of giving me any?

ENGSTRAND: No, I'm blest if I am!

REGINA: Not even of sending me a scrap of stuff for a new dress?

ENGSTRAND: Come to town with me, my lass, and you'll soon get dresses enough.

REGINA: Pooh! I can do that on my own account, if I want to.

ENGSTRAND: No, a father's guiding hand is what you want, Regina. Now, I've got my eye on a capital house in Little Harbour Street. They don't want much ready-money; and it could be a sort of a Sailors' Home, you know.

REGINA: But I will not live with you! I have nothing whatever to do with you. Be off!

ENGSTRAND: You wouldn't stop long with me, my girl. No such luck! If you knew how to play your cards, such a fine figure of a girl as you've grown in the last year or two—

REGINA: Well?

ENGSTRAND: You'd soon get hold of some mate—or maybe even a captain—

REGINA: I won't marry any one of that sort. Sailors have no *savoir vivre*.

ENGSTRAND: What's that they haven't got?

REGINA: I know what sailors are, I tell you. They're not the sort of people to marry.

ENGSTRAND: Then never mind about marrying them. You can make it pay all the same. (*More confidential*) He—the Englishman—the man with the yacht—he came down with three hundred dollars, he did; and she wasn't a bit handsomer than you.

REGINA: (*Making for him*) Out you go!

ENGSTRAND: (*Falling back*) Come, come! You're not going to hit me, I hope.

REGINA: Yes, if you begin talking about mother I shall hit you. Get away with you, I say! (*Drives him back towards the garden door*) And don't slam the doors. Young Mr. Alving—

ENGSTRAND: He's asleep; I know. You're mightily taken up about young Mr. Alving—(*More softly*) Oho! you don't mean to say it's him as—?

REGINA: Be off this minute! You're crazy, I tell you! No, not that way. There comes Pastor Manders. Down the kitchen stairs with you.

ENGSTRAND: (*Towards the right*) Yes, yes, I'm going. But just you talk to him as is coming there. He's the man to tell you what a child owes its father. For I am your father all the same, you know. I can prove it from the church register.

> *He goes out through the second door to the right, which* REGINA *has opened, and closes again after him.* REGINA *glances hastily at herself in the mirror, dusts herself with her pocket handkerchief, and settles her necktie; then she busies herself with the flowers.* PASTOR MANDERS, *wearing an overcoat, carrying an umbrella, and with a small travelling-bag on a strap over his shoulder, comes through the garden door into the conservatory.*

MANDERS: Good-morning, Miss Engstrand.

REGINA: (*Turning round, surprised and pleased*) No, really! Good-morning, Pastor Manders. Is the steamer in already?

MANDERS: It is just in. (*Enters the sitting-room*) Terrible weather we have been having lately.

REGINA: (*Follows him*) It's such blessed weather for the country, sir.

MANDERS: No doubt; you are quite right. We townspeople give too little thought to that. (*He begins to take off his overcoat*)

REGINA: Oh, mayn't I help you?—There! Why, how wet it is? I'll just hang it up in the hall. And your umbrella, too—I'll open it and let it dry.

> *She goes out with the things through the second door on the right.* PASTOR MANDERS *takes off his travelling-bag and lays it and his hat on a chair. Meanwhile* REGINA *comes in again.*

MANDERS: Ah, it's a comfort to get under cover. I hope everything is going on well here?

REGINA: Yes, thank you, sir.

MANDERS: You have your hands full, I suppose, in preparation for to-morrow?

REGINA: Yes, there's plenty to do, of course.

MANDERS: And Mrs. Alving is at home, I trust?

REGINA: Oh dear, yes. She's just upstairs, looking after the young master's chocolate.

MANDERS: Yes, by-the-bye—I heard down at the pier that Oswald had arrived.

REGINA: Yes, he came the day before yesterday. We didn't expect him before to-day.

MANDERS: Quite strong and well, I hope?

REGINA: Yes, thank you, quite; but dreadfully tired with the journey. He has made one rush right through from Paris—the whole way on one train, I believe. He's sleeping a little now, I think; so perhaps we'd better talk a little quietly.

MANDERS: Sh!—as quietly as you please.

REGINA: (*Arranging an arm-chair beside the table.*) Now, do sit down, Pastor Manders, and make yourself comfortable. (*He sits down; she places a footstool under his feet.*) There! Are you comfortable now, sir?

MANDERS: Thanks, thanks, extremely so. (*Looks at her*) Do you know, Miss Engstrand, I positively believe you have grown since I last saw you.

REGINA: Do you think so, sir? Mrs. Alving says I've filled out too.

MANDERS: Filled out? Well, perhaps a little; just enough. (*Short pause*)

REGINA: Shall I tell Mrs. Alving you are here?

MANDERS: Thanks, thanks, there is no hurry, my dear child.—By-the-bye, Regina, my good girl, tell me: how is your father getting on out here?

REGINA: Oh, thank you, sir, he's getting on well enough.

MANDERS: He called upon me last time he was in town.

REGINA: Did he, indeed? He's always so glad of a chance of talking to you, sir.

MANDERS: And you often look in upon him at his work, I daresay?

REGINA: I? Oh, of course, when I have time, I—

MANDERS: Your father is not a man of strong character, Miss Engstrand. He stands terribly in need of a guiding hand.

REGINA: Oh, yes; I daresay he does.

MANDERS: He requires some one near him whom he cares for, and whose judgment he respects. He frankly admitted as much when he last came to see me.

REGINA: Yes, he mentioned something of the sort to me. But I don't know whether Mrs. Alving can spare me; especially now that we've got the new Orphanage to attend to. And then I should be so sorry to leave Mrs. Alving; she has always been so kind to me.

MANDERS: But a daughter's duty, my good girl—Of course, we should first have to get your mistress's consent.

REGINA: But I don't know whether it would be quite proper for me, at my age, to keep house for a single man.

MANDERS: What! My dear Miss Engstrand! When the man is your own father!

REGINA: Yes, that may be; but all the same—Now, if it were in a thoroughly nice house, and with a real gentleman—

MANDERS: Why, my dear Regina—

REGINA: —one I could love and respect, and be a daughter to—

MANDERS: Yes, but my dear, good child—

REGINA: Then I should be glad to go to town. It's very lonely out here; you know yourself, sir, what it is to be alone in the world. And I can assure you I'm both quick and willing. Don't you know of any such place for me, sir?

MANDERS: I? No, certainly not.

REGINA: But, dear, dear sir, do remember me if—

MANDERS: (*Rising*) Yes, yes, certainly, Miss Engstrand.

REGINA: For if I—

MANDERS: Will you be so good as to tell your mistress I am here?

REGINA: I will, at once, sir. (*She goes out to the left*)

MANDERS: (*Paces the room two or three times, stands a moment in the background with his hands behind his back, and looks out over the garden. Then he returns to the table, takes up a book, and looks at the title-page; starts, and looks at several books*) Ha—indeed!

MRS. ALVING *enters by the door on the left; she is followed by* REGINA, *who immediately goes out by the first door on the right.*

MRS. ALVING: (*Holds out her hand*) Welcome, my dear Pastor.

MANDERS: How do you do, Mrs. Alving? Here I am as I promised.

MRS. ALVING: Always punctual to the minute.

MANDERS: You may believe it was not so easy for me to get away. With all the Boards and Committees I belong to—

MRS. ALVING: That makes it all the kinder of you to come so early. Now we can get through our business before dinner. But where is your portmanteau?

MANDERS: (*Quickly*) I left it down at the inn. I shall sleep there to-night.

MRS. ALVING: (*Suppressing a smile*) Are you really not to be persuaded, even now, to pass the night under my roof?

MANDERS: No, no, Mrs. Alving; many thanks. I shall stay at the inn, as usual. It is so conveniently near the landing-stage.

MRS. ALVING: Well, you must have your own way. But I really should have thought we two old people—

MANDERS: Now you are making fun of me. Ah, you're naturally in great spirits to-day—what with to-morrow's festival and Oswald's return.

MRS. ALVING: Yes; you can think what a delight it is to me! It's more than two years since he was home last. And now he has promised to stay with me all the winter.

MANDERS: Has he really? That is very nice and dutiful of him. For I can well believe that life in Rome and Paris has very different attractions from any we can offer here.

MRS. ALVING: Ah, but here he has his mother, you see. My own darling boy—he hasn't forgotten his old mother!

MANDERS: It would be grievous indeed, if absence and absorption in art and that sort of thing were to blunt his natural feelings.

MRS. ALVING: Yes, you may well say so. But there's nothing of that sort to fear with him. I'm quite curious to see whether you know him again. He'll be down presently; he's upstairs just now, resting a little on the sofa. But do sit down, my dear Pastor.

MANDERS: Thank you. Are you quite at liberty—?

MRS. ALVING: Certainly. (*She sits by the table*)

MANDERS: Very well. Then let me show you— (*He goes to the chair where his travelling-bag lies, takes out a packet of papers, sits down on the opposite side of the table, and tries to find a clear space for the papers.*) Now, to begin with, here is— (*Breaking off*) Tell me, Mrs. Alving, how do these books come to be here?

MRS. ALVING: These books? They are books I am reading.

MANDERS: Do you read this sort of literature?

MRS. ALVING: Certainly I do.

MANDERS: Do you feel better or happier for such reading?

MRS. ALVING: I feel, so to speak, more secure.

MANDERS: That is strange. How do you mean?

MRS. ALVING: Well, I seem to find explanation and confirmation of all sorts of things I myself have been thinking. For that is the wonderful part of it, Pastor Manders—there is really nothing new in these books, nothing but what most people think and believe. Only most people either don't formulate it to themselves, or else keep quiet about it.

MANDERS: Great heavens! Do you really believe that most people—?

MRS. ALVING: I do, indeed.

MANDERS: But surely not in this country? Not here among us?

MRS. ALVING: Yes, certainly; here as elsewhere.

MANDERS: Well, I really must say—!

MRS. ALVING: For the rest, what do you object to in these books?

MANDERS: Object to in them? You surely do not suppose that I have nothing better to do than to study such publications as these?

MRS. ALVING: That is to say, you know nothing of what you are condemning?

MANDERS: I have read enough about these writings to disapprove of them.

MRS. ALVING: Yes; but your own judgment—

MANDERS: My dear Mrs. Alving, there are many occasions in life when one must rely upon others. Things are so ordered in this world; and it is well that they are. Otherwise, what would become of society?

MRS. ALVING: Well, well, I daresay you're right there.

MANDERS: Besides, I of course do not deny that there may be much that is attractive in such books. Nor can I blame you for wishing to keep up with the intellectual movements that are said to be going on in the great world—where you have let your son pass so much of his life. But—

MRS. ALVING: But?

MANDERS: (*Lowering his voice*) But one should not talk about it, Mrs. Alving. One is certainly not bound to account to everybody for what one reads and thinks within one's own four walls.

MRS. ALVING: Of course not; I quite agree with you.

MANDERS: Only think, now, how you are bound to consider the interests of this Orphanage, which you decided on founding at a time when—if I understand you rightly—you thought very differently on spiritual matters.

MRS. ALVING: Oh, yes; I quite admit that. But it was about the Orphanage—

MANDERS: It was about the Orphanage we were to speak; yes. All I say is: prudence, my dear lady! And now let us get to business. (*Opens the packet, and takes out a number of papers*) Do you see these?

MRS. ALVING: The documents?

MANDERS: All—and in perfect order. I can tell you it was hard work to get them in time. I had to put on strong pressure. The authorities are almost morbidly scrupulous when there is any decisive step to be taken. But here they are at last. (*Looks through the bundle*) See! here is the formal deed of gift of the parcel of ground known as Solvik in the Manor of Rosenvold, with all the newly constructed buildings, schoolrooms, master's house, and chapel. And here is the legal fiat for the endowment and for the By-laws of the Institution. Will you look at them? (*Reads*) "By-laws for the Children's Home to be known as 'Captain Alving's Foundation.'"

MRS. ALVING: (*Looks long at the paper*) So there it is.

MANDERS: I have chosen the designation "Captain" rather than "Chamberlain." "Captain" looks less pretentious.

MRS. ALVING: Oh, yes; just as you think best.

MANDERS: And here you have the Bank Account of the capital lying at interest to cover the current expenses of the Orphanage.

MRS. ALVING: Thank you; but please keep it—it will be more convenient.

MANDERS: With pleasure. I think we will leave the money in the Bank for the present. The interest is certainly not what we could wish—four per cent, and six months' notice of withdrawal. If a good mortgage could be found later on—of course it must be a first mortgage and an unimpeachable security—then we could consider the matter.

MRS. ALVING: Certainly, my dear Pastor Manders. You are the best judge in these things.

MANDERS: I will keep my eyes open at any rate.—But now there is one thing more which I have several times been intending to ask you.

MRS. ALVING: And what is that?

MANDERS: Shall the Orphanage buildings be insured or not?

MRS. ALVING: Of course they must be insured.

MANDERS: Well, wait a moment, Mrs. Alving. Let us look into the matter a little more closely.

MRS. ALVING: I have everything insured; buildings and movables and stock and crops.

MANDERS: Of course you have—on your own estate. And so have I—of course. But here, you see, it is quite another matter. The Orphanage is to be consecrated, as it were, to a higher purpose.

MRS. ALVING: Yes, but that's no reason—

MANDERS: For my own part, I should certainly not see the smallest impropriety in guarding against all contingencies—

MRS. ALVING: No, I should think not.

MANDERS: But what is the general feeling in the neighbourhood? You, of course, know better than I.

MRS. ALVING: Well—the general feeling—

MANDERS: Is there any considerable number of people—really responsible people—who might be scandalised?

MRS. ALVING: What do you mean by "really responsible people"?

MANDERS: Well, I mean people in such independent and influential positions that one cannot help attaching some weight to their opinions.

MRS. ALVING: There are several people of that sort here, who would very likely be shocked if—

MANDERS: There, you see! In town we have many such people. Think of all my colleagues' adherents! People would be only too ready to interpret our action as a sign that neither you nor I had the right faith in a Higher Providence.

MRS. ALVING: But for your own part, my dear Pastor, you can at least tell yourself that—

MANDERS: Yes, I know—I know; my conscience would be quite easy, that is true enough. But nevertheless we should not escape grave misinterpretation; and that might very likely react unfavourably upon the Orphanage.

MRS. ALVING: Well, in that case—

MANDERS: Nor can I entirely lose sight of the difficult—I may even say painful—position in which *I* might perhaps be placed. In the leading circles of the town, people take a lively interest in this Orphanage. It is, of course, founded partly for the benefit of the town, as well; and it is to be hoped it will, to a considerable extent, result in lightening our Poor Rates. Now, as I have been your adviser, and have had the business arrangements in my hands, I cannot but fear that I may have to bear the brunt of fanaticism—

MRS. ALVING: Oh, you mustn't run the risk of that.

MANDERS: To say nothing of the attacks that would assuredly be made upon me in certain papers and periodicals, which—

MRS. ALVING: Enough, my dear Pastor Manders. That consideration is quite decisive.

MANDERS: Then you do not wish the Orphanage to be insured?

MRS. ALVING: No. We will let it alone.

MANDERS: (*Leaning back in his chair*) But if, now, a disaster were to happen? One can never tell—Should you be able to make good the damage?

MRS. ALVING: No; I tell you plainly I should do nothing of the kind.

MANDERS: Then I must tell you, Mrs. Alving—we are taking no small responsibility upon ourselves.

MRS. ALVING: Do you think we can do otherwise?

MANDERS: No, that is just the point; we really cannot do otherwise. We ought not to expose ourselves to misinterpretation; and we have no right whatever to give offence to the weaker brethren.

MRS. ALVING: You, as a clergyman, certainly should not.

MANDERS: I really think, too, we may trust that such an institution has fortune on its side; in fact, that it stands under a special providence.

MRS. ALVING: Let us hope so, Pastor Manders.

MANDERS: Then we will let it take its chance?

MRS. ALVING: Yes, certainly.

MANDERS: Very well. So be it. (*Makes a note*) Then—no insurance.

MRS. ALVING: It's odd that you should just happen to mention the matter to-day—

MANDERS: I have often thought of asking you about it—

MRS. ALVING: —for we very nearly had a fire down there yesterday.

MANDERS: You don't say so!

MRS. ALVING: Oh, it was a trifling matter. A heap of shavings had caught fire in the carpenter's workshop.

MANDERS: Where Engstrand works?

MRS. ALVING: Yes. They say he's often very careless with matches.

MANDERS: He has so much on his mind, that man—so many things to fight against. Thank God, he is now striving to lead a decent life, I hear.

MRS. ALVING: Indeed! Who says so?

MANDERS: He himself assures me of it. And he is certainly a capital workman.

MRS. ALVING: Oh, yes so long as he's sober—

MANDERS: Ah, that melancholy weakness! But he is often driven to it by his injured leg, he says. Last time he was in town I was really touched by him. He came and thanked me so warmly for having got him work here, so that he might be near Regina.

MRS. ALVING: He doesn't see much of her.

MANDERS: Oh, yes; he has a talk with her every day. He told me so himself.

MRS. ALVING: Well, it may be so.

MANDERS: He feels so acutely that he needs some one to keep a firm hold on him when temptation comes. That is what I cannot help liking about Jacob Engstrand: he comes to you so helplessly, accusing himself and confessing his own weakness. The last time he was talking to me— Believe me, Mrs. Alving, supposing it were a real necessity for him to have Regina home again—

MRS. ALVING: (*Rising hastily*) Regina!

MANDERS: —you must not set yourself against it.

MRS. ALVING: Indeed I shall set myself against it. And besides—Regina is to have a position in the Orphanage.

MANDERS: But, after all, remember he is her father—

MRS. ALVING: Oh, I know very well what sort of a father he has been to her. No! She shall never go to him with my goodwill.

MANDERS: (*Rising*) My dear lady, don't take the matter so warmly. You sadly misjudge poor Engstrand. You seem to be quite terrified—

MRS. ALVING: (*More quietly*) It makes no difference. I have taken Regina into my house, and there she shall stay. (*Listens*) Hush, my dear Mr. Manders; say no more about it. (*Her face lights up with gladness*) Listen! there is Oswald coming downstairs. Now we'll think of no one but him.

OSWALD ALVING, *in a light overcoat, hat in hand, and smoking a large meerschaum, enters by the door on the left; he stops in the doorway.*

OSWALD: Oh, I beg your pardon; I thought you were in the study. (*Comes forward*) Good-morning, Pastor Manders.

MANDERS: (*Staring*) Ah—! How strange—!

MRS. ALVING: Well now, what do you think of him, Mr. Manders?

MANDERS: I—I—can it really be—?

OSWALD: Yes, it's really the Prodigal Son, sir.

MANDERS: (*Protesting*) My dear young friend—

OSWALD: Well, then, the Lost Sheep Found.

MRS. ALVING: Oswald is thinking of the time when you were so much opposed to his becoming a painter.

MANDERS: To our human eyes many a step seems dubious, which afterwards proves—(*Wrings his hand*) But first of all, welcome, welcome home! Do not think, my dear Oswald—I suppose I may call you by your Christian name?

OSWALD: What else should you call me?

MANDERS: Very good. What I wanted to say was this, my dear Oswald —you must not think that I utterly condemn the artist's calling. I have no doubt there are many who can keep their inner self unharmed in that profession, as in any other.

OSWALD: Let us hope so.

MRS. ALVING: (*Beaming with delight*) I know one who has kept both his inner and his outer self unharmed. Just look at him, Mr. Manders.

OSWALD: (*Moves restlessly about the room*) Yes, yes, my dear mother; let's say no more about it.

MANDERS: Why, certainly—that is undeniable. And you have begun to make a name for yourself already. The newspapers have often spoken of you, most favourably. Just lately, by-the-bye, I fancy I haven't seen your name quite so often.

OSWALD: (*Up in the conservatory*) I haven't been able to paint so much lately.

MRS. ALVING: Even a painter needs a little rest now and then.

MANDERS: No doubt, no doubt. And meanwhile he can be preparing himself and mustering his forces for some great work.

OSWALD: Yes.—Mother, will dinner soon be ready?

MRS. ALVING: In less than half an hour. He has a capital appetite, thank God.

MANDERS: And a taste for tobacco, too.

OSWALD: I found my father's pipe in my room—

MANDERS: Aha—then that accounts for it!

MRS. ALVING: For what?

MANDERS: When Oswald appeared there, in the doorway, with the pipe in his mouth, I could have sworn I saw his father, large as life.

OSWALD: No, really?

MRS. ALVING: Oh, how can you say so? Oswald takes after me.

MANDERS: Yes, but there is an expression about the corners of the mouth—something about the lips—that reminds one exactly of Alving: at any rate, now that he is smoking.

MRS. ALVING: Not in the least. Oswald has rather a clerical curve about his mouth, I think.

MANDERS: Yes, yes; some of my colleagues have much the same expression.

MRS. ALVING: But put your pipe away, my dear boy; I won't have smoking in here.

OSWALD: (*Does so*) By all means. I only wanted to try it; for I once smoked it when I was a child.

MRS. ALVING: You?

OSWALD: Yes. I was quite small at the time. I recollect I came up to father's room one evening when he was in great spirits.

MRS. ALVING: Oh, you can't recollect anything of those times.

OSWALD: Yes, I recollect it distinctly. He took me on his knee, and gave me the pipe. "Smoke, boy," he said; "smoke away, boy!" And I smoked as hard as I could, until I felt I was growing quite pale, and the perspiration stood in great drops on my forehead. Then he burst out laughing heartily—

MANDERS: That was most extraordinary.

MRS. ALVING: My dear friend, it's only something Oswald has dreamt.

OSWALD: No, mother, I assure you I didn't dream it. For—don't you remember this?—you came and carried me out into the nursery. Then I was sick, and I saw that you were crying.—Did father often play such practical jokes?

MANDERS: In his youth he overflowed with the joy of life—

OSWALD: And yet he managed to do so much in the world; so much that was good and useful; although he died so early.

MANDERS: Yes, you have inherited the name of an energetic and admirable man, my dear Oswald Alving. No doubt it will be an incentive to you—

OSWALD: It ought to, indeed.

MANDERS: It was good of you to come home for the ceremony in his honour.

OSWALD: I could do no less for my father.

MRS. ALVING: And I am to keep him so long! That is the best of all.

MANDERS: You are going to pass the winter at home, I hear.

OSWALD: My stay is indefinite, sir.—But, ah! it is good to be at home!

MRS. ALVING: *(Beaming)* Yes, isn't it, dear?

MANDERS: *(Looking sympathetically at him)* You went out into the world early, my dear Oswald.

OSWALD: I did. I sometimes wonder whether it wasn't too early.

MRS. ALVING: Oh, not at all. A healthy lad is all the better for it; especially when he's an only child. He oughtn't to hang on at home with his mother and father, and get spoilt.

MANDERS: That's a very disputable point, Mrs. Alving. A child's proper place is, and must be, the home of his fathers.

OSWALD: There I quite agree with you, Pastor Manders.

MANDERS: Only look at your own son—there is no reason why we should not say it in his presence—what has the consequence been for him? He is six or seven and twenty, and has never had the opportunity of learning what a well-ordered home really is.

OSWALD: I beg your pardon, Pastor; there you're quite mistaken.

MANDERS: Indeed? I thought you had lived almost exclusively in artistic circles.

OSWALD: So I have.

MANDERS: And chiefly among the younger artists?

OSWALD: Yes, certainly.

MANDERS: But I thought few of those young fellows could afford to set up house and support a family.

OSWALD: There are many who cannot afford to marry, sir.

MANDERS: Yes, that is just what I say.

OSWALD: But they may have a home for all that. And several of them have, as a matter of fact; and very pleasant, well-ordered homes they are, too. (MRS. ALVING *follows with breathless interest; nods, but says nothing*)

MANDERS: But I'm not talking of bachelors' quarters. By a "home" I understand the home of a family, where a man lives with his wife and children.

OSWALD: Yes; or with his children and his children's mother.

MANDERS: (*Starts; clasps his hands*) But, good heavens—

OSWALD: Well?

MANDERS: Lives with—his children's mother!

OSWALD: Yes. Would you have him turn his children's mother out of doors?

MANDERS: Then it is illicit relations you are talking of! Irregular marriages, as people call them!

OSWALD: I have never noticed anything particularly irregular about the life these people lead.

MANDERS: But how is it possible that a—a young man or young woman with any decency of feeling can endure to live in that way?—in the eyes of all the world!

OSWALD: What are they to do? A poor young artist—a poor girl—marriage costs a great deal. What are they to do?

MANDERS: What are they to do? Let me tell you, Mr. Alving, what they ought to do. They ought to exercise self-restraint from the first; that is what they ought to do.

OSWALD: That doctrine will scarcely go down with warm-blooded young people who love each other.

MRS. ALVING: No, scarcely!

MANDERS: (*Continuing*) How can the authorities tolerate such things! Allow them to go on in the light of day! (*Confronting* MRS. ALVING) Had I not cause to be deeply concerned about your son? In circles where open immorality prevails, and has even a sort of recognised position—!

OSWALD: Let me tell you, sir, that I have been in the habit of spending nearly all my Sundays in one or two such irregular homes—

MANDERS: Sunday of all days!

OSWALD: Isn't that the day to enjoy one's self? Well, never have I heard an offensive word, and still less have I witnessed anything that could be called immoral. No; do you know when and where I have come across immorality in artistic circles?

MANDERS: No, thank heaven, I don't!

OSWALD: Well, then, allow me to inform you. I have met with it when one or other of our pattern husbands and fathers has come to

Paris to have a look round on his own account, and has done the artists the honour of visiting their humble haunts. They knew what was what. These gentlemen could tell us all about places and things we had never dreamt of.

MANDERS: What! Do you mean to say that respectable men from home here would—?

OSWALD: Have you never heard these respectable men, when they got home again, talking about the way in which immorality runs rampant abroad?

MANDERS: Yes, no doubt—

MRS. ALVING: I have too.

OSWALD: Well, you may take their word for it. They know what they are talking about! (*Presses his hands to his head*) Oh! that that great, free, glorious life out there should be defiled in such a way!

MRS. ALVING: You mustn't get excited, Oswald. It's not good for you.

OSWALD: Yes; you're quite right, mother. It's bad for me, I know. You see, I'm wretchedly worn out. I shall go for a little turn before dinner. Excuse me, Pastor: I know you can't take my point of view; but I couldn't help speaking out. (*He goes out by the second door to the right*)

MRS. ALVING: My poor boy!

MANDERS: You may well say so. Then this is what he has come to! (MRS. ALVING *looks at him silently*)

MANDERS: (*Walking up and down*) He called himself the Prodigal Son. Alas! alas! (MRS. ALVING *continues looking at him*)

MANDERS: And what do you say to all this?

MRS. ALVING: I say that Oswald was right in every word.

MANDERS: (*Stands still*) Right? Right! In such principles?

MRS. ALVING: Here, in my loneliness, I have come to the same way of thinking, Pastor Manders. But I have never dared to say anything. Well! now my boy shall speak for me.

MANDERS: You are greatly to be pitied, Mrs. Alving. But now I must speak seriously to you. And now it is no longer your business manager and adviser, your own and your husband's early friend, who stands before you. It is the priest—the priest who stood before you in the moment of your life when you had gone farthest astray.

MRS. ALVING: And what has the priest to say to me?

MANDERS: I will first stir up your memory a little. The moment is well chosen. To-morrow will be the tenth anniversary of your husband's death. To-morrow the memorial in his honour will be unveiled. To-morrow I shall have to speak to the whole assembled multitude. But to-day I will speak to you alone.

MRS. ALVING: Very well, Pastor Manders. Speak.

MANDERS: Do you remember that after less than a year of married life you stood on the verge of an abyss? That you forsook your house and home? That you fled from your husband? Yes, Mrs. Alving—fled, fled, and refused to return to him, however much he begged and prayed you?

MRS. ALVING: Have you forgotten how infinitely miserable I was in that first year?

MANDERS: It is the very mark of the spirit of rebellion to crave for happiness in this life. What right have we human beings to happiness? We have simply to do our duty, Mrs. Alving! And your duty was to hold firmly to the man you had once chosen, and to whom you were bound by the holiest ties.

MRS. ALVING: You know very well what sort of life Alving was leading—what excesses he was guilty of.

MANDERS: I know very well what rumours there were about him; and I am the last to approve the life he led in his young days, if report did not wrong him. But a wife is not appointed to be her husband's judge. It was your duty to bear with humility the cross which a Higher Power had, in its wisdom, laid upon you. But instead of that you rebelliously throw away the cross, desert the back-slider whom you should have supported, go and risk your good name and reputation, and—nearly succeed in ruining other people's reputation into the bargain.

MRS. ALVING: Other people's? One other person's, you mean.

MANDERS: It was incredibly reckless of you to seek refuge with me.

MRS. ALVING: With our clergyman? With our intimate friend?

MANDERS: Just on that account. Yes, you may thank God that I possessed the necessary firmness; that I succeeded in dissuading you from your wild designs; and that it was vouchsafed me to lead you back to the path of duty, and home to your lawful husband.

MRS. ALVING: Yes, Pastor Manders, that was certainly your work.

MANDERS: I was but a poor instrument in a Higher Hand. And what a blessing has it not proved to you, all the days of your life, that I induced you to resume the yoke of duty and obedience! Did not everything happen as I foretold? Did not Alving turn his back on his errors, as a man should? Did he not live with you from that time, lovingly and blamelessly, all his days? Did he not become a benefactor to the whole district? And did he not help you to rise to his own level, so that you, little by little became his assistant in all his undertakings? And a capital assistant, too—oh, I know, Mrs. Alving, that praise is due to you.—But now I come to the next great error in your life.

MRS. ALVING: What do you mean?

MANDERS: Just as you once disowned a wife's duty, so you have since disowned a mother's.

MRS. ALVING: Ah—!

MANDERS: You have been all your life under the dominion of a pestilent spirit of self-will. The whole bias of your mind has been towards insubordination and lawlessness. You have never known how to endure any bond. Everything that has weighed upon you in life you have cast away without care or conscience, like a burden you were free to throw off at will. It did not please you to be a wife any longer, and you left your husband. You found it troublesome to be a mother, and you sent your child forth among strangers.

MRS. ALVING: Yes, that is true. I did so.

MANDERS: And thus you have become a stranger to him.

MRS. ALVING: No! no! I am not.

MANDERS: Yes, you are; you must be. And in what state of mind has he returned to you? Bethink yourself well, Mrs. Alving. You sinned greatly against your husband;—that you recognise by raising yonder memorial to him. Recognize now, also, how you have sinned against your son—there may yet be time to lead him back from the paths of error. Turn back yourself, and save what may yet be saved in him. For (*With uplifted forefinger*) verily, Mrs. Alving, you are a guilt-laden mother!— This I have thought it my duty to say to you. (*Silence*)

MRS. ALVING: (*Slowly and with self-control*) You have now spoken out, Pastor Manders; and to-morrow you are to speak publicly in memory of my husband. I shall not speak to-morrow. But now I will speak frankly to you, as you have spoken to me.

MANDERS: To be sure; you will plead excuses for your conduct—

MRS. ALVING: No. I will only tell you a story.

MANDERS: Well—?

MRS. ALVING: All that you have just said about my husband and me, and our life after you had brought me back to the path of duty—as you called it—about all that you know nothing from personal observation. From that moment you, who had been our intimate friend, never set foot in our house again.

MANDERS: You and your husband left the town immediately after.

MRS. ALVING: Yes; and in my husband's lifetime you never came to see us. It was business that forced you to visit me when you undertook the affairs of the Orphanage.

MANDERS: (*Softly and hesitatingly*) Helen—if that is meant as a reproach, I would beg you to bear in mind—

MRS. ALVING: —the regard you owed to your position, yes; and that I was a runaway wife. One can never be too cautious with such unprincipled creatures.

MANDERS: My dear—Mrs. Alving, you know that is an absurd exaggeration—

MRS. ALVING: Well well, suppose it is. My point is that your judgment as to my married life is founded upon nothing but common knowledge and report.

MANDERS: I admit that. What then?

MRS. ALVING: Well, then, Pastor Manders—I will tell you the truth. I have sworn to myself that one day you should know it—you alone!

MANDERS: What is the truth, then?

MRS. ALVING: The truth is that my husband died just as dissolute as he had lived all his days.

MANDERS: *(Feeling after a chair)* What do you say?

MRS. ALVING: After nineteen years of marriage, as dissolute—in his desires at any rate—as he was before you married us.

MANDERS: And those—those wild oats—those irregularities—those excesses, if you like—you call "a dissolute life"?

MRS. ALVING: Our doctor used the expression.

MANDERS: I do not understand you.

MRS. ALVING: You need not.

MANDERS: It almost makes me dizzy. Your whole married life, the seeming union of all these years, was nothing more than a hidden abyss!

MRS. ALVING: Neither more nor less. Now you know it.

MANDERS: This is—this is inconceivable to me. I cannot grasp it! I cannot realize it! But how was it possible to—? How could such a state of things be kept secret?

MRS. ALVING: That has been my ceaseless struggle, day after day. After Oswald's birth, I thought Alving seemed to be a little better. But it did not last long. And then I had to struggle twice as hard, fighting as though for life or death, so that nobody should know what sort of man my child's father was. And you know what power Alving had of winning people's hearts. Nobody seemed able to believe anything but good of him. He was one of those people whose life does not bite upon their reputation. But at last, Mr. Manders—for you must know the whole story—the most repulsive thing of all happened.

MANDERS: More repulsive than what you have told me!

MRS. ALVING: I had gone on bearing with him, although I knew very well the secrets of his life out of doors. But when he brought the scandal within our own walls—

MANDERS: Impossible! Here!

MRS. ALVING: Yes; here in our own home. It was there *(Pointing towards the first door on the right)*, in the dining-room, that I first came to know of it. I was busy with something in there, and the door was standing ajar. I heard our housemaid come up from the garden, with water for those flowers.

MANDERS: Well—?

MRS. ALVING: Soon after, I heard Alving come in too. I heard him say something softly to her. And then I heard—(*With a short laugh*)—oh! it still sounds in my ears, so hateful and yet so ludicrous—I heard my own servant-maid whisper, "Let me go, Mr. Alving! Let me be!"

MANDERS: What unseemly levity on his part! But it cannot have been more than levity, Mrs. Alving; believe me, it cannot.

MRS. ALVING: I soon knew what to believe. Mr. Alving had his way with the girl; and that connection had consequences, Mr. Manders.

MANDERS: (*As though petrified*) Such things in this house! in this house!

MRS. ALVING: I had borne a great deal in this house. To keep him at home in the evenings, and at night, I had to make myself his boon companion in his secret orgies up in his room. There I have had to sit alone with him, to clink glasses and drink with him, and to listen to his ribald, silly talk. I have had to fight with him to get him dragged to bed—

MANDERS: (*Moved*) And you were able to bear all this!

MRS. ALVING: I had to bear it for my little boy's sake. But when the last insult was added; when my own servant-maid—; then I swore to myself: This shall come to an end! And so I took the reins into my own hand—the whole control—over him and everything else. For now I had a weapon against him, you see; he dared not oppose me. It was then I sent Oswald away from home. He was nearly seven years old, and was beginning to observe and ask questions, as children do. That I could not bear. It seemed to me the child must be poisoned by merely breathing the air of this polluted home. That was why I sent him away. And now you can see, too, why he was never allowed to set foot inside his home so long as his father lived. No one knows what that cost me.

MANDERS: You have indeed had a life of trial.

MRS. ALVING: I could never have borne it if I had not had my work. For I may truly say that I have worked! All the additions to the estate —all the improvements—all the labour-saving appliances, that Alving was so much praised for having introduced—do you suppose he had energy for anything of the sort?—he, who lay all day on the sofa, reading an old Court Guide! No; but I may tell you this too: when he had his better intervals, it was I who urged him on; it was I who had to drag the whole load when he relapsed into his evil ways, or sank into querulous wretchedness.

MANDERS: And it is to this man that you raise a memorial?

MRS. ALVING: There you see the power of an evil conscience.

MANDERS: Evil—? What do you mean?

MRS. ALVING: It always seemed to me impossible but that the truth must come out and be believed. So the Orphanage was to deaden all rumours and set every doubt at rest.

MANDERS: In that you have certainly not missed your aim, Mrs. Alving.

MRS. ALVING: And besides, I had one other reason. I was determined that Oswald, my own boy, should inherit nothing whatever from his father.

MANDERS: Then it is Alving's fortune that—?

MRS. ALVING: Yes. The sums I have spent upon the Orphanage, year by year, make up the amount—I have reckoned it up precisely—the amount which made Lieutenant Alving "a good match" in his day.

MANDERS: I don't understand—

MRS. ALVING: It was my purchase-money. I do not choose that that money should pass into Oswald's hands. My son shall have everything from me—everything.

OSWALD ALVING *enters through the second door to the right; he has taken off his hat and overcoat in the hall.*

MRS. ALVING: (*Going towards him*) Are you back again already? My dear, dear boy!

OSWALD: What can a fellow do out of doors in this eternal rain? But I hear dinner is ready. That's capital!

REGINA: (*With a parcel, from the dining-room*) A parcel has come for you, Mrs. Alving. (*Hands it to her*)

MRS. ALVING: (*With a glance at* MR. MANDERS) No doubt copies of the ode for to-morrow's ceremony.

MANDERS: H'm—

REGINA: And dinner is ready.

MRS. ALVING: Very well. We will come directly. I will just—(*Begins to open the parcel*)

REGINA: (*To* OSWALD) Would Mr. Alving like red or white wine?

OSWALD: Both, if you please.

REGINA: *Bien.* Very well, sir. (*She goes into the dining-room*)

OSWALD: I may as well help to uncork it. (*He also goes into the dining room, the door of which swings half open behind him*)

MRS. ALVING: (*Who has opened the parcel*) Yes, I thought so. Here is the Ceremonial Ode, Pastor Manders.

MANDERS: (*With folded hands*) With what countenance I am to deliver my discourse to-morrow—!

MRS. ALVING: Oh, you will get through it somehow.

MANDERS: (*Softly, so as not to be heard in the dining-room*) Yes; it would not do to provoke scandal.

MRS. ALVING: (*Under her breath, but firmly*) No. But then this long, hateful comedy will be ended. From the day after to-morrow, I shall act in every way as though he who is dead had never lived in this house. There shall be no one here but my boy and his mother. (*From the dining-room comes the noise of a chair overturned, and at the same moment is heard.*)

REGINA: (*Sharply, but in a whisper*) Oswald! take care! are you mad? Let me go!

MRS. ALVING: (*Starts in terror*) Ah—! (*She stares wildly towards the half-open door.* OSWALD *is heard laughing and humming. A bottle is uncorked*)

MANDERS: (*Agitated*) What can be the matter? What is it, Mrs. Alving?

MRS. ALVING: (*Hoarsely*) Ghosts! The couple from the conservatory—risen again!

MANDERS: Is it possible! Regina—? Is she—?

MRS. ALVING: Yes. Come. Not a word—! (*She seizes* PASTOR MANDERS *by the arm, and walks unsteadily toward the dining room*)

Curtain

ACT II.

The same room. The mist still lies heavy over the landscape. MANDERS *and* MRS. ALVING *enter from the dining-room.*

MRS. ALVING: (*Still in the doorway*) *Velbekomme,*[1] Mr. Manders. (*Turns back towards the dining-room*) Aren't you coming too, Oswald?

OSWALD: (*From within*) No, thank you. I think I shall go out a little.

MRS. ALVING: Yes, do. The weather seems a little brighter now. (*She shuts the dining-room door, goes to the hall door, and calls*) Regina!

REGINA: (*Outside*) Yes, Mrs. Alving?

MRS. ALVING: Go down to the laundry, and help with the garlands.

REGINA: Yes, Mrs. Alving.

---

[1] A phrase equivalent to the German *Prosit die Mahlzeit*—"May good digestion wait on appetite."

MRS. ALVING *assures herself that* REGINA *goes; then shuts the door.*

MANDERS: I suppose he cannot overhear us in there?

MRS. ALVING: Not when the door is shut. Besides, he's just going out.

MANDERS: I am still quite upset. I don't know how I could swallow a morsel of dinner.

MRS. ALVING: *(Controlling her nervousness, walks up and down)* Nor I. But what is to be done now?

MANDERS: Yes; what is to be done? I am really quite at a loss. I am so utterly without experience in matters of this sort.

MRS. ALVING: I feel sure that, so far, no mischief has been done.

MANDERS: No; heaven forbid! But it is an unseemly state of things, nevertheless.

MRS. ALVING: It is only an idle fancy on Oswald's part; you may be sure of that.

MANDERS: Well, as I say, I am not accustomed to affairs of the kind. But I should certainly think—

MRS. ALVING: Out of the house she must go, and that immediately. That is as clear as daylight—

MANDER: Yes, of course she must.

MRS. ALVING: But where to? It would not be right to—

MANDERS: Where to? Home to her father, of course.

MRS. ALVING: To whom did you say?

MANDERS: To her— But then, Engstrand is not—? Good God, Mrs. Alving, it's impossible! You must be mistaken after all.

MRS. ALVING: Unfortunately there is no possibility of mistake. Johanna confessed everything to me; and Alving could not deny it. So there was nothing to be done but to get the matter hushed up.

MANDERS: No, you could do nothing else.

MRS. ALVING: The girl left our service at once and got a good sum of money to hold her tongue for the time. The rest she managed for herself when she got to town. She renewed her old acquaintance with Engstrand, no doubt let him see that she had money in her purse and told him some tale about a foreigner who put in here with a yacht that summer. So she and Engstrand got married in hot haste. Why, you married them yourself.

MANDERS: But then how to account for—? I recollect distinctly Engstrand coming to give notice of the marriage. He was quite overwhelmed with contrition and bitterly reproached himself for the misbehaviour he and his sweetheart had been guilty of.

MRS. ALVING: Yes; of course he had to take the blame upon himself.

MANDERS: But such a piece of duplicity on his part! And towards me too! I never could have believed it of Jacob Engstrand. I shall not fail to take him seriously to task; he may be sure of that.—And then the immorality of such a connection! For money—! How much did the girl receive?

MRS. ALVING: Three hundred dollars.

MANDERS: Just think of it—for a miserable three hundred dollars to go and marry a fallen woman!

MRS. ALVING: Then what have you to say of me? I went and married a fallen man.

MANDERS: Why—good heavens!—what are you talking about! A fallen man!

MRS. ALVING: Do you think Alving was any purer when I went with him to the altar than Johanna was when Engstrand married her?

MANDERS: Well, but there is a world of difference between the two cases—

MRS. ALVING: Not so much difference after all—except in the price:—a miserable three hundred dollars and a whole fortune.

MANDERS: How can you compare such absolutely dissimilar cases? You had taken counsel with your own heart and with your natural advisers.

MRS. ALVING: *(Without looking at him)* I thought you understood where what you call my heart had strayed to at the time.

MANDERS: *(Distantly)* Had I understood anything of the kind I should not have been a daily guest in your husband's house.

MRS. ALVING: At any rate, the fact remains that with myself I took no counsel whatever.

MANDERS: Well then, with your nearest relatives—as your duty bade you—with your mother and your two aunts.

MRS. ALVING: Yes, that is true. Those three cast up the account for me. Oh, it's marvellous how clearly they made out that it would be downright madness to refuse such an offer. If mother could only see me now, and know what all that grandeur has come to!

MANDERS: Nobody can be held responsible for the result. This, at least, remains clear: your marriage was in full accordance with law and order.

MRS. ALVING: *(At the window)* Oh, that perpetual law and order! I often think that is what does all the mischief in this world of ours.

MANDERS: Mrs. Alving, that is a sinful way of talking.

MRS. ALVING: Well, I can't help it; I must have done with all this constraint and insincerity. I can endure it no longer. I must work my way out to freedom.

MANDERS: What do you mean by that?

MRS. ALVING: *(Drumming on the window-frame)* I ought never to have concealed the facts of Alving's life. But at that time I dared not do anything else—I was afraid, partly on my own account. I was such a coward.

MANDERS: A coward?

MRS. ALVING: If people had come to know anything, they would have said—"Poor man! with a runaway wife, no wonder he kicks over the traces."

MANDERS: Such remarks might have been made with a certain show of right.

MRS. ALVING: (*Looking steadily at him*) If I were what I ought to be, I should go to Oswald and say, "Listen, my boy: your father led a vicious life—"

MANDERS: Merciful heavens—!

MRS. ALVING: —and then I should tell him all I have told you—every word of it.

MANDERS: You shock me unspeakably, Mrs. Alving.

MRS. ALVING: Yes; I know that. I know that very well. I myself am shocked at the idea. (*Goes away from the window*) I am such a coward.

MANDERS: You call it "cowardice" to do your plain duty? Have you forgotten that a son ought to love and honour his father and mother?

MRS. ALVING: Do not let us talk in such general terms. Let us ask: Ought Oswald to love and honour Chamberlain Alving?

MANDERS: Is there no voice in your mother's heart that forbids you to destroy your son's ideals?

MRS. ALVING: But what about the truth?

MANDERS: But what about the ideals?

MRS. ALVING: Oh—ideals, ideals! If only I were not such a coward!

MANDERS: Do not despise ideals, Mrs. Alving; they will avenge themselves cruelly. Take Oswald's case: he, unfortunately, seems to have few enough ideals as it is; but I can see that his father stands before him as an ideal.

MRS. ALVING: Yes, that is true.

MANDERS: And this habit of mind you have yourself implanted and fostered by your letters.

MRS. ALVING: Yes; in my superstitious awe for duty and the properties, I lied to my boy, year after year. Oh, what a coward—what a coward I have been!

MANDERS: You have established a happy illusion in your son's heart, Mrs. Alving; and assuredly you ought not to undervalue it.

MRS. ALVING: H'm; who knows whether it is so happy after all—? But, at any rate, I will not have any tampering with Regina. He shall not go and wreck the poor girl's life.

MANDERS: No; good God—that would be terrible!

MRS. ALVING: If I knew he was in earnest, and that it would be for his happiness—

MANDERS: What? What then?

MRS. ALVING: But it couldn't be; for unfortunately Regina is not the right sort of woman.

MANDERS: Well, what then? What do you mean?

MRS. ALVING: If I weren't such a pitiful coward, I should say to him, "Marry her, or make what arrangement you please, only let us have nothing underhand about it."

MANDERS: Merciful heavens, would you let them marry! Anything so dreadful—! so unheard of—

MRS. ALVING: Do you really mean "unheard of"? Frankly, Pastor Manders, do you suppose that throughout the country there are not plenty of married couples as closely akin as they?

MANDERS: I don't in the least understand you.

MRS. ALVING: O yes, indeed you do.

MANDERS: Ah, you are thinking of the possibility that—Alas! yes, family life is certainly not always so pure as it ought to be. But in such a case as you point to, one can never know—at least with any certainty. Here, on the other hand—that you, a mother, can think of letting your son—

MRS. ALVING: But I cannot—I wouldn't for anything in the world; that is precisely what I am saying.

MANDERS: No, because you are a "coward," as you put it. But if you were not a "coward," then—? Good God! a connection so shocking!

MRS. ALVING: So far as that goes, they say we are all sprung from connections of that sort. And who is it that arranged the world so, Pastor Manders?

MANDERS: Questions of that kind I must decline to discuss with you, Mrs. Alving; you are far from being in the right frame of mind for them. But that you dare to call your scruples "cowardly"—!

MRS. ALVING: Let me tell you what I mean. I am timid and faint-hearted because of the ghosts that hang about me, and that I can never quite shake off.

MANDERS: What do you say hangs about you?

MRS. ALVING: Ghosts! When I heard Regina and Oswald in there, it was as though ghosts rose up before me. But I almost think we are all of us ghosts, Pastor Manders. It is not only what we have inherited from our father and mother that "walks" in us. It is all sorts of dead ideas, and lifeless old beliefs, and so forth. They have no vitality, but they cling to us all the same, and we cannot shake them off. Whenever

I take up a newspaper, I seem to see ghosts gliding between the lines. There must be ghosts all the country over, as thick as the sands of the sea. And then we are, one and all, so pitifully afraid of the light.

MANDERS: Aha—here we have the fruits of your reading. And pretty fruits they are, upon my word! Oh, those horrible, revolutionary, free-thinking books!

MRS. ALVING: You are mistaken, my dear Pastor. It was you yourself who set me thinking; and I thank you for it with all my heart.

MANDERS: I!

MRS. ALVING: Yes—when you forced me under the yoke of what you called duty and obligation; when you lauded as right and proper what my whole soul rebelled against as something loathsome. It was then that I began to look into the seams of your doctrines. I wanted only to pick at a single knot; but when I had got that undone, the whole thing ravelled out. And then I understood that it was all machine-sewn.

MANDERS: (*Softly, with emotion*) And was that the upshot of my life's hardest battle?

MRS. ALVING: Call it rather your most pitiful defeat.

MANDERS: It was my greatest victory, Helen—the victory over myself.

MRS. ALVING: It was a crime against us both.

MANDERS: When you went astray, and came to me crying, "Here I am; take me!" I commanded you, saying, "Woman, go home to your lawful husband." Was that a crime?

MRS. ALVING: Yes, I think so.

MANDERS: We two do not understand each other.

MRS. ALVING: Not now, at any rate.

MANDERS: Never—never in my most secret thoughts have I regarded you otherwise than as another's wife.

MRS. ALVING: Oh—indeed?

MANDERS: Helen—!

MRS. ALVING: People so easily forget their past selves.

MANDERS: I do not. I am what I always was.

MRS. ALVING: (*Changing the subject*) Well well well; don't let us talk of old times any longer. You are now over head and ears in Boards and Committees, and I am fighting my battle with ghosts, both within me and without.

MANDERS: Those without I shall help you to lay. After all the terrible things I have heard from you today, I cannot in conscience permit an unprotected girl to remain in your house.

MRS. ALVING: Don't you think the best plan would be to get her provided for?—I mean, by a good marriage.

MANDERS: No doubt. I think it would be desirable for her in every respect. Regina is now at the age when— Of course I don't know much about these things, but—

MRS. ALVING: Regina matured very early.

MANDERS: Yes, I thought so. I have an impression that she was remarkably well developed, physically, when I prepared her for confirmation. But in the meantime, she ought to be at home, under her father's eye— Ah! but Engstrand is not— That he—that he— could so hide the truth from me!

A knock at the door into the hall.

MRS. ALVING: Who can this be? Come in!

ENGSTRAND: (*In his Sunday clothes, in the doorway*) I humbly beg your pardon, but—

MANDERS: Aha! H'm—

MRS. ALVING: Is that you, Engstrand?

ENGSTRAND: —there was none of the servants about, so I took the great liberty of just knocking.

MRS. ALVING: Oh, very well. Come in. Do you want to speak to me?

ENGSTRAND: (*Comes in*) No, I'm obliged to you, ma'am; it was with his Reverence I wanted to have a word or two.

MANDERS: (*Walking up and down the room*) Ah—indeed! You want to speak to me, do you?

ENGSTRAND: Yes, I'd like so terrible much to—

MANDERS: (*Stops in front of him*) Well; may I ask what you want?

ENGSTRAND: Well, it was just this, your Reverence: we've been paid off down yonder—my grateful thanks to you, ma'am,—and now everything's finished, I've been thinking it would be but right and proper if we, that have been working so honestly together all this time—well, I was thinking we ought to end up with a little prayer-meeting to-night.

MANDERS: A prayer-meeting? Down at the Orphanage?

ENGSTRAND: Oh, if your Reverence doesn't think it proper—

MANDERS: Oh yes, I do; but—h'm—

ENGSTRAND: I've been in the habit of offering up a little prayer in the evenings, myself—

MRS. ALVING: Have you?

ENGSTRAND: Yes, every now and then—just a little edification, in a manner of speaking. But I'm a poor, common man, and have little enough gift, God help me!—and so I thought, as the Reverend Mr. Manders happened to be here, I'd—

MANDERS: Well, you see, Engstrand, I have a question to put to you first. Are you in the right frame of mind for such a meeting! Do you feel your conscience clear and at ease?

ENGSTRAND: Oh, God help us, your Reverence! we'd better not talk about conscience.

MANDERS: Yes, that is just what we must talk about. What have you to answer?

ENGSTRAND: Why—a man's conscience—it can be bad enough now and then.

MANDERS: Ah, you admit that. Then perhaps you will make a clean breast of it, and tell me—the real truth about Regina?

MRS. ALVING: (*Quickly*) Mr. Manders!

MANDERS: (*Reassuringly*) Please allow me—

ENGSTRAND: About Regina! Lord, what a turn you gave me! (*Looks at* MRS. ALVING) There's nothing wrong about Regina, is there?

MANDERS: We will hope not. But I mean, what is the truth about you and Regina? You pass for her father, eh!

ENGSTRAND: (*Uncertain*) Well—h'm—your Reverence knows all about me and poor Johanna.

MANDERS: Come now, no more prevarication! Your wife told Mrs. Alving the whole story before quitting her service.

ENGSTRAND: Well, then, may—! Now, did she really?

MANDERS: You see we know you now, Engstrand.

ENGSTRAND: And she swore and took her Bible oath—

MANDERS: Did she take her Bible oath?

ENGSTRAND: No; she only swore; but she did it that solemn-like.

MANDERS: And you have hidden the truth from me all these years? Hidden it from me, who have trusted you without reserve, in everything.

ENGSTRAND: Well, I can't deny it.

MANDERS: Have I deserved this of you, Engstrand? Have I not always been ready to help you in word and deed, so far as it lay in my power? Answer me. Have I not?

ENGSTRAND: It would have been a poor look-out for me many a time but for the Reverend Mr. Manders.

MANDERS: And this is how you reward me! You cause me to enter falsehoods in the Church Register, and you withhold from me, year after year, the explanations you owed alike to me and to the truth. Your conduct has been wholly inexcusable, Engstrand; and from this time forward I have done with you!

ENGSTRAND: (*With a sigh*) Yes! I suppose there's no help for it.

MANDERS: How can you possibly justify yourself?

ENGSTRAND: Who could ever have thought she'd have gone and made bad worse by talking about it? Will your Reverence just fancy yourself in the same trouble as poor Johanna—

MANDERS: I!

ENGSTRAND: Lord bless you, I don't mean just exactly the same. But I mean, if your Reverence had anything to be ashamed of in the eyes of the world, as the saying goes. We menfolk oughtn't to judge a poor woman too hardly, your Reverence.

MANDERS: I am not doing so. It is you I am reproaching.

ENGSTRAND: Might I make so bold as to ask your Reverence a bit of a question?

MANDERS: Yes, if you want to.

ENGSTRAND: Isn't it right and proper for a man to raise up the fallen?

MANDERS: Most certainly it is.

ENGSTRAND: And isn't a man bound to keep his sacred word?

MANDERS: Why, of course he is; but—

ENGSTRAND: When Johanna had got into trouble through that Englishman—or it might have been an American or a Russian, as they call them—well, you see, she came down into the town. Poor thing, she'd sent me about my business once or twice before: for she couldn't bear the sight of anything as wasn't handsome; and I'd got this damaged leg of mine. Your Reverence recollects how I ventured up into a dancing saloon, where seafaring men was carrying on with drink and devilry, as the saying goes. And then, when I was for giving them a bit of an admonition to lead a new life—

MRS. ALVING: (*At the window*) H'm—

MANDERS: I know all about that, Engstrand; the ruffians threw you downstairs. You have told me of the affair already. Your infirmity is an honour to you.

ENGSTRAND: I'm not puffed up about it, your Reverence. But what I wanted to say was, that when she came and confessed all to me, with weeping and gnashing of teeth, I can tell your Reverence I was sore at heart to hear it.

MANDERS: Were you indeed, Engstrand? Well, go on.

ENGSTRAND: So I says to her, "The American, he's sailing about on the boundless sea. And as for you, Johanna," says I, "you've committed a grievous sin, and you're a fallen creature. But Jacob Engstrand," says I, "he's got two good legs to stand upon, he has—" You see, your Reverence, I was speaking figurative-like

MANDERS: I understand quite well. Go on.

ENGSTRAND: Well, that was how I raised her up and made an honest woman of her, so as folks shouldn't get to know how as she'd gone astray with foreigners.

MANDERS: In all that you acted very well. Only I cannot approve of your stooping to take money—

ENGSTRAND: Money? I? Not a farthing!

MANDERS: (*Inquiringly to* MRS. ALVING) But—

ENGSTRAND: Oh, wait a minute!—now I recollect. Johanna did have a trifle of money. But I would have nothing to do with that. "No," says I, "that's mammon; that's the wages of sin. This dirty gold—or notes, or whatever it was—we'll just fling that back in the American's face," says I. But he was off and away, over the stormy sea, your Reverence.

MANDERS: Was he really, my good fellow?

ENGSTRAND: He was indeed, sir. So Johanna and I, we agreed that the money should go to the child's education; and so it did, and I can account for every blessed farthing of it.

MANDERS: Why, this alters the case considerably.

ENGSTRAND: That's just how it stands, your Reverence. And I make so bold as to say as I've been an honest father to Regina, so far as my poor strength went; for I'm but a weak vessel, worse luck!

MANDERS: Well, well, my good fellow—

ENGSTRAND: All the same, I bear myself witness as I've brought up the child, and lived kindly with poor Johanna, and ruled over my own house, as the Scripture has it. But it couldn't never enter my head to go to your Reverence and puff myself up and boast because even the likes of me had done some good in the world. No, sir; when anything of that sort happens to Jacob Engstrand, he holds his tongue about it. It don't happen so terrible often, I daresay. And when I do come to see your Reverence, I find a mortal deal that's wicked and weak to talk about. For I said it before, and I say it again—a man's conscience isn't always as clean as it might be.

MANDERS: Give me your hand, Jacob Engstrand.

ENGSTRAND: Oh, Lord! your Reverence—

MANDERS: Come, no nonsense. (*Wrings his hand*) There we are!

ENGSTRAND: And if I might humbly beg your Reverence's pardon—

MANDERS: You? On the contrary, it is I who ought to beg your pardon—

ENGSTRAND: Lord, no, sir!

MANDERS: Yes, assuredly. And I do it with all my heart. Forgive me for misunderstanding you. I only wish I could give you some proof of my hearty regret, and of my good-will towards you—

ENGSTRAND: Would your Reverence do it?

MANDERS: With the greatest pleasure.

ENGSTRAND: Well then, here's the very chance. With the bit of money I've saved here, I was thinking I might set up a Sailors' Home down in the town.

MRS. ALVING: You?

ENGSTRAND: Yes; it might be a sort of Orphanage, too, in a manner of speaking. There's such a many temptations for seafaring folk ashore. But in this Home of mine, a man might feel like as he was under a father's eye, I was thinking.

MANDERS: What do you say to this, Mrs. Alving?

ENGSTRAND: It isn't much as I've got to start with, Lord help me! But if I could only find a helping hand, why—

MANDERS: Yes, yes; we will look into the matter more closely. I entirely approve of your plan. But now, go before me and make everything ready, and get the candles lighted, so as to give the place an air of festivity. And then we will pass an edifying hour together, my good fellow; for now I quite believe you are in the right frame of mind.

ENGSTRAND: Yes, I trust I am. And so I'll say good-bye, ma'am, and thank you kindly; and take good care of Regina for me—(*Wipes a tear from his eye*)—poor Johanna's child. Well, it's a queer thing, now; but it's just like as if she'd growd into the very apple of my eye. It is, indeed. (*He bows and goes out through the hall*)

MANDERS: Well, what do you say of that man now, Mrs. Alving? That was a very different account of matters, was it not?

MRS. ALVING: Yes, it certainly was.

MANDERS: It only shows how excessively careful one ought to be in judging one's fellow creatures. But what a heartfelt joy it is to ascertain that one has been mistaken! Don't you think so?

MRS. ALVING: I think you are, and will always be, a great baby, Manders.

MANDERS: I?

MRS. ALVING: (*Laying her two hands upon his shoulders*) And I say that I have half a mind to put my arms round your neck, and kiss you.

MANDERS: (*Stepping hastily back*) No, no! God bless me! What an idea!

MRS. ALVING: (*With a smile*) Oh, you needn't be afraid of me.

MANDERS: (*By the table*) You have sometimes such an exaggerated way of expressing yourself. Now let me just collect all the documents, and put them in my bag. (*He does so*) There, that's all right. And now, good-bye for the present. Keep your eyes open when Oswald comes back. I shall look in again later. (*He takes his hat and goes out through the hall door*)

MRS. ALVING: (*Sighs, looks for a moment out of the window, sets the room in order a little, and is about to go into the dining-room, but stops at the door with a half-suppressed cry*) Oswald, are you still at table?

OSWALD: (*In the dining room*) I'm only finishing my cigar.

MRS. ALVING: I thought you had gone for a little walk.

OSWALD: In such weather as this?

OSWALD: In such weather as this? (*A glass clinks.* MRS. ALVING *leaves the door open, and sits down with her knitting on the sofa by the window.*)

OSWALD: Wasn't that Pastor Manders that went out just now?

MRS. ALVING: Yes; he went down to the Orphanage.

OSWALD: H'm. (*The glass and decanter clink again*)

MRS. ALVING: (*With a troubled glance*) Dear Oswald, you should take care of that liqueur. It is strong.

OSWALD: It keeps out the damp.

MRS. ALVING: Wouldn't you rather come in here, to me?

OSWALD: I mayn't smoke in there.

MRS. ALVING: You know quite well you may smoke cigars.

OSWALD: Oh, all right then; I'll come in. Just a tiny drop more first.— There! (*He comes into the room with his cigar, and shuts the door after him. A short silence*) Where has the pastor gone to?

MRS. ALVING: I have just told you; he went down to the Orphanage.

OSWALD: Oh, yes; so you did.

MRS. ALVING: You shouldn't sit so long at table, Oswald.

OSWALD: (*Holding his cigar behind him*) But I find it so pleasant, mother. (*Strokes and caresses her*) Just think what it is for me to come home and sit at mother's own table, in mother's room, and eat mother's delicious dishes.

MRS. ALVING: My dear, dear boy!

OSWALD: (*Somewhat impatiently, walks about and smokes*) And what else can I do with myself here? I can't set to work at anything.

MRS. ALVING: Why can't you?

OSWALD: In such weather as this? Without a single ray of sunshine the whole day? (*Walks up the room*) Oh, not to be able to work—!

MRS. ALVING: Perhaps it was not quite wise of you to come home?

OSWALD: Oh, yes, mother; I had to.

MRS. ALVING: You know I would ten times rather forego the joy of having you here, than let you—

OSWALD: (*Stops beside the table*) Now just tell me, mother: does it really make you so very happy to have me home again?

MRS. ALVING: Does it make me happy!

OSWALD: (*Crumpling up a newspaper*) I should have thought it must be pretty much the same to you whether I was in existence or not.

MRS. ALVING: Have you the heart to say that to your mother, Oswald?

OSWALD: But you've got on very well without me all this time.

MRS. ALVING: Yes; I have got on without you. That is true.

A silence. Twilight slowly begins to fall. OSWALD *paces to and fro across the room. He has laid his cigar down.*

OSWALD: (*Stops beside* MRS. ALVING) Mother, may I sit on the sofa beside you?

MRS. ALVING: (*Makes room for him*) Yes, do, my dear boy.

OSWALD: (*Sits down*) There is something I must tell you, mother.

MRS. ALVING: (*Anxiously*) Well?

OSWALD: (*Looks fixedly before him*) For I can't go on hiding it any longer.

MRS. ALVING: Hiding what? What is it?

OSWALD: (*As before*) I could never bring myself to write to you about it; and since I've come home—

MRS. ALVING: (*Seizes him by the arm*) Oswald, what is the matter?

OSWALD: Both yesterday and to-day I have tried to put the thoughts away from me—to cast them off; but it's no use.

MRS. ALVING: (*Rising*) Now you must tell me everything, Oswald!

OSWALD: (*Draws her down to the sofa again*) Sit still; and then I will try to tell you.—I complained of fatigue after my journey—

MRS. ALVING: Well? What then?

OSWALD: But it isn't that that is the matter with me; not any ordinary fatigue—

MRS. ALVING: (*Tries to jump up*) You are not ill, Oswald?

OSWALD: (*Draws her down again*) Sit still, mother. Do take it quietly. I'm not downright ill, either; not what is commonly called "ill." (*Claps his hands above his head*) Mother, my mind is broken down—ruined—I shall never be able to work again! (*With his hands before his face, he buries his head in her lap, and breaks into bitter sobbing*)

MRS. ALVING: (*White and trembling*) Oswald! Look at me! No, no; it's not true.

OSWALD: (*Looks up with despair in his eyes*) Never to be able to work again! Never!—never! A living death! Mother, can you imagine anything so horrible!

MRS. ALVING: My poor boy! How has this horrible thing come upon you?

OSWALD: (*Sitting upright again*) That's just what I cannot possibly grasp or understand. I have never led a dissipated life—never, in any respect. You mustn't believe that of me, mother! I've never done that.

MRS. ALVING: I am sure you haven't, Oswald.

OSWALD: And yet this has come upon me just the same—this awful misfortune!

MRS. ALVING: Oh, but it will pass over, my dear, blessed boy. It's nothing but over-work. Trust me, I am right.

OSWALD: (*Sadly*) I thought so too, at first; but it isn't so.

MRS. ALVING: Tell me everything, from beginning to end.

OSWALD: Yes, I will.

MRS. ALVING: When did you first notice it?

OSWALD: It was directly after I had been home last time, and had got back to Paris again. I began to feel the most violent pains in my head—chiefly in the back of my head, they seemed to come. It was as though a tight iron ring was being screwed round my neck and upwards.

MRS. ALVING: Well, and then?

OSWALD: At first I thought it was nothing but the ordinary headache I had been so plagued with while I was growing up—

MRS. ALVING: Yes, yes—

OSWALD: But it wasn't that. I soon found that out. I couldn't work any more. I wanted to begin upon a big new picture, but my powers seemed to fail me; all my strength was crippled; I could form no definite images; everything swam before me—whirling round and round. Oh, it was an awful state! At last I sent for a doctor—and from him I learned the truth.

MRS. ALVING: How do you mean?

OSWALD: He was one of the first doctors in Paris. I told him my symptoms; and then he set to work asking me a string of questions which I thought had nothing to do with the matter. I couldn't imagine what the man was after—

MRS. ALVING: Well?

OSWALD: At last he said: "There has been something worm-eaten in you from your birth." He used that very word—*vermoulu*.

MRS. ALVING: (*Breathlessly*) What did he mean by that?

OSWALD: I didn't understand either, and begged him to explain himself more clearly. And then the old cynic said—(*Clenching his fist*) Oh—!

MRS. ALVING: What did he say?

OSWALD: He said, "The sins of the fathers are visited upon the children."

MRS. ALVING: (*Rising slowly*) The sins of the fathers—!

OSWALD: I very nearly struck him in the face—

MRS. ALVING: (*Walks away across the room*) The sins of the fathers—

OSWALD: (*Smiles sadly*) Yes; what do you think of that? Of course I assured him that such a thing was out of the question. But do you think he gave in? No, he stuck to it; and it was only when I produced your letters and translated the passages relating to father—

MRS. ALVING: But then—?

OSWALD: Then of course he had to admit that he was on the wrong track; and so I learned the truth—the incomprehensible truth! I ought not to have taken part with my comrades in that light-hearted, glorious life of theirs. It had been too much for my strength. So I had brought it upon myself!

MRS. ALVING: Oswald! No, no; do not believe it!

OSWALD: No other explanation was possible, he said. That's the awful part of it. Incurably ruined for life—by my own heedlessness! All that I meant to have done in the world—I never dare think of it again—I'm not able to think of it. Oh! if I could only live over again, and undo all I have done! (*He buries his face in the sofa.* MRS. ALVING *wrings her hands and walks, in silent struggle, backwards and forwards*)

OSWALD: (*After a while, looks up and remains resting upon his elbow*) If it had only been something inherited—something one wasn't responsible for! But this! To have thrown away so shamefully, thoughtlessly, recklessly, one's own happiness, one's own health, everything in the world—one's future, one's very life—!

MRS. ALVING: No, no, my dear, darling boy; this is impossible! (*Bends over him*) Things are not so desperate as you think.

OSWALD: Oh, you don't know—(*Springs up*) And then, mother, to cause you all this sorrow! Many a time I have almost wished and hoped that at bottom you didn't care so very much about me.

MRS. ALVING: I, Oswald? My only boy! You are all I have in the world! The only thing I care about!

OSWALD: (*Seizes both her hands and kisses them*) Yes, yes, I see it. When I'm at home, I see it, of course; and that's almost the hardest part for me.—But now you know the whole story; and now we won't talk any more about it to-day. I daren't think of it for long together. (*Goes up the room*) Get me something to drink, mother.

MRS. ALVING: To drink? What do you want to drink now?

OSWALD: Oh, anything you like. You have some cold punch in the house.

MRS. ALVING: Yes, but my dear Oswald—

OSWALD: Don't refuse me, mother. Do be kind, now! I must have something to wash down all these gnawing thoughts. (*Goes into the conservatory*) And then—it's so dark here! (MRS. ALVING *pulls a bell-rope on the right*) And this ceaseless rain! It may go on week after week, for months together. Never to get a glimpse of the sun! I can't recollect ever having seen the sun shine all the times I've been at home.

MRS. ALVING: Oswald—you are thinking of going away from me.

OSWALD: H'm—(*Drawing a heavy breath*) I'm not thinking of anything. I cannot think of anything! (*In a low voice*) I let thinking alone.

REGINA: (*From the dining-room*) Did you ring, ma'am?

MRS. ALVING: Yes; let us have the lamp in.

REGINA: Yes, ma'am. It's ready lighted. (*Goes out*)

MRS. ALVING: (*Goes across to Oswald*) Oswald, be frank with me.

OSWALD: Well, so I am, mother. (*Goes to the table*) I think I have told you enough. (REGINA *brings the lamp and sets it upon the table*)

MRS. ALVING: Regina, you may bring us a small bottle of champagne.

REGINA: Very well, ma'am. (*Goes out*)

OSWALD: (*Puts his arm round* MRS. ALVING's *neck*) That's just what I wanted. I knew mother wouldn't let her boy go thirsty.

MRS. ALVING: My own, poor, darling Oswald; how could I deny you anything now?

OSWALD: (*Eagerly*) Is that true, mother? Do you mean it?

MRS. ALVING: How? What?

OSWALD: That you couldn't deny me anything.

MRS. ALVING: My dear Oswald—

OSWALD: Hush!

REGINA: (*Brings a tray with a half-bottle of champagne and two glasses, which she sets on the table*) Shall I open it?

OSWALD: No, thanks. I will do it myself. (REGINA *goes out again*)

MRS. ALVING: (*Sits down by the table*) What was it you meant—that I mustn't deny you?

OSWALD: (*Busy opening the bottle*) First let us have a glass—or two. (*The cork pops; he pours wine into one glass, and is about to pour it into the other*)

MRS. ALVING: (*Holding her hand over it*) Thanks; not for me.

OSWALD: Oh! won't you? Then I will! (*He empties the glass, fills, and empties it again; then he sits down by the table*)

MRS. ALVING: (*In expectancy*) Well?

OSWALD: (*Without looking at her*) Tell me—I thought you and Pastor Manders seemed so odd—so quiet—at dinner to-day.

MRS. ALVING: Did you notice it?

OSWALD: Yes. H'm—(*After a short silence*) Tell me: what do you think of Regina?

MRS. ALVING: What do I think?

OSWALD: Yes; isn't she splendid?

MRS. ALVING: My dear Oswald, you don't know her as I do—

OSWALD: Well?

MRS. ALVING: Regina, unfortunately, was allowed to stay at home too long. I ought to have taken her earlier into my house.

OSWALD: Yes, but isn't she splendid to look at, mother? (*He fills his glass*)

MRS. ALVING: Regina has many serious faults—

OSWALD: Oh, what does that matter? (*He drinks again*)

MRS. ALVING: But I am fond of her, nevertheless, and I am responsible for her. I wouldn't for all the world have any harm happen to her.

OSWALD: (*Springs up*) Mother, Regina is my only salvation!

MRS. ALVING: (*Rising*) What do you mean by that?

OSWALD: I cannot go on bearing all this anguish of soul alone.

MRS. ALVING: Have you not your mother to share it with you?

OSWALD: Yes; that's what I thought; and so I came home to you. But that will not do. I see it won't do. I cannot endure my life here.

MRS. ALVING: Oswald!

OSWALD: I must live differently, mother. That is why I must leave you. I will not have you looking on at it.

MRS. ALVING: My unhappy boy! But, Oswald, while you are so ill as this—

OSWALD: If it were only the illness, I should stay with you, mother, you may be sure; for you are the best friend I have in the world.

MRS. ALVING: Yes, indeed I am, Oswald; am I not?

OSWALD: (*Wanders restlessly about*) But it's all the torment, the gnawing remorse—and then, the great, killing dread. Oh—that awful dread!

MRS. ALVING: (*Walking after him*) Dread? What dread? What do you mean?

OSWALD: Oh, you mustn't ask me any more. I don't know. I can't describe it. (MRS. ALVING *goes over to the right and pulls the bell*)

OSWALD: What is it you want?

MRS. ALVING: I want my boy to be happy—that is what I want. He sha'n't go on brooding over things. (*To* REGINA, *who appears at the door:*) More champagne—a large bottle. (REGINA *goes*)

OSWALD: Mother!

MRS. ALVING: Do you think we don't know how to live here at home?

OSWALD: Isn't she splendid to look at? How beautifully she's built! And so thoroughly healthy!

MRS. ALVING: (*Sits by the table*) Sit down, Oswald; let us talk quietly together.

OSWALD: (*Sits*) I daresay you don't know, mother, that I owe Regina some reparation.

MRS. ALVING: You!

OSWALD: For a bit of thoughtlessness, or whatever you like to call it—very innocent, at any rate. When I was home last time—

MRS. ALVING: Well?

OSWALD: She used often to ask me about Paris, and I used to tell her one thing and another. Then I recollect I happened to say to her one day, "Shouldn't you like to go there yourself?"

MRS. ALVING: Well?

OSWALD: I saw her face flush, and then she said, "Yes, I should like it of all things." "Ah, well," I replied, "it might perhaps be managed"—or something like that.

MRS. ALVING: And then?

OSWALD: Of course I had forgotten all about it; but the day before yesterday I happened to ask her whether she was glad I was to stay at home so long—

MRS. ALVING: Yes?

OSWALD: And then she gave me such a strange look, and asked, "But what's to become of my trip to Paris?"

MRS. ALVING: Her trip!

OSWALD: And so it came out that she had taken the thing seriously; that she had been thinking of me the whole time, and had set to work to learn French—

MRS. ALVING: So that was why—!

OSWALD: Mother—when I saw that fresh, lovely, splendid girl standing there before me—till then I had hardly noticed her—but when she stood there as though with open arms ready to receive me—

MRS. ALVING: Oswald!

OSWALD: —then it flashed upon me that in her lay my salvation; for I saw that she was full of the joy of life.

MRS. ALVING: (*Starts*) The joy of life—? Can there be salvation in that?

REGINA: (*From the dining-room, with a bottle of champagne*) I'm sorry to have been so long, but I had to go to the cellar. (*Places the bottle on the table*)

OSWALD: And now bring another glass.

REGINA: (*Looks at him in surprise*) There is Mrs. Alving's glass, Mr. Alving.

OSWALD: Yes, but bring one for yourself, Regina. (REGINA *starts and gives a lightning-like side glance at* MRS. ALVING) Why do you wait?

REGINA: (*Softly and hesitatingly*) Is it Mrs. Alving's wish?

MRS. ALVING: Bring the glass, Regina. (REGINA *goes out into the dining-room*)

OSWALD: (*Follows her with his eyes*) Have you noticed how she walks? —so firmly and lightly!

MRS. ALVING: This can never be, Oswald!

OSWALD: It's a settled thing. Can't you see that? It's no use saying anything against it. (REGINA *enters with an empty glass, which she keeps in her hand*)

OSWALD: Sit down, Regina. (REGINA *looks inquiringly at* MRS. ALVING)

MRS. ALVING: Sit down. (REGINA *sits on a chair by the dining-room door, still holding the empty glass in her hand*) Oswald—what were you saying about the joy of life?

OSWALD: Ah, the joy of life, mother—that's a thing you don't know much about in these parts. I have never felt it here.

MRS. ALVING: Not when you are with me?

OSWALD: Not when I'm at home. But you don't understand that.

MRS. ALVING: Yes; yes; I think I almost understand it—now.

OSWALD: And then, too, the joy of work! At bottom, it's the same thing. But that, too, you know nothing about.

MRS. ALVING: Perhaps you are right. Tell me more about it, Oswald.

OSWALD: I only mean that here people are brought up to believe that work is a curse and a punishment for sin, and that life is something miserable, something it would be best to have done with, the sooner the better.

MRS. ALVING: "A vale of tears," yes; and we certainly do our best to make it one.

OSWALD: But in the great world people won't hear of such things. There, nobody really believes such doctrines any longer. There, you feel it a positive bliss and ecstasy merely to draw the breath of life. Mother, have you noticed that everything I have painted has turned upon the joy of life?—always, always upon the joy of life?—light and sunshine and glorious air—and faces radiant with happiness. That is why I'm afraid of remaining at home with you.

MRS. ALVING: Afraid? What are you afraid of here, with me?

OSWALD: I'm afraid lest all my instincts should be warped into ugliness.

MRS. ALVING: (*Looks steadily at him*) Do you think that is what would happen?

OSWALD: I know it. You may live the same life here as there, and yet it won't be the same life.

MRS. ALVING: (*Who has been listening eagerly, rises, her eyes big with thought, and says*) Now I see the sequence of things.

OSWALD: What is it you see?

MRS. ALVING: I see it now for the first time. And now I can speak.

OSWALD: (*Rising*) Mother, I don't understand you.

REGINA: (*Who has also risen*) Perhaps I ought to go?

MRS. ALVING: No. Stay here. Now I can speak. Now, my boy, you shall know the whole truth. And then you can choose. Oswald! Regina!

OSWALD: Hush! The Pastor—

MANDERS: (*Enters by the hall door*) There! We have had a most edifying time down there.

OSWALD: So have we.

MANDERS: We must stand by Engstrand and his Sailors' Home. Regina must go to him and help him—

REGINA: No thank you, sir.

MANDERS: (*Noticing her for the first time*) What—? You here? And with a glass in your hand!

REGINA: (*Hastily putting the glass down*) Pardon!

OSWALD: Regina is going with me, Mr. Manders.

MANDERS: Going! With you!

OSWALD: Yes; as my wife—if she wishes it.

MANDERS: But, merciful God—!

REGINA: I can't help it, sir.

OSWALD: Or she'll stay here, if I stay.

REGINA: (*Involuntarily*) Here!

MANDERS: I am thunderstruck at your conduct, Mrs. Alving.

MRS. ALVING: They will do neither one thing nor the other; for now I can speak out plainly.

MANDERS: You surely will not do that! No, no, no!

MRS. ALVING: Yes, I can speak and I will. And no ideals shall suffer after all.

OSWALD: Mother—what is it you are hiding from me?

REGINA: (*Listening*) Oh, ma'am listen! Don't you hear shouts outside. (*She goes into the conservatory and looks out*)

OSWALD: (*At the window on the left*) What's going on? Where does that light come from?

REGINA: (*Cries out*) The Orphanage is on fire!

MRS. ALVING: (*Rushing to the window*) On fire!

MANDERS: On fire! Impossible! I've just come from there.

OSWALD: Where's my hat? Oh, never mind it— Father's Orphanage—!
(*He rushes out through the garden door*)
MRS. ALVING: My shawl, Regina! The whole place is in a blaze!
MANDERS: Mrs. Alving, it is a judgment upon this abode of lawlessness.
MRS. ALVING: Yes, of course. Come, Regina. (*She and* REGINA *hasten out through the hall*)
MANDERS: (*Clasps his hands together*) And we left it uninsured! (*He goes out the same way.*)

ACT III.

The room as before. All the doors stand open. The lamp is still burning on the table. It is dark out of doors; there is only a faint glow from the conflagration in the background to the left. MRS. ALVING, *with a shawl over her head, stands in the conservatory, looking out.* REGINA, *also with a shawl on, stands a little behind her.*

MRS. ALVING: The whole thing burnt!—burnt to the ground!
REGINA: The basement is still burning.
MRS. ALVING: How is it Oswald doesn't come home? There's nothing to be saved.
REGINA: Should you like me to take down his hat to him?
MRS. ALVING: Has he not even got his hat on?
REGINA: (*Pointing to the hall*) No; there it hangs.
MRS. ALVING: Let it be. He must come up now. I shall go and look for him myself. (*She goes out through the garden door*)
MANDERS: (*Comes in from the hall*) Is not Mrs. Alving here?
REGINA: She has just gone down the garden.
MANDERS: This is the most terrible night I ever went through.
REGINA: Yes; isn't it a dreadful misfortune, sir?
MANDERS: Oh, don't talk about it! I can hardly bear to think of it.
REGINA: How can it have happened—?
MANDERS: Don't ask me, Miss Engstrand! How should *I* know? Do you, too—? Is it not enough that your father—?
REGINA: What about him?
MANDERS: Oh, he has driven me distracted—
ENGSTRAND: (*Enters through the hall*) Your Reverence—

MANDERS: (*Turns round in terror*) Are you after me here, too?

ENGSTRAND: Yes, strike me dead, but I must—! Oh, Lord! What am I saying? But this is a terrible ugly business, your Reverence.

MANDERS: (*Walks to and fro*) Alas! alas!

REGINA: What's the matter?

ENGSTRAND: Why, it all came of this here prayer meeting, you see. (*Softly*) The bird's limed, my girl. (*Aloud*) And to think it should be my doing that such a thing should be his Reverence's doing!

MANDERS: But I assure you, Engstrand—

ENGSTRAND: There wasn't another soul except your Reverence as ever laid a finger on the candles down there.

MANDERS: (*Stops*) So you declare. But I certainly cannot recollect that I ever had a candle in my hand.

ENGSTRAND: And I saw as clear as daylight how your Reverance took the candle and snuffed it with your fingers, and threw away the snuff among the shavings.

MANDERS: And you stood and looked on?

ENGSTRAND: Yes; I saw it as plain as a pike-staff, I did.

MANDERS: It's quite beyond my comprehension. Besides, it has never been my habit to snuff candles with my fingers.

ENGSTRAND: And terribly risky it looked, too, that it did! But is there such a deal of harm done after all, your Reverence?

MANDERS: (*Walks restlessly to and fro*) Oh, don't ask me!

ENGTSRAND: (*Walks with him*) And your Reverence hadn't insured it, neither?

MANDERS: (*Continuing to walk up and down*) No, no, no; I have told you so.

ENGSTRAND: (*Following him*) Not insured! And then to go straight away down and set light to the whole thing! Lord, Lord, what a misfortune!

MANDERS: (*Wipes the sweat from his forehead*) Ay, you may well say that, Engstrand.

ENGSTRAND: And to think that such a thing should happen to a benevolent Institution, that was to have been a blessing both to town and country, as the saying goes! The newspapers won't be for handling your Reverence very gently, I expect.

MANDERS: No; that is just what I am thinking of. That is almost the worst of the whole matter. All the malignant attacks and imputations—! Oh, it makes me shudder to think of it!

MRS. ALVING: (*Comes in from the garden*) He is not to be persuaded to leave the fire.

MANDERS: Ah, there you are, Mrs. Alving.

MRS. ALVING: So you have escaped your Inaugural Address, Pastor Manders.

MANDERS: Oh, I should so gladly—

MRS. ALVING: (*In an undertone*) It is all for the best. That Orphanage would have done no one any good.

MANDERS: Do you think not?

MRS. ALVING: Do you think it would?

MANDERS: It is a terrible misfortune, all the same.

MRS. ALVING: Let us speak of it plainly, as a matter of business.—Are you waiting for Mr. Manders, Engstrand?

ENGSTRAND: (*At the hall door*) That's just what I'm a-doing of, ma'am.

MRS. ALVING: Then sit down meanwhile.

ENGSTRAND: Thank you, ma'am; I'd as soon stand.

MRS. ALVING: (*To* MANDERS) I suppose you are going by the steamer?

MANDERS: Yes; it starts in an hour.

MRS. ALVING: Then be so good as to take all the papers with you. I won't hear another word about this affair. I have other things to think of—

MANDERS: Mrs. Alving—

MRS. ALVING: Later on I shall send you a power of attorney to settle everything as you please.

MANDERS: That I will very readily undertake. The original destination of the endowment must now be completely changed, alas!

MRS. ALVING: Of course it must.

MANDERS: I think, first of all, I shall arrange that the Solvik property shall pass to the parish. The land is by no means without value. It can always be turned to account for some purpose or other. And the interest of the money in the Bank I could, perhaps, best apply for the benefit of some undertaking of acknowledged value to the town.

MRS. ALVING: Do just as you please. The whole matter is now completely indifferent to me.

ENGSTRAND: Give a thought to my Sailors' Home, your Reverence.

MANDERS: Upon my word, that is not a bad suggestion. That must be considered.

ENGSTRAND: Oh, devil take considering—Lord forgive me!

MANDERS: (*With a sigh*) And unfortunately I cannot tell how long I shall be able to retain control of these things—whether public opinion may not compel me to retire. It entirely depends upon the result of the official inquiry into the fire—

MRS. ALVING: What are you talking about?

MANDERS: And the result can by no means be foretold.

ENGSTRAND: (*Comes close to him*) Ay, but it can though. For here stands old Jacob Engstrand.

MANDERS: Well well, but—?

ENGSTRAND: (*More softly*) And Jacob Engstrand isn't the man to desert a noble benefactor in the hour of need, as the saying goes.

MANDERS: Yes, but my good fellow—how—?

ENGSTRAND: Jacob Engstrand may be likened to a sort of a guardian angel, he may, your Reverence.

MANDERS: No, no; I really cannot accept that.

ENGSTRAND: Oh, that'll be the way of it, all the same. I know a man as has taken others' sins upon himself before now, I do.

MANDERS: Jacob! (*Wrings his hand*) Yours is a rare nature. Well, you shall be helped with your Sailors' Home. That you may rely upon. (ENGSTRAND *tries to thank him, but cannot for emotion*)

MANDERS: (*Hangs his travelling-bag over ·his shoulder*) And now let us set out. We two will go together.

ENGSTRAND: (*At the dining-room door, softly to* REGINA) You come along too, my lass. You shall live as snug as the yolk in an egg.

REGINA: (*Tosses her head*) Merci! (*She goes out into the hall and fetches* MANDERS' *overcoat*)

MANDERS: Good-bye, Mrs. Alving! and may the spirit of Law and Order descend upon this house, and that quickly.

MRS. ALVING: Good-bye, Pastor Manders. (*She goes up toward the conservatory, as she sees* OSWALD *coming in through the garden door*)

ENGSTRAND: (*While he and* REGINA *help* MANDERS *to get his coat on*) Good-bye, my child. And if any trouble should come to you, you know where Jacob Engstrand is to be found. (*Softly*) Little Harbour Street, h'm—! (*To* MRS. ALVING *and* OSWALD) And the refuge for wandering mariners shall be called "Chamberlain Alving's Home," that it shall! And if so be as I'm spared to carry on that house in my own way, I make so bold as to promise that it shall be worthy of the Chamberlain's memory.

MANDERS: (*In the doorway*) H'm—h'm!—Come along, my dear Engstrand. Good-bye! Good-bye! (*He and* ENGSTRAND *go out through the hall*)

OSWALD: (*Goes towards the table*) What house was he talking about?

MRS. ALVING: Oh, a kind of Home that he and Pastor Manders want to set up.

OSWALD: It will burn down like the other.

MRS. ALVING: What makes you think so?

OSWALD: Everything will burn. All that recalls father's memory is doomed. Here am I, too, burning down. (REGINA *starts and looks at him*)

MRS. ALVING: Oswald! You oughtn't to have remained so long down there, my poor boy.

OSWALD: (*Sits down by the table*) I almost think you are right.

MRS. ALVING: Let me dry your face, Oswald; you are quite wet. (*She dries his face with her pocket-handkerchief*)

OSWALD: (*Stares indifferently in front of him*) Thanks, mother.

MRS. ALVING: Are you not tired, Oswald? Should you like to sleep?

OSWALD: (*Nervously*) No, no—not to sleep! I never sleep. I only pretend to. (*Sadly*) That will come soon enough.

MRS. ALVING: (*Looking sorrowfully at him*) Yes, you really are ill, my blessed boy.

REGINA: (*Eagerly*) Is Mr. Alving ill?

OSWALD: (*Impatiently*) Oh, do shut all the doors! This killing dread—

MRS. ALVING: Close the doors, Regina. (REGINA *shuts them and remains standing by the hall door.* MRS. ALVING *takes her shawl off.* REGINA *does the same.* MRS. ALVING *draws a chair across to* OSWALD'S *and sits by him.*)

MRS. ALVING: There now! I am going to sit beside you—

OSWALD: Yes, do. And Regina shall stay here too. Regina shall be with me always. You will come to the rescue, Regina, won't you?

REGINA: I don't understand—

MRS. ALVING: To the rescue?

OSWALD: Yes—when the need comes.

MRS. ALVING: Oswald, have you not your mother to come to the rescue?

OSWALD: You? (*Smiles*) No, mother; that rescue you will never bring me. (*Laughs sadly*) You! ha ha! (*Looks earnestly at her*) Though, after all, who ought to do it if not you? (*Impetuously*) Why can't you say "thou" to me, Regina? Why don't you call me "Oswald"?

REGINA: (*Softly*) I don't think Mrs. Alving would like it.

MRS. ALVING: You shall have leave to, presently. And meanwhile sit over here beside us. (REGINA *seats herself demurely and hesitatingly at the other side of the table.*)

MRS. ALVING: And now, my poor suffering boy, I am going to take the burden off your mind—

OSWALD: You, mother?

MRS. ALVING: —all the gnawing remorse and self-reproach you speak of.

OSWALD: And you think you can do that?

MRS. ALVING: Yes, now I can, Oswald. A little while ago you spoke of the joy of life; and at that word a new light burst for me over my life and everything connected with it.

OSWALD: (*Shakes his head*) I don't understand you.

MRS. ALVING: You ought to have known your father when he was a young lieutenant. He was brimming over with the joy of life!

OSWALD: Yes, I know he was.

MRS. ALVING: It was like a breezy day only to look at him. And what exuberant strength and vitality there was in him!

OSWALD: Well—?

MRS. ALVING: Well then, child of joy as he was—for he was like a child in those days—he had to live at home here in a half-grown town, which had no joys to offer him—only dissipations. He had no object in life—only an official position. He had no work into which he could throw himself heart and soul; he had only business. He had not a single comrade that could realise what the joy of life meant—only loungers and boon-companions—

OSWALD: Mother—!

MRS. ALVING: So the inevitable happened.

OSWALD: The inevitable?

MRS. ALVING: You told me yourself, this evening, what would become of you if you stayed at home.

OSWALD: Do you mean to say that father—?

MRS. ALVING: Your poor father found no outlet for the overpowering joy of life that was in him. And I brought no brightness into his home.

OSWALD: Not even you?

MRS. ALVING: They had taught me a great deal about duties and so forth, which I went on obstinately believing in. Everything was marked out into duties—into my duties, and his duties, and—I am afraid I made his home intolerable for your poor father, Oswald.

OSWALD: Why have you never spoken of this in writing to me?

MRS. ALVING: I have never before seen it in such a light that I could speak of it to you, his son.

OSWALD: In what light did you see it, then?

MRS. ALVING: (*Slowly*) I saw only this one thing: that your father was a broken-down man before you were born.

OSWALD: (*Softly*) Ah—! (*He rises and walks away to the window*)

MRS. ALVING: And then, day after day, I dwelt on the one thought that by rights Regina should be at home in this house—just like my own boy.

OSWALD: (*Turning round quickly*) Regina—!

REGINA: (*Springs up and asks, with bated breath*) I—?

MRS. ALVING: Yes, now you know it, both of you.

OSWALD: Regina!

REGINA: (*To herself*) So mother was that kind of woman.

MRS. ALVING: Your mother had many good qualities, Regina.

REGINA: Yes, but she was one of that sort, all the same. Oh, I've often suspected it; but—And now, if you please, ma'am, may I be allowed to go away at once?

MRS. ALVING: Do you really wish it, Regina?

REGINA: Yes, indeed I do.

MRS. ALVING: Of course you can do as you like; but—

OSWALD: (*Goes towards* REGINA) Go away now? Your place is here.

REGINA: *Merci*, Mr. Alving!—or now, I suppose, I may say Oswald. But I can tell you this wasn't at all what I expected.

MRS. ALVING: Regina, I have not been frank with you—

REGINA: No, that you haven't indeed. If I'd known that Oswald was an invalid, why— And now, too, that it can never come to anything serious between us— I really can't stop out here in the country and wear myself out nursing sick people.

OSWALD: Not even one who is so near to you?

REGINA: No, that I can't. A poor girl must make the best of her young days, or she'll be left out in the cold before she knows where she is. And I, too, have the joy of life in me, Mrs. Alving!

MRS. ALVING: Unfortunately, you have. But don't throw yourself away, Regina.

REGINA: Oh, what must be, must be. If Oswald takes after his father, I take after my mother, I daresay.—May I ask, ma'am, if Pastor Manders knows all this about me?

MRS. ALVING: Pastor Manders knows all about it.

REGINA: (*Busied in putting on her shawl*) Well then, I'd better make haste and get away by this steamer. The Pastor is such a nice man to deal with; and I certainly think I've as much right to a little of that money as he has—that brute of a carpenter.

MRS. ALVING: You are heartily welcome to it, Regina.

REGINA: (*Looks hard at her*) I think you might have brought me up as a gentleman's daughter, ma'am; it would have suited me better. (*Tosses her head*) But pooh—what does it matter! (*With a bitter side glance at the corked bottle*) I may come to drink champagne with gentlefolks yet.

MRS. ALVING: And if you ever need a home, Regina, come to me.

REGINA: No, thank you, ma'am. Pastor Manders will look after me, I know. And if the worst comes to the worst, I know of one house where I've every right to a place.

MRS. ALVING: Where is that?

REGINA: "Chamberlain Alving's Home."

MRS. ALVING: Regina—now I see it—you are going to your ruin.

REGINA: Oh, stuff! Good-bye. (*She nods and goes out through the hall*)

OSWALD: (*Stands at the window and looks out*) Is she gone?

MRS. ALVING: Yes.

OSWALD: (*Murmuring aside to himself*) I think it was a mistake, this.

MRS. ALVING: (*Goes up behind him and lays her hands on his shoulders*) Oswald, my dear boy—has it shaken you very much?

OSWALD: (*Turns his face towards her*) All that about father, do you mean?

MRS. ALVING: Yes, about your unhappy father. I am so afraid it may have been too much for you.

OSWALD: Why should you fancy that? Of course it came upon me as a great surprise; but it can make no real difference to me.

MRS. ALVING: (*Draws her hands away*) No difference! That your father was infinitely unhappy!

OSWALD: Of course I can pity him, as I would anybody else; but—

MRS. ALVING: Nothing more! Your own father!

OSWALD: (*Impatiently*) Oh, "father,"—"father"! I never knew anything of father. I remember nothing about him, except that he once made me sick.

MRS. ALVING: This is terrible to think of! Ought not a son to love his father, whatever happens?

OSWALD: When a son has nothing to thank his father for? has never known him? Do you really cling to that old superstition?—you who are so enlightened in other ways?

MRS. ALVING: Can it be only a superstition—?

OSWALD: Yes; surely you can see that, mother. It's one of those notions that are current in the world, and so—

MRS. ALVING: (*Deeply moved*) Ghosts!

OSWALD: (*Crossing the room*) Yes; you may call them ghosts.

MRS. ALVING: (*Wildly*) Oswald—then you don't love me, either!

OSWALD: You I know, at any rate—

MRS. ALVING: Yes, you know me; but is that all!

OSWALD: And, of course, I know how fond you are of me, and I can't but be grateful to you. And then you can be so useful to me, now that I am ill.

MRS. ALVING: Yes, cannot I, Oswald? Oh, I could almost bless the illness that has driven you home to me. For I see very plainly that you are not mine: I have to win you.

OSWALD: (*Impatiently*) Yes, yes, yes; all these are just so many phrases. You must remember that I am a sick man, mother. I can't be much taken up with other people; I have enough to do thinking about myself.

MRS. ALVING: (*In a low voice*) I shall be patient and easily satisfied.

OSWALD: And cheerful too, mother!

MRS. ALVING: Yes, my dear boy, you are quite right. (*Goes towards him*) Have I relieved you of all remorse and self-reproach now?

OSWALD: Yes, you have. But now who will relieve me of the dread?

MRS. ALVING: The dread?

OSWALD: (*Walks across the room*) Regina could have been got to do it.

MRS. ALVING: I don't understand you. What is this about dread—and Regina?

OSWALD: Is it very late, mother?

MRS. ALVING: It is early morning. (*She looks out through the conservatory*) The day is dawning over the mountains. And the weather is clearing, Oswald. In a little while you shall see the sun.

OSWALD: I'm glad of that. Oh, I may still have much to rejoice in and live for—

MRS. ALVING: I should think so, indeed!

OSWALD: Even if I can't work—

MRS. ALVING: Oh, you'll soon be able to work again, my dear boy—now that you haven't got all those gnawing and depressing thoughts to brood over any longer.

OSWALD: Yes, I'm glad you were able to rid me of all those fancies. And when I've got over this one thing more— (*Sits on the sofa*) Now we will have a little talk, mother—

MRS. ALVING: Yes, let us. (*She pushes an armchair towards the sofa, and sits down close to him*)

OSWALD: And meantime the sun will be rising. And then you will know all. And then I shall not feel this dread any longer.

MRS. ALVING: What is it that I am to know?

OSWALD: (*Not listening to her*) Mother, did you not say a little while ago, that there was nothing in the world you would not do for me, if I asked you?

MRS. ALVING: Yes, indeed I said so!

OSWALD: And you'll stick to it, mother?

MRS. ALVING: You may rely on that, my dear and only boy! I have nothing in the world to live for but you alone.

OSWALD: Very well, then; now you shall hear—Mother, you have a strong, steadfast mind, I know. Now you're to sit quite still when you hear it.

MRS. ALVING: What dreadful thing can it be—?

OSWALD: You're not to scream out. Do you hear? Do you promise me that? We will sit and talk about it quietly. Do you promise me, mother?

MRS. ALVING: Yes, yes; I promise. Only speak!

OSWALD: Well, you must know that all this fatigue—and my inability to think of work—all that is not the illness itself—

MRS. ALVING: Then what is the illness itself?

OSWALD: The disease I have as my birthright—(*He points to his fore-head and adds very softly*)—is seated here.

MRS. ALVING: (*Almost voiceless*) Oswald! No—no!

OSWALD: Don't scream. I can't bear it. Yes, mother, it is seated here—waiting. And it may break out any day—at any moment.

MRS. ALVING: Oh, what horror—!

OSWALD: Now, quiet, quiet. That is how it stands with me—

MRS. ALVING: (*Springs up*) It's not true, Oswald! It's impossible! It cannot be so!

OSWALD: I have had one attack down there already. It was soon over. But when I came to know the state I had been in, then the dread descended upon me, raging and ravening; and so I set off home to you as fast as I could.

MRS. ALVING: Then this is the dread—!

OSWALD: Yes—it's so indescribably loathsome, you know. Oh, if it had only been as ordinary mortal disease—! For I'm not so afraid of death—though I should like to live as long as I can.

MRS. ALVING: Yes, yes, Oswald, you must!

OSWALD: But this is so unutterably loathsome. To become a little baby again! To have to be fed! To have to— Oh, it's not to be spoken of!

MRS. ALVING: The child has his mother to nurse him.

OSWALD: (*Springs up*) No, never that! That is just what I will not have. I can't endure to think that perhaps I should lie in that state for many years—and get old and grey. And in the meantime you might die and leave me. (*Sits in Mrs. Alving's chair*) For the doctor said it wouldn't necessarily prove fatal at once. He called it a sort of softening of the brain—or something like that. (*Smiles sadly*) I think that expression sounds so nice. It always sets me thinking of cherry-colored velvet—something soft and delicate to stroke.

MRS. ALVING: (*Shrieks*) Oswald!

OSWALD: (*Springs up and paces the room*) And now you have taken Regina from me. If I could only have had her! She would have come to the rescue, I know.

MRS. ALVING: (*Goes to him*) What do you mean by that, my darling boy? Is there any help in the world that I would not give you?

OSWALD: When I got over my attack in Paris, the doctor told me that when it comes again—and it will come—there will be no more hope.

MRS. ALVING: He was heartless enough to—

OSWALD: I demanded it of him. I told him I had preparations to make—(*He smiles cunningly*) And so I had. (*He takes a little box from his inner breast pocket and opens it*) Mother, do you see this?

MRS. ALVING: What is it?

OSWALD: Morphia.

MRS. ALVING: (*Looks at him horror-struck*) Oswald—my boy—

OSWALD: I've scraped together twelve pilules—

MRS. ALVING: (*Snatches at it*) Give me the box, Oswald.

OSWALD: Not yet, mother. (*He hides the box again in his pocket*)

MRS. ALVING: I shall never survive this!

OSWALD: It must be survived. Now if I'd had Regina here, I should have told her how things stood with me—and begged her to come to the rescue at the last. She would have done it. I know she would.

MRS. ALVING: Never!

OSWALD: When the horror had come upon me, and she saw me lying there helpless, like a little newborn baby, impotent, lost, hopeless—past all saving—

MRS. ALVING: Never in all the world would Regina have done this!

OSWALD: Regina would have done it. Regina was so splendidly light-hearted. And she would soon have wearied of nursing an invalid like me.

MRS. ALVING: Then heaven be praised that Regina is not here—

OSWALD: Well then, it is you that must come to the rescue, mother.

MRS. ALVING: (*Shrieks aloud*) I!

OSWALD: Who should do it if not you?

MRS. ALVING: I! your mother!

OSWALD: For that very reason.

MRS. ALVING: I, who gave you life!

OSWALD: I never asked you for life. And what sort of a life have you given me? I will not have it! You shall take it back again!

MRS. ALVING: Help! Help! (*She runs out into the hall*)

OSWALD: (*Going after her*) Do not leave me! Where are you going?

MRS. ALVING: (*In the hall*) To fetch the doctor, Oswald! Let me pass!

OSWALD: (*Also outside*) You shall not go out. And no one shall come in. (*The locking of a door is heard.*)

MRS. ALVING: (*Comes in again*) Oswald! Oswald—my child!

OSWALD: (*Follows her*) Have you a mother's heart for me—and yet can see me suffer from this unutterable dread?

MRS. ALVING: (*After a moment's silence, commands herself, and says:*) Here is my hand upon it.

OSWALD: Will you—

MRS. ALVING: If it should ever be necessary. But it will never be necessary. No, no; it is impossible.

OSWALD: Well, let us hope so. And let us live together as long as we can. Thank you, mother. (*He seats himself in the arm-chair which* MRS. ALVING *has moved to the sofa. Day is breaking. The lamp is still burning on the table*)

MRS. ALVING: (*Drawing near cautiously*) Do you feel calm now?

OSWALD: Yes.

MRS. ALVING: (*Bending over him*) It has been a dreadful fancy of yours, Oswald—nothing but a fancy. All this excitement has been too much for you. But now you shall have a long rest; at home with your mother, my own blessed boy. Everything you point to you shall have, just as when you were a little child.—There now. The crisis is over. You see how easily it passed! Oh, I was sure it would.—And do you see, Oswald, what a lovely day we are going to have? Brilliant sunshine! Now you can really see your home. (*She goes to the table and puts out the lamp. Sunrise. The glacier and the snow-peaks in the background glow in the morning light*)

OSWALD: (*Sits in the arm-chair with his back towards the landscape, without moving. Suddenly he says:*) Mother, give me the sun.

MRS. ALVING: (*By the table, starts and looks at him*) What do you say?

OSWALD: (*Repeats, in a dull, toneless voice*) The sun. The sun.

MRS. ALVING: (*Goes to him*) Oswald, what is the matter with you? (OSWALD *seems to shrink together in the chair; all his muscles relax; his face is expressionless, his eyes have a glassy stare.*)

MRS. ALVING: (*Quivering with terror*) What is this? (*Shrieks*) Oswald! what is the matter with you? (*Falls on her knees beside him and shakes him*) Oswald! Oswald! Look at me! Don't you know me?

OSWALD: (*Tonelessly as before*) The sun.—The sun.

MRS. ALVING: (*Springs up in despair, entwines her hands in her hair and shrieks*) I cannot bear it! (*Whispers, as though petrified*) I cannot bear it! Never! (*Suddenly*) Where has he got them? (*Fumbles hastily in his breast*) Here! (*Shrinks back a few steps and screams:*) No; no; no!—Yes!—No; no! (*She stands a few steps away from him with her hands twisted in her hair, and stares at him in speechless horror*)

OSWALD: (*Sits motionless as before and says*) The sun.—The sun.

THE END

STUDY AND DISCUSSION QUESTIONS

1. (Act I) What are some of the more important aspects of the setting? Does the club foot of Engstrand have any symbolic significance? How does Engstrand feel about Regina? What is his relationship to Pastor Manders? What plan does he have for Regina?

How is Pastor Manders characterized? Do the books on Mrs. Alving's table help to characterize her? Do they have any other significance? What image does Oswald have of his father? What kind of life has Oswald been leading in Paris? Why does Mrs. Alving go to Manders during the first year of her marriage? What is the meaning of Mrs. Alving's exclaimation—"Ghosts! The couple from the conservatory—risen again!"—at the end of the first act?

2.   (Act II) What is the genealogy of Regina? What does Mrs. Alving mean when she says, "Oh, that perpetual law and order! I often think that is what does all the mischief in this world of ours"? How does this statement relate to her relationship with Manders? What are the "ideals" Manders speaks of? What are "the ghosts that hang about" Mrs. Alving? What are the outward manifestations of Oswald's sickness? What is meant by the phrase, "the joy of life"?

3.   (Act III) Who is responsible for the fire at the orphanage? What is Manders' reaction to the fire? What is Mrs. Alving's reaction? Why is it ironic for Oswald to say, "Everything will burn. All that recalls father's memory is doomed. Here I am, too, burning down"? What does Mrs. Alving mean when she says, "And I brought no brightness into his home"? How does Regina react to the truth? What is the meaning of Oswald's request for the sun?

4.   A particular technique Ibsen frequently uses is the echo structure; that is, he will repeat a word, scene, action, symbol, or metaphor. In this play there are a number of such echoes. For instance, the weather seems to be symbolic of the psychological development of some of the characters and particularly of Mrs. Alving. What is Ibsen's purpose for continually emphasizing the weather pattern? Find other echoes in the play and discuss their function.

5.   One of the characteristics of the movement known as Realism is its exploration in the name of truth of the existing institutions and the conventions of thought and feeling. The main purpose of Ibsen and other Realists is to unmask the many illusions that exist in society. F. W. Kaufman ("Ibsen's Conception of Truth") says that Pastor Manders "blinds himself with regard to that part of reality which cannot be caught in his narrow formulas and is thus prevented from any access to the problems which are submitted to him for moral and spiritual advice." What are some of the moral problems that are "submitted" to him? What are the institutions

that are attacked in *Ghosts?* Discuss the importance of Mrs. Alving's facing her hypocrisy and self-deception.

6. Ibsen employs several dramatic techniques in order to strengthen the structure of the play. One of these techniques is the use of irony. For example, before she realizes her genealogy, Regina says that she is "treated almost as a daughter here." Find other uses of irony and the function they perform. Another technique Ibsen uses is paradox; that is, the situation in which a statement or an occurrence seems to be self-contradictory but is at the same time quite logical. Discuss the use Ibsen makes of paradox in *Ghosts.*

7. Elder Olson (*Tragedy and the Theory of Drama*) says the plot's function is to show that "the action and the characters are designed to prove, by example, that in a society in which duty is invariably opposed to pleasure, the good must suffer or become corrupt, while the wicked flourish in hypocrisy." Discuss this statement in relation to the following: the marriage of the Alvings; Mrs. Alving's flight from her husband; Mr. Alving's disease; the birth of Oswald; the significance of the ending.

8. The original draft of *Ghosts* has not been preserved; however, after Ibsen's death some six notes were found that seem to relate to the play. One of the notes as published by Michael Meyer ("Ibsen's Notes to *Ghosts*") states that "The main theme must be: the fine flowing of our spiritual life via literature, art, etc.—and, in contrast, all mankind wandering blindly on the wrong track." Ibsen seems to feel that the moral life that was once in the hands of the Church has passed to the charge of the artist and the philosopher. Discuss this view in relation to *Ghosts.* Using *Ghosts* as a basis of analysis, discuss the complexity of life as the artist conceives it.

9. While discussing the nature of tragedy in the modern world, Joseph Wood Krutch (*The Modern Temper*) states "that the problems of Oswald Alving are more relevant to our life than the problems of Hamlet (or Othello), that the play in which he (Alving) appears is more 'real' than the other more glamorous one, but it is exactly because we find it so that we are condemned. We can believe in Oswald but we cannot believe in Othello, and a light has gone out of the universe." Discuss what Krutch means by "a light has gone out of the universe." Why is Oswald more "real" to us than is Othello? Why are Oswald's problems more relevant to us?

WRITING TOPICS

1. Write an essay explaining the full significance of the title, *Ghosts*. *Or* write an essay explaining the function of the minor characters.

2. "The trouble is that mankind as a whole is a failure. If a human being demands to live and develop according to his nature as a human being, it's regarded as megalomania (a tendency to exaggerate or magnify). All humanity, especially Christians, suffers from megalomania." Write an essay analyzing, in terms of the central theme of *Ghosts*, this quotation by Ibsen (notes on *Ghosts*).

3. Write an essay explaining the significance of the "sun-son" in the play. *Or* discuss in a paper whether or not Pastor Manders is a hypocrite.

4. Halvadan Koht (*Shakespeare and Ibsen*) suggests that one of the most significant influences Shakespeare's works had on Ibsen was that "they inspired him with the passion of search for psychological forces at the bottom of dramatic conflicts. Through them he learned to focus his efforts on the one decisive element of true drama, the study and depiction, merciless and merciful at the same time, of individual characters opposed in battle for life or death, living themselves out, so to speak, according to their innermost essence and for that very reason typically human in their individualities." Write an essay comparing the protagonists of *Othello* and *Ghosts* in the struggle for "their innermost essence."

5. Develop an essay showing how Ibsen transmits the idea of heredity into the Fate of the Greek tragedy. Use either *Oedipus* or *Antigone* as a basis for comparison.

HEDDA GABLER

Henrik Ibsen

Translated from the Norwegian by William Archer

Characters

GEORGE TESMAN
HEDDA TESMAN, *his wife.*
MISS JULIANA TESMAN, *his aunt.*
MRS. ELVSTED
JUDGE BRACK
EILERT LÖVBORG
BERTA, *servant at the Tesmans.*

The scene of the action is Tesman's villa, in the west end of Christiana.

ACT I.

A spacious, handsome, and tastefully furnished drawing-room, decorated in dark colors. In the back, a wide doorway with curtains drawn back, leading into a smaller room decorated in the same style as the drawing-room. In the right-hand wall of the front

Hedda Gabler is reprinted with the permission of Charles Scribner's Sons from Volume X of *The Collected Works of Henrik Ibsen*, translated by William Archer (1906, 1907).

room, a folding door leading out to the hall. In the opposite wall, on the left, a glass door, also with curtains drawn back. Through the panes can be seen part of a veranda outside, and trees covered with autumn foliage. An oval table, with a cover on it, and surrounded by chairs, stands well forward. In front, by the wall on the right, a wide stove of dark porcelain, a high-backed arm-chair, a cushioned foot-rest, and two footstools. A settee, with a small round table in front of it, fills the upper right-hand corner. In front, on the left, a little way from the wall, a sofa. Further back than the glass door, a piano. On either side of the doorway at the back a whatnot with terra-cotta and majolica ornaments.—Against the back wall of the inner room a sofa, with a table, and one or two chairs. Over the sofa hangs the portrait of a handsome elderly man in a General's uniform. Over the table a hanging lamp, with an opal glass shade.—A number of bouquets are arranged about the drawing-room, in vases and glasses. Others lie upon the tables. The floors in both rooms are covered with thick carpets.—Morning light. The sun shines in through the glass door.

MISS JULIANA TESMAN, *with her bonnet on and carrying a parasol, comes in from the hall, followed by* BERTA, *who carries a bouquet wrapped in paper.* MISS TESMAN *is a comely and pleasant-looking lady of about sixty-five. She is nicely but simply dressed in a gray walking-costume.* BERTA *is a middle-aged woman of plain and rather countrified appearance.*

MISS TESMAN: *(Stops close to the door, listens, and says softly)* Upon my word, I don't believe they are stirring yet!

BERTA: *(Also softly)* I told you so, Miss. Remember how late the steamboat got in last night. And then, when they got home!—good Lord, what a lot the young mistress had to unpack before she could get to bed.

MISS TESMAN: Well, well—let them have their sleep out. But let us see that they get a good breath of the fresh morning air when they do appear. *(She goes to the glass door and throws it open)*

BERTA: *(Beside the table, at a loss what to do with the bouquet in her hand)* I declare there isn't a bit of room left. I think I'll put it down here, Miss. *(She places it on the piano)*

MISS TESMAN: So you've got a new mistress now, my dear Berta. Heaven knows it was a wrench to me to part with you.

BERTA: *(On the point of weeping)* And do you think it wasn't hard for me, too, Miss? After all the blessed years I've been with you and Miss Rina.

MISS TESMAN: We must make the best of it, Berta. There was nothing else to be done. George can't do without you, you see—he absolutely can't. He has had you to look after him ever since he was a little boy.

BERTA: Ah, but, Miss Julia, I can't help thinking of Miss Rina lying helpless at home there, poor thing. And with only that new girl, too! She'll never learn to take proper care of an invalid.

MISS TESMAN: Oh, I shall manage to train her. And, of course, you know I shall take most of it upon myself. You needn't be uneasy about my poor sister, my dear Berta.

BERTA: Well, but there's another thing, Miss. I'm so mortally afraid I shan't be able to suit the young mistress.

MISS TESMAN: Oh, well—just at first there may be one or two things——

BERTA: Most like she'll be terrible grand in her ways.

MISS TESMAN: Well, you can't wonder at that—General Gabler's daughter! Think of the sort of life she was accustomed to in her father's time. Don't you remember how we used to see her riding down the road along with the General? In that long black habit—and with feathers in her hat?

BERTA: Yes, indeed—I remember well enough!—But, good Lord, I should never have dreamt in those days that she and Master George would make a match of it.

MISS TESMAN: Nor I.—But by-the-bye, Berta—while I think of it: in future you mustn't say Master George. You must say Dr. Tesman.

BERTA: Yes, the young mistress spoke of that, too—last night—the moment they set foot in the house. Is it true then, Miss?

MISS TESMAN: Yes, indeed it is. Only think, Berta—some foreign university has made him a doctor—while he has been abroad, you understand. I hadn't heard a word about it, until he told me himself upon the pier.

BERTA: Well, well, he's clever enough for anything, he is. But I didn't think he'd have gone in for doctoring people, too.

MISS TESMAN: No, no, it's not that sort of doctor he is. (*Nods significantly*) But let me tell you, we may have to call him something still grander before long.

BERTA: You don't say so! What can that be, Miss?

MISS TESMAN: (*Smiling*) H'm—wouldn't you like to know! (*With emotion*) Ah, dear, dear—if my poor brother could only look up from his grave now, and see what his little boy has grown into! (*Looks around*) But bless me, Berta—why have you done this? Taken the chintz covers off all the furniture?

BERTA: The mistress told me to. She can't abide covers on the chairs, she says.

MISS TESMAN: Are they going to make this their everyday sitting-room then?

BERTA: Yes, that's what I understood—from the mistress. Master George—the doctor—he said nothing.

> GEORGE TESMAN *comes from the right into the inner room, humming to himself, and carrying an unstrapped empty portmanteau. He is a middle-sized, young-looking man of thirty-three, rather stout, with a round, open, cheerful face, fair hair and beard. He wears spectacles, and is somewhat carelessly dressed in comfortable indoor clothes.*

MISS TESMAN: Good morning, good morning, George.

TESMAN: (*In the doorway between the rooms*) Aunt Julia! Dear Aunt Julia! (*Goes up to her and shakes hands warmly*) Come all this way—so early! Eh?

MISS TESMAN: Why, of course I had to come and see how you were getting on.

TESMAN: In spite of your having had no proper night's rest?

MISS TESMAN: Oh, that makes no difference to me.

TESMAN: Well, I suppose you got home all right from the pier? Eh?

MISS TESMAN: Yes, quite safely, thank goodness. Judge Brack was good enough to see me right to my door.

TESMAN: We were so sorry we couldn't give you a seat in the carriage. But you saw what a pile of boxes Hedda had to bring with her.

MISS TESMAN: Yes, she had certainly plenty of boxes.

BERTA: (*To* TESMAN) Shall I go in and see if there's anything I can do for the mistress?

TESMAN: No thank you, Berta—you needn't. She said she would ring if she wanted anything.

BERTA: (*Going towards the right*) Very well.

TESMAN: But look here—take this portmanteau with you.

BERTA: (*Taking it*) I'll put it in the attic. (*She goes out by the hall door*)

TESMAN: Fancy, Auntie—I had the whole of that portmanteau chock full of copies of documents. You wouldn't believe how much I have picked up from all the archives I have been examining—curious old details that no one has had any idea of——

MISS TESMAN: Yes, you don't seem to have wasted your time on your wedding trip, George.

TESMAN: No, that I haven't. But do take off your bonnet, Auntie. Look here! Let me untie the strings—eh?

MISS TESMAN: *(While he does so)* Well well—this is just as if you were still at home with us.

TESMAN: *(With the bonnet in his hand, looks at it from all sides)* Why, what a gorgeous bonnet you've been investing in!

MISS TESMAN: I bought it on Hedda's account.

TESMAN: On Hedda's account? Eh?

MISS TESMAN: Yes, so that Hedda needn't be ashamed of me if we happened to go out together.

TESMAN: *(Patting her cheek)* You always think of everything, Aunt Julia. *(Lays the bonnet on a chair beside the table)* And now, look here —suppose we sit comfortably on the sofa and have a little chat, till Hedda comes. *(They seat themselves. She places her parasol in the corner of the sofa)*

MISS TESMAN: *(Takes both his hands and looks at him)* What a delight it is to have you again, as large as life, before my very eyes, George! My George—my poor brother's own boy!

TESMAN: And it's a delight for me, too, to see you again, Aunt Julia! You, who have been father and mother in one to me.

MISS TESMAN: Oh yes, I know you will always keep a place in your heart for your old aunts.

TESMAN: And what about Aunt Rina? No improvement—eh?

MISS TESMAN: Oh no—we can scarcely look for any improvement in her case, poor thing. There she lies, helpless, as she has lain for all these years. But heaven grant I may not lose her yet awhile. For if I did, I don't know what I should make of my life, George—especially now that I haven't you to look after any more.

TESMAN: *(Patting her back)* There there there——!

MISS TESMAN: *(Suddenly changing her tone)* And to think that here are you a married man, George!—And that you should be the one to carry off Hedda Gabler—the beautiful Hedda Gabler! Only think of it —she, that was so beset with admirers!

TESMAN: *(Hums a little and smiles complacently)* Yes, I fancy I have several good friends about town who would like to stand in my shoes —eh?

MISS TESMAN: And then this fine long wedding-tour you have had! More than five—nearly six months——

TESMAN: Well, for me it has been a sort of tour of research as well. I have had to do so much grubbing among old records—and to read no end of books too, Auntie.

MISS TESMAN: Oh yes, I suppose so. *(More confidentially, and lowering her voice a little*) But listen now, George,—have you nothing—nothing special to tell me?

TESMAN: As to our journey?

MISS TESMAN: Yes.

TESMAN: No, I don't know of anything except what I have told you in my letters. I had a doctor's degree conferred on me—but that I told you yesterday.

MISS TESMAN: Yes, yes, you did. But what I mean is—haven't you any—any—expectations——?

TESMAN: Expectations?

MISS TESMAN: Why you know, George—I'm your old auntie!

TESMAN: Why, of course I have expectations.

MISS TESMAN: Ah!

TESMAN: I have every expectation of being a professor one of these days.

MISS TESMAN: Oh yes, a professor——

TESMAN: Indeed, I may say I am certain of it. But my dear Auntie—you know all about that already!

MISS TESMAN: (*Laughing to herself*) Yes, of course I do. You are quite right there. (*Changing the subject*) But we were talking about your journey. It must have cost a great deal of money, George?

TESMAN: Well, you see—my handsome traveling-scholarship went a good way.

MISS TESMAN: But I can't understand how you can have made it go far enough for two.

TESMAN: No, that's not so easy to understand—eh?

MISS TESMAN: And especially travelling with a lady—they tell me that makes it ever so much more expensive.

TESMAN: Yes, of course—it makes it a little more expensive. But Hedda had to have this trip, Auntie! She really had to. Nothing else would have done.

MISS TESMAN: No no, I suppose not. A wedding-tour seems to be quite indispensable nowadays.—But tell me now—have you gone thoroughly over the house yet?

TESMAN: Yes, you may be sure I have. I have been afoot ever since daylight.

MISS TESMAN: And what do you think of it all?

TESMAN: I'm delighted! Quite delighted! Only I can't think what we are to do with the two empty rooms between this inner parlor and Hedda's bedroom.

MISS TESMAN: (*Laughing*) Oh my dear George, I daresay you may find some use for them—in the course of time.

TESMAN: Why of course you are quite right, Aunt Julia! You mean as my library increases—eh?

MISS TESMAN: Yes, quite so, my dear boy. It was your library I was thinking of.

TESMAN: I am specially pleased on Hedda's account. Often and often, before we were engaged, she said that she would never care to live anywhere but in Secretary Falk's villa.

MISS TESMAN: Yes, it was lucky that this very house should come into the market, just after you had started.

TESMAN: Yes, Aunt Julia, the luck was on our side, wasn't it—eh?

MISS TESMAN: But the expense, my dear George! You will find it very expensive, all this.

TESMAN: (*Looks at her, a little cast down*) Yes, I suppose I shall, Aunt!

MISS TESMAN: Oh, frightfully!

TESMAN: How much do you think? In round numbers?—Eh?

MISS TESMAN: Oh, I can't even guess until all the accounts come in.

TESMAN: Well, fortunately, Judge Brack has secured the most favorable terms for me,—so he said in a letter to Hedda.

MISS TESMAN: Yes, don't be uneasy, my dear boy.—Besides, I have given security for the furniture and all the carpets.

TESMAN: Security? You? My dear Aunt Julia—what sort of security could you give?

MISS TESMAN: I have given a mortgage on our annuity.

TESMAN: (*Jumps up*) What! On your—and Aunt Rina's annuity!

MISS TESMAN: Yes, I knew of no other plan, you see.

TESMAN: (*Placing himself before her*) Have you gone out of your senses, Auntie! Your annuity—it's all that you and Aunt Rina have to live upon.

MISS TESMAN: Well well—don't get so excited about it. It's only a matter of form you know—Judge Brack assured me of that. It was he that was kind enough to arrange the whole affair for me. A mere matter of form, he said.

TESMAN: Yes, that may be all very well. But nevertheless——

MISS TESMAN: You will have your own salary to depend upon now. And, good heavens, even if we did have to pay up a little——! To eke things out a bit at the start——! Why, it would be nothing but a pleasure to us.

TESMAN: Oh Auntie—will you never be tired of making sacrifices for me!

MISS TESMAN: (*Rises and lays her hand on his shoulders*) Have I any other happiness in this world except to smooth your way for you, my dear boy? You, who have had neither father nor mother to depend on.

And now we have reached the goal, George! Things have looked black enough for us, sometimes; but, thank heaven, now you have nothing to fear.

TESMAN: Yes, it is really marvelous how everything has turned out for the best.

MISS TESMAN: And the people who opposed you—who wanted to bar the way for you—now you have them at your feet. They have fallen, George. Your most dangerous rival—his fall was the worst.—And now he has to lie on the bed he has made for himself—poor misguided creature.

TESMAN: Have you heard anything of Eilert? Since I went away, I mean.

MISS TESMAN: Only that he is said to have published a new book.

TESMAN: What! Eilert Lövborg! Recently—eh?

MISS TESMAN: Yes, so they say. Heaven knows whether it can be worth anything! Ah, when your new book appears—that will be another story, George! What is it to be about?

TESMAN: It will deal with the domestic industries of Brabant during the Middle Ages.

MISS TESMAN: Fancy—to be able to write on such a subject as that!

TESMAN: However, it may be some time before the book is ready. I have all these collections to arrange first, you see.

MISS TESMAN: Yes, collecting and arranging—no one can beat you at that. There you are my poor brother's own son.

TESMAN: I am looking forward eagerly to setting to work at it; especially now that I have my own delightful home to work in.

MISS TESMAN: And, most of all, now that you have got the wife of your heart, my dear George.

TESMAN: (*Embracing her*) Oh yes, yes, Aunt Julia. Hedda—she is the best part of it all! (*Looks towards the doorway*) I believe I hear her coming—eh?

HEDDA *enters from the left through the inner room. She is a woman of nine-and-twenty. Her face and figure show refinement and distinction. Her complexion is pale and opaque. Her steel-gray eyes express a cold, unruffled repose. Her hair is of an agreeable medium brown, but not particularly abundant. She is dressed in a tasteful, somewhat loose-fitting morning gown.*

MISS TESMAN: (*Going to meet* HEDDA) Good morning, my dear Hedda! Good morning, and a hearty welcome!

HEDDA: (*Holds out her hand*) Good morning, dear Miss Tesman! So early a call! That is kind of you.

MISS TESMAN: (*With some embarrassment*) Well—has the bride slept well in her new home?

HEDDA: Oh yes, thanks. Passably.

TESMAN: (*Laughing*) Passably! Come, that's good, Hedda! You were sleeping like a stone when I got up.

HEDDA: Fortunately. Of course one has always to accustom one's self to new surroundings, Miss Tesman—little by little. (*Looking towards the left*) Oh—there the servant has gone and opened the veranda door, and let in a whole flood of sunshine.

MISS TESMAN: (*Going towards the door*) Well, then we will shut it.

HEDDA: No no, not that! Tesman, please draw the curtains. That will give a softer light.

TESMAN: (*At the door*) All right—all right.—There now, Hedda, now you have both shade and fresh air.

HEDDA: Yes, fresh air we certainly must have, with all these stacks of flowers——. But—won't you sit down, Miss Tesman?

MISS TESMAN: No, thank you. Now that I have seen that everything is all right here—thank heaven!—I must be getting home again. My sister is lying longing for me, poor thing.

TESMAN: Give her my very best love, Auntie; and say I shall look in and see her later in the day.

MISS TESMAN: Yes, yes, I'll be sure to tell her. But by the by, George— (*Feeling in her dress pocket*)—I had almost forgotten—I have something for you here.

TESMAN: What is it, Auntie? Eh?

MISS TESMAN: (*Produces a flat parcel wrapped in newspaper and hands it to him*) Look here, my dear boy.

TESMAN: (*Opening the parcel*) Well, I declare!—Have you really saved them for me, Aunt Julia! Hedda! isn't this touching—eh?

HEDDA: (*Beside the whatnot on the right*) Well, what is it?

TESMAN: My old morning-shoes! My slippers.

HEDDA: Indeed. I remember you often spoke of them while we were abroad.

TESMAN: Yes, I missed them terribly. (*Goes up to her*) Now you shall see them, Hedda!

HEDDA: (*Going towards the stove*) Thanks, I really don't care about it.

TESMAN: (*Following her*) Only think—ill as she was, Aunt Rina embroidered these for me. Oh you can't think how many associations cling to them.

HEDDA: (*At the table*) Scarcely for me.

364 *Plays by Four Tragedians*

MISS TESMAN: Of course not for Hedda, George.

TESMAN: Well, but now that she belongs to the family, I thought——

HEDDA: (*Interrupting*) We shall never get on with this servant, Tesman.

MISS TESMAN: Not get on with Berta?

TESMAN: Why, dear, what puts that in your head? Eh?

HEDDA: (*Pointing*) Look there! She has left her old bonnet lying about on a chair.

TESMAN: (*In consternation, drops the slippers on the floor*) Why, Hedda——

HEDDA: Just fancy, if any one should come in and see it!

TESMAN: But Hedda—that's Aunt Julia's bonnet.

HEDDA: Is it!

MISS TESMAN: (*Taking up the bonnet*) Yes, indeed it's mine. And, what's more, its not old, Madam Hedda.

HEDDA: I really did not look closely at it, Miss Tesman.

MISS TESMAN: (*Trying on the bonnet*) Let me tell you it's the first time I have worn it—the very first time.

TESMAN: And a very nice bonnet it is too—quite a beauty!

MISS TESMAN: Oh, it's no such great thing, George. (*Looks around her*) My parasol——? Ah, here. (*Takes it*) For this is mine too—(*mutters*)—not Berta's.

TESMAN: A new bonnet and a new parasol! Only think, Hedda!

HEDDA: Very handsome indeed.

TESMAN: Yes, isn't it? Eh? But Auntie, take a good look at Hedda before you go! See how handsome she is!

MISS TESMAN: Oh, my dear boy, there's nothing new in that. Hedda was always lovely. (*She nods and goes towards the right*)

TESMAN: (*Following*) Yes, but have you noticed what splendid condition she is in? How she has filled out on the journey?

HEDDA: (*Crossing the room*) Oh, do be quiet——!

MISS TESMAN: (*Who has stopped and turned*) Filled out?

TESMAN: Of course you don't notice it so much now that she has that dress on. But I, who can see——

HEDDA: (*At the glass door, impatiently*) Oh, you can't see anything.

TESMAN: It must be the mountain air in the Tyrol——

HEDDA: (*Curtly, interrupting*) I am exactly as I was when I started.

TESMAN: So you insist; but I'm quite certain you are not. Don't you agree with me, Auntie?

MISS TESMAN: (*Who has been gazing at her with folded hands*) Hedda is lovely—lovely—lovely. (*Goes up to her, takes her head between both hands, draws it downwards, and kisses her hair*) God bless and preserve Hedda Tesman—for George's sake.

HEDDA: (*Gently freeing herself*) Oh—! Let me go.

MISS TESMAN: (*In quiet emotion*) I shall not let a day pass without coming to see you.

TESMAN: No you won't, will you, Auntie? Eh?

MISS TESMAN: Good-bye—good-bye!

> *She goes out by the hall door.* TESMAN *accompanies her. The door remains half open.* TESMAN *can be heard repeating his message to* AUNT RINA *and his thanks for the slippers.*
> *In the meantime,* HEDDA *walks about the room, raising her arms and clenching her hands as if in desperation. Then she flings back the curtains from the glass door, and stands there looking out. Presently* TESMAN *returns and closes the door behind him.*

TESMAN: (*Picks up the slippers from the floor*) What are you looking at, Hedda?

HEDDA: (*Once more calm and mistress of herself*) I am only looking at the leaves. They are so yellow—so withered.

TESMAN: (*Wraps up the slippers and lays them on the table*) Well you see, we are well into September now.

HEDDA: (*Again restless*) Yes, to think of it!—Already in—in September.

TESMAN: Don't you think Aunt Julia's manner was strange, dear? Almost solemn? Can you imagine what was the matter with her? Eh?

HEDDA: I scarcely know her, you see. Is she not often like that?

TESMAN: No, not as she was to-day.

HEDDA: (*Leaving the glass door*) Do you think she was annoyed about the bonnet?

TESMAN: Oh, scarcely at all. Perhaps a little, just at the moment——

HEDDA: But what an idea, to pitch her bonnet about in the drawing-room! No one does that sort of thing.

TESMAN: Well you may be sure Aunt Julia won't do it again.

HEDDA: In any case, I shall manage to make my peace with her.

TESMAN: Yes, my dear, good Hedda, if you only would.

HEDDA: When you call this afternoon, you might invite her to spend the evening here.

TESMAN: Yes, that I will. And there's one thing more you could do that would delight her heart.

HEDDA: What is it?

TESMAN: If you could only prevail on yourself to say *du* to her. For my sake, Hedda? Eh?

HEDDA: No no, Tesman—you really mustn't ask that of me. I have told you so already. I shall try to call her "Aunt"; and you must be satisfied with that.

TESMAN: Well well. Only I think now that you belong to the family, you——

HEDDA: H'm—I can't in the least see why—— (*She goes up towards the middle doorway*)

TESMAN: (*After a pause*) Is there anything the matter with you, Hedda? Eh?

HEDDA: I'm only looking at my old piano. It doesn't go at all well with all the other things.

TESMAN: The first time I draw my salary, we'll see about exchanging it.

HEDDA: No, no—no exchanging. I don't want to part with it. Suppose we put it there in the inner room, and then get another here in its place. When it's convenient, I mean.

TESMAN: (*A little taken aback*) Yes—of course we could do that.

HEDDA: (*Takes up the bouquet from the piano*) These flowers were not here last night when we arrived.

TESMAN: Aunt Julia must have brought them for you.

HEDDA: (*Examining the bouquet*) A visiting-card. (*Takes it out and reads*) "Shall return later in the day." Can you guess whose card it is?

TESMAN: No. Whose? Eh?

HEDDA: The name is "Mrs. Elvsted."

TESMAN: Is it really? Sheriff Elvsted's wife? Miss Rysing that was.

HEDDA: Exactly. The girl with the irritating hair, that she was always showing off. An old flame of yours I've been told.

TESMAN: (*Laughing*) Oh, that didn't last long; and it was before I knew you, Hedda. But fancy her being in town!

HEDDA: It's odd that she should call upon us. I have scarcely seen her since we left school.

TESMAN: I haven't seen her either for—heaven knows how long. I wonder how she can endure to live in such an out-of-the-way hole—eh?

HEDDA: (*After a moment's thought, says suddenly*) Tell me, Tesman— isn't it somewhere near there that he—that—Eilert Lövborg is living?

TESMAN: Yes, he is somewhere in that part of the country.

BERTA *enters by the hall door.*

BERTA: That lady, ma'am, that brought some flowers a little while ago, is here again. (*Pointing*) The flowers you have in your hand, ma'am.

HEDDA: Ah, is she? Well, please show her in.

BERTA *opens the door for* MRS. ELVSTED, *and goes out herself.*—MRS. ELVSTED *is a woman of fragile figure, with pretty, soft features.*

Her eyes are light blue, large, round, and somewhat prominent,
with a startled, inquiring expression. Her hair is remarkably light,
almost flaxen, and unusually abundant and wavy. She is a couple
of years younger than HEDDA. *She wears a dark visiting dress,*
tasteful, but not quite in the latest fashion.

HEDDA: (*Receives her warmly*) How do you do, my dear Mrs. Elvsted?
It's delightful to see you again.

MRS. ELVSTED: (*Nervously, struggling for self-control*) Yes, it's a very
long time since we met.

TESMAN: (*Gives her his hand*) And we too—eh?

HEDDA: Thanks for your lovely flowers——

MRS. ELVSTED: Oh, not at all—— I would have come straight here
yesterday afternoon; but I heard that you were away——

TESMAN: Have you just come to town? Eh?

MRS. ELVSTED: I arrived yesterday, about midday. Oh, I was quite in
despair when I heard that you were not at home.

HEDDA: In despair! How so?

TESMAN: Why, my dear Mrs. Rysing—I mean Mrs. Elvsted——

HEDDA: I hope that you are not in any trouble?

MRS. ELVSTED: Yes, I am. And I don't know another living creature
here that I can turn to.

HEDDA: (*Laying the bouquet on the table*) Come—let us sit here on
the sofa——

MRS. ELVSTED: Oh, I am too restless to sit down.

HEDDA: Oh no, you're not. Come here. (*She draws* MRS. ELVSTED *down*
upon the sofa and sits at her side)

TESMAN: Well? What is it, Mrs. Elvsted——?

HEDDA: Has anything particular happened to you at home?

MRS. ELVSTED: Yes—and no. Oh—I am so anxious you should not
misunderstand me——

HEDDA: Then your best plan is to tell us the whole story, Mrs. Elvsted.

TESMAN: I suppose that's what you have come for—eh?

MRS. ELVSTED: Yes, yes—of course it is. Well then, I must tell you—if
you don't already know—that Eilert Lövborg is in town, too.

HEDDA: Lövborg——!

TESMAN: What! Has Eilert Lövborg come back? Fancy that, Hedda!

HEDDA: Well well—I hear it.

MRS. ELVSTED: He has been here a week already. Just fancy—a whole
week! In this terrible town, alone! With so many temptations on all
sides.

HEDDA: But, my dear Mrs. Elvsted—how does he concern you so much?

MRS. ELVSTED: (*Looks at her with a startled air, and says rapidly*) He was the children's tutor.

HEDDA: Your children's?

MRS. ELVSTED: My husband's. I have none.

HEDDA: Your step-children's, then?

MRS. ELVSTED: Yes.

TESMAN: (*Somewhat hesitatingly*) Then was he—I don't know how to express it—was he—regular enough in his habits to be fit for the post? Eh?

MRS. ELVSTED: For the last two years his conduct has been irreproachable.

TESMAN: Has it indeed? Fancy that, Hedda!

HEDDA: I hear it.

MRS. ELVSTED: Perfectly irreproachable, I assure you! In every respect. But all the same—now that I know he is here—in this great town—and with a large sum of money in his hands—I can't help being in mortal fear for him.

TESMAN: Why did he not remain where he was? With you and your husband? Eh?

MRS. ELVSTED: After his book was published he was too restless and unsettled to remain with us.

TESMAN: Yes, by the by, Aunt Julia told me he had published a new book.

MRS. ELVSTED: Yes, a big book, dealing with the march of civilization—in broad outline, as it were. It came out about a fortnight ago. And since it has sold so well, and been so much read—and made such a sensation——

TESMAN: Has it indeed? It must be something he has had lying by since his better days.

MRS. ELVSTED: Long ago, you mean?

TESMAN: Yes.

MRS. ELVSTED: No, he has written it all since he has been with us—within the last year.

TESMAN: Isn't that good news, Hedda? Think of that.

MRS. ELVSTED: Ah yes, if only it would last!

HEDDA: Have you seen him here in town?

MRS. ELVSTED: No, not yet. I have had the greatest difficulty in finding out his address. But this morning I discovered it at last.

HEDDA: (*Looks searchingly at her*) Do you know, it seems to me a little odd of your husband—h'm——

MRS. ELVSTED: (*Starting nervously*) Of my husband! What?

HEDDA: That he should send you to town on such an errand—that he does not come himself and look after his friend.

MRS. ELVSTED: Oh no, no—my husband has no time. And besides, I—I had some shopping to do.

HEDDA: (*With a slight smile*) Ah, that is a different matter.

MRS. ELVSTED: (*Rising quickly and uneasily*) And now I beg and implore you, Mr. Tesman—receive Eilert Lövborg kindly if he comes to you! And that he is sure to do. You see you were such great friends in the old days. And then you are interested in the same studies—the same branch of science—so far as I can understand.

TESMAN: We used to be, at any rate.

MRS. ELVSTED: That is why I beg so earnestly that you—you too—will keep a sharp eye upon him. Oh, you will promise me that, Mr. Tesman —won't you?

TESMAN: With the greatest of pleasure, Mrs. Rysing——

HEDDA: Elvsted.

TESMAN: I assure you I shall do all I possibly can for Eilert. You may rely upon me.

MRS. ELVSTED: Oh, how very, very kind of you! (*Presses his hands*) Thanks, thanks, thanks! (*Frightened*) You see, my husband is so very fond of him!

HEDDA: (*Rising*) You ought to write to him, Tesman. Perhaps he may not care to come to you of his own accord.

TESMAN: Well, perhaps it would be the right thing to do, Hedda? Eh?

HEDDA: And the sooner the better. Why not at once?

MRS. ELVSTED: (*Imploringly*) Oh, if you only would!

TESMAN: I'll write this moment. Have you his address, Mrs.—Mrs. Elvsted?

MRS. ELVSTED: Yes. (*Takes a slip of paper from her pocket, and hands it to him*) Here it is.

TESMAN: Good, good. Then I'll go in—— (*Looks about him*) By the by —my slippers? Oh, here. (*Takes the packet, and is about to go*)

HEDDA: Be sure you write him a cordial, friendly letter. And a good long one too.

TESMAN: Yes, I will

MRS. ELVSTED: But please, please don't say a word to show that I have suggested it.

TESMAN: No, how could you think I would? Eh? (*He goes out to the right, through the inner room*)

HEDDA: (*Goes up to* MRS. ELVSTED, *smiles, and says in a low voice*) There! We have killed two birds with one stone.

MRS. ELVSTED: What do you mean?

HEDDA: Could you not see that I wanted him to go?

MRS. ELVSTED: Yes, to write the letter——

HEDDA: And that I might speak to you alone.

MRS. ELVSTED: (*Confused*) About the same thing?

HEDDA: Precisely.

MRS. ELVSTED: (*Apprehensively*) But there is nothing more, Mrs. Tesman! Absolutely nothing!

HEDDA: Oh yes, but there is. There is a great deal more—I can see that. Sit here—and we'll have a cosy, confidential chat. (*She forces* MRS. ELVSTED *to sit in the easy-chair beside the stove, and seats herself on one of the footstools*)

MRS. ELVSTED: (*Anxiously, looking at her watch*) But, my dear Mrs. Tesman—I was really on the point of going.

HEDDA: Oh, you can't be in such a hurry.—Well? Now tell me something about your life at home.

MRS. ELVSTED: Oh, that is just what I care least to speak about.

HEDDA: But to me, dear——? Why, weren't we schoolfellows?

MRS. ELVSTED: Yes, but you were in the class above me. Oh, how dreadfully afraid of you I was then!

HEDDA: Afraid of me?

MRS. ELVSTED: Yes, dreadfully. For when we met on the stairs you used always to pull my hair.

HEDDA: Did I, really?

MRS. ELVSTED: Yes, and once you said you would burn it off my head.

HEDDA: Oh, that was all nonsense, of course.

MRS. ELVSTED: Yes, but I was so silly in those days.—And since then, too—we have drifted so far—far apart from each other. Our circles have been so entirely different.

HEDDA: Well then, we must try to drift together again. Now listen! At school we said *du* to each other; and called each other by our Christian names——

MRS. ELVSTED: No, I am sure you must be mistaken.

HEDDA: No, not at all! I can remember quite distinctly. So now we are going to renew our old friendship. (*Draws the footstool closer to* MRS. ELVSTED) There now! (*Kisses her cheek*) You must say *du* to me and call me Hedda.

MRS. ELVSTED: (*Presses and pats her hands*) Oh, how good and kind you are! I am not used to such kindness.

HEDDA: There, there, there! And I shall say *du* to you, as in the old days, and call you my dear Thora.

MRS. ELVSTED: My name is Thea.

HEDDA: Why, of course! I meant Thea. (*Looks at her compassionately*) So you are not accustomed to goodness and kindness, Thea? Not in your own home?

MRS. ELVSTED: Oh, if I only had a home! But I haven't any; I have never had a home.

HEDDA: (*Looks at her for a moment*) I almost suspected as much.

MRS. ELVSTED: (*Gazing helplessly before her*) Yes—yes—yes.

HEDDA: I don't quite remember—was it not as housekeeper that you first went to Mr. Elvsted's?

MRS. ELSTED: I really went as governess. But his wife—his late wife—was an invalid,—and rarely left her room. So I had to look after the housekeeping as well.

HEDDA: And then—at last—you became mistress of the house.

MRS. ELVSTED: (*Sadly*) Yes, I did.

HEDDA: Let me see—about how long ago was that?

MRS. ELVSTED: My marriage?

HEDDA: Yes.

MRS. ELVSTED: Five years ago.

HEDDA: To be sure; it must be that.

MRS. ELVSTED: Oh those five years——! Or at all events the last two or three of them! Oh, if you[1] could only imagine——

HEDDA: (*Giving her a little slap on the hand*) De? Fie, Thea!

MRS. ELVSTED: Yes, yes, I will try—— Well, if—you could only imagine and understand——

HEDDA: (*Lightly*) Eilert Lövborg has been in your neighborhood about three years, hasn't he?

MRS. ELVSTED: (*Looks at her doubtfully*) Eilert Lövborg? Yes—he has.

HEDDA: Had you known him before, in town here?

MRS. ELVSTED: Scarcely at all. I mean—I knew him by name of course.

HEDDA: But you saw a good deal of him in the country?

MRS. ELVSTED: Yes, he came to us every day. You see, he gave the children lessons; for in the long run I couldn't manage it all myself.

HEDDA: No, that's clear.—And your husband——? I suppose he is often away from home?

MRS. ELVSTED: Yes. Being sheriff, you know, he has to travel about a good deal in his district.

HEDDA: (*Leaning against the arm of the chair*) Thea—my poor, sweet Thea—now you must tell me everything—exactly as it stands.

MRS. ELVSTED: Well then, you must question me.

---

[1] Mrs. Elvsted here uses the formal pronoun *De*, whereupon Hedda rebukes her. In her next speech Mrs. Elvsted says *du*.

HEDDA: What sort of a man is your husband, Thea? I mean—you know
—in everyday life. Is he kind to you?

MRS. ELVSTED: (*Evasively*) I am sure he means well in everything.

HEDDA: I should think he must be altogether too old for you. There is
at least twenty years' difference between you, is there not?

MRS. ELVSTED: (*Irritably*) Yes, that is true, too. Everything about him
is repellent to me! We have not a thought in common. We have no
single point of sympathy—he and I.

HEDDA: But is he not fond of you all the same? In his own way?

MRS. ELVSTED: Oh I really don't know. I think he regards me simply
as a useful property. And then it doesn't cost much to keep me. I am
not expensive.

HEDDA: That is stupid of you.

MRS. ELVSTED: (*Shakes her head*) It cannot be otherwise—not with him.
I don't think he really cares for any one but himself—and perhaps a
little for the children.

HEDDA: And for Eilert Lövborg, Thea.

MRS. ELVSTED: (*Looking at her*) For Eilert Lövborg? What puts that
into your head?

HEDDA: Well, my dear—I should say, when he sends you after him all
the way to town—— (*Smiling almost imperceptibly*) And besides, you
said so yourself, to Tesman.

MRS. ELVSTED: (*With a little nervous twitch*) Did I? Yes, I suppose I
did. (*Vehemently, but not loudly*) No—I may just as well make a clean
breast of it at once! For it must all come out in any case.

HEDDA: Why, my dear Thea——?

MRS. ELVSTED: Well, to make a long story short: My husband did not
know that I was coming.

HEDDA: What! Your husband didn't know it!

MRS. ELVSTED: No, of course not. For that matter, he was away from
home himself—he was traveling. Oh, I could bear it no longer, Hedda!
I couldn't indeed—so utterly alone as I should have been in future.

HEDDA: Well? And then?

MRS. ELVSTED: So I put together some of my things—what I needed
most—as quietly as possible. And then I left the house.

HEDDA: Without a word?

MRS. ELVSTED: Yes—and took the train straight to town.

HEDDA: Why, my dear, good Thea—to think of you daring to do it!

MRS. ELVSTED: (*Rises and moves about the room*) What else could I
possibly do?

HEDDA: But what do you think your husband will say when you go
home again?

MRS. ELVSTED: (*At the table, looks at her*) Back to him?

HEDDA: Of course.

MRS. ELVSTED: I shall never go back to him again.

HEDDA: (*Rising and going towards her*) Then you have left your home —for good and all?

MRS. ELVSTED: Yes. There was nothing else to be done.

HEDDA: But then—to take flight so openly.

MRS. ELVSTED: Oh, it's impossible to keep things of that sort secret.

HEDDA: But what do you think people will say of you, Thea?

MRS. ELVSTED: They may say what they like, for aught *I* care. (*Seats herself wearily and sadly on the sofa*) I have done nothing but what I had to do.

HEDDA: (*After a short silence*) And what are your plans now? What do you think of doing?

MRS. ELVSTED: I don't know yet. I only know this, that I must live here, where Eilert Lövborg is—if I am to live at all.

HEDDA: (*Takes a chair from the table, seats herself beside her, and strokes her hands*) My dear Thea—how did this—this friendship—be- tween you and Eilert Lövborg come about?

MRS. ELVSTED: Oh it grew up gradually. I gained a sort of influence over him.

HEDDA: Indeed?

MRS. ELVSTED: He gave up his old habits. Not because I asked him to, for I never dared do that. But of course he saw how repulsive they were to me; and so he dropped them.

HEDDA: (*Concealing an involuntary smile of scorn*) Then you have reclaimed him—as the saying goes—my little Thea.

MRS. ELVSTED: So he says himself, at any rate. And he, on his side, has made a real human being of me—taught me to think, and to understand so many things.

HEDDA: Did he give you lessons too, then?

MRS. ELVSTED: No, not exactly lessons. But he talked to me—talked about such an infinity of things. And then came the lovely, happy time when I began to share in his work—when he allowed me to help him!

HEDDA: Oh he did, did he?

MRS. ELVSTED: Yes, he never wrote anything without my assistance.

HEDDA: You were two good comrades, in fact?

MRS. ELVSTED: (*Eagerly*) Comrades! Yes, fancy, Hedda—that is the very word he used!—Oh, I ought to feel perfectly happy; and yet I cannot; for I don't know how long it will last.

HEDDA: Are you no surer of him than that?

MRS. ELVSTED: (*Gloomily*) A woman's shadow stands between Eilert Lövborg and me.

HEDDA: (*Looks at her anxiously*) Who can that be?

MRS. ELVSTED: I don't know. Some one he knew in his—in his past. Some one he has never been able wholly to forget.

HEDDA: What has he told you about—about this?

MRS. ELVSTED: He has only once—quite vaguely—alluded to it.

HEDDA: Well! And what did he say?

MRS. ELVSTED: He said that when they parted, she threatened to shoot him with a pistol.

HEDDA: (*With cold composure*) Oh, nonsense! No one does that sort of thing here.

MRS. ELVSTED: No. And that is why I think it must have been that red-haired singing-woman whom he once——

HEDDA: Yes, very likely.

MRS. ELVSTED: For I remember they used to say of her that she carried loaded firearms.

HEDDA: Oh—then of course it must have been she.

MRS. ELVSTED: (*Wringing her hands*) And now just fancy, Hedda—I hear that this singing-woman—that she is in town again! Oh, I don't know what to do——

HEDDA: (*Glancing towards the inner room*) Hush! Here comes Tesman. (*Rises and whispers*) Thea—all this must remain between you and me.

MRS. ELVSTED: (*Springing up*) Oh yes—yes! For heaven's sake——!

GEORGE TESMAN, *with a letter in his hand, comes from the right through the inner room.*

TESMAN: There now—the epistle is finished.

HEDDA: That's right. And now Mrs. Elvsted is just going. Wait a moment—I'll go with you to the garden gate.

TESMAN: Do you think Berta could post the letter, Hedda dear?

HEDDA: (*Takes it*) I will tell her to.

BERTA *enters from the hall.*

BERTA: Judge Brack wishes to know if Mrs. Tesman will receive him.

HEDDA: Yes, ask Judge Brack to come in. And look here—put this letter in the post.

BERTA: (*Taking the letter*) Yes, ma'am.

She opens the door for JUDGE BRACK *and goes out herself.* BRACK *is a man of forty-five; thick-set, but well-built and elastic in his movements. His face is roundish with an aristocratic profile. His hair is*

*short, still almost black, and carefully dressed. His eyes are lively
and sparkling. His eyebrows thick. His moustaches are also thick,
with short-cut ends. He wears a well-cut walking-suit, a little too
youthful for his age. He uses an eye-glass, which he now and then
lets drop.*

JUDGE BRACK: (*With his hat in his hand, bowing*) May one venture to
call so early in the day?

HEDDA: Of course one may.

TESMAN: (*Presses his hand*) You are welcome at any time. (*Introducing
him*) Judge Brack—Miss Rysing——

HEDDA: Oh——!

BRACK: (*Bowing*) Ah—delighted——

HEDDA: (*Looks at him and laughs*) It's nice to have a look at you by
daylight, Judge!

BRACK: Do you find me—altered?

HEDDA: A little younger, I think.

BRACK: Thank you so much.

TESMAN: But what do you think of Hedda—eh? Doesn't she look flourishing? She has actually——

HEDDA: Oh, do leave me alone. You haven't thanked Judge Brack for
the trouble he has taken——

BRACK: Oh, nonsense—it was a pleasure to me——

HEDDA: Yes, you are a friend indeed. But here stands Thea all impatience to be off—so *au revoir* Judge. I shall be back again presently.

(*Mutual salutations.* MRS. ELVSTED *and* HEDDA *go out by the hall
door*)

BRACK: Well, is your wife tolerably satisfied——

TESMAN: Yes, we can't thank you sufficiently Of course she talks of a
little rearrangement here and there; and one or two things are still
wanting. We shall have to buy some additional trifles.

BRACK: Indeed!

TESMAN: But we won't trouble you about these things. Hedda says she
herself will look after what is wanting.—Shan't we sit down? Eh?

BRACK: Thanks, for a moment. (*Seats himself beside the table*) There
is something I wanted to speak to you about, my dear Tesman.

TESMAN: Indeed? Ah, I understand! (*Seating himself*) I suppose it's
the serious part of the frolic that is coming now. Eh?

BRACK: Oh, the money question is not so very pressing; though, for
that matter, I wish we had gone a little more economically to work.

TESMAN: But that would never have done, you know! Think of Hedda, my dear fellow! You, who know her so well——. I couldn't possibly ask her to put up with a shabby style of living!

BRACK: No, no—that is just the difficulty.

TESMAN: And then—fortunately—it can't be long before I receive my appointment.

BRACK: Well, you see—such things are often apt to hang fire for a time.

TESMAN: Have you heard anything definite? Eh?

BRACK: Nothing exactly definite—— (*Interrupting himself*) But by the by—I have one piece of news for you.

TESMAN: Well?

BRACK: Your old friend, Eilert Lövborg, has returned to town.

TESMAN: I know that already.

BRACK: Indeed! How did you learn it?

TESMAN: From that lady who went out with Hedda.

BRACK: Really? What was her name? I didn't quite catch it.

TESMAN: Mrs. Elvsted.

BRACK: Aha—Sheriff Elvsted's wife? Of course—he has been living up in their regions.

TESMAN: And fancy—I'm delighted to hear that he is quite a reformed character!

BRACK: So they say.

TESMAN: And then he has published a new book—eh?

BRACK: Yes, indeed he has.

TESMAN: And I hear it has made some sensation!

BRACK: Quite an unusual sensation.

TESMAN: Fancy—isn't that good news! A man of such extraordinary talents——. I felt so grieved to think that he had gone irretrievably to ruin.

BRACK: That was what everybody thought.

TESMAN: But I cannot imagine what he will take to now! How in the world will he be able to make his living? Eh?

(*During the last words,* HEDDA *has entered by the hall door.*)

HEDDA: (*To* BRACK, *laughing with a touch of scorn*) Tesman is for ever worrying about how people are to make their living.

TESMAN: Well you see, dear—we were talking about poor Eilert Lövborg.

HEDDA: (*Glancing at him rapidly*) Oh, indeed? (*Seats herself in the arm-chair beside the stove and asks indifferently*) What is the matter with him?

TESMAN: Well—no doubt he has run through all his property long ago; and he can scarcely write a new book every year—eh? So I really can't see what is to become of him.

BRACK: Perhaps I can give you some information on that point.

TESMAN: Indeed!

BRACK: You must remember that his relations have a good deal of influence.

TESMAN: Oh, his relations, unfortunately, have entirely washed their hands of him.

BRACK: At one time they called him the hope of the family.

TESMAN: At one time, yes! But he has put an end to all that.

HEDDA: Who knows? (*With a slight smile*) I hear they have reclaimed him up at Sheriff Elvsted's——

BRACK: And then this book that he has published——

TESMAN: Well well, I hope to goodness they may find something for him to do. I have just written to him. I asked him to come and see us this evening, Hedda dear.

BRACK: But my dear fellow, you are booked for my bachelors' party this evening. You promised on the pier last night.

HEDDA: Had you forgotten, Tesman?

TESMAN: Yes, I had utterly forgotten.

BRACK: But it doesn't matter, for you may be sure he won't come.

TESMAN: What makes you think that? Eh?

BRACK: (*With a little hesitation, rising and resting his hands on the back of his chair*) My dear Tesman—and you too, Mrs. Tesman—I think I ought not to keep you in the dark about something that—that——

TESMAN: That concerns Eilert——?

BRACK: Both you and him.

TESMAN: Well, my dear Judge, out with it.

BRACK: You must be prepared to find your appointment deferred longer than you desired or expected.

TESMAN: (*Jumping up uneasily*) Is there some hitch about it? Eh?

BRACK: The nomination may perhaps be made conditional on the result of a competition——

TESMAN: Competition! Think of that, Hedda!

HEDDA: (*Leans further back in the chair*) Aha—aha!

TESMAN: But who can my competitor be? Surely not——?

BRACK: Yes, precisely—Eilᴖrt Lövborg.

TESMAN: (*Clasping his hands*) No, no—it's quite inconceivable! Quite impossible! Eh?

BRACK: H'm—that is what it may come to, all the same.

TESMAN: Well but, Judge Brack—it would show the most incredible lack of consideration for me. (*Gesticulates with his arms*) For—just think—I'm a married man! We have married on the strength of these prospects, Hedda and I; and run deep into debt; and borrowed money from Aunt Julia too. Good heavens, they had as good as promised me the appointment. Eh?

BRACK: Well, well, well—no doubt you will get it in the end; only after a contest.

HEDDA: (*Immovable in her arm-chair*) Fancy, Tesman, there will be a sort of sporting interest in that.

TESMAN: Why, my dearest Hedda, how can you be so indifferent about it?

HEDDA: (*As before*) I am not at all indifferent. I am most eager to see who wins.

BRACK: In any case, Mrs. Tesman, it is best that you should know how matters stand. I mean—before you set about the little purchases I hear you are threatening.

HEDDA: This can make no difference.

BRACK: Indeed! Then I have no more to say. Good-bye! (*To* TESMAN) I shall look in on my way back from my afternoon walk, and take you home with me.

TESMAN: Oh yes, yes—your news has quite upset me.

HEDDA: .(*Reclining, holds out her hand*) Good-bye, Judge; and be sure you call in the afternoon.

BRACK: Many thanks. Good-bye, good-bye!

TESMAN: (*Accompanying him to the door*) Good-bye, my dear Judge! You must really excuse me—— (JUDGE BRACK *goes out by the hall door*)

TESMAN: (*Crosses the room*) Oh Hedda—one should never rush into adventures. Eh?

HEDDA: (*Looks at him, smiling*) Do you do that?

TESMAN: Yes, dear—there is no denying—it was adventurous to go and marry and set up house upon mere expectations.

HEDDA: Perhaps you are right there.

TESMAN: Well—at all events, we have our delightful home, Hedda! Fancy, the home we both dreamed of—the home we were in love with, I may almost say. Eh?

HEDDA: (*Rising slowly and wearily*) It was part of our compact that we were to go into society—to keep open house.

TESMAN: Yes, if you only knew how I had been looking forward to it! Fancy—to see you as hostess—in a select circle! Eh? Well, well, well—for the present we shall have to get on without society, Hedda—only to invite Aunt Julia now and then.—Oh, I intended you to lead such an utterly different life, dear——!

HEDDA: Of course I cannot have my man in livery just yet.

TESMAN: Oh no, unfortunately. It would be out of the question for us to keep a footman, you know.

HEDDA: And the saddle-horse I was to have had——

TESMAN: (*Aghast*) The saddle-horse!

HEDDA: ——I suppose I must not think of that now.

TESMAN: Good heavens, no!—that's as clear as daylight.

HEDDA: (*Goes up the room*) Well, I shall have one thing at least to kill time with in the meanwhile.

TESMAN: (*Beaming*) Oh thank heaven for that! What is it, Hedda? Eh?

HEDDA: (*In the middle doorway, looks at him with covert scorn*) My pistols, George.

TESMAN: (*In alarm*) Your pistols!

HEDDA: (*With cold eyes*) General Gabler's pistols. (*She goes out through the inner room, to the left*)

TESMAN: (*Rushes up to the middle doorway and calls after her*) No, for heaven's sake, Hedda darling—don't touch those dangerous things! For my sake, Hedda! Eh?

ACT II.

The room at the TESMANS *as in the first act, except that the piano has been removed, and an elegant little writing-table with bookshelves put in its place. A smaller table stands near the sofa on the left. Most of the bouquets have been taken away.* MRS. ELVSTED'S *bouquet is upon the large table in front.—It is afternoon.*

HEDDA, *dressed to receive callers, is alone in the room. She stands by the open glass door, loading a revolver. The fellow to it lies in an open pistol-case on the writing-table.*

HEDDA: (*Looks down the garden, and calls*) So you are here again, Judge!

BRACK: (*Is heard calling from a distance*) As you see, Mrs. Tesman!

HEDDA: (*Raises the pistol and points*) Now I'll shoot you, Judge Brack!

BRACK: (*Calling unseen*) No, no, no! Don't stand aiming at me!

HEDDA: This is what comes of sneaking in by the back way.[1] (*She fires*)

---

[1] *Bagveje* means both "back ways" and "underhand courses."

BRACK: (*Nearer*) Are you out of your senses!——

HEDDA: Dear me—did I happen to hit you?

BRACK: (*Still outside*) I wish you would let these pranks alone!

HEDDA: Come in then, Judge.

JUDGE BRACK, *dressed as though for a men's party, enters by the glass door. He carries a light overcoat over his arm.*

BRACK: What the deuce—haven't you tired of that sport, yet? What are you shooting at?

HEDDA: Oh, I am only firing in the air.

BRACK: (*Gently takes the pistol out of her hand*) Allow me, Madam! (*Looks at it*) Ah—I know this pistol well! (*Looks around*) Where is the case? Ah, here it is. (*Lays the pistol in it, and shuts it*) Now we won't play at that game any more to-day.

HEDDA: Then what in heaven's name would you have me do with myself?

BRACK: Have you had no visitors?

HEDDA: (*Closing the glass door*) Not one. I suppose all our set are still out of town.

BRACK: And is Tesman not at home either?

HEDDA: (*At the writing-table, putting the pistol-case in a drawer which she shuts*) No. He rushed off to his aunt's directly after lunch; he didn't expect you so early.

BRACK: H'm—how stupid of me not to have thought of that!

HEDDA: (*Turning her head to look at him*) Why stupid?

BRACK: Because if I had thought of it I should have come a little—earlier.

HEDDA: (*Crossing the room*) Then you would have found no one to receive you; for I have been in my room changing my dress ever since lunch.

BRACK: And is there no sort of little chink that we could hold a parley through?

HEDDA: You have forgotten to arrange one.

BRACK: That was another piece of stupidity.

HEDDA: Well, we must just settle down here—and wait. Tesman is not likely to be back for some time yet.

BRACK: Never mind; I shall not be impatient.

HEDDA *seats herself in the corner of the sofa.* BRACK *lays his overcoat over the back of the nearest chair, and sits down, but keeps his hat in his hand. A short silence. They look at each other.*

HEDDA: Well?

BRACK: (*In the same tone*) Well?

HEDDA: I spoke first.

BRACK: (*Bending a little forward*) Come, let us have a cosy little chat, Mrs. Hedda.

HEDDA: (*Leaning further back in the sofa*) Does it not seem like a whole eternity since our last talk? Of course I don't count those few words yesterday evening and this morning.

BRACK: You mean since our last confidential talk? Our last *tête-à-tête*?

HEDDA: Well, yes—since you put it so.

BRACK: Not a day has passed but I have wished that you were home again.

HEDDA: And I have done nothing but wish the same thing.

BRACK: You? Really, Mrs. Hedda? And I thought you had been enjoying your tour so much!

HEDDA: Oh, yes, you may be sure of that!

BRACK: But Tesman's letters spoke of nothing but happiness.

HEDDA: Oh, Tesman! You see, he thinks nothing so delightful as grubbing in libraries and making copies of old parchments, or whatever you call them.

BRACK: (*With a spice of malice*) Well, that is his vocation in life—or part of it at any rate.

HEDDA: Yes, of course; and no doubt when it's your vocation——. But *I!* Oh, my dear Mr. Brack, how mortally bored I have been.

BRACK: (*Sympathetically*) Do you really say so? In downright earnest?

HEDDA: Yes, you can surely understand it——! To go for six whole months without meeting a soul that knew anything of our circle, or could talk about the things we are interested in.

BRACK: Yes, yes—I, too, should feel that a deprivation.

HEDDA: And then, what I found most intolerable of all——

BRACK: Well?

HEDDA: ——was being everlastingly in the company of—one and the same person——

BRACK: (*With a nod of assent*) Morning, noon, and night, yes—at all possible times and seasons.

HEDDA: I said "everlastingly."

BRACK: Just so. But I should have thought, with our excellent Tesman, one could——

HEDDA: Tesman is—a specialist, my dear Judge.

BRACK: Undeniably.

HEDDA: And specialists are not at all amusing to travel with. Not in the long run at any rate.

BRACK: Not even—the specialist one happens to love?

HEDDA: Faugh—don't use that sickening word!

BRACK: (*Taken aback*) What do you say, Mrs. Hedda?

HEDDA: (*Half laughing, half irritated*) You should just try it! To hear of nothing but the history of civilization morning, noon and night——

BRACK: Everlastingly.

HEDDA: Yes, yes, yes! And then all this about the domestic industry of the middle ages——! That's the most disgusting part of it!

BRACK: (*Looks searchingly at her*) But tell me—in that case, how am I to understand your——? H'm——

HEDDA: My accepting George Tesman, you mean?

BRACK: Well, let us put it so.

HEDDA: Good heavens, do you see anything so wonderful in that?

BRACK: Yes and no—Mrs. Hedda.

HEDDA: I had positively danced myself tired, my dear Judge. My day was done—— (*With a slight shudder*) Oh, no—I won't say that; nor think it, either!

BRACK: You have assuredly no reason to.

HEDDA: Oh, reasons—— (*Watching him closely*) and George Tesman—after all, you must admit that he is correctness itself.

BRACK: His correctness and respectability are beyond all question.

HEDDA: And I don't see anything absolutely ridiculous about him.— Do you?

BRACK: Ridiculous? N—no—I shouldn't exactly say so——

HEDDA: Well—and his powers of research, at all events, are untiring. —I see no reason why he should not one day come to the front, after all.

BRACK: (*Looks at her hesitatingly*) I thought that you, like every one else, expected him to attain the highest distinction.

HEDDA: (*With an expression of fatigue*) Yes, so I did.—And then, since he was bent, at all hazards, on being allowed to provide for me—I really don't know why I should not have accepted his offer?

BRACK: No—if you look at it in that light——

HEDDA: It was more than my other adorers were prepared to do for me, my dear Judge.

BRACK: (*Laughing*) Well, I can't answer for all the rest; but as for myself, you know quite well that I have always entertained a—a certain respect for the marriage tie—for marriage as an institution, Mrs. Hedda.

HEDDA: (*Jestingly*) Oh, I assure you I have never cherished any hopes with respect to you.

BRACK: All I require is a pleasant and intimate interior, where I can make myself useful in every way, and am free to come and go as—as a trusted friend——

HEDDA: Of the master of the house, do you mean?

BRACK: (*Bowing*) Frankly—of the mistress first of all; but, of course, of the master, too, in the second place. Such a triangular friendship—if I may call it so—is really a great convenience for all parties, let me tell you.

HEDDA: Yes, I have many a time longed for some one to make a third on our travels. Oh—those railway-carriage *tête-à-têtes*——!

BRACK: Fortunately your wedding journey is over now.

HEDDA: (*Shaking her head*) Not by a long—long way. I have only arrived at a station on the line.

BRACK: Well, then the passengers jump out and move about a little, Mrs. Hedda.

HEDDA: I never jump out.

BRACK: Really?

HEDDA: No—because there is always some one standing by to——

BRACK: (*Laughing*) To look at your ankles, do you mean?

HEDDA: Precisely.

BRACK: Well, but, dear me——

HEDDA: (*With a gesture of repulsion*) I won't have it. I would rather keep my seat where I happen to be—and continue the *tête-à-tête*.

BRACK: But suppose a third person were to jump in and join the couple.

HEDDA: Ah—that is quite another matter!

BRACK: A trusted, sympathetic friend——

HEDDA: ——with a fund of conversation on all sorts of lively topics——

BRACK: ——and not the least bit of a specialist!

HEDDA: (*With an audible sigh*) Yes, that would be a relief, indeed.

BRACK: (*Hears the front door open, and glances in that direction*) The triangle is completed.

HEDDA: (*Half aloud*) And on goes the train.

GEORGE TESMAN *in a gray walking-suit, with a soft felt hat, enters from the hall. He has a number of unbound books under his arm and in his pockets.*

TESMAN: (*Goes up to the table beside the corner settee*) Ouf—what a load for a warm day—all these books. (*Lays them on the table*) I'm positively perspiring, Hedda. Hallo—are you there already, my dear Judge? Eh? Berta didn't tell me.

BRACK: (*Rising*) I came in through the garden.

HEDDA: What books have you got there?

TESMAN: (*Stands looking them through*) Some new books on my special subjects—quite indispensable to me.

HEDDA: Your special subjects?

BRACK: Yes, books on his special subjects, Mrs. Tesman. (BRACK *and* HEDDA *exchange a confidential smile*)

HEDDA: Do you need still more books on your special subjects?

TESMAN: Yes, my dear Hedda, one can never have too many of them. Of course, one must keep up with all that is written and published.

HEDDA: Yes, I suppose one must.

TESMAN: (*Searching among his books*) And look here—I have got hold of Eilert Lövborg's new book, too. (*Offering it to her*) Perhaps you would like to glance through it, Hedda? Eh?

HEDDA: No, thank you. Or rather—afterwards perhaps.

TESMAN: I looked into it a little on the way home.

BRACK: Well, what do you think of it—as a specialist?

TESMAN: I think it shows quite remarkable soundness of judgment. He never wrote like that before. (*Putting the books together*) Now I shall take all these into my study. I'm longing to cut the leaves——! And then I must change my clothes. (*To* BRACK) I suppose we needn't start just yet? Eh?

BRACK: Oh, dear, no—there is not the slightest hurry.

TESMAN: Well, then, I will take my time. (*Is going with his books, but stops in the doorway and turns*) By the by, Hedda—Aunt Julia is not coming this evening.

HEDDA: Not coming? Is it that affair of the bonnet that keeps her away?

TESMAN: Oh, not at all. How could you think such a thing of Aunt Julia? Just fancy——! The fact is, Aunt Rina is very ill.

HEDDA: She always is.

TESMAN: Yes, but to-day she is much worse than usual, poor dear.

HEDDA: Oh, then it's only natural that her sister should remain with her. I must bear my disappointment.

TESMAN: And you can't imagine, dear, how delighted Aunt Julia seemed to be—because you had come home looking so flourishing!

HEDDA: (*Half aloud, rising*) Oh, those everlasting Aunts!

TESMAN: What?

HEDDA: (*Going to the glass door*) Nothing.

TESMAN: Oh, all right. (*He goes through the inner room, out to the right*)

BRACK: What bonnet were you talking about?

HEDDA: Oh, it was a little episode with Miss Tesman this morning. She had laid down her bonnet on the chair there—(*looks at him and smiles*)—and I pretended to think it was the servant's.

BRACK: (*Shaking his head*) Now, my dear Mrs. Hedda, how could you do such a thing? To that excellent old lady, too!

HEDDA: (*Nervously crossing the room*) Well, you see—these impulses come over me all of a sudden; and I cannot resist them. (*Throws herself down in the easy-chair by the stove*) Oh, I don't know how to explain it.

BRACK: (*Behind the easy-chair*) You are not really happy—that is at the bottom if it.

HEDDA: (*Looking straight before her*) I know of no reason why I should be—happy. Perhaps you can give me one?

BRACK: Well—amongst other things, because you have got exactly the home you had set your heart on.

HEDDA: (*Looks up at him and laughs*) Do you, too, believe in that legend?

BRACK: Is there nothing in it, then?

HEDDA: Oh, yes, there is something in it.

BRACK: Well?

HEDDA: There is this in it, that I made use of Tesman to see me home from evening parties last summer——

BRACK: I, unfortunately, had to go quite a different way.

HEDDA: That's true. I know you were going a different way last summer.

BRACK: (*Laughing*) Oh fie, Mrs. Hedda! Well, then—you and Tesman——?

HEDDA: Well, we happened to pass here one evening; Tesman, poor fellow, was writhing in the agony of having to find conversation; so I took pity on the learned man——

BRACK: (*Smiles doubtfully*) You took pity? H'm——

HEDDA: Yes, I really did. And so—to help him out of his torment—I happened to say, in pure thoughtlessness, that I should like to live in this villa.

BRACK: No more than that?

HEDDA: Not that evening.

BRACK: But afterwards?

HEDDA: Yes, my thoughtlessness had consequences, my dear Judge.

BRACK: Unfortunately that too often happens, Mrs. Hedda.

HEDDA: Thanks! So you see it was this enthusiasm for Secretary Falk's villa that first constituted a bond of sympathy between George Tesman and me. From that came our engagement and our marriage, and our wedding journey, and all the rest of it. Well, well, my dear Judge—as you make your bed so you must lie, I could almost say.

BRACK: This is exquisite! And you really cared not a rap about it all the time?

HEDDA: No, heaven knows I didn't.

BRACK: But now? Now that we have made it so homelike for you?

HEDDA: Uh—the rooms all seem to smell of lavender and dried rose-leaves.—But perhaps it's Aunt Julia that has brought that scent with her.

BRACK: (*Laughing*) No, I think it must be a legacy from the late Mrs. Secretary Falk.

HEDDA: Yes, there is an odor of mortality about it. It reminds me of a bouquet—the day after the ball. (*Clasps her hands behind her head, leans back in her chair and looks at him*) Oh, my dear Judge—you cannot imagine how horribly I shall bore myself here.

BRACK: Why should not you, too, find some sort of vocation in life, Mrs. Hedda?

HEDDA: A vocation—that should attract me?

BRACK: If possible, of course.

HEDDA: Heaven knows what sort of a vocation that could be. I often wonder whether—— (*Breaking off*) But that would never do, either.

BRACK: Who can tell? Let me hear what it is.

HEDDA: Whether I might not get Tesman to go into politics, I mean.

BRACK: (*Laughing*) Tesman? No, really now, political life is not the thing for him—not at all in his line.

HEDDA: No, I daresay not.—But if I could get him into it all the same?

BRACK: Why—what satisfaction could you find in that? If he is not fitted for that sort of thing, why should you want to drive him into it?

HEDDA: Because I am bored, I tell you! (*After a pause*) So you think it quite out of the question that Tesman should ever get into the ministry?

BRACK: H'm—you see, my dear Mrs. Hedda—to get into the ministry, he would have to be a tolerably rich man.

HEDDA: (*Rising impatiently*) Yes, there we have it! It is this genteel poverty I have managed to drop into——! (*Crosses the room*) That is what makes life so pitiable! So utterly ludicrous!—For that's what it is.

BRACK: Now *I* should say the fault lay elsewhere.

HEDDA: Where, then?

BRACK: You have never gone through any really stimulating experience.

HEDDA: Anything serious, you mean?

BRACK: Yes, you may call it so. But now you may perhaps have one in store.

HEDDA: (*Tossing her head*) Oh, you're thinking of the annoyances about this wretched professorship! But that must be Tesman's own affair. I assure you I shall not waste a thought upon it.

BRACK: No, no, I daresay not. But suppose now that what people call —in elegant language—a solemn responsibility were to come upon you? (*Smiling*) A new responsibility, Mrs. Hedda?

HEDDA: (*Angrily*) Be quiet! Nothing of that sort will ever happen!

BRACK: (*Warily*) We will speak of this again a year hence—at the very outside.

HEDDA: (*Curtly*) I have no turn for anything of the sort, Judge Brack. No responsibilities for me!

BRACK: Are you so unlike the generality of women as to have no turn for duties which——?

HEDDA: (*Beside the glass door*) Oh, be quiet, I tell you!—I often think there is only one thing in the world I have any turn for.

BRACK: (*Drawing near to her*) And what is that, if I may ask?

HEDDA: (*Stands looking out*) Boring myself to death. Now you know it. (*Turns, looks towards the inner room, and laughs*) Yes, as I thought! Here comes the Professor.

BRACK: (*Softly, in a tone of warning*) Come, come, come, Mrs. Hedda!

GEORGE TESMAN, *dressed for the party, with his gloves and hat in his hand, enters from the right through the inner room.*

TESMAN: Hedda, has no message come from Eilert Lövborg? Eh?

HEDDA: No.

TESMAN: Then you'll see he'll be here presently.

BRACK: Do you really think he will come?

TESMAN: Yes, I am almost sure of it. For what you were telling us this morning must have been a mere floating rumor.

BRACK: You think so?

TESMAN: At any rate, Aunt Julia said she did not believe for a moment that he would ever stand in my way again. Fancy that!

BRACK: Well, then, that's all right.

TESMAN: (*Placing his hat and gloves on a chair on the right*) Yes, but you must really let me wait for him as long as possible.

BRACK: We have plenty of time yet. None of my guests will arrive before seven or half-past.

TESMAN: Then meanwhile we can keep Hedda company, and see what happens? Eh?

HEDDA: (*Placing* BRACK's *hat and overcoat upon the corner settee*) And at the worst Mr. Lövborg can remain here with me.

BRACK: (*Offering to take his things*) Oh, allow me, Mrs. Tesman!— What do you mean by "at the worst"?

HEDDA: If he won't go with you and Tesman.

TESMAN: (*Looks dubiously at her*) But, Hedda, dear—do you think it would quite do for him to remain with you? Eh? Remember, Aunt Julia can't come.

HEDDA: No, but Mrs. Elvsted is coming. We three can have a cup of tea together.

TESMAN: Oh, yes, that will be all right.

BRACK: (*Smiling*) And that would perhaps be the safest plan for him.

HEDDA: Why so?

BRACK: Well, you know, Mrs. Tesman, how you used to gird at my little bachelor parties. You declared they were adapted only for men of the strictest principles.

HEDDA: But no doubt Mr. Lövborg's principles are strict enough now. A converted sinner——

BERTA *appears at the hall door.*

BERTA: There's a gentleman asking if you are at home, ma'am——

HEDDA: Well, show him in.

TESMAN: (*Softly*) I'm sure it is he! Fancy that!

EILERT LÖVBORG *enters from the hall. He is slim and lean; of the same age as* TESMAN, *but looks older and somewhat worn-out. His hair and beard are of a blackish brown, his face long and pale, but with patches of color on the cheek-bones. He is dressed in a well-cut black visiting suit, quite new. He has dark gloves and a silk hat. He stops near the door, and makes a rapid bow, seeming somewhat embarrassed.*

TESMAN: (*Goes up to him and shakes him warmly by the hand*) Well, my dear Eilert—so at last we meet again!

EILERT LÖVBORG: (*Speaks in a subdued voice*) Thanks for your letter, Tesman. (*Approaching Hedda*) Will you, too, shake hands with me, Mrs. Tesman?

HEDDA: (*Taking his hand*) I am glad to see you, Mr. Lövborg. (*With a motion of her hand*) I don't know whether you two gentlemen——?

LÖVBORG: (*Bowing slightly*) Judge Brack, I think.

BRACK: (*Doing likewise*) Oh, yes,—in the old days——

TESMAN: (*To* LÖVBORG, *with his hands on his shoulders*) And now you must make yourself entirely at home, Eilert! Must'nt he, Hedda?—For I hear you are going to settle in town again? Eh?

LÖVBORG: Yes, I am.

TESMAN: Quite right, quite right. Let me tell you, I have got hold of your new book; but I haven't had time to read it yet.

LÖVBORG: You may spare yourself the trouble.

TESMAN: Why so?

LÖVBORG: Because there is very little in it.

TESMAN: Just fancy—how can you say so?

BRACK: But it has been very much praised, I hear.

LÖVBORG: That was what I wanted; so I put nothing into the book but what every one would agree with.

BRACK: Very wise of you.

TESMAN: Well, but, my dear Eilert——!

LÖVBORG: For now I mean to win myself a position again—to make a fresh start.

TESMAN: (*A little embarrassed*) Ah, that is what you wish to do? Eh?

LÖVBORG: (*Smiling, lays down his hat, and draws a packet, wrapped in paper, from his coat pocket*) But when this one appears, George Tesman, you will have to read it. For this is the real book—the book I have put my true self into.

TESMAN: Indeed? And what is it?

LÖVBORG: It is the continuation.

TESMAN: The continuation? Of what?

LÖVBORG: Of the book.

TESMAN: Of the new book?

LÖVBORG: Of course.

TESMAN: Why, my dear Eilert—does it not come down to our own days?

LÖVBORG: Yes, it does; and this one deals with the future.

TESMAN: With the future! But, good heaven, we know nothing of the future!

LÖVBORG: No; but there is a thing or two to be said about it all the same. (*Opens the packet*) Look here——

TESMAN: Why, that's not your handwriting.

LÖVBORG: I dictated it. (*Turning over the pages*) It falls into two sections. The first deals with the civilizing forces of the future. And here is the second—(*running through the pages towards the end*)—forecasting the probable line of development.

TESMAN: How odd now! I should never have thought of writing anything of that sort.

HEDDA: (*At the glass door, drumming on the pane*) H'm—— I daresay not.

LÖVBORG: (*Replacing the manuscript in its paper and laying the packet on the table*) I brought it, thinking I might read you a little of it this evening.

TESMAN: That was very good of you, Eilert. But this evening——? (*Looking at* BRACK) I don't quite see how we can manage it——

LÖVBORG: Well, then, some other time. There is no hurry.

BRACK: I must tell you, Mr. Lövborg—there is a little gathering at my house this evening—mainly in honor of Tesman, you know——

LÖVBORG: (*Looking for his hat*) Oh—then I won't detain you——

BRACK: No, but listen—will you not do me the favor of joining us?

LÖVBORG: (*Curtly and decidedly*) No, I can't—thank you very much.

BRACK: Oh, nonsense—do! We shall be quite a select little circle. And I assure you we shall have a "lively time," as Mrs. Hed—as Mrs. Tesman says.

LÖVBORG: I have no doubt of it. But nevertheless——

BRACK: And then you might bring your manuscript with you, and read it to Tesman at my house. I could give you a room to yourselves.

TESMAN: Yes, think of that, Eilert,—why shouldn't you? Eh?

HEDDA: (*Interposing*) But, Tesman, if Mr. Lövborg would really rather not! I am sure Mr. Lövborg is much more inclined to remain here and have supper with me.

LÖVBORG: (*Looking at her*) With you, Mrs. Tesman?

HEDDA: And with Mrs. Elvsted.

LÖVBORG: Ah—— (*Lightly*) I saw her for a moment this morning.

HEDDA: Did you? Well, she is coming this evening. So you see you are almost bound to remain, Mr. Lövborg, or she will have no one to see her home.

LÖVBORG: That's true. Many thanks, Mrs. Tesman—in that case I will remain.

HEDDA: Then I have one or two orders to give the servant—— (*She goes to the hall door and rings.* BERTA *enters.* HEDDA *talks to her in a whisper, and points towards the inner room.* BERTA *nods and goes out again.*)

TESMAN: (*At the same time, to* LÖVBORG) Tell me, Eilert—is it this new subject—the future—that you are going to lecture about?

LÖVBORG: Yes.

TESMAN: They told me at the bookseller's that you are going to deliver a course of lectures this autumn.

LÖVBORG: That is my intention. I hope you won't take it ill, Tesman.

TESMAN: Oh no, not in the least! But——?

LÖVBORG: I can quite understand that it must be disagreeable to you.

TESMAN: (*Cast down*) Oh, I can't expect you, out of consideration for me, to——

LÖVBORG: But I shall wait till you have received your appointment.

TESMAN: Will you wait? Yes, but—yes, but—are you not going to compete with me? Eh?

LÖVBORG: No; it is only the moral victory I care for.

TESMAN: Why, bless me—then Aunt Julia was right after all! Oh, yes —I knew it! Hedda! Just fancy—Eilert Lövborg is not going to stand in our way!

HEDDA: (*Curtly*) Our way? Pray leave me out of the question. (*She goes up towards the inner room, where* BERTA *is placing a tray with decanters and glasses on the table.* HEDDA *nods approval, and comes forward again.* BERTA *goes out.*)

TESMAN: (*At the same time*) And you, Judge Brack—what do you say to this? Eh?

BRACK: Well, I say that a moral victory—h'm—may be all very fine——

TESMAN: Yes, certainly. But all the same——

HEDDA: (*Looking at* TESMAN *with a cold smile*) You stand there looking as if you were thunderstruck——

TESMAN: Yes—so I am—I almost think——

BRACK: Don't you see, Mrs. Tesman, a thunderstorm has just passed over?

HEDDA: (*Pointing towards the inner room*) Will you not take a glass of cold punch, gentlemen?

BRACK: (*Looking at his watch*) A stirrup-cup? Yes, it wouldn't come amiss.

TESMAN: A capital idea, Hedda! Just the thing! Now that the weight has been taken off my mind——

HEDDA: Will you not join them, Mr. Lövborg?

LÖVBORG: (*With a gesture of refusal*) No, thank you. Nothing for me.

BRACK: Why bless me—cold punch is surely not poison.

LÖVBORG: Perhaps not for every one.

HEDDA: I will keep Mr. Lövborg company in the meantime.

TESMAN: Yes, yes, Hedda dear, do. (*He and* BRACK *go into the inner room, seat themselves, drink punch, smoke cigarettes, and carry on a lively conversation during what follows.* EILERT LÖVBORG *remains standing beside the stove.* HEDDA *goes to the writing-table*)

HEDDA: (*Raising her voice a little*) Do you care to look at some photographs, Mr. Lövorg? You know Tesman and I made a tour in the Tyrol on our way home? (*She takes up an album, and places it on the table beside the sofa, in the further corner of which she seats herself.* EILERT LÖVBORG *approaches, stops, and looks at her. Then he takes a chair and seats himself to her left, with his back towards the inner room.*)

HEDDA: (*Opening the album*) Do you see this range of mountains, Mr. Lövborg? It's the Ortler group. Tesman has written the name underneath. Here it is: "The Ortler group near Meran."

LÖVBORG: (*Who has never taken his eyes off her, says softly and slowly:*) Hedda—Gabler!

HEDDA: (*Glancing hastily at him*) Ah! Hush!

LÖVBORG: (*Repeats softly*) Hedda Gabler!

HEDDA: (*Looking at the album*) That was my name in the old days—when we two knew each other.

LÖVBORG: And I must teach myself never to say Hedda Gabler again—never, as long as I live.

HEDDA: (*Still turning over the pages*) Yes, you must. And I think you ought to practise in time. The sooner the better, I should say.

LÖVBORG: (*In a tone of indignation*) Hedda Gabler married? And married to—George Tesman!

HEDDA: Yes—so the world goes.

LÖVBORG: Oh, Hedda, Hedda—how could you[1] throw yourself away!

HEDDA: (*Looks sharply at him*) What? I can't allow this!

LÖVBORG: What do you mean?

TESMAN *comes into the room and goes towards the sofa.*

HEDDA: (*Hears him coming and says in an indifferent tone*) And this is a view from the Val d'Ampezzo, Mr. Lövborg. Just look at these peaks! (*Looks affectionately up at* TESMAN) What's the name of these curious peaks, dear?

TESMAN: Let me see. Oh, those are the Dolomites.

HEDDA: Yes, that's it!—Those are the Dolomites, Mr. Lövborg.

TESMAN: Hedda, dear—I only wanted to ask whether I shouldn't bring you a little punch after all? For yourself, at any rate—eh?

HEDDA: Yes, do please; and perhaps a few biscuits.

TESMAN: No cigarettes?

HEDDA: No.

TESMAN: Very well. (*He goes into the inner room and out to the right.* BRACK *sits in the inner room, and keeps an eye from time to time on* HEDDA *and* LÖVBORG)

LÖVBORG: (*Softly, as before*) Answer me, Hedda—how could you go and do this?

HEDDA: (*Apparently absorbed in the album*) If you continue to say *du* to me I won't talk to you.

LÖVBORG: May I not say *du* even when we are alone?

HEDDA: No. You may think it; but you mustn't say it.

LÖVBORG: Ah, I understand. It is an offence against George Tesman, whom you[1]—love.

---

[1] He uses the familiar *du*.

[1] From this point onward Lövborg uses the formal *De*.

HEDDA: (*Glances at him and smiles*) Love? What an idea!

LÖVBORG: You don't love him then!

HEDDA: But I won't hear of any sort of unfaithfulness! Remember that.

LÖVBORG: Hedda—answer me one thing——

HEDDA: Hush!

TESMAN *enters with a small tray from the inner room.*

TESMAN: Here you are! Isn't this tempting? (*He puts the tray on the table*)

HEDDA: Why do you bring it yourself?

TESMAN: (*Filling the glasses*) Because I think it's such fun to wait upon you, Hedda.

HEDDA: But you have poured out two glasses. Mr. Lövborg said he wouldn't have any——

TESMAN: No, but Mrs. Elvsted will soon be here, won't she?

HEDDA: Yes, by the by—Mrs. Elvsted——

TESMAN: Had your forgotten her? Eh?

HEDDA: We were so absorbed in these photographs. (*Shows him a picture*) Do you remember this little village?

TESMAN: Oh, it's that one just below the Brenner Pass. It was there we passed the night——

HEDDA: ——and met that lively party of tourists.

TESMAN: Yes, that was the place. Fancy—if we could only have had you with us, Eilert! Eh? (*He returns to the inner room and sits beside* BRACK)

LÖVBORG: Answer me this one thing, Hedda——

HEDDA: Well?

LÖVBORG: Was there no love in your friendship for me, either? Not a spark—not a tinge of love in it?

HEDDA: I wonder if there was? To me it seems as though we were two good comrades—two thoroughly intimate friends. (*Smilingly*) You especially were frankness itself.

LÖVBORG: It was you that made me so.

HEDDA: As I look back upon it all, I think there was really something beautiful, something fascinating—something daring—in—in that secret intimacy—that comradeship which no living creature so much as dreamed of.

LÖVBORG: Yes, yes, Hedda! Was there not?—When I used to come to your father's in the afternoon—and the General sat over at the window reading his papers—with his back towards us——

HEDDA: And we two on the corner sofa——

LÖVBORG: Always with the same illustrated paper before us——

HEDDA: For want of an album, yes.

LÖVBORG: Yes, Hedda, and when I made my confessions to you—told you about myself, things that at that time no one else knew! There I would sit and tell you of my escapades—my days and nights of devilment. Oh, Hedda—what was the power in you that forced me to confess these things?

HEDDA: Do you think it was any power in me?

LÖVBORG: How else can I explain it? And all those—those roundabout questions you used to put to me——

HEDDA: Which you understood so particularly well——

LÖVBORG: How could you sit and question me like that? Question me quite frankly——

HEDDA: In roundabout terms, please observe.

LÖVBORG: Yes, but frankly nevertheless. Cross-question me about—all that sort of thing?

HEDDA: And how could you answer, Mr. Lövborg?

LÖVBORG: Yes, that is just what I can't understand—in looking back upon it. But tell me now, Hedda—was there not love at the bottom of our friendship? On your side, did you not feel as though you might purge my stains away—if I made you my confessor? Was it not so?

HEDDA: No, not quite.

LÖVBORG: What was your motive, then?

HEDDA: Do you think it quite incomprehensible that a young girl—when it can be done—without any one knowing——

LÖVBORG: Well?

HEDDA: ——should be glad to have a peep, now and then, into a world which——

LÖVBORG: Which——?

HEDDA: ——which she is forbidden to know anything about?

LÖVBORG: So that was it?

HEDDA: Partly. Partly—I almost think.

LÖVBORG: Comradeship in the thirst for life. But why should not that, at any rate, have continued?

HEDDA: The fault was yours.

LÖVBORG: It was you that broke with me.

HEDDA: Yes, when our friendship threatened to develop into something more serious. Shame upon you, Eilert Lövborg! How could you think of wronging your—your frank comrade?

LÖVBORG: (*Clenching his hands*) Oh, why did you not carry out your threat? Why did you not shoot me down?

HEDDA: Because I have such a dread of scandal.

LÖVBORG: Yes, Hedda, you are a coward at heart.

HEDDA: A terrible coward. (*Changing her tone*) But it was a lucky thing for you. And now you have found ample consolation at the Elvsteds'.

LÖVBORG: I know what Thea has confided to you.

HEDDA: And perhaps you have confided to her something about us?

LÖVBORG: Not a word. She is too stupid to understand anything of that sort.

HEDDA: Stupid?

LÖVBORG: She is stupid about matters of that sort.

HEDDA: And I am cowardly. (*Bends over towards him, without looking him in the face, and says more softly:*) But now I will confide something to you.

LÖVBORG: (*Eagerly*) Well?

HEDDA: The fact that I dared not shoot you down——

LÖVBORG: Yes!

HEDDA: ——that was not my most arrant cowardice—that evening.

LÖVBORG: (*Looks at her a moment, understands, and whispers passionately*) Oh, Hedda! Hedda Gabler! Now I begin to see a hidden reason beneath our comradeship! You and I——! After all, then, it was your craving for life——

HEDDA: (*Softly, with a sharp glance*) Take care! Believe nothing of the sort! (*Twilight has begun to fall. The hall door is opened from without by* BERTA)

HEDDA: (*Closes the album with a bang and calls smilingly:*) Ah, at last! My darling Thea,—come along!

MRS. ELVSTED *enters from the hall. She is in evening dress. The door is closed behind her.*

HEDDA: (*On the sofa, stretches out her arms towards her*) My sweet Thea—you can't think how I have been longing for you! (MRS. ELVSTED, *in passing, exchanges slight salutations with the gentlemen in the inner room, then goes up to the table and gives* HEDDA *her hand.* EILERT LÖVBORG *has risen. He and* MRS. ELVSTED *greet each other with a silent nod*)

MRS. ELVSTED: Ought I to go in and talk to your husband for a moment?

HEDDA: Oh, not at all. Leave those two alone. They will soon be going.

MRS. ELVSTED: Are they going out?

HEDDA: Yes, to a supper-party.

MRS. ELVSTED: (*Quickly, to* LÖVBORG) Not you?

LÖVBORG: No.

HEDDA: Mr. Lövborg remains with us.

MRS. ELVSTED: (*Takes a chair and is about to seat herself at his side*) Oh, how nice it is here!

HEDDA: No, thank you, my little Thea! Not there! You'll be good enough to come over here to me. I will sit between you.

MRS. ELVSTED: Yes, just as you please. (*She goes round the table and seats herself on the sofa on* HEDDA's *right.* LÖVBORG *re-seats himself on his chair*)

LÖVBORG: (*After a short pause, to* HEDDA) Is not she lovely to look at?

HEDDA: (*Lightly stroking her hair*) Only to look at?

LÖVBORG: Yes. For we two—she and I—we are two real comrades. We have absolute faith in each other; so we can sit and talk with perfect frankness——

HEDDA: Not round about, Mr. Lövborg?

LÖVBORG: Well——

MRS. ELVSTED: (*Softly clinging close to* HEDDA) Oh, how happy I am, Hedda! For, only think, he says I have inspired him, too.

HEDDA: (*Looks at her with a smile*) Ah! Does he say that, dear?

LÖVBORG: And then she is so brave, Mrs. Tesman!

MRS. ELVSTED: Good heavens—am I brave?

LÖVBORG: Exceedingly—where your comrade is concerned.

HEDDA: Ah, yes—courage! If one only had that!

LÖVBORG: What then? What do you mean?

HEDDA: Then life would perhaps be livable, after all. (*With a sudden change of tone*) But now, my dearest Thea, you really must have a glass of cold punch.

MRS. ELVSTED: No, thanks—I never take anything of that kind.

HEDDA: Well, then, you, Mr. Lövborg.

LÖVBORG: Nor I, thank you.

MRS. ELVSTED: No, he doesn't, either.

HEDDA: (*Looks fixedly at him*) But if I say you shall?

LÖVBORG: It would be no use.

HEDDA: (*Laughing*) Then I, poor creature, have no sort of power over you?

LÖVBORG: Not in that respect.

HEDDA: But seriously, I think you ought to—for your own sake.

MRS. ELVSTED: Why, Hedda——!

LÖVBORG: How so?

HEDDA: Or rather on account of other people.

LÖVBORG: Indeed?

HEDDA: Otherwise people might be apt to suspect that—in your heart of hearts—you did not feel quite secure—quite confident in yourself.

MRS. ELVSTED: (*Softly*) Oh, please, Hedda——!

LÖVBORG: People may suspect what they like—for the present.

MRS. ELVSTED: (*Joyfully*) Yes, let them!

HEDDA: I saw it plainly in Judge Brack's face a moment ago.

LÖVBORG: What did you see?

HEDDA: His contemptuous smile, when you dared not go with them into the inner room.

LÖVBORG: Dared not? Of course I preferred to stop here and talk to you.

MRS. ELVSTED: What could be more natural, Hedda?

HEDDA: But the Judge could not guess that. And I saw, too, the way he smiled and glanced at Tesman when you dared not accept his invitation to this wretched little super-party of his.

LÖVBORG: Dared not! Do you say I dared not?

HEDDA: I don't say so. But that was how Judge Brack understood it.

LÖVBORG: Well, let him.

HEDDA: Then you are going with them?

LÖVBORG: I will stay here with you and Thea.

MRS. ELVSTED: Yes, Hedda—how can you doubt that?

HEDDA: (*Smiles and nods approvingly to* LÖVBORG) Firm as a rock; Faithful to your principles, now and forever! Ah, that is how a man should be! (*Turns to* MRS. ELVSTED *and caresses her*) Well, now, what did I tell you, when you came to us this morning in such a state of distraction——

LÖVBORG: (*Surprised*) Distraction!

MRS. ELVSTED: (*Terrified*) Hedda—oh, Hedda——!

HEDDA: You can see for yourself! You haven't the slightest reason to be in such mortal terror—— (*Interrupting herself*) There! Now we can all three enjoy ourselves!

LÖVBORG: (*Who has given a start*) Ah—what is all this, Mrs. Tesman?

MRS. ELVSTED: Oh, my God, Hedda! What are you saying? What are you doing?

HEDDA: Don't get excited! That horrid Judge Brack is sitting watching you.

LÖVBORG: So she was in mortal terror! On my account!

MRS. ELVSTED: (*Softly and piteously*) Oh, Hedda—now you have ruined everything!

LÖVBORG: (*Looks fixedly at her for a moment. His face is distorted*) So that was my comrade's frank confidence in me?

MRS. ELVSTED: (*Imploringly*) Oh, my dearest friend—only let me tell you——

LÖVBORG: (*Takes one of the glasses of punch, raises it to his lips, and says in a low, husky voice*) Your health, Thea! (*He empties the glass, puts it down, and takes the second*)

MRS. ELVSTED: (*Softly*) Oh, Hedda, Hedda—how could you do this?

HEDDA: *I* do it? *I*? Are you crazy?

LÖVBORG: Here's to your health, too, Mrs. Tesman. Thanks for the truth. Hurrah for the truth! (*He empties the glass and is about to re-fill it.*)

HEDDA: (*Lays her hand on his arm*) Come, come—no more for the present. Remember you are going out to supper.

MRS. ELVSTED: No, no, no!

HEDDA: Hush! They are sitting watching you.

LÖVBORG: (*Putting down the glass*) Now, Thea—tell me the truth——

MRS. ELVSTED: Yes.

LÖVBORG: Did your husband know that you had come after me?

MRS. ELVSTED: (*Wringing her hands*) Oh, Hedda—do you hear what he is asking?

LÖVBORG: Was it arranged between you and him that you were to come to town and look after me? Perhaps it was the Sheriff himself that urged you to come? Aha, my dear—no doubt he wanted my help in his office! Or was it at the cardtable that he missed me?

MRS. ELVSTED: (*Softly, in agony*) Oh, Lövborg, Lövborg——!

LÖVBORG: (*Seizes a glass and is on the point of filling it*) Here's a glass for the old Sheriff, too!

HEDDA: (*Preventing him*) No more just now. Remember, you have to read your manuscript to Tesman.

LÖVBORG: (*Calmly, putting down the glass*) It was stupid of me all this, Thea—to take it in this way, I mean. Don't be angry with me, my dear, dear comrade. You shall see—both you and the others—that if I was fallen once—now I have risen again! Thanks to you, Thea.

MRS. ELVSTED: (*Radiant with joy*) Oh, heaven be praised——!

BRACK *has in the meantime looked at his watch. He and* TESMAN *rise and come into the drawing room.*

BRACK: (*Takes his hat and overcoat*) Well, Mrs. Tesman, our time has come.

HEDDA: I suppose it has.

LÖVBORG: (*Rising*) Mine too, Judge Brack.

MRS. ELVSTED: (*Softly and imploringly*) Oh, Lövborg, don't do it!

HEDDA: (*Pinching her arm*) They can hear you!

MRS. ELVSTED: (*With a suppressed shriek*) Ow!

LÖVBORG: (*To* BRACK) You were good enough to invite me.

BRACK: Well, are you coming after all?

LÖVBORG: Yes, many thanks.

BRACK: I'm delighted——

LÖVBORG: (*To* TESMAN, *putting the parcel of MS. in his pocket*) I should like to show you one or two things before I send it to the printers.

TESMAN: Fancy—that will be delightful. But, Hedda dear, how is Mrs. Elvsted to get home? Eh?

HEDDA: Oh, that can be managed somehow.

LÖVBORG: (*Looking towards the ladies*) Mrs. Elvsted? Of course, I'll come again and fetch her. (*Approaching*) At ten or thereabouts, Mrs. Tesman? Will that do?

HEDDA: Certainly. That will do capitally.

TESMAN: Well, then, that's all right. But you must not expect me so early, Hedda.

HEDDA: Oh, you may stop as long—as long as ever you please.

MRS. ELVSTED: (*Trying to conceal her anxiety*) Well, then, Mr. Löv-borg—I shall remain here until you come.

LÖVBORG: (*With his hat in his hand*) Pray do, Mrs. Elvsted.

BRACK: And now off goes the excursion train, gentlemen! I hope we shall have a lively time, as a certain fair lady puts it.

HEDDA: Ah, if only the fair lady could be present unseen——!

BRACK: Why unseen?

HEDDA: In order to hear a little of your liveliness at first hand, Judge Brack.

BRACK: (*Laughing*) I should not advise the fair lady to try it.

TESMAN: (*Also laughing*) Come, you're a nice one, Hedda! Fancy that!

BRACK: Well, good-bye, good-bye, ladies.

LÖVBORG: (*Bowing*) About ten o'clock, then.

BRACK, LÖVBORG, *and* TESMAN *go out by the hall door. At the same time,* BERTA *enters from the inner room with a lighted lamp, which she places on the drawing-room table; she goes out by the way she came.*

MRS. ELVSTED: (*Who has risen and is wandering restlessly about the room*) Hedda—Hedda—what will come of all this?

HEDDA: At ten o'clock—he will be here. I can see him already—with vine-leaves in his hair—flushed and fearless——

MRS. ELVSTED: Oh, I hope he may.

HEDDA: And then, you see—then he will have regained control over himself. Then he will be a free man for all his days.

MRS. ELVSTED: Oh, God!—if he would only come as you see him now!

HEDDA: He will come as I see him—so, and not otherwise! (*Rises and approaches* THEA) You may doubt him as long as you please; *I* believe in him. And now we will try——

MRS. ELVSTED: You have some hidden motive in this, Hedda!

HEDDA: Yes, I have. I want for once in my life to have power to mould a human destiny.

MRS. ELVSTED: Have you not the power?

HEDDA: I have not—and have never had it.

MRS. ELVSTED: Not your husband's?

HEDDA: Do you think that is worth the trouble? Oh, if you could only understand how poor I am. And fate has made you so rich! (*Clasps her passionately in her arms*) I think I must burn your hair off, after all.

MRS. ELVSTED: Let me go! Let me go! I am afraid of you, Hedda!

BERTA: (*In the middle doorway*) Tea is laid in the dining-room, ma'am.

HEDDA: Very well. We are coming.

MRS. ELVSTED: No, no, no! I would rather go home alone! At once!

HEDDA: Nonsense! First you shall have a cup of tea, you little stupid. And then—at ten o'clock—Eilert Lövborg will be here—with vine-leaves in his hair. (*She drags* MRS. ELVSTED *almost by force towards the middle doorway*)

ACT III.

The room at the TESMANS'. *The curtains are drawn over the middle doorway, and also over the glass door. The lamp, half turned down, and with a shade over it, is burning on the table. In the stove, the door of which stands open, there has been a fire, which is now nearly burnt out.*

MRS. ELVSTED, *wrapped in a large shawl, and with her feet upon a foot-rest, sits close to the stove, sunk back in the armchair.* HEDDA, *fully dressed, lies sleeping upon the sofa, with a sofa-blanket over her.*

MRS. ELVSTED: (*After a pause, suddenly sits up in her chair, and listens eagerly. Then she sinks back again wearily, moaning to herself*) Not yet!—Oh, God—oh, God—not yet!

BERTA *slips cautiously in by the hall door. She has a letter in her hand.*

MRS. ELVSTED: (*Turns and whispers eagerly*) Well—has any one come?
BERTA: (*Softly*) Yes, a girl has just brought this letter.
MRS. ELVSTED: (*Quickly, holding out her hand*) A letter! Give it to me!
BERTA: No, it's for Dr. Tesman, ma'am.
MRS. ELVSTED: Oh, indeed.
BERTA: It was Miss Tesman's servant that brought it. I'll lay it here on the table.
MRS. ELVSTED: Yes, do.
BERTA: (*Laying down the letter*) I think I had better put out the lamp. It's smoking.
MRS. ELVSTED: Yes, put it out. It must soon be daylight now.
BERTA: (*Putting out the lamp*) It is daylight already, ma'am.
MRS. ELVSTED: Yes, broad day! And no one come back yet——!
BERTA: Lord bless you, ma'am—I guessed how it would be.
MRS. ELVSTED: You guessed?
BERTA: Yes, when I saw that a certain person had come back to town—and that he went off with them. For we've heard enough about that gentleman before now.
MRS. ELVSTED: Don't speak so loud. You will waken Mrs. Tesman.
BERTA: (*Looks towards the soft and sighs*) No, no—let her sleep, poor thing. Shan't I put some wood on the fire?
MRS. ELVSTED: Thanks, not for me.
BERTA: Oh, very well. (*She goes softly out by the hall door*).
HEDDA: (*Is awakened by the shutting of the door, and looks up*) What's that——?
MRS. ELVSTED: It was only the servant——
HEDDA: (*Looking about her*) Oh, we're here—! Yes, now I remember. (*Sits erect upon the sofa, stretches herself, and rubs her eyes*) What o'clock is it, Thea?
MRS. ELVSTED: (*Looks at her watch*) It's past seven.
HEDDA: When did Tesman come home?
MRS. ELVSTED: He has not come.
HEDDA: Not come home yet?
MRS. ELVSTED: (*Rising*) No one has come.

HEDDA: Think of our watching and waiting here till four in the morning——

MRS. ELVSTED: (*Wringing her hands*) And how I watched and waited for him!

HEDDA: (*Yawns, and says with her hand before her mouth*) Well, well —we might have spared ourselves the trouble.

MRS. ELVSTED: Did you get a little sleep?

HEDDA: Oh, yes; I believe I have slept pretty well. Have you not?

MRS. ELVSTED: Not for a moment. I couldn't, Hedda!—not to save my life.

HEDDA: (*Rises and goes towards her*) There, there, there! There's nothing to be so alarmed about. I understand quite well what has happened.

MRS. ELVSTED: Well, what do you think? Won't you tell me?

HEDDA: Why, of course, it has been a very late affair at Judge Brack's——

MRS. ELSTED: Yes, yes—that is clear enough. But all the same——

HEDDA: And then, you see, Tesman hasn't cared to come home and ring us up in the middle of the night. (*Laughing*) Perhaps he wasn't inclined to show himself either—immediately after a jollification.

MRS. ELVSTED: But in that case—where can he have gone?

HEDDA: Of course, he has gone to his aunts' and slept there. They have his old room ready for him.

MRS. ELVSTED: No, he can't be with them; for a letter has just come for him from Miss Tesman. There it lies.

HEDDA: Indeed? (*Looks at the address*) Why, yes, it's addressed in Aunt Julia's own hand. Well, then, he has remained at Judge Brack's. And as for Eilert Lövborg—he is sitting, with vine-leaves in his hair, reading his manuscript.

MRS. ELVSTED: Oh, Hedda, you are just saying things you don't believe a bit.

HEDDA: You really are a little blockhead, Thea.

MRS. ELVSTED: Oh, yes, I suppose I am.

HEDDA: And how mortally tired you look.

MRS. ELVSTED: Yes, I am mortally tired.

HEDDA: Well, then, you must do as I tell you. You must go into my room and lie down for a little while.

MRS. ELVSTED: Oh, no, no—I shouldn't be able to sleep.

HEDDA: I am sure you would.

MRS. ELVSTED: Well, but your husband is certain to come soon now; and then I want to know at once——

HEDDA: I shall take care to let you know when he comes.

MRS. ELVSTED: Do you promise me, Hedda?

HEDDA: Yes, rely upon me. Just you go in and have a sleep in the meantime.

MRS. ELVSTED: Thanks; then I'll try to. (*She goes off through the inner door*)

(HEDDA *goes up to the glass door and draws back the curtains. The broad daylight streams into the room. Then she takes a little hand-glass from the writing-table, looks at herself in it, and arranges her hair. Next she goes to the hall door and presses the bell-button*).
BERTA *presently appears at the hall door.*

BERTA: Did you want anything, ma'am?

HEDDA: Yes; you must put some more wood in the stove. I am shivering.

BERTA: Bless me—I'll make up the fire at once. (*She rakes the embers together and lays a piece of wood upon them; then stops and listens*) That was a ring at the front door, ma'am.

HEDDA: Then go to the door. I will look after the fire.

BERTA: It'll soon burn up. (*She goes out by the hall door*)

HEDDA *kneels on the foot-rest and lays some more pieces of wood in the stove.*
After a short pause, GEORGE TESMAN *enters from the hall. He looks tired and rather serious. He steals on tiptoe towards the middle doorway and is about to slip through the curtains.*

HEDDA: (*At the stove, without looking up*) Good morning.

TESMAN: (*Turns*) Hedda! (*Approaching her*) Good heavens—are you up so early? Eh?

HEDDA: Yes, I am up very early this morning.

TESMAN: And I never doubted you were still sound asleep! Fancy that, Hedda!

HEDDA: Don't speak so loud. Mrs. Elvsted is resting in my room.

TESMAN: Has Mrs. Elvsted been here all night?

HEDDA: Yes, since no one came to fetch her.

TESMAN: Ah, to be sure.

HEDDA: (*Closes the door of the stove and rises*) Well, did you enjoy yourselves at Judge Brack's?

TESMAN: Have you been anxious about me? Eh?

HEDDA: No, I should never think of being anxious. But I asked if you had enjoyed yourself.

TESMAN: Oh, yes,—for once in a way. Especially the beginning of the evening; for then Eilert read me part of his book. We arrived more than an hour too early—fancy that! And Brack had all sorts of arrangements to make—so Eilert read to me.

HEDDA: (*Seating herself by the table on the right*) Well? Tell me, then——

TESMAN: (*Sitting on a footstool near the stove*) Oh, Hedda, you can't conceive what a book that is going to be! I believe it is one of the most remarkable things that have ever been written. Fancy that!

HEDDA: Yes, yes; I don't care about that——

TESMAN: I must make a confession to you, Hedda. When he had finished reading—a horrid feeling came over me.

HEDDA: A horrid feeling?

TESMAN: I felt jealous of Eilert for having had it in him to write such a book. Only think, Hedda!

HEDDA: Yes, yes, I am thinking!

TESMAN: And then how pitiful to think that he—with all his gifts—should be irreclaimable, after all.

HEDDA: I suppose you mean that he has more courage than the rest?

TESMAN: No, not at all—I mean that he is incapable of taking his pleasures in moderation.

HEDDA: And what came of it all—in the end?

TESMAN: Well, to tell the truth, I think it might best be described as an orgy, Hedda.

HEDDA: Had he vine-leaves in his hair?

TESMAN: Vine-leaves? No, I saw nothing of the sort. But he made a long, rambling speech in honor of the woman who had inspired him in his work—that was the phrase he used.

HEDDA: Did he name her?

TESMAN: No, he didn't; but I can't help thinking he meant Mrs. Elvsted. You may be sure he did.

HEDDA: Well—where did you part from him?

TESMAN: On the way to town. We broke up—the last of us at any rate—all together; and Brack came with us to get a breath of fresh air. And then, you see, we agreed to take Eilert home; for he had had far more than was good for him.

HEDDA: I daresay.

TESMAN: But now comes the strange part of it, Hedda; or, I should rather say, the melancholy part of it. I declare I am almost ashamed—on Eilert's account—to tell you——

HEDDA: Oh, go on——!

TESMAN: Well, as we were getting near town, you see, I happened to drop a little behind the others. Only for a minute or two—fancy that!

HEDDA: Yes, yes, yes, but——?

TESMAN: And then, as I hurried after them—what do you think I found by the wayside? Eh?

HEDDA: Oh, how should I know!

TESMAN: You mustn't speak of it to a soul, Hedda! Do you hear! Promise me, for Eilert's sake. (*Draws a parcel, wrapped in paper, from his coat pocket*) Fancy, dear—I found this.

HEDDA: Is not that the parcel he had with him yesterday?

TESMAN: Yes, it is the whole of his precious, irreplaceable manuscript! And he had gone and lost it, and knew nothing about it. Only fancy, Hedda! So deplorably——

HEDDA: But why did you not give him back the parcel at once?

TESMAN: I didn't dare to—in the state he was then in——

HEDDA: Did you not tell any of the others that you found it?

TESMAN: Oh, far from it! You can surely understand that, for Eilert's sake, I wouldn't do that.

HEDDA: So no one knows that Eilert Lövborg's manuscript is in your possession?

TESMAN: No. And no one must know it.

HEDDA: Then what did you say to him afterwards?

TESMAN: I didn't talk to him again at all; for when we got in among the streets, he and two or three of the others gave us the slip and disappeared. Fancy that!

HEDDA: Indeed! They must have taken him home then.

TESMAN: Yes, so it would appear. And Brack, too, left us.

HEDDA: And what have you been doing with yourself since?

TESMAN: Well, I and some of the others went home with one of the party, a jolly fellow, and took our morning coffee with him; or perhaps I should rather call it our night coffee—eh? But now, when I have rested a little, and given Eilert, poor fellow, time to have his sleep out, I must take this back to him.

HEDDA: (*Holds out her hand for the packet*) No—don't give it to him! Not in such a hurry, I mean. Let me read it first.

TESMAN: No, my dearest Hedda, I mustn't, I really mustn't.

HEDDA: You must not?

TESMAN: No—for you can imagine what a state of despair he will be in when he wakens and misses the manuscript. He has no copy of it, you must know! He told me so.

HEDDA: (*Looking searchingly at him*) Can such a thing not be reproduced? Written over again?

TESMAN: No, I don't think that would be possible. For the inspiration, you see——

HEDDA: Yes, yes—I suppose it depends on that—— (*Lightly*) But, by the by—here is a letter for you.

TESMAN: Fancy——!

HEDDA: (*Handing it to him*) It came early this morning.

TESMAN: It's from Aunt Julia! What can it be? (*He lays the packet on the other footstool, opens the letter, runs his eye through it, and jumps up*) Oh, Hedda—she says the poor Aunt Rina is dying!

HEDDA: Well, we were prepared for that.

TESMAN: And that if I want to see her again, I must make haste. I'll run in to them at once.

HEDDA: (*Suppressing a smile*) Will you run?

TESMAN: Oh, my dearest Hedda—if you could only make up your mind to come with me! Just think!

HEDDA: (*Rises and says wearily, repelling the idea*) No, no, don't ask me. I will not look upon sickness and death. I loathe all sorts of ugliness.

TESMAN: Well, well, then——! (*Bustling around*) My hat——? My overcoat——? Oh, in the hall——. I do hope I mayn't come too late, Hedda? Eh?

HEDDA: Oh, if you run——

BERTA *appears at the hall door.*

BERTA: Judge Brack is at the door, and wishes to know if he may come in.

TESMAN: At this time! No, I can't possibly see him.

HEDDA: But I can. (*To* BERTA) Ask Judge Brack to come in.

BERTA *goes out.*

HEDDA: (*Quickly, whispering*) The parcel, Tesman! (*She snatches it up from the stool*)

TESMAN: Yes, give it to me!

HEDDA: No, no, I will keep it till you come back. (*She goes to the writing-table and places it in the bookcase.* TESMAN *stands in a flurry of haste, and cannot get his gloves on*)

JUDGE BRACK *enters from the hall.*

HEDDA: (*Nodding to him*) You are an early bird, I must say.

BRACK: Yes, don't you think so? (*To* TESMAN) Are you on the move, too?

TESMAN: Yes, I must rush off to my aunts'. Fancy—the invalid one is lying at death's door, poor creature.

BRACK: Dear me, is she indeed? Then on no account let me detain you. At such a critical moment——

TESMAN: Yes, I must really rush—— Good-bye! Good-bye! (*He hastens out by the hall door*)

HEDDA: (*Approaching*) You seem to have made a particularly lively night of it at your rooms, Judge Brack.

BRACK: I assure you I have not had my clothes off, Mrs. Hedda.

HEDDA: Not you, either?

BRACK: No, as you may see. But what has Tesman been telling you of the night's adventures?

HEDDA: Oh, some tiresome story. Only that they went and had coffee somewhere or other.

BRACK: I have heard about that coffee-party already. Eilert Lövborg was not with them, I fancy?

HEDDA: No, they had taken him home before that.

BRACK: Tesman too?

HEDDA: No, but some of the others, he said.

BRACK: (*Smiling*) George Tesman is really an ingenuous creature, Mrs. Hedda.

HEDDA: Yes, heaven knows he is. Then is there something behind all this?

BRACK: Yes, perhaps there may be.

HEDDA: Well then, sit down, my dear Judge, and tell your story in comfort. (*She seats herself to the left of the table.* BRACK *sits near her, at the long side of the table*)

HEDDA: Now then?

BRACK: I had special reasons for keeping track of my guests—or rather of some of my guests—last night.

HEDDA: Of Eilert Lövborg among the rest, perhaps?

BRACK: Frankly—yes.

HEDDA: Now you make me really curious——

BRACK: Do you know where he and one or two of the others finished the night, Mrs. Hedda?

HEDDA: If it is not quite unmentionable, tell me.

BRACK: Oh no, it's not at all unmentionable. Well, they put in an appearance at a particularly animated *soirée*.

HEDDA: Of the lively kind?

BRACK: Of the very liveliest——

HEDDA: Tell me more of this, Judge Brack——

BRACK: Lövborg, as well as the others, had been invited in advance.

I knew all about it. But he declined the invitation; for now, as you know, he has become a new man.

HEDDA: Up at the Elvsteds', yes. But he went after all, then?

BRACK: Well, you see, Mrs. Hedda—unhappily the spirit moved him at my rooms last evening——

HEDDA: Yes, I hear he found inspiration.

BRACK: Pretty violent inspiration. Well, I fancy that altered his purpose; for we menfolk are unfortunately not always so firm in our principles as we ought to be.

HEDDA: Oh, I am sure you are an exception, Judge Brack. But as to Lövborg——?

BRACK: To make a long story short—he landed at last in Mademoiselle Diana's rooms.

HEDDA: Mademoiselle Diana's?

BRACK: It was Mademoiselle Diana that was giving the soirée, to a select circle of her admirers and her lady friends.

HEDDA: Is she a red-haired woman?

BRACK: Precisely.

HEDDA: A sort of a—singer?

BRACK: Oh yes—in her leisure moments. And moreover a mighty huntress—of men—Mrs. Hedda. You have no doubt heard of her. Eilert Lövborg was one of her most enthusiastic protectors—in the days of his glory.

HEDDA: And how did all this end?

BRACK: Far from amicably, it appears. After a most tender meeting, they seem to have come to blows——

HEDDA: Lövborg and she?

BRACK: Yes. He accused her or her friends of having robbed him. He declared that his pocketbook had disappeared—and other things as well. In short, he seems to have made a furious disturbance.

HEDDA: And what came of it all?

BRACK: It came to a general scrimmage, in which the ladies as well as the gentlemen took part. Fortunately the police at last appeared on the scene.

HEDDA: The police too?

BRACK: Yes. I fancy it will prove a costly frolic for Eilert Lövborg, crazy being that he is.

HEDDA: How so?

BRACK: He seems to have made a violent resistance—to have hit one of the constables on the head and torn the coat off his back. So they had to march him off to the police-station with the rest.

HEDDA: How have you learnt all this?

BRACK: From the police themselves.

HEDDA: (*Gazing straight before her*) So that is what happened. Then he had no vine-leaves in his hair.

BRACK: Vine-leaves, Mrs. Hedda?

HEDDA: (*Changing her tone*) But tell me now, Judge—what is your real reason for tracking out Eilert Lövborg's movements so carefully?

BRACK: In the first place, it could not be entirely indifferent to me if it should appear in the police-court that he came straight from my house.

HEDDA: Will the matter come into court then?

BRACK: Of course. However, I should scarcely have troubled so much about that. But I thought that, as a friend of the family, it was my duty to supply you and Tesman with a full account of his nocturnal exploits.

HEDDA: Why so, Judge Brack?

BRACK: Why, because I have a shrewd suspicion that he intends to use you as a sort of blind.

HEDDA: Oh, how can you think such a thing!

BRACK: Good heavens, Mrs. Hedda—we have eyes in our head. Mark my words! This Mrs. Elvsted will be in no hurry to leave town again.

HEDDA: Well, even if there should be anything between them, I suppose there are plenty of other places where they could meet.

BRACK: Not a single home. Henceforth, as before, every respectable house will be closed against Eilert Lövborg.

HEDDA: And so ought mine to be, you mean?

BRACK: Yes. I confess it would be more than painful to me if this personage were to be made free of your house. How superfluous, how intrusive, he would be, if he were to force his way into——

HEDDA: ——into the triangle?

BRACK: Precisely. It would simply mean that I should find myself homeless.

HEDDA: (*Looks at him with a smile*) So you want to be the one cock in the basket[1]—that is your aim.

BRACK: (*Nods slowly and lowers his voice*) Yes, that is my aim. And for that I will fight—with every weapon I can command.

HEDDA: (*Her smile vanishing*) I see you are a dangerous person—when it comes to the point.

BRACK: Do you think so?

HEDDA: I am beginning to think so. And I am exceedingly glad to think—that you have no sort of hold over me.

---

[1] *Eneste hane i kurven*—a proverbial saying.

BRACK: (*Laughing equivocally*) Well well, Mrs. Hedda—perhaps you are right there. If I had, who knows what I might be capable of?

HEDDA: Come, come now, Judge Brack! That sounds almost like a threat.

BRACK: (*Rising*) Oh, not at all! The triangle, you know, ought, if possible, to be spontaneously constructed.

HEDDA: There I agree with you.

BRACK: Well, now I have said all I had to say; and I had better be getting back to town. Good-bye, Mrs. Hedda. (*He goes towards the glass door*)

HEDDA: (*Rising*) Are you going through the garden?

BRACK: Yes, it's a short cut for me.

HEDDA: And then it is a back way, too.

BRACK: Quite so. I have no objection to back ways. They may be piquant enough at times.

HEDDA: When there is ball practice going on, you mean?

BRACK: (*In the doorway, laughing to her*) Oh, people don't shoot their tame poultry, I fancy.

HEDDA: (*Also laughing*) Oh, no, when there is only one cock in the basket—— (*They exchange laughing nods of farewell. He goes. She closes the door behind him*)

> HEDDA, *who has become quite serious, stands for a moment looking out. Presently she goes and peeps through the curtain over the middle doorway. Then she goes to the writing-table, takes* LÖV-BORG'S *packet out of the bookcase, and is on the point of looking through its contents.* BERTA *is heard speaking loudly in the hall.* HEDDA *turns and listens. Then she hastily locks up the packet in the drawer, and lays the key on the inkstand.*
> *tears open the hall door. He looks somewhat confused and irritated.*

LÖVBORG: (*Looking towards the hall*) And I tell you I must and will come in! There! (*He closes the door, turns, sees* HEDDA, *at once regains his self-control, and bows*)

HEDDA: (*At the writing-table*) Well, Mr. Lövborg, this is rather a late hour to call for Thea.

LÖVBORG: You mean rather an early hour to call on you. Pray pardon me.

HEDDA: How do you know that she is still here?

LÖVBORG: They told me at her lodgings that she had been out all night.

HEDDA: (*Going to the oval table*) Did you notice anything about the people of the house when they said that?
LÖVBORG: (*Looks inquiringly at her*) Notice anything about them?
HEDDA: I mean, did they seem to think it odd?
LÖVBORG: (*Suddenly understanding*) Oh yes, of course! I am dragging her down with me! However, I didn't notice anything.—I suppose Tesman is not up yet?
HEDDA: No—I think not——
LÖVBORG: When did he come home?
HEDDA: Very late.
LÖVBORG: Did he tell you anything?
HEDDA: Yes, I gathered that you had had an exceedingly jolly evening at Judge Brack's.
LÖVBORG: Nothing more?
HEDDA: I don't think so. However, I was so dreadfully sleepy——

MRS. ELVSTED *enters through the curtains of the middle doorway.*

MRS. ELVSTED: (*Going towards him*) Ah, Lövborg! At last——!
LÖVBORG: Yes, at last. And too late!
MRS. ELVSTED: (*Looks anxiously at him*) What is too late?
LÖVBORG: Everything is too late now. It is all over with me.
MRS. ELVSTED: Oh no, no—don't say that!
LÖVBORG: You will say the same when you hear——
MRS. ELVSTED: I won't hear anything!
HEDDA: Perhaps you would prefer to talk to her alone? If so, I will leave you.
LÖVBORG: No, stay—you too. I beg you to stay.
MRS. ELVSTED: Yes, but I won't hear anything, I tell you.
LÖVBORG: It is not last night's adventures that I want to talk about.
MRS. ELVSTED: What is it then——?
LÖVBORG: I want to say that now our ways must part.
MRS. ELVSTED: Part!
HEDDA: (*Involuntarily*) I knew it!
LÖVBORG: You can be of no more service to me, Thea.
MRS. ELVSTED: How can you stand there and say that! No more service to you! Am I not to help you now, as before? Are we not to go on working together?
LÖVBORG: Henceforward I shall do no work.
MRS. ELVSTED: (*Despairingly*) Then what am I to do with my life?
LÖVBORG: You must try to live your life as if you had never known me.
MRS. ELVSTED: But you know I cannot do that!

LÖVBORG: Try if you cannot, Thea. You must go home again——

MRS. ELVSTED: (*In vehement protest*) Never in this world! Where you are, there will I be also! I will not let myself be driven away like this! I will remain here! I will be with you when the book appears.

HEDDA: (*Half aloud, in suspense*) Ah yes—the book!

LÖVBORG: (*Looks at her*) My book and Thea's; for that is what it is.

MRS. ELVSTED: Yes, I feel that it is. And that is why I have a right to be with you when it appears! I will see with my own eyes how respect and honor pour in upon you afresh. And the happiness—the happiness—oh, I must share it with you!

LÖVBORG: Thea—our book will never appear.

HEDDA: Ah!

MRS. ELVSTED: Never appear!

LÖVBORG: Can never appear.

MRS. ELVSTED: (*In agonizing foreboding*) Lövborg—what have you done with the manuscript?

HEDDA: (*Looks anxiously at him*) Yes, the manuscript——?

MRS. ELVSTED: Where is it?

LÖVBORG: Oh Thea—don't ask me about it!

MRS. ELVSTED: Yes, yes, I will know. I demand to be told at once.

LÖVBORG: The manuscript——. Well then—I have torn the manuscript into a thousand pieces.

MRS. ELVSTED: (*Shrieks*) Oh no, no——!

HEDDA: (*Involuntarily*) But that's not——

LÖVBORG: (*Looks at her*) Not true, you think?

HEDDA: (*Collecting herself*) Oh well, of course—since you say so. But it sounded so improbable——

LÖVBORG: It is true, all the same.

MRS. ELVSTED: (*Wringing her hands*) Oh God—oh God, Hedda—torn his own work to pieces!

LÖVBORG: I have torn my own life to pieces. So why should I not tear my life-work too——?

MRS. ELVSTED: And you did this last night?

LÖVBORG: Yes, I tell you! Tore it into a thousand pieces—and scattered them on the fjord—far out. There there is cool sea-water at any rate—let them drift upon it—drift with the current and the wind. And then presently they will sink—deeper and deeper—as I shall, Thea.

MRS. ELVSTED: Do you know, Lövborg, that what you have done with the book—I shall think of it to my dying day as though you had killed a little child.

LÖVBORG: Yes, you are right. It is a sort of child-murder.

MRS. ELVSTED: How could you, then——! Did not the child belong to me too?

HEDDA: (*Almost inaudibly*) Ah, the child——

MRS. ELVSTED: (*Breathing heavily*) It is all over then. Well well, now I will go, Hedda.

HEDDA: But you are not going away from town?

MRS. ELVSTED: Oh, I don't know what I shall do. I see nothing but darkness before me. (*She goes out by the hall door*)

HEDDA: (*Stands waiting for a moment*) So you are not going to see her home, Mr. Lövborg?

LÖVBORG: I? Through the streets? Would you have people see her walking with me?

HEDDA: Of course I don't know what else may have happened last night. But is it so utterly irretrievable?

LÖVBORG: It will not end with last night—I know that perfectly well. And the thing is that now I have no taste for that sort of life either. I won't begin it anew. She has broken my courage and my power of braving life out.

HEDDA: (*Looking straight before her*) So that pretty little fool has had her fingers in a man's destiny. (*Looks at him*) But all the same, how could you treat her so heartlessly?

LÖVBORG: Oh, don't say that it was heartless!

HEDDA: To go and destroy what has filled her whole soul for months and years! You do not call that heartless!

LÖVBORG: To you I can tell the truth, Hedda.

HEDDA: The truth?

LÖVBORG: First promise me—give me your word—that what I now confide to you Thea shall never know.

HEDDA: I give you my word.

LÖVBORG: Good. Then let me tell you that what I said just now was untrue.

HEDDA: About the manuscript?

LÖVBORG: Yes. I have not torn it to pieces—nor thrown it into the fjord.

HEDDA: No, no——. But—where it is then?

LÖVBORG: I have destroyed it none the less—utterly destroyed it, Hedda!

HEDDA: I don't understand.

LÖVBORG: Thea said that what I had done seemed to her like a child-murder.

HEDDA: Yes, so she said.

LÖVBORG: But to kill his child—that is not the worst thing a father can do to it.

HEDDA: Not the worst?

LÖVBORG: No. I wanted to spare Thea from hearing the worst.

HEDDA: Then what is the worst?

LÖVBORG: Suppose now, Hedda, that a man—in the small hours of the morning—came home to his child's mother after a night of riot and debauchery, and said: "Listen—I have been here and there—in this place and in that. And I have taken our child with me—to this place and to that. And I have lost the child—utterly lost it. The devil knows into what hands it may have fallen—who may have had their clutches on it."

HEDDA: Well—but when all is said and done, you know—this was only a book——

LÖVBORG: Thea's pure soul was in that book. ·

HEDDA: Yes, so I understand.

LÖVBORG: And you can understand, too, that for her and me together no future is possible?

HEDDA: What path do you mean to take then?

LÖVBORG: None. I will only try to make an end of it all—the sooner the better.

HEDDA: (*A step nearer him*) Eilert Lövborg—listen to me.—Will you not try to—to do it beautifully?

LÖVBORG: Beautifully? (*Smiling*) With vine-leaves in my hair, as you used to dream in the old days——?

HEDDA: No, no. I have lost my faith in the vine-leaves. But beautifully nevertheless! For once in a way!—Good-bye! You must go now—and do not come here any more.

LÖVBORG: Good-bye, Mrs. Tesman. And give George Tesman my love. (*He is on the point of going*)

HEDDA: No, wait! I must give you a memento to take with you. (*She goes to the writing-table and opens the drawer and the pistol-case; then returns to* LÖVBORG *with one of the pistols*)

LÖVBORG: (*Looks at her*) This? Is this the memento?

HEDDA: (*Nodding slowly*) Do you recognize it? It was aimed at you once.

LÖVBORG: You should have used it then.

HEDDA: Take it—and do you use it now.

LÖVBORG: (*Puts the pistol in his breast pocket*) Thanks!

HEDDA: And beautifully, Eilert Lövborg. Promise me that!

LÖVBORG: Good-bye, Hedda Gabler. (*He goes out by the hall door*)

HEDDA *listens for a moment at the door. Then she goes up to the writing-table, takes out the packet of manuscript, peeps under the cover, draws a few of the sheets half out, and looks at them. Next she goes over and seats herself in the arm-chair beside the stove, with the packet in her lap. Presently she opens the stove door, and then the packet.*

HEDDA: (*Throws one of the quires into the fire and whispers to herself*) Now I am burning your child, Thea!—Burning it, curly-locks! (*Throwing one or two more quires into the stove*) Your child and Eilert Lövborg's. (*Throws the rest in*) I am burning—I am burning your child.

ACT IV.

The same rooms at the TESMANS'. *It is evening. The drawing-room is in darkness. The back room is lighted by the hanging lamp over the table. The curtains over the glass door are drawn close.*

HEDDA, *dressed in black, walks to and fro in the dark room. Then she goes into the back room and disappears for a moment to the left. She is heard to strike a few chords on the piano. Presently she comes in sight again, and returns to the drawing-room.*

BERTA *enters from the right, through the inner room, with a lighted lamp, which she places on the table in front of the corner settee in the drawing-room. Her eyes are red with weeping, and she has black ribbons in her cap. She goes quietly and circumspectly out to the right.* HEDDA *goes up to the glass door, lifts the curtain a little aside, and looks out into the darkness.*

Shortly afterwards, MISS TESMAN, *in mourning, with a bonnet and veil on, comes in from the hall.* HEDDA *goes towards her and holds out her hand.*

MISS TESMAN: Yes, Hedda, here I am, in mourning and forlorn; for for now my poor sister has at last found peace.

HEDDA: I have heard the news already, as you see. Tesman sent me a card.

MISS TESMAN: Yes, he promised he would. But nevertheless I thought that to Hedda—here in the house of life—I ought myself to bring the tidings of death.

HEDDA: That was very kind of you.

MISS TESMAN: Ah, Rina ought not to have left us just now. This is not the time for Hedda's house to be a house of mourning.

HEDDA: (*Changing the subject*) She died quite peacefully, did she not, Miss Tesman?

MISS TESMAN: Oh, her end was so calm, so beautiful. And then she had the unspeakable happiness of seeing George once more—and bidding him good-bye.—Has he not come home yet?

HEDDA: No. He wrote that he might be detained. But won't you sit down?

MISS TESMAN: No thank you, my dear, dear Hedda. I should like to, but I have so much to do. I must prepare my dear one for her rest as well as I can. She shall go to her grave looking her best.

HEDDA: Can I not help you in any way?

MISS TESMAN: Oh, you must not think of it! Hedda Tesman must have no hand in such mournful work. Nor let her thoughts dwell on it either—not at this time.

HEDDA: One is not always mistress of one's thoughts——

MISS TESMAN: (*Continuing*) Ah yes, it is the way of the world. At home we shall be sewing a shroud; and here there will soon be sewing too, I suppose—but of another sort, thank God!

GEORGE TESMAN *enters by the hall door.*

HEDDA: Ah, you have come at last!

TESMAN: You here, Aunt Julia? With Hedda? Fancy that!

MISS TESMAN: I was just going, my dear boy. Well, have you done all you promised?

TESMAN: No; I'm really afraid I have forgotten half of it. I must come to you again to-morrow. To-day my brain is all in a whirl. I can't keep my thoughts together.

MISS TESMAN: Why, my dear George, you mustn't take it in this way.

TESMAN: Mustn't——? How do you mean?

MISS TESMAN: Even in your sorrow you must rejoice, as I do—rejoice that she is at rest.

TESMAN: Oh yes, yes—you are thinking of Aunt Rina.

HEDDA: You will feel lonely now, Miss Tesman.

MISS TESMAN: Just at first, yes. But that will not last very long, I hope. I daresay I shall soon find an occupant for poor Rina's little room.

TESMAN: Indeed? Who do you think will take it? Eh?

MISS TESMAN: Oh, there's always some poor invalid or other in want of nursing, unfortunately.

HEDDA: Would you really take such a burden upon you again?

MISS TESMAN: A burden! Heaven forgive you, child—it has been no burden to me.

HEDDA: But suppose you had a total stranger on your hands——

MISS TESMAN: Oh, one soon makes friends with sick folk; and it's such an absolute necessity for me to have some one to live for. Well, heaven be praised, there may soon be something in *this* house, too, to keep an old aunt busy.

HEDDA: Oh, don't trouble about anything here.

TESMAN: Yes, just fancy what a nice time we three might have together, if——?

HEDDA: If——?

TESMAN: (*Uneasily*) Oh, nothing. It will all come right. Let us hope so—eh?

MISS TESMAN: Well well, I daresay you two want to talk to each other. (*Smiling*) And perhaps Hedda may have something to tell you, too, George. Good-bye! I must go home to Rina. (*Turning at the door*) How strange it is to think that now Rina is with me and with my poor brother as well!

TESMAN: Yes, fancy that, Aunt Julia! Eh? (MISS TESMAN *goes out by the hall door*)

HEDDA: (*Follows* TESMAN *coldly and searchingly with her eyes*) I almost believe your Aunt Rina's death affects you more than it does your Aunt Julia.

TESMAN: Oh, it's not that alone. It's Eilert I am so terribly uneasy about.

HEDDA: (*Quickly*) Is there anything new about him?

TESMAN: I looked in at his rooms this afternoon, intending to tell him the manuscript was in safe keeping.

HEDDA: Well, did you not find him?

TESMAN: No. He wasn't at home. But afterwards I met Mrs. Elvsted, and she told me that he had been here early this morning.

HEDDA: Yes, directly after you had gone.

TESMAN: And he said that he had torn his manuscript to pieces—eh?

HEDDA: Yes, so he declared.

TESMAN: Why, good heavens, he must have been completely out of his mind! And I suppose you thought it best not to give it back to him, Hedda?

HEDDA: No, he did not get it.

TESMAN: But of course you told him that we had it?

HEDDA: No. (*Quickly*) Did you tell Mrs. Elvsted?

TESMAN: No; I thought I had better not. But you ought to have told him. Fancy, if, in desperation, he should go and do himself some injury!

Let me have the manuscript, Hedda! I will take it to him at once. Where is it?

HEDDA: (*Cold and immovable, leaning on the arm-chair*) I have not got it.

TESMAN: Have not got it? What in the world do you mean?

HEDDA: I have burnt it—every line of it.

TESMAN: (*With a violent movement of terror*) Burnt! Burnt Eilert's manuscript!

HEDDA: Don't scream so. The servant might hear you.

TESMAN: Burnt! Why, good God——! No, no, no! It's impossible!

HEDDA: It is so, nevertheless.

TESMAN: Do you know what you have done, Hedda? It's unlawful appropriation of lost property. Fancy that! Just ask Judge Brack, and he'll tell you what it is.

HEDDA: I advise you not to speak of it—either to Judge Brack, or to any one else.

TESMAN: But how could you do anything so unheard-of? What put it into your head? What possessed you? Answer me that—eh?

HEDDA: (*Suppressing an almost imperceptible smile*) I did it for your sake, George.

TESMAN: For my sake!

HEDDA: This morning, when you told me about what he had read to you——

TESMAN: Yes yes—what then?

HEDDA: You acknowledged that you envied him his work.

TESMAN: Oh, of course I didn't mean that literally.

HEDDA: No matter—I could not bear the idea that any one should throw you into the shade.

TESMAN: (*In an outburst of mingled doubt and joy*) Hedda! Oh, is this true? But—but—I never knew you show your love like that before. Fancy that!

HEDDA: Well, I may as well tell you that—just at this time—— (*Impatiently, breaking off*) No, no; you can ask Aunt Julia. She will tell you, fast enough.

TESMAN: Oh, I almost think I understand you, Hedda! (*Clasps his hands together*) Great heavens! do you really mean it! Eh?

HEDDA: Don't shout so. The servant might hear.

TESMAN: (*Laughing in irrepressible glee*) The servant! Why, how absurd you are, Hedda. It's only my old Berta! Why, I'll tell Berta myself.

HEDDA: (*Clenching her hands together in desperation*) Oh, it is killing me,—it is killing me, all this!

TESMAN: What is, Hedda? Eh?

HEDDA: *(Coldly, controlling herself)* All this—absurdity—George.

TESMAN: Absurdity! Do you see anything absurd in my being over-joyed at the news! But after all—perhaps I had better not say anything to Berta.

HEDDA: Oh——why not that too?

TESMAN: No, no, not yet! But I must certainly tell Aunt Julia. And then that you have begun to call me George too! Fancy that! Oh, Aunt Julia will be so happy—so happy!

HEDDA: When she hears that I have burnt Eilert Lövborg's manuscript —for your sake?

TESMAN: No, by the by—that affair of the manuscript—of course no-body must know about that. But that you love me so much, Hedda— Aunt Julia must really share my joy in that! I wonder, now, whether this sort of thing is usual in young wives? Eh?

HEDDA: I think you had better ask Aunt Julia that question too.

TESMAN: I will indeed, some time or other. *(Looks uneasy and down-cast again)* And yet the manuscript—the manuscript! Good God! it is terrible to think what will become of poor Eilert now.

MRS. ELVSTED, *dressed as in the first act, with hat and cloak, enters by the hall door.*

MRS. ELVSTED: *(Greets them hurriedly, and says in evident agitation)* Oh, dear Hedda, forgive my coming again.

HEDDA: What is the matter with you, Thea?

TESMAN: Something about Eilert Lövborg again—eh?

MRS. ELVSTED: Yes! I am dreadfully afraid some misfortune has hap-pened to him.

HEDDA: *(Seizes her arm)* Ah,—do you think so?

TESMAN: Why, good Lord—what makes you think that, Mrs. Elvsted?

MRS. ELVSTED: I heard them talking of him at my boarding-house—just as I came in. Oh, the most incredible rumors are afloat about him to-day.

TESMAN: Yes, fancy, so I heard too! And I can bear witness that he went straight home to bed last night. Fancy that!

HEDDA: Well, what did they say at the boarding-house?

MRS. ELVSTED: Oh, I couldn't make out anything clearly. Either they knew nothing definite, or else——. They stopped talking when they saw me; and I did not dare to ask.

TESMAN: *(Moving about uneasily)* We must hope—we must hope that you misunderstood them, Mrs. Elvsted.

MRS. ELVSTED: No, no; I am sure it was of him they were talking. And I heard something about the hospital or——

TESMAN: The hospital?

HEDDA: No—surely that cannot be!

MRS. ELVSTED: Oh, I was in such mortal terror! I went to his lodgings and asked for him there.

HEDDA: You could make up your mind to that, Thea!

MRS. ELVSTED: What else could I do? I really could bear the suspense no longer.

TESMAN: But you didn't find him either—eh?

MRS. ELVSTED: No. And the people knew nothing about him. He hadn't been home since yesterday afternoon, they said.

TESMAN: Yesterday! Fancy, how could they say that?

MRS. ELVSTED: Oh, I am sure something terrible must have happened to him.

TESMAN: Hedda dear—how would it be if I were to go and make inquiries——?

HEDDA: No, no—don't you mix yourself up in this affair.

JUDGE BRACK, *with his hat in his hand, enters by the hall door, which* BERTA *opens, and closes behind him. He looks grave and bows in silence.*

TESMAN: Oh, is that you, my dear judge? Eh?

BRACK: Yes. It was imperative I should see you this evening.

TESMAN: I can see you have heard the news about Aunt Rina?

BRACK: Yes, that among other things.

TESMAN: Isn't it sad—eh?

BRACK: Well, my dear Tesman, that depends on how you look at it.

TESMAN: (*Looks doubtfully at him*) Has anything else happened?

BRACK: Yes.

HEDDA: (*In suspense*) Anything sad, Judge Brack?

BRACK: That, too, depends on how you look at it, Mrs. Tesman.

MRS. ELVSTED: (*Unable to restrain her anxiety*) Oh! it is something about Eilert Lövborg!

BRACK: (*With a glance at her*) What makes you think that, Madam? Perhaps you have already heard something——?

MRS. ELVSTED: (*In confusion*) No, nothing at all, but——

TESMAN: Oh, for heaven's sake, tell us!

BRACK: (*Shrugging his shoulders*) Well, I regret to say Eilert Lövborg has been taken to the hospital. He is lying at the point of death.

MRS. ELVSTED: (*Shrieks*) Oh God! oh God——!

TESMAN: To the hospital! And at the point of death!

HEDDA: (*Involuntarily*) So soon then——

MRS. ELVSTED: (*Wailing*) And we parted in anger, Hedda!

HEDDA: (*Whispers*) Thea—Thea—be careful!

MRS. ELVSTED: (*Not heeding her*) I must go to him! I must see him alive!

BRACK: It is useless, Madam. No one will be admitted.

MRS. ELVSTED: Oh, at least tell me what has happened to him? What is it?

TESMAN: You don't mean to say that he has himself—— Eh?

HEDDA: Yes, I am sure he has.

TESMAN: Hedda, how can you——?

BRACK: (*Keeping his eyes fixed upon her*) Unfortunately you have guessed quite correctly, Mrs. Tesman.

MRS. ELVSTED: Oh, how horrible!

TESMAN: Himself, then! Fancy that!

HEDDA: Shot himself!

BRACK: Rightly guessed again, Mrs. Tesman.

MRS. ELVSTED: (*With an effort at self-control*) When did it happen, Mr. Brack?

BRACK: This afternoon—between three and four.

TESMAN: But, good Lord, where did he do it? Eh?

BRACK: (*With some hesitation*) Where? Well—I suppose at his lodgings.

MRS. ELVSTED: No, that cannot be; for I was there between six and seven.

BRACK: Well then, somewhere else. I don't know exactly. I only know that he was found——. He had shot himself—in the breast.

MRS. ELVSTED: Oh, how terrible! That he should die like that!

HEDDA: (*To* BRACK) Was it in the breast?

BRACK: Yes—as I told you.

HEDDA: Not in the temple?

BRACK: In the breast, Mrs. Tesman.

HEDDA: Well, well—the breast is a good place, too.

BRACK: How do you mean, Mrs. Tesman?

HEDDA: (*Evasively*) Oh, nothing—nothing.

TESMAN: And the wound is dangerous, you say—eh?

BRACK: Absolutely mortal. The end has probably come by this time.

MRS. ELVSTED: Yes, yes, I feel it. The end! The end! Oh, Hedda——!

TESMAN: But tell me, how have you learnt all this?

BRACK: (*Curtly*) Through one of the police. A man I had some business with.

HEDDA: (*In a clear voice*) At last a deed worth doing!

TESMAN: (*Terrified*) Good heavens, Hedda! what are you saying?

HEDDA: I say there is beauty in this.

BRACK: H'm, Mrs. Tesman——

TESMAN: Beauty! Fancy that!

MRS. ELVSTED: Oh, Hedda, how can you talk of beauty in such an act!

HEDDA: Eilert Lövborg has himself made up his account with life. He has had the courage to do—the one right thing.

MRS. ELVSTED: No, you must never think that was how it happened! It must have been in delirium that he did it.

TESMAN: In despair!

HEDDA: That he did not. I am certain of that.

MRS. ELVSTED: Yes, yes! In delirium! Just as when he tore up our manuscript.

BRACK: (*Starting*) The manuscript? Has he torn that up?

MRS. ELVSTED: Yes, last night.

TESMAN: (*Whispers softly*) Oh, Hedda, we shall never get over this.

BRACK: H'm, very extraordinary.

TESMAN: (*Moving about the room*) To think of Eilert going out of the world in this way! And not leaving behind him the book that would have immortalized his name.

MRS. ELVSTED: Oh, if only it could be put together again!

TESMAN: Yes, if it only could! I don't know what I would not give——

MRS. ELVSTED: Perhaps it can, Mr. Tesman.

TESMAN: What do you mean?

MRS. ELVSTED: (*Searches in the pocket of her dress*) Look here. I have kept all the loose notes he used to dictate from.

HEDDA: (*A step forward*) Ah——!

TESMAN: You have kept them, Mrs. Elvsted! Eh?

MRS. ELVSTED: Yes, I have them here. I put them in my pocket when I left home. Here they still are——

TESMAN: Oh, do let me see them!

MRS. ELVSTED: (*Hands him a bundle of papers*) But they are in such disorder—all mixed up.

TESMAN: Fancy, if we could make something out of them, after all! Perhaps if we two put our heads together——

MRS. ELVSTED: Oh yes, at least let us try——

TESMAN: We will manage it! We must! I will dedicate my life to this task.

HEDDA: You, George? Your life?

TESMAN: Yes, or rather all the time I can spare. My own collections must wait in the meantime. Hedda—you understand, eh? I owe this to Eilert's memory.

HEDDA: Perhaps.

TESMAN: And so, my dear Mrs. Elvsted, we will give our whole minds to it. There is no use in brooding over what can't be undone—eh? We must try to control our grief as much as possible, and——

MRS. ELVSTED: Yes, yes, Mr. Tesman, I will do the best I can.

TESMAN: Well then, come here. I can't rest until we have looked through the notes. Where shall we sit? Here? No, in there, in the back room. Excuse me, my dear Judge. Come with me, Mrs. Elvsted.

MRS. ELVSTED: Oh, if only it were possible!

TESMAN *and* MRS. ELVSTED *go into the back room. She takes off her hat and cloak. They both sit at the table under the hanging lamp, and are soon deep in an eager examination of the papers.* HEDDA *crosses to the stove and sits in the arm-chair. Presently* BRACK *goes up to her.*

HEDDA: (*In a low voice*) Oh, what a sense of freedom it gives one, this act of Eilert Lövborg's.

BRACK: Freedom, Mrs. Hedda? Well, of course, it is a release for him——

HEDDA: I mean for me! It gives me a sense of freedom to know that a deed of deliberate courage is still possible in this world,—a deed of spontaneous beauty.

BRACK: (*Smiling*) H'm—my dear Mrs. Hedda——

HEDDA: Oh, I know what you are going to say. For you are a kind of specialist, too, like—you know!

BRACK: (*Looking hard at her*) Eilert Lövborg was more to you than perhaps you are willing to admit to yourself. Am I wrong?

HEDDA: I don't answer such questions. I only know that Eilert Lövborg has had the courage to live his life after his own fashion. And then—the last great act, with its beauty! Ah! that he should have the will and the strength to turn away from the banquet of life—so early.

BRACK: I am sorry, Mrs. Hedda,—but I fear I must dispel an amiable illusion.

HEDDA: Illusion?

BRACK: Which could not have lasted long in any case.

HEDDA: What do you mean?

BRACK: Eilert Lövborg did not shoot himself—voluntarily.

HEDDA: Not voluntarily?

BRACK: No. The thing did not happen exactly as I told it.

HEDDA: (*In suspense*) Have you concealed something? What is it?

BRACK: For poor Mrs. Elvsted's sake I idealized the facts a little.

HEDDA: What are the facts?

BRACK: First, that he is already dead.

HEDDA: At the hospital?

BRACK: Yes—without regaining consciousness.

HEDDA: What more have you concealed?

BRACK: This—the event did not happen at his lodgings.

HEDDA: Oh, that can make no difference.

BRACK: Perhaps it may. For I must tell you—Eilert Lövborg was found shot in—in Mademoiselle Diana's boudoir.

HEDDA: (*Makes a motion as if to rise, but sinks back again*) That is impossible, Judge Brack! He cannot have been there again to-day.

BRACK: He was there this afternoon. He went there, he said, to demand the return of something which they had taken from him. Talked wildly about a lost child——

HEDDA: Ah—so that was why——

BRACK: I thought probably he meant his manuscript; but now I hear he destroyed that himself. So I suppose it must have been his pocketbook.

HEDDA: Yes, no doubt. And there—there he was found?

BRACK: Yes, there. With a pistol in his breast-pocket, discharged. The ball had lodged in a vital part.

HEDDA: In the breast—yes.

BRACK: No— in the bowels.

HEDDA: (*Looks up at him with an expression of loathing*) That, too! Oh, what curse is it that makes everything I touch turn ludicrous and mean?

BRACK: There is one point more, Mrs. Hedda—another disagreeable feature in the affair.

HEDDA: And what is that?

BRACK: The pistol he carried——

HEDDA: (*Breathless*) Well? What of it?

BRACK: He must have stolen it.

HEDDA: (*Leaps up*) Stolen it! That is not true! He did not steal it!

BRACK: No other explanation is possible. He must have stolen it—— Hush!

TESMAN *and* MRS. ELVSTED *have risen from the table in the back room, and come into the drawing-room.*

TESMAN: (*With the papers in both his hands*) Hedda, dear, it is almost impossible to see under that lamp. Think of that!

HEDDA: Yes, I am thinking.

TESMAN: Would you mind our sitting at your writing-table—eh?

HEDDA: If you like (*Quickly*) No, wait! Let me clear it first!

TESMAN: Oh, you needn't trouble, Hedda. There is plenty of room.

HEDDA: No, no, let me clear it, I say! I will take these things in and put them on the piano. There! (*She has drawn out an object, covered with sheet music, from under the bookcase, places several other pieces of music upon it, and carries the whole into the inner room, to the left.* TESMAN *lays the scraps of paper on the writing-table, and moves the lamp there from the corner table. He and* MRS. ELVSTED *sit down and proceed with their work.* HEDDA *returns*)

HEDDA: (*Behind* MRS. ELVSTED'S *chair, gently ruffling her hair*) Well, my sweet Thea,—how goes it with Eilert Lövborg's monument?

MRS. ELVSTED: (*Looks dispiritedly up at her*) Oh, it will be terribly hard to put in order.

TESMAN: We must manage it. I am determined. And arranging other people's papers is just the work for me.

HEDDA *goes over to the stove, and seats herself on one of the foot-stools.* BRACK *stands over her, leaning on the arm-chair.*

HEDDA: (*Whispers*) What did you say about the pistol?

BRACK: (*Softly*) That he must have stolen it.

HEDDA: Why stolen it?

BRACK: Because every other explanation ought to be impossible, Mrs. Hedda.

HEDDA: Indeed?

BRACK: (*Glances at her*) Of course, Eilert Lövborg was here this morning. Was he not?

HEDDA: Yes.

BRACK: Were you alone with him?

HEDDA: Part of the time.

BRACK: Did you not leave the room whilst he was here?

HEDDA: No.

BRACK: Try to recollect. Were you not out of the room a moment?

HEDDA: Yes, perhaps just a moment—out in the hall.

BRACK: And where was your pistol-case during that time?

HEDDA: I had it locked up in——

BRACK: Well, Mrs. Hedda?

HEDDA: The case stood there on the writing-table.

BRACK: Have you looked since, to see whether both the pistols are there?

HEDDA: No.

BRACK: Well, you need not. I saw the pistol found in Lövborg's pocket, and I knew it at once as the one I had seen yesterday—and before, too.

HEDDA: Have you it with you?

BRACK: No; the police have it.

HEDDA: What will the police do with it?

BRACK: Search till they find the owner.

HEDDA: Do you think they will succeed.

BRACK: (*Bends over her and whispers*) No, Hedda Gabler—not so long as I say nothing.

HEDDA: (*Looks frightened at him*) And if you do not say nothing,—what then?

BRACK: (*Shrugs his shoulders*) There is always the possibility that the pistol was stolen.

HEDDA: (*Firmly*) Death rather than that.

BRACK: (*Smiling*) People say such things—but they don't do them.

HEDDA: (*Without replying*) And supposing the pistol was not stolen, and the owner is discovered? What then?

BRACK: Well, Hedda—then comes the scandal.

HEDDA: The scandal!

BRACK: Yes, the scandal—of which you are so mortally afraid. You will, of course, be brought before the court—both you and Mademoiselle Diana. She will have to explain how the thing happened—whether it was an accidental shot or murder. Did the pistol go off as he was trying to take it out of his pocket, to threaten her with? Or did she tear the pistol out of his hand, shoot him, and push it back into his pocket? That would be quite like her; for she is an able-bodied young person, this same Mademoiselle Diana.

HEDDA: But *I* have nothing to do with all this repulsive business.

BRACK: No. But you will have to answer the question: Why did you give Eilert Lövborg the pistol? And what conclusions will people draw from the fact that you did give it to him?

HEDDA: (*Lets her head sink*) That is true. I did not think of that.

BRACK: Well, fortunately, there is no danger, so long as I say nothing.

HEDDA: (*Looks up at him*) So I am in your power, Judge Brack. You have me at your beck and call, from this time forward.

BRACK: (*Whispers softly*) Dearest Hedda—believe me—I shall not abuse my advantage.

HEDDA: I am in your power none the less. Subject to your will and your demands. A slave, a slave then. (*Rises impetuously*) No, I cannot endure the thought of that! Never!

BRACK: (*Looks half-mockingly at her*) People generally get used to the inevitable.

HEDDA: (*Returns his look*) Yes, perhaps. (*She crosses to the writing-table. Suppressing an involuntary smile, she imitates* TESMAN's *intonations*) Well? Are you getting on, George? Eh?

TESMAN: Heaven knows, dear. In any case it will be the work of months.

HEDDA: (*As before*) Fancy that! (*Passes her hands softly through* MRS. ELVSTED's *hair*) Doesn't it seem strange to you, Thea? Here are you sitting with Tesman—just as you used to sit with Eilert Lövborg?

MRS. ELVSTED: Ah, if I could only inspire your husband in the same way!

HEDDA: Oh, that will come, too—in time.

TESMAN: Yes, do you know, Hedda—I really think I begin to feel something of the sort. But won't you go and sit with Brack again?

HEDDA: Is there nothing I can do to help you two?

TESMAN: No, nothing in the world. (*Turning his head*) I trust to you to keep Hedda company, my dear Brack.

BRACK: (*With a glance at* HEDDA) With the very greatest of pleasure.

HEDDA: Thanks. But I am tired this evening. I will go in and lie down a little on the sofa.

TESMAN: Yes, do dear—eh?

HEDDA *goes into the back room and draws the curtains. A short pause. Suddenly she is heard playing a wild dance on the piano.*

MRS. ELVSTED: (*Starts from her chair*) Oh—what is that?

TESMAN: (*Runs to the doorway*) Why, my dearest Hedda—don't play dance-music to-night! Just think of Aunt Rina! And of Eilert, too!

HEDDA: (*Puts her head out between the curtains*) And of Aunt Julia. And of all the rest of them.—After this, I will be quiet. (*Closes the curtains again*)

TESMAN: (*At the writing-table*) It's not good for her to see us at this distressing work. I'll tell you what, Mrs. Elvsted,—you shall take the empty room at Aunt Julia's, and then I will come over in the evenings, and we can sit and work there—eh?

HEDDA: (*In the inner room*) I hear what you are saying, Tesman. But how am *I* to get through the evenings out here?

TESMAN: (*Turning over the papers*) Oh, I daresay Judge Brack will be so kind as to look in now and then, even though I am out.

BRACK: (*In the arm-chair, calls out gaily*) Every blessed evening, with all the pleasure in life, Mrs. Tesman! We shall get on capitally together, we two!

HEDDA: (*Speaking loud and clear*) Yes, don't you flatter yourself we will, Judge Brack? Now that you are the one cock in the basket——

A shot is heard within. TESMAN, MRS. ELVSTED, *and* BRACK *leap to their feet.*

TESMAN: Oh, now she is playing with those pistols again. (*He throws back the curtains and runs in, followed by* MRS. ELVSTED. HEDDA *lies stretched on the sofa, lifeless. Confusion and cries.* BERTA *enters in alarm from the right*)

TESMAN: (*Shrieks to* BRACK) Shot herself! Shot herself in the temple! Fancy that!

BRACK: (*Half-fainting in the arm-chair*) Good God!—people don't do such things.

STUDY AND DISCUSSION QUESTIONS

1.   (Act I) Read the stage directions carefully. What season is it? Why is the whole play set in the living room? What is the dramatic purpose of General Gabler's portrait? What is the function of the dialogue between Juliana Tesman and Berta? Between George and Juliana? What aspects of George's character are emphasized? How is Hedda characterized? What do the "morning-shoes" symbolize? How does Hedda react to Juliana's hints of pregnancy? What function does Mrs. Elvsted serve? In what ways does Mrs. Elvsted contrast with Hedda? What is Judge Brack's dramatic function? What is the symbolic significance of the pistols?

2.   (Act II) What is the purpose of the opening scene between Brack and Hedda? Is there anything significant in the fact that he disarms her so easily? What is the relationship between Brack and Hedda? Why did Hedda marry George Tesman? What is the meaning of the "train" metaphor? Why is Hedda bored? What function does Eilert serve? Why is Hedda jealous of Mrs. Elvsted? Why does Hedda induce Eilert to take a drink? What is the meaning of the vision Hedda has of Eilert "with vine-leaves in his hair"?

3.   (Act III) What is the function of the dialogue between Hedda and Mrs. Elvsted? What effect does George's account of Eilert's actions have on Hedda? Why won't Hedda visit the dying Aunt Rina? What does the manuscript symbolize? Why does Hedda burn the manuscript?

4.   (Act IV) What is the significance of Aunt Rina's death? How does Hedda react to Juliana's statement, "it's such an absolute necessity for me to have someone to live for"? What is Tesman's reaction to Hedda's burning the manuscript? How is Eilert's death contrasted with Rina's? How does his death affect Hedda? Mrs. Elvsted? Tesman? What is Brack's purpose in blackmailing Hedda? Why does Hedda commit suicide? What is the meaning of Brack's final comment: "people don't do such things"?

5. The structure of *Hedda Gabler* is based primarily on the various groups of characters that are on stage at one time. For example, in the first act there are eight scenes or eight different groups of characters, with each group having a specific function in relation to the protagonist. Take a particular act and analyze its structure in terms of the characters involved. Determine also the dramatic function of each scene.

6. A physical characteristic that Ibsen seems to be particularly concerned with is the abundance and color of hair. Which characters have dark hair? Which have light hair? Why does Ibsen differentiate characters on the basis of hair color? Are there certain personality characteristics that are similar to a particular group? Does this technique have any thematic significance?

7. The character of Hedda Gabler has elicited many differing responses from critics. Jeannette Lee sees Hedda as "a pistol, deadly, simple, passionless, and straight," while Caroline W. Mayerson suggests that she is "spiritually sterile." Do you agree with either of these interpretations of Hedda's character? If not, how do you see her? Does the character of George Tesman provide any redeeming qualities for Hedda?

8. Soon after Ibsen had finished *Hedda Gabler* he stated his intention in writing the play: "What I principally wanted to do was to depict human beings, human emotions, and human destinies, upon a groundwork of certain of the social conditions and principles of the present day." How does this statement compare or contrast with his intention in *Ghosts* and with the following motifs: the failure of marriage; the hypocrisy of society; the biological inheritance; convention vs. individual freedom.

9. Joseph Wood Krutch in *The Modern Temper* states, "No increased powers of expression, no greater gift for words, could have transformed Ibsen into Shakespeare. The materials out of which the latter created his works—his conception of human dignity, his sense of the importance of human passions, his vision of the amplitude of human life—simply did not and could not exist for Ibsen. . . ." Discuss some of the changes in the nature of man that would bring about this difference suggested by Krutch. Compare

Hedda Gabler and *Othello* in relation to the three criteria Krutch suggests here.

WRITING TOPICS

1. Write an essay on one of the following topics: (a) the full significance of the title, (b) the forces that play upon Hedda, (c) the thematic function of the symbols.

2. "Hedda is an unscrupulous thirster after life; her temperature slumbers beneath a cold-blooded attitude, until her lust spies an ignoble goal, when she pursues it at feverish heat. She is not a woman, but a vampire; she shuns every quality of womanhood; she desires only to remain unbridled; she abhors any reference to her pregnant state—a state which might account for her cerebral restlessness, and her neurotic irritability." Write an essay defending or attacking all or part of this statement.

3. Theodore Jorgenson in *Henrik Ibsen: A Study in Art and Personality* says that *Hedda Gabler* is "a play of forces within the personality and in the environment. It is possible to distinguish three different social groups that appear in more or less clearly outlined form." Write an essay explaining the characteristics of "the three different social groups."

4. In a speech given by Ibsen in 1898, the dramatist pointed out his purpose for writing: "My task has been the description of humanity. To be sure, whenever such a description is felt to be reasonably true, the reader will read his own feelings and sentiments into the work of the poet. These are then attributed to the poet; but incorrectly so. Every reader remolds the work beautifully and neatly, each according to his own personality. Not only those who write but also those who read are poets. They are collaborators. They are often more poetical than the poet himself." Write an essay defining your "own feelings and sentiments" about *Hedda Gabler*. *Or* if the central theme of *Hedda Gabler* is the contrast of the superficially magnificent people in the world with the superficially inert, what evidence could you present in an essay to prove this?

5. Write an essay on one of the following topics: (a) comparison of Hedda to Mrs. Alving; (b) comparison of Ibsen to Sophocles or Shakespeare in terms of some technique or tragic vision; (c) comparison of the use of symbols in *Ghosts* and *Hedda Gabler*.

Strindberg

At first glance the similarities between Henrik Ibsen and August Strindberg may seem striking indeed. They were very close in age, both were Scandinavian, both wrote for the same sort of theater, and in their best work both employed the techniques of realism. The *principal* difference between them is one of degree rather than kind, and it is much the same as the difference between realism and naturalism in drama. If the reader is to understand fully the work of both dramatists, he must understand the distinction between the two terms.

The realism practiced by Ibsen was an attempt to recreate upon the stage a close imitation of life. That is, the characters, settings, plots, and conflicts were clearly recognizable by the audience and had an immediacy and relevance to their own lives. However, the realist was under no obligation to propound a particular philosophy or world view in his drama; his main concern was with fidelity to life and experience as he knew it.

The naturalist playwright operated under the same fundamental assumptions, but he went a step further. He sought to imitate not only patterns of life and life-like speech, but to communicate certain attitudes he held to be basic to all human existence. Naturalism was highly influenced by scientific strides in biology and psychology during the nineteenth century. Its most vocal spokesman, Emile Zola, maintained that the role of the dramatist was to "bring the theatre into closer relation with the great movement toward truth and experimental science." Man was not exempt from the natural laws of the universe, and scientific determinism, a determinism that took into account both the biological laws of heredity and the sociological-psychological effects of environment, became the guiding philosophy of the naturalistic school of drama. Thus the objectivity of the realist became the almost clinical detachment of the naturalist, who dramatized the lives of his characters with the dispassion of a scientist dissecting a laboratory specimen.

Naturalism in drama, then, is essentially a mechanistic attitude toward what life is like. In characterization it denies free will and the effectiveness of human reason, substituting for them basic physical drives and forces beyond the individual's control. In setting it tends to focus on the lower social classes, since they demonstrate most obviously the results of environmental pressures and instinctive drives. In theme it frequently deals with the inexorable working out of raw passions in the lives of doomed characters. Naturalism deliberately uncovers the sordid, ostensibly in the interest of truth. But the fact is that naturalistic drama is its own kind of propaganda, and though it was instrumental in challenging all that was sentimental and romantic in the older drama, it had no special claim to the truth.

Certain of the plays of August Strindberg are among the finest examples of naturalism. In his work he added to the typical characteristics of naturalism a talent for keen psychological analysis of character. He surpassed Ibsen in his ability to create the tightly woven plot that virtually does away with exposition and in its place dramatizes the climax. His concept of tragedy as the product of a variety of forces, not the least of which is the bewildering complexity of human character, has had a lasting influence on modern tragic drama.

Strindberg (1849-1912): A Biographical Note. August Strindberg was born of poor parents in Stockholm, Sweden, and his early years were filled with misery and personal unhappiness. After a succession of false starts at various careers, he attracted the attention of King Charles V of Sweden for one of his plays and was awarded a small stipend. After the king died, Strindberg found a position in the Royal Library, which he kept from 1874-1882. During that time he studied and wrote avidly. He fell in love with the wife of a baron and they were later married, but their domestic life was violent. Some of its conflict is reflected in Strindberg's collection of realistic short stories, *Married*. In 1891 they were divorced, but he went on to two more unsuccessful marriages. Many of his plays are devoted to the eternal struggle between the sexes, and he became famous for his misogyny. Strindberg's influence on modern drama has been considerable. The American dramatist, Eugene O'Neill, considered him "the greatest interpreter of the characteristic spiritual conflicts that constitute the drama."

THE FATHER

August Strindberg
Translated by Elizabeth Sprigge

Characters

THE CAPTAIN
LAURA, *his wife.*
BERTHA, *their daughter.*
DOCTOR ÖSTERMARK
THE PASTOR
THE NURSE
NÖJD
THE ORDERLY

The whole play takes place in the central living-room of the Captain's home. He is a cavalry officer in a remote country district of Sweden.
It is about 1886, shortly before Christmas.
At the back of the room, towards the right, a door leads to the hall. In the left wall there is a door to other rooms, and in the right-hand corner another, smaller door, covered in the same wall-paper as the walls, opens on to a staircase leading to the Captain's room above.
In the centre of the room stands a large round table on which are newspapers, magazines, a big photograph album and a lamp. On the right are a leather-covered sofa, arm chairs and a smaller table.

The Father is reprinted by permission of Collins-Knowlton-Wing, Inc. Copyright © 1955 by Elizabeth Sprigge.

*On the left is a writing-bureau with a pendulum clock upon it.
Arms, guns and gun-bags hang on the walls, and military coats on
pegs by the door to the hall.*

ACT I

Early evening. The lamp on the table is lighted. The CAPTAIN *and
the* PASTOR *are sitting on the sofa talking. The* CAPTAIN *is in un-
dress uniform with riding-boots and spurs; the* PASTOR *wears black,
with a white cravat in place of his clerical collar, and is smoking a
pipe.
The* CAPTAIN *rises and rings a bell. The* ORDERLY *enters from the
hall.*

ORDERLY: Yes, sir?

CAPTAIN: Is Nöjd there?

ORDERLY: Nöjd's in the kitchen, sir, waiting for orders.

CAPTAIN: In the kitchen again, is he? Send him here at once.

ORDERLY: Yes, sir. (*Exit.*)

PASTOR: Why, what's the trouble?

CAPTAIN: Oh, the ruffian's been at his tricks again with one of the
servant girls! He's a damn nuisance, that fellow!

PASTOR: Was it Nöjd you said? Didn't he give some trouble back in
the spring?

CAPTAIN: Ah, you remember that, do you? Look here, you give him a
bit of a talking to, there's a good chap. That might have some effect.
I've sworn at him and thrashed him, without making the least impression.

PASTOR: So now you want me to preach to him. How much impression
do you think God's word is likely to make on a trooper?

CAPTAIN: Well, my dear brother-in-law, it makes none at all on me, as
you know, but . . .

PASTOR: As I know only too well.

CAPTAIN: But on him? Worth trying anyhow.

Enter NÖJD.

What have you been up to now, Nöjd?

NÖJD: God bless you, sir, I can't talk about that—not with Pastor here.

PASTOR: Don't mind me, my lad.

NÖJD: Well you see, sir, it was like this. We was at a dance at Gabriel's, and then, well then Ludwig said as . . .

CAPTAIN: What's Ludwig got to do with it? Stick to the point.

NÖJD: Well then Emma said as we should go in the barn.

CAPTAIN: I see. I suppose it was Emma who led you astray.

NÖJD: Well, not far from it. What I mean is if the girl's not game, nothing don't happen.

CAPTAIN: Once and for all—are you the child's father or are you not?

NÖJD: How's one to know?

CAPTAIN: What on earth do you mean? Don't you know?

NÖJD: No, you see, sir, that's what you never can know.

CAPTAIN: You mean you weren't the only man?

NÖJD: That time I was. But you can't tell if you've always been the only one.

CAPTAIN: Are you trying to put the blame on Ludwig? Is that the idea?

NÖJD: It's not easy to know who to put the blame on.

CAPTAIN: But, look here, you told Emma you would marry her.

NÖJD: Oh well, you always have to say that, you know.

CAPTAIN: *(to the PASTOR)* This is atrocious.

PASTOR: It's the old story. Come now, Nöjd, surely you are man enough to know if you are the father.

NÖJD: Well, sir, it's true, I did go with her, but you know yourself, Pastor, that don't always lead to nothing.

PASTOR: Look here, my lad, it's you we are talking about. And you are not going to leave that girl destitute with a child. You can't be forced to marry her, but you must make provision for the child. That you must do.

NÖJD: So must Ludwig then.

CAPTAIN: If that's how it is, the case will have to go before the Magistrate. I can't settle it, and it's really nothing to do with me. Dismiss!

PASTOR: One moment, Nöjd. Ahem. Don't you think it's rather a dirty trick to leave a girl destitute with a child like that? Don't you think so —eh?

NÖJD: Yes, if I knew I was the father, it would be, but I tell you, Pastor, you never can know that. And it wouldn't be much fun slaving all your life for another chap's brat. You and the Captain must see that for yourselves.

CAPTAIN: That will do, Nöjd.

NÖJD: Yes, sir, thank you, sir.

CAPTAIN: And keep out of the kitchen, you scoundrel! *(Exit NÖJD.)*

Why didn't you haul him over the coals?

PASTOR: What do you mean? Didn't I?

CAPTAIN: No, you just sat there muttering to yourself.

PASTOR: As a matter of fact, I scarcely knew what to say to him. It's hard on the girl, of course, but it's hard on the boy too. Supposing he's not the father? The girl can nurse the baby for four months at the orphanage, and after that it will be taken care of for good. But the boy can't nurse the child, can he? Later on, the girl will get a good place in some respectable family, but if the boy is cashiered, his future may be ruined.

CAPTAIN: Upon my soul, I'd like to be the magistrate and judge this case! Maybe the boy is responsible—that's what you can't know. But one thing you *can* know—if anybody's guilty, the girl is.

PASTOR: Well, I never sit in judgment. Now what was it we were talking about when this blessed business interrupted us? Yes, Bertha and her confirmation, wasn't it?

CAPTAIN: It's not just a question of confirmation, but of her whole future. The house is full of women, all trying to mould this child of mine. My mother-in-law wants to turn her into a spiritualist; Laura wants her to be an artist; the governess would have her a Methodist, old Margaret a Baptist, and the servant girls a Salvation Army lass. You can't make a character out of patchwork. Meanwhile I . . . I, who have more right than all the rest to guide her, am opposed at every turn. So I must send her away.

PASTOR: You have too many women running your house.

CAPTAIN: You're right there. It's like going into a cage of tigers. They'd soon tear me to pieces, if I didn't hold a red-hot poker under their noses. It's all very well for you to laugh, you blackguard. It wasn't enough that I married your sister; you had to palm off your old stepmother on me too.

PASTOR: Well, good Lord, one can't have stepmothers in one's house!

CAPTAIN: No, you prefer mothers-in-law—in someone else's house, of course.

PASTOR: Well, well, we all have our burdens to bear.

CAPTAIN: I daresay, but I have more than my share. There's my old nurse too, who treats me as if I still wore a bib. She's a good old soul, to be sure, but she shouldn't be here.

PASTOR: You should keep your women-folk in order, Adolf. You give them too much rope.

CAPTAIN: My dear fellow, can you tell me how to keep women in order?

PASTOR: To tell the truth, although she's my sister, Laura was always a bit of a handful.

CAPTAIN: Laura has her faults, of course, but they are not very serious ones.

PASTOR: Oh come now, I know her!

CAPTAIN: She was brought up with romantic ideas and has always found it a little difficult to come to terms with life. But she is my wife and . . .

PASTOR: And because she is your wife she must be the best of women. No, brother-in-law, it's she not you who wears the trousers.

CAPTAIN: In any case, the whole household has gone mad. Laura's determined Bertha shan't leave her, and I won't let her stay in this lunatic asylum.

PASTOR: So Laura's determined, is she? Then there's bound to be trouble, I'm afraid. As a child she used to lie down and sham dead until they gave in to her. Then she would calmly hand back whatever she'd set her mind on, explaining it wasn't the thing she wanted, but simply to get her own way.

CAPTAIN: So she was like that even then, was she? Hm. As a matter of fact, she does sometimes get so overwrought I'm frightened for her and think she must be ill.

PASTOR: What is it you want Bertha to do that's such a bone of contention? Can't you come to some agreement?

CAPTAIN: Don't think I want to turn her into a prodigy—or into some image of myself. But I will not play pander and have my daughter fitted for nothing but the marriage market. For then, if she didn't marry after all, she'd have a wretched time of it. On the other hand, I don't want to start her off in some man's career with a long training that would be entirely wasted if she did marry.

PASTOR: Well, what do you want then?

CAPTAIN: I want her to be a teacher. Then, if she doesn't marry she'll be able to support herself, and at least be no worse off than those unfortunate schoolmasters who have to support families on their earnings. And if she does marry, she can educate her own children. Isn't that reasonable?

PASTOR: Reasonable, yes—but what about her artistic talent? Wouldn't it be against the grain to repress that?

CAPTAIN: No. I showed her attempts to a well-known painter who told me they were nothing but the usual sort of thing learnt at school. Then, during the summer, some young jackanapes came along who knew better and said she was a genius—whereupon the matter was settled in Laura's favour.

PASTOR: Was he in love with Bertha?

CAPTAIN: I take that for granted.

PASTOR: Well, God help you, old boy, I don't see any solution. But it's a tiresome business, and I suppose Laura has supporters . . . *(indicates other rooms)* in there.

CAPTAIN: You may be sure of that. The whole household is in an uproar, and between ourselves the method of attack from that quarter is not exactly chivalrous.

PASTOR: *(rising)* Do you think I haven't been through it?

CAPTAIN: You too?

PASTOR: Yes, indeed.

CAPTAIN: But to me the worst thing about it is that Bertha's future should be decided in there from motives of sheer hate. They do nothing but talk about men being made to see that women can do this and do that. It's man versus woman the whole day long . . . Must you go? Won't you stay to supper? I don't know what there is, but do stay. I'm expecting the new doctor, you know. Have you seen him yet?

PASTOR: I caught a glimpse of him on my way here. He looks a decent, reliable sort of man.

CAPTAIN: That's good. Do you think he may be my ally?

PASTOR: Maybe. It depends how well he knows women.

CAPTAIN: But won't you stay?

PASTOR: Thank you, my dear fellow, but I promised to be home this evening, and my wife gets anxious if I'm late.

CAPTAIN: Anxious! Furious, you mean. Well, as you please. Let me help you on with your coat.

PASTOR: It's certainly very cold to-night. Thank you. You must look after yourself, Adolf. You seem a bit on edge.

CAPTAIN: On edge? Do I?

PASTOR: Yes. You aren't very well, are you?

CAPTAIN: Did Laura put this into your head? For the last twenty years she's been treating me as if I had one foot in the grave.

PASTOR: Laura? No, it's just that I'm . . . I'm worried about you. Take my advice and look after yourself. Goodbye, old man. By the way, didn't you want to talk about the confirmation?

CAPTAIN: By no means. But I give you my word this shall take its own course—and be chalked up to the official conscience. I am neither a witness to the truth, nor a martyr. We have got past that sort of thing. Goodbye. Remember me to your wife.

PASTOR: Goodbye, Adolf. Give my love to Laura. *(Exit* PASTOR. *The* CAPTAIN *opens the bureau and settles down to his accounts.)*

CAPTAIN: Thirty-four—nine, forty-three—seven, eight, fifty-six.

LAURA: *(entering from the next room.)* Will you please . . .

CAPTAIN: One moment!—sixty-six, seventy-one, eighty-four, eighty-nine, ninety-two, a hundred. What is it?

LAURA: Am I disturbing you?

CAPTAIN: Not in the least. Housekeeping money, I suppose?

LAURA: Yes, housekeeping money.

CAPTAIN: If you put the accounts down there, I will go through them.

LAURA: Accounts?

CAPTAIN: Yes.

LAURA: Do you expect me to keep accounts now?

CAPTAIN: Of course you must keep accounts. Our position's most precarious, and if we go bankrupt, we must have accounts to show. Otherwise we could be accused of negligence.

LAURA: It's not my fault if we're in debt.

CAPTAIN: That's what the accounts will show.

LAURA: It's not my fault the tenant farmer doesn't pay.

CAPTAIN: Who was it recommended him so strongly? You. Why did you recommend such a—shall we call him a scatterbrain?

LAURA: Why did you take on such a scatterbrain?

CAPTAIN: Because I wasn't allowed to eat in peace, sleep in peace or work in peace till you got him here. You wanted him because your brother wanted to get rid of him; my mother-in-law wanted him because I didn't; the governess wanted him because he was a Methodist, and old Margaret because she had known his grandmother as a child. That's why, and if I hadn't taken him I should be in a lunatic asylum by now, or else in the family vault. However, here's the housekeeping allowance and your pin money. You can give me the accounts later.

LAURA: *(with an ironic bob.)* Thank you so much.—By the way, do you keep accounts yourself—of what you spend outside the household?

CAPTAIN: That's none of your business.

LAURA: True. As little my business as the future of my own child. Did you gentlemen come to any decision at this evening's conference?

CAPTAIN: I had already made my decision, so I merely had to communicate it to the only friend I have in the family. Bertha is going to live in town. She will leave in a fortnight's time.

LAURA: Where, if I may ask, is she going to stay?

CAPTAIN: At Sävberg's—the solicitor's.

LAURA: That Freethinker!

CAPTAIN: According to the law as it now stands, children are brought up in their father's faith.

LAURA: And the mother has no say in the matter?

CAPTAIN: None whatever. She sells her birthright by legal contract and surrenders all her rights. In return the husband supports her and her children.

LAURA: So she has no rights over her own child?

CAPTAIN: None at all. When you have sold something, you don't expect to get it back and keep the money too.

LAURA: But supposing the father and mother were to decide things together . . . ?

CAPTAIN: How would that work out? I want her to live in town; you want her to live at home. The mathematical mean would be for her to stop at the railway station, midway between home and town. You see? It's a deadlock.

LAURA: Then the lock must be forced. . . . What was Nöjd doing here?

CAPTAIN: That's a professional secret.

LAURA: Which the whole kitchen knows.

CAPTAIN: Then doubtless you know it too.

LAURA: I do.

CAPTAIN: And are ready to sit in judgment?

LAURA: The law does that.

CAPTAIN: The law doesn't say who the child's father is.

LAURA: Well, people know that for themselves.

CAPTAIN: Discerning people say that's what one never can know.

LAURA: How extraordinary! Can't one tell who a child's father is?

CAPTAIN: Apparently not.

LAURA: How perfectly extraordinary! Then how can the father have those rights over the mother's child?

CAPTAIN: He only has them when he takes on the responsibility—or has it forced on him. But of course in marriage there is no doubt about the paternity.

LAURA: No doubt?

CAPTAIN: I should hope not.

LAURA: But supposing the wife has been unfaithful?

CAPTAIN: Well, such a supposition has no bearing on our problem. Is there anything else you want to ask me about?

LAURA: No, nothing.

CAPTAIN: Then I shall go up to my room. Please let me know when the doctor comes. (*Closes the bureau and rises.*)

LAURA: I will.

CAPTAIN: (*going out by the wall-papered door.*) As soon as he comes, mind. I don't want to be discourteous, you understand. (*Exit.*)

LAURA: I understand. (*She looks at the bank-notes she is holding.*)

MOTHER-IN-LAW: (*off.*) Laura!

LAURA: Yes, Mother?

MOTHER-IN-LAW: Is my tea ready?

LAURA: (*at the door to the next room.*) It's coming in a moment.

(*The* ORDERLY *opens the hall door.*)

ORDERLY: Dr. Östermark.

Enter DOCTOR. *Exit* ORDERLY, *closing the door.*

LAURA: (*shaking hands*) How do you do, Dr. Östermark. Let me welcome you to our home. The Captain is out, but he will be back directly.

DOCTOR: I must apologize for calling so late, but I have already had to pay some professional visits.

LAURA: Won't you sit down?

DOCTOR: Thank you.

LAURA: Yes, there is a lot of illness about just now, but I hope all the same that you will find this place suits you. It is so important for people in a lonely country district like this to have a doctor who takes a real interest in his patients. I have heard you so warmly spoken of, Dr. Östermark, I hope we shall be on the best of terms.

DOCTOR: You are too kind, dear lady. I hope, however, for your sake that my visits here will not often be of a professional nature. I take it that the health of your family is, on the whole, good, and that . . .

LAURA: Yes, we have been fortunate enough not to have any serious illnesses, but all the same things are not quite as they should be.

DOCTOR: Indeed?

LAURA: No, I'm afraid not really at all as one could wish.

DOCTOR: Dear, dear, you quite alarm me!

LAURA: In a family there are sometimes things which honour and duty compel one to keep hidden from the world.

DOCTOR: But not from one's doctor.

LAURA: No. That is why it is my painful duty to tell you the whole truth from the start.

DOCTOR: May we not postpone this conversation until I have had the honour of meeting the Captain?

LAURA: No. You must hear what I have to say before you see him.

DOCTOR: Does it concern him then?

LAURA: Yes, him. My poor, dear husband.

DOCTOR: You are making me most uneasy. Whatever your trouble, Madam, you can confide in me.

LAURA: (*taking out her handkerchief.*) My husband's mind is affected. Now you know, and later on you will be able to judge for yourself.

DOCTOR: You astound me. The Captain's learned treatise on mineralogy, for which I have the greatest admiration, shows a clear and powerful intellect.

LAURA: Does it? I shall be overjoyed if we—his relatives—are mistaken.

DOCTOR: It is possible, of course, that his mind is disturbed in other ways. Tell me . . .

LAURA: That is exactly what we fear. You see, at times he has the most peculiar ideas, which wouldn't matter much for a scientist, if they weren't such a burden on his family. For instance, he has an absolute mania for buying things.

DOCTOR: That is significant. What kind of things?

LAURA: Books. Whole cases of them, which he never reads.

DOCTOR: Well, that a scholar should buy books isn't so alarming.

LAURA: You don't believe what I am telling you?

DOCTOR: I am convinced, Madam, that you believe what you are telling me.

LAURA: Well, then, is it possible for anyone to see in a microscope what's happening on another planet?

DOCTOR: Does he say he can do that?

LAURA: Yes, that's what he says.

DOCTOR: In a microscope?

LAURA: In a microscope. Yes.

DOCTOR: That is significant, if it is so.

LAURA: If it is so! You don't believe me, Doctor. And here have I let you in to the family secret.

DOCTOR: My dear lady, I am honoured by your confidence, but as a physician I must observe and examine before giving an opinion. Has the Captain shown any symptoms of instability, any lack of will power?

LAURA: Has he, indeed! We have been married twenty years, and he has never yet made a decision without going back on it.

DOCTOR: Is he dogmatic?

LAURA: He certainly lays down the law, but as soon as he gets his own way, he loses interest and leaves everything to me.

DOCTOR: That is significant and requires careful consideration. The will, you see, Madam, is the backbone of the mind. If it is injured, the mind falls to pieces.

LAURA: God knows how I have schooled myself to meet his every wish during these long hard years. Oh, if you knew what I have been through with him, if you only knew!

DOCTOR: I am profoundly distressed to learn of your trouble, Madam, and I promise I will do what I can. You have my deepest sympathy and I beg you to rely on me implicitly. But now you have told me this, I am going to ask one thing of you. Don't allow anything to prey on the patient's mind. In a case of instability, ideas can sometimes take hold and grow into an obsession—or even monomania. Do you follow me?

LAURA: . . . You mean don't let him get ideas into his head.

DOCTOR: Precisely. For a sick man can be made to believe anything. He is highly susceptible to suggestion.

LAURA: I see . . . I understand. Yes, indeed. (*A bell rings within.*) Excuse me. That's my mother ringing. I won't be a moment . . . Oh, here's Adolf!

As LAURA *goes out, the* CAPTAIN *enters by the wall-papered door.*

CAPTAIN: Ah, so you have arrived, Doctor! You are very welcome.

DOCTOR: How do you do, Captain. It's a great honour to meet such a distinguished scientist.

CAPTAIN: Oh please! Unfortunately, my military duties don't give me much time for research . . . All the same, I do believe I am now on the brink of a rather exciting discovery.

DOCTOR: Really?

CAPTAIN: You see, I have been subjecting meteoric stones to spectrum analysis, and I have found carbon—an indication of organic life. What do you say to that?

DOCTOR: Can you see that in a microscope?

CAPTAIN: No, in a spectroscope, for heaven's sake!

DOCTOR: Spectroscope! I beg your pardon. Then you will soon be telling us what is happening on Jupiter.

CAPTAIN: Not what is happening, what *has* happened. If only that blasted Paris bookseller would send my books. I really think the whole book-trade must be in league against me. Think of it, for two months I've not had one single answer to my orders, my letters or my abusive telegrams! It's driving me mad. I can't make out what's happened.

DOCTOR: Well, what could it be but ordinary carelessness? You shouldn't let it upset you.

CAPTAIN: Yes, but the devil of it is I shan't be able to get my article finished in time.—I know they're working on the same lines in Berlin . . . However, that's not what we should be talking about now, but about you. If you would care to live here, we can give you a small suite of rooms in that wing. Or would you prefer your predecessor's house?

DOCTOR: Whichever you please.

CAPTAIN: No, whichever *you* please. You have only to say.

DOCTOR: It's for you to decide, Captain.

CAPTAIN: Nothing of the kind. It's for you to say which you prefer. I don't care one way or the other.

DOCTOR: But I really can't . . .

CAPTAIN: For Christ's sake, man, say what you want! I haven't any opinion, any inclination, any choice, any preference at all. Are you such a milksop that you don't know what you want? Make up your mind, or I shall lose my temper.

DOCTOR: If I am to choose, I should like to live here.

CAPTAIN: Good!—Thank you. (*Rings.*) Oh dear me!—I apologise, Doctor, but nothing irritates me so much as to hear people say they don't care one way or the other.

The NURSE *enters.*

Ah, it's you, Margaret. Look here, my dear, do you know if the rooms in the wing are ready for the doctor?

NURSE: Yes, Captain, they're ready.

CAPTAIN: Good. Then I won't detain you, Doctor, for you must be tired. Goodnight, and once again—welcome. I look forward to seeing you in the morning.

DOCTOR: Thank you. Goodnight.

CAPTAIN: By the way, I wonder if my wife told you anything about us—if you know at all how the land lies?

DOCTOR: Your good lady did suggest one or two things it might be as well for a newcomer to know. Goodnight, Captain.

The NURSE *shows the* DOCTOR *out and returns.*

CAPTAIN: What is it, old girl? Anything the matter?

NURSE: Now listen, Mr. Adolf, dear.

CAPTAIN: Yes, go on, Margaret, talk. You're the only one whose talk doesn't get on my nerves.

NURSE: Then listen, Mr. Adolf. Couldn't you go halfway to meet the mistress in all this bother over the child? Think of a mother . . .

CAPTAIN: Think of a father, Margaret.

NURSE: Now, now, now! A father has many things besides his child, but a mother has nothing but her child.

CAPTAIN: Quite so, my friend. She has only one burden, while I have three and bear hers too. Do you think I'd have been stuck in the army all my life if I hadn't had her and her child to support?

NURSE: I know, but that wasn't what I wanted to talk about.

CAPTAIN: Quite. What you want is to make out I'm in the wrong.

NURSE: Don't you believe I want what's best for you, Mr. Adolf?

CAPTAIN: I'm sure you do, my dear, but you don't know what is best for me. You see, it's not enough to have given the child life. I want to give her my very soul.

NURSE: Oh, that's beyond me, but I do think you ought to come to terms.

CAPTAIN: Margaret, you are not my friend.

NURSE: Not your friend! Ah God, what are you saying, Mr. Adolf? Do you think I ever forget you were my baby when you were little?

CAPTAIN: Well, my dear, am I likely to forget it? You have been like a mother to me, and stood by me against all the others. But now that things have come to a head, you're deserting—going over to the enemy.

NURSE: Enemy?

CAPTAIN: Yes, enemy. You know perfectly well how things are here. You've seen it all from beginning to end.

NURSE: Aye, I've seen plenty. But, dear God, why must two people torment the lives out of each other? Two people who are so good and kind to everyone else. The mistress never treats me wrong or . . .

CAPTAIN: Only me. I know. And I tell you, Margaret, if you desert me now, you'll be doing a wicked thing. For a net is closing round me, and that doctor is no friend of mine.

NURSE: Oh, goodness, Mr. Adolf, you believe the worst of everyone! But that's what comes of not having the true faith. That's your trouble.

CAPTAIN: While you and the Baptists have found the one true faith, eh? You're lucky.

NURSE: Aye, luckier than you, Mr. Adolf. Humble your heart and you will see how happy God will make you in your love for your neighbour.

CAPTAIN: Isn't it strange—as soon as you mention God and love, your voice grows hard and your eyes fill with hate. No, Margaret, I'm sure you haven't found the true faith.

MARGARET: However proud you are and stuffed with book-learning, that won't get you anywhere when the pinch comes.

CAPTAIN: How arrogantly thou speakest, O humble heart! I'm well aware that learning means nothing to creatures like you.

NURSE: Shame on you! Still, old Margaret loves her great big boy best of all. And when the storm breaks, he'll come back to her, sure enough, like the good child he is.

CAPTAIN: Forgive me, Margaret. You see, you really are the only friend I have here. Help me, for something is going to happen. I don't know what, but I know it's evil, this thing that's on its way. (*A scream from within*) What's that? Who's screaming?

BERTHA *runs in.*

BERTHA: Father, Father! Help me! Save me!

CAPTAIN: What is it? My darling, tell me.

BERTHA: Please protect me. I know she'll do something terrible to me.

CAPTAIN: Who? What do you mean? Tell me at once.

BERTHA: Grandmother. But it was my fault. I played a trick on her.

CAPTAIN: Go on.

BERTHA: Yes, but you mustn't tell anyone. Promise you won't.

CAPTAIN: Very well, but what happened? (*Exit* NURSE.)

BERTHA: You see, sometimes in the evening she turns the lamp down and makes me sit at the table holding a pen over a piece of paper. And then she says the spirits write.

CAPTAIN: Well, I'll be damned! And you never told me.

BERTHA: I'm sorry, I didn't dare. Grandmother says spirits revenge themselves on people who talk about them. And then the pen writes, but I don't know if it's me doing it or not. Sometimes it goes well, but sometimes it doesn't work at all. And when I get tired nothing happens, but I have to make something happen all the same. This evening I thought I was doing rather well, but then Grandmother said it was all out of Stagnelius* and I had been playing a trick on her. And she was simply furious.

CAPTAIN: Do you believe there are spirits?

BERTHA: I don't know.

CAPTAIN: But I know there are not.

BERTHA: Grandmother says you don't understand, and that you have worse things that can see into other planets.

CAPTAIN: She says that, does she? And what else does she say?

BERTHA: That you can't work miracles.

CAPTAIN: I never said I could. You know what meteorites are, don't you?—stones that fall from other heavenly bodies. Well, I examine these and see if they contain the same elements as the earth. That's all I do.

BERTHA: Grandmother says there are things she can see and you can't.

CAPTAIN: My dear, she is lying.

BERTHA: Grandmother doesn't lie.

CAPTAIN: How do you know?

BERTHA: Then Mother does too.

CAPTAIN: Hm!

BERTHA: If you say Mother is a liar, I'll never believe a word you say again.

---

* Erik Johan Stagnelius, Swedish poet and dramatist. (1793-1823.)

CAPTAIN: I didn't say that, so now you must believe me. Listen. Your happiness, your whole future depends on your leaving home. Will you do this? Will you go and live in town and learn something useful?

BERTHA: Oh yes, I'd love to live in town—anywhere away from here! It's always so miserable in there, as gloomy as a winter night. But when you come home, Father, it's like a spring morning when they take the double windows down.

CAPTAIN: My darling, my beloved child!

BERTHA: But, Father, listen, you must be kind to Mother. She often cries.

CAPTAIN: Hm! . . . So you would like to live in town?

BERTHA: Oh yes!

CAPTAIN: But supposing your mother doesn't agree?

BERTHA: She must.

CAPTAIN: But supposing she doesn't?

BERTHA: Then I don't know what will happen. But she must, she must!

CAPTAIN: Will you ask her?

BERTHA: No, you must ask her—very nicely. She wouldn't pay any attention to me.

CAPTAIN: Hm! . . . Well now, if you want this and I want it and she doesn't want it, what are we to do then?

BERTHA: Oh, then the fuss will begin all over again! Why can't you both . . .

Enter LAURA

LAURA: Ah, so you're here, Bertha! Well now, Adolf, as the question of her future is still to be decided, let's hear what she has to say herself.

CAPTAIN: The child can hardly have anything constructive to say about the development of young girls, but you and I ought to be able to sum up the pros and cons. We've watched a good number grow up.

LAURA: But as we don't agree, Bertha can give the casting vote.

CAPTAIN: No. I won't allow anyone to interfere with my rights—neither woman nor child. Bertha, you had better leave us. (*Exit* BERTHA.)

LAURA: You were afraid to hear her opinion because you knew she would agree with me.

CAPTAIN: I know she wants to leave home, but I also know you have the power to make her change her mind.

LAURA: Oh, have I much power?

CAPTAIN: Yes, you have a fiendish power of getting your own way, like all people who are unscrupulous about the means they employ.

How, for instance, did you get rid of Dr. Norling? And how did you get hold of the new doctor?

LAURA: Yes, how did I?

CAPTAIN: You ran the old doctor down until he had to leave, and then you got your brother to canvass for this one.

LAURA: Well, that was quite simple and perfectly legal. Then is Bertha to leave home?

CAPTAIN: Yes, in a fortnight's time.

LAURA: I warn you I shall do my best to prevent it.

CAPTAIN: You can't.

LAURA: Can't I? Do you expect me to give up my child to be taught by wicked people that all she has learnt from her mother is nonsense? So that I would be despised by my own daughter for the rest of my life.

CAPTAIN: Do you expect me to allow ignorant and bumptious women to teach my daughter that her father is a charlatan?

LAURA: That shouldn't matter so much to you—now.

CAPTAIN: What on earth do you mean?

LAURA: Well, the mother's closer to the child, since the discovery that no one can tell who the father is.

CAPTAIN: What's that got to do with us?

LAURA: You don't know if you are Bertha's father.

CAPTAIN: Don't know?

LAURA: How can you know what nobody knows?

CAPTAIN: Are you joking?

LAURA: No, I'm simply applying your own theory. How do you know I haven't been unfaithful to you?

CAPTAIN: I can believe a good deal of you, but not that. And if it were so, you wouldn't talk about it.

LAURA: Supposing I were prepared for anything, for being turned out and ostracised, anything to keep my child under my own control. Supposing I am telling the truth now when I say: Bertha is my child but not yours. Supposing . . .

CAPTAIN: Stop it!

LAURA: Just supposing . . . then your power would be over.

CAPTAIN: Not till you had proved I wasn't the father.

LAURA: That wouldn't be difficult. Do you want me to?

CAPTAIN: Stop.

LAURA: I should only have to give the name of the real father—with particulars of place and time, of course. For that matter—when was Bertha born? In the third year of our marriage . . .

CAPTAIN: Will you stop it now, or . . .

LAURA: Or what? Very well, let's stop. All the same, I should think twice before you decide anything. And, above all, don't make yourself ridiculous.

CAPTAIN: I find the whole thing tragic.

LAURA: Which makes you still more ridiculous.

CAPTAIN: But not you?

LAURA: No, we're in such a strong position.

CAPTAIN: That's why we can't fight you.

LAURA: Why try to fight a superior enemy?

CAPTAIN: Superior?

LAURA: Yes. It's odd, I have never been able to look at a man without feeling myself his superior.

CAPTAIN: One day you may meet your master—and you'll never forget it.

LAURA: That will be fascinating.

Enter NURSE.

NURSE: Supper's ready. Come along now, please.

LAURA: Yes, of course. (*The* CAPTAIN *lingers and sits down in an armchair near the sofa.*) Aren't you coming?

CAPTAIN: No, thank you, I don't want any supper.

LAURA: Why not? Has anything upset you?

CAPTAIN: No, but I'm not hungry.

LAURA: Do come, or they'll start asking questions, and that's not necessary. Do be sensible. You won't? Well, stay where you are then! (*Exit.*)

NURSE: Mr. Adolf, whatever is it now?

CAPTAIN: I don't know yet. Tell me—why do you women treat a grown man as if he were a child?

NURSE: Well, goodness me, you're all some woman's child, aren't you? —All you men, big or small . . .

CAPTAIN: While no woman is born of man, you mean. True. But I must be Bertha's father. You believe that, Margaret, don't you? Don't you?

NURSE: Lord, what a silly boy you are! Of course you're your own child's father. Come along and eat now. Don't sit here sulking. There now, come along, do.

CAPTAIN: (*rising.*) Get out, woman! To hell with the hags (*At the hall door.*) Svärd! Svärd!

ORDERLY: (*entering*) Yes, sir?

CAPTAIN: Have the small sleigh got ready at once. (*Exit* ORDERLY.)

NURSE: Now listen, Captain . . .

CAPTAIN: Get out, woman! Get out, I say!

NURSE: God preserve us, whatever's going to happen now?

CAPTAIN: (*putting on his cap*) Don't expect me home before midnight. (*Exit.*)

NURSE: Lord Jesus! What *is* going to happen?

ACT II

The same as before, late that night. The DOCTOR *and* LAURA *are sitting talking.*

DOCTOR: My conversation with him has led me to the conclusion that your suspicions are by no means proved. To begin with, you were mistaken in saying that he had made these important astronomical discoveries by using a microscope. Now I have learnt that it was a spectroscope. Not only is there no sign in this of mental derangement—on the contrary, he has rendered a great service to science.

LAURA: But I never said that.

DOCTOR: I made a memorandum of our conversation, Madam, and I remember questioning you on this vital point, because I thought I must have misheard. One must be scrupulously accurate when bringing charges which might lead to a man being certified.

LAURA: Certified?

DOCTOR: I presume you are aware that if a person is certified insane, he loses both his civil and his family rights.

LAURA: No, I didn't know that.

DOCTOR: There is one other point I should like to be clear about. He spoke of not getting any replies from his book-sellers. May I ask whether—from the best of intentions, of course—you have been intercepting his correspondence?

LAURA: Yes, I have. It is my duty to protect the family. I couldn't let him ruin us all and do nothing about it.

DOCTOR: Excuse me, I do not think you understand the possible consequences of your action. If he realises you have been interfering with his affairs behind his back, his suspicions will be aroused and might even develop into a persecution mania. Particularly, as by thwarting his will, you have already driven him to the end of his tether. Surely you know how enraging it is to have your will opposed and your dearest wishes frustrated.

LAURA: Do I not!

DOCTOR: Then think what this means to him.

LAURA: (*rising*) It's midnight and he's not back yet. Now we can expect the worst.

DOCTOR: Tell me what happened this evening after I saw him. I must know everything.

LAURA: He talked in the wildest way and said the most fantastic things. Can you believe it—he even suggested he wasn't the father of his own child!

DOCTOR: How extraordinary! What can have put that into his head?

LAURA: Goodness knows, unless it was an interview he had with one of his men about maintenance for a child. When I took the girl's part, he got very excited and said no one could ever tell who a child's father was. God knows I did everything I could to calm him, but I don't believe anything can help him now. (*Weeps.*)

DOCTOR: This can't go on. Something must be done—without rousing his suspicions. Tell me, has he had any such delusions before?

LAURA: As a matter of fact, he was much the same six years ago, and then he actually admitted—in a letter to his doctor—that he feared for his reason.

DOCTOR: I see, I see. A deep-seated trouble. But . . . er . . . the sanctity of family life . . . and so forth . . . I mustn't probe too far . . . must keep to the surface. Unfortunately what is done cannot be undone, yet the remedy should have been applied to what is done . . . Where do you think he is now?

LAURA: I can't imagine. He has such wild notions these days . . .

DOCTOR: Would you like me to stay until he comes in? I could explain my presence by saying—well, that your mother is ill and I came to see her.

LAURA: That's a very good idea. Please stand by us, Doctor. If you only knew how worried I am! . . . But wouldn't it be better to tell him straight out what you think of his condition?

DOCTOR: We never do that with mental patients, unless they bring the subject up themselves, and rarely even then. Everything depends on how the case develops. But we had better not stay here. May I go into some other room, to make it more convincing?

LAURA: Yes, that will be best, and Margaret can come in here. She always waits for him. (*At the door.*) Margaret! Margaret! She is the only one who can manage him.

NURSE: (*entering*) Did you call, Madam? Is Master back?

LAURA: No, but you are to wait here for him. And when he comes, tell him that my mother is unwell and the doctor is with her.

NURSE: Aye, aye. Leave all that to me.

LAURA: (*opening the door*) If you will be so good as to come in here, Doctor . . .

DOCTOR: Thank you.

(*They go out. The* NURSE *sits at the table, puts on her glasses and picks up her hymn-book.*)

NURSE: Ah me! Ah me! (*Reads softly:*)

> *A sorrowful and grievous thing*
> *Is life, so swiftly passing by,*
> *Death shadows with his angel's wing*
> *The whole earth, and this his cry:*
> *'Tis Vanity, all Vanity!*

Ah me! Ah me!

> *All that on earth his life and breath,*
> *Falls low before his awful might,*
> *Sorrow alone is spared by Death,*
> *Upon the yawning grave to write:*
> *'Tis Vanity, all Vanity!*

Ah me! Ah me!

During the last lines, BERTHA *enters, carrying a tray with a coffee-pot and a piece of embroidery.*

BERTHA: (*softly*) Margaret, may I sit in here with you? It's so dismal up there.

NURSE: Saints alive! Bertha, are you still up?

BERTHA: Well, you see, I simply must get on with Father's Christmas present. And here's something nice for you.

NURSE: But, sweetheart, this won't do. You have to be up bright and early, and it's past twelve now.

BERTHA: Oh, that doesn't matter! I daren't stay up there all alone. I'm sure there are ghosts.

NURSE: There now! What did I tell you? Mark my words, there's no good fairy in this house. What was it? Did you hear something, Bertha?

BERTHA: Oh Margaret, someone was singing in the attic!

NURSE: In the attic? At this time of night?

BERTHA: Yes. It was such a sad song; the saddest I ever heard. And it seemed to come from the attic—you know, the one on the left where the cradle is.

NURSE: Oh dear, dear, dear! And such a fearful night too. I'm sure the chimneys will blow down. "Alas, what is this earthly life? Sorrow, trouble, grief and strife. Even when it seems most fair, Nought but tribulation there."—Ah, dear child, God grant us a happy Christmas!

BERTHA: Margaret, is it true Father's ill?

NURSE: Aye, that's true enough.

BERTHA: Then I don't expect we shall have a Christmas party. But why isn't he in bed if he's ill?

NURSE: Well, dearie, staying in bed doesn't help his kind of illness. Hush! I hear someone in the porch. Go to bed now—take the tray with you, or the Master will be cross.

BERTHA: *(going out with the tray)* Goodnight, Margaret.

NURSE: Goodnight, love. God bless you.

Enter the CAPTAIN.

CAPTAIN: *(taking off his overcoat.)* Are you still up? Go to bed.

NURSE: Oh, I was only biding till . . .

The CAPTAIN *lights a candle, opens the bureau, sits down at it and takes letters and newspapers from his pocket.*

Mr. Adolf . . .

CAPTAIN: What is it?

NURSE: The old mistress is ill. Doctor's here.

CAPTAIN: Anything serious?

NURSE: No, I don't think so. Just a chill.

CAPTAIN: *(rising)* Who was the father of your child, Margaret?

NURSE: I've told you often enough, it was that heedless fellow Johansson.

CAPTAIN: Are you sure it was he?

NURSE: Don't talk so silly. Of course I'm sure, seeing he was the only one.

CAPTAIN: Yes, but was he sure he was the only one? No, he couldn't be sure, only you could be. See? That's the difference.

NURSE: I don't see any difference.

CAPTAIN: No, you don't see it, but it's there all the same. *(Turns the pages of the photograph album on the table.)* Do you think Bertha's like me?

NURSE: You're as like as two peas in a pod.

CAPTAIN: Did Johansson admit he was the father?

NURSE: Well, he was forced to.

CAPTAIN: How dreadful!—Here's the doctor.

Enter DOCTOR.

Good evening, Doctor. How is my mother-in-law?

DOCTOR: Oh, it's nothing much. Just a slight sprain of the left ankle.

CAPTAIN: I thought Margaret said it was a chill. There appear to be different diagnoses of the case. Margaret, go to bed. (*Exit* NURSE. *Pause.*) Won't you sit down, Dr. Östermark?

CAPTAIN: Is it true that if you cross a mare with a zebra you get striped foals?

DOCTOR: (*astonished*) Perfectly true.

CAPTAIN: And that if breeding is then continued with a stallion, the foals may still be striped?

DOCTOR: That is also true.

CAPTAIN: So, in certain circumstances, a stallion can sire striped foals, and vice versa.

DOCTOR: That would appear to be the case.

CAPTAIN: So the offspring's resemblance to the father proves nothing.

DOCTOR: Oh . . .

CAPTAIN: You're a widower, aren't you? Any children?

DOCTOR: Ye-es.

CAPTAIN: Didn't you sometimes feel rather ridiculous as a father? I myself don't know anything more ludicrous than the sight of a man holding his child's hand in the street, or hearing a father say: "My child." "My wife's child," he ought to say. Didn't you ever see what a false position you were in? Weren't you ever haunted by doubts—I won't say suspicions, as a gentleman I assume your wife was above suspicion?

DOCTOR: No, I certainly wasn't. There it is, Captain, a man—as I think Goethe says—must take his children on trust.

CAPTAIN: Trust, where a woman's concerned? A bit of a risk.

DOCTOR: Ah, but there are many kinds of women!

CAPTAIN: The latest research shows there is only one kind . . . when I was a young fellow and not, if I may say so, a bad specimen, I had two little experiences which afterwards gave me to think. The first was on a steamer. I was in the saloon with some friends, and the young stewardess told us—with tears running down her cheeks—how her sweetheart had been drowned at sea. We condoled with her and I ordered champagne. After the second glass I touched her foot, after the fourth her knee, and before morning I had consoled her.

DOCTOR: One swallow doesn't make a summer.

CAPTAIN: My second experience was a summer swallow. I was staying at Lysekil and got to know a young married woman who was there with her children—her husband was in town. She was religious and high-minded, kept preaching at me and was—or so I thought—the soul of virtue. I lent her a book or two which, strange to relate, she returned. Three months later, I found her card in one of those books with a pretty outspoken declaration of love. It was innocent—as innocent, that's to say, as such a declaration from a married woman could be—to a stranger who had never made her any advances. Moral: don't believe in anyone too much.

DOCTOR: Don't believe too little either.

CAPTAIN: The happy mean, eh? But you see, Doctor, that woman was so unaware of her motives she actually told her husband of her infatuation for me. That's where the danger lies, in the fact that women are unconscious of their instinctive wickedness. An extenuating circumstance, perhaps, but that can only mitigate the judgment, not revoke it.

DOCTOR: You have a morbid turn of mind, Captain. You should be on your guard against this.

CAPTAIN: There's nothing morbid about it. Look here. All steam-boilers explode when the pressure-gauge reaches the limit, but the limit isn't the same for all boilers. Got that? After all, you're here to observe me. Now if I were not a man I could sniff and snivel and explain the case to you, with all its past history. But as unfortunately I am a man, like the ancient Roman I must cross my arms upon my breast and hold my breath until I die. Goodnight.

DOCTOR: If you are ill, Captain, there's no reflection on your manhood in telling me about it. Indeed, it is essential for me to hear both sides of the case.

CAPTAIN: I thought you were quite satisfied with one side.

DOCTOR: You're wrong. And I should like you to know, Captain, that when I heard that Mrs. Alving* blackening her late husband's memory, I thought what a damned shame it was that the fellow should be dead.

CAPTAIN: Do you think if he'd been alive he'd have said anything? Do you think if any husband rose from the dead he'd be believed?

* Reference to Mrs. Alving in Ibsen's GHOSTS.

Goodnight, Doctor. Look how calm I am. It's quite safe for you to go to bed.

DOCTOR: Then I will bid you goodnight. I wash my hands of the whole business.

CAPTAIN: So we're enemies?

DOCTOR: By no means. It's just a pity we can't be friends. Goodnight.
(*The* CAPTAIN *shows the* DOCTOR *out by the hall door, then crosses to the other and slightly opens it.*)

CAPTAIN: Come in and let's talk. I knew you were eavesdropping.

Enter LAURA, *embarrassed. The* CAPTAIN *sits at the bureau.*

It's very late, but we'd better have things out now. Sit down. (*She sits. Pause.*) This evening it was I who went to the post office and fetched the mail, and from my letters it is clear to me that you have been intercepting my correspondence—both in and out. The result of this has been a loss of time which has pretty well shattered the expectations I had for my work.

LAURA: I acted from the best of intentions. You were neglecting your military duties for this other work.

CAPTAIN: Scarcely the best of intentions. You knew very well that one day I should win more distinction in this field than in the Army, but what you wanted was to stop me winning laurels of any kind, because this would stress your own inferiority. Now, for a change, I have intercepted letters addressed to you.

LAURA: How chivalrous!

CAPTAIN: In keeping with the high opinion you have of me. From these letters it appears that for a long time now you've been setting my old friends against me, by spreading rumous about my mental condition. So successful have your efforts been that now scarcely one person from Colonel to kitchen-maid believes I am sane. The actual facts about my condition are these. My reason is, as you know, un-affected, and I am able to discharge my duties both as soldier and father. My emotions are still pretty well under control, but only so long as my will-power remains intact. And you have so gnawed and gnawed at my will that at any moment it may slip its cogs, and then the whole bag of tricks will go to pieces. I won't appeal to your feelings, because you haven't any—that is your strength. I appeal to your own interests.

LAURA: Go on.

CAPTAIN: By behaving in this way you have made me so full of suspicion that my judgment is fogged and my mind is beginning to stray. This means that the insanity you have been waiting for is on its way and may come at any moment. The question you now have to decide is whether it is more to your advantage for me to be well or ill. Consider. If I go to pieces, I shall have to leave the Service, and where will you be then? If I die, you get my life-insurance. But if I take my own life, you get nothing. Is it therefore to your advantage that I should live my life out.

LAURA: Is this a trap?

CAPTAIN: Certainly. You can avoid it or stick your head in it.

LAURA: You say you'd kill yourself, but you never would.

CAPTAIN: Are you so sure? Do you think a man can go on living when he has nothing and nobody to live for?

LAURA: Then you give in?

CAPTAIN: No, I offer peace.

LAURA: On what terms?

CAPTAIN: That I may keep my reason. Free me from doubt and I will give up the fight.

LAURA: Doubt about what?

CAPTAIN: Bertha's parentage.

LAURA: Are there doubts about that?

CAPTAIN: Yes, for me there are, and it was you who roused them.

LAURA: I?

CAPTAIN: Yes. You dropped them like henbane in my ear, and circumstances encouraged them to grow. Free me from uncertainty. Tell me straight out it is so, and I will forgive you in advance.

LAURA: I can scarcely admit to guilt that isn't mine.

CAPTAIN: What can it matter to you, when you know I won't reveal it? Do you think any man would proclaim his shame from the housetops?

LAURA: If I say it isn't so, you still won't be certain, but if I say it is, you will believe me. You must want it to be true.

CAPTAIN: Strangely enough I do. Perhaps because the first supposition can't be proved, while the second can.

LAURA: Have you any grounds for suspicion?

CAPTAIN: Yes and no.

LAURA: I believe you want to make out I'm guilty, so you can get rid of me and have absolute control of the child. But you won't catch me in any such trap.

CAPTAIN: Do you think, if I were convinced of your guilt, I should want to take on another man's child?

LAURA: No, I'm sure you wouldn't. So evidently you were lying when you said you'd forgive me in advance.

CAPTAIN: (*rising*) Laura, save me and my reason! You can't have understood what I was saying. If the child's not mine, I have no rights over her, nor do I want any. And that's how you'd like it, isn't it? But that's not all. You want complete power over the child, don't you, with me still there to support you both?

LAURA: Power, that's it. What's this whole life and death struggle for if not power?

CAPTAIN: For me, as I don't believe in a life to come, this child was my life and death, my conception of immortality—the only one, perhaps, that's valid. If you take her away, you cut my life short.

LAURA: Why didn't we separate sooner?

CAPTAIN: Because the child bound us together, but the bond became a chain. How was that? I never thought of this before, but now memories return, accusing, perhaps condemning. After two years of marriage we were still childless—you know best why. Then I was ill and almost died. One day, between bouts of fever, I heard voices in the next room. You and the lawyer were discussing the property I still owned then. He was explaining that as there were not children, you could not inherit, and he asked if by any chance you were pregnant. I did not hear your reply. I recovered and we had a child. Who is the father?

LAURA: You are.

CAPTAIN: No, I am not. There's a crime buried here that's beginning to stink. And what a fiendish crime! You women, who were so tender-hearted about freeing black slaves, kept the white ones. I have slaved for you, your child, your mother, your servants. I have sacrificed career and promotion. Tortured, beaten, sleepless—my hair has gone grey through the agony of mind you have inflicted on me. All this I have suffered in order that you might enjoy a care-free life and, when you were old, relive it in your child. This is the lowest form of theft, the cruellest slavery. I have had seventeen years of penal servitude—and I was innocent. How can you make up to me for this?

LAURA: Now you really are mad.

CAPTAIN: (*sitting*) So you hope. I have watched you trying to conceal your crime, but because I didn't understand I pitied you. I've soothed your conscience, thinking I was chasing away some nightmare. I've heard you crying out in your sleep without giving your words a second thought. But now . . . now! The other night—Bertha's birthday—comes back to me. I was still up in the early hours, reading, and you suddenly screamed as if someone were trying to strangle you. "Don't! Don't!" you cried. I knocked on the wall—I didn't want to hear any more. For a long time I have had vague suspicions. I did not want them confirmed. That is what I have suffered for you. What will you do for me?

LAURA: What can I do? Swear before God and all that I hold sacred that you are Bertha's father?

CAPTAIN: What good would that do? You have already said that a mother can and ought to commit any crime for her child. I implore you by the memory of the past, I implore you as a wounded man begs to be put out of his misery, tell me the truth. Can't you see I'm helpless as a child? Can't you hear me crying to my mother that I'm hurt? Forget I'm a man, a soldier whose word men—and even beasts—obey. I am nothing but a sick creature in need of pity. I renounce every vestige of power and only beg for mercy on my life.

LAURA: (*laying her hand on his forehead*) What? You, a man, in tears?

CAPTAIN: Yes, a man in tears. Has not a man eyes? Has not a man hands, limbs, senses, opinions, passions? Is he not nourished by the same food as a woman, wounded by the same weapons, warmed and chilled by the same winter and summer? If you prick us, do we not bleed? If you tickle us, do we not laugh? If you poison us, do we not die? Why should a man suffer in silence or a soldier hide his tears? Because it's not manly? Why isn't it manly?

LAURA: Weep, then, my child, and you shall have your mother again. Remember, it was as your second mother that I came into your life. You were big and strong, yet not fully a man. You were a giant child who had come into the world too soon, or perhaps an unwanted child.

CAPTAIN: That's true. My father and mother had me against their will, and therefore I was born without a will. That is why, when you and I became one, I felt I was completing myself—and that is why you dominated. I—in the army the one to command—became at home the one to obey. I grew up at your side, looked up to you as a superior being and listened to you as if I were your foolish little boy.

LAURA: Yes, that's how it was, and I loved you as if you were my little boy. But didn't you see how, when your feelings changed and you came to me as a lover, I was ashamed? The joy I felt in your embraces was followed by such a sense of guilt my very blood seemed tainted. The mother become the mistress—horrible!

CAPTAIN: I saw, but I didn't understand. I thought you despised my lack of virility, so I tried to win you as a woman by proving myself as a man.

LAURA: That was your mistake. The mother was your friend, you see, but the woman was your enemy. Sexual love is conflict. And don't imagine I gave myself. I didn't give. I only took what I meant to take. Yet you did dominate me . . . I felt it and wanted you to feel it.

CAPTAIN: You always dominated me. You could hypnotise me when I was wide awake, so that I neither saw nor heard, but simply obeyed. You could give me a raw potato and make me think it was a peach; you could make me take your ridiculous ideas for flashes of genius. You could corrupt me—yes, make me do the shabbiest things. You never had any real intelligence, yet, instead of being guided by me, you would take the reins into your own hands. And when at last I woke to the realisation that I had lost my integrity, I wanted to blot out my humiliation by some heroic action—some feat, some discovery— even by committing *hara-kiri*. I wanted to go to war, but I couldn't. It was then that I gave all my energies to science. And now—now when I should be stretching out my hand to gather the fruit, you chop off my arm. I'm robbed of my laurels; I'm finished. A man cannot live without repute.

LAURA: Can a woman?

CAPTAIN: Yes—she has her children, but he has not . . . Yet you and I and everyone else went on living, unconscious as children, full of fancies and ideals and illusions, until we woke up. Right—but we woke topsy-turvy, and what's more, we'd been woken by someone who was talking in his own sleep. When women are old and stop being women, they grow beards on their chins. What do men grow, I wonder, when they are old and stop being men? In this false dawn, the birds that crowed weren't cocks, they were capons, and the hens that answered their call were sexless, too. So when the sun should have risen for us, we found ourselves back among the ruins in the full moonlight, just as in the good old times. Our light morning sleep had only been troubled by fantastic dreams—there had been no awakening.

LAURA: You should have been a writer, you know.

CAPTAIN: Perhaps.

LAURA: But I'm sleepy now, so if you have any more fantasies, keep them till to-morrow.

CAPTAIN: Just one thing more—a fact. Do you hate me?

LAURA: Sometimes—as a man.

CAPTAIN: It's like race-hatred. If it's true we are descended from the ape, it must have been from two different species. There's no likeness between us, is there?

LAURA: What are you getting at?

CAPTAIN: In this fight, one of us must go under.

LAURA: Which?

CAPTAIN: The weaker naturally.

LAURA: Then is the stronger in the right?

CAPTAIN: Bound to be as he has the power.

LAURA: Then I am in the right.

CAPTAIN: Why, what power have you?

LAURA: All I need. And it will be legal power to-morrow when I've put you under restraint.

CAPTAIN: Under restraint?

LAURA: Yes. Then I shall decide my child's future myself out of reach of your fantasies.

CAPTAIN: Who will pay for her if I'm not there?

LAURA: Your pension.

CAPTAIN: (*moving towards her menacingly*) How can you have me put under restraint?

LAURA: (*producing a letter*) By means of this letter, an attested copy of which is already in the hands of the authorities.

CAPTAIN: What letter?

LAURA: (*retreating*) Your own. The one in which you told the doctor you were mad. (*He stares at her in silence*) Now you have fulfilled the unfortunately necessary functions of father and bread-winner. You are no longer needed, and you must go. You must go, now that you realise my wits are as strong as my will—you won't want to stay and acknowledge my superiority.

The CAPTAIN *goes to the table, picks up the lighted lamp and throws it at* LAURA, *who escapes backward through the door.*

ACT III

The same. The following evening. A new lamp, lighted, is on the table. The wall-papered door is barricaded with a chair. From the room above comes the sound of pacing footsteps. The NURSE *stands listening, troubled. Enter* LAURA *from within.*

LAURA.   Did he give you the keys?

NURSE: Give? No, God help us, I took them from the coat Nöjd had out to brush.

LAURA: Then it's Nöjd who's on duty?

NURSE: Aye, it's Nöjd.

LAURA: Give me the keys.

NURSE: Here you are, but it's not better than stealing. Hark at him up there! To and fro, to and fro.

LAURA: Are you sure the door's safely bolted?

NURSE: It's bolted safe enough. (*Weeps.*)

LAURA: (*opening the bureau and sitting down at it*) Pull yourself together, Margaret. The only way we can protect ourselves is by keeping calm. (*A knock at the hall door.*) See who that is.

NURSE: (*opening door*) It's Nöjd.

LAURA: Tell him to come in.

NÖJD: (*entering*) Despatch from the Colonel.

LAURA: Give it to me. (*Reads.*) I see . . . Nöjd, have you removed the cartridges from all the guns and pouches?

NÖJD: Yes, Ma'am, just as you said.

LAURA: Wait outside while I write to the Colonel. (*Exit* NÖJD. LAURA *writes. Sound of sawing above.*)

NURSE: Listen, Madam. Whatever is he doing now?

LAURA: Do be quiet. I'm writing.

NURSE: (*muttering.*) Lord have mercy on us! What will be the end of all this?

LAURA: (*holding out the note*) Here you are. Give it to Nöjd. And, remember, my mother's to know nothing of all this. (*Exit* NURSE *with note.* LAURA *opens the bureau drawers and takes out papers.*)

Enter PASTOR.

PASTOR: My dear Laura! As you probably gathered, I have been out all day and only just got back. I hear you've been having a terrible time.

LAURA: Yes, brother, I've never been through such a night and day in all my life!

PASTOR: Well, I see you're looking none the worse for it.

LAURA: No, thank heaven, I wasn't hurt. But just think what might have happened!

PASTOR: Tell me all about it. I've only heard rumours. How did it begin?

LAURA: It began by him raving about not being Bertha's father, and ended by him throwing the lighted lamp in my face.

PASTOR: But this is appalling. He must be quite out of his mind. What in heaven's name are we to do?

LAURA: We must try to prevent further violence. The doctor has sent to the hospital for a strait-jacket. I have just written a note to the Colonel, and now I'm trying to get some idea of the state of our affairs, which Adolf has so shockingly mismanaged. (*Opens another drawer.*)

PASTOR: It's a miserable business altogether, but I always feared something of the kind might happen. When fire and water meet, there's bound to be an explosion. (*Looks in drawer.*) Whatever's all this?

LAURA: Look! This is where he's kept everything hidden.

PASTOR: Good heavens! Here's your old doll! And there's your christening cap . . . and Bertha's rattle . . . and your letters . . . and that locket . . . (*Wipes his eyes.*) He must have loved you very dearly, Laura. I never kept this kind of thing.

LAURA: I believe he did love me once, but times changes everything.

PASTOR: What's this imposing document? (*Examines it.*) The purchase of a grave! Well, better a grave than the asylum! Laura, be frank with me. Aren't you at all to blame?

LAURA: How can I be to blame because someone goes out of his mind?

PASTOR: We—ell! I will say no more. After all, blood's thicker than water.

LAURA: Meaning what, if I may ask?

PASTOR: (*gazing at her*) Oh come now!

LAURA: What?

PASTOR: Come, come! You can scarcely deny that it would suit you down to the ground to have complete control of your daughter.

LAURA: I don't understand.

PASTOR: I can't help admiring you.

LAURA: Really?

PASTOR: And as for me—I shall be appointed guardian to that Free-thinker whom, as you know, I always regarded as a tare among our wheat.

LAURA *gives a quick laugh which she suppresses.*

LAURA: You dare say that to me, his wife?

PASTOR: How strong-willed you are, Laura, how amazingly strong-willed! Like a fox in a trap that would gnaw off its own leg rather than be caught. Like a master-thief working alone, without even a conscience for accomplice. Look in the mirror! You daren't.

LAURA: I never use a mirror.

PASTOR: No. You daren't look at yourself. Let me see your hand. Not one tell-tale spot of blood, not a trace of that subtle poison. A little innocent murder that the law cannot touch. An unconscious crime. Unconscious? A stroke of genius that. Listen to him up there! Take care, Laura! If that man gets loose, he will saw you in pieces too.

LAURA: You must have a bad conscience to talk like that. Pin the guilt on me if you can.

PASTOR: I can't.

LAURA: You see? You can't, and so—I am innocent. And now, you look after your charge and I'll take care of mine.

Enter DOCTOR.

Ah, here is the Doctor! (*Rises*) I'm so glad to see you, Doctor. I know I can count on you to help me, although I'm afraid not much can be done now. You hear him up there. Are you convinced at last?

DOCTOR: I am convinced there has been an act of violence. But the question is—should that act of violence be regarded as an outbreak of temper or insanity?

PASTOR: But apart from this actual outbreak, you must admit that he suffers from fixed ideas.

DOCTOR: I have a notion, Pastor, that *your* ideas are even more fixed.

PASTOR: My firmly rooted convictions of spiritual . . .

DOCTOR: Convictions apart, it rests with you, Madam, to decide if your husband is to be fined or imprisoned or sent to the asylum. How do you regard his conduct?

LAURA: I can't answer that now.

DOCTOR: Oh? Have you no—er—firmly rooted conviction of what would be best for the family? And you, Pastor?

PASTOR: There's bound to be a scandal either way. It's not easy to give an opinion.

LAURA: But if he were only fined for violence he could be violent again.

DOCTOR: And if he were sent to prison he would soon be out again. So it seems best for all parties that he should be treated as insane. Where is the nurse?

LAURA: Why?

DOCTOR: She must put the strait-jacket on the patient. Not at once, but after I have had a talk with him—and not then until I give the order. I have the—er—garment outside. (*Goes out to hall and returns with a large parcel.*) Kindly call the nurse.

LAURA *rings. The* DOCTOR *begins to unpack the strait-jacket.*

PASTOR: Dreadful! Dreadful!

Enter NURSE.

DOCTOR: Ah, Nurse! Now please pay attention. You see this jacket. When I give you the word I want you to slip it on the Captain from behind. So as to prevent any further violence, you understand. Now it has, you see, unusually long sleeves. That is to restrict his movements. These sleeves must be tied together behind his back. And now here are two straps with buckles, which afterwards you must fasten to the arm of a chair—or to whatever's easiest. Can you do this, do you think?

NURSE: No, Doctor, I can't. No, not that.

LAURA: Why not do it yourself, Doctor?

DOCTOR: Because the patient distrusts me. You, Madam, are the proper person, but I'm afraid he doesn't trust you either. (LAURA *grimaces*.) Perhaps you, Pastor . . .

PASTOR: I must beg to decline.

Enter NÖJD.

LAURA: Did you deliver my note?

NÖJD: Yes, Madam.

DOCTOR: Oh, it's you, Nöjd! You know the state of things here, don't you? You know the Captain has had a mental breakdown. You must help us look after the patient.

NÖJD: If there's aught I can do for Captain, he knows I'll do it.

DOCTOR: You are to put this jacket on him.

NURSE: He's not to touch him. Nöjd shan't hurt him. I'd rather do it myself, gently, gently. But Nöjd can wait outside and help me if need be—yes, that's what he'd best do.

A pounding on the paper-covered door.

DOCTOR: Here he is! (*To* NURSE.) Put the jacket on that chair under your shawl. And now go away, all of you, while the Pastor and I talk to him. That door won't hold long. Hurry!

NURSE: (*going out*) Lord Jesus help us!

LAURA *shuts the bureau and follows the* NURSE. NÖJD *goes out to the hall. The paper-covered door bursts open, the lock broken and the chair hurled to the floor. The* CAPTAIN *comes out, carrying a pile of books.*

CAPTAIN: (*putting the books on the table.*) Here it all is. You can read it in every one of these volumes. So I wasn't mad after all. (*Picks one up.*) Here it is in the Odyssey, Book I, page 6, line 215 in the Uppsala translation. Telemachus speaking to Athene: "My mother says I am Odysseus' son; but for myself I cannot tell. It's a wise child that knows its own father."* And that's the suspicion Telemachus has about Penelope, the most virtuous of women. Fine state of affairs, eh? (*Takes up another book.*) And here we have the Prophet Ezekiel: "The fool saith, Lo, here is my father; but who can tell whose loins have engendered him?" That's clear enough. (*Picks up another.*) And what's this? A history of Russian literature by Merzlyakov. Alexander Pushkin, Russia's greatest poet, was mortally wounded—but more by the rumours of his wife's unfaithfulness than by the bullet he received in his breast at the duel. On his deathbed he swore she was innocent. Jackass! How could he swear any such thing? I *do* read my books, you see! Hullo, Jonas, are you here? And the Doctor, of course. Did I ever tell you what I said to the English lady who was deploring the habit Irishmen have of throwing lighted lamps in their wives' faces? "God, what women!" I said. "Women?" she stammered. "Of course," I replied. "When things get to such a pass that a man who has loved, has worshipped a woman, picks up a lighted lamp and flings it in her face, then you may be sure . . ."

PASTOR: Sure of what?

CAPTAIN: Nothing. You can never be sure of anything—you can only believe. That's right, isn't it, Jonas? One believes and so one is saved. Saved, indeed! No. One can be damned through believing. That's what I've learnt.

DOCTOR: But, Captain . . .

CAPTAIN: Hold your tongue! I don't want any chat from you. I don't want to hear you relaying all the gossip from in there like a telephone. In there—you know what I mean. Listen to me, Jonas. Do you imagine you're the father of your children? I seem to remember you had a tutor in the house, a pretty boy about whom there was quite a bit of gossip.

PASTOR: Take care, Adolf!

CAPTAIN: Feel under your wig and see if you don't find two little nobs. Upon my soul, he's turning pale! Well, well! It was only talk, of course, but my God, how they talked! But we married men are all figures of fun, every man Jack of us. Isn't that right, Doctor? What about your own marriage bed? Didn't you have a certain lieutenant in your house, eh? Wait now, let me guess. He was called . . . (*Whispers in the* DOCTOR's *ear.*) By Jove, he's turned pale too! But don't worry. She's dead and buried, so what was done can't be done again. As a matter of fact, I knew him, and he's now—look at me, Doctor—no, straight in the eyes!

---

* English translation E. V. Rieu. Penguin Classics.

He is now a major of Dragoons. Good Lord, I believe *he* has horns too!
DOCTOR: *(angrily)* Be so good as to change the subject, Captain.
CAPTAIN: See! As soon as I mention horns he wants to change the subject.
PASTOR: I suppose you know, brother-in-law, that you're not in your right mind?
CAPTAIN: Yes, I do know. But if I had the handling of your decorated heads, I should soon have you shut up too. I am mad. But how did I become mad? Doesn't that interest you? No, it doesn't interest anyone. *(Takes the photograph album from the table.)* Christ Jesus, there is my daughter! Mine? That's what we can never know. Shall I tell you what we should have to do so as to know? First marry, in order to be accepted by society, then immediately divorce; after that become lovers and finally adopt the children. That way one could at least be sure they were one's own adopted children. Eh? But what good's that to me? What's good's anything now you have robbed me of my immortality? What can science or philosophy do for me when I have nothing left to live for? How can I live without honour? I grafted my right arm and half my brain and spinal cord on to another stem. I believed they would unite and grow into a single, more perfect tree. Then someone brought a knife and cut below the graft, so now I'm only half a tree. The other part, with my arm and half my brain, goes on growing. But I wither—I am dying, for it was the best part of myself I gave away. Let me die. Do what you like with me. I'm finished.

The DOCTOR *and* PASTOR *whisper, then go out. The* CAPTAIN *sinks into a chair by the table.* BERTHA *enters.*

BERTHA: *(going to him)* Are you ill, Father?
CAPTAIN: *(looking up stupidly at word "Father")* Me?
BERTHA: Do you know what you did? You threw a lamp at Mother.
CAPTAIN: Did I?
BERTHA: Yes. Supposing she'd been hurt!
CAPTAIN: Would that have mattered?
BERTHA: You're not my father if you talk like that.
CAPTAIN: What d'you say? Not your father? How d'you know? Who told you? Who is your father, then? Who?
BERTHA: Not you, anyway.
CAPTAIN: Anyone but me! Who then? Who? You seem well informed. Who told you? That I should live to hear my own child tell me to my face I am not her father! Do you realise you're insulting your mother by saying this? Don't you understand that, if it's true, *she* is disgraced?

BERTHA: You're not to say anything against Mother, I tell you!

CAPTAIN: Yes, all in league against me, just as you've always been.

BERTHA: Father!

CAPTAIN: Don't call me that again!

BERTHA: Father, Father!

CAPTAIN: (*drawing her to him*) Bertha, my beloved child, yes, you *are* my child. Yes, yes, it must be so—it *is* so. All that was only a sick fancy —it came on the wind like an infection or a fever. Look at me! Let me see my soul in your eyes . . . But I see *her* soul as well. You have two souls. You love me with one and hate me with the other. You must love me and only me. You must have only one soul or you'll have no peace —neither shall I. You must have only one mind, fruit of my mind. You must have only one will—mine!

BERTHA: No, no! I want to be myself.

CAPTAIN: Never! I am a cannibal, you see, and I'm going to eat you. Your mother wanted to eat me, but she didn't succeed. I am Saturn who devoured his children because it was foretold that otherwise they would devour him. To eat or to be eaten—that is the question. If I don't eat you, you will eat me—you've shown your teeth already. (*Goes to the rack.*) Don't be afraid, my darling child. I shan't hurt you. (*Takes down a revolver.*)

BERTHA: (*dodging away from him*) Help! Mother, help! He wants to kill me!

NURSE: (*hurrying in*) What in heaven's name are you doing, Mr. Adolf?

CAPTAIN: (*examining the revolver*) Did you remove the cartridges?

NURSE: Well, I did just tidy them away, but sit down here and take it easy and I'll soon fetch them back. (*She takes the* CAPTAIN *by the arm and leads him to a chair. He slumps down. She picks up the strait-jacket and goes behind the chair.* BERTHA *creeps out.*) Mr. Adolf, do you remember when you were my dear little boy, and I used to tuck you up at night and say your prayers with you? And do you remember how I used to get up in the night to get you a drink when you were thirsty? And how, when you had bad dreams and couldn't go to sleep again, I'd light the candle and tell you pretty stories. Do you remember?

CAPTAIN: Go on talking. Margaret. It soothes my mind. Go on talking.

NURSE: Aye, that I will, but you listen carefully. D'you remember how once you took a great big kitchen knife to carve a boat with, and I came in and had to trick the knife away from you? You were such a silly little lad, one had to trick you, you never would believe what anyone did was for your own good . . . "Give me that snake," I said, "or else he'll bite you." And then, see, you let go of the knife. (*Takes the revolver from his hand.*) And then, too, when it was time for you to dress yourself, and you wouldn't. I had to coax you, and say you should have a golden coat and be dressed just like a prince. Then I took your little tunic, that was just made of green wool, and held it up in front of you and said: "In with your arms, now, both together." (*Gets the jacket on.*) And then I said: "Sit nice and still now, while I button it up behind." (*Ties the sleeves behind him.*) And then I said: "Up with you, and walk across the floor like a good boy, so Nurse can see how it fits." (*Leads him to the sofa.*) And then I said: "Now you must go to bed."

CAPTAIN: What's that? Go to bed, when I'd just been dressed? My God! What have you done to me? (*Tries to get free.*) Oh you fiendish woman, what devilish cunning! Who would have thought you had the brains for it? (*Lies down on the sofa.*) Bound, fleeced, outwitted and unable to die!

NURSE: Forgive me, Mr. Adolf, forgive me! I had to stop you killing the child.

CAPTAIN: Why didn't you let me kill her? If life's hell and death's heaven, and children belong to heaven?

NURSE: What do you know of the hereafter?

CAPTAIN: It's the only thing one does know. Of life one knows nothing. Oh, if one had known from the beginning!

NURSE: Humble your stubborn heart, Mr. Adolf, and cry to God for mercy! Even now it's not too late. It wasn't too late for the thief on the Cross, for Our Saviour said: "To-day shalt thou be with me in paradise."

CAPTAIN: Croaking for a corpse already, old crow? (*She takes her hymn-book from her pocket. He calls*) Nöjd! Are you there, Nöjd?

Enter NÖJD.

Throw this woman out of the house or she'll choke me to death with her hymn-book. Throw her out of the window, stuff her up the chimney, do what you like only get rid of her!

NÖJD: (*staring at the* NURSE) God save you, Captain—and that's from the bottom of my heart—but I can't do that, I just can't. If it were six men now, but a woman!

CAPTAIN: What? You can't manage one woman?

NÖJD: (*staring at the* NURSE) God save you, Captain—and that's from laying hands on a woman.

CAPTAIN: What is this something? Haven't they laid hands on me?

NÖJD: Yes, but I just can't do it, Sir. Same as if you was to tell me to hit Pastor. It's like religion, it's in your bones. I can't do it.

Enter LAURA. *She signs to* NÖJD, *who goes out.*

CAPTAIN: Omphale! Omphale! Playing with the club while Hercules spins your wool.

LAURA: (*approaching the sofa*) Adolf, look at me! Do you believe I'm your enemy?

CAPTAIN: Yes, I do. I believe all you women are my enemies. My mother did not want me to come into the world because my birth would give her pain. She was my enemy. She robbed my embryo of nourishment, so I was born incomplete. My sister was my enemy when she made me knuckle under to her. The first woman I took in my arms was my enemy. She gave me ten years of sickness in return for the love I gave her. When my daughter had to choose between you and me, she became my enemy. And you, you, my wife, have been my mortal enemy, for you have not let go your hold until there is no life left in me.

LAURA: But I didn't mean this to happen. I never really thought it out. I may have had some vague desire to get rid of you—you were in my way—and perhaps, if you see some plan in my actions, there was one, but I was unconscious of it. I have never given a thought to my actions—they simply ran along the rails you laid down. My conscience is clear, and before God I feel innocent, even if I'm not. You weighed me down like a stone, pressing and pressing till my heart tried to shake off its intolerable burden. That's how it's been, and if without meaning to I have brought you to this, I ask your forgiveness.

CAPTAIN: Very plausible, but how does that help me? And whose fault is it? Perhaps our cerebral marriage is to blame. In the old days one married a wife. Now one goes into partnership with a business woman or sets up house with a friend. Then one rapes the partner or violates the friend. What becomes of love, the healthy love of the senses? It dies of neglect. And what happens to the dividends from those love shares, payable to holder, when there's no joint account? Who is the holder when the crash comes? Who is the bodily father of the cerebral child?

LAURA: Your suspicions about our daughter are entirely unfounded.

CAPTAIN: That's the horror of it. If they had some foundation, there would at least be something to catch hold of, to cling to. Now there are only shadows, lurking in the undergrowth, peering out with grinning faces. It's like fighting with air, a mock battle with blank cartridges. Reality, however deadly, puts one on one's mettle, nerves body and soul for action, but as it is . . . my thoughts dissolve in fog, my brain grinds a void till it catches fire . . . Put a pillow under my head. Lay something over me. I'm cold. I'm terribly cold.

LAURA *takes off her shawl and spreads it over him. Exit* NURSE.

LAURA: Give me your hand, my dear.

CAPTAIN: My hand! Which you have bound behind my back. Omphale, Omphale! But I can feel your shawl soft against my mouth. It's warm and gentle like your arms and smells of vanilla like your hair when you were young. When you were young, Laura, and we used to walk in the birch woods. There were primroses and thrushes—lovely, lovely! Think how beautiful life was then—and what it has become! You did not want it to become like this, neither did I. Yet it has. Who then rules our lives?

LAURA: God.

CAPTAIN: The God of strife then—or nowadays the Goddess!

Enter NURSE *with a pillow.*

Take away this cat that's lying on me. Take it away! (NURSE *removes the shawl and puts the pillow under his head.*) Bring my uniform. Put my tunic over me. (*The* NURSE *takes the tunic from a peg and spreads it over him.*) (*To* LAURA.) Ah, my tough lion's skin that you would take from me! Omphale! Omphale! You cunning woman, lover of peace and contriver of disarmament. Wake, Hercules, before they take away your club! You would trick us out of our armour, calling it tinsel. It was iron, I tell you, before it became tinsel. In the old days the smith forged the soldier's coat, now it is made by the needlewoman. Omphale! Omphale! Rude strength has fallen before treacherous weakness. Shame on you, woman of Satan, and a curse on all your sex! (*He raises himself to spit at her, but sinks back again.*) What sort of a pillow have you given me, Margaret? How hard and cold it is! So cold! Come and sit beside me on this chair. (*She does so.*) Yes, like that. Let me put my head on your lap. Ah, that's warmer! Lean over me so I can feel your breast. Oh how sweet it is to sleep upon a woman's breast, be she mother or mistress! But sweetest of all a mother's.

LAURA: Adolf, tell me, do you want to see your child?

CAPTAIN: My child? A man has no children. Only women have children. So the future is theirs, while we die childless. O God, who holds all children dear!

NURSE: Listen! He's praying to God.

CAPTAIN: No, to you, to put me to sleep. I'm tired, so tired. Good night, Margaret. "Blessed art thou among women." (*He raises himself, then with a cry falls back on the* NURSES's *knees.*)

LAURA: (*at the door, calling.*) Doctor!

Enter DOCTOR *and* PASTOR.

Help him, Doctor—if it's not too late! Look, he has stopped breathing!
DOCTOR: (*feeling his pulse.*) It is a stroke.
PASTOR: Is he dead?
DOCTOR: No, he might still wake—but to what, who can say?
PASTOR: ". . . once to die, but after this the judgment."*
DOCTOR: No judgment—and no recriminations. You who believe that a God rules over human destiny must lay this to his charge.
NURSE: Ah Pastor, with his last breath he prayed to God!
PASTOR: (*to* LAURA.) Is this true?
LAURA: It is true.
DOCTOR: If this be so, of which I am as poor a judge as of the cause of his illness, in any case my skill is at an end. Try yours now, Pastor.
LAURA: Is that all you have to say at this deathbed, Doctor?
DOCTOR: That is all. I know no more. Let him who knows more, speak.

BERTHA *comes in and runs to* LAURA.

BERTHA: Mother! Mother!
LAURA: My child! My own child!
PASTOR: Amen.

END

STUDY AND DISCUSSION QUESTIONS

1. (Act I) What is the dramatic function of the first scene? What is the function of the Pastor? What contradiction exists between the Captain's army life and his home life? How are women characterized in this act? What is the conflict in the Captain's home? What are some of the references that indicate the antagonism between Laura and Adolf has been going on for some time? What is the Doctor's reaction to Laura's charges concerning her husband? What is the significance of Adolf's scientific research? What is the dramatic function of the Nurse? How is Bertha characterized? How effective are Laura's schemes to drive her husband insane?

---

* HEBREWS: ix, 27.

2. (Act II) What is the function of the scene between Laura and the Doctor? What function does the grandmother serve? Why is the play set on Christmas Eve? What experience has Adolf had with women in the past? Why is Adolf willing to compromise with Laura? What is the ultimate reason for the conflict between husband and wife? Why could Laura love Adolf as a child and not as a husband? What is the meaning of the following comment by Adolf: "Yet you and I and everyone else went on living, unconscious as children, full of fancies and ideals and illusions, until we woke up."? What is the symbolic significance of Adolf throwing the lamp?

3. (Act III) How does the Nurse react to Laura's scheme? How do Nöjd and the Pastor react? Does the straitjacket serve as a symbol? Why does Adolf present examples from literature to satisfy his suspicion? What is Bertha's reaction to her father's accusation? Why doesn't Nöjd help Adolf? What is the significance of the shawl? Of the army coat? How do the Pastor and the Doctor react to the apparent death of the Captain?

4. Even though the play has act divisions, it is remarkable for its compactness. The central argument over the education of Bertha is only the end result of a long struggle between the opposing sexes. Discuss the details that underscore the fact that the struggle has been a prolonged affair.

5. There is a great deal of imagery in *The Father*, most of it concentrated on "the emasculated warrior, the tokens of power, the demonic female, sleep and awakening." Trace some of these patterns of imagery to see how they function in relation to the central theme.

6. The men in the play generally represent some great social power (church, military, science), but they all appear to be helpless in the face of Laura's power. Discuss how she gets control over each of these powers and the significance of this control in terms of the theme.

7. Aristotle defines tragedy as "an imitation of an action that is serious, complete, and of a certain magnitude; in language embellished with each kind of artistic ornament, the several kinds being found in separate parts of the play; in the form of action, not narrative; through pity and fear effecting the proper purgation of these emotions." Analyze *The Father* according to this definition of tragedy. What conclusions can you make about modern tragedy?

8. Carl E. W. Dahlström ("Strindberg's *The Father* as Tragedy") suggests "that the Greek writers of tragedy and Shakespeare were the most significant tragic poets that Strindberg could possibly copy or emulate." Compare *The Father* to Greek tragedy (*Oedipus* or *Antigone*) in terms of plot, character, diction, thought, and spectacle. In his "Forward to *Miss Julie*," Strindberg says that "people recently complained about my tragedy *The Father*, that it was so sad." A. C. Bradley in *Shakespearean Tragedy* says that "of all Shakespeare's tragedies . . . not even excepting *King Lear*, *Othello* is the most painfully exciting and the most terrible. From the moment when the temptation of the hero begins, the reader's heart and mind are held in a vice, experiencing the extremes of pity and fear, sympathy and repulsion, sickening hope and dreadful expectation." Compare *The Father* with *Othello* for the quality of the emotions they elicit in the reader.

WRITING TOPICS

1. Write an essay on one of the following topics: (a) the full significance of the title, (b) the antagonist, (c) the universality of the play, (d) the dramatic function of the minor characters.

2. "Life as perpetual prison, inferno, explosive storehouse of hypocrisy and hatred—these are basic themes throughout Strindberg's dramas." Write an essay developing what you consider to be the most characteristic of the above themes in *The Father*.

3. Laura is a "semisocial animal whose chief characteristic is brute cunning. She does not have sufficient intelligence to recognize enough to move warily in the social jungle. She is amoral and thus without scruples of any kind." Write an essay attacking or defending all or part of the above statement.

4. Write an essay analyzing *The Father* for the elements of naturalism (see Glossary and Introduction to this section). Also single out qualities in the play that transcend naturalism.

5. Reread question 8 (Study and Discussion Questions) and write an essay comparing and contrasting *The Father* with a play by Sophocles or one by Shakespeare (choose just one or two aspects such as character or some dramatic technique). *Or* compare and contrast the theme of feminism in *The Father* and *Hedda Gabler*.

MISS JULIE
A Tragedy in One Act

August Strindberg
Translated by Elizabeth Sprigge

Characters

MISS JULIE, *aged 25.*
JEAN, *the valet, aged 30.*
KRISTIN, *the cook, aged 35.*

*Scene: The large kitchen of a Swedish manor house in a country
district in the eighties.*
Midsummer eve.
The kitchen has three doors, two small ones into JEAN'S *and*
KRISTIN'S *bedrooms, and a large, glass-fronted double one, opening
on to a courtyard. This is the only way to the rest of the house.*
*Through these glass doors can be seen part of a fountain with a
cupid, lilac bushes in flower and the tops of some Lombardy pop-
lars. On one wall are shelves edged with scalloped paper on which
are kitchen utensils of copper, iron and tin.*
*To the left is the corner of a large tiled range and part of its chim-
ney-hood, to the right the end of the servants' dinner table with
chairs beside it.*

Miss Julie is reprinted by permission of Collins-Knowlton-Wing, Inc. Copyright
© 1955 by Elizabeth Sprigge.

The stove is decorated with birch boughs, the floor strewn with twigs of juniper. On the end of the table is a large Japanese.spice jar full of lilac.
There are also an ice-box, a scullery table and a sink.
Above the double door hangs a big old-fashioned bell; near it is a speaking-tube.
A fiddle can be heard from the dance in the barn near-by.
KRISTIN *is standing at the stove, frying something in a pan. She wears a light-coloured cotton dress and a big apron.*
JEAN *enters, wearing livery and carrying a pair of large riding-boots with spurs, which he puts in a conspicuous place.*

JEAN: Miss Julie's crazy again to-night, absolutely crazy.
KRISTIN: Oh, so you're back, are you?
JEAN: When I'd taken the Count to the station, I came back and dropped in at the Barn for a dance. And who did I see there but our young lady leading off with the gamekeeper. But the moment she sets eyes on me, up she rushes and invites me to waltz with her. And how she waltzed—I've never seen anything like it! She's crazy.
KRISTIN: Always has been, but never so bad as this last fortnight since the engagement was broken off.
JEAN: Yes, that was a pretty business, to be sure. He's a decent enough chap, too, even if he isn't rich. Oh, but they're choosy! (*Sits down at the end of the table.*) In any case, it's a bit odd that our young—er—lady would rather stay at home with the yokels than go with her father to visit her relations.
KRISTIN: Perhaps she feels a bit awkward, after that bust-up with her fiancé.
JEAN: Maybe. That chap had some guts, though. Do you know the sort of thing that was going on, Kristin? I saw it with my own eyes, though I didn't let on I had.
KRISTIN: You saw them . . . ?
JEAN: Didn't I just! Came across the pair of them one evening in the stable-yard. Miss Julie was doing what she called "training" him. Know what that was? Making him jump over her riding-whip—the way you teach a dog. He did it twice and got a cut each time for his pains, but when it came to the third go, he snatched the whip out of her hand and broke it into smithereens. And then he cleared off.
KRISTIN: What goings on! I never did!
JEAN: Well, that's how it was with that little affair . . . Now, what have you got for me, Kristin? Something tasty?
KRISTIN: (*serving from the pan to his plate*) Well, it's just a little bit of kidney I cut off their joint.

JEAN: (*smelling it*) Fine! That's my special delice. (*Feels the plate.*) But you might have warmed the plate.

KRISTIN: When you choose to be finicky you're worse than the Count himself. (*Pulls his hair affectionately.*)

JEAN: (*crossly*) Stop pulling my hair. You know how sensitive I am.

KRISTIN: There, there! It's only love, you know.

(JEAN *eats.* KRISTIN *brings a bottle of beer.*)

JEAN: Beer on Midsummer Eve? No thanks! I've got something better than that. (*From a drawer in the table brings out a bottle of red wine with a yellow seal.*) Yellow seal, see! Now get me a glass. You use a glass with a stem of course when you're drinking it straight.

KRISTIN: (*giving him a wine-glass*) Lord help the woman who gets you for a husband, you old fusser! (*She puts the beer in the ice-box and sets a small saucepan on the stove.*)

JEAN: Nonsense! You'll be glad enough to get a fellow as smart as me. And I don't think it's done you any harm people calling me your fiancé. (*Tastes the wine.*) Good. Very good indeed. But not quite warmed enough. (*Warms the glass in his hand.*) We bought this in Dijon. Four frances the litre without the bottle, and duty on top of that. What are you cooking now? It stinks.

KRISTIN: Some bloody muck Miss Julie wants for Diana.

JEAN: You should be more refined in your speech, Kristin. But why should you spend a holiday cooking for that bitch? Is she sick or what?

KRISTIN: Yes, she's sick. She sneaked out with the pug at the lodge and got in the usual mess. And that, you know, Miss Julie won't have.

JEAN: Miss Julie's too high-and-mighty in some respects, and not enough in others, just like her mother before her. The Countess was more at home in the kitchen and cowsheds than anywhere else, but would she ever go driving with only one horse? She went round with her cuffs filthy, but she had to have the coronet on the cuff-links. Our young lady—to come back to her—hasn't any proper respect for herself or her position. I mean she isn't refined. In the Bar just now she dragged the gamekeeper away from Anna and made him dance with her—no waiting to be asked. We wouldn't do a thing like that. But that's what happens when the gentry try to behave like the common people—they become common . . . Still she's a fine girl. Smashing! What shoulders! And what—er—etcetera!

KRISTIN: Oh come off it! I know what Clara says, and she dresses her.

JEAN: Clara? Pooh, you're all jealous! But I've been out riding with her . . . and as for her dancing!

KRISTIN: Listen, Jean. You will dance with me, won't you, as soon as I'm through.

JEAN: Of course I will.

KRISTIN: Promise?

JEAN: Promise? When I say I'll do a thing I do it. Well, thanks for the supper. It was a real treat. (*Corks the bottle.*) (JULIE *appears in the doorway, speaking to someone outside.*)

JULIE: I'll be back in a moment. Don't wait. (JEAN *slips the bottle into the drawer and rises respectfully.*)

JULIE *enters and joins* KRISTIN *at the stove.*

   Well, have you made it? (KRISTIN *signs that* JEAN *is near them.*)

JEAN: (*gallantly*) Have you ladies got some secret?

JULIE: (*flipping his face with her handkerchief*) You're very inquisitive.

JEAN: What a delicious smell! Violets.

JULIE: (*coquettishly*) Impertinence! Are you an expert of scent too? I must say you know how to dance. Now don't look. Go away. (*The music of a schottische begins.*)

JEAN: (*with impudent politeness*) Is it some witches' brew you're cooking on Midsummer Eve? Something to tell your stars by, so you can see your future?

JULIE: (*sharply*) If you could see that you'd have good eyes. (*To* KRISTIN.) Put it in a bottle and cork it tight. Come and dance this schottische with me, Jean.

JEAN: (*hesitating*) I don't want to be rude, but I've promised to dance this one with Kristin.

JULIE: Well, she can have another, can't you, Kristin? You'll lend me Jean, won't you?

KRISTIN: (*bottling*) It's nothing to do with me. When you're so condescending, Miss, it's not his place to say no. Go on, Jean, and thank Miss Julie for the honour.

JEAN: Frankly speaking, Miss, and no offence meant, I wonder if it's wise for you to dance twice running with the same partner, specially as those people are so ready to jump to conclusions.

JULIE: (*flaring up*) What did you say? What sort of conclusions? What do you mean?

JEAN: (*meekly*) As you choose not to understand, Miss Julie, I'll have to speak more plainly. It looks bad to show a preference for one of your retainers when they're all hoping for the same unusual favour.

JULIE: Show a preference! The very idea! I'm surprised at you. I'm doing the people an honour by attending their ball when I'm mistress of the house, but if I'm really going to dance, I mean to have a partner who can lead and doesn't make me look ridiculous.

JEAN: If those are your orders, Miss, I'm at your service.

JULIE: (*gently*) Don't take it as an order. To-night we're all just people enjoying a party. There's no question of class. So now give me your arm. Don't worry, Kristin. I shan't steal your sweetheart. (JEAN *gives* JULIE *his arm and leads her out.*)

> *Left alone,* KRISTIN *plays her scene in an unhurried, natural way, humming to the tune of the schottische, played on a distant violin. She clears* JEAN'S *place, washes up and puts things away, then takes off her apron, brings out a small mirror from a drawer, props it against the jar of lilac, lights a candle, warms a small pair of tongs and curls her fringe. She goes to the door and listens, then turning back to the table finds* MISS JULIE'S *forgotten handkerchief. She smells it, then meditatively smooths it out and folds it.*

Enter JEAN.

JEAN: She really *is* crazy. What a way to dance! With people standing grinning at her too from behind the doors. What's got into her, Kristin?

KRISTIN: Oh, it's just her time coming on. She's always queer then. Are you going to dance with me now?

JEAN: Then you're not wild with me for cutting that one.

KRISTIN: You know I'm not—for a little thing like that. Besides, I know my place.

JEAN: (*putting his arm round her waist*) You're a sensible girl, Kristin, and you'll make a very good wife . . .

Enter JULIE, *unpleasantly surprised.*

JULIE: (*with forced gaiety*) You're a fine beau—running away from your partner.

JEAN: Not away, Miss Julie, but as you see back to the one I deserted.

JULIE: (*changing her tone*) You really can dance, you know. But why are you wearing your livery on a holiday. Take it off at once.

JEAN: Then I must ask you to go away for a moment, Miss. My black coat's here. (*Indicates it hanging on the door to his room.*)

JULIE: Are you so shy of me—just over changing a coat? Go into your room then—or stay here and I'll turn my back.

JEAN: Excuse me then, Miss. (*He goes to his room and is partly visible as he changes his coat.*)

JULIE: Tell me, Kristin, is Jean your fiancé? You seem very intimate.

KRISTIN: My fiancé? Yes, if you like. We call it that.

JULIE: Call it?

KRISTIN: Well, you've had a fiancé yourself, Miss, and . . .

JULIE: But we really were engaged.

KRISTIN: All the same it didn't come to anything.

JEAN *returns in his black coat.*

JULIE: Très gentil, Monsieur Jean. Très gentil.

JEAN: Vous voulez plaisanter, Madame.

JULIE: Et vous voulez parler français. Where did you learn it?

JEAN: In Switzerland, when I was sommelier at one of the biggest hotels in Lucerne.

JULIE: You look quite the gentleman in that get-up. Charming. (*Sits at the table.*)

JEAN: Oh, you're just flattering me!

JULIE: (*annoyed*) Flattering you?

JEAN: I'm too modest to believe you would pay real compliments to a man like me, so I must take it you are exaggerating—that this is what's known as flattery.

JULIE: Where on earth did you learn to make speeches like that? Perhaps you've been to the theatre a lot.

JEAN: That's right. And travelled a lot too.

JULIE: But you come from this neighbourhood, don't you?

JEAN: Yes, my father was a labourer on the next estate—the District Attorney's place. I often used to see you, Miss Julie, when you were little, though you never noticed me.

JULIE: Did you really?

JEAN: Yes. One time specially I remember . . . but I can't tell you about that.

JULIE: Oh do! Why not? This is just the time.

JEAN: No, I really can't now. Another time perhaps.

JULIE: Another time means never. What harm is now?

JEAN: No harm, but I'd rather not. (*Points to* KRISTIN, *now fast asleep.*) Look at her.

JULIE: She'll make a charming wife, won't she? I wonder if she snores.

JEAN: No, she doesn't, but she talks in her sleep.

JULIE: (*cynically*) How do you know she talks in her sleep?

JEAN: (*brazenly*) I've heard her. (*Pause. They look at one another.*)

JULIE: Why don't you sit down?

JEAN: I can't take such a liberty in your presence.

JULIE: Supposing I order you to.

JEAN: I'll obey.

JULIE: Then sit down. No, wait a minute. Will you get me a drink first?

JEAN: I don't know what's in the ice-box. Only beer, I expect.

JULIE: There's no only about it. My taste is so simple I prefer it to wine. (JEAN *takes a bottle from the ice-box, fetches a glass and plate and serves the beer.*)

JEAN: At your service.

JULIE: Thank you. Won't you have some yourself?

JEAN: I'm not really a beer-drinker, but if it's an order . . .

JULIE: Order? I should have thought it was ordinary manners to keep your partner company.

JEAN: That's a good way of putting it. (*He opens another bottle and fetches a glass.*)

JULIE: Now drink my health. (*He hesitates.*) I believe the man really is shy. (JEAN *kneels and raises his glass with mock ceremony.*)

JEAN: To the health of my lady!

JULIE: Bravo! Now kiss my shoe and everything will be perfect. (*He hesitates, then boldly takes hold of her foot and lightly kisses it.*) Splendid. You ought to have been an actor.

JEAN: (*rising*) We can't go on like this, Miss Julie. Someone might come in and see us.

JULIE: Why would that matter?

JEAN: For the simple reason that they'd talk. And if you knew the way their tongues were wagging out there just now, you . . .

JULIE: What were they saying? Tell me. Sit down.

JEAN: (*sitting*) No offence meant, Miss, but . . . well, their language wasn't nice, and they were hinting . . . oh, you know quite well what. You're not a child, and if a lady's seen drinking alone at night with a man—and a servant at that—then . . .

JULIE: Then what? Besides, we're not alone. Kristin's here.

JEAN: Yes, asleep.

JULIE: I'll wake her up. (*Rises.*) Kristin, are you asleep? (KRISTIN *mumbles in her sleep.*) Kristin! Goodness, how she sleeps!

KRISTIN: (*in her sleep*) The Count's boots are cleaned—put the coffee on—yes, yes, at once . . . (*Mumbles incoherently.*)

JULIE: (*tweaking her nose*) Wake up, can't you!

JEAN: (*sharply*) Let her sleep.

JULIE: What?

JEAN: When you've been standing at the stove all day you're likely to be tired at night. And sleep should be respected.

JULIE: (*changing her tone*) What a nice idea. It does you credit. Thank you for it. (*Holds out her hand to him.*) Now come out and pick some lilac for me. (*During the following* KRISTIN *goes sleepily into her bedroom.*)

JEAN: Out with you, Miss Julie?

JULIE: Yes.

JEAN: It wouldn't do. It really wouldn't.

JULIE: I don't know what you mean. You can't possibly imagine that . . .

JEAN: I don't, but others do.

JULIE: What? That I'm in love with the valet?

JEAN: I'm not a conceited man, but such a thing's been known to happen, and to these rustics nothing's sacred.

JULIE: You, I take it, are an aristocrat.

JEAN: Yes, I am.

JULIE: And I am coming down in the world.

JEAN: Don't come down, Miss Julie. Take my advice. No one will believe you came down of your own accord. They'll all say you fell.

JULIE: I have a higher opinion of our people than you. Come and put it to the test. Come on. (*Gazes into his eyes.*)

JEAN: You're very strange, you know.

JULIE: Perhaps I am, but so are you. For that matter everything is strange. Life, human beings, everything, just scum drifting about on the water until it sinks—down and down. That reminds me of a dream I sometimes have, in which I'm on top of a pillar and can't see any way of getting down. When I look down I'm dizzy; I have to get down but I haven't the courage to jump. I can't stay there and I long to fall, but I don't fall. There's no respite. There can't be any peace at all for me until I'm down, right down on the ground. And if I did get to the ground I'd want to be under the ground . . . Have you ever felt like that?

JEAN: No. In my dream I'm lying under a great tree in a dark wood. I want to get up, up to the top of it, and look out over the bright landscape where the sun is shining and rob that high nest of its golden eggs. And I climb and climb, but the trunk is so thick and smooth and it's so far to the first branch. But I know if I can once reach that first branch I'll go to the top just as if I'm on a ladder. I haven't reached it yet, but I shall get there, even if only in my dreams.

JULIE: Here I am chattering about dreams with you. Come on. Only into the park. (*She takes his arm and they go towards the door.*)

JEAN: We must sleep on nine midsummer flowers tonight; then our dreams will come true, Miss Julie. (*They turn at the door. He has a hand to his eye.*)

JULIE: Have you got something in your eye? Let me see.

JEAN: Oh, it's nothing. Just a speck of dust. It'll be gone in a minute.

JULIE: My sleeve must have rubbed against you. Sit down and let me see to it. (*Takes him by the arm and makes him sit down, bends his head back and tries to get the speck out with the corner of her handkerchief.*) Keep still now, quite still. (*Slaps his hand.*) Do as I tell you. Why, I believe you're trembling, big, strong man though you are! (*Feels his biceps.*) What muscles!

JEAN: (*warning*) Miss Julie!

JULIE: Yes, Monsieur Jean?

JEAN: Attention. Je ne suis qu'un homme.

JULIE: Will you stay still! There now. It's out. Kiss my hand and say thank you.

JEAN: (*rising*) Miss Julie, listen. Kristin's gone to bed now. Will you listen?

JULIE: Kiss my hand first.

JEAN: Very well, but you'll have only yourself to blame.

JULIE: For what?

JEAN: For what! Are you still a child at twenty-five? Don't you know it's dangerous to play with fire?

JULIE: Not for me. I'm insured.

JEAN: (*bluntly*) No, you're not. And even if you are, there's still stuff here to kindle a flame.

JULIE: Meaning yourself?

JEAN: Yes. Not because I'm me, but because I'm a man and young and . . .

JULIE: And good-looking? What incredible conceit! A Don Juan perhaps? Or a Joseph? Good Lord, I do believe you are a Joseph!

JEAN: Do you?

JULIE: I'm rather afraid so. (JEAN *goes boldly up and tries to put his arms round her and kiss her. She boxes his ears.*) How dare you!

JEAN: Was that in earnest or a joke?

JULIE: In earnest.

JEAN: Then what went before was in earnest too. You take your games too seriously and that's dangerous. Anyhow I'm tired of playing now and beg leave to return to my work. The Count will want his boots first thing and it's past midnight now.

JULIE: Put those boots down.

JEAN: No. This is my work, which it's my duty to do. But I never undertook to be your playfellow and I never will be. I consider myself too good for that.

JULIE: You're proud.

JEAN: In some ways—not all.

JULIE: Have you even been in love?

JEAN: We don't put it that way, but I've been gone on quite a few girls. And once I went sick because I couldn't have the one I wanted. Sick, I mean, like those princes in the Arabian Nights who couldn't eat or drink for love.

JULIE: Who was she? (*No answer.*) Who was she?

JEAN: You can't force me to tell you that.

JULIE: If I ask as an equal, ask as a—friend? Who was she?

JEAN: You.

JULIE: (*sitting*) How absurd!

JEAN: Yes, ludicrous if you like. That's the story I wouldn't tell you before, see, but now I will . . . Do you know what the world looks like from below? No, you don't. No more than the hawks and falcons do whose backs one hardly ever sees because they're always soaring up aloft. I lived in a labourer's hovel with several other children and a pig, out in the grey fields where there isn't a single tree. But from the window I could see the wall round the Count's park with apple-trees above it. That was the Garden of Eden, guarded by many terrible angels with flaming swords. All the same I and the other boys managed to get to the tree of life. Does all this make you despise me?

JULIE: Goodness, all boys steal apples!

JEAN: You say that now, but all the same you do despise me. However, one time I went into the Garden of Eden with my mother to weed the onion beds. Close to the kitchen garden there was a Turkish pavilion hung all over with jasmine and honeysuckle. I hadn't any idea what it was used for, but I'd never seen such a beautiful building. People used to go in and then come out again, and one day the door was left open. I crept up and saw the walls covered with pictures of kings and emperors, and the windows had red curtains with fringes— you know now what the place was, don't you? I . . . (*Breaks off a piece of lilac and holds it for* JULIE *to smell. As he talks, she takes it from him.*) I had never been inside the manor, never seen anything but the church, and this was more beautiful. No matter where my thoughts went, they always came back—to that place. The longing went on growing in me to enjoy it fully, just once. Enfin, I sneaked in, gazed and admired. Then I heard someone coming. There was only one way out for the gentry, but for me there was another and I had no choice but to take it. (JULIE *drops the lilac on the table.*) Then I took to my heels, plunged through the raspberry canes, dashed across the strawberry beds and found myself on the rose terrace. There I saw a pink dress and a pair of white stockings—it was you. I crawled into a weed pile and lay there right under it among prickly thistles and damp rank earth. I watched you walking among the roses and said to myself: "If it's true that a thief can get to heaven and be with the angels, it's pretty strange that a labourer's child here on God's earth mayn't come in the park and play with the Count's daughter."

JULIE: *(sentimentally)* Do you think all poor children feel the way you did?

JEAN: *(taken aback, then rallying) All* poor children? . . . Yes, of course they do. Of course.

JULIE: It must be terrible to be poor.

JEAN: *(with exaggerated distress)* Oh yes, Miss Julie, yes. A dog may lie on the Countess's sofa, a horse may have his nose stroked by a young lady, but a servant . . . *(change of tone)* well, yes, now and then you meet one with guts enough to rise in the world, but how often? Anyhow, do you know what I did? Jumped in the millstream with my clothes on, was pulled out and got a hiding. But the next Sunday, when Father and all the rest went to Granny's, I managed to get left behind. Then I washed with soap and hot water, put my best clothes on and went to church so as to see you. I did see you and went home determined to die. But I wanted to die beautifully and peacefully, without any pain. Then I remembered it was dangerous to sleep under an elder bush. We had a big one in full bloom, so I stripped it and climbed into the oats-bin with the flowers. Have you ever noticed how smooth oats are? Soft to touch as human skin . . . Well, I closed the lid and shut my eyes, fell asleep, and when they woke me I was very ill. But I didn't die, as you see. What I meant by all that I don't know. There was no hope of winning you—you were simply a symbol of the hopelessness of ever getting out of the class I was born in.

JULIE: You put things very well, you know. Did you go to school?

JEAN: For a while. But I've read a lot of novels and been to the theatre. Besides, I've heard educated folk talking—that's what's taught me most.

JULIE: Do you stand round listening to what we're saying?

JEAN: Yes, of course. And I've heard quite a bit too! On the carriage box or rowing the boat. Once I heard you, Miss Julie, and one of your young lady friends . . .

JULIE: Oh! Whatever did you hear?

JEAN: Well, it wouldn't be nice to repeat it. And I must say I was pretty startled. I couldn't think where you had learnt such words. Perhaps, at bottom, there isn't as much difference between people as one's led to believe.

JULIE: How dare you! We don't behave as you do when we're engaged.

JEAN: (*looking hard at her*) Are you sure? It's no use making out so innocent to me.

JULIE: The man I gave my love to was a rotter.

JEAN: That's what you always say—afterwards.

JULIE: Always?

JEAN: I think it must be always. I've heard the expression several time in similar circumstances.

JULIE: What circumstances?

JEAN: Like those in question. The last time . . .

JULIE: (*rising*) Stop. I don't want to hear any more.

JEAN: Nor did *she*—curiously enough. May I go to bed now please?

JULIE: (*gently*) Go to bed on Midsummer Eve?

JEAN: Yes. Dancing with that crowd doesn't really amuse me.

JULIE: Get the key of the boathouse and row me out on the lake. I want to see the sun rise.

JEAN: Would that be wise?

JULIE: You sound as though you're frightened for your reputation.

JEAN: Why not? I don't want to be made a fool of, nor to be sent packing without a character when I'm trying to better myself. Besides, I have Kristin to consider.

JULIE: So now it's Kristin.

JEAN: Yes, but it's you I'm thinking about too. Take my advice and go to bed.

JULIE: Am I to take orders from you?

JEAN: Just this once, for your own sake. Please. It's very late and sleepiness goes to one's head and makes one rash. Go to bed. What's more, if my ears don't deceive me, I hear people coming this way. They'll be looking for me, and if they find us here, you're done for.

The CHORUS *approaches, singing. During the following dialogue the song is heard in snatches, and in full when the peasants enter.*

> *Out of the wood two women came,*
> *Tridiri-ralla, tridiri-ra.*
> *The feet of one were bare and cold,*
> *Tridiri-ralla-la.*
>
> *The other talked of bags of gold,*
> *Tridiri-ralla, tridiri-ra.*
> *But neither had a sou to her name,*
> *Tridiri-ralla-la.*
>
> *The bridal wreath I give to you,*
> *Tridiri-ralla, tridiri-ra.*
> *But to another I'll be true,*
> *Tridiri-ralla-la.*

JULIE: I know our people and I love them, just as they do me. Let them come. You'll see.

JEAN: No, Miss Julie, they don't love you. They take your food, then spit at it. You must believe me. Listen to them, just listen to what they're singing . . . No, don't listen.

JULIE: *(listening.)* What are they singing?

JEAN: They're mocking—you and me.

JULIE: Oh no! How horrible! What cowards!

JEAN: A pack like that's always cowardly. But against such odds there's nothing we can do but run away.

JULIE: Run away? Where to? We can't get out and we can't go into Kristin's room.

JEAN: Into mine then. Necessity knows no rules. And you can trust me. I really am your true and devoted friend.

JULIE: But supposing . . . supposing they were to look for you in there?

JEAN: I'll bolt the door, and if they try to break in I'll shoot. Come on. *(Pleading)* Please come.

JULIE: *(tensely)* Do you promise . . . ?

JEAN: I swear!

JULIE *goes quickly into his room and he excitedly follows her. Led by the fiddler, the peasants enter in festive attire with flowers in their hats. They put a barrel of beer and a keg of spirits, garlanded with leaves, on the table, fetch glasses and begin to carouse. The scene becomes a ballet. They form a ring and dance and sing and mime:* "Out of the wood two women came." *Finally they go out, still singing.*

JULIE *comes in alone. She looks at the havoc in the kitchen, wrings her hands, then takes out her powder puff and powders her face.*

JEAN *enters in high spirits.*

JEAN: Now you see! And you heard, didn't you? Do you still think it's possible for us to stay here?

JULIE: No, I don't. But what can we do?

JEAN: Run away. Far away. Take a journey.

JULIE: Journey? But where to?

JEAN: Switzerland. The Italian lakes. Ever been there?

JULIE: No. Is it nice?

JEAN: Ah! Eternal summer, oranges, evergreens . . . ah!

JULIE: But what would we do there?

JEAN: I'll start a hotel. First-class accommodation and first-class customers.

JULIE: Hotel?

JEAN: There's life for you. New faces all the time, new languages—no time for nerves or worries, no need to look for something to do—work rolling up of its own accord. Bells ringing night and day, trains whistling, buses coming and going, and all the time gold pieces rolling on to the counter. There's life for you!

JULIE: For *you*. And I?

JEAN: Mistress of the house, ornament of the firm. With your looks, and your style . . . oh, it's bound to be a success! Terrific! You'll sit like a queen in the office and set your slaves in motion by pressing an electric button. The guests will file past your throne and nervously lay their treasure on your table. You've no idea the way people tremble when they get their bills. I'll salt the bills and you'll sugar them with your sweetest smiles. Ah, let's get away from here! (*Produces a time-table.*) At once, by the next train. We shall be at Malmö at six-thirty, Hamburg eight-forty next morning, Frankfurt-Basle the following day, and Como by the St. Gothard pass in—let's see—three days. Three days!

JULIE: That's all very well. But Jean, you must give me courage. Tell me you love me. Come and take me in your arms.

JEAN: (*reluctantly*) I'd like to, but I daren't. Not again in this house. I love you—that goes without saying. You can't doubt that, Miss Julie, can you?

JULIE: (*shyly, very feminine*) Miss? Call me Julie. There aren't any barriers between us now. Call me Julie.

JEAN: (*uneasily*) I can't. As long as we're in this house, there are barriers between us. There's the past and there's the Count. I've never been so servile to anyone as I am to him. I've only got to see his gloves on a chair to feel small. I've only to hear his bell and I shy like a horse. Even now, when I look at his boots, standing there so proud and stiff, I feel my back beginning to bend. (*Kicks the boots.*) It's those old, narrow-minded notions drummed into us as children . . . but they can soon be forgotten. You've only got to get to another country, a republic, and people will bend themselves double before my porter's livery. Yes, double they'll bend themselves, but I shan't. I wasn't born to bend. I've got guts, I've got character, and once I reach that first branch, you'll watch me climb. Today I'm valet, next year I'll be proprietor, in ten years I'll have made a fortune, and then I'll go to Roumania, get myself decorated and I may, I only say *may*, mind you, end up as a Count.

JULIE: (*sadly*) That would be very nice.

JEAN: You see in Roumania one can buy a title, and then you'll be a Countess after all. My Countess.

JULIE: What do I care about all that? I'm putting those things behind me. Tell me you love me, because if you don't . . . if you don't, what am I?

JEAN: I'll tell you a thousand times over—later. But not here. No sentimentality now or everything will be lost. We must consider this thing calmly like reasonable people. (*Takes a cigar, cuts and lights it.*) You sit down there and I'll sit here and we'll talk as if nothing has happened.

JULIE: My God, have you no feelings at all?

JEAN: Nobody has more. But I know how to control them.

JULIE: A short time ago you were kissing my shoe. And now . . .

JEAN: (*harshly*) Yes, that was then. Now we have something else to think about.

JULIE: Don't speak to me so brutally.

JEAN: I'm not. Just sensibly. One folly's been committed, don't let's have more. The Count will be back at any moment and we've got to settle our future before that. Now, what do you think of my plans? Do you approve?

JULIE: It seems a very good idea—but just one thing. Such a big undertaking would need a lot of capital. Have you got any?

JEAN: (*chewing his cigar*) I certainly have. I've got my professional skill, my wide experience and my knowledge of foreign languages. That's capital worth having, it seems to me.

JULIE: But it won't buy even one railway ticket.

JEAN: Quite true. That's why I need a backer to advance some ready cash.

JULIE: How could you get that at a moment's notice?

JEAN: You must get it, if you want to be my partner.

JULIE: I can't. I haven't any money of my own. (*Pause.*)

JEAN: Then the whole thing's off.

JULIE: And . . . ?

JEAN: We go on as we are.

JULIE: Do you think I'm going to stay under this roof as your mistress? With everyone pointing at me. Do you think I can face my father after this? No. Take me away from here, away from this shame, this humiliation. Oh my God, what have I done? My God, my God! (*Weeps.*)

JEAN: So that's the tune now, is it? What have you done? Same as many before you.

JULIE: (*hysterically*) And now you despise me. I'm falling, I'm falling.

JEAN: Fall as far as me and I'll lift you up again.

JULIE: Why was I so terribly attracted to you? The weak to the strong, the falling to the rising? Or was it love? Is that love? Do you know what love is?

JEAN: Do I? You bet I do. Do you think I never had a girl before?

JULIE: The things you say, the things you think!

JEAN: That's what life's taught me, and that's what I am. It's no good getting hysterical or giving yourself airs. We're both in the same boat now. Here, my dear girl, let me give you a glass of something special. (*Opens the drawer, takes out the bottle of wine and fills two used glasses.*)

JULIE: Where did you get that wine?

JEAN: From the cellar.

JULIE: My father's burgundy.

JEAN: Why not, for his son-in-law?

JULIE: And I drink beer.

JEAN: That only shows your taste's not so good as mine.

JULIE: Thief!

JEAN: Are you going to tell on me?

JULIE: Oh God! The accomplice of a petty thief! Was I blind drunk? Have I dreamt this whole night? Midsummer Eve, the night for innocent merrymaking.

JEAN: Innocent, eh?

JULIE: Is anyone on earth as wretched as I am now?

JEAN: Why should *you* be? After such a conquest. What about Kristin in there? Don't you think she has any feelings?

JULIE: I did think so, but I don't any longer. No. A menial is a menial . . .

JEAN: And a whore is a whore.

JULIE: (*falling to her knees, her hands clasped*) O God in heaven, put an end to my miserable life! Lift me out of this filth in which I'm sinking. Save me! Save me!

JEAN: I must admit I'm sorry for you. When I was in the onion bed and saw you up there among the roses, I . . . yes, I'll tell you now . . . I had the same dirty thoughts as all boys.

JULIE: You, who wanted to die because of me?

JEAN: In the oats-bin? That was just talk.

JULIE: Lies, you mean.

JEAN: (*getting sleepy*) More or less. I think I read a story in some paper about a chimney-sweep who shut himself up in a chest full of lilac because he'd been summonsed for not supporting some brat . . .

JULIE: So this is what you're like.

JEAN: I had to think up something. It's always the fancy stuff that catches the women.

JULIE: Beast!

JEAN: Merde!

JULIE: Now you have seen the falcon's back.

JEAN: Not exactly its *back*.

JULIE: I was to be the first branch.

JEAN: But the branch was rotten.

JULIE: I was to be a hotel sign.

JEAN: And I the hotel.

JULIE: Sit at your counter, attract your clients and cook their accounts.

JEAN: I'd have done that myself.

JULIE: That any human being can be so steeped in filth!

JEAN: Clean it up then.

JULIE: Menial! Lackey! Stand up when I speak to you.

JEAN: Menial's whore, lackey's harlot, shut your mouth and get out of here! Are you the one to lecture me for being coarse? Nobody of my kind would ever be as coarse as you were tonight. Do you think any servant girl would throw herself at a man that way? Have you ever seen a girl of my class asking for it like that? I haven't. Only animals and prostitutes.

JULIE: *(broken)* Go on. Hit me, trample on me—it's all I deserve. I'm rotten. But help me! If there's any way out at all, help me.

JEAN: *(more gently)* I'm not denying myself a share in the honour of seducing you, but do you think anybody in my place would have dared look in your direction if you yourself hadn't asked for it? I'm still amazed . . .

JULIE: And proud.

JEAN: Why not? Though I must admit the victory was too easy to make me lose my head.

JULIE: Go on hitting me.

JEAN: *(rising)* No. On the contrary I apologise for what I've said. I don't hit a person who's down—least of all a woman. I can't deny there's a certain satisfaction in finding that what dazzled one below was just moonshine, that that falcon's back is grey after all, that there's powder on the lovely cheek, that polished nails can have black tips, that the handkerchief is dirty although it smells of scent. On the other hand it hurts to find that what I was struggling to reach wasn't high and isn't real. It hurts to see you fallen so low you're lower than your own cook. Hurts like when you see the last flowers of summer lashed to pieces by rain and turned to mud.

JULIE: You're talking as if you're already my superior.

JEAN: I am. I might make you a Countess, but you could never make me a Count, you know.

JULIE: But I am the child of a Count, and you could never be that.

JEAN: True, but I might be the father of Counts if . . .

JULIE: You're a thief. I'm not.

JEAN: There are worse things that being a thief—much lower. Besides, when I'm in a place I regard myself as a member of the family to some extent, as one of the children. You don't call it stealing when children pinch a berry from overladen bushes. (*His passion is roused again.*) Miss Julie, you're a glorious woman, far too good for a man like me. You were carried away by some kind of madness, and now you're trying to cover up your mistake by persuading yourself you're in love with me. You're not, although you may find me physically attractive, which means your love's no better than mine. But I wouldn't be satisfied with being nothing but an animal for you, and I could never make you love me.

JULIE: Are you sure?

JEAN: You think there's a chance? Of my loving you, yes, of course. You're beautiful, refined (*takes her hand*) educated, and you can be nice when you want to be. The fire you kindle in a man isn't likely to go out. (*Puts his arm round her.*) You're like mulled wine, full of spices, and your kisses . . . (*He tries to pull her to him, but she breaks away.*)

JULIE: Let go of me! You won't win me that way.

JEAN: Not that way, how then? Not by kisses and fine speeches, not by planning the future and saving you from shame? How then?

JULIE: How? How? I don't know. There isn't any way. I loathe you—loathe you as I loathe rats, but I can't escape from you.

JEAN: Escape with me.

JULIE: (*pulling herself together*) Escape? Yes, we must escape. But I'm so tired. Give me a glass of wine. (*He pours it out. She looks at her watch.*) First we must talk. We still have a little time. (*Empties the glass and holds it out for more.*)

JEAN: Don't drink like that. You'll get tipsy.

JULIE: What's that matter?

JEAN: What's it matter? It's vulgar to get drunk. Well, what have you got to say?

JULIE: We've got to run away, but we must talk first—or rather, I must, for so far you've done all the talking. You've told me about your life, now I want to tell you about mine, so that we really know each other before we begin this journey together.

JEAN: Wait. Excuse my saying so, but don't you think you may be sorry afterwards if you give away your secrets to me?

JULIE: Aren't you my friend?

JEAN: On the whole. But don't rely on me.

JULIE: You can't mean that. But anyway everyone knows my secrets. Listen. My mother wasn't well-born; she came of quite humble people, and was brought up with all those new ideas of sex-equality and women's rights and so on. She thought marriage was quite wrong. So when my father proposed to her, she said she would never become his *wife* . . . but in the end she did. I came into the world, as far as I can make out, against my mother's will, and I was left to run wild, but I had to do all the things a boy does—to prove women are as good as men. I had to wear boy's clothes; I was taught to handle horses—and I wasn't allowed in the dairy. She made me groom and harness and go out hunting; I even had to try to plough. All the men on the estate were given the women's jobs, and the women the men's, until the whole place went to rack and ruin and we were the laughing-stock of the neighbourhood. At last my father seems to have come to his senses and rebelled. He changed everything and ran the place his own way. My mother got ill—I don't know what was the matter with her, but she used to have strange attacks and hide herself in the attic or the garden. Sometimes she stayed out all night. Then came the great fire which you have heard people talking about. The house and the stables and the barns—the whole place burnt to the ground. In very suspicious circumstances. Because the accident happened the very day the insurance had to be renewed, and my father had sent the new premium, but through some carelessness of the messenger it arrived too late. (*Refills her glass and drinks.*)

JEAN: Don't drink any more.

JULIE: Oh, what does it matter? We were destitute and had to sleep in the carriages. My father didn't know how to get money to rebuild, and then my mother suggested he should borrow from an old friend of hers, a local brick manufacturer. My father got the loan and, to his surprise, without having to pay interest. So the place was rebuilt. (*Drinks.*) Do you know who set fire to it?

JEAN: Your lady mother.

JULIE: Do you know who the brick manufacturer was?

JEAN: Your mother's lover?

JULIE: Do you know whose the money was?

JEAN: Wait . . . no, I don't know that.

JULIE: It was my mother's.

JEAN: In other words the Count's, unless there was a settlement.

JULIE: There wasn't any settlement. My mother had a little money of her own which she didn't want my father to control, so she invested it with her—friend.

JEAN: Who grabbed it.

JULIE: Exactly. He appropriated it. My father came to know all this. He couldn't bring an action, couldn't pay his wife's lover, nor prove it was his wife's money. That was my mother's revenge because he made himself master in his own house. He nearly shot himself then—at least there's a rumour he tried and didn't bring it off. So he went on living, and my mother had to pay dearly for what she'd done. Imagine what those five years were like for me. My natural sympathies were with my father, yet I took my mother's side, because I didn't know the facts. I'd learnt from her to hate and distrust men—you know how she loathed the whole male sex. And I swore to her I'd never become the slave of any man.

JEAN: And so you got engaged to that attorney.

JULIE: So that he should be my slave.

JEAN: But he wouldn't be.

JULIE: Oh yes, he wanted to be, but he didn't have the chance. I got bored with him.

JEAN: Is that what I saw—in the stable-yard?

JULIE: What did you see?

JEAN: What I saw was him breaking off the engagement.

JULIE: That's a lie. It was I who broke it off. Did he say it was him? The cad.

JEAN: He's not a cad. Do you hate men, Miss Julie?

JULIE: Yes . . . most of the time. But when that weakness comes, oh . . . the shame!

JEAN: Then do you hate me?

JULIE: Beyond words. I'd gladly have you killed like an animal.

JEAN: Quick as you'd shoot a mad dog, eh?

JULIE: Yes.

JEAN: But there's nothing here to shoot with—and there isn't a dog. So what do we do now?

JULIE: Go abroad.

JEAN: To make each other miserable for the rest of our lives?

JULIE: No, to enjoy ourselves for a day or two, for a week, for as long as enjoyment lasts, and then—to die . . .

JEAN: Die? How silly! I think it would be far better to start a hotel.

JULIE: (*without listening*) . . . die on the shores of Lake Como, where the sun always shines and at Christmas time there are green trees and glowing oranges.

JEAN: Lake Como's a rainy hole and I didn't see any oranges outside the shops. But it's a good place for tourists. Plenty of villas to be rented by—er—honeymoon couples. Profitable business that. Know why? Because they all sign a lease for six months and all leave after three weeks.

JULIE: (*naïvely*) After three weeks? Why?

JEAN: They quarrel, of course. But the rent has to be paid just the same. And then it's let again. So it goes on and on, for there's plenty of love although it doesn't last long.

JULIE: You don't want to die with me?

JEAN: I don't want to die at all. For one thing I like living and for another I consider suicide's a sin against the Creator who gave us life.

JULIE: You believe in God—*you?*

JEAN: Yes, of course. And I go to church every Sunday. Look here, I'm tired of all this. I'm going to bed.

JULIE: Indeed! And do you think I'm going to leave things like this? Don't you know what you owe the woman you've ruined?

JEAN: (*taking out his purse and throwing a silver coin on the table.*) There you are. I don't want to be in anybody's debt.

JULIE: (*pretending not to notice the insult*) Don't you know what the law is?

JEAN: There's no law unfortunately that punishes a woman for seducing a man.

JULIE: But can you see anything for it but to go abroad, get married and then divorce?

JEAN: What if I refuse this mésalliance?

JULIE: Mésalliance?

JEAN: Yes, for me. I'm better bred than you, see! Nobody in my family committed arson.

JULIE: How do you know?

JEAN: Well, you can't prove otherwise, because we haven't any family records outside the Registrar's office. But I've seen your family tree in that book on the drawing-room table. Do you know who the founder of your family was? A miller who let his wife sleep with the King one night during the Danish war. I haven't any ancestors like that. I haven't any ancestors at all, but I might become one.

JULIE: This is what I get for confiding in someone so low, for sacrificing my family honour . . .

JEAN: Dishonour! Well, I told you so. One shouldn't drink, because then one talks. And one shouldn't talk.

JULIE: Oh, how ashamed I am, how bitterly ashamed! If at least you loved me!

JEAN: Look here—for the last time—what do you want? Am I to burst into tears? Am I to jump over your riding whip? Shall I kiss you and carry you off to Lake Como for three weeks, after which . . . What am I to do? What do you want? This is getting unbearable, but that's what comes of playing around with women. Miss Julie, I can see how miserable you are; I know you're going through hell, but I don't understand you. We don't have scenes like this; we don't go in for hating each other. We make love for fun in our spare time, but we haven't all day and all night for it like you. I think you must be ill. I'm sure you're ill.

JULIE: Then you must be kind to me. You sound almost human now.

JEAN: Well, be human yourself. You spit at me, then won't let me wipe it off—on you.

JULIE: Help me, help me! Tell me what to do, where to go.

JEAN: Jesus, as if I knew!

JULIE: I've been mad, raving mad, but there must be a way out.

JEAN: Stay here and keep quiet. Nobody knows anything.

JULIE: I can't. People do know. Kristin knows.

JEAN: They don't know and they wouldn't believe such a thing.

JULIE: (*hesitating*) But—it might happen again.

JEAN: That's true.

JULIE: And there might be—consequences.

JEAN: (*in panic*) Consequences! Fool that I am I never thought of that. Yes, there's nothing for it but to go. At once. I can't come with you. That would be a complete giveaway. You must go alone—abroad—anywhere.

JULIE: Alone? Where to? I can't.

JEAN: You must. And before the Count gets back. If you stay, we know what will happen. Once you've sinned you feel you might as well go on, as the harm's done. Then you get more and more reckless and in the end you're found out. No. You must go abroad. Then write to the Count and tell him everything, except that it was me. He'll never guess that—and I don't think he'll want to.

JULIE: I'll go if you come with me.

JEAN: Are you crazy, woman? "Miss Julie elopes with valet." Next day it would be in the headlines, and the Count would never live it down.

JULIE: I can't go. I can't stay. I'm so tired, so completely worn out. Give me orders. Set me going. I can't think any more, can't act . . .

JEAN: You see what weaklings you are. Why do you give yourselves airs and turn up your noses as if you're the lords of creation? Very well, I'll give you your orders. Go upstairs and dress. Get money for the journey and come down here again.

JULIE: *(softly)* Come up with me.

JEAN: To your room? Now you've gone crazy again. *(Hesitates a moment.)* No! Go along at once. *(Takes her hand and pulls her to the door.)*

JULIE: *(as she goes)* Speak kindly to me, Jean.

JEAN: Orders always sound unkind. Now you know. Now you know. *(Left alone, JEAN sighs with relief, sits down at the table, takes out a note-book and pencil and adds up figures, now and then aloud. Dawn begins to break.)*

KRISTIN *enters dressed for church, carrying his white dickey and tie.*

KRISTIN: Lord Jesus, look at the state the place is in! What have you been up to? *(Turns out the lamp.)*

JEAN: Oh, Miss Julie invited the crowd in. Did you sleep through it? Didn't you hear anything?

KRISTIN: I slept like a log.

JEAN: And dressed for church already.

KRISTIN: Yes, you promised to come to Communion with me today.

JEAN: Why, so I did. And you've got my bib and tucker, I see. Come on then. *(Sits. KRISTIN begins to put his things on. Pause. Sleepily.)* What's the lesson today?

KRISTIN: It's about the beheading of John the Baptist, I think.

JEAN: That's sure to be horribly long. Hi, you're choking me! Oh Lord, I'm so sleepy, so sleepy!

KRISTIN: Yes, what have you been doing up all night? You look absolutely green.

JEAN: Just sitting here talking with Miss Julie.

KRISTIN: She doesn't know what's proper, that one. *(Pause.)*

JEAN: I say, Kristin.

KRISTIN: What?

JEAN: It's queer really, isn't it, when you come to think of it? Her.

KRISTIN: What's queer?

JEAN: The whole thing. (*Pause.*)

KRISTIN: (*looking at the half-filled glasses on the table.*) Have you been drinking together too?

JEAN: Yes.

KRISTIN: More shame you. Look me straight in the face.

JEAN: Yes.

KRISTIN: Is it possible? Is it possible?

JEAN: (*after a moment*) Yes, it is.

KRISTIN: Oh! This I would never have believed. How low!

JEAN: You're not jealous of her, surely?

KRISTIN: No, I'm not. If it had been Clara or Sophie I'd have scratched your eyes out. But not of her. I don't know why; that's how it is though. But it's disgusting.

JEAN: You're angry with her then.

KRISTIN: No. With you. It was wicked of you, very very wicked. Poor girl. And, mark my words, I won't stay here any longer now—in a place where one can't respect one's employers.

JEAN: Why should one respect them?

KRISTIN: You should know since you're so smart. But you don't want to stay in the service of people who aren't respectable, do you? I wouldn't demean myself.

JEAN: But it's rather a comfort to find out they're no better than us.

KRISTIN: I don't think so. If they're not better there's nothing for us to live up to. Oh and think of the Count! Think of him. He's been through so much already. No, I won't stay in the place any longer. A fellow like you too! If it had been that attorney now or somebody of her own class.

JEAN: Why, what's wrong with . . .

KRISTIN: Oh, you're all right in your own way, but when all's said and done there is a difference between one class and another. No, this is something I'll never be able to stomach. That our young lady who was so proud and so down on men you'd never believe she'd let one come near her should go and give herself to one like you. She who wanted to have poor Diana shot for running after the lodge-keeper's pug. No, I must say. . . ! Well, I won't stay here any longer. On the twenty-fourth of October I quit.

JEAN: And then?

KRISTIN: Well, since you mention it, it's about time you began to look around, if we're ever going to get married.

JEAN: But what am I to look for? I shan't get a place like this when I'm married.

KRISTIN: I know you won't. But you might get a job as porter or caretaker in some public institution. Government rations are small but sure, and there's a pension for the widow and children.

JEAN: That's all very fine, but it's not in my line to start thinking at once about dying for my wife and children. I must say I had rather bigger ideas.

KRISTIN: You and your ideas! You've got obligations too, and you'd better start thinking about them.

JEAN: Don't *you* start pestering me about obligations. I've had enough of that. (*Listens to a sound upstairs.*) Anyway we've plenty of time to work things out. Go and get ready now and we'll be off to church.

KRISTIN: Who's that walking about upstairs?

JEAN: Don't know—unless it's Clara.

KRISTIN: (*going*) You don't think the Count could have come back without our hearing him?

JEAN: (*scared*) The Count? No, he can't have. He'd have rung for me.

KRISTIN: God help us! I've never known such goings on. (*Exit.*)

The sun has now risen and is shining on the treetops. The light gradually changes until it slants in through the windows. JEAN *goes to the door and beckons.* JULIE *enters in travelling clothes, carrying a small bird-cage covered with a cloth which she puts on a chair.*

JULIE: I'm ready.

JEAN: Hush! Kristin's up.

JULIE: (*in a very nervous state*) Does she suspect anything?

JEAN: Not a thing. But, my God, what a sight you are!

JULIE: Sight? What do you mean?

JEAN: You're white as a corpse and—pardon me—your face is dirty.

JULIE: Let me wash then. (*Goes to the sink and washes her face and hands.*) There. Give me a towel. Oh! The sun is rising!

JEAN: And that breaks the spell.

JULIE: Yes. The spell of Midsummer Eve . . . But listen Jean. Come with me. I've got the money.

JEAN: (*sceptically*) Enough?

JULIE: Enough to start with. Come with me. I can't travel alone today. It's Midsummer Day, remember. I'd be packed into a suffocating train among crowds of people who'd all stare at me. And it would stop at every station while I yearned for wings. No, I can't do that, I simply can't. There will be memories too; memories of Midsummer

Days when I was little. The leafy church—birch and lilac—the gaily spread dinner table, relatives, friends—evening in the park—dancing and music and flowers and fun. Oh, however far you run away—there'll always be memories in the baggage car—and remorse and guilt.

JEAN: I will come with you, but quickly now then, before it's too late. At once.

JULIE: Put on your things. (*Picks up the cage.*)

JEAN: No luggage mind. That would give us away.

JULIE: No, only what we can take with us in the carriage.

JEAN: (*fetching his hat*) What on earth have you got there? What is it?

JULIE: Only my greenfinch. I don't want to leave it behind.

JEAN: Well, I'll be damned! We're to take a bird-cage along, are we? You're crazy. Put that cage down.

JULIE: It's the only thing I'm taking from my home. The only living creature who cares for me since Diana went off like that. Don't be cruel. Let me take it.

JEAN: Put that cage down, I tell you—and don't talk so loud. Kristin will hear.

JULIE: No, I won't leave it in strange hands. I'd rather you killed it.

JEAN: Give the little beast here then and I'll wring its neck.

JULIE: But don't hurt it, don't . . . no, I can't.

JEAN: Give it here. I *can.*

JULIE: (*taking the bird out of the cage and kissing it*) Dear little Serena, must you die and leave your mistress?

JEAN: Please don't make a scene. It's *your* life and future we're worrying about. Come on, quick now!! (*He snatches the bird from her, puts it on a board and picks up a chopper.* JULIE *turns away.*) You should have learnt how to kill chickens instead of target-shooting. Then you wouldn't faint at a drop of blood.

JULIE: (*screaming*) Kill me too! Kill me! You who can butcher an innocent creature without a quiver. Oh, how I hate you, how I loathe you! There is blood between us now. I curse the hour I first saw you. I curse the hour I was conceived in my mother's womb.

JEAN: What's the use of cursing. Let's go.

JULIE: (*going to the chopping-block as if drawn against her will*) No, I won't go yet. I can't . . . I must look. Listen! There's a carriage. (*Listens without taking her eyes off the board and chopper.*) You don't think I can bear the sight of blood. You think I'm so weak. Oh, how I should like to see your blood and your brains on a chopping-block! I'd like to see the whole of your sex swimming like that in a sea of blood. I think I could drink out of your skull, bathe my feet in your broken breast and eat your heart roasted whole. You think I'm weak. You think I love you, that my womb yearned for your seed and I want to carry your offspring under my heart and nourish it with my blood. You think I want to bear your child and take your name. By the way, what is your name? I've never heard your surname. I don't suppose you've got one. I should be "Mrs. Hovel" or "Madam Dunghill." You dog wearing my collar, you lackey with my crest on your buttons! I share you with my cook; I'm my own servant's rival! Oh! Oh! Oh! . . . You think I'm coward and will run away. No, now I'm going to stay— and let the storm break. My father will come back . . . find his desk broken open . . . his money gone. Then he'll ring that bell—twice for the valet—and then he'll send for the police . . . and I shall tell everything. Oh how wonderful to make an end of it all—a real end! He has a stroke and dies and that's the end of all of us. Just peace and quietness . . . eternal rest. The coat of arms broken on the coffin and the Count's line extinct . . . But the valet's line goes on in an orphanage, wins laurels in the gutter and ends in jail.

JEAN: There speaks the noble blood! Bravo, Miss Julie. But now, don't let the cat out of the bag.

KRISTIN *enters dressed for church, carrying a prayer-book.* JULIE *rushes to her and flings herself into her arms for protection.*

JULIE: Help me, Kristin! Protect me from this man!

KRISTIN: (*unmoved and cold*) What goings-on for a feast day morning! (*Sees the board.*) And what a filthy mess. What's it all about? Why are you screaming and carrying on so?

JULIE: Kristin, you're a woman and my friend. Beware of that scoundrel!

JEAN: (*embarrassed*) While you ladies are talking things over, I'll go and shave. (*Slips into his room.*)

JULIE: You must understand. You must listen to me.

KRISTIN: I certainly don't understand such loose ways. Where are you off to in those travelling clothes? And he had his hat on, didn't he, eh?

JULIE: Listen, Kristin. Listen, I'll tell you everything.

KRISTIN: I don't want to know anything.

JULIE: You must listen.

KRISTIN: What to? Your nonsense with Jean? I don't care a rap about that; it's nothing to do with me. But if you're thinking of getting him to run off with you, we'll soon put a stop to that.

JULIE: (*very nervously*) Please try to be calm, Kristin, and listen. I can't stay here, nor can Jean—so we must go abroad.

KRISTIN: Hm, hm!

JULIE: (*brightening*) But you see, I've had an idea. Supposing we all three go—abroad—to Switzerland and start a hotel together . . . I've got some money, you see . . . and Jean and I could run the whole thing—and I thought you would take charge of the kitchen. Wouldn't that be splendid? Say yes, do. If you come with us everything will be fine. Oh do say yes! (*Puts her arms round* KRISTIN.)

KRISTIN: (*coolly thinking*) Hm, hm.

JULIE: (*presto tempo*) You've never travelled, Kristin. You should go abroad and see the world. You've no idea how nice it is travelling by train—new faces all the time and new countries. On our way through Hamburg we'll go to the zoo—you'll love that—and we'll go to the theatre and the opera too . . . and when we get to Munich there'll be the museums, dear, and pictures by Rubens and Raphael— the great painters, you know . . . You've heard of Munich, haven't you? Where King Ludwig lived—you know, the king who went mad. . . . We'll see his castles—some of his castles are still just like in fairy-tales . . . and from there it's not far to Switzerland—and the Alps. Think of the Alps, Kristin dear, covered with snow in the middle of summer . . . and there are oranges there and trees that are green the whole year round . . . (JEAN *is seen in the door of his room, sharpening his razor on a strop which he holds with his teeth and his left hand. He listens to the talk with satisfaction and now and then nods approval.* JULIE *continues, tempo prestissimo.*)

And then we'll get a hotel . . . and I'll sit at the desk, while Jean receives the guests and goes out marketing and writes letters . . . There's life for you! Trains whistling, buses driving up, bells ringing upstairs and downstairs . . . and I shall make out the bills—and I shall cook them too . . . you've no idea how nervous travellers are when it comes to paying their bills. And you—you'll sit like a queen in the kitchen . . . of course there won't be any standing at the stove for you. You'll always have to be nicely dressed and ready to be seen, and with your looks—no, I'm not flattering you—one fine day you'll catch yourself a husband . . . some rich Englishman, I shouldn't wonder—they're the ones who are easy (*slowing down*) to catch . . . and then we'll get rich and build ourselves a villa on Lake Como . . . of course it rains there a little now and then—but (*dully*) the sun must shine there too sometimes—even though it seems gloomy and if not—then we can come home again—come back (*pause*) here—or somewhere else . . .

KRISTIN: Look here, Miss Julie, do you believe all that yourself?

JULIE: (*exhausted*) Do I believe it?

KRISTIN: Yes.

JULIE: (*wearily*) I don't know. I don't believe anything any more. (*Sinks down on the bench; her head in her arms on the table.*) Nothing. Nothing at all.

KRISTIN: (*turning to* JEAN) So you meant to beat it, did you?

JEAN: (*disconcerted, putting the razor on the table*) Beat it? What are you talking about? You've heard Miss Julie's plan, and though she's tired now with being up all night, it's a perfectly sound plan.

KRISTIN: Oh, is it? If you thought I'd work for that . . .

JEAN: (*interrupting*) Kindly use decent language in front of your mistress. Do you hear?

KRISTIN: Mistress?

JEAN: Yes.

KRISTIN: Well, well, just listen to that!

JEAN: Yes, it would be a good thing if you did listen and talked less. Miss Julie is your mistress and what's made you lose your respect for her now ought to make you feel the same about yourself.

KRISTIN: I've always had enough self-respect——

JEAN: To despise other people.

KRISTIN: —not to go below my own station. Has the Count's cook ever gone with the groom or the swineherd? Tell me that.

JEAN: No, you were lucky enough to have a high-class chap for your beau.

KRISTIN: High-class all right—selling the oats out of the Count's stable.

JEAN: You're a fine one to talk—taking a commission on the groceries and bribes from the butcher.

KRISTIN: What the devil . . . ?

JEAN: And now you can't feel any respect for your employers. You, you!

KRISTIN: Are you coming to church with me? I should think you need a good sermon after your fine deeds.

JEAN: No, I'm not going to church today. You can go alone and confess your own sins.

KRISTIN: Yes, I'll do that and bring back enough forgiveness to cover yours too. The Saviour suffered and died on the cross for all our sins, and if we go to Him with faith and a penitent heart, He takes all our sins upon Himself.

JEAN: Even grocery thefts?

JULIE: Do you believe that, Kristin?

KRISTIN: That is my living faith, as sure as I stand here. The faith I learnt as a child and have kept grace ever since, Miss Julie. "But where sin abounded, grace did much more abound."

JULIE: Oh, if I had your faith! Oh, if . . .

KRISTIN: But you see you can't have it without God's special grace, and it's not given to all to have that.

JULIE: Who is it given to then?

KRISTIN: That's the great secret of the workings of grace, Miss Julie. God is no respector of persons, and with Him the last shall be first . . .

JULIE: Then I suppose He does respect the last.

KRISTIN: (*continuing*) . . . and it is easier for a camel to go through the eye of a needle than for a rich man to enter into the kingdom of God. That's how it is, Miss Julie. Now I'm going—alone, and on my way I shall tell the groom not to let any of the horses out, in case anyone should want to leave before the Count gets back. Goodbye. (*Exit.*)

JEAN: What a devil! And all on account of a greenfinch.

JULIE: (*wearily*) Never mind the greenfinch. Do you see any way out of this, any end to it?

JEAN: (*pondering*) No.

JULIE: If you were in my place, what would you do?

JEAN: In your place? Wait a bit. If I was a woman—a lady of rank who had—fallen. I don't know. Yes, I do know now.

JULIE: (*picking up the razor and making a gesture*) This?

JEAN: Yes. But *I* wouldn't do it, you know. There's a difference between us.

JULIE: Because you're a man and I'm a woman? What is the difference?

JEAN: The usual difference—between man and woman.

JULIE: (*holding the razor*) I'd like to. But I can't. My father couldn't either, that time he wanted to.

JEAN: No, he didn't want to. He had to be revenged first.

JULIE: And now my mother is revenged again, through me.

JEAN: Didn't you ever love your father, Miss Julie?

JULIE: Deeply, but I must have hated him too—unconsciously. And he let me be brought up to despise my own sex, to be half woman, half man. Whose fault is what's happened? My father's, my mother's or my own? My own? I haven't anything that's my own. I haven't one single thought that I didn't get from my father, one emotion that didn't come from my mother, and as for this last idea—about all people's being equal—I got that from him, my fiancé—that's why I call him a cad. How can it be my fault? Push the responsibility on to Jesus, like Kristin does? No, I'm too proud and—thanks to my father's teaching—too intelligent. As for all that about a rich person not being able to get into heaven, it's just a lie, but Kristin, who has money in the savings-bank, will certainly not get in. Whose fault is it? What does it matter whose fault it is? In any case I must take the blame and bear the consequences.

JEAN: Yes, but . . . (*There are two sharp rings on the bell.* JULIE *jumps to her feet.* JEAN *changes into his livery.*) The Count is back. Supposing Kristin . . . (*Goes to the speaking-tube, presses it and listens.*)

JULIE: Has he been to his desk yet?

JEANS This is Jean, sir. (*Listens.*) Yes, sir. (*Listens.*) Yes, sir, very good, sir. (*Listens.*) At once, sir? (*Listens.*) Very good, sir. In half an hour.

JULIE: (*in panic*) What did he say? My God, what did he say?

JEAN: He ordered his boots and his coffee in half an hour.

JULIE: Then there's half an hour . . . Oh, I'm so tired! I can't do anything. Can't be sorry, can't run away, can't stay, can't live—can't die. Help me. Order me, and I'll obey like a dog. Do me this last service—save my honour, save his name. You know what I ought to do, but haven't the strength to do. Use your strength and order me to do it.

JEAN: I don't know why—I can now—I don't understand . . . It's just as if this coat made me—I can't give you orders—and now that the Count has spoken to me—I can't quite explain, but . . . well, that devil of a lackey is bending my back again. I believe if the Count came down now and ordered me to cut my throat, I'd do it on the spot.

JULIE: Then pretend you're him and I'm you. You did some fine acting before, when you knelt to me and played the aristocrat. Or . . . Have you ever seen a hypnotist at the theatre? (*He nods.*) He says to the person "Take the broom," and he takes it. He says "Sweep," and he sweeps . . .

JEAN: But the person has to be asleep.

JULIE: (*as if in a trance*) I am asleep already . . . the whole room has turned to smoke—and you look like a stove—a stove like a man in black with a tall hat—your eyes are glowing like coals when the fire is low—and your face is a white patch like ashes. (*The sunlight has now reached the floor and lights up* JEAN.) How nice and warm it is! (*She holds out her hands as though warming them at a fire.*) And so light—and so peaceful.

JEAN: (*putting the razor in her hand*) Here is the broom. Go now while it's light—out to the barn—and . . . (*Whispers in her ear.*)

JULIE: (*walking*) Thank you. I am going now—to rest. But just tell me that even the first can receive the gift of grace.

JEAN: The first? No, I can't tell you that. But wait . . . Miss Julie, I've got it! You aren't one of the first any longer. You're one of the last.

JULIE: That's true. I'm one of the very last. I *am* the last. Oh! . . . But now I can't go. Tell me again to go.

JEAN: No, I can't now either. I can't.

JULIE: And the first shall be last.

JEAN: Don't think, don't think. You're taking my strength away too and making me a coward. What's that? I thought I saw the bell move . . . To be so frightened of a bell. Yes, but it's not just a bell. There's somebody behind it—a hand moving it—and something else moving the hand—and if you stop your ears—if you stop your ears—yes, then it rings louder than ever. Rings and rings until you answer—and then it's too late. Then the police come and . . . and . . . (*The bell rings twice loudly.* JEAN *flinches, then straightens himself up.*) It's horrible. But there's no other way to end it . . . Go!

JULIE *walks firmly out through the door.*

CURTAIN

STUDY AND DISCUSSION QUESTIONS

1.   Why is the play set on Midsummer Eve? What is the function of the initial dialogue between Jean and Kristin? How is Julie characterized before she comes on stage? What is the significance of Kristin's reference to Julie's dog? How is the class struggle portrayed? What is Jean's background? What is the significance of Julie's dream? Of Jean's dream? Describe the tale that Jean tells of his childhood. What does it mean? Why does Jean want to go to Switzerland? What does Jean mean when he says, "Fall down to my level, and I'll lift you up again"? What is the dramatic function of the Count? What is Kristin's attitude toward Julie after the seduction? Compare Jean's treatment of Kristin and Julie. What is significant about the killing of the greenfinch? What role does religion play in the drama? What is the meaning of Julie's comment, "And the first shall be last"? What do the Count's boots and bell symbolize? Why does Julie apparently commit suicide?

2.   There are a great many recurring images and objects in the play —trees, bushes, flowers, boots, wine, beer, far off places, dreams, fire, dirt and the Bible. Trace some of these images and objects to determine their dramatic function

3.   Julie is described in the "Author's Foreword" as "a modern character, not that the half-woman, the man-hater, has not existed al-

ways, but because now that she has been discovered she has stepped to the front and begun to make a noise." Why does Strindberg describe her as "the half-woman"? In what ways are her dual sensibilities emphasized? Does she have any romantic characteristics? What ideas does she express? Is she a tragic figure?

4. Jean is described in the "Author's Foreword" as "a race-builder, a man of marked characteristics." What does the author mean by "race-builder"? In what ways is Jean a progressive type? What effect does his self-assurance have? How is he both polished and vulgar? What is his attitude toward his master? How is he like his master? What is the significance of his thievery? Is he a realist or a romantic? Why?

5. In "An Approach to Tragedy" Carl E. W. L. Dahlström says that regardless of the kind of *dramatis personae* employed in a tragedy —human or divine—the struggle always reflects human difficulties, with man never equal to all the circumstances in which he finds himself. The very essence of tragedy carries in it the thought of at least a major defeat of the prime figure, no matter how noble his intentions, how valiant his struggles. According to the tragic poet, the life of sensation-consciousness is something that man cannot endeavor to put in order without blundering and thus also not without enduring pain, suffering, sacrifice, and disaster. That is to say, life is for the most part too much for man. In the efforts to succeed, whether he is seeking material supremacy or spiritual, a man at some point errs and suffers defeat." Discuss this concept of tragedy in relation to *Miss Julie*.

6. Compare the theme, construction, dialogue, character, and symbol of *The Father* with *Miss Julie*.

7. "This thesis, a product of post-Darwinian biology in the mid-nineteenth century, held that man belongs entirely in the order of nature and does not have a soul or any other connection with a religious or spiritual world beyond nature; that man is therefore merely a higher-order animal whose character and fortunes are determined by two kinds of natural forces, heredity and environment. He inherits his personal traits and his compulsive instincts, especially hunger and sex, and he is subject to the economic and social forces in the environment into which he is born." (M. A. Abrams, *A Glossary of Literary Terms*.) Discuss the elements of naturalism in *Miss Julie* according to the above definition. Also point out those elements, such as symbolism and expressionism (see Glossary), that seem to transcend naturalism.

WRITING TOPICS

1. Write an essay discussing fully the reasons for Julie's tragic fate. *Or* write a character analysis of Julie or Jean (use questions 3 and 4 under Study and Discussion Questions as a guide).

2. Write an essay on one of the following themes in *Miss Julie:* (a) the "battle of the sexes," (b) the class struggle, (c) the element of feminism.

3. Read the definition of naturalism offered in question 7 under Study and Discussion Questions. Write an essay analyzing *Miss Julie* for those aspects that are NOT naturalistic, such as symbolism and expressionism.

4. Analyze the concept of tragedy as presented by Dahlström in question 5 under Study and Discussion Questions, and write an essay defending or attacking *Miss Julie* as a tragedy.

5. Write an essay comparing *Miss Julie* with one of the Greek tragedies you have read (limit your analysis to structure and character).

Sophocles:
OEDIPUS THE KING
and ANTIGONE

Selected Bibliography
and Research Topics

BIBLIOGRAPHY

Adams, Robert M. *Strains in Discord: Studies in Literary Openness.* New York: Cornell University Press, 1958 (*"Oedipus Rex* and The Bacchae," pp. 19-38).

Bowra, C. M. *Sophoclean Tragedy.* London: Oxford University Press, 1944.

Brown, John Mason. "The Glory That Was Greece." *Saturday Review,* vol. 35 (December 20, 1952), 24-25.

Campbell, Lewis. *Tragic Drama in Aeschylus, Sophocles, and Shakespeare.* London: John Murray, 1904 (Chapter X).

Earp, F. R. *The Style of Sophocles.* Cambridge: Cambridge University Press, 1944.

Ehrenberg, Victor. *Sophocles and Pericles.* Oxford: Basil Blackwell, 1954 (Chapters II and III).

Fowler, Harold N. "Sophocles" from *A History of Ancient Greek Literature.* New York: The Macmillan Co., 1928.

Freud, Sigmund. *The Interpretation of Dreams.* New York: Basic Books, Inc., 1954 (*"Oedipus Rex"*).

Haigh, A. E. "Sophocles" from *The Tragic Drama of the Greeks.* New York: Oxford University Press, 1946.

Heidegger, Martin. "The Ode on Man in Sophocles' *Antigone*" from *An Introduction to Metaphysics.* New Haven: Yale University Press, 1959.

Jones, John. *"Antigone* and *Oedipus the King"* from *On Aristotle and Greek Tragedy.* New York: Oxford University Press, 1962.

Kitto, H. D. F. *Greek Tragedy* (Chapters V-VII, X, XIII). New York: Barnes & Noble, Inc., 1957.

————. *Form and Meaning in Drama* (Chapters IV-VI). New York: Barnes & Noble, Inc., 1957.

————. *Sophocles: Dramatist and Philosopher: Three Lectures.* London: Oxford University Press, 1958.

Knox, Bernard M. W. "Sophocles' *Oedipus"* from *Tragic Themes in Western Literature.* New Haven: Yale University Press, 1955.

————. *The Heroic Temper: Studies in Sophoclean Tragedy.* Berkeley: University of California Press, 1964.

Lattimore, Richard. *The Poetry of Greek Tragedy* (pp. 81-102). Balitmore: The Johns Hopkins Press, 1958.

Lucas, D. L. *The Greek Tragic Poets* (Chapter IV). Boston: The Beacon Press, 1952.

MacGregor, Marshall. "Want of Thought" from *Studies and Diversions in Greek Literature.* London: Edward Arnold and Co., 1937.

Mackail, J. W. *Lectures on Greek Poetry* ("Sophocles"). London: Longmans, Green and Company, 1926.

Musurillo, Herbert. "Tragic Wisdom: Aeschyles and Sophocles" from *Symbol and Myth in Ancient Poetry.* New York: Fordham University Press, 1961.

Rexroth, Kenneth. "Sophocles: The Theban Plays." *Saturday Review,* vol. 48 (November 13, 1965), 40.

Rose, H. J. "Athens and the Drama" from *A Handbook of Greek Literature.* New York: The Macmillan Co., 1928.

Segal, Charles Paul. "Sophocle's Praise of Man and the Conflicts of *Antigone."* *Arion,* III, No. 2 (Summer, 1964), 46-66.

Sheppard, J. T. *"Antigone"* from *The Wisdom of Sophocles.* London: George Allen and Unwin Ltd., 1947.

Whitman, Cedric H. *Sophocles: A Study of Heroic Humanism.* Cambridge, Mass.: Harvard University Press, 1951.

Wilson, Edmund. "Sophocles, Babbitt, and Freud." *The New Republic,* LXV (December 3, 1930), 68-70.

Woodward, Thomas (ed.). *Sophocles* (Twentieth Century Views). Englewood Cliffs, New Jersey: Prentice-Hall, Inc., 1966.

Young, Sherman A. *"Antigone"* from *The Women of Greek Drama.* New York: Exposition Press, 1953.

RESEARCH TOPICS

CHARACTER. The character and motives of Oedipus and Antigone have been thoroughly discussed by the various scholars in the articles listed in the Bibliography. Write a research paper that analyzes the character and motives of Oedipus or Antigone within the thematic structure of the play (for Antigone consult Haigh, Norwood, Sheppard, Young, Rose, and Wilson; for Oedipus see Lattimore, Adams, Freud, Kitto, Knox, and Whitman).

STRUCTURE. *Oedipus the King* and *Antigone* have been proclaimed masterpieces of unity (each element contributing to the whole). Read the articles by Kitto, Bowra, and Waldock and then write a paper demonstrating why *Oedipus* or *Antigone* is structurally unified. Take into consideration the plot, verse, theme, and climax.

THEME. Ehrenberg states that the "unwritten laws" are the chief antagonists of *Oedipus* and *Antigone*. (1) Write a research paper comparing and contrasting the various theories of Ehrenberg, Kitto, Wilson, Lattimore, Bowra, and Whitman on the antagonistic elements in *Oedipus* or *Antigone*. (2) Select what you consider an interesting interpretation by one of the critics and compare and contrast this interpretation with one or two others.

TECHNIQUE. Herbert Musurillo contends that in *Oedipus* Sophocles achieves his greatest symbolic masterpiece. Musurillo says that in the early part of the play "Sophocles lays down a series of fundamental images, then the most important of these, the predominant images, are taken up and developed like musical themes and allowed to acquire deeper connotations as the play comes to a close." Read Musrillo's article and discuss some of these images, citing speaker and page to substantiate your analysis and, at the same time, show the relationship of these images to the central theme. This kind of analysis can also be applied to *Antigone*.

TRAGEDY. Critic Kenneth Rexroth contends that the unique artistic experience of Attic tragedy was contemporary with the glory of Athenian power (the wars with Persia and Sparta). This glory lasted less than three generations. He further contends that the men and women in the tragedies of Sophocles are as human as ourselves but purer, simpler, and more beautiful, the inhabitants of a kind of Utopia. After doing some research on the Periclean Age write a paper that takes into consideration the following: (a) the effect of the age upon dramatic literature, (b) view each of the characters in *Oedipus* or *Antigone* in context of Rexroth's contention and show the degree to which each displays the vivid human traits of his own Utopian existence.

Shakespeare:

ROMEO AND JULIET

and OTHELLO

Selected Bibliography

and Research Topics

BIBLIOGRAPHY

Babcock, Weston. "Iago—An Extraordinary Honest Man." *Shakespeare Quarterly*, XVI (1965), 297-301.

Bonnard, Georges A. "*Romeo and Juliet:* A Possible Significance?" *Review of English Studies*, Vol. II, New Series, No. 8 (October, 1951), 319-327.

Bowling, Lawrence Edward. "The Thematic Framework of *Romeo and Juliet*." *Modern Language Association Publication*, LXIV (1949), 208-220.

Bradley, A. C. *Shakespearean Tragedy*. London: The Macmillan Company (2nd Edition), 1952.

Brooke, Stopford A. "Romeo and Juliet" from *On Ten Plays of Shakespeare*. New York: Barnes & Noble, Inc., 1961.

Bush, Geoffrey. *Shakespeare and the Natural Condition*. Cambridge: Harvard University Press, 1956.

Cain, H. Edward. "Crabbed Age and Youth in *Romeo and Juliet*." *The Shakespeare Association Bulletin*, IX (October, 1934), 186-191.

Cambell, Lily B. *Shakespeare's Tragic Heroes: Slaves of Passion*. New York: Cambridge University Press, 1930.

Charlton, H. B. *Shakespearian Tragedy*. New York: Cambridge University Press, 1948.

Clemen, Wolfgang. "Romeo and Juliet" from *The Development of Shakespeare's Imagery*. London: Methuen and Co. Ltd., 1953.

Dean, Leonard F. (ed.). *A Casebook on Othello*. New York: Thomas Y. Crowell Company, 1961.

Elliott, G. R. *Flaming Minister*. Durham: Duke University Press, 1953.

Goddard, Harold C. "Romeo and Juliet" from *The Meaning of Shakespeare*. Chicago: The University of Chicago Press, 1951.

Granville-Barker, Harley. *Preface to Othello*. Princeton: Princeton University Press, 1958.

Harbage, Alfred. *Shakespeare: A Reader's Guide*. New York: Farrar, Straus & Giroux, Inc., 1963.

Harrison, G. B. "Romeo and Juliet" from *Shakespeare's Tragedies*. New York: Oxford University Press, 1953.

Harrison, Thomas P. "Hang up Philosophy." *The Shakespeare Association Bulletin*, XXII (October, 1947), 203-209.

Heilman, Robert B. *Magic in the Web: Action and Language in Othello*. Lexington: University of Kentucky Press, 1956.

Henry, William A. "Theme and Image in *Romeo and Juliet*." *Shakespeare Quarterly*, XI (Winter, 1962), 13-17.

Holloway, John. *The Story of Night*. London: Routledge and Kegan Paul, Ltd. 1961.

Hubler, Edward. "The Damnation of Othello." *Shakespeare Quarterly*, IX (1958), 295-300.

Hunt, Hugh. "Romeo and Juliet" from *Old Vic Prefaces*. London: Routledge and Kegan Paul, Ltd., 1954.

Laird, David. "The Generation of Style in *Romeo and Juliet*." *Journal of English and Germanic Philology*, LXIII (April, 1964), 204-213.

Lawlor, John. *The Tragic Sense in Shakespeare*. London: Chatto and Windus, 1960.

Levin, Harry. "Form and Formality in *Romeo and Juliet*." *Shakespeare Quarterly*, XI (Winter, 1960), 3-11.

McArthur, Herbert. "Romeo's Loquacious Friend." *Shakespeare Quarterly*, X (Winter, 1959), 34-44.

Nicoll, Allardyce. *Studies in Shakespeare*. New York: Harcourt, Brace, & World, Inc., 1927.

Nowottny, Winifred M. T. "Justice and Love in *Othello*." *The University of Toronto Quarterly*, XXI (1951-52), 330-344.

Ribner, Irving. *Patterns in Shakespearian Tragedy*. London: Methuen, 1960.

Rosenberg, Marvin. *The Masks of Othello: The Search for the Identity of Othello, Iago, and Desdemona by Three Centuries of Actors and Critics*. Berkeley: University of California Press, 1961.

Sewall, Richard B. "The Tragic Form" from *Essays in Criticism*, IV. Oxford, England: Basil Blackwell, 1954.

Shapiro, Stephen A. *"Romeo and Juliet: Reversals, Contraries, Transformations, and Ambivalence." College English*, XXV (April, 1964), 498-501.

Siegel, Paul N. "Christianity and the Religion of Love in *Romeo and Juliet.*" *Shakespeare Quarterly*, XII (Autumn, 1961), 371-392.

Smith, Robert Metcalf. "Three Interpretations of *Romeo and Juliet.*" *The Shakespeare Association Bulletin*, XXIII (April, 1948), 60-77.

Spurgeon, Caroline F. E. *Shakespeare's Imagery and What It Tells Us.* London: Cambridge University Press, 1935.

Stauffer, Donald A. "The School of Love" from *Shakespeare's World of Images.* New York: W. W. Norton & Company, Inc., 1949.

Stoll, Elmer Edgar. "Romeo and Juliet" from *Shakespeare's Young Lovers.* New York: Oxford University Press, 1937.

————. *Othello: An Historical and Comparative Study.* Minneapolis: University of Minnesota Press, 1915.

Tillyard, E. M. W. *The Elizabethan World Picture.* London: Chatto and Windus, 1943.

Traversi, Derek. *An Approach to Shakespeare.* New York: Doubleday & Company, Inc., 1956.

West, Robert H. "The Christianness of *Othello.*" *Shakespeare Quarterly*, XV (1964), 333-43.

Wilcox, John. "Othello's Crucial Moment." *The Shakespeare Association Bulletin*, XXIV (1949), 181-92.

Williams, Philip. "Rosemary Theme in *Romeo and Juliet.*" *Modern Language Notes*, LXVIII (June, 1953), 400-403.

RESEARCH TOPICS

CHARACTER. Several of the critics and scholars listed in the Bibliography have conflicting interpretations of the characters of Othello and Iago. (1) Read the selections by Bradley, Stoll, and Hubler and write a paper agreeing or disagreeing with their theories on Othello. (2) Read the selections by Heilman, Rosenberg, and Babcock and write a paper on Iago's function in the play. (3) Read the articles by Harrison, McArthur, Brooke, Goddard, and Hunt and write a paper in which you agree or disagree with their analysis on the roles performed by the minor characters in *Romeo and Juliet.* (4) Write a paper on the function of the minor characters in *Othello* (see Heilman, Nowottny, Stoll, Rosenberg, and Granville-Barker).

STRUCTURE. Harry Levin in "Form and Formality in *Romeo and Juliet*" discusses many of the conventions Shakespeare uses in the play. (1) Write a paper showing how a knowledge of these conventions helps in the understanding of the play. (2) Read Stephen Shapiro's article concerning the "geographical centers" of *Romeo and Juliet* and write a paper explaining the insights of the article (this type of analysis can also be applied to *Othello*). (3) Read the article by Bowling that discusses the use of "paradox" in *Romeo and Juliet* and write a paper evaluating his analysis in relation to your reading of the play. (4) Read the article by Wilcox concerning the structural climax in *Othello* and write a paper analyzing his thesis.

THEME. Using the articles from the Bibliography that would support your material, write an interpretation of either *Romeo and Juliet* or *Othello* (for *Romeo and Juliet* see the articles by Smith, Williams, Siegel, Harrison, Cain, and Stoll; for *Othello* consult the articles by Nicoll, Charlton, Nowottny, Heilman, Stoll, and Shaw).

TECHNIQUE. Several of the critics suggest that an important technique employed by Shakespeare is the use of imagery and style to convey a particular aspect of character to them. (1) Read the materials by Laird, Henry, Hunt, Clemen, and Spurgeon on *Romeo and Juliet* and write a paper attacking or supporting their interpretations. (2) Read the articles by Shaw, West, Wilcox, Clemen, and Spurgeon and write a paper on one of the techniques which they suggest is successful in *Othello*.

COMPARATIVE STUDY. Using the articles by Harrison, Bonnard, Granville-Barker, and Heilman as a basis of proof, write a comparative study on the use of time in *Romeo and Juliet* and *Othello* (some other aspect such as theme, character, imagery, or artistic development may also be used).

Ibsen:

GHOSTS and
HEDDA GABLER

Selected Bibliography

and Research Topics

BIBLIOGRAPHY

Archer, William. *The Old Drama and the New.* London: The Macmillan Company, 1922.

Arestad, Sverre. "Ibsen's Concept of Tragedy." *Modern Language Association Publication,* LXXIV, 3 (June, 1959), 285-297.

Bentley, Eric. "Ibsen, Pro and Con" from *In Search of Theater.* New York: Vintage Books, 1959.

Blau, Herbert. *"Hedda Gabler:* The Irony of Decadence." *Educational Theater Journal,* vol. 5 (May, 1953), 112-116.

Bradbrook, M. C. *Ibsen, the Norwegian: A Revaluation.* New York: The Macmillan Company, 1948.

Brustein, Robert. "Henrik Ibsen" from *The Theatre of Revolt.* Boston: Little, Brown and Company, 1964.

Bull, Francis. *Ibsen: The Man and the Dramatist.* Taylorian Lecture: Oxford, 1954.

Corrigan, R. W. "The Sun Always Rises: Ibsen's *Ghosts* as Tragedy?". *Educational Theatre Journal,* XI (1959), 172-180.

Dobree, Bonamy. "Henrik Ibsen" from *The Lamp and the Lute.* London: Frank Cross and Company, 1929.

Down, Brian W. *Ibsen: The Intellectual Background.* New York: The Macmillan Company, 1947.

————. *A Study of Six Plays by Ibsen.* New York: Cambridge University Press, 1950.

Engelstad, C. F. "Henrik Ibsen and the Modern Theater." *World Theater*, VI, 1 (1957), 5-26.

Fergusson, Francis. *"Ghosts:* The Theater of Modern Realism" from *The Idea of a Theater*. Princeton: Princeton University Press, 1949.

Gilman, R. "The Search for Ibsen." *Commonweal*, LXXIV (1961), 473-5.

Huneker, James. "Henrik Ibsen" from *Iconoclasts*. New York: Charles Scribner's Sons, 1905.

Kaufmann, F. W. "Ibsen's Conception of Truth." *Germanic Review*, XXXII (April, 1957), 83-92.

Keldalh, Erling E. "The Social Conditions and Principles of *Hedda Gabler*." *Educational Theater Journal*, vol. 13 (October, 1961), 207-13.

Knight, G. Wilson. *Henrik Ibsen*. New York: Grove Press, Inc., 1962.

Koht, Halvdan. "Shakespeare and Ibsen." *Journal of English and Germanic Philology*, XLIV, No. 1 (January, 1945), 79-86.

Lavin, Janko. "The Law of Adjustment" from *Ibsen: An Approach*. London: Methuen and Company, Ltd., 1950.

Lowenthal, Leo. "Henrik Ibsen" from *Literature and the Image of Man*. Boston: Beacon Press, 1957.

Lucas, F. L. *The Drama of Ibsen and Strindberg*. New York: The Macmillan Company, 1962.

Mayerson, Caroline W. "Thematic Symbols in *Hedda Gabler*." *Scandinavian Studies*, 22:4 (November, 1950), 151-160.

McFarlane, James Walter. "Henrik Ibsen" from *Ibsen and the Temper of Norwegian Literature*. London: Oxford University Press, 1960.

Northam, John. *Ibsen's Dramatic Method*. London: Faber and Faber, Ltd., 1953.

Rose, Henry. *Henrik Ibsen: Poet, Mystic and Moralist*. New York: Dodd Mead & Co., 1913.

Shaw, G. B. *The Quintessence of Ibsenism*. New York: Hill & Wang, Inc., 1957.

Sondel, B. S. *Zola's Naturalistic Theory with Particular Reference to the Drama*. Chicago: University of Chicago Press, 1939.

Spacks, Patricia Meyer. "The World of Hedda Gabler." *Tulane Drama Review*, Vol. 7 (Fall, 1962), 155-64.

Stuart, D. C. *The Development of Dramatic Art*. New York: The Macmillan Company, 1928.

Tennant, P. F. D. *Ibsen's Dramatic Technique*. Cambridge: Bowes and Bowes, 1948.

Thompson, Alan. "Ibsen the Detestable." *Theatre Arts*, XXXVI, viii (1952), 22-23.

Valency, Maurice. *The Flower and the Castle: An Introduction to the Modern Drama: Ibsen and Strindberg*. New York: The Macmillan Company, 1963.

Weigand, Hermann L. *The Modern Ibsen*. New York: E. P. Dutton & Co., Inc., 1960.

RESEARCH TOPICS

CHARACTER. "All of Ibsen's characters," says Dobree, "have shorn themselves from every support of life, every hope is taken until there is nothing left between them and the universe. Then the only question is a metaphysical one, 'What is the value of existence?' " (1) Discuss whether this statement is applicable to Hedda (or Mrs. Alving). Depending on the character under analysis, you might look at the articles by Valency, Huneker, Bradbrook, Shaw, Corrigan, and Bentley to help with the characterization. (2) Read the articles by Boyesen, Mayerson, Weigand, and Keldalh and write an analysis of the dramatic function of the minor characters in either *Ghosts* or *Hedda Gabler*.

TECHNIQUE. Several of the critics cited in the Bibliography suggest that the technique of Ibsen is a combination of classicism, realism, and naturalism. (1) Read the articles by Tennant, Northam, Valency, Weigand, Archer, Stuart, and Sondel and write a paper explaining how Ibsen employs the various techniques mentioned above. (2) Read the articles by Spacks, Mayerson, and Rose and write a paper analyzing Ibsen's use of symbols to develop his theme.

THEME. Both *Ghosts* and *Hedda Gabler* are attacks on society, but many of the critics do not agree on what the criticisms are or what they mean. For example, Patricia Spacks believes that *Hedda Gabler* is a study of an abnormal society, while Huneker and Rose suggest the Hedda's environment is normal but Hedda is not. (1) Write a paper discussing Ibsen's attack on society in either play. (2) Compare and contrast the various points of view on theme as suggested by the following critics: *Ghosts*—McFarlane, Shaw, Rose, and Gilman; *Hedda Gabler*—Bradbrook, Mayerson, Valency, and Keldalh.

TRAGEDY. There is considerable discussion among critics regarding Ibsen's conformity to Aristotle's definition of tragedy (see Introduction for the definition). Read the articles by Lavin, Corrigan, Arestad, and Sewall (see Shakespeare Bibliography) and write a paper analyzing either *Ghosts* or *Hedda Gabler* for their classical elements of tragedy.

COMPARATIVE STUDIES. It is obvious that *Ghosts* and *Hedda Gabler* are similar in many respects. For example, environmental and hereditary elements function similarly in both plays. (1) Using some of the articles in the Bibliography, write a comparative study (using theme, symbol, character) of *Ghosts* and *Hedda Gabler*. (2) Write a research paper on the influence of Shakespeare on Ibsen (see the article by Koht). (3) Write a paper on the role of Fate in the works of Sophocles, Shakespeare, and Ibsen (use the articles in the various Bibliographies as source material).

Strindberg:

THE FATHER and
MISS JULIE

Selected Bibliography

and Research Topics

BIBLIOGRAPHY

Benston, Alice S. "From Naturalism to the Dream Play: A Study of the Evolution of Strindberg's Unique Theatrical Form." *Modern Drama*, vol. 7, No. 4 (Feb., 1965), 383-398.

Bentley, Eric. *In Search of Theater*. New York: Random House, Inc., 1953, pp. 134-143.

Bjorkman, E. and Erichsen, N. *Eight Famous Plays*. Editor's Preface to *Miss Julie*. New York: Charles Scribner's Sons, 1949.

Block, Haskell M. "Strindberg and the Symbolist Drama." *Modern Drama*, vol. 5 (1961), 314-322.

Brustein, Robert (ed.). *Strindberg: Selected Plays and Prose*. New York: Holt, Rinehart & Winston, Inc., 1964, pp. ix-lxiv.

————. "Male and Female in August Strindberg." *Tulane Drama Review*, VII, ii, 130-174.

Cargill, A. "The Freudians" from *Intellectual America*. New York: The Macmillan Co., 1941.

Clark, B. H. and G. Freedley (eds.). *History of Modern Drama*. New York: The Meredith Publishing Co., 1947.

Dahlström, C. E. W. L. "Strindberg and the Naturalistic Tragedy." *Scandinavian Studies*, vol. 30, No. 1 (1958), 1-11.

————. "Strindberg's *Fadern* as an Expressionistic Drama." *Scandinavian Studies*, Vol. 14, No. 3 (August, 1940), 83-94.

————. *Strindberg's Dramatic Expression.* Ann Arbor: University of Michigan, 1930.

Freedman, Morris. "Strindberg's Positive Nihilism." *Drama Studies,* V (1963), 288-296.

Gassner, John (ed.). *Treasury of the Theatre: Ibsen to Ionesco.* New York: Holt, Rinehart & Winston, Inc., 1965, pp. 75-77.

Gustafson, Alrik. *A History of Swedish Literature.* Minneapolis: University of Minnesota Press, 1961.

Huneker, J. G. "August Strindberg" from *Iconoclasts.* New York: Charles Scribner's Sons, 1905.

Kaufmann, R. J. "Strindberg: The Absence of Irony." *Drama Studies,* III (1963), 243-276.

Krutch, J. W. "Modernism" from *Modern Drama.* Ithaca: Cornell University Press, 1953.

Lamm, Martin. "Strindberg and the Theatre." *Tulane Drama Review,* VI (Nov., 1961).

Lucus, F. L. *The Drama of Ibsen and Strindberg.* New York: The Macmillan Company, 1962.

Lyons, Charles L. "The Archetypal Action of Male Submission in Strindberg's *The Father.*" *Scandinavian Studies,* XXXVI, No. 3 (August, 1964), 218-232.

Madsen, Borge Gedso. *Strindberg's Naturalistic Theater: Its Relation to French Naturalism.* Seattle: University of Washington Press, 1962.

McGill, V. L. *August Strindberg.* New York: Atheneum Publishers, 1964.

Meyer, Richael (trans.). *The Plays of Strindberg.* vol. I. New York: Random House, Inc., 1964, pp. 15-26.

Morgan, Margery M. "Strindberg and the English Theater." *Modern Drama,* VII, 161-173.

Mortenson, B. M. E. and B. W. Downs. *Strindberg.* New York: Cambridge University Press, 1964.

Muller, H. J. "Naturalistic Tragedy" from *Spirit of Tragedy.* New York: Random House, Inc., 1956.

Nicoll, A. "Strindberg and the Play of the Subconscious" from *World Drama.* New York: Harcourt, Brace & World, Inc., 1960.

Paulson, Arvid. "*The Father:* A Survey of Critical Opinion of August Strindberg's Tragedy and Leading American Performances of It During the Past Half Century." *Scandinavian Studies* (1964), 247-259.

Scobbie, Irene. "The Drama of Ibsen and Strindberg." *Modern Drama,* V (1961).

————. "Strindberg and Lagerkvist." *Modern Drama,* VIII (Sept., 1964).

Spivack, C. K. "The Many Hells of August Strindberg." *Twentieth Century Literature,* IX (1962), 10-16.

Sprinchorn, Evert (ed.). "The Ironic Strindberg" and "Toward a New Art Form" from *The Genius of Scandinavian Theatre.* New York: New American Library, 1964.

Thompson, Alan R. *The Anatomy of Drama.* Berkeley: University of California Press, 1946, pp. 341-356.

Valency, Maurice J. *The Flower and the Castle.* New York: Macmillan, 1963.

White, Kenneth S. "Strindberg and the Naturalistic Theater." *Modern Drama,* vol. 5, No. 3 (December, 1962), 314-322.

Williams, Raymond. *Drama from Ibsen to Eliot.* London: Chatto and Williams, 1965.

Young, Vernon. "The History of *Miss Julie.*" *Hudson Review,* VIII (Spring, 1955).

RESEARCH TOPICS

CHARACTER. "The characters of *The Father* are drawn entirely out of perspective, with an almost complete disregard for conventional proportion or verisimulitude, with an eye to their essential, not their accidental relationships." (1) Using the articles by Brustein, Dahlström, Lyons, McGill, and Mortensen as source material, write a paper analyzing this statement by Maurice Valency in relation to *The Father* (it may also be applied to *Miss Julie*). (2) Write a research paper, using the articles mentioned above, analyzing the dramatic function of the minor characters in *The Father.*

TECHNIQUE. Strindberg's plays are considered by many to be a mixture of naturalism, realism, expressionism, and symbolism. (1) Read the articles by Dahlström, White, and Block and write a paper analyzing *The Father* or *Miss Julie* for one or more of the elements cited above. (2) Write a paper analyzing *The Father* or *Miss Julie* for the use of imagery or irony (check the Bibliography for pertinent material).

THEME. Several of the critics have conflicting views on the theme of *The Father* and *Miss Julie.* For example, Raymond Williams describes the theme of *The Father* as a "revealed truth" rather than an "everyday experience," while Alan Thompson explains the theme of the play as a conflict between strife (man) and instinct (woman). Consult the articles by Benston, Block, Brustein, Dahlström, Kaufmann, Lamm, and Nicoll and write a paper on the central theme of either *The Father* or *Miss Julie.*

TRAGEDY. "In *The Father* Strindberg deliberately attempted to write a modern Greek tragedy. . . . This led him back to the simplicity of the dramatic unities, the whole action taking place within twenty-four hours, in one room, and a very small number of characters—eight —being introduced." Write a paper analyzing the influence of naturalism on the classical concept of tragedy as presented by Strindberg (see Clark, Dahlström, Huneker, Krutch, Muller, and White).

COMPARATIVE STUDIES. "The difference between *Miss Julie* and *The Father* is thus largely a matter of the type of experience which Strindberg chose to reproduce in these plays. The former is ostensibly an interpretation of the life of the outer world; the latter interprets the inner life. Both are, in their fashion, realistic; they differ principally in the order of reality which they are intended to transmit, and the order of illusion they are intended to produce." (1) Write a comparison and contrast of *Miss Julie* and *The Father* in terms of the above statement. (2) Write a paper comparing some dramatic technique of Ibsen and Strindberg (the articles by Scobbie, Valency, Lucus, Gustafson will be useful as far as determining an area of interest). (3) Following the suggestions of Benston and Dahlström that *The Father* and *Othello* have many similarities, write a paper comparing the protagonists of the two plays. (4) Write a paper comparing one of Strindberg's plays with a Greek tragedy: consider such things as characterization, theme, structure, and technique. (5) Read a play by O'Neill (such as *Desire under the Elms*) and write a paper analyzing the influence Strindberg had on his work.

Glossary of Useful Terms

ANTAGONIST

The antagonist is the character who opposes the protagonist and draws him into the conflict. The antagonist is usually a person or a group, but may also be represented by a group of persons, nature, environment, or an abstract force.

CHARACTERIZATION

Characterization is the representation of the personalities of the figures in a play. There are several classifications of characters:

1. *developing characters*—characters who come to a new awareness or deeper understanding of themselves as a result of the conflict.
2. *flat characters*—characters who display one side of their personalities, and have a single identifying trait.
3. *foil characters*—characters who provide a contrast to the protagonist and thus help develop and convey his character.
4. *parallel characters*—characters whose function is to develop the protagonist's personality through analogy with their own.
5. *static characters*—characters who remain essentially unchanged throughout the play.
6. *stock characters*—characters who, by their actions, speech, and appearance, signal a predetermined response in the reader and audience.

CLIMAX

The point of maximum interest or highest action in the play is traditionally defined as the climax. It is more precise to think of climax as the point at which the protagonist makes or has made for him a crucial decision growing out of the conflict.

COINCIDENCE

When characters within a story or novel seem to meet by chance at a given time or place or when events seem to happen for the convenience

525

of plot or theme development, a coincidence occurs. If the dramatist is too obvious in his use of coincidence the plot seems improbable and weak.

CONFLICT

Conflict is the clash of wills, desires, ideas, or physical actions. It may be mental, physical, emotional, or moral, and as a rule it manifests itself in one or more of three forms: a character at odds with another person or group, with an external force (nature, "fate"), or with an internal force (something in his own nature).

CONSISTENCY

Successful creation of character results from a dramatist's strict attention to consistency. Drama, unlike life, demands characters whose actions grow naturally out of the personalities established for them. A character depicted as a selfish person must act selfishly throughout the play. This does not mean that a character cannot undergo change. Many times such a change may be the central issue resolved in the play. But the change must be consistent with the character as he has been developed.

CONVENTIONS

Art is never reality and any art form necessarily differs from reality. Each art form asks us, therefore, to accept certain conditions which are different from reality. These conditions are called conventions. For example, in a play a character may speak his thoughts aloud and not be heard by other figures on the stage (aside), or he may express his thoughts aloud on an empty stage (soliloquy).

DENOUEMENT

Denouement is that part of the play in which the mysteries or complications of the plot are unraveled or resolved.

DEUS EX MACHINA

Deus ex machina means "God from a machine." The term originated in Greek drama with the practice of lowering a god to the stage by means of ropes. It grew to mean any improbable device used to bring a plot to a satisfactory conclusion.

DRAMATIC IRONY

Dramatic irony is that condition in which the audience knows that the state of affairs is the tragic opposite of what the characters understand it to be. This sort of irony is not necessarily related to an element of surprise but rather to the complexity, contradictions, and misunderstandings common to the human experience.

EXPOSITION

Exposition is generally that opening conversation of a play calculated to set the time and place and to clarify the position of the characters relative to both. Exposition may be found at any point in a play but it is usually employed at the beginning of acts or as a substitute for action taking place off stage.

EXPRESSIONISM

The expressionist dramatist presents not a realistic picture of life, but rather life as he (or his characters) subjectively and emotionally conceive it to be. Thus reality will be distorted for the purpose of representing the dramatist's feelings about it. Stage settings, for example, may not be realistic or accurate but more a reflection of a state of mind.

FORESHADOWING (ADUMBRATION)

Foreshadowing is the attempt on the part of the dramatist to interest his audience in the conflict which is the heart of the play. It is generally found at the beginning of a play, and consists of subtle suggestions that arouse curiosity and give hints of the struggle which is to come.

MELODRAMA

A drama in which clearly recognizable character types (villains and heroes) are set in conflict in sensational situations. Melodrama employs action, mystery, and suspense for their own effects.

MOTIVATION

Motivation is the gradual unfolding of the reasons for a character's behavior. Motivation is closely allied to consistency. If a character changes in a play, the reasons for the change must be logical and consistent with the presentation and development of his personality.

NATURALISM

Naturalism is the technique of portraying an accurate, objective picture of life that includes everything and selects nothing. It is a manner of regarding man as a creature determined by environmental and hereditary forces and bereft of free will and reason.

PLAUSIBILITY

Plausibility implies the balanced and full development of a character. The plausible character is generally a "round" or developing character, for the dramatist must convince his audience that the character is or could be a person in real life.

PLOT

Plot is the sequence in which a dramatist arranges incidents and events for the artistic purposes of his play. It is the sum total of all the things which the characters do or which happen to them in the course of the drama. In a good plot the emphasis is upon causality; that is, an event grows logically and naturally out of those events which precede it.

POETIC JUSTICE (JUST RETRIBUTION)

Poetic justice embodies the idea of punishment for the evil and reward for the good. Though it is obvious that life does not have such a just arrangement, the doctrine is defended by those who feel that the moral function of literature is primary.

PRECEDENT ACTION

Precedent action is that action which, by implication, occurred prior to the beginning of the play. It is usually explained in the exposition and it may or may not be a part of the foreshadowing.

PROTAGONIST

The protagonist is the central character in a play. He is the focal figure around whom the main action and the conflict revolve.

REALISM

Realism is the precise representation of the familiar details, experiences, and circumstances of every-day life. Realism is more selective than naturalism and less prone to adopt a rigid philosophic attitude toward the scenes and characters depicted.

SENTIMENTALITY

Sentimentality is an excess of tender emotions, disproportionate to what is warranted by any particular situation or character. Sentimental drama tends to overlook or forgive evil; it strives to elicit sympathy or tears when a colder, more objective judgment is in fact called for. James Joyce once defined sentiment as "unearned emotion."

SETTING

The time and place at which a drama occurs constitute its setting. It may serve to establish the mood or atmosphere of the play, and may function as an antagonist.

SUSPENSE

Suspense is the uncertainty generated in the audience as a direct result of the clash of forces which make up the conflict of a play. The quality of dramatic suspense is often characterized as a curious kind of pleasurable anxiety.

SYMBOL

A symbol is any object, person, action, setting, or characteristic which means something more than it simply denotes or describes. Symbols draw together the concrete and the abstract by making the former suggestive of the latter. There are three types of symbols. The *natural symbol* resembles and partakes of the higher quality it suggests; thus a rose, fragile and beautiful itself, represents beauty generally. The *private symbol* is unique to its user and becomes meaningful to his audience only through repeated use and ultimate acceptance (the hair color and texture in *Hedda Gabler*). The *conventional symbol* (which may embrace the category of natural symbol) is generally recognized and accepted by any audience and is readily accessible to any writer (a dove as a symbol of peace).

THEME

Theme is the controlling idea particularized in a play. It may be a moral, a message, a belief, an attitude, or a world view, but it is invariably the central insight the playwright wishes to communicate.

VERISIMILITUDE

Verisimilitude is that quality which gives a play the appearance of truth. Verisimilitude implies close attention to minute detail, but a play need not be realistic to achieve verisimilitude. Subjects which are imaginative, fantastic, or highly improbable can be represented as though they were in fact true.